Tower

Genealogy

An Account of the Descendants of

JOHN TOWER

of

Hingham, Massachusetts

Compiled Under the Direction of

Charlemagne Tower

Late of Philadelphia, Deceased.

HERITAGE BOOKS
2010

HERITAGE BOOKS

AN IMPRINT OF HERITAGE BOOKS, INC.

Books, CDs, and more—Worldwide

For our listing of thousands of titles see our website
at
www.HeritageBooks.com

A Facsimile Reprint
Published 2010 by
HERITAGE BOOKS, INC.
Publishing Division
100 Railroad Ave. #104
Westminster, Maryland 21157

Originally published
Cambridge:
John Wilson and Son
University Press
1891

International Standard Book Numbers
Paperbound: 978-0-7884-1337-7
Clothbound: 978-0-7884-8382-0

INTRODUCTION.

———◆———

THIS Genealogy, as it titlepage indicates, was prepared under the direction of Mr. Charlemagne Tower, late of Philadelphia, deceased. His attention was called to his ancestry while he was a student at Harvard College. He was then able to follow on his own line the generations backward toward the early settlement of Massachusetts to Ambrose Tower[3], who appeared in that part of Concord afterwards made into the town of Lincoln; but there did not appear anything of record to connect Ambrose with any other of the family of Tower. The interest however continued present to his mind, inducing him to make further and continued research; and when some years following his own graduation his younger brother, Francis Marion Tower, became a member of the same college, he took up the research in sympathy with his elder brother's wishes, and succeeded in finding evidence which established the connection of Ambrose[3], through his father Benjamin[2], with the immigrant John[1]. This evidence was found among the old papers which had been preserved in the dwelling-house now standing upon the later homestead of John Tower[1], and occupying a space contiguous to the dwelling-house which John Tower built, and which he occupied until his death.

The discovery here made deepened the interest which he had already felt in the subject, and some progress was made in the beginning of a Genealogy; but the large and ever-increasing demands of his profession, and the large business enterprises growing out of it so completely absorbed his time and energies that the genealogical work was suspended and held in abeyance for several years.

It was not until the close of our Civil War that Mr. Tower again found opportunity to resume the work. At this time, while his son was pursuing his collegiate studies at Cambridge, and his daughters were receiving instruction in Massachusetts schools, Mr. Tower had occasion to make frequent visits to the home of his ancestors, and the interest so long lying latent among his large cares became again awakened into resolution to pursue the subject to such completion as time and circumstance would permit.

The increased attention to genealogical pursuits which had then been given, provided facilities for pursuing the work not before available, and he was enabled by liberal compensation to obtain aid in his undertaking.

Mr. Tower was much interested in the early history of the several colonies, out of which has grown our now common country, and had made a large collection of the earlier laws many of which it is now difficult or impossible to find. The laws of a free people are supposed to indicate the average intelligence and wisdom of those who frame them, and they are indices along the road of progress on which a free people are constantly moving in the process of development and growth. The underlying principles are eternal, varying in their application as conditions and circumstances shall change, and only to be subverted and lost when the virtue and intelligence necessary to the existence of free institutions shall become impaired and lost.

Since Mr. Tower's death, his widow has presented this collection to the Pennsylvania Historical Society, and the Society has published the titles to them in an elegant quarto volume. It is a fitting monument to the industry and perseverance of the collector of these ancient colonial laws.

In the manner Mr. Tower has presented John Tower [1], the immigrant from Old England, and the founder of the family, will be seen the interest he had in the relation his ancestor bore to the troubled times in which the immigration occurred, and the equally troubled times following the immigration, when new conditions called for new application of old methods or the invention of entirely new ones to meet changed and ever-varying circumstances. The conflict was then, as now, between the conservatism which sees safety in the old and often tried ways, and the theory of the dreamer and enthusiast reaching out with more assurance than knowledge into the sea of adventure with faith that the continent of golden hopes may be safely reached. The struggle was then, as now ; and many a bark went down, as they will continue to go down, in overwhelming storm, from their imperfect structure and equipment, before one shall be found so completely constructed and manned as to reach the haven of promise and assurance.

The present volume of Genealogy is confined to the descendants of John Tower [1], of the Tower name, and of the children of the females who have borne the Tower name. Much however has been collected and arranged in the many lines of the females, probably sufficient to make two volumes of the size of the present one. Work in this direction was interrupted by Mr. Tower's somewhat sudden death. He had attained and completed the full age of eighty years, yet from his ability to labor in these later years he may well have indulged hopes of being able to continue to labor until he had completed and prepared the whole work for publication.

It is hoped that these quite large collections may be availed of in the preparation of the genealogies of the families to which they belong, of the greater number of which no genealogy has as yet been published. It is now thought best to publish so much of the work as has been prepared, and which is in a suitable condition for publication.

The account of the first five generations brings the history down to the close of the Revolutionary War. This account will show the work they did in subduing the wilderness and preparing for themselves comfortable habitations, as well as the work they did in other industrial pursuits which were necessary for the comfort of the people.

Many of the family rendered service in the wars with the Indians, and later with their neighbors, the French, while in the Revolutionary War most of those of the name within the age of military service were soldiers either in the Continental Army or in answering the constant demands made upon the militia.

They were all educated in the common schools, but none of the name had availed himself of a college education until the sixth generation, from which we find three graduates, — two from Brown, and one from Harvard College.

During the Revolutionary War, and more particularly at its close, there was a large emigration from the older towns of Massachusetts and from Rhode Island, especially from the towns on the seaboard, to the western part of Massachusetts and extending into Vermont, and subsequently continued into the unsettled and fertile portions of New York.

Many of the descendants of John Tower were engaged in this movement. They had become acquainted with much of the outlying wilderness during frequent marches to Crown Point and Ticonderoga, the objective points of the opposing forces during the Old French and the early part of the Revolutionary War. In the older portions of the State the lands had been subjected to division, so that there was little left to provide for the wants of all the members so constantly appearing in their somewhat prolific families. The long years of the continuance of the latter war had sufficed to sweep from the ocean almost every vestige of the commerce the colonies had enjoyed under the protecting flag of the mother country. Peace brought to a close all privateering adventure, wherein the hardihood of the few remaining sailors had found exercise.

The promising field for labor and enterprise was westward in the wilderness, and here they went to repeat the work of their ancestors in subduing it. Here they succeeded in making themselves comfortable homes, from which succeeding generations have gone throughout the whole extent of our domain, and they are now found in nearly every State in the Union.

Much has been collected showing what acquisitions they made ; but the limits proposed for this volume will prevent a proper presentation of what the descendants of the later generations have done to improve their temporal condition, or to show their advancement in intellectual work, or how well they have borne their part in the various callings of business and enterprise, in scientific pursuits, or in the learned professions.

It is hoped that the publication of this volume will lead some other member or members of the family to continue it to such completion as will lead to the publication of the large amount of material which Mr. Tower had collected.

Appended hereto is a brief account of Mr. Tower as it appears in the publication of the Pennsylvania Historical Society hereinbefore mentioned, with slight correction and change.

Mr. Tower's descent from John Tower is shown fully in the Genealogy. His father, Reuben Tower, a well-known and public-spirited man, born at Rutland, Worcester County, Massachusetts, on the 15th day of February, 1787, and married in the Township of Paris on the 15th day of February, 1808, was active in the development of the public improvements of his time, in the State of New York, notably in connection with the Chenango Canal ; and was also a member of the Legislature of New York in 1828. He died at the age of forty-five, on the 14th of March, 1832, in St. Augustine, Florida, where he had gone for his health. His mother, Deborah Taylor (Pearce) Tower, was born at Little Compton, in Rhode Island, on the 6th day of July, 1785.

Mr. Tower's education was begun in his native place, and carried on subsequently at the Oxford Academy in Chenango County, and at the Clinton Academy, and the Utica Academy in Oneida County, New York. It is worthy of note that he taught school in the common schools of the townships of Paris and Marshall, in Oneida County, for two consecutive years, when he was but fourteen and fifteen years of age ; and in 1825 he was assistant teacher in the Utica Academy. He was also shortly after engaged in business as a clerk with Messrs. Hart and Gridley, merchants, in Utica. In 1826 his father took him to Cambridge, Massachusetts, and placed him under the tutorship of Rev. Caleb Stetson, to prepare him for admission to Harvard University. He entered the Freshman class at Harvard in February, 1827, and was graduated there in the year 1830. Among his classmates was Charles Sumner, between whom and Mr. Tower a very close friendship grew up, which continued through many years, and lasted until Mr. Sumner's death.

After graduation Mr. Tower began, in 1831, the study of the law, in the office of Hon. Harmanus Bleeker, in Albany, New York. The death of his father occurring in the next year, his family interests recalled him

to Waterville, Oneida County, New York, the home of his family, where
he continued his studies. He went later to New York City, and finished
his study of the law in the office of Messrs. John L. and James L.
Graham. He was admitted to practice in the Supreme Court of the
State of New York, at Utica, in October, 1836. He began the profession in New York City in the office of Messrs. Graham and Sanford, continued it later in Waterville, and was engaged at the latter
place for some years in manufacturing and commercial pursuits. Re-
turning however to his practice, he won a foremost place at the bar
of Oneida County.

Some legal questions that arose in connection with his practice took
him to Pennsylvania in 1846, for the examination of the title to large
bodies of mineral land lying chiefly in the County of Schuylkill. Result-
ing from this, Mr. Tower married Amelia Malvina Bartle, the daughter
of Lambert B. Bartle and Sarah (Herring) Bartle, his wife, at Orwigsburg, on the 14th day of June, 1847, by whom he had one son and six
daughters. His legal interests induced him to take up his residence
in Pennsylvania, which he did in the Spring of 1848, at Orwigsburg, at
that time the county-seat of Schuylkill County, where he lived until
1850, when, upon the removal of the county-seat to Pottsville, he also
moved his residence to that place. He lived in Pottsville from 1850 to
1875.

Mr. Tower's career at the bar in Pennsylvania brought him in con-
tact with some of the most difficult and intricate questions of law, more
especially upon the subject of titles to lands. The great coal-fields of
the State had become the subject of wide-spread litigation, which led to
the trial of cases that frequently involved estates of large value, and the
conduct of which called into action the best legal talent of the day. Mr.
Tower's life during this period of more than twenty-five years was exceedingly active and laborious. It was his custom to prepare his cases
for trial, not only with a wonderful nicety of detail, so that in coming
before the court he was prepared to meet the most exacting inquiry, but
he would also go out upon the lands themselves, which often lay in
a mountainous country, almost inaccessible by reason of thick forests
and heavy undergrowth, and would run the lines and establish the
monuments himself, in company with his engineers.

His excellent training in early life, his patient labor and untiring industry, as well as his good judgment in questions of law, and his able
treatment of them, won for him a standing at the bar among the foremost lawyers in Pennsylvania. While his devotion to the interests of
his clients, and his sterling integrity as a man, brought him a very wide
practice. his opinion upon questions of title was esteemed so highly
that it is not unusual, even now, to hear him quoted in open court
as authority.

Mr. Tower was the leading counsel in the famous trials that arose out of questions relating to the Munson and Williams estate, in Schuylkill County, comprising a large body of coal lands, the litigation in regard to which he carried along for more than twenty-five years. He mastered it, and perfected the title to these lands, which are now the property of the Philadelphia and Reading Coal and Iron Company ; and his footsteps may be traced through many other great legal battles in different counties of Pennsylvania.

At the breaking out of the War of the Rebellion, Mr. Tower's loyalty to the Union was instant and decisive. Although he was fifty-two years of age, and long accustomed to the sedentary habits of his profession, he determined to take the field. He enlisted a body of two hundred and seventy men within one week, at Pottsville, and proceeded with them to Harrisburg, where they were mustered into the service of the United States on the 21st day of April, 1861. They were divided into two whole companies and part of a third, and attached to the Sixth Regiment of Pennsylvania Volunteers, in the three months' campaign. Mr. Tower, having asked to be made captain, received his commission at the time of their entering the service, and commanded, throughout its term, one of his companies, — Company H, Sixth Regiment. He was under the command of Gen. Robert Patterson, and moved into Virginia by way of Chambersburg and Hagerstown, crossing the Potomac River at Williamsport, June 21, 1861, and taking part in the action at Falling Waters, very early in the war. Mr. Tower provided uniforms for his whole company at his own expense. He was mustered out of service with his men at the end of their term of service at Harrisburg, on the 26th of July, 1861, whence he returned to his family. Afterwards he paid a bounty of five dollars a man to a full company, recruited for three years by Capt. Henry Pleasants (his second lieutenant in the three months' campaign, — later Brigadier-General). This was Company C, Forty-Eighth Regiment Pennsylvania Volunteers, which performed much honorable service and became distinguished in the war.

On the 15th of August, 1861, Mr. Tower's men, who had served under him in the campaign, marched to his residence in Pottsville, and presented him with an exceedingly handsome sword, bearing this inscription : —

> Presented by the Tower Guards, of Pottsville, Pa.,
> To Capt. Charlemagne Tower,
> As a token of their respect for him as a man and
> soldier, and of their esteem for him as a friend.
> *August* 10, 1861.

Mr. Tower was appointed United States Provost Marshal for the Tenth Congressional District of Pennsylvania on the 18th of April,

1863, which commission he held until his resignation on the 1st of May, 1864, during a period of great national anxiety and many difficulties that at this time grew out of the carrying on of the war. His administration was soldierly, vigorous, and consistent, and won for him high distinction at Washington.

Mr. Tower continued in the practice of his profession after his return from the war, until 1875, when he retired from activity at the bar, and in the fall of that year moved to Philadelphia, in order to devote himself to his private interests in various industries and enterprises, which had grown to be very large. During his residence in Pennsylvania he had become owner of large bodies of coal land, and was director in several corporations in which he was a party in interest. He was part-owner in the well-known Coxe and Tower lands, on the Green Mountains, in Schuylkill County. He was one of the original proprietors of the Honey Brook Coal Company, and for many years one of its managers ; and he took an active part, in conjunction with Mr. Charles Parrish and Mr. John Taylor Johnston, in transforming that successful enterprise into the Lehigh and Wilkes-Barre Coal Company. He was also actively interested in the construction and management of the Northern Pacific Railroad, and a member of its board of directors for several years. The assistance given by him to this road, by both personal attention to its affairs and financial support, frequently, when it became necessary, was of very great value to the company, and Mr. Tower may fairly be said to have contributed largely to its ultimate success. His judgment and foresight in business affairs placed him among the few men who never lost confidence in the value of this road, or in the great future development of the country through which it has been built.

The greatest and most successful undertaking, perhaps, of Mr. Tower's long business career was his development of the iron resources of Minnesota, in the district now well known to the world as the Vermilion Range. The presence of large deposits of iron ore in that country having been brought to his attention about the year 1875, he made a thorough investigation of their quantity and value by sending out several expeditions to explore them and report to him ; the result of which having proved extremely favorable, he concluded to proceed with their actual development. The enterprise was a daring one. These ore deposits lay in St. Louis County, Minnesota, some ninety miles northeast from Duluth, and about seventy miles in a direct line north from the north shore of Lake Superior. The country was densely wooded, was traversed by many small streams and broken by long stretches of swamp that in the summer season were almost impassable. Provisions, as well as materials and supplies, could only be transported in midwinter, laboriously, over the frozen ground and on the snow, frequently at a temperature of forty degrees Fahrenheit below zero, and in the summer carried upon the backs of men, or over a circuitous route by Indians in canoes. The opening and working of the iron mines at this great distance from the outskirts of civilization implied a formidable expenditure ; but this was far surpassed by the necessity of constructing a railroad seventy miles long to the nearest water communication, the shore of Lake Superior, and equipping it, in order to transport the product of the mines to market, and the construction of sufficient dock and harbor facilities for vessels to receive it at the water's edge. Many experienced business men, consulted in regard to the enterprise, drew back from an undertaking fraught with so many and so great dangers. But Mr. Towers's courage was supported by his judgment derived from careful and systematic investigation, and he determined, at the age of seventy-three, to carry out his purpose single-handed. After having acquired title to the lands which contained the ore deposits, and also to a body of land lying upon Lake Superior, known then as Burlington Bay and Agate Bay, which he afterwards called Two Harbors, he formed in 1883 two companies, the Minnesota Iron Company and the Duluth and Iron Range Railroad Company, the former of which owned the latter. He built the railroad from the mines at Lake Vermilion to Two Harbors, on Lake Superior, seventy miles ; erected large docks, roundhouses, machine shops, and saw-mills, and provided equipment for the transportation of the ore, besides carrying along the development of the mines in order that their product might be ready for shipment at the completion of the railroad. The iron ore lay in veins, tilted into a position almost vertical, extending for more than a mile in a northeasterly and southwesterly direction, and varying in thickness from forty to one hundred and fifty feet. The ore was a hard specular hematite, yielding by analysis sixty-eight per cent of metallic iron, and from one thirty-thousandth to one fifty-thousandth of phosphorus, free from sulphur and all refractory substance.

Mr. Tower carried along this enterprise with vigor and determination until August, 1884, when the railroad was completed and put into operation, and the first shipments of ore were made from Two Harbors to Cleveland. These shipments met with great favor after having been largely distributed among the iron and steel manufacturers of Illinois, Ohio, and Pennsylvania, and almost from its commencement Mr. Tower's enterprise was proved to be successful. The country opened very rapidly, and soon after a considerable town, called Tower, grew up on the shore of Lake Vermilion, and another at Two Harbors ; whilst along the line of the railroad lumbering interests, the quarrying of granite, and various industries sprang up with the increase of population. In 1886 the raiload line was constructed along the shore of Lake Superior, twenty-seven miles, to Duluth. The annual shipments of ore from the mines at Tower, which in 1884, at the opening of the railroad, were sixty-eight thousand tons, increased in 1885 to two hundred and twenty-five thousand tons, in 1886 to three hundred thousand tons, and in 1887 to four hundred thousand tons. This industry, planted by the energy and courage of a single man in a remote and difficult country, placed the State of Minnesota, hitherto unknown as a mineral-producing district, in the space of four years among the foremost iron markets of the United States, employed fifteen hundred men in its mines, and gave support, directly and indirectly, to more than five thousand people. It is not too much to say that this was one of the most remarkable developments ever made in the United States. Its value to Minnesota, and indeed to the whole country of the Northwest, in the benefits that are likely to be derived from it, is almost incalculable. Mr. Tower in it erected a proud monument to himself as a man and a benefactor of his fellow-man that will endure and grow greater as time goes on.

In the year 1887 it was found that valuable deposits of iron ore existed throughout a long stretch of country lying to the east and northeast of the Minnesota Iron Company's property at Tower. These were explored after the opening of the railroad, and they had been acquired by various individual owners and companies, who were ready to open new mines upon the extension to them of the railroad by which they might reach a market with their product. Mr. Tower concluded that, having carried out successfully his own undertaking, he did not wish singly to build the road to an unlimited extent in order to supply the demands that naturally arose as the country was more fully explored ; neither did he wish to separate his railroad from the mines at Tower by transferring its ownership from the Minnesota Iron Company. He therefore concluded to make a combination with a syndicate formed in New York and Chicago, which already had large interests to the east of him.

These gentlemen bought from him his entire property in May, 1887, which he then transferred to them, retaining, however, an interest considerably smaller than his former holding in the new organization which they formed, called the Minnesota Mining and Railroad Syndicate. This arrangement was highly advantageous in a financial sense to Mr. Tower, who now had the gratification of having proved the wisdom of his foresight, and of having seen his great undertaking carried through to an eminently successful issue, and in a very short time. He retained the presidency of the Minnesota Iron Company, at the request of the syndicate, until October, 1887, when he resigned his office ; whereupon the Board of Directors, composed of the new owners, passed the following resolution, which they had handsomely engraved and sent to him :

Resolved, That in thus severing, at his request, the active connection of Mr. Tower with the Company, we desire to place upon the permanent records of the organization our high appreciation of the great service he has performed in developing and rendering successful the enterprise. Mr. Tower came to its support in its infancy, and has been, from the beginning, its promoter and ruling spirit, giving to it always, unselfishly, the benefit of his ripe judgment and business experience, as well as unlimited aid from his own financial resources. During all the years of his connection with it, including years of general financial distress and anxiety, he has never faltered, and the full measure of prosperity which the Company now enjoys is largely due to his personal efforts, and is a sufficient tribute at once to his business capacity and his patient courage. We exceedingly regret that Mr. Tower feels compelled to retire from the service of the Company, but beg to assure him that he carries with him the gratitude and best wishes of the Board and of all interested in the property.

Mr. Tower was a man of cultivated tastes, a lover of books, particularly of those relating to the history of America. He was one of the first to recognize the importance of the comparative study of American colonial law. His unrivalled collection on this subject was begun nearly forty years ago, and was latterly supplemented with many rare and costly works belonging to the general field of *Americana*. He was a member of the Board of Overseers of Harvard University from 1884 until his death. He died at his summer residence in Waterville, Oneida County, New York, on the 24th of July, 1889, in the eighty-first year of his age.

Mr. Tower's life was one of integrity, patient labor, and of great good to others with whom he has lived. His influence extended very widely throughout the United States. As a citizen, in peace and in war, and as a professional man, in business and in private life, his career made him one of the remarkable men of his country and of his time.

July, 1891

THE TOWER GENEALOGY.

JOHN TOWER [1], son of Robert and Dorothy (Damon) Tower, bapt. May 17, 1609; mar. Margaret Ibrook, Feb. 13, 1638–9, in Charlestown, Mass. She was b. in England, date not known, and was dau. of Richard Ibrook. Childr. all born in Hingham, Mass.

2.	I.	JOHN [2]	bapt.	Dec. 13, 1639.
	II.	JONATHAN [2]	"	Aug. 1, 1641 ; died, unmar.
3.	III.	IBROOK [2]	"	Feb. 7, 1643–4.
4.	IV.	JEREMIAH [2]	"	March 9, 1645–6.
5.	V.	ELIZABETH [2]	"	Oct. 9, 1648.
6.	VI.	SARAH [2]	"	July 16, 1650.
7.	VII.	HANNAH [2]	"	July 17, 1652.
8.	VIII.	BENJAMIN [2]	"	Nov. 5, 1654.
9.	IX.	JEMIMA [2]	born	April 25, 1660.
10.	X.	SAMUEL [2]	"	Jan. 26, 1661–2.

John Tower [1], died in Hingham, Mass., Feb. 13, 1701–2, ag. 92 y. 9 m. 0 d.

Margaret (Ibrook) Tower, died in Hingham, Mass., May 15, 1700, ag. about 83.

John Tower was born in the parish of Hingham, in the county of Norfolk, in the eastern part of England. An examination of the parish records shows the following entries : —

"Robert Tower and Dorothy Damon were married, Aug. 31, 1607."
"John, child of Robert Tower, was baptized May 14, 1609."
"Dorithe, the wife of Robert Tower, was buried Nov. 10, 1629."
"Robert Tower was buried, May 1, 1634."

This is the whole record of the family of Robert Tower as found in the Hingham parish records, and the name of Tower is nowhere else found in them, and all attempts to find the ancestry of Robert Tower have been unsuccessful.

The name is a significant one, and we find it in other parts of England, in Scotland, Wales, and Ireland ; but in most cases the name is spelled with the terminal "s," — "Towers," — and in Scotland we meet with the spelling "Towar." Descendants of the families of these several localities are now to be found in this country ; but by far the greater part who bear the name are the descendants of John Tower, and these have preserved the ancestral spelling of the name for more than two hundred and fifty years, with only occasional corruptions in spelling and pronunciation, — as in "Tour" and "Tore."

That the parents of John Tower were in comparatively humble circumstances in life we may infer from the fact that they failed to give their only child so much instruction as would enable him to write his name ; or else his omission to write his name to the various instruments he was called upon to execute during his long and somewhat eventful life must have arisen from some physical cause or accident. His contemporaries in emigration, many of whom were born and reared in the same parish, were for the most part instructed in the elements of knowledge ; they could write, and some of them with an elegance of penmanship not surpassed at the present day. The earlier records, both of the proprietors and town, bear evidence of this.

The causes which led John Tower to leave a comfortable home in England for the hardships of a life in the wilderness, were probably those which induced so many others to emigrate during the period between 1630 and 1640. The story has been so often told in history that it is only necessary to mention it briefly in a personal narrative.

The long contest both in civil and ecclesiastical affairs in England must reach a result either in suppression or success. The advocates for a change seemed to see their opportunity in emigration, and embraced it. Among the parishes in sympathy with the Puritanic movement was that of Hingham, where Robert Peck had been installed as rector a few years before John Tower was born, and under whose ministry John Tower had passed the whole period of his life.

Robert Peck had become so decided in the expression of his opinions as to call for admonition and reform from his superior, Bishop Wren; and under the more forceful administration of Laud, he was reduced to the alternative of submission or flight. He chose the latter, and with many of his parishioners, among whom was John Tower, came to New England in 1637. The chronicler says that many of these sold out their possessions at a great sacrifice. It does not appear from any record what the possessions of John Tower were. In this emigration it was the practice of young men who wished to come, and who were without the means to defray the expense of a passage and to establish themselves, to bind themselves to service to others in better condition for these purposes. The ancestors of some of our now opulent people came into New England as servants.

John Tower, however, seems to have had means sufficient to pay his passage, and to establish himself in the colony.

In a record kept by Daniel Cushing, a town clerk, who made many records of the early settlement of Hingham and of those who came from England, we find the following : —

"1637 — John Tower and Samuel Lincoln came from Old Hingham, and both settled at New Hingham."

A few persons were here as early as 1633, but large accessions were made in 1635 by people from Old Hingham and from neighboring parts of Norfolk county, — when a church was gathered, and the proprietors received from the colony a grant of the land in the limits of the township.

The Rev. Peter Hobart had been called to be the pastor of the church. He was a few years the senior of John Tower, was born in the same parish, educated at, and graduated from, Magdalen College, and seems to have imbibed under the ministrations of his teacher, Robert Peck, the Puritanic sentiment of religious faith and practice.

When John Tower arrived in New England he was not a stranger to the people among whom he came. Some were of his own parish, — among whom all the years of his life had been passed, and among whom he was to live through all the rest of his life, — and the following year many more came, the most of them from Old Hingham.

The land within the township was granted to those designated as proprietors, which included all such as should thereafter be admitted ; and these lands were given or granted to the several proprietors by vote, and the vote, being recorded in the proprietors' records, is the evidence of the grant and the title to the land.

These lands were granted for several and distinct purposes, which grew out of their situation and want. They needed a compact settlement for social and religious purposes, — they had been accustomed to village life in Old England for many generations,— and for suitable and mutual aid in protection from the savages they must live near together.

A colonial ordinance limited the granting of house-lots to a distance of half a mile from the meeting-house. In the laying out of the house-lots in Hingham this ordinance received such liberal interpretation as to extend about one mile. John Tower's house-lot was about one fourth of a mile from the meeting-house. These house-lots were limited in size to the supposed wants of the occupants, varying from three to ten acres. John Tower had a lot of three acres, sufficient for a residence and centrally situated, but of little value for agricultural purposes. For this latter and most important purpose, lands of greater extent were granted to all to whom house-lots were granted.

These lots were at a distance varying from one to three miles from the house-lot. As the earlier settlers of Massachusetts brought with them a stock of cattle, the lands which would furnish these cattle with an immediate supply of food were of the greatest value. These lands were the salt meadows bordering upon the many indentations of the sea, and the fresh meadows bordering upon the running streams, and where the industrious beaver had by constructed dams converted wooded swamps into a condition for bearing crops of coarse and luxuriant grass. As these lands were quite limited in area, they were granted in small parcels, that all might be accommodated. There was another value these lands had, in the long and coarse grass which grew upon the immediate banks of the creeks, and which was used for thatching the roofs of the earlier dwellings.

It is to be understood that these lands were granted without any consideration, except the terms as expressed in the several votes of the proprietors, and were to be held in fee-simple, free from conditions of servitude, and subject to the obligations as the proprietors had made by their recorded votes, as follow : —

1635, Sept. 18–28. " It is agreed upon that every man that is admitted to be a townsman and have lots granted them shall bear charges both to church and commonwealth proportionable to their abilities, and in case they shall sell their lots they shall first tender them to the town ; and in case the town shall refuse to give what it shall be worth, or find a chapman to buy it, then it shall be lawful for them to sell it; always provided it be to an honest man that shall be placed into the said lot or lots."

" It is likewise agreed upon by a joint and general vote of the freemen that all cedar and pine swamps be in common, and preserved to the town's use, although any should fall into any man's lot."

The Proprietors' Records show the following grants of land as made to John Tower (page 68), 1637 : —

" The several parcels of land and meadow legally given unto John Tower by the town of Hingham.

" Given unto John Tower by the town for a house-lot, three acres of land lying on Bachelor Street, bounded with the land of William Ludkin,

Northwestward, and with the land of Thomas Shaw, Southeastward, butting upon the street Eastward, and upon the common Westward.

"Given unto John Tower by the town for a great lot, ten acres of land lying upon the great plain in the first furlong to the eastward of the centre, butting upon the highways eastward and westward, bounded with the land of John Tucker Northward, and with the land of Thomas Barnes southward.

"Given unto John Tower by the town for a planting lot, three acres of land lying in the plain neck, and one acre more at the end of the same for an addition, bounded with the land of William Ludkin southwestward, and with the land of Henry Rust northeastward, butting upon the common northward and southward."

"Given unto John Tower by the town, one acre and half of Salt Marsh on the north side of Layford Lyking river, next unto Ralph Woodward."

This last-named grant John Tower lost through the failure of the Hingham proprietors to maintain their title to the same against the Hull proprietors, in an issue before the colonial authorities. He received satisfaction for the loss by the following grant : —

"1647. Given unto John Tower by the town, one acre and half of Salt Marsh at Conyhassett : it is the 29 lot in the first division, bounded with the meadow of James Buck northward, and with the meadow of Daniel Cushing westward, and with the cove, Eastward and Southward, — which meadow was given for satisfaction for meadow given him at Nantascutt.

"1647. Given unto him one acre of Salt Marsh at Conyhassett. It is the 30th lot in the third division, bounded with the meadow of Mr. Bozoon Allen northward, and with the meadow of Matthew Hawke southward ; with the river eastward, and with the town's land westward ; and he is to have all the abovesaid parcels of land and meadow to him and his heirs forever, be they more or less, as they were measured.

"1649. Given unto John Tower by the town, a small parcel of upland lying between Bachelor Street and the Salt Marsh of Thomas Loring."

John Tower does not appear to have built a house upon the lot granted him for that purpose by the town, as he sold it the next year. We find in the town records the following : —

"1638. Edward Cooper have bo't three acres of upland of John Tower, next to William Ludkin, which was given him by the town for a house-lot."

In this same year, 1638, John Tower made purchase of several parcels of land of Thomas Shaw, who owned the adjoining house-lot, and upon which he had erected a house, but who had removed to Barnstable, in Plymouth Colony. This sale appears upon the Town Records, and it would seem that the sale was satisfactory to the town, and that the provisions of the vote in making the grant of the land had been complied with in obtaining for a purchaser "an honest man." The deed of the several parcels of land was made many years subsequent to the sale, for in the Suffolk Records of Deeds, book 8, page 146, and dated June 30, 1665, is found recorded the deed of Thomas Shaw to John Tower, conveying the several parcels of land as they appear in the town records in 1638. The deed is acknowledged before Thomas Hinckley, assistant in the government of New Plymouth, and recorded May 10, 1673, thirty-five years after the sale. It recites as follows : —

" Thomas Shaw, sometime of Hingham, but now of Barnstable, in the Gov. of New Plymouth, planter, in consideration of a valuable sum of money conveys to John Tower, of Hingham, yeoman, 'All that my dwelling house and house lot adjoining to it, with another parcel of planting ground, and my great lot, as also a parcel of marsh Meadow, all lying and being in Hingham aforesaid, and as it was given and granted to me by the inhabitants of the said Hingham, together with all and singular the profits, common, privileges, and appurtenances to all and every the said premises belonging or any ways appertaining, the said house lot lying or being at the place there commonly called Bachelor's Street, and containing three acres, be it more or less, bounded northwestward by the land of said John Tower, southeastward with the land of Joseph Phippen, southwestward by the common, and northeastward by said Bachelor Street. The other parcel of planting land aforesaid, lying and being at a place called the "Old Planters' Hill," containing three acres, be it more or less, bounded southerly by the land of Joseph Andrews, westerly by the sea, easterly by the land of Thomas Wakely, and northerly by the lands of Thomas Wakely, — my great lot aforesaid, lying and being at the place there commonly called the great plain, and containing twelve acres, be it more or less, bounded easterly, westerly, and southerly by the highway, and northerly by the lands of Thomas Chubbuck, — and the parcels of Marsh meadow aforesaid, lying and being at the place commonly called the home meadow, containing three acres, be it more or be it less, bounded northerly by the cove, westerly by the upland, southerly by the Marsh of Thomas Loring, and easterly by the cove.' "

Other grants and purchases of lands were made to and by John Tower, which will be noticed as we proceed. He also sold lands, though but few of these sales are found in the records.

That John Tower was in sympathy with the whole movement which led to the settlement of New England will appear from the fact that on Dec. 13, 1638, he made application to be made a free-man of the Massachusetts Bay Colony. As none but members of the churches could be admitted as freemen, it would appear that he had qualified himself for admission, as his application was granted on the 13th of March, 1638–9.

He had already taken some part in the business of the town, and had been joined with some of the principal inhabitants in a committee for important business, as the record recites : —

"1638, Dec. 5. By a joint consent and general vote the freemen have chosen and deputed Mr. Joseph Hull, Anthony Eames, Samuel Ward, John Porter, and Joseph Andrews to Join with John Otis and John Tower, as they were measured, to lay out the great lots to the eastward of the river in order with 'convenientsie' as may be, with all expedition."

Pending the petition of John Tower for admission to the free-dom of the colony, another petition of more importance to this genealogy had been granted, as appears by Rev. Peter Hobart's record, wherein, under date of Feb. 13, 1638–9, we find : "John Tower and Margaret Ibrook married at Charlestown."

Margaret Ibrook was the daughter of Richard Ibrook, of whom we have but brief account. He was among the early settlers of Hingham, having a grant of a house-lot on what is now Lincoln Street, but known in the earlier records as "Broad Cove." The two lots next to his northward were granted to William Cockram and to William Cockerill, respectively, who appear to be sons-in-law of Richard Ibrook.

Richard Ibrook came to Hingham with his wife — whose name I have been unable to learn — and three unmarried daughters, — Ellen, Margaret, and Rebecca. Ellen married Joshua Hobart, a brother of Rev. Peter Hobart, 1638 ; Margaret married John Tower, as above ; and Rebecca married Rev. Peter Hobart. She was his second wife. There appear to be no means for finding the dates of the births of either Ellen or Margaret. Rev. Nehemiah Hobart, a grandson of Rev. Peter and Rebecca (Ibrook) Hobart, has the following among his records, namely : —

"1693, Sept. 9. Died my Hond Grandmother, Rebecca Hobart, ae. 73, lived in New England 55 years."

This would give the date of her coming 1638, three years sub-sequent to the date of the grant of a house-lot to her father.

The following records are found in Rev. Peter Hobart's Diary : —

"1642, Oct. 3 — Brother Cockram sayled for England."
"1651, Nov. 14 — Mr. Ibrook dyed."
"1664, April 4 — Mother Ibrook dyed."

Richard Ibrook left no son, and the name disappears as a surname and has been preserved as a given name among the descendants of his daughters, as Ibrook Tower, Ibrook Hobart, and Ibrook Whipple.

The fact that John Tower made a considerable purchase of land soon after his arrival, and made it for a valuable consideration, would show that he, like many others of the settlers of Hingham, was possessed of property in England, and that he, like them, was compelled to make large sacrifice in the sale of it.

And now, in the year 1639, at the age of thirty years, we find John Tower a member of one of the early towns of the Massachusetts Bay Colony, a member of the church gathered there, and brought by his marriage into relationship to the minister of it, and to his brother, a leader in the affairs of town, church and state, and a member of the chartered corporation to which he has been elected a freeman.

An inventory of his possessions in realty will show a house-lot centrally situated, on which is his dwelling-house, probably of limited dimensions and rude construction, with a thatch-covered roof, to which his bride will bring such household furnishings as maidens of that period were accustomed to prepare from wheel and loom for so reasonably an anticipated contingency. Next is his planting lot in the plain neck of four acres, more than a mile distant from his home, as the way then was. The salt-marsh of one and one-half acres on the north side of the river of quaint name, now known as Wear, or Weir, river, could be reached by land travel only by a circuitous route of some ten miles ; but as this soon passed from his possession, it was probably of little use to him. The salt-marsh given to him by the town instead of this, and another piece in the vicinity, were still farther from his home. The salt-marsh of three acres which he bought of Thomas Shaw was near his home, while the lot of three acres at " Old Planter's Hill " was about two miles away.

The great lots granted and purchased, containing together twenty-two acres, were more than two miles from his home. In addition to these he had a common right to the lands not granted. These lands as they became cleared of the forest were made available for the pasturage of cattle and sheep. As the planters brought much stock with them, we may suppose that John Tower had such supply as would enable him to carry on the work of subduing the forest and so cultivating the soil thus cleared as to supply the means of supporting his family.

To the business man of the present day it would appear that in the allotment of lands to the several inhabitants, of which John

Tower's is a very good illustration, all the laws of economy, in the expenditure of time and force in their cultivation, were set at defiance. The daily travel to and from these lands consumed no small portion both of time and energy, and became a total loss when these elements for subduing a wilderness were of so much importance. This sacrifice was made, as before stated, in obedience to former habits of life and work in England, the importance the early settlers attached to convenience for social religious worship, and the management of those common affairs which grew out of their new condition, and which taxed their ability to conduct. After the Pequot war of 1636, a year after the settlement of the town, the danger from the savages passed away for the period of more time than is allotted to one generation, and did not appear again until King Philip's war, in 1675; and this war, so devastating to all the colonies of New England, brought but little loss to the town of Hingham.

We can form some picture of the life of John Tower at this period when we think of him as occupying a home about midway in the settlement which extended irregularly about one mile on either side of him, whose inhabitants had common objects and common pursuits in subduing the wilderness and gaining a living from the products of the soil.

It was an aid to the settlers in the clearing of the land of forest that timber had an early value. The business of building vessels sprang into considerable importance in Boston soon after its settlement, and the ready means for transporting timber from Hingham to Boston by water gave the town advantages over other places before roads were constructed. The exception of the cedar and pine swamps in all particular grants shows the value placed upon that species of timber.

That John Tower engaged in this work of preparing timber, and that he and others, probably owing to imperfectly defined boundaries, trespassed upon the common land, would appear from the following order in the first volume of the Town Records : —

"1641, Sept. 4. — These bills be discharged for eight pence a tree, — John Tower, ten trees; Stephen Payne, six trees; George Lane, fifteen trees; Anthony Eames, four trees; Thomas Nichols, four trees; Nicholas Jacob, John Foulsham, thirty trees.

"It is likewise ordered and agreed upon that every tree that is not now brought in and submitted to the fine of eight pence a tree to the town's use, having so lawful a warning of their agreement, upon their tender shall pay ten shillings for every tree so proved according to the former order, although it be now repealed. Further, it is agreed that all those fines of

8 pence a tree are to be paid into the town's use by the 29th of September next, and are to be employed to the buying of a drum.

" All these have tendered themselves to the pleasure of the town of 8 pence a tree as followeth, — John Sutton, Thomas Barnes, Richard Osborne, Thomas Gill, Andrew Lane, for twenty oak-trees, and promise payment as aforesaid."

There had been a previous order passed, Feb. 20, 1640–41, in relation to the preservation of trees, —

" That from the date hereof, thenceforth there shall be no tree or trees cut or felled upon the way, upon the pain of twenty shillings, to be levied to the use of the town, because all good trees are to be preserved for the shading of cattle in the summer time, and for the exercising of the military affairs."

The passage of this order within five or six years of a settlement in the wilderness, together with the later one calling trespassers to account, indicates the value that the timber had reached, and the rapidity with which the work of clearing the land had been carried on.

The value of the price, eight pence, of a tree, and that of the fines imposed, will be seen by comparing these sums with the product of a day's work of a laborer as fixed by a colonial law.

" It is ordered that laborers shall not take above 12^d a day for their work, nor above 6^d and meat and drink."

It would require two thirds of a day's work of a laboring man to pay for a tree; and the severity of a fine of ten shillings will be appreciated when it is seen that it measures the value of ten days' work.

The conditions of the life of John Tower and of his fellow-townsmen may be imagined, by remembering how distant most of their lands, adapted to cultivation, were from their several homes, and the amount of travel involved in their ordinary rounds of daily industry.

On any bright, early morning would be seen emerging from their several homesteads all the able working male members of the family, with such force of teams as they might possess, wending their way to their respective allotments, making the old woods vocal with their varied forms of industry, in felling trees, preparing and hauling such as were suitable for building either houses or ships, to the several landings for transportation, making the land fit for cultivation by burning the brush and the wood worthless for timber, and with narrow and pointed harrows, constructed of logs, scarifying the surface, whereupon they scattered the seeds of rye, barley, and wheat, waiting in hope and patience for their fruition in fields of harvest. Following which came the heavy team-work of removing the stumps into huge heaps, that wind and sun might fit them for a holocaust of flame, leaving the land root-tenant-less for the plough, rude in construction, with mould-board thick studded in broad-headed nails and such scraps of iron as their scanty means might furnish; not easy of draught, but turning up the virgin soil to air and sunlight, and making it ready for that best of all New England crops, Indian corn, congenial to soil and climate, and stimulated to its growth by the migratory alewives, so opportune in season and abundant in supply as to warrant an especial grant of privilege by the order that "Thomas Loring, Clement Bates, Nicholas Jacob, and Joseph Andrews shall have the river called Layford's Liking, to build, erect, and set up a wear to take the fish that usually cometh into the said river, called by the name of alewives; . . . to charge the freemen 2/ 6^d per thousand for the fish," — with the provision that "the grant shall continue seven years." And that a fair distribution of this lively fertilizer might be enjoyed, the land in the vicinity of this wear was granted in small parcels, varying from one to five acres; John Tower having four acres, so that his transportation of this ferti-lizer was made convenient, while calling for some ten thousand fish for the suitable dressing of an acre of land at a cost of 25s., to be accounted for in a crop of fifty bushels to the acre, which at the oft-regulated price of 2s. per bushel would make a disburse-ment of the value of one fourth part of the crop for this fertilizing element in its production, — a rule of proportion recognized in New England for more than two centuries in the elements of the cost of a crop of Indian corn; namely, the use of the land, the preparation of the same, the fertilizer, and the labor of cultivation, — each severally representing one quarter part of the cost of the crop whenever disjointed capital and labor made bargain for mu-tual benefit, — an early recognition of the principle that labor should share in the profits of an undertaking whenever it became one of the instruments of production, and abandoned only when labor increased its demands beyond the power of capital to supply.

There seems to be nothing of importance to note during the five or six years following John Tower's marriage, excepting his giv-ing hostage of good citizenship to the commonwealth in the birth of three sons, who made their appearance with the accustomed regularity of the earlier New England families. We have every reason to suppose that he was improving his condition by his in-dustry, though from the daily travel of so long distances to the

place of labor much of that industry was wasted ; and it is a matter
of curiosity to the historian to note the fact that often in communities and people, habits of work and business which grew out of
necessity will continue long after the necessity has passed away,
even when the accustomed habit is attended with disadvantage
and loss ; and so for nearly two centuries the descendants of John
Tower and others continued to cultivate the lands of their ancestors after the primitive method, to be abandoned only when
the increased facilities for transportation from more fertile
regions made these lands valueless for cultivation as formerly
conducted.

In the year 1644 John Tower was involved with others of his
townsmen in a serious difficulty, to which not only the inhabitants of the town, but the whole colony, became parties, and
which raised important questions both in civil and ecclesiastical
affairs. The occasion of this difficulty was the election of a
person by the military company of the town, to be presented to
the colonial authorities for their approval.

It would seem that previous to this time the company had not
had a captain, but was under the command of Lieutenant Anthony
Eames ; but being directed to present one or more persons for the
office of captain, an election was held, and Lieutenant Eames was
chosen ; but before he received approbation or commission there
was some occasion of offence taken, whereupon the company chose
Bozoon Allen. Both of these were men of influence in the town
and church, and such only were deemed worthy to hold a military
office of the importance of a captain.

The friends or partisans of both Eames and Allen attended the
meeting of the next General Court and presented their respective
claims, evidently under much excitement of feeling. The General Court did not make an appointment, and the Hingham people
returned home, both parties apparently equally excited and un-
satisfied with the result, and bringing with them different and conflicting reports of the opinions of the magistrates and deputies.
Some of the magistrates appear to have favored Eames's claims on
account of his office and former service, thinking that Allen's
knowledge of military affairs was what he had obtained from
Eames, under whom he had been trained. The deputies however
were not so generally agreed to this, and so the matter was not
decided.

After their return home Allen's friends appointed a training-
day, — " without the lieutenant's knowledge," — and when they
were assembled, the lieutenant made his appearance and claimed
the authority to exercise them by virtue of his office. The major-

ity of the company refused to obey him, but recognized Allen as their commander, who exercised them two or three days.

In the dispute between Eames and his opponents, Eames was reminded of the advice given him by the magistrates that he " should go home and honorably lay down his authority." This Eames denied ; and the contest waxing warm, the lie was given.

The greater part of the contestants were freemen, and consequently members of the church, and the affair was taken cognizance of by the church. Among those most earnest in their opposition to Eames were Joshua Hobart and his two brothers, and all brothers of the minister, Peter Hobart, of whom Allen was an especial friend. In this hearing John Tower testified that one magistrate did advise Eames to lay down his authority, and at the conclusion of the hearing the minister was disposed to excommunicate Eames. Whereupon Eames made complaint to the magistrates, who sent warrant to the constable to attach the principal offenders, — John Tower, the three Hobarts, and one other, — and to bring them before the said magistrates. This being done, they were ordered to give bonds, with sureties, for their appearance. John Tower denied the authority of the court in the premises, and was accordingly committed and sent to prison.

Rev. Peter Hobart was so indignant at the arrest of his relatives by the magistrates in a matter which he considered purely ecclesiastical and within his own jurisdiction that he appeared before the magistrates' court and protested against the action of the court in sending the summons, and against their jurisdiction in the case, with so much vehemence that " the magistrates told him that were it not for respect to his ministry they would commit him."

Before the return day at the next magistrates' court, a session of the General Court was held, and a petition of Peter Hobart and eighty others of Hingham was presented, asking the court to consider the matter of the complaint of their petition, " to this effect, that whereas some of them had been bound over and others committed by some of the magistrates for words spoken concerning the power of the General Court, and their liberties and the liberties of the church," etc., and requesting the court to hear their case. Under this petition the court proceeded to hear the case, the deputy-governor (Winthrop) being made the defendant or impeached. To the charges of the petition the deputy-governor made answer, when the court proceeded to hear " the whole cause." The result of this hearing at the " meeting house in Boston," in the presence of " diverse of the elders and a great assembly of people," as stated by Winthrop, is as follows : —

"Two of the magistrates and many of the deputies were of opinion that the magistrates exercised too much power, and that the people's liberty was thereby in danger; and other of the deputies (being about half) and all the rest of the magistrates were of a different judgment, and that authority was overmuch slighted, which, if not timely remedied, would endanger the commonwealth and bring us to a mere democracy. By occasion of this difference there was not so orderly carriage at the hearing as was meet, each side striving unseasonably to enforce the evidence, and declaring their judgments thereupon. . . . So the best part of two days was spent in this public agitation and examination of witnesses, etc."

The magistrates and deputies in their several chambers spent much time and debate before they could reach any agreement. The magistrates were for censuring the petitioners and for imposing heavy fines upon "those who were bound over and others that were parties to the disturbance at Hingham," to which the deputies would not consent; but "the deputies being thus hard held to it, *and growing weary of the court,* for it began on the 14th of May and brake not up (save one week) till the 5" of July, finally compromised the matter, after refusing to join with the magistrates in calling in the help of the elders; "for they knew that many of the elders understood the cause, and were more careful to uphold the honor and power of the magistrates than themselves were liked of."

It would be interesting to the student of history to have a full sketch of the several findings of the magistrates and deputies upon the issues made in the case; but for the purpose of this personal biography it is proposed to present only what is necessary to show how John Tower was affected by them. To the magistrates' findings the deputies return as follows: —

10. "We find that the public charge and accusation of John Folsom and John Tower against the deputy-governor, the premises considered, are causeless and unjust, and that some things in the petition and explanation of it are false and scandalous, for which all the petitioners ought to receive their due censure.

"To the charge by John Folsom of the deputy-governor, 14 deputies assent that it is unjust, and 13 deputies dissent; 6 stand neuter."

"To the charge by John Tower of the deputy-governor 17 deputies vote the negative that his charge is not unjust, and 14 affirm, and 2 stand neuter."

And again the deputies return to the magistrates: —

"We find that Mr. Bellingham did legally give advice to Lieut. Eames, namely, that he, said Lieut. Eames, should go home and go into the field and honorably lay down his place, Capt. Robert Keayne, contrary, dissenting."

To this return of the deputies the magistrates reply : —

" To the 2ᵈ we answer, that what advise Mr. Bellingham gave according to his apprehension while the matter was in agitation was not illegal, but how legal or convenient it was to cross the advise of the magistrates and his own also, or whether it were so or no, we rather leave, that have heard it to consider of, than positively to determine it, not being, as we conceive, pertinent to the case as it concerns Mr. Bellingham."

1645, June 28. — The magistrates vote to fine certain of the persons engaged in the Hingham disturbance in several sums, varying from £2 to £20, John Tower being fined £5. They also impose a fine of 20s. each upon the petitioners, excepting therefrom three, " Mr. Peter Hobart, John Folsom, and John Tower ; " the aggregate of the fines being £155 10s.

The deputies do not agree to the magistrates' apportionment of fines, but present a list, wherein the aggregate of fines amounts to £105, John Tower's name not being in the list.

Further correspondence takes place between the magistrates and deputies, and as they fail to agree, arbitration is proposed ; but before this is agreed upon, the deputies present a new list, still continuing the fine of £5 to Lieutenant Eames, and " John Tower's censure for his delinquency is, that he should bear his imprisonment, provided he bear no other censure, either as petitioner or otherwise."

" The house of deputies do agree that £53 10s. should be laid upon all the petitioners by an equal rate by the poll towards the payment of the charge of the court upon the case, excepting John Tower and the rest of those delinquents that are fined as is above mentioned &c."

" The magistrates agree to these fines above mentioned all but for Lieut. Eames, whom we judge to bear his own charge and have an admonition for laying down his place without consent of authority and other failings."

"The deputies do concur with our honored magistrates' last return concerning Lieut. Eames rather than nothing be imposed upon him."

And thus ended this case by the imposition of fines and the acquittal of the deputy-governor. Something more grew out of it in the process of collecting the fines, but nothing immediately affecting John Tower, only as his sympathy may have been enlisted for his brother-in-law, Rev. Peter Hobart, who continued still to raise questions, as John Tower had done, as to the authority of the court, for which he was arrested and heavily fined.

The questions raised in this trial are of great interest to the student of history, but are not suitable for a discussion here, except as they have a bearing upon John Tower's case and the offence he is charged with committing, with the degree of blame then held to pertain to the offence. He is charged with causing the disturbance by the testimony he gave in the church, and by his contempt of authority in refusing to give bond for his appearance, and for signing the petition bringing charges against the deputy-governor.

To understand the degree of guilt incurred by the commission of these offences in the early period of the history of the Massachusetts Bay Colony, it will be necessary to remember how it was constituted by its charter, which gave authority for the choice of governor and assistants by the freemen of the corporation. These were first chosen in England, and came to New England, bringing their charter with them. The governor, assistants, and freemen were authorized to make rules and regulations for the government of those who should come to inhabit the colony, " for the imposition of lawful fines, mulcts, imprisonments, or other lawful correction according to the course of other corporations in this our realm of England."

" Willing, commanding, and requiring . . . That all such orders, statutes, and ordinances, instructions and directions as shall be so made by the governor, deputy-governor of the said company, and such of the assistants and freemen as aforesaid, and published in writing under the common seal, shall be carefully and duly observed, kept, and performed, and put in execution according to the true intent and meaning of the same."

But from the first the assistants seemed inclined to take to themselves all the authority belonging to themselves and the freemen, without consulting the freemen.

The first court was a court of assistants, and was held at Charlestown, Aug. 23, 1630 ; and among the orders passed was the following very important one : —

" It was ordered that the governor and deputy-governor shall always be justices of the peace, and that Sir Richard Salstonstall, Mr. Johnson, Mr. Endicot, and Mr. Ludlow shall be justices of the peace for the present time, in all things to have like power that justices of peace hath in England for reformation of abuses and punishing of offenders, and that any justice of the peace may imprison an offender, but not inflict any corporal punishment without the presence and consent of some one of the assistants."

1630, Oct. 19, a General Court was held, whereat, contrary to the charter, power is conferred upon the governor, deputy-governor, and assistants to make laws and choose officers to execute them. The court of assistants soon exercise their conferred authority, and in a number of cases they make the law and punish a breach of it at the same time.

It is evident that the authorities mean to be obeyed and respected, and some of the severest penalties are inflicted upon those who dare to oppose or call in question their authority; as at a court of assistants, May 3, 1631, —

"Thomas Walford of Charlestown is fined 40s. and is enjoined he and his wife to depart out of the limits of this patent before the 20th day of October next, under pain of confiscation of his goods for his contempt of authority and confronting of officers."

It must be said to the credit of the impartiality of this court that one of their number, the fiery and pugnacious Endicott, is tried by a jury and assessed in damages of 40s. for "battery" on Thomas Dexter.

1631, June 14. — At a court of assistants, "It is ordered that Philip Ratliffe shall be whipped, have his ears cut off, fined £40, and banished out of the limits of this jurisdiction, for uttering malicious and scandalous speeches against the government and church of Salem, as appeareth by a particular thereof proved upon oath."

1631, Sept. 6. — At a court of assistants, "It is ordered that Henry Lyon shall be whipped and banished the plantation, before the 6th day of October next, for writing into England falsely and maliciously against the government and execution of Justice here.

"Thomas Knower was set in the bilbowes for threatening the court that if he should be punished, he would have it tried in England whether he was lawfully punished or not."

1632, Oct. 3. — "Edward Burton is fined £5 for his contempt of authority in refusing to come to court when summoned by the governor, and 40s. for drunkenness."

1633, Sept. 3. — "Capt. John Stone, for his outrage in confronting authority, abusing Mr. Ludlow, both in words and behavior, assaulting him and calling him a 'just ass,' is fined £100 and prohibited coming within the patent without leave from the government, under penalty of death."

1634, April 1. — "It is ordered that John Lee shall be whipped and fined for calling Mr. Ludlow false-hearted knave and hard-hearted knave, etc."

So far the court of assistants seems to have carried on the work of government without any code of laws or of procedure, adapting penalties to the several cases as the discretion of the court might see fit, imposing the heavier penalty upon any one who should be impelled by a sense of injustice suffered to give expression to his feelings as to the decision, or to the magistrate who makes the decision.

It is necessary to know the value and power of the money of the times to appreciate what the fines measure. This can be done by comparing them with the value of a laboring man's day's work as fixed by the same authority, which was 12*d*. a day. Therefore a fine of 40*s*. for drunkenness inflicted upon Edward Burton would represent forty days' work; while his fine of £5 for contempt of authority would represent a hundred days' work, — sufficient, one would suppose, effectually to guard the most exacting magistrate from an undue measure of suffering, were it not for the often recurrence of these entries in the earlier records.

What was the exercise of authority by Mr. Ludlow which threw the valiant Captain Stone into so much of manifest disrespect as to result in the fine of £100 — representing nearly seven years of a laboring man's work — and banishment from the colony, does not appear of record; but it does appear that there was a conflict going on between the principal men, including the magistrates and the great body of the freemen. The former seemed to be moving to establish and carry on the new government by and through an aristocracy of talent and wealth, while the great body of the freemen were not content to be shut out from their share in its conduct; and in 1634, at the General Court held in May, several agreements were made, curtailing the power of the magistrates and the exercise of it in the magistrates' courts. It was ordered —

" That none but the General Court hath power to make and establish laws, nor to elect and appoint officers, as governor, deputy-governor, assistants, secretary, captain, lieutenants, ensigns, or any of like moment, or to remove such upon misdemeanor, as also to set out the duties and powers of the said officers.

" That none but the General Court hath power to raise moneys and taxes, to dispose of lands, uses, to give and confirm proprieties."

It would seem that some of the more recent acts of the court of assistants had given occasion for these and some other orders; as —

" It is agreed that there shall be £10 fine set upon the court of assistants and Mr. Mayhew for breach of an order of court against employing Indians to shoot with pieces, the one half to be paid by Mr. Pynchon and Mr. Mayhew, offending therein, the other half by the court of assistants then in being, who gave leave thereunto."

This fine of £10 was remitted by the court.

The severity of Captain Stone's punishment would seem to be the occasion of the order, —

"It is agreed that no trial shall pass upon any for life or banishment but by a jury summoned [or by the General Court]. . . . It is likewise ordered that there shall be four General Courts held yearly, to be summoned by the governor for the time being, and not to be dissolved without the consent of the major part of the court."

This court seems to have resented an indignity offered to the governor ; as, —

"It is ordered that John Lee shall be whipped and fined £40 for speaking reproachfully of the governor, saying he was but a lawyer's clerk, and what understanding had he more than himself ; also taxing the court for making laws to pick men's purses," etc.

And at a later court, Nov. 7, 1634, mercy was blended with justice in the order, — "There is £30 of John Lee's fines remitted him."

But still the offences against the magistrates continue, and at the next General Court —

"It is ordered that Mr. Israel Stoughton shall be disabled for bearing any public office in the Commonwealth within this jurisdiction, for the space of three years, for affirming the assistants were no magistrates."

It is very evident from the foregoing extracts that the members of the Massachusetts Bay Colony, and those subjected to its authority, were not satisfied with the method of its management, or the seemingly arbitrary rules to which its conduct was subjected, and that there was call for the establishment of some fundamental rules.

In an article written by Francis C. Gray, and published in the Massachusetts Historical Collections, 3d series, vol. viii., this matter is ably presented, showing how these rules, or "Body of Liberties," had their rise, progress, and completion, after several years of agitation and delay. This delay was caused principally by the magistrates, and was occasioned, in part, by doubts whether the provisions of the charter could be construed to warrant the establishment of such rules, and whether an attempt to do this might not cause a revocation thereof, together with the tendency among the magistrates to continue a form of government so largely dependent upon their wisdom.

It was fortunate for the Massachusetts Bay Colony that John Winthrop was governor when the charter, with the attendant large immigration, came to its shores. He had been brought up to a knowledge of law in England, was puritanic in his principles, and mellowed more than usual with a mild and humane spirit. For the good of the colony he made large sacrifices of time and wealth, and of his stores of wisdom and experience he gave freely. He knew the limitations of power given by the charter, and that to frame the ideal government he and his associates dreamed of, would lead to its revocation so soon as authority in England should take notice of it. What they had already done had led to the issue of the warrant by which they were called to show cause in the king's court why it should not be revoked. Nothing but the growing trouble between the king and parliament, and the subsequent condition of civil war, prevented its loss.

Winthrop would have such rules as were necessary grow up by practice as their wants demanded, without embodying them into written laws, trusting to the wisdom and integrity of the administrators that no one should suffer wrong ; and in default of their own wisdom they could appeal to the laws of God, and by the help of the learned and pious ministers they had means for their interpretation.

But such a plan for the growth of a people was not to come so easily. Contention for principles and forms would come in, and all the repressing force of fines and punishments could not keep out their expression ; and the age was not one to tolerate freedom of expression. Truth in civil and ecclesiastical affairs was a matter not to be tolerated in progress, but to be reached in its end ; and being once arrived at and secured, was no further to be questioned.

It has been seen how the suppression of expression had been attended by severe punishments and heavy penalties, imposed by the magistrates without any fixed rules, until the people had become somewhat restless ; and at a court, May 6, 1635, —

"The deputies having conceived great danger to our state, in regard that our magistrates for want of positive laws in many cases might proceed according to their discretion, it was agreed that some men should be appointed to frame a body of grounds of laws, in resemblance to a Magna Charta, which being allowed by some of the ministers and the General Court, should be received for fundamental laws."

But such was the opposition of the magistrates that nearly eight years passed before the Body of Liberties, prepared by Rev. Nathaniel Ward, of Ipswich, was finally adopted, and became the fundamental law of the colony under the charter.

In 1644 — the year in which the difficulty at Hingham took place — another important change was made in the colonial government.

The assistants and deputies had formerly sat in the same chamber and voted as one body ; but the memorable trial of the claims of Captain Keayne and of the widow Saunders to the same pig caused these two bodies to divide and sit in separate chambers, and to have a negative vote upon each other in case of disagreement.

In considering the Hingham case it is important to keep in mind this disagreement between the deputies, representing the great body of the freemen, and the magistrates, who for the most part were of the wealthy and influential families of the colony, and who by their abilities and character had given direction to all the colonial affairs, and whose heavy fines and severe punishments had repressed opposition to their authority.

As the difficulty at Hingham began in military affairs, and became transferred to the church, it is of importance to know what the rules and regulations were in relation to both. In military affairs, as in all others, the assistants from the first in their court — composed of the governor, deputy-governor, and assistants, and denominated the court of assistants — assumed the whole regulation. But in 1634, as has already been stated, the General Court had resumed the appointment of the military as well as other officers, — though subsequently they delegated this authority to the council for life when the General Court was not in session.

From the beginning there seems to be large demand for military preparation and exercise, —

"1631, April 12. It is ordered that every captain shall train his company on Saturday in every week."

"1631, July 26. — Order for a watch in Boston, and for a monthly training of Capt. Underhill's company in Boston and Roxbury, and also for those in Charlestown and Mystic."

"1631–32, March 6. — Order for the arming of every person under a penalty of a year's service in default."

"1632, Nov. 7. — Several are fined for absence at training or for their men being absent ; among them are Mr. Matthew Cradock's men at divers times."

"1633, Nov. 5. — Ensign Morris is discharged of his place, and Mr. Thomas Mootham chosen in his room. Sergeant Stoughton is chosen· Ensign to Capt. Mason."

"1633–4, March 4. — Mr. Nathaniel Turner is chosen Captain of the military company at Saugus. . . . Mr. Richard Morris is chosen Lieutenant to Capt. Underhill."

1634, May. — The General Court having resumed the functions belonging to it, —

"Mr. Robert Harding, William Baulston, and Ralph Sprague are chosen Sergeants to Capt. Underhill and John Oliver, chosen Corporal to the said Captain."

"1634, Sept. 3. — Capt. Underhill, Capt. Patrick, Capt. Mason, Capt. Frask, Capt. Turner, Lieutenant Feakes, and Lieut. Morris appointed a committee."

"It is ordered that the captains shall train their bands once every month, giving a week's warning before (except in July and August), and that the captains shall have liberty to train all such unskilful men as are at their own hands so often as they please, provided that they exceed not three days in a week.

" Sergeant Perkins is chosen Ensign to the company at Roxbury.

" It is ordered that every captain shall be maintained by his own company ; and where any company consists of two towns or more, the several towns shall contribute to the maintenance of that captain proportionally to the number of soldiers in town."

"1634, Sept. 25. — Mr. Edward Gibbons is chosen Ensign to Capt. Underhill. . . . It is ordered that Lieut. Morris shall train the company at Roxbury."

And that military officers shall be properly submissive and respectful to the authority which has created them, —

" It is ordered that Ensign Jennison shall be fined the sum of £20 for upbraiding the court with injustice, uttering these words: ' I pray God deliver me from this court ; ' professing he had waited from court to court, and could not have justice done him."

" 1634. Nov. 7. — Mr. John Benjamin, William Pancry, and Henry Goldston are (by reason of their age and infirmities) dismissed from training, only they are to have in readiness at all times sufficient arms for themselves, besides for their servants."

" 1634–5, March 4. — It is ordered that all forfeitures for want of arms, or not observing training days, shall be distrained by the clerk of the band where the offence is committed, who, together with the captain and other officers, shall have power to buy therewith drum-heads and such arms as poor men want and are not able to provide themselves of.

" It is further ordered that every man of or above the age of sixteen years who hath been or shall hereafter be resident within this jurisdiction by the space of six months (as well servants, as others), and not enfranchised, shall take the oath of residents before the governor, deputy-governor, or two of the next assistants, who shall have power to convent him for that purpose, and upon his refusal, to bind him over to the next court of assistants, and upon his refusal the second time, to be punished at the discretion of the court.

" A committee " was " appointed to have full charge of all military affairs, the order to continue till the end of the next General Court.

" It is ordered, from this day forward the captains shall receive maintenance out of the treasury, and not from their companies."

" 1635, Sept. 2. The order whereby " military officers are to have their maintenance out of the treasury " is repealed. It is ordered that every company shall maintain their own officers.

" Further it was agreed that Charlestown and Watertown shall be two distinct companies, and to have officers of their own."

" 1636, Sept. 28. The commission for military affairs is committed to the standing council till the court in May next, and so forward until the General Court shall take other orders."

" 1636, Dec. 7. It is ordered that all military men in this Jurisdiction shall be ranked into three regiments; viz., Boston, Roxbury, Dorchester, Weymouth, Hingham, to be one regiment, whereof John Winthrop, senior, Esq.. shall be colonel, and Thomas Dudley, Esq., lieutenant-colonel, etc., and the governor for the time being shall be chief general. And each several regiment shall make choice of such men as they shall think most fit and safe for the service and trust of those places of colonel and lieutenant-colonel, and present them by their deputies to the next session of this court; and for the captains and lieutenants of the several companies the several towns shall make choice of some principal man, or two or three in each town, and present them to the council, who shall appoint one of them to the said office in each company."

" 1636–7, March 9. All persons of any trained band, both freemen and others, who have taken the oath of residents, or shall take the same, and being no covenant servant in household with any other, shall have their votes in nomination of those persons who are to be appointed captains or other inferior officers of the same band, provided they nominate none but such as shall be freemen; for it is the intent and order of the court that no person shall henceforth be chosen to any office in the commonwealth but such as is a freeman. Any one magistrate may administer the said oath.

" Order for watches to be kept in every town on account of danger from the Indians, to which every person above the age of 18 years is subject (except magistrates and elders of churches)."

" 1637, Apr. 18. Apportionment of 160 soldiers for the Pequot war among the several towns — Capt. Traske and Lieut. Davenport to have command.

" Mr. John Spencer is discharged from being captain at Newbury, and Edward Woodman is chosen lieutenant at Newbury. Several orders in relation to the conduct of the expedition against the Pequots, and commanders chosen."

" 1637, Nov. 2. The court did discharge Capt. Underhill for any further service, and gave him a quarter's pay for a gratuity.

" Capt. Underhill, being convented for having his hand to the seditious writing, is disfranchised, and put off the captain's place."

" 1637, Nov. 20. Fifty-nine persons in Boston, and seventeen in other towns, disarmed, on account of the dangerous errors into which they were supposed to be led, etc."

" 1638, June 8. The military company of Boston may present two or three to the council to choose a captain out of them, if the council like them."

" 1640, July 30. John Tower for his disturbance of the peace, and the offence thereby against the Commonwealth, is fined five pounds."

This was at a " quarter court," or court of assistants. The record does not show any particular act of John Tower by which the peace was disturbed.

" 1640, Oct. 7." Ordering the number of trainings in the year to be ten, and following to the year 1644, there are several orders of the court, regulating the duty of the companies, providing fines for neglect of trainings and failure in equipments, and allowing the companies to select such times for training, as shall best suit their convenience, and give as little loss of time in their agricultural pursuits as may be consistent with a proper perfomance of the military duty.

" 1643, May 10. It is ordered that warrants should be sent to the towns to send the nnmber of males from 16 years old to 60."

This continued to be the limit of age for military service for many years.

The foregoing extracts from the records in relation to military affairs in the earlier years of the colony will the better enable us to perceive the character and extent of offence given by the military company in Hingham, of which John Tower was a member. This unfortunate affair came to have in its progress another and fully as important a cause of offence, which brought the minister and the church of which John Tower was a member, and from his marriage connection with the minister, Peter Hobart, undoubtedly a sympathizer, into relations of offence with the authorities.

Just what the civil and ecclesiastical relations were in the colony it would be difficult to determine : the charter made no recognition of them ; and yet the establishment of churches and the institution of religious worship, according to doctrines and forms generally recognized, were paramount even to the ideal commonwealth they wished to found. The emigrants were mostly of that body of the church denominated Independents in England, recognizing every church gathered to be free to manage its own affairs, without any outside controlling ecclesiastical power. Anything from outside must come in the form of advice, and not in that of direction from other churches.

The civil power seems to have been exercised to protect the churches in what they generally agreed to recognize as fundamental truths, and to aid them in keeping these unimpaired by heretical opinions and practices.

All the freemen must be members of some of the churches, but all the members of the churches did not become freemen, and in consequence had no voice in the civil government and no vote in the choice of civil officers. So many of the church members failed to become freemen that the civil authorities made complaint to the churches, urging measures for its correction.

As the churches held and exercised the right of excommunicating any member for fault of doctrine or practice, and without any appeal, it raised the perplexing question whether a person excommunicated from the church was any longer a freeman, and if holding either civil or military office, whether his expulsion from the church must of necessity determine the tenure of his office.

That this or some other occasion did cause this question to be raised, will be seen by reference to the earlier colonial laws.

"Every church hath also free liberty of admission, recommendation, dismission, and expulsion or disposal of their officers and members upon due cause, with free exercise of the discipline and censures of Christ, according to the rules of the word."

This law was subsequently modified by this provision : —

"But no church censure shall degrade or depose any man from any civil dignity, office, or authority he shall have in the commonwealth."

This was a very grave question, and probably the moving cause of feeling and action on the part of the magistrates, making it of more consequence than the military part of the matter. There is nothing of record of any particular act of John Tower in the military proceedings ; but we may infer that he was in sympathy with his brother-in-law, Joshua Hobart, the principal offender, and upon whom the heaviest fine was imposed. But he seems to have been censured for the testimony he gave in the church and, in common with the others, for being a petitioner.

Under the orderly proceedings of courts as they are now constituted for the trial of offences it seems somewhat difficult to understand the proceedings of the General Court in the Hingham case. Under the petition, Winthrop, the deputy-governor, was put upon trial, he claiming that he might have pleaded to the petition and demurred in law, yet consented to the trial, and was acquitted. One would suppose that that would be the end of the proceedings, and that the court of assistants would proceed to hear the case against John Tower and others who were before that court on complaint. Nothing, however, of this kind was done, but the General Court proceeded to pass upon the guilt or innocence of the petitioners, and to determine who should be convicted. But just what offence was found, does not appear from the record. A brief review of the military trouble will show that the company in Hingham, composed of all the male members of the town between the ages of sixteen and sixty, had so grown in numbers as to be a full company, independent of any other town, and entitled to be commanded by a captain, — an officer of great dignity and importance to those whom he should be called upon to command and instruct. It is seen that formerly the military officers had been chosen and appointed by the General Court ; but in 1636 a law was passed empowering the several companies to choose their own officers and present them to the General Court, or such committee as the General Court should appoint for their commissions. The companies were authorized to choose one, two, or three persons to be thus presented. The Hingham company first presented the name of Lieutenant Eames, who had held that office for several years ; but becoming dissatisfied with that nomination, they sent another name, Bozoon Allen, which would seem to be in compliance with the law. Moreover, the law says that " the council *shall* appoint one of them." This the Council and the General Court neglected to do. It seems that the people of Hingham had become greatly excited in the matter of their proposed captain, and numbers of both parties attended the session of the General Court to urge the claims of their respective candidates. The magistrates and deputies were at variance. The former thought it would be a slight to Eames to have him passed over; while the latter, seeing so large an expression of feeling and so many in numbers for Allen, believed it for the best that this expression should be regarded ; and so nothing was done. The parties came home, bringing different reports of what the magistrates and deputies had said in the case; and acting upon these, much irregularity and tumult took place in the training of the company and in matters of speech, so unworthy of members of the same church as to call for such action as churches were authorized to take by law.

It would be difficult to show, under any provision of law then existing, that the court of assistants had jurisdiction in church matters ; but the law did give the church full and exclusive jurisdiction therein. The testimony which John Tower gave in the church that " authority did advise Lieut. Eames to lay down his place, and that one magistrate did advise him to do so," is fully confirmed by the finding of the deputies, with only one dissenting vote. It will be seen that the magistrates evade this finding and refuse to consider it, and yet they propose to fine John Tower £5 for bearing testimony to it. To this the deputies will not agree, and so the fine is not imposed. In the imposition of the costs of the court upon the petitioners, three being excepted, of whom John Tower is one, the General Court evidently do not intend to encourage the making of complaints against the exercise of authority. In the great contest which John Quincy Adams carried on in the House of Representatives at Washington, vindicating the right of petition, this effectual way of suppressing such petitions, by assessing the cost of entertaining them upon the petitioners, never seemed to occur to his opponents, and Mr. Adams did not probably enlighten them as to this early case in the history of his State.

It is a little remarkable in this very singular trial before the General Court that while Winthrop is fully acquitted, John Tower is exempt from all imposition of fine and costs, to which the rest are subjected and to which he was similarly liable. Because he had suffered imprisonment, he is allowed to offset so much of fine and cost by so much of imprisonment, thus showing that the imprisonment was unwarranted; at the same time the magistrate who inflicted it is sustained for the act.

In bringing the already lengthy presentation of this case to a close, it may be proper to say that the military company in Hingham was still further proceeded against by a denial of its right to a captain; neither was Lieutenant Eames vindicated by the continuance of his authority as lieutenant, but the company was put under the charge of Lieutenant Torrey, of Weymouth. This continued about one year, when Major Gibbons was ordered to take charge of the company. He commanded it for a few years, when the company was once more restored to favor, and permitted to elect its officers, which it proceeded to do by the choice of the same Bozoon Allen for captain, and the heavily fined Joshua Hobart as lieutenant, soon after to succeed Allen as captain.

The early settlers in the several towns on the coast of Massachusetts Bay do not seem to have remained wholly satisfied with their situation, but were often looking into the great wilderness beyond for more favorable places for settlement, where they could find upon the streams wide expanse of meadow, prolific of food for their cattle. It is true these settlements were exposed to danger from the savages, and did suffer severely; but the more adventurous colonists took this risk for the advantages which they afforded. In 1653 Lancaster was incorporated. A number of the early settlers were from Hingham, Scituate, and Weymouth, and in 1654 John Tower's name is found among them. He was probably there then, but did not remain. The following agreement is found upon the Lancaster records: —

"That such of them as were not inhabitants, and who were not yet come up to build, improve, and inhabit, would by the will of God come up to build, plant, and inhabit within a year, otherwise to forfeit all they had expended, forfeit also their land, and pay five pounds for the use of the plantation."

This was signed by "John Towers," April 18, 1654. He does not seem to have proceeded any further in this matter. We next find him engaged in an enterprise of some importance as an undertaking, though in its results it did not bring any pecuniary advantage to him, but rather entailed loss. This was the purchase of a tract of land from the Indians in what is now the State of Rhode Island. A copy of the first deed is here given. There are four other deeds, and the quantity of land embraced within the descriptions in the several deeds is about twenty-four square miles. This land would appear to be within what are now the towns of Cranston, Scituate, and Johnston.

Know all men to Whom Theis p'sents shall come That we Petnowatuk, Mattarnnahamen, Woumpapagun, Sepatanchihimit, living upon and belonging to a certain tract of Land, caled by the name of Toushkenuck, have for a good and valuable consideration by us In hand Reaceaved and pay'd by John Tower of Hingham in the Matathussetts, Wherewith we doe acknowledge ourselves to be fully Contented and satisfyed, have given, granted, Bargained, sould, Infefed and Confirmed, and by theis p'sents doe give, grant, sell, Infef, and confirm Unto the above-mentioned John Tower, Senior, the aforesayd tract of Land as before specifyed Lying bounded as it doth further appear as by a Draught which the aforesayd Indians made and confirmed under their hands, Containing two Miles Broade, bounded by Pautuxsitt River, and to begin at a place called Mossonakisett, and so to run two miles by Pautuxsitt River, and to run three miles in Length, the bound & Runing withe Midest of the River called Mokshontatak River, unto the aforesayd John Tower, Senior, and to his heirs forever. And we the aforesayed Petnowatuk, Matavnnahamen, Woumpapagun, and Sepatanchihimit doe covenant and grant by these p'sents That we, the aforesayd Indians, are the true and proper owners of the aforesayd Barganed premises at the Tyme of the Bargan and Salle thereof, and that the aforesayd premises, with all the apurtenances, are free and Cleare and frely and clearlye aquitted, exonarited and discharged for and from all former bargans, sales, gifts, grants, titels, Morgages, and Ingagm'ts, and farly aquitted of and for all manner of Salles, Actions, Atachm'ts, Judgm'ts, executions, and Incombrances whatsoever that may Arise conserning the same. And we the aforsayd Petnowatuk, Matavnnahamen, Woumpapagum, and Sepatanchihimit doe covenant and grant by these p'sents for us and our heires all the aforesayd premises, with thir apurtnances, to warrant, aquitt, and defend against all persons whatsoever that may lay clame and Challeng any Way to the Mollestation of the aforesayd John Tower & fre possession of the same, according to Those premises and p'sent. And that it is and shall be lawful for the Sayd John

Tower or his heirs or assignes to Inrole and Record or cause to be Inroled and Recorded The tittell an tenor of theis p'sents according to the true intent and meaning thereof. And according to Usual Manner [worn away] and Recording deeds and Covenants made and proved ; in Witness we the sayd Petnowatuk, Matarnnahamen, Woumpapagun, Sepatanchihmit, have hereunto set our hands and Seales This seavententh day of June, one thousand six hundred and sixty one.

Sealled and dellived	The ♂ Mark
in the p'sence of us	of Petnowatuk [Seal]
	The M Mark
JOSEPH PECK, Senior	of Matarnnahamen [Seal]
NATHANIEL BAKER	The ⚓ Mark
WILLIAM CARPENTER.	of Woumpapagun [Seal]
	The ⊙ Mark
	of Sepatanchichimitt [Seal].

Nathaniel Baker came before me the 19th, 1st, 1662–3, and did Testifie upon oath that he see the Indians herein named Seale and deliver this Deed, whereunto he subscribed his name as wittnes. It was delivered to John Tower the elder.

RI. BELLINGHAM, *Dep. Gov*

Entered and recorded in the 375 & 376 pages of the third book of Records of the Notary Publicke of the Massachusetts Colonie of New England the 12th of March, 1662.

p. ROBERT HOWARD, *Not : publ. colonia p'd.*

It appears that the lands conveyed to John Tower by the Indians had other claimants, who rested their title upon prior deeds from the Indians. The earliest deed was that of " Canonicus " and " Miantonomi " to Roger Williams. His associates, William Harris and others, claimed that Mr. Williams obtained this deed for them as well as for himself, he acting as their agent. After the description of the land there is this additional clause, —

" We do freely give unto him all that land from those rivers reaching to Pawtuxet river, as also the grass and meadows upon the said Pawtuxet river."

In 1659 the brother of Miantonomi, who was killed by Uncas in 1643, gave a confirmatory deed to the men of Providence and Pawtuxet ; namely, —

" All the lands between Pawtucket river and Pawtuxet river up the streams, without limit, for the use of cattle ; and I also do for summer and winter feeding of their cattle and ploughing, and all other necessary improvements, as for farms, and all manner of plantations whatsoever."

In the same year other Indians, describing themselves as chief sachems of the Indians of those parts, made a confirmatory deed to the same grantees of the same lands.

The Narragansetts, of whom these Indians were chiefs, were more advanced in the work of agriculture than any of the other Indian tribes in New England; and it seems that upon some parts of these lands granted by the chiefs there were individuals of the tribe residing who had cultivated the same. It was one of the theories of Roger Williams and his associates that the Indians had full title to the land, and that any title by patent from any European power was invalid unless confirmed by a deed from the Indians themselves, which could alone give good title to the purchasers. Whether all these Indians who granted lands to John Tower by their several deeds were chiefs of the tribe, does not appear. They are not the same who convey apparently the same lands to the men of Providence and Pawtuxet. Pumham, who signs one of John Tower's deeds, was a noted chief.

As a result of these conflicting claims, a controversy took place, and William Harris, representing the original proprietors, —

"In June, 1677, undertook a voyage to England to petition the King for the appointment of a special commission to hear and determine these claims. . . .

"In his petition he gives a summary of the difficulties and dangers that surrounded the Pawtuxet purchase. He states that he and his twelve partners had purchased the land about forty years before; that their purchase or parts of it were claimed by the town of Providence, the town of Warwick, the colony of New Plymouth, and two parties of the province of Massachusetts Bay. . . . All these various claims depended upon the extent of the original purchase of Providence. . . . The prayer of this petition was granted, and the governors of the four New England colonies were directed to appoint commissioners to hear the matter in dispute. The gentlemen appointed upon this commission were Thomas Hinckley and James Cudworth, of Plymouth; Simon Lynde and Daniel Henchman, of Massachusetts; George Dennison and Daniel Wetherel, of Connecticut; and John Coggeshall and Peleg Sanford, of Rhode Island. They met in Boston on the third of October, 1677, and empannelled a jury, — four of whom belonged to Massachusetts, two to Plymouth, three to Connecticut, and three to Rhode Island. They then adjourned to Providence, where they met on the 17th of November.

"Five cases were there entered and tried before the jury. William Harris, Thomas Field, and Nathaniel Waterman were the plaintiffs. The defendants were John Tours, of Hingham; the town of Warwick; John Harrod and partners; Edmund Caverly, Gregory Dexter, Arthur Fenner, and the town of Providence." *

* Staple's Annals of Providence.

Judgment was given for the plaintiff in all these cases, and execution issued for possession and costs. An appeal was taken by the defendants in the second case, and another commission appointed to hear the case, by which the former judgment was affirmed.

As William Harris had difficulty in obtaining possession of the lands according to the verdict, he again went to England; but was taken by pirates and carried to Algiers, where he remained some time, but was finally redeemed. He then went to England, and to London a few days after reaching there. Some thirty years after, his heirs petition for execution of the decree, reciting that the authorities have neglected to give them possession of the land. There is no evidence that they were kept out of possession by any act of John Tower, though it is doubtful whether he paid the costs awarded in the judgment. In the inventory of the estate of William Harris, recorded in the probate office in Providence, is entered as due from John Tower the sum of £18. There is no evidence of its payment, and it is here presented as a matter of consideration to some of his descendants who have strong impressions of the existence of a large fortune held in abeyance in England, and waiting only the presentation of the family claim for its payment, whether this ancient debt, with its accumulated interest, does not present an obligation of duty running as concurrently strong as the promise of fortune.

The judgment in this matter, so adverse to John Tower, must have caused him loss, both in time and in the means necessary to obtain the deeds from the Indians. Tradition has preserved the story that he had large acquaintance and much influence with the Indians.

In the years intervening from the time John Tower received grants of land from the town, near the time of the first settlement, he continued to receive other grants, and also to obtain additional land by purchase, as under date of Jan. 1, 1650-1, —

"By a general vote of the town, John Tower hath that great lot given him which was formerly given unto Thomas Gill."

1657, March 25, William Cockram, of Southhold, in the county of Suffolk, mariner, gives power of attorney to his son, William Cockram, Jr., to convey land ; and Sept. 27, 1657, William Cockram, Jr., conveys land and marsh in Hingham to John Tower. William Cockram was brother-in-law to John Tower.

In the year 1664 John Tower made purchase of a considerable tract of land in Hingham, as appears by deed of Edward Wilder

and Elizabeth, his wife, recorded in Suffolk Deeds, book viii. page
147, with the following description : —

" All that said dwelling-house situate in Hingham aforesaid, with all
houses, out-houses, barns, buildings, stables, cowhouses, orchards, gardens,
foldyards, with the lands thereunto adjoining, containing five acres, be it
more or less, which was given by the inhabitants of the town of Hingham
unto Martha Wilder, my mother, for a house-lot, and is bounded with
the highway that leadeth from the plain to the common northward, and
with the land of Michael Pearse eastward, and with the land that was
formerly John Benson's westward, and the land that was formerly
Edward Gilman's, southward ; and another house-lot, containing three
acres of land, be it more or less, lately purchased of John Benson, and is
bounded with the aforesaid house-lot of five acres eastward, and with the
common westward, and with the aforesaid highway northward, and with a
parcel of land lately given by the town to the said Edward Wilder southward ; and another parcel of land containing four acres, be it more or less,
lately purchased of Edward Gilman, and is bounded with the land of
Michael Pearse, formerly the land of Stephen Paine, eastward, and with
the aforesaid house-lot of five acres northward, and with the aforesaid parcel of land lately given by the town to the said Edward Wilder westward,
and with a little brook southward, which runneth between the said four
acres of land and the land of Edward Wilder, which he purchased of Samuel Ward ; and another parcel of land lying to the westward of the aforesaid four acres, which was given me by the town of Hingham ; and it is
bounded with the aforesaid house-lot that was John Benson's northward,
and the common land westward ; and three acres of salt marsh, lying and
being in the township of Hingham, aforesaid, in Cohasset Marshes ; being
the first lot in the 2nd division, which was given me by the town of Hingham, and is bounded with the meadow of Henry Chamberlain and the Cove
northward, and with the town's land southward and westward, and with
the meadow of John Page eastward ; with all the privileges . . . (always
excepting the privilege of commons of the aforesaid house-lot of three acres,
that was formerly John Benson's)."

This deed is dated May 16, 1664, and acknowledged before
Eleazer Lusher, May 17, 1664, and recorded May 10, 1673.

The tract of land described in the foregoing deed extended from
what is now Main Street, at Cole's Corner, to the brook at Tower's
Bridge, and, allowing for the large area of an acre, as seems to
be given in the allotment of house-lots, as we find by those which
can now be identified, must have contained about thirty acres,
all of which was capable of cultivation. These house-lots of Martha Wilder and John Benson were the extreme house-lots granted
by the town, under the law limiting the distance from the meeting-
house to which house-lots could be granted, and were about one
mile from John Tower's residence. He seems to have come into

possession of considerable tracts of other lands, as appears by subsequent conveyances, though the deeds of purchase, like many of the deeds of that period, fail to be recorded.

At the time of this purchase John Tower's ten children were all born, the eldest three sons had attained their majority, though none were then married, and he was well equipped with a force of labor sufficient for the clearing and cultivation of his extensive lands. He soon after built a dwelling-house at the southern boundary of his recent purchase, where he lived during the remainder of his days. Three of his sons had their dwelling-houses upon this land, where they spent their lives, and a portion of the same, including the lot where he built his house, is now owned by Lucy A. Tower, the widow of a descendant, and is now occupied by her. The house built by John Tower was taken down about the beginning of the present century. There does not appear upon the records any deed of conveyance of his original lot, the birthplace of all his children; but as there is no subsequent recognition of ownership of it by him, it may be inferred that he sold it.

During these years John Tower appears to have done service to the town in several offices of labor and trust, to which he was chosen; and he also had several controversies with the town, growing out of alleged encroachments, incident to imperfectly defined boundaries and to the clearing of the lands of wood and timber. He also had complaints against the town for loss and damage suffered in his lands needed and taken for public uses.

In 1657 he was one of the way-wardens; in 1659 he was one of the constables.

In 1665 a committee having large powers was chosen, as appears by the following vote : —

"By a joint consent and general vote of the town, Daniel Cushing, Matthew Cushing, John Jacob, John Tower, and Edmund Hobart are chosen to get the best evidence they can concerning highways formerly laid out, or about land formerly left for highways; and they are impowered by the town to lay out highways accordingly where they see it most convenient for the use of the town."

In 1684 "the town renewed and continued the power of the above said committee for laying out highways in Hingham till the town shall see cause to call in their power."

At about this time John Tower seems to have been compelled to a summary process to maintain or enforce some claim, as the following record shows : —

"The town hath fined John Tower and John Magoon twenty shillings apiece, for the use of the town, for quarrelling and striking one another in a public town meeting."

What the occasion of this fierce encounter was, does not appear, but from some other transactions which can be incidentally learned, it would seem to have arisen from a claim of a right of way by one, through the lands of the other.

Edmund Pitts, aged fifty-one years or thereabouts, and John Tucker, aged twenty-nine years or thereabouts, these deponents testifieth, and saith that they being present when Simon Peck bought of John Tower that house and land, whereupon John Magoon now dwelleth, these deponents did then hear the said John Tower and said Simon Peck agree and conclude that he, the said John Tower, should have a way through the said land unto the said John Tower's salt-marsh meadow, both to cart and carry hay, to drive and fetch cattle for egress and regress, he the said Tower and his heirs and assigns forever, without molestation or denial; and this we are ready to testify upon oath when legally called thereunto.

Dated this 20th of June, 1665.

"EM" PITT.
JOHN TUCKER.

The said Edmund Pitts and John Tucker were sworn in Hingham to the truth of what is above written on the nineteenth day of May, Anno Dom. sixteen hundred and eighty-four, before me,

DANIEL CUSHING, *Commissioner.*

In the same year John Tower brings a claim before the town for compensation for loss sustained and damage suffered by default and action of the town, as the following from the Town Records will show: —

At a town meeting, John Tower, Sen., of Hingham, desired of the town satisfaction for a small parcel of upland, taken of the westward end of his great lot of land lying on the great plain in said Hingham, near the digged way, for the enlarging the country road; also he desired satisfaction for salt-marsh, that, he said, was granted by the said town at "Nantascut" to William Cockerill; and he then said that the said William Cockerill had given or sold his said marsh to him, and the town left that matter to the selectmen to be issued with the said John Tower; and on the eighteenth day of March, 1666, the selectmen of the town and the said John Tower viewed some brushy meadow lying in the woods in Hingham, near to Ridge Hills, but did not lay out any while they were there, but as they were coming home proposed to the said Tower what they thought to allow of said brushy meadow in satisfaction for said upland and marsh, and he seemed to be content therewith; but some of the selectmen went after to lay out what the selectmen agreed with him, and the said John Tower denied their agreement, and claimed more than was agreed upon; and the persons that went to lay it out returned and did nothing, but concluded that what had been formerly done was nothing in reference to that matter. And at a town meeting in said Hingham on the 24th day of January, 1670, the said John Tower renewed his motion to the town for satisfaction for said upland and marsh-land, and the town hearing how said selectmen had acted about it, the town then chose Lieut. John Smith, John Jacob, John Leavitt, Thomas Lincoln, husbandman, and Daniel Cushing, to measure or set out to John Tower, Sen., a parcel of brushy meadow at a place called "Ridge Hills," according to their agreement with the said Tower on the town's behalf, on the aforesaid eighteenth of March, they at that time being selectmen of the town. The said five men above named, or the major part of them, have, since they were chosen, laid out a piece of brushy meadow which contained by estimation about six acres of land or thereabout, and it is bounded with the Ridge Hill and with the meadow of John Prince, toward the northeast, and with the main brook toward the northwest, and with the town's land toward the southeast and also toward the southwest, which said piece of brushy meadow is laid out in full satisfaction for the said John Tower's upland, and also for the said marsh-land that the said John Tower said was granted to the said William Cockerill.

Entered and recorded by

DANIEL CUSHING, *Town Clerk.*

It would seem that other causes of disagreement, leading to litigation then pending, were existing between the town and John Tower, as we find under date of Oct. 16, 1668 : —

"By a joint consent of the town, John Tower, Sen., is released from the four actions that are now depending in the Commissioners' Courts, provided that he pay all the charges that the town hath been out about them which he did promise to pay."

Just what the causes of these actions may have been, does not appear by any especial statement of the same. It may be inferred that the following agreement by the town may have had an office in the settlement of the same.

"It was agreed upon by the town that John Tower, Sen., should have the wood which he hath cut upon the common at the end of his wood lot, at Straits Pond, for six pence the cord, but he is to be at the charge of measuring his lot, and satisfy Edmund Hobart and John Jacob, who were appointed by the town to bound out those wood lots. He was charged with cutting 25 cords of wood upon the common."

The trespass here made by John Tower upon the town's common seems to have been accidental rather than intentional, and grew out of imperfectly defined boundaries. The merely nominal price of sixpence a cord for the wood would seem also to show the town meant that John Tower should get benefit enough to compensate him for his payment of costs in the actions. The large quantity of wood allowed tends to confirm this.

It does not appear of record that this particular lot was granted to John Tower by the town, and he probably acquired it by purchase, by a deed which failed to be recorded. The failure to record deeds in the early settlement of Massachusetts was quite common, and instances can be found in the registry of deeds where a deed has been recorded more than a century after it was given.

1671, Dec. 11, John Tower, Sen., of Hingham, etc., planter, and Margaret his wife, in consideration of £50, convey to Stephen French, of Weymouth, —

Three lots of land; that is to say, one lot containing six acres of land, which was given by the inhabitants of the town of Hingham to Mr. Richard Ibrook for a planting lot; and another lot, containing six acres of land, which was given by the inhabitants of the town of Hingham to Wm. Cockerum, for a planting lot; and another lot, containing six acres of land, which was given to Wm. Cockerill for a planting lot : the said three lots lieth all in one piece of land in Hingham, and is bounded by the line that runneth between Hingham and Weymouth westward, and with the common land eastward and southward, and with the land of John Fearing and with the common lands northward.

JOHN TOWER   (Seal)
his T mark
MARGARET TOWER (Seal)

This deed was recorded April 30, 1685.

The land probably came to Margaret Tower either by gift or inheritance from her father and brothers-in-law.

Attention is called to the consideration named in this deed, — namely, £50, — remembering that the wages of a laboring man is by regulation 2s. a day, and that £50 at that rate will represent five hundred days' work, which at their present value of one dollar and fifty cents a day will amount to seven hundred and fifty dollars, — a price far in excess of the value of the lands at the present day.

It will be remembered that John Tower was to pay the costs in certain actions commenced by the town, and the sum demanded for certain wood ; and May 3, 1669, —

"At a publick town meeting Deacon Leavitt, in the behalf of the town, did demand of John Tower, Sen., two pounds ten shillings and fourpence, which was the charge of the courts about the actions the town sued him in, and twelve shillings and sixpence for 25 cords of wood, which he cut upon the common, which he promised and engaged to pay, as appears by his agreement with the town upon the 16th day of Octob<u>r</u> 1668; and this pay being demanded of him, he promised to pay it if the town did appoint any to receive it. The town then upon the second day of February did appoint the selectmen to receive it for the use of the town."

It would seem that John Tower had learned some caution in his controversies with the town and those pretending to represent it, and he meant to be sure that full and explicit authority was granted them before he would treat with them; and as the town did not give such authority to Deacon Leavitt, it would seem that John Tower was using proper discretion in refusing to make payment to him.

A matter of much importance to all the inhabitants of Hingham had been under agitation for some time, and that was the disposition of the lands within the limits of the town which had not already been granted. It will be remembered that few new settlers came after 1640; while many left and were engaged in forming new settlements.

The result of this agitation was a conclusion to draw a line around and at some distance from the grants already made, and to divide the remaining land among the proprietors as their several claims could be determined or adjusted. Much difficulty was found in this work. Some, in addition to their own grants, had purchased in whole or in part of those who had left, and those remaining had purchased or exchanged with others. It was finally determined to make seven hundred shares, and to distribute them among the proprietors. The greatest number of shares allotted to any one was thirty-five, and this number was given to Daniel Cushing; and the smallest number was two shares. Several persons had that number by inheritance and by the division of estates. To John Tower were allotted eight shares.

There was dissatisfaction with the allotments, and probably no allotment could have been made giving complete contentment. John Tower was one of the complainants, as will hereafter be seen.

The territory divided was made in four distinct parcels or lots, which were designated first, second, third divisions, and second part of the third division. The most of this land is within the limits of the present town of Cohasset, and makes the greater part of that town.

The first and most important of the divisions commenced at Bound Brook, which made the boundary between Hingham and

Scituate; then on a line extending from said Bound Brook, in a northerly direction, about two and one fourth miles, being nearly identical with the present Main Street of Cohasset. The several lots were laid out at right angles with said line, and were about one mile in length. There were eighty-three lots, several of the smaller shares being put in one lot.

At a town meeting held Jan. 24, 1669–70, —

"It was voted that no man shall sell his land that shall fall to him by the division of the commons to any person or persons living out of town, unless he shall sell with it his whole seat of land which he has in the town, and the vote passed in the affirmative; but three men dissented from the vote; as namely, Humphrey Johnson, John Tower, and William Woodcock."

Dec. 6, 1670, the lots in the several divisions were drawn in numbers. John Tower drew the sixty-sixth lot in the first division, containing fifteen acres, two roods, and thirty-two rods; and if the lot was just one mile in depth, it would call for a frontage upon the street of nearly one hundred and twenty-nine and one half feet.

On the same day the lots in the second division were drawn, and John Tower's was the forty-second lot, and contained twenty-three acres and sixteen rods.

March 10, 1670–71, the lots in the third division and in the second part of the third division were drawn, and John Tower drew the seventieth lot, containing seventeen acres and two roods. This lot is in the present limits of Hingham, and is bounded southerly by the patent line formerly separating the colonies of Plymouth and Massachusetts Bay. His lot in the second part of the third division contained sixteen acres, one rood, and twenty-eight rods.

The whole quantity of land embraced in these divisions, including the land left for roads, was about ten square miles; and the whole quantity drawn by John Tower was seventy-two acres, two roods, and thirty-six rods. His lots were from three to five miles from his residence.

John Tower was much dissatisfied with his share of the lands, as the following petition will show : —

1673, May 9. — Honored General Court now sitting in Boston. The   of John Tower, Sen., of Hingham,

Humbly Sheweth — That whereas your petitioner has been an inhabitant and freeman of the town of Hingham about 35 years, and in and about the years 68 and 69 the said town had several meetings, and the major part of the said town's people did amply agree of and settle a division of the common that belonged to the said town, excepting some part of the said common that was to lie common property for the use of the proprietors, and some exceptions made about the wood, and the same day it was also agreed upon the manner of the division of the aforesaid common, which was that the land, wood, and timber was to be divided according to the house lots, heads, and estates of the proprietors or inhabitants aforesaid;

And at another town meeting after it was agreed how they should be valued or rated as by the town's book or records thereof may appear, and yet notwithstanding all what before said to be legally and amply done by the town in the premises, your petitioner has nor cannot receive any benefit or allowance according to the aforesaid town acts as to heads and estates, and on nothing was his just proportion as to house-lots.

Although your petitioner has used all fair means and profert as far as he was capable for the obtaining the same, it is positively denied him. And further, your petitioner is denied by the clerk any copy authenticated of the town's book records, the said clerk being prohibited to give me any that is authentic, so that I cannot sue at common law, nor any other way proceed for want of the copies of the town records as before said, and am wholly left destitute of being able to do anything for myself excepting what this Honorable General Court shall please to grant me, to whom I make this humble supplication for that favor to be granted me, that I may but have a hearing of my just complaint wherein I am so great a sufferer.

And if the Honored Court shall appoint any other persons to examine the premises, I humbly crave that there may be the respect had that the matter be committed or left unto unconcerned persons no ways interested as to persons or case; in which I shall be happy and ever bound to pray for the prosperity of this Honored General Court, and subscribe myself your poor petitioner for my redress.

HINGHAM, May 9th, 1673.

JOHN T TOWER, Sen., his mark.

In answer to this petition the magistrates —

Refer the petitioner to a due course of law against the town or clerk, their brethren.

EDWARD RAWSON, *Secretary.*

The Deputies hereto consenting, May 9th, 1673.
Consented to. The Deputies.

WILLIAM TORREY, *Clerk.*

It does not appear that John Tower availed himself of the means of redress to which his attention was called by the action of the General Court upon his petition, and he probably rested in his dissatisfaction with the several votes of the town by which the common lands were distributed, instead of engaging in dilatory and expensive litigation.

In 1675 came on the cruel and devastating war of King Philip, involving so many of the towns and settlements of New England in partial or complete destruction, and causing a loss of life unparalleled in its history. Hingham, from its situation on the seaboard, suffered but small loss of property in this war, but gave freely of the lives and services of her sons in defence of the colony.

John Tower's home was on the extreme outskirt of the town, and in any inroad of the savages would be the most exposed to attacks. It would seem that it was considered by the town authorities to be so unsafe and untenable that he had been ordered to remove his family into one of the forts near the more compactly settled portion of the town. He was not inclined to yield ready obedience to the order, and once more addressed the colonial authorities, in the following petition : —

March 10, 1675-76. John Tower, Sen., of Hingham, is bold to inform your Honors that he hath at his own proper charge fortified his house, and to beg your favor that his four sons and one or two persons more, that he may hire at his own cost, may be allowed him for the garrisoning his house, and may not be called off by the committee of the town for to come into any other garrison, my sons having deserted their own dwellings and brought their goods into my fortification. I shall then acknowledge your Honors' favor herein, and be thereby further obliged to pray for a blessing on your councils.

Your humble servant,

Jⁿ T TOWER, Sen.

It would seem that this favor was granted, and that John Tower remained in his fortified house. Only one irruption of the Indians is known to have taken place in the vicinity of his house, and John Jacob was slain within one half of a mile of it, — the only person killed in town by the Indians in this war, and within three quarters of a mile of his own house. The houses of Joseph Jones and Anthony Sprague were burned, they having probably been vacated by their owners.

The number belonging to John Tower's family and sheltered within his fortified house appears to be as follows : himself and wife and seven children (his son Jonathan probably having died before this time, though no record of his death appears), including his oldest son John[2], with wife Sarah and infant son Benjamin[3]; son Ibrook[2], with wife Margaret and children, Richard[3], Daniel[3], John[3], Rachel[3]; son Jeremiah[2], with wife Elizabeth and

children, Jeremiah [3] and Mary [3]; daughter Hannah [2], with son
Joseph Cowell [3]; and his unmarried children, Benjamin [2], Jemima [2],
and Samuel [2], — making twenty persons in all, of whom eight are
children of tender years, and one, Samuel [2], a lad of fourteen
years. All of these were to be accommodated in one house of
moderate dimensions, and defended by John Tower, then sixty-
seven years of age, his four sons, and one or two hired men. It
will be seen by turning to the history of King Philip's war that
the Indians at this particular time had become savagely aggres-
sive, and were attacking the settlements all through the colonies,
with a last desperate effort for their destruction, as the only hope
of their own salvation.

Tradition in the family has preserved something of this time of
peril, showing also that previously John Tower had been in a position of influence and intercourse with the Indians. When occasion required some one to go outside of the fortification, the duty
was assigned to "old John Tower;" as they would all say:
"You go, old John Tower; the Indians all know you, and they
won't hurt you."

It is probable that John Tower's sons, besides the garrison service for the protection of their own and their father's family, did
service in the field. In the journal kept by the especial colonial
treasurer for the war, there is an account with Benjamin Tower,
showing a payment made to him for specified service. Jeremiah
Tower probably died in the service, as there is no record of his
death in the town records of deaths, or in the diary of his uncle,
Rev. Peter Hobart. The omission of the record would indicate
that he died away from home, and that the time and place were
unknown. Administration was granted upon his estate January
30, 1676–77, and the following abstract from a deed shows a
conveyance of land by John Tower. It is dated January 31,
1676–77 : —

Whereas Jeremiah Tower, of Hingham, in New England, weaver,
have lately built a dwelling house upon part of the land of John Tower,
Sen., of Hingham, aforesaid, lately purchased of Edward Wilder, and
was formerly the land of John Benson. Know all men by these presents that I, the said John Tower and Margaret my wife, as well for and
in consideration of the fatherly love and good will and affection which
we have and bear unto the aforesaid Jeremiah Tower, our well-beloved
son, as also for divers other good causes and considerations unto us at this
present especially moving, have given, etc. . . . unto our said son, Jeremiah Tower, his heirs and assigns forever, the land on which the said
dwelling house now standeth, and so much more adjoining to it as shall
make up the land on which the said dwelling house now standeth, two

acres of land, which two acres of land lieth in the township of Hingham aforesaid, and is part of a lot formerly John Benson's, and part of a lot formerly Edward Wilder's, and the said two acres of land is bounded with the land of the said John Tower, northward and southward, and with the land of Edmund Pitts, lately purchased of Michael Pearse, eastward, and with the common land westward.

his
JOHN T TOWER (Seal.)
mark.

Signed, sealed, and
delivered in presence of
the county court.   Entered and compared, March 29, 1677.
J. ADDINGTON, *Clerk.*   Js. ADDINGTON, *Clerk.*

In 1674 John Tower conveys his land in the "plain neck" to Daniel Cushing.

In 1677 another division of the common lands in Hingham was made among the proprietors, and John Tower received twelve acres. This was called the "fourth" division. It lies next to the Weymouth line. This is the last division of the common lands in which John Tower had part. The other divisions were made subsequent to his death.

1680, Oct. 9. John Tower was taxed with the other inhabitants of Hingham in a rate for the building of a new meeting-house, — an event of some importance when the cost is considered, and the impoverished condition of the country so near the close of King Philip's war, the cost and devastation of which lay so heavily upon the colonies.

The sum raised by this rate was £436 14s. 11d. This was imposed upon one hundred and forty-three different persons, making an average tax of £3 1s. 1d. John Tower's tax was £2 17s. 6d., — a little less than the average. The whole tax, measured by the wages of laboring men at 2s. 6d. a day, would call for three thousand four hundred and fifty-four days work nearly; and estimating this work at the price for the same at the present time, — namely, one dollar and a half a day, — it would require nearly five thousand one hundred and eighty-one dollars. John Tower's part would call for twenty-three days' work, at a present value of thirty-four and one half dollars. On the completion of the meeting-house, as there was no private ownership within the walls, the people had their seats assigned them by a committee appointed for that purpose. A record of the seating on the day it was first occupied for religious services, Jan. 8, 1682, new style, has been preserved. Respect appears to have been paid to age and station in this assignment, and John Tower, with four other aged men, had the seat directly under the pulpit. The old meeting-house still gathers within its walls the descendants of its builders, and though no one of the name of Tower is a constant attendant, yet on any bright Sunday morning some fifty of his descendants may be found where he came to worship more than two hundred years ago. The oldest of these are in the seventh generation, and among the youngest may be found those in the eleventh.

And now, having passed the threescore and ten years of his life in a sphere of activity attendant upon a new settlement and amid the formation of a new government taxing the powers of the wisest properly to provide for, he appears to have passed the remaining years of his long life in comparative quiet and rest. He lived long enough to witness the abrogation of the charter under whose constructive provisions he had wrestled with authority and had suffered, and now found himself, with the others, subjected to a tyranny claiming a right and power to divest him of all title to his hard-earned possessions.

This, however, did not wholly prevent him from having transactions in real estate, both in buying and selling, some of which are made matter of record.

He seems to have continued in making provision for his children in deeds of gift of lands; as in May 26, 1684, he conveys to his youngest son, Samuel, " in consideration of the natural love and affection that I have and do bear unto my loving son Samuel, . . . one acre of my salt-marsh meadow lying on the westward part of my salt-marsh meadow which I formerly purchased of Thomas Shaw."

At the same date he conveys to his son Benjamin, for a similar consideration, " my two acres of land . . . which I had of Mr. Joseph Peck, . . . and is bounded with the street sometimes called Bachelor Street."

Dec. 28, 1686. Theodore Atkinson and Mary his wife, in consideration of £37, convey to John Tower " all that his piece or parcel of land situate in Boston, containing fifty foot square, bounded Westerly by land of John Atkinson, Northeasterly by land of Theodore Atkinson, Southerly by a highway fourteen feet wide, that is to be laid out on the south side of said land."

July 1, 1691. John Tower, Sen., and Margaret his wife convey to their son Benjamin Tower, in consideration of £10 10s., " one acre and a quarter of upland and a piece of salt-marsh meadow" in Hingham. " The upland is bounded westerly with the orchard of the said John and Margaret Tower, northerly with the land of Matthew Whiting and land of the grantors, southerly with the land of Samuel Tower, and easterly with the land of John Stodder. . . . The said salt-marsh meadow is bounded southerly with the salt-marsh meadow of the grantors, northerly with the meadow of Eyebrook Tower, easterly with the low-water mark in the pond, westerly with the upland of Jeremiah Bate."

Among the papers belonging to John Tower which have been preserved is the following: —

Some time in the year 1691, I being present as a witness to the deed of sale that John Tower, Sen., made to his son Samuel Tower, I then and there heard John Tower, Sen., object against the signing of this deed, because that his son Benjamin had a way to his land that he had sold him that lay at the east side of his orchard, whereupon Samuel Tower said, let not that hinder, for if his Brother Benjamin would get a *written* made, he would sign it.

JOHN STODDER, Jun.

John Tower lived long enough to witness the union of the two colonies of Plymouth and Massachusetts Bay under one charter government, and the advent of a royal governor, in 1692, with whom and with whose several successors his descendants were to wrestle in questions of rights, liberty, and governmental policy, as he had already often contended with authority under the old charter for the same things. That sturdy hold upon the possibility of an independent commonwealth which Winthrop and his associates brought with them never relinquished its grasp until attainment and security came to reward their tenacity and fidelity.

It will be noticed that John Tower invariably made his mark when his signature was required to deeds or other instruments of writing, while his wife always signed her name; and specimens of her written name have been preserved, made a few years only before her death.

John Tower left no will, nor is there any settlement of his estate in the Probate Court. It would seem that he gave his property to his children before he died, a few of the deeds of gift being recorded; but from the extent of his possessions it appears that the greater part failed to be put on record.

At the time of the death of John Tower three of his children had deceased; namely, John [2], Jonathan [2], and Jeremiah [2]. The other seven children were probably living. There had been born to his John [2] six children, of whom three were living. To his son Ibrook [2] twelve children; ten appear to be living. To his son Jeremiah [2], three children, two of whom were living. To his son Benjamin [2], twelve children, ten of whom were living. To his son Samuel [2], five children, all of whom were living. To his daughter Elizabeth [2] Roberts, the baptism of one son is recorded, and there is no record of his death. To his daughter Sarah [2] Curtis there appears to be one daughter who is living. To his daughter Hannah [2] Whipple, eight children, seven of whom were living. The whole number of the children living at his death was seven, grandchildren thirty-nine, and great-grandchildren thirteen. As it is not proposed to follow the daughters in the line of their descendants in this work, a brief description of them will be given under the heads of the several families to which they belong. Elizabeth [2], the eldest daughter of John Tower, married William Roberts, who is supposed to be the son of Robert Roberts, of Boston. They appear to have had only one son, Thomas, baptized June 20, 1669. William Roberts served as a soldier in King Philip's war. Sarah [2], the second daughter, married a Curtis. The only evidence of the marriage or of any issue is derived from the following deed, recorded in Suffolk Registry of Deeds, book 27, page 60, and dated Sept. 16, 1708, which recites that "Eyebrook Tower, Cooper, Benjamin Tower, Weaver, and Samuel Tower, Cooper, in consideration of the natural love and affection which they have and do bear unto Militiah, the wife of Joseph Maudesly, of Dorchester, in the county aforesaid, yeoman, their kinswoman, do convey unto her a piece of land situate in Boston, which John Tower bo't of Theodore Atkinson, all of which said land and premises were heretofore the estate and inheritance of their father, John Tower, late of Hingham, aforesaid, yeoman, who in his lifetime gave the same to his daughter, Sarah Curtis, mother of the said Militiah, by word only, without deed."

In the same Registry of Deeds, book 28, page 149, is the record of a deed from Joseph Maudesly and Militiah, his wife, to Theodore Atkinson, dated Sept. 8, 1714.

In the History of Dorchester published by Ebenezer Clapp, 1859, on page 293, is the following : —

"1725, Sept. 26. About a fortnight ago Joseph Maudsly, Mr. John Preston, Mr. Soper, and Mrs. Butts's son, on a fishing voyage, turned into a cove to the eastward in their vessel, with Joseph Maudsly's servant boy ; also Mr. Hunnewell, of Boston, went in with them, also Mr. Cox strove to go in ; but the fog hindered him, and the Indians barbarously murdered all that went in but the boy. [The boy was rdeemed in 1728.]"

Joseph Maudesly was the son of Thomas and Mary (Lawrence) Maudesly, and was born in Dorchester April 17, 1681. His will is dated April 20, 1707, and allowed by the Probate Court Oct. 8, 1725. There appears to be no issue of this marriage. The name

Maudesly is variously spelled, and is now written Moseley. Militiah Maudesly married, second, Charles King, of Dorchester, March 29, 1727. He died, and administration upon his estate was granted to his widow Jan 20, 1728–9. She married, third, Henry Freeborn, of Dorchester, Jan. 29, 1729–30.

The records afford but little knowledge of Jemima, the youngest daughter of John Tower. When the people of the town had their seats assigned them on the opening of the new meetinghouse, she had a seat among the maids. She was then nearly twenty-three years old. It is conjectured that she is the person intended in the following record of marriage, found in the first volume of the Town Records : —

"1705, Dec. 17. Mar. Thomas Garnet & *Judith* Tower, by Mr. John Norton."

The name of Judith does not appear among the children of John Tower or of his sons, nor was there a widow of that name. At the date of this marriage Jemima Tower was forty-six years old, and Thomas Garnet was forty-one. Neither birth nor baptism of children of Thomas Garnet are found in the Hingham Records, nor is there any record of his death or that of his wife.

Third Generation.   Tower.

1. JOHN [2], JOHN [1].

JOHN [2], son of John [1] and Margaret (Ibrook) Tower, bapt. Dec. 13, 1639; mar. Sarah Hardin, May 14, 1669. She was born   and was dau. of John Hardin, of Braintree, Mass. Childr.

11.	I.	BENJAMIN [3] born Jan. 25, 1673–4, in Hingham.			
	II.	GIDEON [3]	" Jan. 26, 1676–7	" "	d. in Braintree Oct. 26, 1698, ag. 21 y. 9 m.
	III.	SARAH [3]	" Oct. 21, 1679	" "	
	IV.	JOHN [3]	" June 18, 1682	" "	
12.	V.	JOSEPH [3]	" Feb. 27, 1685–6	" Braintree.	
13.	VI.	MARY [3]	" April 26, 1690.		

John Tower [2] died in Braintree, Aug. 30, 1693, ag. 53 y. 8 m. 17 d.   Sarah (Hardin) Tower died   Oct. 16, 1729.

John Tower [2], the oldest son of John Tower [1], lived in Hingham some fourteen years after his marriage, when he removed to Braintree, where he died a few years before his father's death. In Dec. 27, 1682, at a town meeting in Hingham, it was voted to sell the wood at a place called " Couper's Islands " to such of the proprietors of the adjoining meadows as " will have a part of it, . . . they paying ten pounds in money." This money the town gave to John Tower, Jr., "toward the paying of his purchase of land he bought in Plymouth Colony." It does not appear that he settled upon this land, but soon after went to Braintree.

3.   **Third Generation.**   **Tower.**

1. IBROOK [2], JOHN [1].

IBROOK [2], son of John [1] and Margaret (Ibrook) Tower, bapt. Feb. 7, 1643-4, mar. Margaret Hardin, of Braintree, April 24, 1668. She was b. 1647, and was dau. of John Hardin, of Braintree, Mass. Childr. all born in Hingham.

14.	I.	RICHARD [8]	born July 20, 1669.	
	II.	DANIEL [8]	" June 15, 1671; died Nov., 1690, ag. 19 y. 5 m.	
15.	III.	JOHN [8]	" March 21, 1672-3.	
16.	IV.	RACHEL [8]	" March 16, 1674-5.	
17.	V.	MARY [8]	" Aug. 16, 1677.	
18.	VI.	PATIENCE [8]	" March 21, 1678-9.	
19.	VII.	HEZEKIAH [8]	bapt. Oct. 9, 1681.	
	VIII.	ELIZABETH [8]	born June 9, 1682; mar. Merritt.	
20.	IX.	CONTENT [8]	" Feb. 3, 1683-4.	
	X.	NEHEMIAH [8]	" Nov. 4, 1685.	
21.	XI.	LYDIA [8]	" Nov. 25, 1687.	
22.	XII.	DANIEL [8]	bapt. July 24, 1692.	

Margaret (Harding) Tower died in Hingham (Cohasset), Nov. 19, 1705. Ibrook Tower [2] mar. 2d, Patience, widow of Daniel Hobart, and previously the widow of Benjamin Jones, Aug. 6, 1712.

Ibrook Tower [2] died in Cohasset Nov. 22, 1732, ag. 88 y. 9 m.

Patience ( ) (Jones) (Hobart) Tower died Dec. 22, 1747.

Ibrook Tower [2], the third son of John Tower, had the land which his father drew in the first division of land made by the proprietors in 1670. The deed is not recorded. Ibrook Tower probably went upon this land and built himself a house soon after the termination of King Philip's war, and was among the earlier settlers of what was then the village, and has since 1770 been the district and town of Cohasset.

He was frequently called upon to fill various municipal offices, and in 1699 he was one of the selectmen of the town. In addition to the agricultural pursuits common to all the people he was also a cooper, — an occupation for which the people of Hingham early became noted.

The raising of sheep early became an object of importance. This industry suffered loss from the depredations of wolves, and the records of the town show disbursements made for their destruction. In a list of debts due from the town in 1670–71 is one to " John Stodder and Ibrook Tower for killing a wolf, £1 ;" and again the same year is the entry, " Paid to John Stodder, Ibrook Tower, and Purden Varlow for killing of a wolf, 9s." In 1672, " Paid Ibrook Tower, about killing a wolf, 2s. 10d."

In making his home at Cohasset, Ibrook Tower and the others, who began the settlement there, were some four or five miles removed from the school and meeting-house, — those desirable adjuncts to a New England town. For some thirty years this young settlement went on without any better facilities for the education of the children and for their own attendance upon the Sunday services of the sanctuary. And yet under these disadvantages the sons and grandsons of Ibrook Tower obtained so much of the rudiments of learning as to be able to write, for they invariably sign their names to all instruments requiring their signature. The daughters and granddaughters were not so fortunate ; and when the occasion calls for their signature it is often made with the mark, — a matter of frequent occurrence at this period of New England history among the females.

In the years 1717–21 a precinct was formed of Cohasset, a meeting-house was built and a minister ordained, and soon after a school-house was built, and the people were relieved of their long and wearisome journeys over the imperfectly formed roads through the woods which separated their newer village from the parent town.

The first minister of the newly formed parish was Rev. Nehemiah Hobart, a grandson of Rev. Peter Hobart, and a relative of Ibrook Tower, who early became a member of the church gathered there.

In 1720, at the age of seventy-six years, Ibrook Tower makes his will, of which the following are extracts : —

" Gives to his wife Patience all the personal estate she brought in marriage," etc. Gives her " eight pounds per annum every year she remains my widow, £3 10s. to be paid by my son Hezekiah, £4 10s. by my son Daniel."

He sets apart certain pieces of land as security for the payment, with directions for the sale of the same in the event of the failure of said payment.

" And further 't is my will that my said wife, in lieu of the west end of my former dwelling-house and leanto, cellar and oven liberty, shall have the use and improvement of my now dwelling-house and a spot for a garden, with apples for her own use, with liberty of ingress, egress, and regress, during her being my widow. . . ."

Gives " to son Hezekiah . . . all my part and parcels of lands in the third division and second division, and all that part of the lots whereon my dwelling-house now stands, beginning at the fence standing upon Deer Hill, and thence running to the highway dividing between the first and second divisions, which is the end of said lot, together with an acre of my tillage land adjoining to said lot ; also one half part of my salt-marsh at Cooper's island. . . ."

Gives " to son Daniel all the rest of my housing and lands not hereby otherwise disposed of. . . ." Gives to Hezekiah and Daniel " all my cooper's tools."

Gives to his " six daughters, — Rachel Bates, Mary Whiton, Elizabeth Merritt, Content Souther, Patience James, and Lydia Franklin seven pounds apiece ; £15 to be paid by Hezekiah, and £27 by Daniel." Gives " to two grandsons, John Tower and Elisha Tower, £5 apiece in bills of credit or current money." Discharges his daughter Esther from all book debts. Nominates sons Hezekiah and Daniel to be executors.

In explanation of the provisions of Ibrook Tower's will, it should be stated that as a preliminary arrangement to his marriage with the widow Patience Hobart a deed of trust was made by Ibrook Tower, with the following provisions ; namely, she is to have her own personal property for her own disposal, and if she survive him and continue his widow —

" She shall have the use, benefit, and improvement of the west end of the house wherein the said Ibrook Tower dwells, and the leanto contiguous thereto, and the cellar under the same, with liberty to bake in the oven in a low room of the said house, with free egress and regress to the said house, and the use and privilege of the well, and of a yard for the convenient putting of Firewood for the use of said house ; and also a small spot of ground for a garden, and what apples she shall want for her own use out of the orchard."

Eight pounds were to be paid to her annually, in addition ; and this is made a charge upon the following lands : —

" Eight acres near ' Cooper's Island ; ' three acres bounded with land of Richard Tower, deceased, southeast, southwest on land of Lazarus Beal ; eight acres bounded southeast on ' Scituate Pond ; ' west on land of Aaron Pratt, east and northwest on the highway ; two acres bounded southeast on the ' Ironworks,' northwest upon said Pratt's land, south on Mordecai Lincoln's land, and eastward upon land of Thomas Andrews." Dated July 9, 1712.

4

Schedule of Patience Hobart's Personal Property.

"Money, £40. One Bed, Bedstead and Curtains, One pr. of Bed Blankets, Eight pr. of Sheets, Four Coverlets, Three pr. of Pillowbeers, Ten Napkins, Two Table Cloths, Six Towels, Three Chests, One Trunk, One Box, Two Iron Kettles, One Iron Pot, Three Chairs, Three Pewter Basins, One Quart Pot, One Pint Pot, One Baker Cup, One Candle Stick, One Frying Pan, One Warming Pan, A Box Iron & Heaters, A Washing Tub, Brewing Tub, One Meat Tub, One Spring Wheel, Two Beer Vessels."

In the condition of household furnishings at the present time the foregoing schedule of this widow would indicate destitution rather than comfort. It is only by a comparison of the cost of its production then that its real value can be seen. £40 in money at the rate of labor at 2s. a day would call for four hundred days' labor, which at the present prices would yield $600; and the household utensils at a similar value would give an outfit of elegance and abundance which few laboring-men of the present day can afford.

This will was allowed Dec. 31, 1731, and on this day an inventory was returned, showing lands, swamps, and meadows in Hingham, about seventy-four acres, valued at £988, and personal property to the amount of £45 2s.

As there will be repeated occasion to mention values of estates and commodities, it seems necessary to state that these values vary from year to year, owing to a constant and continued depreciation of the currency as compared to specie; and the specie currency of New England was in comparison to that of England as 3 to 4. That is, the Spanish piece of eight reals, or the dollar, was rated in New England at 6s., while in England it was 4s. 6d., making a pound sterling $4.44⅔, while a pound in New England currency was $3.33⅓, — a rate it retained so long as values were reckoned in the denomination of pounds, etc. The ratio between gold and silver was 15 to 1, which ratio it retained in the United States until near the middle of the present century, when by statute it was changed so as to be 16 to 1.

The emission of bills of credit in all the New England colonies under the delusion that the increase of money would bring increasing prosperity was attended all along the years of the first half of the eighteenth century with a continued depreciation. Reckoning was generally made in this currency, which was called "old tenor." Massachusetts redeemed its bills in specie, paying 6s. in specie for 45s. in currency. She was enabled to do this with the specie paid to her by Great Britain in remuneration for the expenses she incurred in the reduction of Louisburg in 1745. Though this currency was redeemed, yet business transactions continued to be reckoned and stated in it for several years afterwards, even to the time of the Revolution, when a currency created by the exigency of the times was made both by State and the United States, which depreciated to a much greater extent than the " old tenor " did.

It is not always certain whether values are stated in specie or currency, but it may generally be found that these values are given in " old tenor," reckoned at its comparative worth, when the contrary is not stated.

When Ibrook Tower made his will, in 1720, the comparative value of "old tenor" to specie was about 6 to 8. When the will was allowed, the ratio was about 6 to 17, — making a loss to the legatees of more than one half of the provision made for them.

At the time Ibrook Tower made his will four of his children had died, — Daniel [3] of small-pox in the ill-fated Canada expedition under Phips, at the age of nineteen years; Richard [3] in 1702; John [3] in 1711; and the date of Nehemiah's death is not known. Richard [3] and John [3] left issue, and provision is made for a son of each in the will.

The other children of Richard and John seem to be dissatisfied with the neglect of their grandfather to make provision for them, and claim a legal right to some part of the estate, as will appear from a petition to the Probate Court, from which the following extracts are made : —

1732, June 15. Petition of Rachel Stephenson, daughter of Richard Tower, son of Ibrook Tower, Esther Marbel, Cornelius Tower, Martha Tower, Elizabeth Tower, Ann Tower, children of John Tower, son of Ibrook Tower, deceased, humbly showeth . . . that no provision was made for them by Ibrook Tower in his will . . . refers to a law of the Province, passed in the 12$\frac{th}{}$ year of William the 3$\frac{rd}{}$, and to a resolve of the General Court, passed in 1718, May 28$\frac{th}{}$. Ask that their share of said estate may be set out to them.

Signed by   CORNELIUS TOWER,

RACHEL STEPHENSON,

her
ESTHER m MARBEL,
mark

her
MARTHA w TOWER,
mark

ELIZABETH TOWER,

her
ANN ɩ TOWER.
mark

The following indorsement is written upon the petition : —

"Jan'y 9, 1732–3, This matter continued to this day six weeks."

There being no other paper on file in the case, it does not appear what disposition was made of it.

The law referred to is as follows : —

" Be it therefore enacted by the authority aforesaid that any child or children not having a legacy given them in the will of their father or mother, every such child shall have a proportion of the estate of their parents given and set out unto them, as the law directs, for the distribution of the estates of intestates.

" Provided such child or children have not had an equal proportion of his estate bestowed on them by the father in his lifetime.

" At a great and general court begun and held at Boston on the 28th day of May, 1718, a petition being moved upon the second section or paragraph in the act providing for posthumous children, and such as have no legacy given them by will, made in the twelfth year of King William, viz. : Whether the said act doth as well extend to the grandchildren, in case of the death of the father or mother, as to the child himself, if living,

" Resolved in the affirmative, and that the law is so to be understood and practised, any usage or custom to the contrary notwithstanding."

The homestead of Ibrook Tower has remained in the possession of his descendants to the present time. Memorial-stones in the Cohasset Cemetery mark the place of his burial and that of his first wife, with the following inscriptions : —

<table>
<tr><td>Here Lyes Ye
Body of Mr.
Ibrook Tower who
Died November
Ye 22 " 1732 in
Ye 88 year
(of his age.)</td><td>Here Lyes the
Body of Mrs.
Margaret Tower,
wife of Mr.
Ibrook Tower who
died November
Ye 19 " 1705 in
Ye 59 year
of her age.</td></tr>
</table>

Ibrook Tower attained a greater age than any of the other children of John Tower, and he is the only one of the number whose place of burial is marked by a stone.

4.   **Third Generation.**   **Tower.**

1. JEREMIAH [2], JOHN [1].

Jeremiah [2], son of John [1] and Margaret (Ibrook) Tower, bapt. March 9, 1645–6 ; mar. widow Elizabeth Rowlands Nov. 1670. Childr. all born in Hingham.

23.   I. JEREMIAH [3] born Sept. 10, 1671.
24.   II. MARY [3]   "   Nov. 3, 1672.
      III. PETER [3]   "   April 30, 1674 ; died Dec. 1691, ag. 17 y. 7 m.

Jeremiah Tower [3] died ab. 1676, ag. 30 yrs.

Elizabeth (   ) (Rowland) Tower died in Providence, R. 1., Aug. 9, 1723.

The date of Jeremiah Tower's death is not recorded. It took place some time in 1676, and it is very probable that it occurred while in the service of the country during King Philip's war. He was the first of the descendants of John Tower to die. Administration upon his estate was granted to his widow, Elizabeth Tower, by the County Court at Boston, Jan. 30, 1676–7.

His estate was appraised at Hingham by John Smith and John Jacob, Jan. 22, 1676, a copy of which is here given for the purpose of showing the possessions of a householder and their value at that time. It should be remembered that Jeremiah Tower had been married six years only, and died at the early age of thirty years. In estimating values at this early period, and before any depreciation of the currency had taken place, it should be kept in mind, as has been before stated, that the value of a day's wages of a laboring-man was 2s.

	£	s.	d.
One Feather Bed and Bolster and Two Pillows	4	0	0
One Rug £2, Seven Sheets 20/, One pr. Vallents Curtains 16/	3	16	0
One Bedstead 20/, One Chest 16/, Desk 2/	1	18	0
One Box 2/, One Looking Glass 8/, One Basket 2/		12	0
One Hat Case 18d., Eight Pewter Platters £1 12/	1	13	6
One Salt Cellar 10d., Other Old Pewter 5/ 2d.		6	0
One Kettle and Two Brass Skillets		10	0
One Iron Pot and Pot Hooks		10	0
Table Linen 20/, One Trunk 8/, Six Boxes 12/	2	0	0
Five Pillow Beers 10/, Books £1 10/	2	0	0
Keeler, Old Tubs 4/, One Pillow 2/ 6d., Six Towels 3/		9	6
One Pair of Tongs & Fire Pan 2/ 6d., One Warming Pan 8/		10	6
One Pair of Bellows 1/, Two Pairs of Spinning Wheels 4/		5	0
Four Chairs 4/, One Jug & Some Small Things 2/, One Blanket 5/		11	0
His Clothing £2 10/, One Coverlet £1, One pr. Blankets £1 10	5	0	0
Ticking for Bed & Bolster 18/, Five yards of White Karsey £1 5/	2	3	0
One Axe, Old Hoes, & a pr. of Fetters 6/, Books 4/		10	0
One Smoothing Iron with Heaters 5/, One Beer Vessel 2/		7	0
Earthen Ware and Some Small Things 4/ 8d.		4	8
Two Meat Tubs, One Pail & Two Sieves 12/, One Roast Iron 1/ 6d.		13	6
One Cradle and Cradle Cloth 6/, One Meal Bag 2/		8	0
One Pike 2/, Part of a Musket 11/ 6d., Meat in the House 2d.		13	8
Two Looms with Slaize & Harness, and all other Working Geer	8	2	6
One Heifer £2, One Horse £1 10/, Two Swine & Two Pigs £2	5	10	0
Houses & Lands given him by his father, John Tower, Senior, which there is no deed for	12	0	0
	£54	13	10

This apparently small value of Jeremiah Tower's property at the time of his decease will be better understood and enhanced when we see that, measured by the value of a day's labor, it will represent nearly 547 days, which, reckoned at the present rate of $1.50 per day, will amount to 820\frac{50}{100}$ nearly. This would be considered a very respectable property at the present day for a laboring-man to save from his earnings, which were encumbered with the support of a family. It would seem that Jeremiah Tower was a weaver by occupation, and that more than one seventh part of the value of all his possessions was invested in the implements of his trade.

5. Roberts.   Third Generation.   Tower.

1. ELIZABETH [2], JOHN [1].
Elizabeth [2], dau. of John and Margaret (Ibrook) Tower, bapt. Oct. 9, 1648 ; mar. William Roberts at Boston, Oct. 9, 1667. Child.

I. THOMAS [3], bapt. June 20, 1669, in Hingham ; died in Hingham Feb. 16, 1735-6.

6. Curtiss.   Third Generation.   Tower.

1. SARAH [2], JOHN [1].
Sarah [2], dau. of John [1] and Margaret (Ibrook) Tower, bapt. July 16, 1650; mar.   Curtiss.   Child.

I. MILITIAH [3], born   ; mar., 1st, Joseph Maudesly, of Dorchester; 2d, Charles King, March 29, 1727, in Dorchester; 3d, Henry Freeborn, Jan. 9, 1729–30, in Dorchester.

7. Whipple, Cowell.   Third Generation.   Tower.

1. HANNAH [2], JOHN [1].
Hannah [2], dau. of John [1] and Margaret (Ibrook) Tower, bapt. July 17, 1652; mar.   Cowell.   Child.

I. JOSEPH [3], born Dec. 29, 1673, in Hingham.

Hannah (Tower) Cowell [2] mar., 2d, David Whipple, in Hingham, Nov. 13, 1677, by Capt. Joshua Hobart. D. Whipple, born Sept. 28, 1656, was son of John and Sarah Whipple. Childr.

	II.	ISRAEL [3]	born	Aug. 16, 1678,	in Providence, R. I.		
11.	III.	DEBORAH [3]	"		"	"	"
	IV.	JEREMIAH [3]	"	June 27, 1683	"	"	"
	V.	WILLIAM [3]	"	May 29, 1685	"	"	"
	VI.	SARAH [3]	"	Nov. 16, 1687	"	"	"
	VII.	HANNAH [3]	"	Jan. 9, 1690	"	"	"

died in Rehoboth Oct. 16, 1708, ag. 18 y. 9 m.
7 d.

	VIII.	ABIGAIL [3]	"	Oct. 20, 1692, in Providence, R. I. ; died

David Whipple died in Rehoboth Dec. 18, 1710, ag. 54 y. 2 m. 20 d.

Hannah (Tower) (Cowell) Whipple [2] d.   1722, ag. 70 y.

As it is not proposed to continue the record of the descendants in the female line, a brief description will be given of some of those in these lines who by their abilities and virtues have been of service to the communities in which they have lived.

Hannah Tower is the only daughter of John Tower whose descendants can be traced to the present time. After her marriage to David Whipple she went with her husband to reside in what is now Cumberland, R. I., but formerly a part of Attleborough Gore. David Whipple bought the land on which William Blackstone had built his residence when he felt compelled to leave the " Lords Brethren " of Boston as he had left the " Lords Bishops " of England. Here, on the beautiful height on the banks of the river bearing the name of its earliest settler, came Hannah (Tower) Whipple to dwell, and here she lived until her death in 1722. The place where she lived is now the flourishing manufacturing village of Lonsdale, — one of the many places where the waters of the river are arrested for available power, from its source, until it loses itself in the tide-waters.

In her will, dated May 28, 1720, Hannah Tower names her children then living, and gives them severally certain legacies. Joseph Cowell, the son of her first union, removed to that part of Dorchester which afterwards was made a part of Wrentham, where he died in 1761, at the age of eighty-seven years. His son David graduated from Harvard College in 1732. He is the earliest descendant of John Tower who graduated from a college, preceding by sixty-eight years the graduation of any descendant bearing the name of Tower. He was settled as the minister of the Presbyterian Church of Trenton, N. J., where he was ordained in 1736, and where he remained in the ministry until his death, which took place in 1760. He was an overseer of Princeton College, and did efficient service in that capacity, and in an interregnum he filled the office of president for a short time. He did not marry.

Ebenezer Cowell [4], son of Joseph [3], removed to Trenton, where he was during the Revolutionary War. He was a gunsmith by trade, and early in the war made a contract, for the manufacture of arms, with a committee of Congress. He was largely engaged in the repair of guns during the war, and on the capture of the Hessians at Trenton in 1776 the thousand stand taken there passed under his inspection for necessary repairs.

Some of his descendants have filled the learned professions, while others in the line of mercantile pursuits in Philadelphia and elsewhere have acquired wealth and distinction. His daughter Lois gave personal service and contributed of her ample means to help the sick of Philadelphia during the scourge of yellow fever which afflicted that city in 1793, and died that year, a victim to the disease.

John M. Cowell, a great-grandson of Ebenezer, now a resident of Philadelphia, has compiled a genealogy of the family, comprising biographical notices of many members of it, — a work of much labor and research, and valuable not only as a memorial of private worth, but of interest to our general history. It is hoped that it may receive publication.

Joseph Cowell [4], son of Joseph [3], lived in Massachusetts and had two children, — Samuel [5] and Olive [5], who married Benjamin Hawes. Olive was a woman of much ability. That able scholar, Rev. Dr. Emmons, of Franklin, Mass., said that " she was the ablest female theologian he ever met." In an interview with Mrs. Ide — the daughter of Dr. Emmons and wife of Rev. Dr. Ide, of Medway, Mass., who at the advanced age of eighty-nine years remembered Olive Hawes and related many of the sayings of her father in illustration of the esteem in which he held her — was seen the evidence of impression made in early life by this able woman.

Benjamin Cowell [6], the grandson of Joseph [4], was a graduate of Brown University. He was for many years clerk of the United States District Court for Rhode Island, and subsequently was Chief Justice of the Court of Common Pleas for that State. He wrote and published several works, among which were, " The Deity of Christ," and " The Spirit of Seventy-Six." Of his sons, Rev. Samuel [7] has been a life-long minister of the Episcopal Church, and his grandson, Dr. Joseph H. [8], is a graduate of Brown University and a practising physician in East Saginaw, Mich.

Of the descendants through Olive Hawes [5] was her grandson, Oliver H. Kollock [7], a graduate of Brown University and a prac-

tising lawyer at the South, whose son Cornelius [8] is also a graduate of Brown University, and is now a physician in South Carolina. Many other descendants of Hannah Tower, both through
the Cowell and Whipple alliance, who are now living, might be
named, to show how well they have improved their advantages,
making themselves a power and use to both church and state.

8. **Third Generation.** **Tower.**

1. BENJAMIN [2], JOHN [1].

Benjamin [2], son of John [1] and Margaret (Ibrook) Tower, bapt.
Nov. 5, 1654; mar. Deborah Garnet (Gardner), in Hingham,
September, 1680. She was born in Hingham July 5, 1657, and
was dau. of John and Mary Garnet. Childr. all born in Hingham.

25.	I.	ABIGAIL [3]	bapt.	May 22, 1681.
	II.	RUTH [3]	"	Sept. 2, 1682; died Nov. 2, 1682.
	III.	NATHANIEL [3] born		Sept. 12, 1683; died Nov. 24, 1700, ag. 17 y. 2 m. 12 d.
26.	IV.	DEBORAH [3]	"	Feb. 4, 1684–5.
27.	V.	BENJAMIN [3]	"	Sept. 2, 1686.
28.	VI.	CHRISTIAN [3]	"	March 16, 1687–8.
29.	VII.	SARAH [3]	"	Dec. 18, 1689.
30.	VIII.	JAEL [3]	"	Oct. 26, 1691.
31.	IX.	THOMAS [3]	"	June 27, 1693.
32.	X.	HANNAH [3]	"	March 14, 1694–5.
33.	XI.	PETER [3]	"	July 17, 1697.
34.	XII.	AMBROSE [3]	"	Jan., 1699–1700.

Benjamin Tower [2] died in Hingham March 24, 1721–2, ag.
68 y. 4 m. 19 d.

Deborah (Garnet) Tower died in Hingham 1728 or 9, ag. 71
or 72 y.

Among the papers of Benjamin Tower which have been preserved are several unrecorded deeds. One of these, bearing date
April 8, 1692, recites that John Stodder, of Hingham, etc., —

"In consideration of about . . . [torn] and three quarters of one
acre of land lying between the house of Benjamin Tower, weaver, of
said Hingham, and the house of Samuel Tower, which said land the said
Benjamin Tower grant and confirm unto the said John Stodder, as may
fully appear by a deed under the hand and seal of said Benjamin Tower,
it beareth date with these presents, wherewith the said John Stodder is
fully satisfied . . . have granted, etc., unto the said Benjamin Tower
. . . all that his about one acre and half of land being in said Hingham,
and lying on the south end of his land, that he bought of Michael Pearse,
and was formerly the land of Stephen Paine, and the said acre and half

of land is bounded with the land of said Tower west, and with a small brook between the said land and Wilder's land south, and with the land of said Stodder east and north, and stones set in the ground for standing bounds."

Another deed, bearing date Dec. 7, 1713, recites, —

"Whereas Benjamin Tower and Benjamin Garnet, both of Hingham," etc., "be the owners of the eleventh lot of land on the great plain in said Hingham, in the first furlong eastward from the centre or country road, said Tower is owner of the north half, and said Garnet is owner of the south half, . . . the said Benjamin Garnet for and in consideration of ten pounds" conveys to "Benjamin Tower all the south side of said lot."

Benjamin Tower's will is dated July 2, 1717. He died March 24, 1721-2. It was proved and allowed April 28, 1722.

He gives "unto Deborah Tower, my well-beloved wife, the use and benefit of all my estate, both real and personal, during her natural life, except that I hereafter dispose of; and in case she stand in need in the time of her widowhood for her maintenance, I do hereby give her full power to sell any part of my estate not disposed of."

"I do give to my son Peter Tower all the tackling that I use in my trade of weaving, and the loom, he paying to every one of his brothers and sisters five shillings apiece in one year after my decease."

He names his children Benjamin, Thomas, Peter, and Ambrose, sons; and Abigail Hollis, Deborah Corthell, Christian Pratt, Sarah Whiton, Jael Stubs, Hannah Tower, daughters; and makes them equally residuary devisees and legatees. Inventory, dated April 16, 1722: —

	£	s.	d.
The Mansion House, with the land adjoining, and other out-houses, and all the other lands in the town of Hingham .	150	0	0
Wearing apparel £10 4s., Province Bills £1 3s., Books £1 10s.	12	17	0
Stock, Oxen, Cows, Sheep, Horsekind	24	0	0
Farmer's Tools, Plows, and Yokes and Chains	4	17	0
Weaving Tacklen £8; Provision and Grain £3 10s..	11	10	0
Iron Ware and Brass Ware £2 5s.; Beds & Bedding £10 . .	12	5	0
Tables, Chest, and Boxes £1 10s.; Chairs, Tubs, & other housel stuff, £5	6	10	0
Woollen Cloth 15s.; Horse-tackling, Saddle, Bridle, & Pilyon 17s.	1	12	0
	£223	11	0

(Signed)   BENJAMIN GARNET,
SAMUEL TOWRE.

Subjecting the foregoing sum to the tests of depreciation and the comparative value of labor, it would represent at the present day $1,642$\frac{50}{100}$.

There does not appear of record any division of the real estate of Benjamin Tower [2]. His will gave his widow power to sell. There is only one deed on record showing that she availed herself of that power. In book xxx., page 193, Suffolk Registry of Deeds, dated Oct. 12, 1726, is recorded a deed reciting that —

" Deborah Tower, widow and relict of Benjamin Tower, late of Hingham, deceased," in consideration of £30 " paid by my son, Peter Tower, of Hingham, aforesaid, weaver," conveys " a piece or part of the home lot of land where I now dwell, in the township of Hingham, abovesaid, containing by estimation two acres, be it more or less, bounded as followeth : northerly and easterly with the land of Jacob Stodder, southerly with the other part of the said home lot, and the southeast corner bounds is a white oak tree, and the line runs from said white oak tree to the southeast corner of the dwelling-house of the said Deborah Tower, and westerly partly with said dwelling-house, and partly with the town's common land or highway."

The dwelling-house mentioned here is undoubtedly the dwelling-house that John Tower built about the year 1664, and which he fortified in King Philip's war. On this site one or more dwelling-houses have succeeded the original, and the one standing there at the present time was built near the commencement of the present century. It is now owned and occupied by the widow of William Tower [6], to whom it came by devise successively from former generations.

9. Garnet or Gardner. Third Generation. Tower.

1. JEMIMA [2], JOHN [1].

Jemima [2], dau. of John [1] and Margaret (Ibrook) Tower, born April 25, 1660 ; mar. Thomas Garnet in Hingham Dec. 17, 1705, by Rev. John Norton. T. Garnet bapt. in Hingham June 5, 1664, and was son of John and Mary Garnet. Childr. none.

10. Third Generation. Tower.

1. SAMUEL [2], JOHN [1].

Samuel [2], son of John [1] and Margaret (Ibrook) Tower, born Jan. 26, 1661-2 ; mar. Silence Damon, of Scituate, Dec. 14, 1683, by Robert Pike, assistant. She was born 1663, and was dau. of John and Martha (Howland) Damon. Childr. all born in Hingham.

35.   I.   Silence[8]   born Aug. 27, 1684.
36. II.   Margaret[8] "   March 18, 1686-7.
37. III. Samuel[8]   bapt. Dec. 15, 1689.
38. IV.   Ruth[8]   "   July 13, 1691.
39.   V.   Martha[8]   born July 20, 1693.

Silence (Damon) Tower died in Hingham Nov. 15, 1702, ag. 39. Samuel Tower[2] mar. 2d, Deborah Hayward (Howard) Jan. 20, 1704, by Major Samuel Eells. She was born in Hingham Nov. 24, 1672, and was dau. of Daniel and Deborah (Pitt) Hayward. Childr.

40.   VI.   Daniel[8] born Nov. 22, 1704.
     VII.   Sarah[8]   · "   1706 ; unmar. ; died in Hingham, 1744,
                                         ag. 38.
33. VIII.   Ann[8]   "   1708.
41.   IX.   Joshua[8]   "   Feb. 10, 1709-10.
42.   X.   Joseph[8]   "   Aug. 28, 1712.
      XI.   Deborah[8] "   1715; died unmar., in Hingham, March
                                         9, 1809, ag. 94.

Samuel Tower[2] died in Hingham March 21, 1723–4, ag. 62 y. 1 m. 25 d.

Deborah (Hayward) Tower died in Hingham Jan. 30, 1742, ag. 69 y. 2 m. 6d.

Samuel Tower[2] was several times chosen by his fellow-townsmen to fill various town offices. In 1694, May 16, at a town meeting appears the following vote of the town in answer to his request: —

" Samuel Tower, having sown some tobacco seed in a small piece of the town's land, desired that he might have the use of the said piece of land till his tobacco be ripe, and he would give to the town one pound of good tobacco ready cut ; and upon that condition the town granted him his request."

1706, May 1. "The town passed a vote to allow Corporal Samuel Tower forty shillings out of the town treasury for money the said Tower lost in the country rate when he was constable, by money being then brought from tale to weight."

1707–8, March 18. Samuel Tower was chosen one of the selectmen.

1715–16, March 12. He is again chosen one of the selectmen.

Among the papers preserved are several copies of the rates assessed upon polls and estates.

He seems to have been a considerable land-owner, though there are but few conveyances on record wherein he appears as grantor or grantee. He probably received from his father by gift the greater part of his lands. He and his brother Benjamin had the home lands of their father, except what was given to Jeremiah.

His will is dated March 14, 1723–4, and proved and allowed April 21, 1724. He is called a " cooper." He gives to his " eldest son Samuel two acres of land adjoining to his dwelling-house as it is now fenced in." Gives to his " son Daniel one acre and half of land bounded northerly on the land I gave to my son Samuel." Gives to his " sons Joshua and Joseph the sum of ten pounds, to be paid by my executors when they shall arrive at the age of twenty-one years." Gives to each of his " daughters, Sarah Tower, Ann Tower, and Deborah Tower, the sum of ten pounds, to be paid . . . upon marriage, or when they shall arrive at the age of twenty-one years." Gives to each of his " grandchildren, Elijah and Abigail Whiton, the sum of five shillings."

Give to his " beloved wife Deborah Tower all my household stuff for her own forever, with the benefit and improvement of the residue and re-mainder of my estate, both real and personal . . . for the maintenance of my children during the time she remains my widow; and if she marry she shall have one hundred pounds paid out of my estate. I do also empower her to sell land for the maintenance of the children if necessity calls for it.

" My mind and will is that what of my estate as shall be left at her marriage or decease, the one half thereof shall be equally divided ' be-tween ' my four sons, . . . and the other half equally divided ' between ' my six daughters and granddaughter, Martha Whiton, only with the reserve that my sons . . . shall have liberty to keep the lands, they pay-ing to my daughters and granddaughter their proportion of the same."

Nominates his wife and " cousin," Peter Tower, to be executors.

Peter Tower was his nephew, and he afterwards married Anna, the daughter of his uncle Samuel.

On the third Tuesday of August, 1742, a warrant was issued from the Superior Court for the County of Suffolk for the division and partition of the estate of Samuel Tower, late of Hingham, cooper, deceased. The commissioners proceed to divide the same " into two equal parts ; " viz. : —

" For his four sons' half we have bounded out about ten acres and a half on the south side of his homestead, with the dwelling-house thereon, by a line running from the highway at the west end of said land, near fourteen feet north of the middle of the breadth ; as far eastward as be-tween Jacob Sprague's northeast corner of his fence and Isaac Whiton's land, and from thence to Ripley's meadow, at nine rods of a brook ; also, the south part of his Salt Meadow 'by the Mill Pond, containing about one acre and three quarters ; also, his half of the second lot in the north division of the small ' *Sheers*,' so-called, at the west side thereof ; also, four elevenths parts of all his right in the land in said Hingham, lately called the undivided commons. And for the other half of the deceased estate for his six daughters and granddaughter we have set out the rest of the home land on the north side of the line above described, containing about nine acres and a half ; also, the north part of the Salt Marsh abovesaid, containing about one acre, one quarter, and twenty-two rods ; also, his half of the fifth lot in the south division of said small shares on the east side thereof ; also, seven elevenths parts of his shares in the said undivided common land, as so lately called ; also, all his land in the first part of the 'third division,' southwestward of ' Prospect Hill,' so called, being about ten acres and half in partnership with the heirs of Joshua Hersey, deceased.

" And then his four sons' half we have divided as followeth : To the heirs of his eldest son, Samuel Tower, deceased, a part of the small shares, etc. . . . Also two acres and twenty rods of swamp land, more or less, at the east end of the southward half of the homestead, bounded westerly with the land now set to Joshua Tower by a north and south line, at 12¾ rods eastward of Jacob Sprague's northeast corner.

" To his son Daniel Tower a part of the small shares.

" To his son Joshua Tower about six acres, one quarter, and twenty rods, more or less, in the south side, or half of the homestead, bounded easterly with the swamp of Samuel Tower's heirs, . . . and westerly with two acres, being twenty-one rods and two thirds in length eastward from the highway, now set to Joseph Tower, by a line north and south. . . .

" To his son Joseph Tower the two acres of land at the west end of the south side of the homestead as aforesaid, with the dwelling-house standing thereon. . . . "

The north part of the homestead, which was assigned to his daughter and granddaughter, was set off to the heirs of three deceased daughters ; the heirs of Ruth Garnet having three acres, one quarter, and ten rods at the east end, the heirs of Margaret Whiton, deceased, having three and one half acres and thirty rods in the middle part, and the heirs of Sarah Tower, deceased, having about two and one half acres and twenty rods at the west end, bounding upon the highway.

The following account of the division of Samuel Tower's estate is found among the family papers : —

	£	s.	d.
Samuel Tower's part, —			
West half of the " Shares " land	148	0	0
¾ and ½ acre, — Swamp in the Home Place	8	10	0
$\frac{1}{11}$ of Commons	20	0	0
	£176	10	0

Daniel Tower's part, —	£	s.	d.
East half of the " Share " land	148	0	0
1 acre and 10 rods, — Swamp in the Home Place	8	10	0
$\frac{1}{11}$ of Commons	20	0	0
	£176	10	0

Joshua Tower's part, —			
6 acres, 1 quarter, and 20 rods next to Joseph in the Home Place	80	0	0
One half of all the Salt Marsh and Island adjoining.	76	10	0
$\frac{1}{11}$ of Commons	20	0	0
	£176	10	0

Joseph Tower's part, —			
The House	60	0	0
Two acres adjoining	54	0	0
Cedar Swamp	42	7	6
$\frac{1}{11}$ of Commons	20	0	0
	£176	7	6

The heirs of Silence Sprague, —			
$4\frac{1}{2}$ acres, north part of Prospect Hill	42	0	0
$\frac{1}{4}$ part of the Salt Marsh and Island	38	5	0
$\frac{1}{11}$ of Commons	20	0	0
	£100	5	0

The heirs of Margaret Whiton, —			
$\frac{1}{4}$ part of the Salt Marsh	38	5	0
1 acre and 20 rods of upland next the 3d part	27	0	0
1 acre and $\frac{1}{2}$ and 20 rods, Fresh Meadow, adjoining	7	10	0
1 acre of Woody Swamp, adjoining the Meadow	8	0	0
$\frac{1}{11}$ of Commons	20	0	0
	£100	15	0

The heirs of Ruth Garnet, —			
3 acres, 1 quarter, and 10 rods of woody swamp in the east end of the homestead	26	10	0
16 acres, 1 third, and 7 rods next the cross line in the south part of the share lands, swamp and upland	54	10	0
$\frac{1}{11}$ of Commons	20	0	0
	£101	0	0

Martha Barnes', —			
$5\frac{1}{2}$ acres south part at Prospect Hill	81	0	0
$\frac{1}{11}$ of Commons	20	0	0
	£101	0	0

The heirs of Sarah Tower, —	£	s.	d.
2½ acres north side of the house, and 20 rods in the front .	80	15	0
$\frac{1}{11}$ of Commons	20	0	0
	£100	15	0

Ann Tower, —			
The east side of the remainder of the south Share land . .	81	0	0
$\frac{1}{11}$ of Commons	20	0	0
	£101	0	0

Deborah Tower, —			
The west side of the remainder of the south Share land . .	81	0	0
$\frac{1}{11}$ of Commons	20	0	0
	£101	0	0

At the date of this division the currency was so depreciated as to be worth a little less than one fourth of its nominal value.

By the foregoing division it will be seen that Samuel Tower had about twenty acres of land in his homestead, with a frontage of about four hundred and sixty feet upon the street. This land was probably his portion of his father's land, purchased of Edward Wilder. Of this gift from John Tower to his son no deed either of preservation or record remains. The warrant for the division from which the foregoing extracts have been made, is probably a copy of the original warrant made before the return to the court from which it issued, as it bears no indorsement of action of the court either for its acceptance or rejection. It is dated Dec. 5, 1743, and signed by Abel Cushing, Jacob Beal, Thomas Andrews, Jo⁵. Lincoln, Thep⁵. Cushing.

In the description of the lands of Samuel Tower as they are set out to the devisees under his will, by the foregoing commission, mention is made of certain " small shares," without naming where they are situated. As there are no such lands designated in the division of Hingham lands, the following lengthy recital in an old deed, not recorded, but found among the papers which have come down from Samuel Tower, has some historical as well as local interest.

Whereas the Court of Plymouth in New England, in America, heretofore granted to Timothy Hatherly, late of Scituate, in the County of Plymouth, now in his Majesties province of the Massachusetts Bay, in New England, a tract of land containing three miles square, lying and being in said Plymouth Colony, as it was then called, near to the pond of fresh water commonly called " Accord Pond," which said tract of land is commonly called by the name of the shares, having been formerly cast into forty shares, and have lately been divided into four parts by the proprietors of the whole tract of land ;

The first part of the said tract of land as it is now divided into four parts is the eastward part, and lieth next to the line of Scituate township. The first, third, and fourth parts of the said tract of land as it was divided by the proprietors of the whole tract of land belonged to, and was then in the possession of, Captain John Jacob and his partners. The second part of the said tract of land as it is now divided, is in the possession of divers other persons, in which said second part of the said tract of land Michael Peerse, of Scituate, having a single share, which amounts to as much as a forty part of the whole tract of land of three miles square, which single share of the aforesaid tract of land of three miles square, containing one fortieth part of the said whole tract of land, and lieth in the second part of said tract of land as it is now divided into four parts by the proprietors.

The aforesaid Michael Peerse heretofore sold to Ephraim Wilder and Isaac Wilder, as appears by deed of sale under the hand and seal of Michael Peerse, bearing date the first day of November, 1675, which said single share of the said tract of land of three miles square, sold by the said Michael Peerse to the said Ephraim and Isaac Wilder, do now belong to Jabez Wilder and Thomas Wilder, son of the said Isaac Wilder, (viz. :) Ephraim's part of said share to Jabez Wilder, and Isaac Wilder's part of said share to the said Thomas Wilder.

And the proprietors of the said second part of the said tract of land of three miles square, judging it not to be convenient to have their shares to run at such a length, they divided their second part of the said tract of land with a cross line about the middle of the length of their shares of their said second part of their said tract of land, and so every proprietor have his share in the said second part of the said tract of land of three miles square, lying in two parts, which they have divided by lot amongst themselves ; every man drew but one lot for both parts of his share in the said second part of the said tract of land.

And by a mutual agreement of the proprietors, because the land was not timbered alike, that such persons as had the north lot in the first part of their division should have a better lot in the second part of the division, and by that means the second lot in the first part of their division, and the fifth lot in their second part of their division, were to go together for one man's share of the second part of the said tract of land, and do amount to the fortieth part of the whole tract of land of three miles square, which said second and fifth lots in their said division of their land fell to be the share of the said Ephraim Wilder and Isaac Wilder, which they have by their purchasing of a share of the abovesaid Michael Peerse.

The first part of the second lot in their said division of their land which fell to Ephraim and Isaac Wilder is bounded with the " Patent Line " northward, and with the land of Josiah Loring and Thomas Lincoln, carpenter, Eastward, and with the land of James Whiton, Senior, westward, and with the cross line (that divide between the two parts of their division of their said lots now made of their second part of the said tract of land) southward, the said fifth lot in their second part of the division of their land now made, and fell to Ephraim and Isaac Wilder, is bounded with the land that fell to Captain John Smith and John Ripley eastward, and with the land of Josiah Loring and Thomas Lincoln, carpenter, westward, and with the lands late in the possession of Robert Stutson southward, and with the said cross line that divide between the two parts of their said division northward.

And all persons proprietors of the said second part of said tract of land have mutually agreed among themselves that they shall have the liberty for themselves, their heirs and assigns, each of them, to pass through one another's shares with carts or otherwise without molestation. . . .

Now know all men by these presents that Jabez Wilder, of Hingham, in the County of Suffolk, in New England, yeoman, and Mary Wilder, his wife, for and in consideration of the sum of twelve pounds and ten shillings in current money of New England, to them in hand at and before the sealing hereof, well and truly paid by Samuel Tower, of said Hingham, cooper, the receipt whereof they the said Jabez Wilder and Mary his wife doth hereby acknowledge, and themselves therewith fully satisfied, contented, and paid, and thereof, and of every part and parcel thereof, doth clearly acquit, exonerate, and discharge the said Samuel Tower, his heirs, executors, and administrators forever, by these presents, have given, granted, bargained, sold, aliened, enfeoffed, and confirmed, and by these presents do fully, clearly, and absolutely give, grant, bargain, sell, alien, enfeoff, and confirm unto the said Samuel Tower, his heirs and assigns forever, the moiety or one half part of the above-said single share (viz.): the one half of that their brother, Ephraim and Isaac Wilder, purchased of the above-said Michael Peerse (to wit) that moiety or one half of said single share that did belong to the said Ephraim Wilder, according as it is now lotted and laid by the above-said proprietors in two parts and lots (to wit) the one half of the above-said second lot of land in the first part of their division, and the one half of the above-said fifth lot in the second part of their division, which said two lots, being counted together, make one single share of the second part of the said tract of land, each of the said lots being bounded as aforesaid, etc.

Dated May 1, 1696, and signed,   JABEZ WILDER [Seal]

MARY w WILDER [Seal]
mark

May 4, 1696, acknowledged before DANIEL CUSHING, *Justice of the Peace*

The foregoing comprises about one half part of the deed, the covenants being omitted. The land granted by this deed lies in what was afterwards the township of Abington, and by the sub-division of this town it is now in the town of Rockland, which contains the greater part of the tract of three miles square. Many of the descendants of Samuel Tower have continued here, and to-day some of them are living upon this tract of land, in a flourishing town of nearly five thousand inhabitants.

It will be seen that the quantity of land belonging to one share was one hundred and forty-four acres, and Samuel Tower buying one half a share would, on the division of it, be entitled to seventy-two acres.

It will also be noticed that the share was originally granted to Michael Peerse, known in his time by his prowess as the fighting Michael Peerse. The year following the date of his deed to the Wilders, he and his whole company fell into an ambush and were slain by the Indians.

Samuel Tower seems to have come into possession of other lands in the former Plymouth Colony probably through his second marriage, as among his papers is found a lease under date of Feb. 20, 1712, whereby he leases for a term of ten years to Thomas Hathaway, of Dartmouth, in the county of Bristol, —

All that his messuage or tenement lying in the township of Dartmouth; . . . and the leased premises are the moiety or one half part of all the lands, housing, orchards, meadow, and marsh that Daniel Howard, late of Hingham, dec⁴., had in right of his father, John Howard, of Dartmouth, aforesaid, dec⁴, etc.

(Signed,)   SAMUEL TOWER [Seal]

THOMAS HATHAWAY [Seal]

Witnesses, SAMUEL TOWER, JR.
THOMAS TOWER.

By an unrecorded deed, dated April 14, 1716, John Lewis, of Hingham, blacksmith, conveys to Samuel Tower, —

"All that my piece or parcel of swamp lying and being at a place called ' olives ' swamp, on the south side of the training-field in Hingham, . . . and contains by estimation six acres . . . and is butted and bounded northerly with the land or meadow of Matthew Cushing, dec⁴, Easterly with the meadow of John Smith and Peter Ripley, Southerly with a brook that bounds the said swamp from the land of John Wilder, and westerly partly with the land of Jacob Stodder, and partly with the land of Samuel Tower." The consideration named in the deed is " forty-three pounds of the current money of New England."

This price, allowing for depreciation of New England currency, and subjected to the comparative value of days' work, would represent at the present time 415\frac{25}{100}$.

By another unrecorded deed, dated Sept. 1, 1719, John Norton, son of Rev. John Norton, deceased, in consideration of £25 lawful money of New England, conveys to Samuel Tower —

All my salt-marsh lying in the home meadows in the township of Hingham, which salt-marsh my father Norton, late deceased, purchased of Thomas Jewell, and contains by estimation one acre.

(Signed)   JOHN NORTON [Seal]

Witnesses,
  SAMUEL THAXTER, JUN?
  NATHA^{LL} FEARING.

The consideration named in this deed, £25, allowing for depreciation, and subjected as before-mentioned, would represent at the present time $214, — which is probably more than four times the value of this identical piece of land.

Deborah Tower, widow of Samuel Tower, who died Jan. 30, 1741–2, by her last will gives to her "three sons, namely, Daniel, Joshua, and Joseph, in pewter, twenty shillings apiece;" to her "daughter Anna Tower, wife of Peter Tower, one bed and the furniture belonging to the same;" to her "daughter Deborah Tower, my best bed and furniture belonging to the same, also my cow; and further my mind and will is that all the remainder of my estate, both household stuff and movables, shall be, equally with my quick stock, divided between my two daughters abovementioned, Anna and Deborah. . . ." She names her son-in-law, Peter Tower, executor. The will is dated Jan. 14, 1741–2. Among the papers preserved is a bond of Deborah Tower to Peter Tower, dated Sept. 13, 1742, the condition being the payment by Deborah Tower of one half part of the funeral charges and one half part of the debts of " Deborah Tower, late of Hingham, deceased."

her
(Signed)   DEBORAH ◯ TOWER.
mark

In presence of MATTHEW TOWER.
  THEOPHILUS CUSHING.

---

11.   **Fourth Generation.**   **Tower.**

2. BENJAMIN [3], JOHN [2], JOHN [1].

Benjamin [3], son of John [2] and Sarah (Hardin) Tower, born Jan. 25, 1673–4; mar. Deborah Whipple in Rehoboth. She was born Sept. 12, 1681, and was dau. of David and (7) Hannah [2] (Tower) Whipple. Childr. born in Cumberland, R. I.

43.	I.	GIDEON [4]	born	Feb. 24, 1699–1700.
44.	II.	PATIENCE [4]	"	April 10, 1702.
45.	III.	SARAH [4]	"	Aug. 16, 1704.
46.	IV.	MARGARET [4]	"	Oct. 26, 1706.
47.	V.	ZIPPORAH [4]	"	Dec. 17, 1709.
48.	VI.	JOHN [4]	"	Nov. 23, 1711.

	VII.	HANNAH [4] born		Jan. 2, 1713-14 ; mar. Wm. Hancock, of Wrentham, July 19, 1733. He was son of Anthony and Ruth Hancock.
49.	VIII.	BENJAMIN [4]	"	Feb. 25, 1715-16.
	IX.	HESTER [4]	"	Jan. 15, 1717-18.
50.	X.	JOSEPH [4]	"	Sept. 13, 1721.
	XI.	ENOCH [4]	"	Dec. 3, 1724.

Benjamin Tower died about 1743, ag. about 69.
Deborah (Whipple) Tower died about 1755, ag. about 74.

Having given so extended an account of the several members of the family in the first two generations, a brief account only can be given of the many following in the succeeding ones. Benjamin Tower[3], who was born in Hingham, went in early life with his parents to the neighboring town of Braintree. He married his cousin, Deborah Whipple, who resided in that part of the old town of Rehoboth known subsequently as Attleborough Gore, and on the adjustment of the boundary line between Massachusetts and Rhode Island it became the town of Cumberland in the latter State.

He seems to have resided in the northern part of the town, in the vicinity of what is known as " Tower " Hill. His lands are described in the records of the Attleborough proprietors as " one quarter of a whole share purchased of Benjamin Robinson," as by " deed bearing date Feb. 10, 1713." Then follow several grants, — " $6\frac{1}{2}$ acres, . . . being his first lot granted in 1714. . . . Likewise $6\frac{1}{4}$ acres of land, being his second lot adjoining his house-lot, and laid out March 4, 1717-18, and six acres of land drawn on division, 1735." He seems also to have acquired other land in the neighborhood by purchase, — as in 1720 from his brother-in-law, William Whipple ; and in 1724 Job Whipple, of Providence, conveys to Benjamin Tower lands in Attleborough, namely, " three small lots, . . . 6 acres adjoining land of said Tower, on the southeast part of his homestead, and eight acres lying at the end of said Tower's on the east side of a highway by ' Abbott's Run,' and four acres lying on the northeast part of said Tower's lot."

In 1731 John Wilkinson, of Smithfield, conveys to Benjamin Tower " one acre of ' Fresh Meadow,' being on the run commonly called ' Abbott's Run ; ' also two acres adjoining the above meadow." He appears to have had other lands ; and in 1729 he gives to his son Gideon by deed " my four lots in Wrentham, . . . adjoining each other . . . ' at Hoop Pole Hill,' and containing 42 acres." This deed is signed " Benjamin X Tower, his mark."

In 1734 he grants land in Wrentham to his son Gideon Tower, and his son-in-law, William Hancock, both of Wrentham. He also gives land to his sons John and Benjamin, and other land to Gideon.

Benjamin Tower died in 1743. His will is dated Dec. 27, 1742, and proved and allowed Aug. 16, 1743. No memorial-stone marks his grave or that of his wife. The burial-ground nearest to his old homestead is known as the "Ballou" Cemetery, situated opposite to the ancient meeting-house known as the "Ballou" meeting-house. This meeting-house is probably the most ancient of the meeting-houses in Rhode Island; and though the exact date of the building of it is not known, yet tradition carries it back to the early part of the eighteenth century, and it was probably built in the lifetime of Benjamin Tower, and by his aid and contribution. It is now remote from any village, and is only occasionally used for religious services. A descendant of Benjamin Tower has conducted religious services in this meeting-house, as will be seen by the following extract from a letter of the Rev. Adin Ballou : —

"HOPEDALE, MASS., *June* 16, 1884.

"Concerning the ancient Meeting House, we have striven in vain to ascertain the exact date of its erection. We are certain of one important fact, — the date of the deed donating the site by my great grandfather, James Ballou [3]. This was March 22, 1749. But that deed says the house had already been built on the site with his consent. We conjecture that it was built between 1740 and 1749. Obadiah Ballou, brother of James, gave the burial-ground also in 1749. The church structure was first called the 'Elder Cook' meeting-house, because two 'Elder Cooks,' Josiah and Nathaniel, were the first pastors who preached in it successively. After their death 'Elder Abner Ballou' preached in it through a long pastorate of between thirty and forty years. This gave it the title it has long borne. It derives its title, not from me at all, though I preached my first discourse in it about the middle of July, 1821, and have preached in it occasionally many times since.

"It has been repeatedly repaired, from generation to generation; and though at least 140 years old, promises to outlast the present century."

Rev. Adin Ballou is a descendant of Benjamin Tower [3], as will be seen by this Genealogy.

This old meeting-house is worthy of preservation as a specimen of the rude structures our fathers were wont to build for religious purposes; and it was probably in keeping with their circumstances and surroundings, as they lived in a sparsely settled agricultural community.

The external appearance of the building suggests rather a two-story dwelling-house than a public building. It has entrances on two sides. The interior shows the frame of oaken timber as it was put in place on the day it was built. There are galleries on three sides, supported by the same oaken timbers, whose roughness is unrelieved by any plastered or finished ceiling. The preacher's desk occupies nearly all the space on the other side of the house, projecting about two feet from the same, showing a frontage of plain pine boards in a vertical parallelogram of about fifteen by six feet, and the fronts of the galleries are finished in the same manner. All the wood-work is guiltless of paint, exhibiting the original color of the wood, except as time has darkened it.

The seating accommodation of the house is by the old oaken benches, with upright backs and somewhat narrow seats, which are placed so near together as to suggest the question of a smaller size of people than the present generation, did not tradition contradict it by the tales of their feats of strength and endurance.

Benjamin Tower, by his will, gives his wife one half of his personal property and the improvement of his homestead lot, and six acres of land.

He gives to his son Gideon " one shilling ; and that, with what I formerly gave him, shall be his full part of my estate." To his son John a quarter right in the undivided land in Attleborough, " with what I have formerly given him, shall be his full share."

He gives to his son Joseph " the whole of my home-lot, together with a six-acre lot," etc., conditioned on his paying his five sisters five pounds each ; to his grandson, Nathan Carpenter, " that lives with me, . . . my gun, sword, cartouch-box, and chest."

He directs his " son Gideon to sell all his interest in land eastward at a place called ' Sheepsent,' . . . the proceeds to be divided equally among my children."

His widow Deborah died in 1755. In the record of deeds for Cumberland, R. I., is a " plat " of land, containing between forty and fifty acres, divided into four parts, and marked respectively, Gideon, John, Benjamin, and Joseph, with the following recital : " Land formerly a part of the homestead of Benjamin Tower, late of Cumberland, deceased, . . . given to us by our honored mother, Deborah Tower, deceased, by her last will and testament. . . . Division according to a plan made by Thomas Wilmarth, surveyor." Dated May 24, 1755.

2. JOSEPH [3], JOHN [2], JOHN [1].

Joseph [3], son of John [2] and Sarah (Hardin) Tower, born Feb. 27, 1685–6; mar. Ruth Thayer. Childr. born in Braintree.

	I.	RUTH [4]	born March 6, 1711.
51.	II.	HANNAH [4]	" Sept. 18, 1713.
	III.	SARAH [4]	" Feb. 18, 1715–16.
52.	IV.	JOHN [4]	" Feb. 7, 1717–18.
	V.	MARGARET [4]	" Aug. 21, 1721.
53.	VI.	GIDEON [4]	" 1723.
54.	VII.	JOSEPH [4]	
55.	VIII.	MARY [4]	

Ruth (Thayer) Tower died in Braintree March 28, 1752.

Joseph Tower [3] mar., 2d, Elizabeth Arnold, in Braintree, int. pub. March 27, 1756; and mar., 3d, widow Hannah Jones, in Braintree. Int. pub. September, 1759.

Joseph Tower [3] lived in Braintree, where he probably died. His wife, Ruth (Thayer) Tower, died in Braintree March 28, 1752. In the Braintree records of marriage intentions are the following: Joseph Tower and Elizabeth Arnold, March 27, 1756, and Joseph Tower and widow Hannah Jones, September, 1759. No record of his death or of these later wives appears in the Braintree records. There appears to be neither will nor administration upon his estate. He probably lived in that part of Braintree which is now included in the town of Randolph.

A few transactions in real estate to which he was a party are found in the Suffolk Registry of Deeds. Oct. 27, 1742, Joseph Tower conveys to Richard and Stanley Sylvester, laborers, for the consideration of " £25 lawful money of the Province," forty-two acres of woodland lying in the southernmost precinct of Braintree.

July 16, 1743, Richard and Stanley Sylvester re-convey the same land to Joseph Tower, of Braintree, set-work cooper.

April 6, 1742, Joseph Tower, of Braintree, conveys to Samuel Allen, of Braintree, blacksmith, consideration £25, ten acres of land in " Moor's Farm," so-called, reserving a right of way to the " Great Meadow."

Feb. 2, 1731–2, Christopher Dyer, of Braintree, conveys to Joseph Tower, of Braintree, consideration £180, " one messuage or tenement, containing fifty acres, lying and being in Braintree, aforesaid, bounded northerly by land of Isaac Royal and John

Kinsley, east by lands of Deacon Samuel White, south by land of Joshua Hayward, and west by the fifteenth lot in the sixth division, together with one single share of land and one third part of a single share, both lying in the fore-mentioned fifteenth lot, which lots are known by the name of the ' Great Pond lots.' "

May 15, 1744. "Joseph Tower and John Tower, both of Braintree, husbandmen," convey to Josiah Thayer and Caleb Thayer, both of said Braintree, husbandmen, consideration £10, two acres of land in Braintree. Ruth Tower and Rachel Tower release dower.

Feb. 19, 1749–50. Joseph Tower, of Braintree, set-work cooper, conveys to David Holbrook et als., of Braintree, consideration £100, twenty acres, chiefly pasture land, at " Moor's Farm."

Jan. 28, 1761. Joseph Tower, of Braintree, yeoman, conveys to Benjamin Hayden, consideration £14 11s. 4d., four acres of meadow and swamp land in Braintree, near " Monekquot " river. This deed is acknowledged Aug. 29, 1761. This is the latest transaction of Joseph Tower which appears of record. At the date of the acknowledgment he was in the seventy-sixth year of his age, and probably the date of his death was not far from this time.

---

13. Spear.   **Fourth Generation.**   **Tower.**

2. MARY [3], JOHN [2], JOHN [1].

Mary [3], dau. of John [2] and Sarah (Hardin) Tower, born April 26, 1690; mar. Ebenezer Spear in Braintree Jan. 12, 1726–7, by Rev. Samuel Niles. E. Spear born in Braintree June 27, 1680, and was son of Ebenezer and Rachel (Deering) Spear. Child.

     I.   GIDEON [4], born May 24, 1730, in Braintree.

---

14.   **Fourth Generation.**   **Tower.**

3. RICHARD [3], IBROOK [2], JOHN [1].

Richard [3], son of Ibrook [2] and Margaret (Hardin) Tower, born July 20, 1669; mar. Abigail Farrar. She was born in Hingham Jan. 27, 1669–70, and was dau. of John and Mary (Hilliard) Farrar. Childr. all born in Hingham (Cohasset).

56.	I.	ABIGAIL [4]	born March 14, 1693–4.
57.	II.	RACHEL [4]	" Feb. 24, 1696–7.
58.	III.	ELISHA [4]	" May 22, 1700.
	IV.	OBADIAH [4]	" March 31, 1702.

Richard Tower [3] died in Hingham (Cohasset) Dec. 21, 1702, ag. 33 y. 5 m. 1 d.

Abigail (Farrar) Tower died in Hingham, Oct. 5, 1745, ag. 75 y. 8 m. 8 d.

| 15. | Fourth Generation. | Tower. |

3. JOHN [3], IBROOK [2], JOHN [1].

John [3], son of Ibrook [2] and Margaret (Hardin) Tower, born March 21, 1672–3 ; mar. Hester Canterbury in Hingham Jan. 15, 1695–6, by Rev. John Norton. She was born in Hingham Nov. 19, 1671, and was dau. of Cornelius and Anna Canterbury. Childr. all born in Hingham (Cohasset).

59.	I.	JOHN [4]	born Jan. 21, 1696–7.
	II.	HESTER [4]	" Sept. 2, 1698 ; died May 9, 1700, ag. 1 y. 8 m. 7 d.
60.	III.	ESTHER [4]	" Sept. 22, 1700.
61.	IV.	CORNELIUS [4]	" Feb. 5, 1701–2.
62.	V.	MARTHA [4]	" Jan. 14, 1703–4.
37.	VI.	ELIZABETH [4]	" Sept. 18, 1705.
	VII.	MARY [4]	" July 21, 1707 ; died Aug.17, 1730, ag. 23 y. 26 d.
	VIII.	NEHEMIAH [4]	" March 8, 1708–9 ; unmar. ; died 1749–50, ag. 40 y.
	IX.	ANN [4]	mar. John Harding, of Eastham, Nov. 16, 1737.

John Tower [3] died in Cohasset, Dec. 9, 1711, ag. 38 y. 8 m. 18 d.

Hester (Canterbury) Tower died in Cohasset, Dec. 25, 1729, ag. 58 y. 1 m. 6 d.

Nehemiah Tower's [4] death probably took place near the time when administration was granted upon his estate to his brother John, Feb. 23, 1749–50. He is called "shipwright."

| 16. Bates. | Fourth Generation. | Tower. |

3. RACHEL [3], IBROOK [2], JOHN [1].

Rachel [3], dau. of Ibrook [2] and Margaret (Hardin) Tower, born March 16, 1674–5 ; mar. Joshua Bates in Hingham (Cohasset), Jan. 15, 1695–6, by Rev. John Norton. J. Bates, born Aug. 14, 1671, was son of Joseph and Esther (Hilliard) Bates. Childr. all born in Hingham (Cohasset).

I.	RACHEL [4]	born July 14, 1696.
II.	JOSHUA [4]	" June 15, 1698.
III.	BATHSHEBA [4]	" Feb. 9, 1699–1700 ; mar. Perry.
IV.	ELIZABETH [4]	" Nov. 23, 1703 ; mar. Ebenezer Woodward.
V.	SOLOMON [4]	" April 13, 1706.
VI.	ISAAC [4]	" March 3, 1707–8.
VII.	JACOB [4]	" Aug. 20, 1710.

Joshua Bates died in Hingham (Cohasset) April, 1757, ag. 85 y. 8 m.

Rachel (Tower) Bates died

Of Ibrook Tower's children, Richard and John died in early manhood. His daughter Rachel[3] mar. Joshua Bates[3], a descendant of Clement Bates, one of the earlier settlers of Hingham. Joshua Bates resided in that part of Hingham which is now the town of Cohasset. The descendants of Joshua and Rachel (Tower) Bates have been and are now numerous in Cohasset and the neighboring towns. Some of them by intermarriage have again taken the name of Tower; some have gone out in the many different lines of emigration which at times have gone from older seaboard towns to subdue the wilderness of western New England, and in continuation, borne by the ever-increasing wave, the later descendants have been swept through all the States to the Pacific ocean.

In the old French and Indian war Massachusetts largely supplied the forces for carrying on the yearly expeditions against the French at Ticonderoga and Crown Point. The men engaged in these expeditions became familiar with the various parts of the wilderness through which their route lay; and at the close of the war, emigration for the settlement of portions of this region commenced. The hill-towns in Massachusetts west of the Connecticut river, and portions of Vermont, received early attention, calling for hardy enterprise and persevering industry.

The War of the Revolution found the same field for action in the first years of its progress as in the French war; and Ticonderoga and Crown Point were again the objective points of attack and defence, and again the tramp of the New England militia resounded through the woods until the time of the capture of Burgoyne.

At the close of the war many of the men of the seaboard towns found their old occupations in commercial and fishing pursuits gone; and the lands in the older settlements having been all appropriated, there seemed to be nothing left for them to do but to seek new fields for their work and enterprise. Those who held small allotments of land sold them for the most they could get; and the younger men, who had nothing of property, put into the common stock their contribution of energy and hope.

And again the Western movement begins, — not this time in martial array, but the patient ox is harnessed to the heavy wagon, laden with the household utensils and implements of anticipated labor, covered with the folds of amply protecting canvas, under which the women and children find protection from the weather,

until after many days they find rest for their weariness in the
forest solitude of their new home.

Abner Bates [5], James Bates, and Nehemiah Bates, grandsons of
Joshua and Rachel (Tower) went to Chesterfield, Mass., which
from the nativity of many of its early settlers was at first called
New Hingham.   Levi Bates, Theophilus Bates, and Phineas Bates,
brothers, and Josiah Bates, a cousin of the former named, all
great-grandsons of Joshua [3] and Rachel [3] (Tower), went to Springfield, Vt., in the early settlement of that town.   They had obtained
a knowledge of the locality through the many marches and counter-
marches, during the War of the Revolution, which they made from
the seaboard to Ticonderoga and Crown Point.   Fort No. 4, now
Charlestown, N. H., was an objective point of rendezvous; thence
directly across the Connecticut, the trail ran over the high hills
and through the wilderness, now converted by the labors of these
pioneers into the productive and beautiful farms of the mountain
town.   Their descendants made closer the connection with the
Tower family by frequent intermarriages.

Some of the descendants are remembered by their ability and
sacrifices in the line of their calling.   The names of Rev. Dexter
Bates and his brother, Rev. Lewis Bates, will readily occur.   Both
of them were early workers in the Methodist Episcopal Church in
the period of frontier life, when the minister required large physical endowments as well as mental equipment to meet the demands made upon him.   In all respects these brothers were well
prepared, and wrought with great efficiency in their Master's
service.   The following anecdote in the life of Father Taylor, the
sailor preacher, will show to what unusual service these frontier
preachers were sometimes called : —

"It was on the occasion of the camp-meeting, some sixty years ago.
Just after the meeting had commenced, rumors of war had reached the camp.
A gang of dissolute fellows, headed by a notorious bully, had signified their
intention of breaking up the camp-meeting.   The brethren, however, paid
but little heed to these threats, and proceeded with their exercises.   One
morning, just as the forenoon services were to commence, an excited and
almost breathless brother rushed up to the preacher's stand with the news
that the gang of roughs were on the march for the camp-ground.   Some
confusion ensued, when up sprang Father Taylor, shouting in stentorian
tones : 'Who will go with me and fight these Philistines?'   The first
man to respond was Rev. Lewis Bates.   He was a man of large stature
and herculean strength.   Father Taylor was then in his prime, and very
tough, wiry, and muscular.   Several stalwart brethren at once volunteered,
and in less than five minutes' time were on the way to meet the foe.   When
just on the outskirts of the grounds they encountered the band of ruffians,

headed by their leader, a huge, wicked-looking fellow. ' Now,' says Brother Bates, ' I will tackle that leader myself ; and the rest of you make the best use of your fists and cudgels.' The two giants approached and clinched. In an instant the bully was thrown to the ground with great violence, and the heavy foot of Brother Bates was placed upon his throat. In the mean time Father Taylor and his aids made such a vigorous assault upon the rest of the gang that they fled for dear life. Brother Bates now addressed the prostrate bully, who was writhing and choking under the heavy pressure, ' Beg for mercy, you scoundrel ! ' And he did beg, and solemnly promised never to disturb another camp-meeting ; upon which he was released."

Rev. Lewis Bates continued in the ministry, in contests with other and not so easily defeated foes, until a late period in life, dying at the ripe age of eighty-five years. His sons — Rev. George W. Bates and Rev. Lewis B. Bates — are worthy sons of so distinguished a father.

In this connection, it is proper to name Rev. Joshua Bates[7], D.D., late president of Middlebury College, of Vermont, and his son so well remembered in educational work, the late Joshua Bates[8], the life-long teacher and master of the Brimmer School, of Boston.

| 17. Whiton. | Fourth Generation. | Tower. |

3. MARY[3], IBROOK[2], JOHN[1].

Mary[3], dau. of Ibrook[2] and Margaret (Hardin) Tower, born Aug. 16, 1677 ; mar. John Whiton, of Hingham, Feb. 3, 1703–4, by Rev. John Norton. J. Whiton born in Hingham Jan. 10, 1679–80, and was son of Matthew and Deborah (Pitt) (Hayward) Whiton. Childr. all born in Hingham.

I.	JOHN[4]	born Nov. 7, 1704; died Nov. 15,1725, ag. 21 y. 8 m.
II.	DEBORAH[4]	" March 3, 1705–6 ; mar. Solomon Bates, of Scituate, May 1, 1730.
III.	MARGARET[4]	" Feb. 3, 1707–8; mar. John Collamore, of Scituate, April 27, 1732.
IV.	JOSHUA[4]	" April 14, 1710; settled in Scituate; wife, Silence.
V.	ANN[4]	" June 18, 1711; unmar.; died Sept. 13, 1799, ag. 88 y. 2 m. 26 d.
VI.	LYDIA[4]	" May 26,1714; died Oct. 19, 1734, ag. 20 y. 4 m. 23 d.
VII.	MARY[4]	" 1716.

| 18. James Farrar. | Fourth Generation. | Tower. |

3. PATIENCE[3], IBROOK[2], JOHN[1].

Patience[3], dau. of Ibrook[2] and Margaret (Hardin) Tower, born March 21, 1678–9; mar. William Farrar Jan. 31, 1700–1701, by

Rev. J. Norton. William Farrar born in Hingham Nov. 17, 1677, and was son of John and Mary (Hilliard) Farrar. Child.

> I.   PATIENCE [4]   born Feb. 7, 1701–2.

William Farrar died Dec. 23, 1702, ag. 25 y. 1 m. 6 d.

Patience (Tower) Farrar mar., 2d, Thomas James, of Hingham, May 30, 1704, by Rev. John Wilson, of Braintree. Thomas James born in Hingham Dec. 9, 1669, and was son of Francis and Elizabeth James. Childr.

II.	THOMAS [4]	born Jan. 11, 1704–5.
III.	ELIZABETH [4]	" Aug. 20, 1706; mar. Abisha Stetson, of Kingston, Aug. 21, 1730.
IV.	PHILIP [4]	" July 25, 1708.
V.	JOHN [4]	" 1712.
VI.	JANE [4]	" Sept. 27, 1714; mar. Jeremiah Lane, June 27, 1734.
VII.	SARAH [4]	" Sept. 27, 1714; died Nov. 28, 1714.
VIII.	MARGARET [4]	" March 19, 1715–16; mar. Samuel Drew, of Hingham, March 1, 1737.
IX.	CONTENT [4]	" 1718; mar. Samuel Harding, of Eastham, Oct. 3, 1739.

Thomas James died in Hingham (Cohasset) July 31, 1724, ag. 54 y. 7 m. 22 d.

Patience (Tower) (Farrar) James died subsequent to 1750.

Of the descendants of Patience [3], a daughter of Ibrook Tower, may be named Ruth James [5], who married Joseph Loring, of Hingham. Her sons, Josiah [6] and Benjamin [6], twins, and bachelors through their lives, were noted stationers in Boston, and Colonel Benjamin made a gift to the people of his native town, who have built a memorial hall nearly opposite to his birthplace, which bears his family name. Two other sons, Elijah [6] and George [6] were largely engaged in the fruit trade of Southern Europe. Elijah conducted the business in Boston, while George lived in Spain, and died there in 1843 at the age of seventy-one. He married a Spanish lady of gentle birth, and his descendants have allied themselves with the distinguished families of Spain. A grandson, George Loring [8], has been entitled to the distinction of " The Marquis de Casa Loring, member of the Cortes, deputy from the province of Malaga."

19.   **Fourth Generation.**   **Tower.**

3. HEZEKIAH [3], IBROOK [2], JOHN [1].

Hezekiah [3], son of Ibrook [2] and Margaret (Hardin) Tower, bapt. Oct. 9, 1681; mar. Elizabeth Whiton, of Hingham, Jan. 13, 1703–4, by Rev. John Norton. She was born in Hingham March

31, 1684, and was dau. of Matthew and Deborah (Pitt) (Hayward) Whiton. Childr. all born in Hingham (Cohasset).

63.   I.   ELIZABETH [4] born June 11, 1705.
64.   II.   SUSANNAH [4]   "   April 16, 1707.
65.   III.   DAVID [4]   "   Aug. 28, 1708.
66.   IV.   LYDIA [4]   "   May 1, 1713.
    V.   RUTH [4]   "   Oct. 28, 1717; died March 23, 1770, ag. 52 y. 4 m. 23 d.

Elizabeth (Whiton) Tower died
Hezekiah Tower [3] died in Hingham (Cohasset) subsequent to 1765.

Hezekiah Tower [3] lived in that part of Hingham which is now Cohasset. He owned lands and probably resided near " Scituate Pond," — so called, the old record says, " not because it lieth within the town of Scituate, but because the way leading thereto passes this pond." For many years afterwards it colloquially bore the name of " Kiah TORE's Pond," " Tore " being a corrupt pronunciation of Tower, which at one time was quite prevalent. The written name, however, seldom followed that pronunciation.

The date of the death of Hezekiah Tower and that of his wife does not appear of record. There is neither will nor administration upon his estate.

In 1754, at the age of seventy-three, he conveys to his son David Tower " a certain piece of land, being my homestead, lying nigh to a pond called Scituate Pond, . . . and is part of the first lot in the second part of the third division, on the northwest side of the pond aforesaid, and contains by estimation seven acres, be it more or less, . . . reserving to myself one acre in the westerly corner of the land aforesaid, whereon the dwelling-house of John Burbank now standeth." In this deed Hezekiah Tower and his son David are called " coopers."

In 1747–8, January 7, he made a conveyance to his son David of about fourteen acres of land in the eightieth lot of the second division. This lot is situated near the former lot.

In 1758, March 15, he made another conveyance to his son David of three acres of land, near the last-named lot.

In 1765, March 4, he conveys to his grandson, Abner Tower, three acres of land in the second division, " lying northwest on the land of David Tower, which he purchased of me. . . . Also that my piece or parcel of meadow which I purchased of my father, Ibrook Tower, in the township of Scituate, . . . being a part of that which is called the threescore acres."

In 1765, Oct. 1, he conveys to Lydia Tower, widow of Abner Tower, and to her two sons, Ephraim and Elijah, about twelve acres of land in the second division. This land is "bounded southeast with land of me, the said Hezekiah Tower. . . ." This deed was acknowledged Nov. 24, 1766. He was then in his eighty-sixth year.

Much of the land and many of the dwellings are now owned and occupied by the descendants of Ibrook Tower through the female lines.

20. Souther.   Fourth Generation.   Tower.

3. CONTENT [3], IBROOK [2], JOHN [1].

Content [3], dau. of Ibrook [2] and Margaret (Hardin) Tower, born Feb. 3, 1683–4; mar. Joseph Souther April 22, 1708, by Rev. John Norton. Childr. all born in Cohasset.

I.	HANNAH [4]	born March 16, 1708–9; died Oct. 17, 1725, ag. 16 y. 7 m. 1 d.
II.	SAMUEL [4]	" Oct. 15, 1711; died July 20, 1713, ag. 1 y. 9 m. 5 d.
III.	SARAH [4]	" May 28, 1714; mar. Joseph Blake Nov. 1, 1734.
IV.	MARY [4]	" March 3, 1715–16; mar. James Cushing, of Scituate, Jan. 21, 1738–9.
V.	JOSEPH [4]	" Nov. 20, 1721.
VI.	ELIZABETH [4]	bapt. Nov. 4, 1722; mar. Micah Jepson Sept. 5, 1744.
VII.	DANIEL [4]	" Aug. 13, 1727, *s. p.*

Content (Tower) Souther died in Cohasset Dec. 18, 1730, ag. 46 y. 10 m. 15 d.

Joseph Souther died in Cohasset July 22, 1740.

Content Tower [3], daughter of Ibrook [2], married Joseph Souther. He is the first of the name found in the Hingham records, and those who have since resided in Hingham and its vicinity bearing the name are his descendants, many of whom continued to follow his business of a ship-builder until that business was abandoned here.

A descendant, Francis Lincoln Souther, was shot at the battle of Big Bethel, and died of his wounds at Fortress Monroe June 9, 1861. He was probably the first Massachusetts soldier killed in battle in the War of the Rebellion. The longevity of one family in this line of descent may be worthy of preservation. The record is as follows. Childr. of John and Deborah (Leavitt) Souther.

I. JOHN [6] born Sept. 13, 1781; died in Boston March 28, 1878, ag. 96 y. 6 m. 14 d.
II. DEBORAH [6] " Sept. 29, 1783; " " 1866, ag. 86.
III. POLLY [6] " Feb. 5, 1787; " " Boston June 13, 1881, ag. 94 y. 4 m. 8 d.
IV. LYDIA [6] " June 17, 1789; " " Quincy Oct. 14,1889, ag. 100 y. 3 m. 27 d.
V. HARRIET [6] " Nov. 28, 1791; " " Hingham Oct. 18, 1880, ag. 88 y. 10 m. 14 d.
VI. LEAVITT [6] " May 1, 1794; " " Hingham July 27, 1865, ag. 71 y. 2 m. 26 d.
VII. HANNAH [6] " Feb. 7, 1798; " " Hingham July 2, 1889, ag. 91 y. 4 m. 23 d.

21. Franklin.   Fourth Generation.   Tower.

3. LYDIA [3], IBROOK [2], JOHN [1].

Lydia [3], dau. of Ibrook [2] and Margaret (Hardin) Tower, born Nov. 25, 1687; mar. John Franklin March 15, 1711–12. Childr. born in Hingham.

I. SARAH [4] born April 14, 1713; mar. John Curtis, of Scituate, June 29, 1732.
II. LYDIA [4] " Jan. 3, 1714–15; died Feb. 4, 1715–16; ag. 1 y. 1 m. 1 d.
III. LYDIA [4] " Sept. 18, 1717.
IV. ELIZABETH [4] " Oct. 17, 1720.
V. MARGARET [4] " Jan. 25, 1722–23.
VI. MARY [4] " March 14, 1724–25.

22.   Fourth Generation.   Tower.

3. DANIEL [0], IBROOK [2], JOHN [1].

Daniel [3], son of Ibrook [2] and Margaret (Hardin) Tower, born July 24, 1692; mar. Sarah Lincoln, of Cohasset. Int. pub. Feb. 25, 1715–16. She was born July 14, 1694, and was dau. of Mordecai and Sarah (Jones) Lincoln. Childr. born in Cohasset.

67. I. SARAH [4] born June 24, 1717.
68. II. DANIEL [4] " June 23, 1720.
    III. ABRAHAM [4] " Jan. 31, 1722–23; died May 9, 1736, ag. 13 y. 3 m. 9 d.
69. IV. JOB [4] " Sept. 8, 1726.
    V. MORDECAI [4] " Aug. 6, 1729; " June 10, 1736, ag. 6 y. 10 m. 4 d.
    VI. THANKFUL [4] " Sept., 1732; " May 2, 1733, ag. 8 m.
    VII. THANKFUL [4] " Oct. 2, 1734; " Nov. 18, 1743, ag. 9 y. 1 m. 16 d.

Sarah (Lincoln) Tower died in Cohasset July 7, 1754, ag. 59 y. 11 m. 23 d.

Daniel Tower[3] mar., 2d, Persis Curtis, of Hanover, Feb. 26, 1755; she was born in Hanover,   1707.

Daniel Tower[3] died in Cohasset Feb. 21, 1774, ag. 81 y. 7 m.

Persis (Curtis) Tower died in Hanover June 24, 1787, ag. 80 y

In Daniel Cushing's record of the early immigration to Hingham we find the following: —

"1637. John Tower and Samuel Lincoln came from Old Hingham, and both settled in New Hingham."

Daniel Tower[3] was the grandson of the first, and his wife Sarah was the granddaughter of the last named. Her mother was Sarah Jones, of Hull, the daughter of Abraham Jones. The name Abraham in the Tower and Lincoln families among those descending from Abraham Jones has been handed down through successive generations to the present time. Our late martyred President, we have ample evidence to believe, was one of the descendants.

Daniel Tower[3] came by inheritance into the possession of a part of his father's homestead, which we have already noticed was upon land allotted to John Tower in the first division of the Cohasset lands in 1670. It has been handed down through successive generations, and is now owned and occupied by Abraham H. Tower and his brothers Henry C. and Newcomb B. Tower.

Daniel Tower's will is dated Aug. 1, 1771, in which he names his wife Persis, and to whom he gives —

"All the movables she brought at our marriage . . ." and other personal property, on the condition that she shall relinquish dower in his real estate. He gives to his son Daniel "my dwelling-house, barn, and all my homestead adjoining in the first division of Cohasset uplands. . . ." Gives to his son Job "my dwelling-house and barn which he now lives in, with all my land there adjoining. . . ." He gives the rest of his lands in equal parts to his sons Daniel and Job. He mentions his daughter Sarah Whitcomb.

He gives "my negro woman Philis her freedom at my decease; also my son Daniel shall support her out of the estate I have given him, if she should come to want; also that she shall dwell with which of my sons she shall be pleased to dwell with; also at Philis' decease my son Daniel shall be at the charge to bury her."

23.   **Fourth Generation.**   **Tower.**

4. JEREMIAH[3], JEREMIAH[2], JOHN[1].

Jeremiah[3], son of Jeremiah[2] and Elizabeth (Rowlands) Tower, born Sept. 10, 1671; mar. Hannah Hobart, in Hingham, Jan. 3,

1698–9, by Rev. John Norton. She was bapt. in Hingham June 20, 1675, and was dau. of John and Hannah (Burr) Hobart. Childr. born in Hingham.

	I.	ELIZABETH[4]	born	Sept. 1, 1699 ; died Sept. 6, 1749, ag. 50 y. 5 d.
70.	II.	PETER[4]	"	Sept. 14, 1701.
71.	III.	HANNAH[4]	"	April 11, 1705.
	IV.	ROWLANDS[4]	"	Nov. 29, 1707; died Jan. 21, 1723–4, ag. 16 y. 1 m. 22 d.

Jeremiah Tower[3] died in Hingham April 20, 1743, ag. 71 y. 7 m. 10 d.

Hannah (Hobart) Tower died in Hingham Sept. 12, 1749, ag. 74 y. 2 m. 23 d.

24. Sprague.   Fourth Generation.   Tower.

4. MARY[3], JEREMIAH[2], JOHN[1].

Mary[3], dau. of Jeremiah[2], and Elizabeth (Rowlands) Tower, born Nov. 3, 1672; mar. William Sprague, of Providence, R. I. Int. pub. Nov. 5, 1709. He was born in Hingham July 2, 1650, and was son of William and Millesant Sprague. Childr. born in Providence.

	I.	ROWLAND[4]	born
	II.	PETER[4]	"
	III.	MARY[4]	"
	IV.	JUDAH[4]	"

William Sprague died in Providence, R. I.,   1723, ag. 73.

Mary (Tower) Sprague was the second wife of William Sprague, who removed from Hingham to Providence, R. I., where he died in 1723. He names several children by his former marriage, his wife Mary and her children, Rowland, Peter, Mary, and Judah. To his sons Rowland and Peter, he gives his homestead when they come to the age of twenty-one years ; and to his daughters Mary and Judah he gives one hundred acres of land without the seven-mile limit when they come to the age of eighteen years.

The homestead given to Rowland and Peter was situated mostly in Cranston. Rowland sold his portion to Peter, who by his will, after making provision for his wife, his daughter Amey, and grandson Abner, gives all the rest and residue of his property to his son William. The inventory of his personal property, made in 1790, shows the extent of his business as a farmer, while the prices of the products of the farm may be interesting and instructive by way of comparison with the prices of the same products at the present time. The following are selected for this purpose :

12 bu. of potatoes, 12s.; that is 16⅔ cents per bu.

630 lbs. of pork, £10 10s.; about 5½ cents per lb.

55 lbs. of salt beef, 11s. 6d.; about 3½ cents per lb.

80 lbs. of new milk cheese, £1 10s.; about 6¼ cents per lb.

61 lbs. of hog's lard, £1 5s. 5d.; about 7 cents per lb.

6 lbs. of butter, 3s. 6d.; nearly 10 cents per lb.

44 bu. of corn, £6 12s.; 50 cents per bu.

7 bu. of barley, 18s. 8d.; about 44 cents per bu.

3½ bu. of rye, 15s. 9d.; 75 cents per bu.

½ ton of English hay, 24s.; eight dollars per ton.

It will be seen that the price of Indian corn, then the great staple for bread, is about the same as at the present time; while all the other products of the farm, which then, as now, were necessary for the support of a family, were held at a greatly reduced rate.

William Sprague[5], the son of Peter[4] and the residuary devisee under his father's will, died April 1, 1795, and by his will, after making provision for his wife and children, Sarah and Peter, gives all the rest and residue of his property to his sons Abner[6] and William[6].

William Sprague[6] died in Cranston in 1836. In addition to his work as a farmer on the old homestead, he was one of the pioneer manufacturers who have made the State of Rhode Island so noted and prosperous. He is remembered as a man of great capacity for labor, of indomitable energy and persevering industry, united with business qualifications in an eminent degree. The result of these valuable equipments is seen in the provisions of his will, wherein he makes liberal provision for his children and grandchildren, and gives all the rest and residue of his estate, "including mills and machinery, bleaching and printing-works, to his sons William[7] and Amasa[7]."

With what success these sons conducted the business coming to them by this devise has already become a part of the history of Rhode Island, in the great wealth accumulated, and the high and honorable distinction attained by the capacity which these brothers evinced in the management of the great interests committed to them. William was elected to several offices of public trust, and became the Governor of the State and a Member of Congress.

They were men of large stature and well proportioned. Amasa is remembered as a man of inflexible determination. He had the direct management of the printing-mills in Cranston; and being much annoyed by the rumsellers in the neighborhood in the effects of their business upon the operatives in the mills, he determined to break them up, and followed up this determination so closely as exceedingly to anger the men engaged therein. On his way home one night he was waylaid and brutally murdered. The murderers were arrested and tried. One was executed, and one was sentenced to State prison for life, where he died. The sons of Amasa[7], Amasa[8] and William[8], succeeded to the business and wealth of their father, and William followed closely the career of his uncle in the offices to which he has been elected. At the commencement of the War of the Rebellion he was Governor of Rhode Island. He rendered the government efficient aid by the promptness with which he organized troops and early sent them forward, going himself as their commander.

It would be pleasant could this brief sketch of enterprise, industry, and thrift stop here. But the sequel to the story is the old one so often found in the history of wealth gained in our country. The great fortune of this family, gained by the industry and enterprise of a few generations, and amounting in its accumulations to millions, has within the last twenty-five years passed from the possession of these brothers.

Some portions of it probably remain among other descendants. One thing worthy of notice is that the real estate coming from Peter Sprague[4] must, from its situation, lie, in part at least, in the very land which his ancestor, John Tower, bought of the Indians.

---

25. Hollis.   **Fourth Generation.**   **Tower.**

8. ABIGAIL[3], BENJAMIN[2], JOHN[1].

Abigail[3], dau. of Benjamin[2] and Deborah (Garnet) Tower, bapt. May 22, 1681 ; mar. Samuel Hollis, of Weymouth. Childr. all born in Weymouth.

73.	I.	SAMUEL[4] born	Jan. 12, 1711.
	II.	ABIGAIL[4] "	March 20, 1712.
72.	III.	DEBORAH[4] "	March 21, 1713.
	IV.	THOMAS[4] "	May 20, 1714.
	V.	THOMAS[4] "	May 5, 1715.
	VI.	BENJAMIN[4] "	Nov. 5, 1716.
	VII.	JOHN[4] "	April 5, 1718; mar. Jerusha Clark Sept. 28, 1738.
	VIII	STEPHEN[4] "	April 5, 1721.
	IX.	JAEL[4] "	Jan. 3, 1722.
75.	X.	LYDIA[4] "	June 5, 1723.
	XI.	STEPHEN[4] "	March 22, 1725; mar. Nabby Porter Dec. 18, 1783. She was born in Weymouth April 7, 1753, and was dau. of Matthew and Sarah (Pratt) Porter.

Samuel Hollis died in Weymouth Nov. 15, 1740.

8. DEBORAH[3], BENJAMIN[2], JOHN[1].

Deborah[3], dau. of Benjamin[2] and Deborah (Garnet) Tower, b.
Feb. 4, 1684–5 ; mar. Robert Corthell in Hingham, Oct. 13, 1708, by
Rev. John Norton. R. Corthell born in Scotland. Childr. born in
Hingham.

I.	MARY[4]	born	Nov. 13, 1709.
II.	DEBORAH[4]	"	Aug. 24, 1711.
III.	JOHN[4]	"	March 23, 1712–13.
IV.	DANIEL[4]	"	July 27, 1715.
V.	ABIGAIL[4]	"	Sept. 21, 1717.
VI.	ROBERT[4]	"	May 21, 1720.
VII.	HANNAH[4]	"	Feb. 28, 1724.

Robert Corthell died March 5, 1737–8, ag. 51.

Robert Corthell was the first of the name whom we find in
Hingham. Tradition loves to dwell upon the story of his abduc-
tion from Scotland in childhood. The name is not often found
in our early history, and those of this vicinity and in Maine can
generally trace their descent from Robert and Deborah (Tower)
Corthell.

Of those who have interested themselves in this genealogy may
be named John K. Corthell[8], of Hingham, whose son, Charles
Loring[9], graduated from West Point in 1884, and is now a lieutenant in the 4th Regt. U. S. Artillery. He is the second in
descent from John Tower[1], among the graduates from this
military academy.

William P. Corthell[7], born 1814, of Whitman, in this commonwealth, a town recently formed from the south part of Abington,
was a representative from Abington to the Massachusetts legislature in 1850 and 1853. He was one of the selectmen of Abington
from 1850 to 1856, was a special commissioner for the county of
Plymouth in 1860 and 1861, and one of the county commissioners
for the same county from 1862 to 1877, inclusive, — a period of
fifteen years. He was one of the selectmen of South Abington,
now Whitman, for ten years.

William J. Corthell[7], born 1826, resides in Gorham, Me. He
graduated from Waterville College in 1857. He has been engaged
in teaching the greater part of his life. He was county superintendent of schools for three years, and State superintendent for a
like period. He has been municipal judge for the city of Calais,
Me., and he also was representative from that city for six years,
and senator from Washington county for two years, in the legislature of Maine.

27.   **Fourth Generation.**   **Tower.**

8. BENJAMIN[3], BENJAMIN[2], JOHN[1].

Benjamin[3], son of Benjamin[2] and Deborah (Garnet) Tower, born Sept. 2, 1686 ; mar. Margaret (   ). Childr.

> I. JEMIMA[4] born Jan. 2, 1711, in Weymouth; mar. William Prouty, of Scituate, Nov. 15, 1733.
>
> 72. II. BENJAMIN[4] "   July 14, 1712, in Weymouth.

Margaret Tower died in Weymouth July 11, 1717.

Benjamin Tower[3] mar., 2d, Bethiah Woodward, in Scituate, May 6, 1718, by Rev. N. Eells. Childr.

> 73. III. DEBORAH[4] born Feb. 16, 1718–19.
>
>   IV. BETHIAH[4] "   Jan. 16, 1720–21.
>
> 74. V. JAMES[4] "   Feb. 16, 1722–23.
>
> 75. VI. JONATHAN[4] " Nov. 3, 1724.

Bethiah (Woodward) Tower died

Benjamin Tower[3] mar., 3d, Rebecca Whiton, in Hingham. Int. pub. Sept. 21, 1744. She was born in Hingham Dec. 6, 1691, and was dau. of James and Abigail Whiton.

Benjamin Tower[3] lived in Weymouth and Scituate, dying in the latter place. There does not appear to be record either of his death or of his place of burial. He received grants of lands in Weymouth, as will be seen from papers presented to the Weymouth Historical Society by Mrs. Orcutt.

Dec. 22, 1769, John Shaw, of Weymouth, conveys to Jonathan Derby, Jun., " a piece of swamp containing half a share, originally granted to Benjamin Tower."

The descendants of Benjamin Tower[3], many of them, continue to reside in that part of Scituate where he lived, now the town of Norwell. Other descendants are to be found in the neighboring town of Hanover, formerly a part of Scituate.

The name of John Tower, of Hanover, Mass., is found on the rolls of soldiers doing duty in the War of the Revolution, but there does not appear on the records, either of Scituate or Hanover, the birth or baptism of one of this name. The records of baptism of Rev. David Barnes, of the second parish of Scituate, are missing. Rev. Mr. Deane, a successor of Dr. Barnes in the ministerial office, and the compiler of the History of Scituate, was unable to find them. This John Tower was undoubtedly a grandson of Benjamin.[3]

In a roll of the soldiers enlisted for three years, preserved in the Massachusetts Archives, is the name of John Tower, of Hanover. On a pay-roll for six months' service his name appears in Col. John Bailey's regiment as engaged during the war, and again in another roll his name appears as entitled to a credit of forty-five months and eighteen days. His subsequent history is unknown.

28. Pratt.   Fourth Generation.   Tower.

8. CHRISTIAN[3], BENJAMIN[2], JOHN[1].

Christian[3], dau. of Benjamin[2] and Deborah (Garnet) Tower, born March 16, 1687–8; mar. Samuel Pratt, of Weymouth, Jan. 10, 1716–17, by Rev. Peter Thatcher, of Boston. S. Pratt born in Weymouth Nov. 16, 1670, and was son of Samuel and Hannah Pratt. Childr. born in Weymouth.

I.	LYDIA[4]	born Dec. 21, 1719.
II.	SARAH[4]	" Oct. 27, 1721.
III.	JOSEPH[4]	" Oct. 22, 1723.
IV.	MICAH[4]	" Nov. 13, 1726.
V.	BENJAMIN[4]	" Nov. 2, 1730.

Samuel Pratt died in Weymouth Oct. 14, 1744, ag. 73 y. 10 m. 28 d.

Christian (Tower) Pratt died in Weymouth October, 1765, ag. 77 y. 7 m.

29. Whiting.   Fourth Generation.   Tower.

8. SARAH[3], BENJAMIN[2], JOHN[1].

Sarah[3], dau. of Benjamin[2] and Deborah (Garnet) Tower, born Dec. 18, 1689; mar. Benjamin Whiting, in Hingham, April 19, 1716, by Rev. John Norton. B. Whiting born in Hingham May 21, 1693, and was son of James and Abigail Whiting. Childr.

I.	BENJAMIN[4]	born Dec. 28, 1716.
II.	THOMAS[4]	" Jan. 29, 1718–19.
III.	WILLIAM[4]	" March 28, 1720.
IV.	JACOB[4]	" Aug. 10, 1723.
V.	NATHANIEL[4]	" 1725; died 1725.
VI.	SARAH[4]	" Oct. 22, 1726.
VII.	LEMUEL[4]	" Aug. 7, 1729.
VIII.	ABEL[4]	" May 7, 1733, *s. p.*

Benjamin Whiting died Jan. 22, 1783, ag. 89 y. 8 m. 1 d.

30. Stubbs.   Fourth Generation.   Tower.

8. JAEL[3], BENJAMIN[2], JOHN[1].

Jael[3], dau. of Benjamin[2] and Deborah (Garnet) Tower, born Oct. 26, 1691; mar. Richard Stubbs, in Hingham, Feb. 16,

1715–16, by Samuel Thaxter, Esq. R. Stubbs born in Hull June 10, 1692, and was son of Richard and Margaret (Reed) Stubbs. Childr. born in Hull.

    I. RICHARD [4] born Nov. 9, 1717.
    II. MARY [4]   " July 3, 1718.
    III. HANNAH [4] " Oct. 21, 1722.
    IV. JAEL [4]   " Dec. 26, 1724.

Richard Stubbs, the husband of Jael [3] (Tower), removed to Hull, where he appears to have been engaged in seafaring pursuits, which his descendants followed. Some of them made their homes on Cape Cod, and others removed to Falmouth, now Portland, Me.

The following letter was written by Richard Stubbs to his wife's parents on the occasion of his reported death. It is the earliest written letter found among the family papers. It shows the dangers to which he was exposed in the calling he followed, and in which many of the men of New England were early engaged :

JUNE 9, 1716.

HONORED FATHER AND MOTHER, — I present these lines a token of my Respect and Deuty, hoping thaye will come to your view while in perfect health, for the which I Desire to Bles god thaye Left me.

I suppose you have heard what was reported concerning my Being Drowned. But it has pleased god to deal Better with Me, which I desire forever to Bles god, for I was urgd to go with them, and it is not in my power to give you any Reson I did not go, saue of all Mity power of god In keeping Me Back from Distructtion.

Remember My Kind Loue to all my Brothers and Sisters, and to all my frends. I have but Littel nuse to send you. We have But a small matter as yet, thare has Bin no Man Mortelly hurt uppon the uoieg as I have hard of. the 3 Bots stoue and spyled, one of which the harponeear and Bowman, with the stroke of the whale, dropt the bottom of the bot, the other 4 tosed into the are, and when thaye came to water again it is reported thaye ware forty feet a part, and yet no man hurt. No more at present. I remain your deutifull child to Till Death.

RICHARD STUBS.

31.   **Fourth Generation.**   **Tower.**

8. THOMAS [3], BENJAMIN [2], JOHN [1].

Thomas [3], son of Benjamin [2] and Deborah (Garnet) Tower, born June 27, 1693 ; mar. Elizabeth Woodward, in Weymouth, March 6, 1717. Childr. born in Hingham.

76. I. NATHANIEL [4] born March 13, 1718–19.
77. II. SHADRACH [4] " Feb. 5, 1720–21.
    III. ELIZABETH [4] " July 30, 1723.
78. IV. THOMAS [4]   " July 6, 1725.
    V. LYDIA [4] bapt. Jan. 4, 1729–30.
    VI. BETHIA [4]   " Aug. 7, 1730; died Dec. 1, 1730.

Elizabeth (Woodward) Tower died April 13, 1740.

Thomas Tower [3] mar., 2d, widow Dorothy (Cobb) Groce, July 11, 1745. She was born   1701, and was daughter of Richard and Esther (Bate) Cobb, and widow of Isaac Groce.

Thomas Tower [3] died in Hingham July 12, 1768, ag. 75 y. 15 d.

32. Garnett or Gardner.   Fourth Generation.   Tower.

8. HANNAH [3], BENJAMIN [2], JOHN [1].

Hannah [3], dau. of Benjamin [2] and Deborah (Garnet) Tower, born March 14, 1694–5; mar. Nathaniel Garnett, in Hingham, Nov. 20, 1728, by Rev. E. Gay. N. Garnett born in Hingham July 26, 1701, and was son of James and Elizabeth (Ward) Garnett. Childr.

> I.   HANNAH [4]   born Sept. 4, 1729.
> II. DEBORAH [4]   " Sept. 16, 1731.
> III. NATHANIEL [4] " April 25, 1733.
> IV. NOAH [4]   " Jan. 20, 1735–6.

33.   Fourth Generation.   Tower.

8. PETER [3], BENJAMIN [2] }
10. ANN [3], SAMUEL [2]   } JOHN [1].

Peter [3], son of Benjamin [2] and Deborah (Garnet) Tower, born July 17, 1697; mar. Ann Tower, in Hingham, Feb. 1, 1727–8, by Rev. E. Gay. She was born in Hingham   1708, and was dau. of Samuel [2] and Deborah (Howard) Tower. Childr. born in Hingham.

79.	I.	SAMUEL [4]	born March 17, 1728–9.
	II.	RICHARD [4]	" Sept. 2, 1730; died Sept. 3, 1730.
80.	III.	ISAIAH [4]	" Sept. 2, 1731.
81.	IV.	JOSHUA [4]	" April 25, 1733.
	V.	JEREMIAH [4]	" March 24, 1738; died Sept. 16, 1738.
	VI.	JESSE [4]	" Nov. 17, 1739; died Feb. 22, 1744–5, ag. 5 y. 3 m. 5 d.
	VII.	JESSE [4]	" Dec. 1, 1745.
	VIII.	STEPHEN [4]	bapt. Aug. 25, 1750; died Sept. 30, 1751.
82.	IX.	LABAN [4]	born Aug. 3, 1751.

Peter Tower [3] died in Hingham April 19, 1781, ag. 83 y. 9 m. 2 d.

Ann (Tower) Tower [3] died in Hingham Sept. 6, 1801, ag. 94 y.

Peter Tower [3] and his wife Anna Tower [3] came into possession of the old homestead of John Tower [1], their grandfather, on which they lived and died. They carefully preserved the papers of their grandfather and those of their parents. These papers embrace many deeds of lands; and as these were not recorded, it is through this preservation that the business of the two earlier generations is known.

The following deed of Deborah, widow of Benjamin Tower [2], to her son Peter [3] conveys a portion of the John Tower homestead :

Oct. 13, 1726. " Deborah Tower, widow and relict of Benjamin Tower, late of Hingham, deceased, in consideration of £30 paid by my son, Peter Tower, of Hingham, aforesaid, weaver, . . ." conveys " a piece or part of the home-lot where I now dwell, in the township of Hingham, abovesaid, containing by estimation two acres, be it more or less, bounded as followeth : Northerly and Easterly with the land of Jacob Stodder, Southerly with the other part of the said home-lot, and the Southeast corner bounds is a White Oak Tree; and the line runs from said White Oak Tree to the Southeast corner of the dwelling-house of the said Deborah Tower, and Westerly partly with the said dwelling-house, and partly with the town's common land or highway."

It will be noticed that Peter Tower is called weaver, — following the occupation of his father. He would seem to have added to this also that of cooper, — a business which early acquired prominence in Hingham, and gained for it the name of " Bucket Town." This appellation, though sometimes used in disparagement of the people, was in reality a tribute to their skill and industry. They were all more or less husbandmen, and drew from the soil their food and clothing. But when snow and ice covered the fields, making labor therein unprofitable, they found employment in the small shop or the vacant room in the house, where they converted the cedars of the swamps and the pines of the forests into various utensils of domestic use, in the work of which there was found place and occasion for the available force of the several families, all of which during the winter season were hives of industry.

The distribution of the products of this industry gave employment to traders both on land and sea. The small schooner, laden with wooden-ware, was well known in all the ports along the coast from Maine to Georgia, and the West India ports were not strangers to their sails.

Although the times were not rife with inventions, yet there was one labor-saving machine, the product of their skill, which deserves notice. This was a washing-machine, constructed wholly of wood and known by the name of the " Dumb Betty." It had a local habitation, and was hardly known outside of the town and its immediate vicinity. But among the townspeople it was held to be essential to the proper performance of the week's washing; and a household would be considered deficient in its equipments were it wanting in one of these implements, whereby the strength of the man or the large boy could come in to relieve the oft-burdened and weaker force of the woman.

In the present day of the professional in this important household work and the abounding laundries the "Dumb Betty" has become extinct, or if preserved at all, it is relegated to the lumber-room of the garret, among the discarded spinning-wheels and antiquated hand-looms.

Many of the descendants of John Tower are called coopers for some two centuries; but the introduction of machinery operated by power has completely superseded the old method of individual hand-work, and one after another those little shops, formerly so common as adjuncts to the dwelling-house, have disappeared, and at the present time the only man in town plying this ancient vocation is Nelson Corthell, now seventy-five years old. He is a lineal descendant of Robert and Deborah [3] (Tower) Corthell.

Peter Tower [3], with his varied occupations of weaver, cooper, and husbandman, added thereto that of trader, as an old memorandum-book preserved among his papers will show.

The following, copied from an indenture found among his papers, will show how instruction was given in the trades, and how much of time and labor was required to pay for that instruction: —

"This indenture, made this twelfth day of March, one thousand seven hundred & thirty & three or four, Witnesseth that I, Samuel Tower, of Hingham, cooper, in the county of Suffolk, in the province of Massachusetts Bay, in New England, have placed and bound my son, Matthew Tower, as an apprentice to Peter Tower, weaver, of the same town, county, & province abovesaid, and Ann, his wife, to serve them in their lawful business (viz.: in any out-door work), from the day of the date hereof until July the twelfth, one thousand seven hundred & forty & three, during which said term of time he the said apprentice is to behave himself well towards his said master and mistress, their lawful commands gladly to do. He shall not waste the estate of his said master and mistress, or suffer it to be wasted by others, but shall in all things as a good and faithful apprentice demean himself towards his said master and mistress during the said term of time.

"And in consideration whereof the said Peter Tower and Ann his wife do promise for themselves, their heirs, executors, administrators, or assigns, in manner following; that is to say, that they or their heirs, executors, administrators, or assigns will provide for the said apprentice both in sickness and health, and provide meat, drink, apparel, washing, and lodging fitting for such an apprentice during the said term of time. And the said

Peter Tower doth promise to teach and instruct him in the art & mystery of a weaver, and to teach and instruct or cause him to be taught or instructed in the art or mystery of a set-work cooper; and also to practice him in his reading and *wrighting*, and learn or cause him to be learned to cypher as far as the rule of three, or golden rule.

"And at the expiration of the said term of time to give the said apprentice two suits of apparel, one of them a new one, suitable for all parts of his body, both linen and woollen. But if the said Peter Tower shall be taken away before the expiration of the said term of time, then the said apprentice is to learn but one of the abovesaid trades, and that is to be which he shall choose."

Peter Tower's will is dated Oct. 19, 1769, and was allowed in the Probate Court for Suffolk County, April 25, 1781.

He gives to "wife, Anna, the use and improvement of all my estate, . . . except what I shall give unto Deborah Tower. . . . Gives to his son Isaiah the whole of the land where he now lives, eastward of the burying-yard; to his sister Deborah a living in the old part of his house during the widowhood of his wife. Gives to his four sons, Samuel, Isaiah, Joshua, and Laban, all the remainder of his estate, to be divided equally between them, deducting the value of Isaiah's former devise."

By the division of Peter Tower's real estate Joshua and Laban came into possession of the old John Tower homestead. Samuel, the oldest son, removed to Worthington, Mass., in the early settlement of that town, and Isaiah had a specific devise of real estate, the greater part of which remains in the ownership of his descendants and those connected with them by marriage.

It will be noticed that Peter Tower's nine children were all sons.

34.   Fourth Generation.   Tower.

8. AMBROSE[3], BENJAMIN[2], JOHN[1].
   Ambrose[3], son of Benjamin[2] and Deborah (Garnet) Tower, b. Jan., 1699–1700; mar. Mary (   ); mar., 2d, Elizabeth (   ).

Childr.

83.	I.	JOSEPH[4]	born Sept. 25, 1723, in Hull, Mass.
84.	II.	AMBROSE[4]	" 1727.
85.	III.	JONATHAN[4]	" 1729.
86.	IV.	MARY[4]	" 1731.
	V.	ELIZABETH[4]	" 1734, unmar.; died in Concord, Mass., Feb. 19, 1814, ag. 80.
87.	VI.	BENJAMIN[4]	bapt. March 18, 1738–9.
	VII.	LYDIA[4]	born Nov. 12, 1742.
	VIII.	SARAH[4]	" 1744, unmar.; died in Concord, Mass., May 14, 1807, ag. 64.

Ambrose Tower [3] removed from Hingham quite early. There appears to be no record of either of his marriages. He was in Hull when his oldest son was born. He afterwards removed to Concord, Mass., and resided in that part of the town which was set off and made the town of Lincoln. There appear to be no conveyances of real estate to or from him, and at his death there was neither will nor administration upon his estate. The following will show that he was at one time somewhat embarrassed in his circumstances. The first paper is a summons from the " Inferior Court of Common Pleas, to be holden at Boston on the first Tuesday of July next, then and there to answer unto Peter Tower, of Hingham, etc., weaver, in an action of debt " of £58. The summons is dated June 18, 1733. On the 20th of June, 1733, Ambrose Tower signs a bond in the penal sum of £44 to secure the payment of £22 " in good bills of credit, or current lawful silver money, on or before the 30th day of this instant June." On the back of the bond the receipt of two payments is indorsed, April 21, 1736, £3, and July 1, 1736, £3 19s. 5d.

Most of those bearing the name of Tower now residing in Middlesex County are the descendants of Ambrose. Others of his descendants have gone out into all parts of the country, and are to-day filling positions of honor and trust.

35. Sprague.   Fourth Generation.   Tower.

10. SILENCE [3], SAMUEL [2], JOHN [1].
Silence [3], dau. of Samuel [2] and Silence (Damon) Tower, b. Aug. 27, 1684; mar. William Sprague, in Hingham, April 23, 1707, by Rev. John Norton. William Sprague b. in Hingham, Dec. 24, 1675, and was son of William and Deborah (Lane) Sprague.

Childr.

I.	SILENCE [4]	born Sept. 7, 1708, in Hingham; mar. John Woker, in Weymouth, Feb. 19, 1729.	
II.	WILLIAM [4]	" Jan. 29, 1710.	
III.	JEDEDIAH [4]	" March 18, 1712–13.	
IV.	JOSHUA [4]	" in Abington, Mass.	
V.	JOANNA [4]	" " " "	; mar. John Nash, in Weymouth, May 28, 1740.
VI.	LYDIA [4]	"	mar. Wm. Wales, of Braintree, Jan. 11, 1753. He was born in Braintree Feb. 3, 1722–3, and was son of Joseph and Hannah Wales.

36. Whiting. Fourth Generation. Tower.

10. MARGARET[3], SAMUEL[2], JOHN[1].

Margaret[3], dau. of Samuel[2] and Silence (Damon) Tower, b.
March 18, 1686-7 ; mar. Samuel Whiting, of Scituate, Mass.,
March 11, 1711-12. He was b.
Nov. 12, 1685, and was son of James and Abigail Whiting.

Childr. born in Scituate.

I.	SAMUEL[4]	born March 8, 1712-13.
II.	DANIEL[4]	" 1714; died Oct. 13, 1714.
III.	MOSES[4]	" Dec. 2, 1715; died Aug. 8, 1717, ag. 1 y. 8 m. 6 d.
IV.	DESIRE[4]	" April 6, 1717; died young.
V.	HANNAH[4]	bapt. Dec. 7, 1718.
VI.	KEZIA[4]	born June 5, 1720.
VII.	DANIEL[4]	" Nov.15, 1722.
VIII.	ABIGAIL[4]	" 1724.
IX.	MARGARET[4]	" "

Margaret (Tower) Whiting died in Scituate April 3, 1738, ag.
51 y. 16 d.

Samuel Whiting mar., 2d, Elizabeth (Garnet) Williams Oct.
4, 1738.

37. Fourth Generation. Tower.

10. SAMUEL[3], SAMUEL[2], JOHN[1].

Samuel[3], son of Samuel[2] and Silence (Damon) Tower, bapt.
Dec. 15, 1689; mar. Lydia Whiting, in Hingham,
Nov. 26, 1719, by Rev. E. Gay. She was b. in Hingham
April 2, 1693, and was dau. of Matthew and Deborah (Howard)
Whiting.

Childr. born in Hingham.

	I.	SAMUEL[4]	born Oct. 11, 1720; died May 28, 1721.
88.	II.	MATTHEW[4]	" July 11, 1722.
89.	III.	SILENCE[4]	bapt. Sept. 27, 1724.
90.	IV.	LYDIA[4]	" Oct. 8, 1727.

Lydia (Whiting) Tower died in Hingham Oct. 3, 1727, ag. 34 y.
6 m. 1 d.

15. Samuel Tower[3] mar., 2d, Elizabeth Tower[4], in Hingham,
Oct. 6, 1729, by Samuel Thaxter, Esq. She was b. in Hingham
Sept. 18, 1705, and was dau. of John[3] and Hester (Canter-
bury) Tower.

Child.

V. ELIJAH[4] & [5] born Feb. 6, 1729-30.

Samuel Tower [3] died in Hingham March 13, 1733–4, ag. 44,
6 m. 1 d.

Elizabeth (Tower) Tower died in Hingham Sept. 5, 1747, ag.
41 y. 11 m. 18 d.

38. Garnet (or Gardner).   Fourth Generation.   Tower.

10. RUTH [3], SAMUEL [2], JOHN [1].
Ruth [3], dau. of Samuel [2] and Silence (Damon) Tower, b.
July 13, 1691; mar. Samuel Gardner, in Hingham,
Feb. 4, 1712–13.   He was b. in Hingham
Aug. 14, 1684, and was son of Francis and Joanna (May)
Gardner.

Childr. born in Hingham.

I.	SAMUEL [4]	born Nov. 13, 1713.
II.	RUTH [4]	"	March 14, 1714–15; died March 19, 1714–15.
III.	HOSEA [4]	"	Feb. 27, 1715–16; d. Nov. 25, 1744, ag. 28 y. 8 m. 29 d.
IV.	THOMAS [4]	"	Dec. 6, 1717.
V.	RUTH [4]	"	May 7, 1719.
VI.	HANNAH [4]	"	Feb. 27, 1720–21.
VII.	HOPESTILL [4]	"	Aug. 2, 1726.

Ruth (Tower) Gardner died in Hingham Oct. 12, 1726, ag.
35 y. 2 m. 29 d.

Samuel Gardner mar., 2d, Ann Clark, in Hingham, Dec. 12,
1728, by Rev. E. Gay.

Samuel Gardner died in Hingham Nov. 5, 1774, ag. 85 y. 3 m.
23 d.

39. Whiting.   Fourth Generation.   Tower.

10. MARTHA [3], SAMUEL [2], JOHN [1].
Martha [3], dau. of Samuel [2] and Silence (Damon) Tower, b.
July 20, 1693; mar. Joseph Whiting, in Hingham,
Dec. 10, 1713, by Rev. John Norton. J. Whiting b. in Hingham
March 23, 1686–7, and was son of James and Abigail Whiting.

Childr.

I.	ELIJAH [4]	born	, 1714.
II.	ABIGAIL [4]	"	, 1716.
III.	MARTHA [4]	"	, 1718.

Martha (Tower) Whiting died in Rehoboth, Mass., Sept. 19,
1719, ag. 26 y. 1 m. 30 d.

40.   **Fourth Generation.**   **Tower.**

10. DANIEL [3], SAMUEL [2], JOHN [1].
    Daniel [3], son of Samuel [2] and Deborah (Howard) Tower, b.
    Nov. 22, 1704; mar. Silence Gross, in Hingham,
    Jan. 20, 1736–7, by Rev. E. Gay. She was b. in Hingham,
        1713, and was dau. of Edmund and Martha (Bacon)
    Gross.

Childr.

91.	I.	ALICE [4]	born Dec. 5, 1737.
92.	II.	RACHEL [4]	" Jan. 19, 1741.

Daniel Tower [3] died in Hingham Dec. 3, 1791, ag. 87 y. 11 d.
Silence (Gross) Tower died in Hingham May 5, 1798, ag. 85.

Daniel Tower [3] also was a cooper, and appears to have lived
upon the part of the homestead set off to him in the division of his
father's estate. He was a soldier in the old French war of 1756–
63. He was in Capt. Ebenezer Beal's company, which marched
to the relief of Fort William Henry in 1757. In the following
year he was in Captain Ward's company, serving therein five
months and fourteen days, for the reduction of Canada, and receiving for pay £9 18s. 3d. The next year he was in Capt.
Jotham Gay's company, and served thirty weeks and four days,
continuing in the same company the next year from January 1st
to June 21st.
    There appears to be neither will nor settlement of his estate;
but March 18, 1791, several months previous to his death, he conveyed to his grandson, Bela Tower, cooper, " a piece of land lying
in the South Parish, in Hingham, containing one quarter of an
acre, with my dwelling-house standing thereon."

41.   **Fourth Generation.**   **Tower.**

10. JOSHUA [3], SAMUEL [2], JOHN [1].
    Joshua [3], son of Samuel [2] and Deborah (Howard) Tower, b.
    Feb. 10, 1709–10; mar. Jerusha Sprague, in Hingham,
    Aug. 30, 1731, by Rev. E. Gay. She was b. in Hingham
    Dec. 1, 1712, and was dau. of James and Elizabeth (Fearing)
    Sprague.

Childr., all born in Rehoboth, Mass.

I.	JERUSHA [4]	born Feb. 4, 1731–2; died
II.	JAMES [4]	" June 30, 1733.
III.	{ JERUSHA [4]	" July 31, 1741.
IV.	{ DEBORAH [4]	" " " "

7

Jerusha (Sprague) Tower died subsequent to 1757.

Joshua Tower [3] mar., 2d, Huldah Bliss, dau. of Elisha Bliss.

Childr. born in Rehoboth.

V. JOSHUA [4] born March 26, 1760.
VI. HULDAH [4] " Dec. 23, 1761.
VII. EZRA [4] " Oct. 7, 1769.

Joshua Tower [3] and his father-in-law, James Sprague, removed to Rehoboth previous to 1740, as in this year James Sprague conveys to Joshua Tower, his son-in-law, " my new dwelling-house," adjoining land of said Tower.

1786, July 18, Elisha Bliss makes a conveyance to Ezra Tower, minor, " son of my loving daughter, Huldah Tower, widow."

Nov. 7, 1792, Huldah Tower, of Rehoboth, widow, and Ezra Tower, of "*Skohary*," county of *Montgomery*, State of New York, make a conveyance of land.

No further trace of the descendants of Joshua Tower has been found. We find, however, that his son James [4] was a soldier in the old French war, serving in Colonel Carpenter's regiment at Lake George in 1755.

42.　　　　　　**Fourth Generation.**　　　　　　**Tower.**

10. JOSEPH [3], SAMUEL [2], JOHN [1].

Joseph [3], son of Samuel [2] and Deborah (Howard) Tower, b. Aug. 28, 1712; mar. Deborah Taylor, of Scituate. Int. pub. Nov. 10, 1739. She was b.
　　　　　1721.

Childr. bapt. in Hingham.

	I.	JOSEPH [4]	bapt. March 22, 1740–41; died April 12, 1741.
93.	II.	DESIRE [4]	" Oct. 24, 1742.
94.	III.	JOSEPH [4]	" July 28, 1745.
	IV.	ABNER [4]	" October, 1749.
	V.	RACHEL [4]	" September, 1756; died
95.	VI.	RACHEL [4]	" August, 1766.

Joseph Tower [3] died in Hingham Feb. 21, 1783, ag. 70 y. 5 m. 24 d.

Deborah (Taylor) Tower died in Hingham Feb. 12, 1806, ag. 85.

Joseph Tower [3] was a cooper, and seems to have led a quiet and uneventful life, living upon the estate set off to him in the division of his father's estate. A valuation of estates in Hingham in 1751 for the assessment of taxes has been preserved among the Tower papers. Joseph Tower's real estate is valued at £10, and his personal estate at £2.

In 1782, a few months before his death, he conveys to his son-in-law, Amos Dunbar, cordwainer, —

"A piece of land lying in Hingham, containing half an acre, . . . with the house standing thereon."

There appears to be neither will nor settlement of his estate. He had previously, in 1773 and in 1774, made three several conveyances of portions of his homestead.

In the old French war he served in Captain Ward's company, where he is credited with 24 days' travel and 6 months and 16 days' service, with wages earned of £11 16s. 7d., and stands charged with a gun, not returned, of the value of £3.

43. **Fifth Generation.** **Tower.**

11. GIDEON [4], BENJAMIN [3], JOHN [2], JOHN [1].
Gideon [4], son of Benjamin [3] and Deborah (Whipple) Tower, b. Feb. 24, 1699–1700 ; mar. Mary Ray, in Wrentham, Mass., Oct. 2, 1729, by Rev. Henry Messinger.   She was b. Aug. 22, 1710, and was dau. of Samuel and Miriam Ray.

Childr.

	I.	DEBORAH [5] born April 5, 1731.
96.	II.	PATIENCE [5] "	May 23, 1733.
	III.	MARY [5] "	" " "
	IV.	GIDEON [5] "	July 23, 1735; died in the army, in the War of the Revolution.
97.	V.	ENOCH [5] "	Dec. 20, 1737.
98.	VI.	ICHABOD [5] "	Feb. 18, 1740.
99.	VII.	LEVI [5] "	July 19, 1742.
100.	VIII.	REUBEN [5] "	Nov. 9, 1745.
101.	IX.	SAMUEL [5] "	May 2, 1747.
102.	X.	LYDIA [5] "	Aug. 4, 1752.

Gideon Tower [4] died in Cumberland, R. I., Dec. 29, 1772, ag. 72 y. 10 m. 5 d.
Mary (Ray) Tower died in Cumberland, R. I., May 29, 1794, ag. 83.

44. Carpenter. **Fifth Generation.** **Tower.**

11. PATIENCE [4], BENJAMIN [3], JOHN [2], JOHN [1].
Patience [4], dau. of Benjamin [3] and Deborah (Whipple)Tower, b. April 10, 1702; mar. Nathan Carpenter, of Rehoboth, Dec. 26, 1723.   He was son of Samuel Carpenter, Jun., of Rehoboth.

45. Sabin.   Fifth Generation.   Tower.

11. SARAH[4], BENJAMIN[3], JOHN[2], JOHN[1].
Sarah[4], dau. of Benjamin[3] and Deborah (Whipple) Tower, b.
Aug. 16, 1704 ; mar. Elisha Sabin, of Dudley, Mass. Int. pub.
June 19, 1732. He was b. in Pomfret, Conn.,
May 16, 1705, and was son of Benjamin Sabin.

Childr. born in Dudley, Mass.

I.	ELISHA[5]	born	Oct. 12, 1733.
II.	MARY[5]	"	June 12, 1735.
III.	SARAH[5]	"	March 24, 1736; died 1741.
IV.	EUNICE[5]	"	Sept. 18, 1737.
V.	ESTHER[5]	"	April 7, 1741.
VI.	GIDEON[5]	"	March 20, 1743.
VII.	JESSE[5]	"	Jan. 18, 1746 ; mar. Rhoda Waters April 16, 1772.
VIII.	ZILPHA[5]	"	July 10, 1747.

Elisha Sabin died Sept. 26, 1760, ag. 55 y. 4 m. 10 d.
Sarah (Tower[4]) Sabin died subsequent to her husband's death.

46. Bartlett.   Fifth Generation.   Tower.

11. MARGARET[4], BENJAMIN[3], JOHN[2], JOHN[1].
Margaret[4], dau. of Benjamin[3] and Deborah (Whipple)
Tower, b.
Oct. 26, 1706 ; mar. Jeremiah Bartlett,
May 15, 1730, by Jonathan Sprague, Jun.

Childr. born in Attleborough, Mass.

I.	ALLES[5]	born	April 23, 1731; mar. Stephen Staples.
II.	SARAH[5]	"	Dec. 18, 1733.
III.	MARGARET[5]	"	July 31, 1735.
IV.	JEREMIAH[5]	"	Aug. 16, 1741; died Aug. 20, 1800, ag. 59 y. 4 d.
V.	SUSANNAH[5]	"	Oct. 26, 1743.
VI.	ABIGAIL[5]	"	June 30, 1745.

Margaret (Tower) Bartlett died in Cumberland, R. I., April
9, 1787, ag. 80 y. 5 m. 14 d.

47. Jackson.   Fifth Generation.   Tower.

11. ZIPPORAH[4], BENJAMIN[3], JOHN[2], JOHN[1].
Zipporah[4], dau. of Benjamin[3] and Deborah (Whipple) Tower, b.
Dec. 17, 1709 ; mar. Joseph Jackson
Jan. 28, 1730–31.

Childr.

I.	MARY [5]		born May 15, 1732, in Wrentham, Mass.; mar. Perez Bradford, Jan. 24, 1750, in Attleborough, by John Dexter, J. P.
II.	BENJAMIN [5]	"	Mar. 25, 1735, in Cumberland, R. I.; mar. Lydia Peake, Dec. 29, 1756.
III.	JOSEPH [5]	"	Feb. 24, 1737.
IV.	JEREMIAH [5]	"	Aug. 2, 1739.
V.	ZIPPORAH [5]	"	May 14, 1742.
VI.	NEHEMIAH [5]	"	Sept. 11, 1744.
VII.	ELEAZER [5]	"	Aug. 10, 1747.
VIII.	MICHAEL [5]	"	June 7, 1750.
IX.	MORRIS [5]		
X.	CHLOE [5]		mar. William Ross, of Providence, R. I., Feb. 1, 1781, by John Dexter, J. P.

48.   **Fifth Generation.**   **Tower.**

11. JOHN [4], BENJAMIN [3], JOHN [2], JOHN [1].

John [4], son of Benjamin [3] and Deborah (Whipple) Tower, b. Nov. 23, 1711; mar. Hannah Hancock, in Wrentham, Mass., Nov. 22, 1739, by Rev. Elias Haven. She was b. July 3, 1709, and was dau. of Anthony and Ruth Hancock.

Childr. born in Cumberland, R. I.

103.	I.	JONATHAN [5]	born	Dec. 12, 1740.
104.	II.	FREELOVE [5]	"	Aug. 28, 1742.
	III.	HANNAH [5]	"	Aug. 5, 1744; mar. James Streeter Oct. 21, 1764.
	IV.	MOLLY [5]	"	Sept. 19, 1746; " Benjamin Knowlton, Dec., 1764.
	V.	JOHN [5]	"	Sept. 7, 1748.
105.	VI.	DEBORAH [5]	"	Aug. 26, 1750.
106.	VII.	GIDEON [5]	"	April 30, 1753.

49.   **Fifth Generation.**   **Tower.**

11. BENJAMIN [4], BENJAMIN [3], JOHN [2], JOHN [1].

Benjamin [4], son of Benjamin [3] and Deborah (Whipple) Tower, b. Feb. 25, 1715–16; mar. Ruth

Childr. none.

Benjamin Tower [4] died in Cumberland, R. I., Feb. 12, 1792, ag. 75 y. 11 m. 18 d.

50.   **Fifth Generation.**   **Tower.**

11. JOSEPH [4], BENJAMIN [3], JOHN [2], JOHN [1].

Joseph [4], son of Benjamin [3] and Deborah (Whipple) Tower, b. Sept. 13, 1721; mar. Judith Briggs, of Taunton, Mass. Int. pub. April, 1743.

Childr. born in Cumberland, R. I.

	I.	BENJAMIN [5]	born	Sept. 22, 1744.
107.	II.	JOSEPH [5]	"	April 28, 1746.
108.	III.	NATHANIEL [5]	"	June 23, 1748.
	IV.	JOSUHA [5]	"	June 30, 1750.
	V.	LUCY [5]	"	Oct. 13, 1752.
	VI.	WILLIAM [5]	"	March 6, 1755.

Joseph Tower [4] died at sea about 1761.

51.   Hayden.   Fifth Generation.   Tower.

12. HANNAH [4], JOSEPH [3], JOHN [2], JOHN [1].
Hannah [4], dau. of Joseph [3] and Ruth (   ) Tower, b.
Sept. 18, 1713; mar. Daniel Hayden, in Braintree,
Nov. 11, 1736, by Rev. Elisha Eaton.

Childr. born in Braintree, Mass.

I.	DANIEL [5] born	
II.	} Twins	{ died. Jan 17, 1739–40.
III.		{ " Nov. 27, 1748.

Hannah (Tower) Hayden died in Braintree, Feb. 28, 1757, ag.
43 y. 5 m. 10 d.

52.   Fifth Generation.   Tower.

12. JOHN [4], JOSEPH [3], JOHN [2], JOHN [1].
John [4], son of Joseph [3] and Ruth (   ) Tower, b.
Feb. 7, 1717–18; mar. Rachel Hayden, in Braintree,
June 23, 1741, by Rev. Elisha Eaton.   She was b. in Braintree
Dec. 22, 1724, and was dau. of Ebenezer and Mary (Hollis)
Hayden.

Childr. born in Braintree.

	I.	RACHEL [5]	born Jan. 24, 1741–2; mar. Silas Lovell. Int. pub. Sept. 28, 1759.
	II.	JOHN [5]	" May, 1743; died May, 1743.
	III.	SARAH [5]	" May, 1745; " May, 1749.
109.	IV.	JAMES [5]	" Dec., 1746.
	V.	JOHN [5]	" May 29, 1749; died.

Rachel (Hayden) Tower died in Braintree, July 18, 1750, ag.
25 y. 6 m. 26 d.
John Tower [4] mar., 2d, widow Rebecca (Staples) French.

Childr. born in Braintree.

110.	VI.	JOHN [5]	born	1752.
111.	VII.	SARAH [5].		
	VIII.	REBECCA [5].		

John Tower[4] died in the army, 1759, ag. 41.

Rebecca (Staples) (French) Tower mar., 3d, Ebenezer Hayden in Braintree. Int. pub. Feb. 15, 1765.

John Tower[4] was a soldier in the old French war. He was a corporal in Capt. Peter Thayer's company, which marched for the relief of Fort William Henry. In 1758 he served in Captain Ward's company, Colonel William's regiment, six months and twenty-three days, and received for pay £12 5s. 7d. He was at Frontenac. In 1759 he was in Capt. Jotham Gay's company, serving for a period of seven weeks and four days. His pay was £3 8s. 2d. Mrs. Mehitable Orcutt, his granddaughter, says "he was wounded in the knee at a fort, and did not return." Administration was granted upon his estate, Aug. 7, 1759, to his widow, Rebecca Tower.

53.   **Fifth Generation.**   **Tower.**

12.   GIDEON[4], JOSEPH[3], JOHN[2], JOHN[1].

     Gideon[4], son of Joseph[3] and Ruth (   ) Tower, b.
         1723 ; mar. Lydia Sylvester. She was b.
         1727, and was dau. of Benjamin and Elizabeth Sylvester.

Childr.

112.	I.	GIDEON[5]	born Feb. 29, 1752.
113.	II.	LYDIA[5]	"
114.	III.	MARGARET[5]	"
	IV.	SARAH[5]	"
	V.	RICHARD SYLVESTER[5]	"
115.	VI.	RUTH[5]	"
116.	VII.	BENJAMIN[5]	"
117.	VIII.	ABIGAIL[5]	" Sept. 12, 1772.

Gideon Tower[4] died in Randolph, Oct. 16, 1803, ag. 80 y.

Lydia (Sylvester) Tower died in Randolph, March 16, 1810, ag. 83 y.

Gideon Tower[4] was a member of Capt. William Arbuthnot's company at the capitulation of Fort William Henry. He lived in the west part of Randolph, Mass.

54.   **Fifth Generation.**   **Tower.**

12.   JOSEPH[4], JOSEPH[3], JOHN[2], JOHN[1].

     Joseph[4], son of Joseph[3] and Ruth (   ) Tower, b.
         mar. Rebecca

Childr. born in Braintree.

    I.   REBECCA[5] born   ; mar. Luther Spear. Int. pub. in Braintree Nov. 14, 1778.

II. JANE [5]   born   ; mar. Eli Spear. Int. pub. in
                                             Braintree Nov. 14, 1778.
   III. ABRAHAM [5] "
   IV. ELIZABETH [5] "
118.   V. ISAAC [5]   "   Feb. 22, 1767.
119. VI. RUTH [5]   "
   VII. RHODA [5]   "
   VIII. MARY [5]   "
120. IX. JOSEPH [5]   "   1780.

Joseph Tower [4] died in Randolph Sept. 7, 1801.

Joseph Tower [4], of Braintree, was in Capt. Peter Thayer's
company, which marched for the relief of Fort William Henry.
He afterwards served in Captain Ward's company for five months
and eleven days, with pay £9 14s. 2d.

Joseph Tower also served in the War of the Revolution, though
he was forty-five years old at its commencement. He went as
sergeant in Capt. Seth Turner's company on the 19th of April,
1775, on four days' service. On the 4th of March, 1776, he was
called out and performed fifteen days' service as a lieutenant in
Capt. Eliphalet Sawen's company, for which he received £3 17s.
On the 14th of June, the same year, he served as lieutenant in
the same company for four days. Tradition says he was at the
surrender of Burgoyne.

His will was dated Dec. 18, 1800, and allowed Oct. 6, 1801. He
names his wife, Rebecca, his sons Isaac and Joseph, and his daughters Jenny, Rebecca, and Ruth. The other children, Abraham,
Elizabeth, Rhoda, and Mary, probably had died previously without
issue. The inventory of his estate shows property, real and
personal, to the value of 3335\frac{56}{100}$.

---

55. Chessman.   Fifth Generation.   Tower.

12. MARY [4], JOSEPH [3], JOHN [2], JOHN [1].
    Mary [4], dau. of Joseph [3] and Ruth (   ) Tower, b.
      ; mar. Samuel Chessman in Braintree,
    July 23, 1747. He was b. in Braintree
    March 15, 1722–3, and was son of George and Jane (   )
    Chessman.

Childr. born in Braintree.

   I. MARY [5]   born Feb. 24, 1747–8.
  II. RUTH [5]   "   July 5, 1750; died
 III. SAMUEL [5]   "   May 6, 1752; mar. Martha French, of Stoughton.
                Int. pub. April 19, 1777.

IV. RUTH[5] born Nov. 2, 1754; mar. Atkins Clark. Int. pub. in
Braintree Feb. 22, 1772.
V. NOAH[5] " April 28, 1757; mar. Mary Holbrook. Int. pub. in
Braintree Sept. 24, 1780.
VI. HANNAH[5] " Feb. 5, 1760.
VII. NAOMI[5] " Sept. 3, 1767.

56. Joy. **Fifth Generation.** **Tower.**

14. ABIGAIL[4], RICHARD[3], IBROOK[2], JOHN[1].
Abigail[4], dau. of Richard[3] and Abigail (Farrow) Tower, b.
March 14, 1693–4 ; mar. Prince Joy, of Hingham. Int. pub.
Sept. 26, 1713. He was b. in Hingham
March 19, 1690–91, and was son of Joseph and Elizabeth
(Andrews) Joy.

Childr. born in Hingham.

I. ABIGAIL[5] born March 22, 1713–14.
II. SUSANNA[5] " July 1, 1715 ; mar. Paul Packard, of Bridgewater, Oct.
23, 1744.
III. AMOS[5] " Aug. 1, 1720.
IV. JOSEPH[5] " April 25, 1725.
V. SUBMIT[5] " July 10, 1728; mar. Matthew Gannet, of Scituate,
April 25, 1745.

Abigail (Tower) Joy died in Cohasset, Aug. 26, 1728, ag. 34 y.
5 m. 12 d.
Prince Joy mar., 2d, Hannah Orcutt, dau. of John Orcutt,
Jan. 2, 1728–9. He died in Cohasset March 4, 1755, ag.
63 y. 11 m. 16 d.

57. Stephenson. **Fifth Generation.** **Tower.**

14. RACHEL[4], RICHARD[3], IBROOK[2], JOHN[1].
Rachel[4], dau. of Richard[3] and Abigail (Farrar) Tower, b.
Feb. 24, 1696–7 ; mar. John Stephenson, in Boston,
July 22, 1717, by Samuel Checkley, Esq.

Childr. born in Cohasset.

I. JOHN[5] born Aug. 6, 1718.
II. JESSE[5] " Jan. 29, 1720–21.
III. OBADIAH[5] " Oct. 22, 1724; died Oct. 23, 1750, ag. 26 y. 1 d.
IV. REUBEN[5] " Oct. 2, 1726.
V. LUKE[5] " June 17, 1728; died Dec. 31, 1750, ag. 22 y. 6 m. 14 d.
VI. LUTHER[5] " July 13, 1730.
VII. LUCITANUS[5] " April 13, 1732.
VIII. SOLON[5] " Sept. 14, 1734.
IX. SARAH[5] " June 16, 1736.
X. JEROME[5] bapt. June 25, 1738.
XI. THOMAS[5] "

58.   **Fifth Generation.**   **Tower.**

14. ELISHA [4], RICHARD [3], IBROOK [2], JOHN [1].
Elisha [4], son of Richard [3] and Abigail (Farrar) Tower, b.
May 22, 1700; mar. Abigail Joy, in Boston,
July 6, 1724, by Penn Townsend, Esq. She was b. in Hingham
Dec. 29, 1701, and was dau. of Joseph and Elizabeth(   ) Joy.

Childr. born in Cohasset.

	I.	OBADIAH [5]	born Feb. 25, 1724–5 ; died March 5, 1724–5.
	II.	LYDIA [5]	" May 14, 1726.
121.	III.	ELISHA [5]	" June 30, 1728.
122.	IV.	ABIGAIL [5]	" Aug. 5, 1730.
	V.	OBADIAH [5]	" Feb. 3, 1732–3.
	VI.	RICHARD [5]	" March 3, 1734–5.
	VII.	DESIRE [5]	" Aug. 20, 1737 ; died May 22, 1759, ag. 21 9 m. 2 d.
123.	VIII.	JETHRO [5]	Twins " Aug. 12, 1740. Sylvanus died, unmarried, 1762, ag. 22.
	IX.	SYLVANUS [5]	

Abigail (Joy) Tower died, and Elisha Tower [4] mar., 2d, Esther
Tower,
Sept. 18, 1760, by Samuel Cushing, J. P. She was the widow
of his cousin John [4].

Obadiah Tower's [5] name is found on the roll of Capt. Obadiah
Beal's company, of Cohasset, which marched to Dorchester March
4, 1776, and again on the roll of Capt. Thomas Nash's company
in Col. David Cushing's regiment, called out for service at Hull
in 1777.

59.   **Fifth Generation.**   **Tower.**

15. JOHN [4], JOHN [3], IBROOK [2], JOHN [1].
John [4], son of John [3] and Hester (Canterbury) Tower, b.
Jan. 21, 1696–7; mar. Esther Cobb, of Boston,
Jan. 2, 1722–3. She was dau. of Richard and Hester Cobb.

Childr. born in Cohasset.

	I.	SUSANNAH [5]	born March 11, 1723–4.
	II.	JOHN [5]	" Dec. 20, 1725.
124.	III.	SILENCE [5]	" June 9, 1728.
	IV.	MICAH [5]	" June 23, 1731.
125.	V.	RICHARD [5]	" Sept. 10, 1733.
	VI.	MARY [5]	bapt. Nov. 13, 1737.
	VII.	MERCY [5]	" Jan. 24, 1757, adult.
126.	VIII.	EUNICE [5]	born Dec. 1, 1744.
	IX.	REUBEN [5]	" June 3, 1747.

John Tower [5], great-grandson of Ibrook Tower, was not married, and all the record of his death is from the settlement of his estate. Administration was granted to John Wheelwright, of Scituate, April 11, 1809. The inventory of his estate shows household furniture and live stock $120, and one half of the real estate, including the dwelling-house and barn in common and undivided with John Wheelwright.

He was a soldier in the War of the Revolution, doing duty in Lieut. Obadiah Beal's company from Dec. 12, 1775, to April 3, 1776.

60. Marble.   Fifth Generation.   Tower.

15. ESTHER [4], JOHN [3], IBROOK [2], JOHN [1].

Esther [4], dau. of John [3] and Hester (Canterbury) Tower, b. Sept. 22, 1700; mar. John Marble, in Cohasset, Sept. 7, 1724, by Rev. N. Hobart. John Marble was son of Gershom.

Childr. born in Cohasset.

	I.	GERSHOM [5]	born May 15, 1725;	died	July 1751, ag. 26 y. 2 m.
	II.	MARY [5]	" Nov. 26, 1726;	"	Aug. 18, 1751, ag. 24 y. 9 m. 8 d.
126.	III.	NOAH [5]	" Sept. 4, 1730.		
	IV.	NEHEMIAH [5]	" Nov. 10, 1734;	"	Oct. 21, 1736, ag. 1 y. 11 m. 11 d.

John Marble died at Cape Cod April, 1738.

61.   Fifth Generation.   Tower.

15. CORNELIUS [4], JOHN [3], IBROOK [2], JOHN [1].

Cornelius [4], son of John [3] and Hester (Canterbury) Tower, b. Feb. 5, 1701–2; mar. Hannah Higgins, of Eastham, Mass. Int. pub. April 1, 1732.

Childr. born in Cohasset.

	I.	NEHEMIAH [5]	born Oct. 15, 1732; died Jan. 23, 1735–6, ag. 3 y. 3 m. 8 d.
127.	II.	ELKANAH [5]	" Sept. 3, 1734.
125.	III.	HANNAH [5]	" Sept. 16, 1736.
128.	IV.	SILENCE [5]	" Oct. 24, 1738.
129.	V.	ISAAC [5]	" May 10, 1744.
	VI.	CORNELIUS [5]	bapt. March 17, 1751.
	VII.	BENJAMIN [5]	" July 7, 1754.

Cornelius Tower [4] served as a soldier in the old French war. His name appears in Col. Thomas Clapp's regiment, where his

age is given as fifty-six years. His name also appears in Capt.
Josiah Thatcher's company in Colonel Thomas's regiment from
April 6 to November 1, at Halifax, 1759, where he was discharged
December 20th, the same year. There is no further record of
him, and it is supposed he died soon after.

62. Pritchard.   Fifth Generation.   Tower.

15. MARTHA [4], JOHN [3], IBROOK [2], JOHN [1].
    Martha [4], dau. of John [3] and Hester (Canterbury) Tower, b.
    Jan. 14, 1703–4 ; mar. John Pritchard, in Cohasset,
    July 8, 1733, by Rev. N. Hobart.

Childr. born in Cohasset.

122.	I.	OLIVER [5] born	March 22, 1733–4.
	II.	PRICE [5] "	Feb. 18, 1736–7.
	III.	MARY [5] "	March, 1740; died Oct. 25, 1752, ag. 12 y. 7 m.

John Pritchard died in Cohasset, 1772.
Martha (Tower) Pritchard died in Cohasset, 1776, ag. 72.

63. Burbank.   Fifth Generation.   Tower.

19. ELIZABETH [4], HEZEKIAH [3], IBROOK [2], JOHN [1].
    Elizabeth [4], dau. of Hezekiah [3] and Elizabeth (Whiton) Tower, b.
    June 11, 1705 ; mar. John Burbank, in Cohasset,
    June 28, 1728, by Rev. N. Hobart.

Childr. born in Cohasset.

	I.	ELIZABETH [5] born	Dec. 30, 1728; died Oct. 13, 1730, ag. 1 y. 9 m. 13 d.
	II.	LYDIA [5] "	Aug. 4, 1730; died July 21, 1748, ag. 17 y. 10 m. 17 d.
	III.	ELIZABETH [5] "	Feb. 19, 1731–2; died Dec. 18, 1737, ag. 5 y. 9 m. 29 d.
	IV.	JOHN [5] "	Dec. 6, 1733; died Dec. 10, 1737, ag. 4 y. 4 d.
	V.	TIMOTHY [5] "	Aug. 30, 1735; died Jan. 26, 1757, ag. 21 y. 4 m. 27 d.
	VI.	REBECCA [5] "	Jan. 14, 1736–7.
132.	VII.	ELIZABETH [5] bapt.	Dec. 31, 1738.
	VIII.	JANE [5]	born June 10, 1740; mar. James Newell, of Scituate, May 15, 1760.
	IX.	DEBORAH [5] "	March 6, 1741–2 ; died .
	X.	DEBORAH [5] "	Dec. 23, 1743.
	XI.	RUTH [5] "	Aug. 30, 1735.
	XII.	SUSANNAH [5] "	Sept. 6, 1747.
	XIII.	JOHN [5] "	June 15, 1749.

64. Worrick, Sutton. Fifth Generation. Tower.

19. SUSANNAH [4], HEZEKIAH [3], IBROOK [2], JOHN [1].
Susannah [4], dau. of Hezekiah [3] and Elizabeth (Whiton)
Tower, b.
April 16, 1707 ; mar. Ray Sutton, of Scituate,
Aug. 1, 1734, by Rev. N. Hobart. R. Sutton was b.
1710.

Childr.

I. SUSANNAH [5] bapt. Oct. 19, 1735; died Dec. 18, 1737, ag. 2 y. 1 m.
30 d.
II. SARAH [5]   " Sept. 18, 1737; " Nov. 7, 1737.

Ray Sutton died in Cohasset, Sept. 20, 1737, ag. 27.
Susannah [4] (Tower) Sutton mar., 2d, widower Chasling
Worrick, of Cohasset,
Nov. 22, 1739, by Rev. N. Hobart.

Childr.

	III.	HEZEKIAH [5] born Aug. 9, 1740.
134.	IV.	LYDIA [5]	" Nov. 17, 1742.
	V.	ESTHER [5]	" May 13, 1745.
	VI.	JESSE [5]	bapt. Sept. 11, 1748.

Chasling Worrick died April 7, 1749.

65. Fifth Generation. Tower.

19. DAVID [4], HEZEKIAH [3], IBROOK [2], JOHN [1].
David [4], son of Hezekiah [3] and Elizabeth (Whiton) Tower, b.
Aug. 28, 1708 ; mar. Susanna Tucker, in Cohasset,
Dec. 17, 1730, by Rev. N. Hobart. She was b.
Nov. 12, 1710, and was dau. of Joshua and Hannah Tucker.

Childr. born in Cohasset.

130.	I.	HANNAH [5]	born Feb. 4, 1731-2.
	II.	Son [5]	" March 7, 1732-3; died March 8, 1732-3.
131.	III.	SUSANNAH [5]	" May 15, 1734.
132.	IV.	ROBERT [5]	" 1735.
	V.	MARY [5]	bapt. Jan. 2, 1736-7; unmar.
133.	VI.	PHEBE [5]	" July 2, 1739.
134.	VII.	ABNER [5]	born April 17, 1741.
	VIII.	LYDIA [5]	" Dec. 31, 1744; died Oct. 19, 1753, ag. 8 y. 9 m. 19 d.
135.	IX.	RACHEL [5]	" July 31, 1746.

   X. Ephraim[5] born Sept. 21, 1748; died Oct. 5, 1754, ag. 4 y.
          14 d.
   XI. David[5]   " Nov. 16, 1750;   " Jan. 25, 1755, ag. 4 y.
          2 m. 9 d.

Susanna (Tucker) Tower died May 12, 1762, ag. 51 y. 6 m.

David Tower[4] mar., 2d, widow Joanna Leavitt (Abraham, Jun.),

Aug. 30, 1763, by Rev. John Brown. She was bapt. in Hingham

Aug. 9, 1719, and was dau. of John and Joanna (Bisbee) Leavitt. David Tower[4] died

Nov. 7, 1765, ag. 57 y. 2 m. 10 d.

66. Vickery.   **Fifth Generation.**   **Tower.**

19. Lydia[4], Hezekiah[3], Ibrook[2], John[1].
   Lydia[4], dau. of Hezekiah[3] and Elizabeth (Whiton) Tower, b.
   May 1, 1713; mar. George Vickery,
   May 1, 1735, by Rev. N. Hobart. G. Vickery b.
   Nov. 12, 1713, and was son of George and Elizabeth Vickery.

67. Whitcomb.   **Fifth Generation.**   **Tower.**

22. Sarah[4], Daniel[3], Ibrook[2], John[1].
   Sarah[4], dau. of Daniel[3] and Sarah (Lincoln) Tower, b.
   June 24, 1717; mar. John Whitcomb, in Cohasset,
   Aug. 29, 1734, by Rev. N. Hobart. J. Whitcomb b.
        1711, and was son of Israel and Mary (Stoddard)
   Whitcomb.

              Childr.

   I.   Child   born Dec. 25, 1734; died Jan. 2, 1734–5.
   II. John[5]   "   1735.
   III. Elizabeth[5]
   IV. Sarah[5]
   V. Thankful[5]   mar. Elijah Stoddard.
   VI. Mary[5]   "   Joseph Beal, of Cohasset.

John Whitcomb died about 1787.
Sarah[4] (Tower) Whitcomb died about 1802, ag. 85 y.

68.   **Fifth Generation.**   **Tower.**

22. Daniel[4], Daniel[3], Ibrook[2], John[1].
   Daniel[4], son of Daniel[3] and Sarah (Lincoln) Tower, b.
   June 23, 1720; mar. Bethiah Nichols, of Cohasset,

Jan. 5, 1741-2, by Rev. E. Gay. She was b. in Cohasset
May 12, 1724, and was dau. of Roger and Bethiah (Winslow)
Nichols.

Childr. born in Cohasset.

	I.	ABRAHAM [5]	born June, 1741; died March 4, 1741-2.
	II.	SARAH [5]	" May 30,1743; mar. James Cushing, Jun., of Scituate, Dec. 8, 1763.
	III.	MORDECAI [5]	" May 24, 1745; drowned at sea.
	IV.	BETHIAH [5]	" April 20, 1747; mar. John Pratt, of Cohasset, *s. p.*
	V.	DANIEL [5]	" Oct. 5, 1749; died young.
136.	VI.	ABRAHAM [5] ⎫ Twins	" April 18, 1752.
137.	VII.	ISAAC [5] ⎬	
138.	VIII.	SAMUEL [5]	" April 30, 1754.
139.	IX.	LEVI [5]	" July 25, 1756.
140.	X.	PERSIS [5]	" Aug. 1, 1759.
	XI.	MARY [5]	bapt. June 21, 1761; died.
141.	XII.	MARY [5]	" May 27, 1764.
142.	XIII.	BETHIAH [5]	" Jan. 24, 1768.
143.	XIV.	DANIEL [5]	born July 29, 1771.

Daniel Tower [4] died in Cohasset, Jan. 28, 1800, ag. 79 y. 7 m.
5 d.

Bethiah (Nichols) Tower died in Cohasset, April 27, 1813,
ag. 88 y. 11 m. 15 d.

Daniel Tower's [4] will is dated October, 1799, and allowed April 1,
1800. He gives his wife Bethiah the improvement of all his estate
both real and personal, with some exceptions, during her natural
life. He names his daughters, Sarah Cushing, Persis Hall, Bethiah
Lothrop, and Mary Bates, to whom he gives legacies. He gives to
his son-in-law, James Cushing, " all the real estate I purchased of
him lying in the township of Scituate."

He names his sons Abraham, Isaac, Samuel, and Levi, and his
grandson Daniel Nichols Tower, and makes them residuary
devisees of his estate, and makes a contingent gift to his said
grandson.

The inventory of his estate shows sixty-seven acres of homestead, which indicates the purchase of land in addition to the original grant to his great-grandfather, John Tower, on which his
grandfather, Ibrook, settled. The valuation of his whole estate is
$4,787.

69.   **Fifth Generation.**   **Tower.**

22. JOB [4], DANIEL [3], IBROOK [2], JOHN [1].
Job [4], son of Daniel [3] and Sarah (Lincoln) Tower, b.
Sept. 8, 1726 ; mar. Mary Pratt in Boston
Nov. 19, 1749, by Jonas Clark, Esq.   She was b. in Cohasset
June 13, 1726, and was dau. of Aaron and Mary Pratt.

Childr. born in Cohasset.

144.	I.	MOLLY [5]	born	Feb. 3, 1753.
145.	II.	THANKFUL [5]	"	July 25, 1755.
	III.	OBADIAH [5]	"	Oct. 17, 1757; died
	IV.	MARGARET [5]	"	Dec. 24, 1759; "
146.	V.	MERIEL [5]	bapt.	Nov. 28, 1762.
	VI.	MARGARET [5]	"	Nov. 17, 1765; "
147.	VII.	SARAH [5]		
148.	VIII.	BETTY [5]	"	Oct. 21, 1770.

Job Tower [4] died in Cohasset about 1793, ag. about 66.
Mary (Pratt) Tower died in Cohasset, Feb. 19, 1806, ag.
79 y. 9 m. 4 d.

70.   **Fifth Generation.**   **Tower.**

23. PETER [4], JEREMIAH [3], JEREMIAH [2], JOHN[1].
Peter [4], son of Jeremiah [3] and Hannah (Hobart) Tower, b.
Sept. 14, 1701 ; mar. Patience Garnet, in Hingham
May 11, 1727, by Rev. E. Gay.   She was b. in Hingham
Sept. 3, 1703, and was dau. of Stephen and Sarah (Warren)
Garnet.

Childr. born in Hingham.

149.	I.	PETER [5]	bapt.	Jan. 19, 1728-9.
150.	II.	PATIENCE [5]	"	Dec. 10, 1730.
151.	III.	SARAH [5]	"	Oct. 22, 1732.
	IV.	HANNAH [5]	"	Dec. 22, 1734; died Dec. 25, 1734.
	V.	HANNAH [5]	"	March 28, 1736 ; mar. Benj. Bicknell, of Wey-
				mouth. Int. pub. Dec. 12, 1766, *s. p.* She
				died previous to 1769.
152.	VI.	MALACHI [5]	"	March 19, 1737-8.
153.	VII.	MARY [5]	"	Feb. 24, 1739-40.
154.	VIII.	LUCY [5]	"	March 28, 1742.

Peter Tower [4] died in Hingham April 21, 1768, ag. 66 y.
7 m. 7 d.
Patience (Garnet) Tower died in Hingham previous to the
death of her husband.

71. Dunbar.   Fifth Generation.   Tower.

23. HANNAH [4], JEREMIAH [3], JEREMIAH [2], JOHN [1].
    Hannah [4], dau. of Jeremiah [3] and Hannah (Hobart) Tower, b.
    April 11, 1705 ; mar. Jonathan Dunbar, in Boston
    April 10, 1729, by S. Checkley, Esq.

Childr. born in Hingham.

I.   HANNAH [5]   born Nov. 30, 1729.
II. JONATHAN [5] "   Feb. 23, 1730–31.
III. MARY [5]   "   April 16, 1734.
IV. RUTH [5]   "   April 12, 1736; mar. David Garner June 6, 1781.

Hannah (Tower) Dunbar died in Hingham, Nov. 28, 1740, ag.
35 y. 7 m. 17 d.

72.   Fifth Generation.   Tower.

27. BENJAMIN [4], BENJAMIN [3], BENJAMIN [2], JOHN [1].
    Benjamin [4], son of Benjamin [3] and Margaret (   ) Tower, b.
25. July 14, 1712 ; mar. Deborah Hollis [4].   Int. pub.
    Jan. 13, 1739–40.   She was b.
    Mar. 21, 1713–14, and was dau. of Abigail [3] (Tower) and
    Samuel Hollis.

Childr.

I.   DAVID [5]   bapt. July 10, 1743.
II. ABIGAIL [5]   "   May 4, 1746.
III. ESTHER [5]   "   Aug. 6, 1749.

David Tower [5] does not appear to have left descendants, or at
least no record of them has been discovered ; neither is there
found any record of his marriage or death. At the commencement of the Revolutionary War he was thirty-two years old, and
appears at that time to be a resident of Abington. His name is
on the roll of Capt. Wm. Reed's company, with thirty others,
on the 19th of April, 1775, with a record of one month and
one day's service, and a marching distance of ninety-five miles.
And again we find him doing duty in the same company in October, 1775, at Roxbury. As we do not meet with his name again
in any of the records, we may reasonably infer that he died
without issue during the war.

73. Hollis.   Fifth Generation.   Tower.

27. DEBORAH [4], BENJAMIN [3], BENJAMIN [2], JOHN [1].
    Deborah [4], dau. of Benjamin [3] and Bethiah(Woodward)Tower, b.

25. Feb. 16, 1718–19; mar. Samuel Hollis [4], of Weymouth,
     Jan. 15, 1735–6. He was b. in Weymouth
     Jan. 12, 1711–12, and was son of Abigail [3] (Tower) and
     Samuel Hollis.

Childr. born in Weymouth.

I.	BETHIAH [5]	born Dec. 13, 1736; died July 12, 1737.
II.	SAMUEL [5]	"	June 5, 1739.
III.	JOSHUA [5]	"	Feb. 11, 1742.
IV.	BETHIAH [5]	"	Aug. 14, 1744.

74.   **Fifth Generation.**   **Tower.**

27. JAMES [4], BENJAMIN [3], BENJAMIN [2], JOHN [1].
     James [4], son of Benjamin [3] and Bethiah (Woodward) Tower, b.
     Feb. 6, 1722–3; mar. Mary Day in Hingham
     Jan. 16, 1745–6, by Rev. E. Gay. She was bapt. in Hingham
     Feb. 15, 1729–30, and was dau. of James and Mary (Sherlock)
         Day.

Childr. born in Scituate, Mass.

155	I.	MARGARET [5]	born	1746.
156.	II.	LYNDE [5]	"	1749.
157.	III.	BETHIA [5]	"	1752.
158.	IV.	MATTHEW [5]	"	Dec. 1, 1755.
159.	V.	BENJAMIN [5]	"	July 4, 1756.
	VI.	DEBORAH [5]	"	; mar. John Webb, of Weymouth, Nov. 25, 1786.

Mary (Day) Tower died
James Tower [4] mar., 2d, Lucy Dunbar. Int. pub.
April 9, 1780. She was b. in Hingham

Childr.

	VII.	JOHN [5]	born Oct. 19, 1781; unmar.; died 1814, ag. 33.
160.	VIII.	POLLY [5]	" Oct. 11, 1783.	
161.	IX.	SOLOMON [5]	" Oct. 25, 1785.	
162.	X.	DAVID [5]	" July 6, 1788.	
163.	XI.	LUCY [5]	" Oct. 14, 1791.	
	XII.	RACHEL [5]	" May 20, 1794; mar. Thomas Stoddard, of Scituate, Oct. 17, 1825, *s. p.*

James Tower [4] died   1796, ag. 73.
Lucy (Dunbar) Tower mar., 2d, Theophilus Corthell, of Scituate,
May 29, 1800.

James Tower [4] was a soldier in the old French war. He was in Captain Parker's company. The following certificate is found in the Massachusetts Archives : —

SUFFOLK COUNTY, May 25th, 1758.

These are to certify that James Tower, aged thirty-seven years, born at Scituate, came before me, one of his Majesty's Justices of the Peace for the said county, and acknowledged to have voluntarily enlisted himself to serve his Majesty, King George the Second, in the abovesaid service; and that he also acknowledged he had heard read unto him the second and sixth sections of the articles of war against mutiny and desertion, and took the oath of fidelity mentioned in the articles of war.

JO? WILLIAMS.

James Tower [4] served also in the War of the Revolution. He was in Capt. Jotham Loring's company of Hingham on the 19th of April, 1775, and did thirteen days' duty. He was in Capt. Seth Stower's company, on duty in Hull from May 22 to Aug. 1, 1776, and is credited with one month and twenty-seven days' time. In a pay-roll of Capt. Jabez Wilder's half company, James Tower is credited with six days in February, 1778, doing duty at Hull.

In the muster-roll of the independent company stationed at Hingham, commanded by Capt. James Lincoln, from May 5, 1775, to Jan. 1, 1776, is the name of James Tower, with a credit for seven months and four days, and thirty-six miles of travel, with a payment of £16 5s. 8½d.

He was in Capt. Job Cushing's company at Tiverton, R. I., July, 1779, and is credited with thirty-nine days' service. In 1781 he was in Capt. Elijah Baker's company in Rhode Island, and served three months and twenty-four days. On the 4th of March, 1776, he was in Capt. Pyam Cushing's company for four days' service at Dorchester, marching thirty-six miles. In 1778 he was in Capt. Elias Whiton's company, doing guard duty in Boston one month and twenty days, for which service he received £3 6s. 8d. In 1779 he was on the same duty in Capt. Caleb Champney's company for two months and twenty-six days.

It will be seen by referring to the date of his birth that he was fifty-two years old when hostilities began, and fifty-eight years old when his last term of duty was performed.

75.   **Fifth Generation.**   **Tower.**

27. JONATHAN [4], BENJAMIN [3], BENJAMIN [2], JOHN [1].
    Jonathan [4], son of Benjamin [3] and Bethiah (Woodward) Tower, b.

25. Nov. 3, 1724 ; mar. Lydia Hollis [4], in Weymouth,
    Dec. 18, 1746. She was b. in Weymouth
    June 5, 1723, and was dau. of Abigail [3] (Tower) and Samuel
    Hollis.

Childr.

I.   LYDIA [5]   bapt. April 17, 1748.

164.   II.   JONATHAN [5] "   Aug. 26, 1753.

Jonathan Tower [4] died about 1759, ag. 35.

Jonathan Tower [4] was a soldier in the old French war. He
served in Capt. Asa Foster's company, Col. Ebenezer Nichols'
regiment, from May 24 to Oct. 24, 1758, and is reported " dead."
There is a tradition among his descendants living in Vermont
that he died among the mountains near Wallingford, Vt.

76.   **Fifth Generation.**   **Tower.**

31. NATHANIEL [4], THOMAS [3], BENJAMIN [2], JOHN [1].
    Nathaniel [4], son of Thomas [3] and Elizabeth(Woodward)Tower, b.
    March 13, 1718–19 ; mar. Sarah Teague, in Hingham, Mass.,
    July 31, 1740, by Rev. E. Gay. She was b. in Hingham
    June 9, 1722, and was dau. of Daniel and Sarah (Pray)
    Teague.

Childr.

165.   I.   SARAH [5]   born April 22, 1742.

166.   II.   NATHANIEL [5] "   Oct. 7, 1744.

167.   III.   AMBROSE [5]   "   Jan. 31, 1746–7.

168.   IV.   BETTE [5]   "   Feb. 18, 1760.

Nathaniel Tower [4] died in Hingham, Sept. 6, 1767, ag. 48 y.
    5 m. 23 d.

77.   **Fifth Generation.**   **Tower**

31. SHADRACH [4], THOMAS [3], BENJAMIN [2], JOHN [1].
    Shadrach [4], son of Thomas [3] and Elizabeth (Woodward)
    Tower, b.
    Feb. 5, 1720–21 ; mar. Ruth Cobb, in Hingham, Mass.,
    May 16, 1744, by Rev. E. Gay. She was b.
    May 14, 1718, and was dau. of Richard and Ruth (Beal) Cobb.

Childr. born in Hingham.

I.   KESIA [5]   born March 31, 1745; died Jan. 8, 1761, ag.
                15 y. 9 m. 8 d.

II.   RICHARD COBB [5] "   Nov. 8, 1746.

III. Moses [5]   born May 18, 1748; died Nov. 21, 1757, ag. 9 y.
6 m. 3 d.

169. IV. Martin [5]   "   June 10, 1750.

V. Elizabeth [5]   "   May 9, 1752.

170. VI. Thomas Gross [5]   "   Aug. 12, 1754.

VII. Ruth [5]   "   Nov. 22, 1757; died in Dorchester, Oct.
11, 1820, ag. 62 y. 10 m. 19 d.

Shadrach Tower [4] died April 1, 1760, ag. 39 y. 1 m. 27 d.

Ruth (Cobb) Tower mar., 2d, Ebenezer Brown, of Dorchester, May 29, 1768, by Rev. E. Gay.

78.   **Fifth Generation.**   **Tower.**

31. Thomas [4], Thomas [3], Benjamin [2], John [1].

Thomas [4], son of Thomas [3] and Elizabeth (Woodward) Tower, b.
July 6, 1725; mar. Ruth Teague, in Hingham, Mass.
Nov. 21, 1749, by Rev. E. Gay. She was b. in Hingham
Jan. 24, 1727–8, and was dau. of Daniel and Sarah (Pray)
Teague.

Childr. None.

Thomas Tower [4] died Aug. 7, 1759, ag. 34 y. 1 m. 1 d.

79.   **Fifth Generation.**   **Tower.**

33. Samuel [4] { Peter [3], Benjamin [2] } John [1].
            { Anna [3], Samuel [2] }

Samuel [4], son of Peter [3] and Anna [3] (Tower) Tower, b.
March 17, 1728–9; mar. Hannah Collamore, of Scituate,
Feb. 12, 1761.

Childr., all but the last named, born in Hingham.

171. I. Samuel [5]   bapt. Dec. 22, 1761.

172. II. Ann [5]   born Sept. 10, 1763.

III. Jesse [5]   "   Aug. 1, 1765; unmar.; died in Deruyter, N.Y.,
Aug., 1825, ag. 60.

173. IV. Shubael [5]   "   Sept. 28, 1767.

174. V. Hannah [5]   "   Feb. 13, 1770.

VI. Obadiah [5]   "   Oct. 13, 1774; died May 7, 1794, ag. 19 y. 6 m.
24 d.

175. VII. Peter [5]   "   Sept. 26, 1776.

VIII. Jotham [5]   "   Nov. 21, 1778; died June 23, 1780.

IX. Joshua [5]   bapt. May 21, 1780, in Worthington, Mass.

Samuel Tower [4] died in Worthington, Oct. 7, 1811, ag. 82 y.
5 m. 27 d.

Hannah (Collamore) Tower died in Worthington, July 3, 1818,
ag. 78.

Samuel Tower's[4] name is found on the roll of Capt. Pyam Cushing's company, " assembled to guard the shores from March 11 to March 29, 1776 ; " and again at two different times in the same company in the month of June of the same year he was doing duty at Hull.   He removed from Hingham to Worthington, Mass., during the War of the Revolution, and became one of the early settlers of that town.   His farm was situated on the highest part of that elevated region, and here, where he built his dwelling-house and farm-buildings, nothing now remains but the cellar and the remnant of the stone chimney fallen therein.   A tree has taken root in the deserted cellar, and has already attained considerable dimensions.   No sound of industry breaks the solitude, and the farm bids fair in a few years to relapse into its condition of forest from which Samuel Tower and his helping sons reclaimed it scarcely a century ago.   His children and grandchildren went out of Worthington into other fields, to repeat the lesson of subduing the wilderness for which their early experience so well fitted them.   The earliest record in Worthington of Samuel Tower's family is the baptism of his youngest son, May 21, 1780, and under the date of Nov. 4, 1780, is found " admitted to the church in Worthington, wife of Samuel Tower."   Memorial-stones in the cemetery record the death of Samuel Tower and his wife Hannah Tower.   His will, dated July 6, 1806, makes provision for his wife, and especial provision for his infirm son Jesse[5].   He names his surviving sons, Samuel, Shubael, and Peter, and his daughters, Anna Alford and Hannah Hall.

The inventory of his estate, taken Oct. 6, 1812, shows the area of his farm, 139 acres, which, with the buildings thereon, has a value of $973.   This, and the farm-stock, products, and household furniture, of a value of 198\frac{21}{100}$, make the sum total of a life of industry prolonged to more than fourscore years in the more primitive pursuits of life.   And yet, modest as this sum appears, it is questionable whether it does not compare favorably with the average result of a wage-earner of the present day, amid all the advantages of science and invention as applied to human labor.

80.   **Fifth Generation.**   **Tower.**

33. ISAIAH [4], PETER [3], BENJAMIN [2], JOHN [1].
Isaiah [4], son of Peter [3] and Anna [3] (Tower) Tower, b.
Sept. 2, 1731 ; mar. Lydia Gill, in Hingham,
Dec. 18, 1760, by Rev. E. Gay.   She was b. in Hingham
Sept. 1, 1738, and was dau. of Samuel and Rebecca (Leavitt)
Gill.

Childr. born in Hingham.

176.	I.	LYDIA [5] born May 26, 1761.	
177.	II.	ISAIAH [5] " April 12, 1766.	
	III.	CELIA [5] " May 27, 1772; died Aug. 21, 1775, ag. 3 y. 2 m. 25 d.	

Isaiah Tower [4] died in Hingham, Feb. 2, 1811, ag. 79 y. 3 m. 27 d.

Lydia (Gill) Tower died in Hingham, Feb. 27, 1815, ag. 76 y. 5 m. 15 d.

Isaiah Tower [4] was a private in Capt. Pyam Cushing's company, which marched to Dorchester on the 4th of March, 1776, when he is credited with thirty-six miles of travel and four days service; and in the same company again from the 11th to the 29th of March, guarding the shores; and again in the same company at Hull at two different times in June in the same year.

Isaiah Tower [4] was a weaver by trade, as were his father and grandfather before him. He lived at the corner of Main and High Streets in Hingham, where he built a house about the year 1752, according to tradition in the family. The lot on which the house stands became by descent and division of property the estate of his grandson, Leavitt Tower [6], who occupied it during his life, which closed in 1882; and by his will it passed to the wife of his nephew. The house has been added to since it was built, and is well preserved.

---

81. **Fifth Generation.** **Tower.**

33. JOSHUA [4], PETER [3], BENJAMIN [2], JOHN [1].

Joshua [4], son of Peter [3] and Anna [3] (Tower) Tower, b. April 25, 1733; mar. Lucy Dunbar, in Hingham, Jan. 30, 1776, by Rev. D. Shute. She was b. in Hingham July 29, 1749, and was dau. of Solomon and Rachel (Damon) Dunbar.

Childr.

I. LUCY [5] born 1776; died 1779.

Joshua Tower [4] died in Hingham, Sept. 30, 1810, ag. 76 y. 4 m. 25 d.

Lucy (Dunbar) Tower died in Hingham, Dec. 16, 1776, ag. 27 y. 4 m. 18 d.

Joshua Tower [4] was a soldier in the War of the Revolution. He was a private in Capt. Jotham Loring's company, called into service on the 19th of April, 1775, and credited with thirteen days service.

In 1776 Joshua Tower was chosen and commissioned as second lieutenant of the third company in the second Suffolk regiment, of which company Pyam Cushing was the captain. He marched with his company on the 4th of March to Dorchester to relieve that part of the army which left their lines in Roxbury to take possession of Dorchester Heights, causing the British troops to evacuate Boston. After the evacuation the company returned to Hingham, having completed four days service and thirty-six miles travel. From the 11th to the 29th of March of the same year he was on duty at intervals guarding the shores. The roll of the company contains seventy-eight names, including the officers, and eight of these are the names of Tower. · In June of the same year he was twice called to Hull with his company. In 1777 he went from Hingham with a lieutenant's command to join the company of Capt. Moses French, at Providence, R. I., in General Spencer's expedition.

Among his papers is preserved a roll of the forty-two men under his command, and, including himself, six are of the name of Tower, — all his neighbors and relatives. On this paper are several indorsements: " Marched from Hingham May 17th; arrived at Providence the 19th, about 10 o'clock. . . . July 8, at Providence at night, a mighty rain. . . . July 11, General Prescott taken prisoner, brought off Rhode Island by Col. Barton, of Providence." Two other papers, containing reports of the main guard at two different times, are signed by Captain Grant, officer of the day.

Among his papers are many deeds of land which he purchased, and in some of which he is a grantee with his brother Samuel; and in 1803 the brothers, Isaiah, Joshua, and Laban, make partition of lands which they held in common, by a deed in which they all join. None of these deeds have been recorded, though much of the land has been since subdivided and passed by many successive conveyances.

Joshua Tower's will is dated March 12, 1810, and proved and allowed Nov. 6, 1810. In this he gives " to my youngest brother, Laban Tower, all my homestead and buildings thereon, together with all my other freehold estate whatsoever;" and he makes him his residuary legatee. By the devise under this will Laban Tower [4] becomes the sole owner of the homestead of John Tower [1].

82.   Fifth Generation.   Tower.

33. LABAN [4], PETER [3], BENJAMIN [2], JOHN [1].
Laban [4], son of Peter [3] and Anna [3] (Tower) Tower, b.
Aug. 3, 1751; mar. Esther Cushing, in Weymouth, Mass.,
May 2, 1776, by Rev. S. Williams. She was b. in Weymouth
June 10, 1757, and was dau. of Frederick and Grace (Bate)
Cushing.

Childr. born in Hingham.

178. I. GRACE [5] born March 23, 1777.
179. II. LUCY [5]   "   May 19, 1780.

Laban Tower [4] died in Hingham, July 30, 1824, ag. 72 y. 11 m.
27 d.
Esther (Cushing) Tower died in Hingham, May 30, 1828,
ag. 70 y. 11 m. 13 d.

Laban Tower [4], the youngest of Peter [3] and Anna [3] (Tower)
Tower's nine sons, was a soldier in the War of the Revolution, and
the following is something of the record of his service. On the
19th of April, 1775, under Capt. Jotham Loring, he is credited
with thirteen days service. He served in Capt. James Lincoln's
company of guards in Hingham in 1776, and was with Capt. Pyam
Cushing at Hull in June of that year. In the same year his name
appears on a roll of men drafted from Hingham, Braintree, and
other towns, under Lieut. Theophilus Wilder, of Hingham. In
the months of December, 1776, and January and February, 1777,
he was a sergeant doing duty in Capt. Theophilus Wilder's company, and from May to July, 1777, he was with his brother's command in Rhode Island, and in 1778 he was with Capt. Jabez
Wilder's half company, doing duty at Hull, and in the same year
he was in Capt. Elias Whiton's company doing guard duty.
Laban Tower was a cooper by trade, and pursued his calling upon
the old homestead, where he lived, and which by the will of his
brother Joshua became his sole property. By his will, dated July
28, 1824, and proved and allowed September 7 of the same year,
he gave his homestead and all his other lands to his wife for and
during her life, with remainder to his grandson William Tower [6].
The homestead remained in the possession of William Tower until
his death, April 12, 1879, and the dwelling-house and a portion
of the land are now owned and occupied by his widow, Lucy A.
Tower.

83.   **Fifth Generation.**   **Tower.**

34. JOSEPH [4], AMBROSE [3], BENJAMIN [2], JOHN [1].
Joseph [4], son of Ambrose [3] and Mary Tower, b.
Sept. 5, 1723; mar. Hepzibah Gibbs in Sudbury,
July 21, 1748, by Rev. Israel Loring. She was b. in Sudbury
Feb. 25, 1730, and was dau. of Isaac and Thankful (Wheeler)
Gibbs.

Childr.

	I.	JOSEPH [5]	born April 11, 1750; died, 1776, in the army at the siege of Boston.
180.	II.	ISAAC [5]	" Feb. 2, 1752.
181.	III.	THANKFUL [5]	" Feb. 9, 1754.
182.	IV.	JEDUTHAN [5]	" May 17, 1756.
183	V.	JONATHAN [5]	" Aug. 7, 1758.
	VI.	POLLY [5]	" Dec. 17, 1760; mar. Abijah Potter, of Brookfield, Mass., May 4, 1784.
184.	VII.	LURANY [5]	" Jan. 4, 1763.
185.	VIII.	JUSTUS [5]	" Oct. 16, 1765.
186.	IX.	JONAS [5]	" March 8, 1768.
187.	X.	JOHN [5]	" May 13, 1770.
188.	XI.	JOTHAM [5]	" Jan. 28, 1774.
	XII.	JOSEPH [5]	" April 12, 1776; died in Rutland, Mass., 1780, ag. 4 yrs.

Joseph Tower [4] died in Rutland, Mass.,   1779, ag. 56.
Hepzibah (Gibbs) Tower died in Waterville, N. Y., Jan. 16,
1816, ag. 85 y. 10 m. 22 d.

Joseph Tower [4] in the early part of his manhood resided in
Weston, Mass., and was a member of the church there. He removed to Sudbury in 1748, and resided there nearly twenty years.
He afterwards removed to and resided in the towns of Princeton,
Lancaster, Shrewsbury, and Rutland. He was a millwright by
occupation, and the demand for experience and skill in providing
the progressive settlements with saw and grist mills explains his
frequent removals. At the time of his death he was the owner of
a mill in Rutland. It will be noticed that the names of all his
nine sons begin with the same letter of the alphabet, the I and J
then having the same visible representative, though distinguished
by difference of sound.

84.   **Fifth Generation.**   **Tower.**

34. AMBROSE [4], AMBROSE [3], BENJAMIN [2], JOHN [1].
Ambrose [4], son of Ambrose [3] and Mary (   ) Tower, d.
1727; mar. Jerusha Clapp in Sudbury, Mass.,

Oct. 10, 1751, by Rev. Israel Loring. She was b.
May 14, 1728, and was dau. of John and Abigail (Easterbrook)
Clapp.

Childr. born in Sudbury.

189.	I.	SILENCE [5]	born	Aug. 31, 1754.
190.	II.	SILAS [5]	"	Aug. 15, 1756.
191.	III.	ABEL [5]	"	June 16, 1758.
192.	IV.	ASAHEL [5]	"	Oct. 9, 1760.
	V.	MARY [5]	"	May 31, 1764.
	VI.	SARAH [5]	"	Oct. 5, 1766; mar. Samuel Childs.
193.	VII.	JERUSHA [5]	"	July 16, 1769.
194.	VIII.	DANIEL [5]	"	Feb. 3, 1772.

Jerusha (Clapp) Tower died Jan. 30, 1782, ag. 53 y. 8 m. 16 d.
Ambrose Tower [4] mar., 2d, Elizabeth Davis.
He died in Sudbury, April 1, 1788, ag. 61.

Ambrose Tower [4] resided in Sudbury, Mass. He was a soldier
in the old French war, and was in Capt. Josiah Richardson's
company of Sudbury in 1757. He was a landholder, owning lands
in both Middlesex and Worcester counties; but previous to his
death he seems to have conveyed his real estate to his sons, making one conveyance to Silas in 1783, and in 1787 he conveys his
homestead to Abel. In the administration upon his estate in
1788 the inventory shows only personal property.

85.　　　　　　　**Fifth Generation.**　　　　　　　**Tower.**

34. JONATHAN [4], AMBROSE [3], BENJAMIN [2], JOHN [1].
Jonathan [4], son of Ambrose [3] and Mary (   ) Tower, b.
1729; mar. Eunice Allen, in Lincoln, Mass.,
March 8, 1759, by Rev. Wm. Lawrence. She was b.
Jan. 28, 1732-3, and was dau. of Benjamin and Eunice
(   ) Allen.

Childr. born in Lincoln.

195.	I.	BEULAH [5]	born	Aug. 27, 1760.
196.	II.	EUNICE [5]	"	Oct. 16, 1762.
197.	III.	JONATHAN [5]	"	Oct. 16, 1764.
	IV.	BENJAMIN [5]	"	Jan. 23, 1767.
	V.	LUCY [5]	"	Sept. 2, 1769.
198.	VI.	DANIEL [5]	"	Oct. 18, 1771.
199.	VII.	NATHAN [5]	"	April 26, 1775.

Jonathan Tower [4] died in Lincoln,　　　1777. ag. 48.
Eunice (Allen) Tower died in Lincoln,　　　1779, ag. 46.

Jonathan Tower[4] was a soldier in the old French war; he was in Capt. Ebenezer Curtis's company in 1757. He was a shoemaker by trade, and the tradition in the family is that he died of the small-pox, being infected through the repairing of a shoe. He appears to have died intestate, and there was no administration upon his estate.

86. Parmenter. Fifth Generation. Tower.

34. MARY[4], AMBROSE[3], BENJAMIN[2], JOHN[1].

Mary[4], dau. of Ambrose[3] and Mary (   ) Tower, b. 1731; mar. Samuel Parmenter, of Sudbury, Nov. 14, 1751, by Rev. D. Bliss. S. Parmenter b. May 11, 1722, and was son of David and Abigail (Brewer) Parmenter.

Childr.

I.	PERSIS[5]	born Nov. 17, 1753.
II.	JONAS[5]	" Oct. 8, 1757.
III.	EZRA[5]	" June 26, 1760.
IV.	ELIZABETH[5]	" May 7, 1762.
V.	ABIGAIL[5]	" Sept. 28, 1764.
VI.	MARY[5]	" Jan. 23, 1767.
VII.	ABIGAIL[5]	" July 2, 1771.
VIII.	DAVID[5]	" Feb. 13, 1775.

87. Fifth Generation. Tower.

34. BENJAMIN[4], AMBROSE[3], BENJAMIN[2], JOHN[1].

Benjamin[4], son of Ambrose[3] and Elizabeth (   ) Tower, bapt. March 18, 1738–9; mar. Anne Vorce in Sudbury, Mass., Jan. 7, 1761, by Rev. Israel Loring. She was b. in Sudbury, Dec. 12, 1737, and was dau. of Mark and Prudence (   ) Vorce.

Childr. born in Sudbury.

200.	I.	PETER[5]	born June 1, 1761.
201.	II.	RUTH[5]	" Oct. 27, 1762.
	III.	CATHERINE[5]	" Jan. 17, 1765; mar. Bemis, of Royalston, Mass.
202.	IV.	AUGUSTUS[5]	" June 23, 1767.
	V.	JONAS[5]	" July 4, 1769; died at sea.
	VI.	NAHUM[5]	" April 14, 1772; unmar.; died in Sudbury.
203.	VII.	REUBEN[5]	" June 3, 1774.
204.	VIII.	ABIGAIL W.[5]	" Feb. 3, 1780; mar. Sweet, of Roxbury.

Benjamin Tower[4] died July 24, 1790, ag. about 51.

Anne (Vorce) Tower died in Stow, Jan. 29, 1824, ag. 86 y. 1 m. 17 d.

Benjamin Tower [4] was a soldier in the old French war. He was in Capt. Thomas Williams's company at Albany in 1756, and in Capt. Josiah Richardson's company in 1757, and in Capt. Nicholas Dakin's company in 1758. He also served in the War of the Revolution. In a list of names of men who enlisted to serve for three years is the name of Benjamin Tower, of Sudbury. In a descriptive list of men engaged to serve in the Continental army for nine months, agreeable to a resolve of the General Court of Massachusetts Bay, is the name of Benjamin Tower, who enlisted June 9, 1779. His age is forty-one; height five feet nine inches; complexion, sandy; residence, Sudbury; regiment, How, company, Rice. At Springfield, Aug. 22, 1779, he joins with other soldiers in an acknowledgment " that we . . . have received of Capt. James Tisdale one gun, one bayonet, one scabbard, one worm, two flints, which we promise to be accountable for to him." In an account of the balance drawn between the United States and the Sixth Massachusetts Regiment, in the settlement of clothing account from Jan. 1, 1778, to Dec. 31, 1782, Benjamin Tower has a credit of $29.39. In the record of invalid pensioners called for by a resolution of the Senate in consequence of the destruction of the papers of the War Office in 1801 and 1814, is the name of Benjamin Tower. The pension commenced March 4, 1789, under a law of June 7, 1785. Administration was granted on his estate to his oldest son, Peter Tower [5], March 6, 1793.

---

88.   **Fifth Generation.**   **Tower.**

37. MATTHEW [4], SAMUEL [3], SAMUEL [2], JOHN [1].
Matthew [4], son of Samuel [3] and Lydia (Whiting) Tower, b. July 11, 1722 ; mar. Lydia Wilder, in Hingham, May 15, 1745, by Rev. E. Gay. She was b. in Hingham, Nov. 24, 1725, and was dau. of Ephraim and Mary (Lane) Wilder.

Childr.

205.   I.   MATTHEW [5] born Jan. 15, 1746–7.
      II.   LYDIA [5]   "   Dec. 28, 1748.

Matthew Tower [4] died in Abington   1749, ag. 27.
Lydia (Wilder) Tower mar., 2d, Joseph Richards in Abington, May 10, 1750. He was b. Dec. 17, 1727, and was son of Joseph and Mercy Richards.

Matthew Tower [4] was a short time before his father's death apprenticed to his father's cousin Peter Tower [3], to learn the two

trades of weaver and set-work cooper. Soon after attaining his
majority he removed to Abington, a town adjoining his native
town of Hingham. He died soon after, the exact date whereof
we have no record. Administration was granted upon his estate
to his widow, who subsequently married Joseph Richards of that
town.

89. Lazell.   Fifth Generation.   Tower.

37. SILENCE[4], SAMUEL[3], SAMUEL[2], JOHN[1].
Silence[4], dau. of Samuel[3] and Lydia (Whiting) Tower, bapt.
Sept. 27, 1724 ; mar. Israel Lazell, in Hingham,
June 5, 1753, by Rev. E. Gay. I. Lazell was b. in Hingham,
Jan. 8, 1703–1704, and was son of Israel and Rachel (Lincoln)
    Lazell.

Childr.

I. SILENCE[5] bapt. March 17, 1754.
II. HANNAH[5]   "   June, 1756.

Israel Lazell died   1770, ag. 66.

90. Lane.   Fifth Generation.   Tower.

37. LYDIA[4], SAMUEL[3], SAMUEL[2], JOHN[1].
Lydia[4], dau. of Samuel[3] and Lydia (Whiting) Tower, bapt.
Oct. 8, 1727 ; mar. Daniel Lane in Hingham,
May 19, 1746, by Rev. E. Gay. D. Lane, b. in Hingham
May 28, 1724, and was son of Jonathan and Abigail (An-
    drews) Lane.
    Childr., all but the first-named, born in Abington.

I. LYDIA[5]   born July 11, 1746; mar. Jacob Smith, Jun., of Ab-
                    ington. Int. pub. March 29, 1767.
II. SUSANNAH[5] " Aug. 1, 1748 ; mar. Philip Shaw, of Abington,
                    Dec. 15, 1776.
III. DANIEL[5]   " Feb. 25, 1750–51.
IV. OLIVE[5]   " April 8, 1754; died
V. RUTH[5]   " June 27, 1756; unmar.; died Jan. 24, 1840, ag.
                    83 y. 6 m. 28 d.
VI. CHLOE[5]   " Sept. 2, 1758; mar. Benj. Vining, of Abington,
                    Nov. 20, 1782.
VII. CHRISTIANA[5] " Nov. 29, 1760; died
VIII. CALEB[5]   " Nov. 4, 1763; died June 17, 1840, ag. 76 y.
                    7 m. 13 d.
IX. CHARLES   " April 19, 1766.
X. NABBY[5]   " Dec. 11, 1768.

Lydia (Tower) Lane died
Daniel Lane mar., 2d, Bethiah Cushing, in Abington,
Aug. 14, 1773.
Daniel Lane died in Abington, March 13, 1816, ag. 91 y. 9 m.
14 d.

91. Sprague.   Fifth Generation.   Tower.

40. ALICE[4], DANIEL[3], SAMUEL[2], JOHN[1].
Alice[4], dau. of Daniel[3] and Silence (Gross) Tower, b.
Dec. 5, 1737 ; mar. Jacob Sprague in Hingham
Oct. 1, 1767, by Rev. D. Shute. J. Sprague b. in Hingham
June, 1737, and was son of Jacob and Priscilla (Knight)
Sprague.

Childr. born in Hingham.

206.   I. BELA TOWER[5] born May 28, 1760.
       II. JACOB[5]   "
      III. CHARLES[5]   "   ; died in the West Indies.
       IV. ASA[5]   "
        V. SALLY[5]   "   Sept.   , 1772; unmar.; died in Hingham
                                    March 12, 1859, ag. 86 y. 6 m.
       VI. ABIGAIL[5]   "   1774; unmar.; died in Hingham,
                                    Aug. 13, 1857, ag. 83.

Jacob Sprague died in Halifax, N. S.
Alice (Tower) Sprague died in Hingham, Feb. 18, 1816, ag.
78 y. 2 m. 7 d.

92. Ward.   Fifth Generation.   Tower.

40. RACHEL[4], DANIEL[3], SAMUEL[2], JOHN[1].
Rachel[4], dau. of Daniel[3] and Silence (Gross) Tower, b.
Jan. 19, 1741–2 ; mar. Benjamin Ward in Hingham,
June 6, 1761, by Rev. D. Shute. B. Ward b. in Hingham
Jan. 12, 1741–2, and was son of Edward and Susannah
(Ward) Ward.

Childr. born in Hingham.

     I. DEBORAH[5] born Oct. 11, 1764.
    II. CHLOE[5]   "   May 6, 1767.
   III. EDWARD[5] bapt. July, 1769; died July 3, 1797, ag. 28.
    IV. BENJAMIN[5] "   May   , 1777.
     V. FEARING[5]   "   July , 1780.

Rachel (Tower) Ward died in Hingham, April 23, 1798,
ag. 56 y. 3 m. 4 d.

93. Farrar.   Fifth Generation.   Tower.

42. DESIRE[4], JOSEPH[3], SAMUEL[2], JOHN[1].

Desire[4], dau. of Joseph[3] and Deborah (Taylor) Tower, bapt.
Oct. 24, 1742; mar. David Farrar, in Hingham,
Dec. 14, 1780, by Rev. D. Shute. D. Farrar b. in Hingham
Sept. 1, 1750, and was son of David and Sarah (Pratt) Farrar.

Childr. none.

David Farrar died previous to 1809.
Desire (Tower) Farrar died in Hingham, Dec. 15, 1815,
ag. 73 y. 1 m. 21 d.

94.   Fifth Generation.   Tower.

42. JOSEPH[4], JOSEPH[3], SAMUEL[2], JOHN[1].

Joseph[4], son of Joseph[3] and Deborah (Taylor) Tower, bapt.
July 28, 1745; mar. Sarah Hersey, in Hingham,
July 30, 1767, by Rev. E. Gay. She was b. in Hingham
Aug. 10, 1745, and was dau. of Jonathan and Mary (May)
Hersey.

Childr.

207.	I.	ABNER[5]	born Nov. 28, 1767, in Hingham.
208.	II.	SARAH[5]	"	
209.	III.	PYAM[5]	"	
210.	IV.	EZEKIEL[5]	"	Dec. , 1781.
	V.	LUTHER[5]	"	; died ag. 20.
	VI.	JULETTE[5]	"	1783; mar. Amos Remington. She died in Worthington, Mass., Feb. 10, 1809, ag. 26.

Joseph Tower[4] died in Worthington, April 20, 1823, ag. 77 y.
8 m. 23 d.
Sarah (Hersey) Tower died in Worthington, Sept. 22, 1839,
ag. 94 y. 1 m. 12 d.

Joseph Tower[4] was a soldier in the War of the Revolution. He
was a private in Capt. Jotham Loring's company, called into service on the 19th of April, 1775, and credited for thirteen days
time. In March, 1776, he was a member of Capt. Pyam Cushing's
company, guarding the shores. In 1777 he was with Lieut. Joshua
Tower in Rhode Island. Near the close of the war he, like many
others, removed from Hingham, finding a new home in the town
of Worthington, Mass., where and in the vicinity many of his

descendants are now living. The dwelling-house he built is gone, and the farm upon which he settled and lived has passed into the hands of strangers. Memorial-stones in the cemetery record the date of his death and that of his wife, and the great age to which her life was prolonged.

95. Dunbar.   **Fifth Generation.**   **Tower.**

42. RACHEL [4], JOSEPH [3], SAMUEL [2], JOHN [1].
Rachel [4], dau. of Joseph [3] and Deborah (Taylor) Tower, bapt. Aug. , 1766 ; mar. Amos Dunbar in Hingham May 16, 1779, by Rev. D. Shute.

Childr.

I.	PELEG [5]	bapt. March , 1780 ; mar. Olive Whiton in Hingham Feb. 15, 1805.
II.	DEBORAH [5]	" Nov. , 1783.
III.	AMOS [5]	" ; mar. Abigail Gray, of Hanover, Int. pub. March 20, 1808.
IV.	JOSEPH [5]	born 1790.
V.	EMMA [5]	" 1793.

Amos Dunbar died in Hingham July 2, 1809.
Rachel [4] (Tower) Dunbar died Aug. 29, 1839, ag. 83.

96. Jencks.   **Sixth Generation.**   **Tower.**

43. PATIENCE [5], GIDEON [4], BENJAMIN [3], JOHN [2], JOHN [1].
Patience [5], dau. of Gideon [4] and Mary (Ray) Tower, b. May 23, 1733 ; mar. Jeremiah Jencks in Cumberland, R. I., March 22, 1753, by Job Bartlett, J. P.

Childr.

I.	ANTHONY [6]	born Sept. 2, 1755.
II.	GIDEON [6]	" Jan. 7, 1759.
III.	JEDEDIAH [6]	" April 13, 1761.
IV.	LEVI [6]	" Oct. 8, 1763.
V.	ANANIAS [6]	" Dec. 17, 1766.
VI.	DESIRE [6]	" July 1, 1772.

97.   **Sixth Generation.**   **Tower.**

43. ENOCH [5], GIDEON [4], BENJAMIN [3], JOHN [2], JOHN [1].
Enoch [5], son of Gideon [4] and Mary (Ray) Tower, b. Dec. 20, 1737 ; mar. Lucy Lovett in Cumberland, R. I., Dec. 9, 1762, by Nathaniel Cook, elder.

Childr. born in Cumberland, R. I.

	I.	GIDEON [6]	born Dec. 15, 1763; died
	II.	BENJAMIN [6]	" April 21, 1765; mar. Martha Gully in Charlton Feb. 22, 1795.
211.	III.	WANTON [6]	" Jan. 4, 1768.
	IV.	ELIPHALET [6]	" Nov. 12, 1771.
212.	V.	LOIS [6]	" Dec. 15, 1773.
213.	VI.	CYNTHIA [6]	

Lucy (Lovett) Tower died, and Enoch Tower[5] mar., 2d, Ellis White Sept. 10, 1797 ; and, 3d, he mar. Ruth Kirby, dau. of John Kirby, of Newport, R. I., Oct. 19, 1800.

Enoch Tower[5] died in Cumberland, R. I., April 16, 1807, ag. 69 y. 3 m. 27 d.

98.   **Sixth Generation.**   **Tower.**

43. ICHABOD[5], GIDEON[4], BENJAMIN[3], JOHN[2], JOHN[1].
Ichabod[5], son of Gideon[4] and Mary (Ray) Tower, b. Feb. 28, 1740 ; mar. Mary Pullen in Cumberland, R. I., Oct. 16, 1768, by Elder Nathaniel Cook.

Childr.

	I.	AMY [6]	born Oct. 29, 1769.
214.			
215.	II.	DAVID [6]	" May 27, 1771.
	III.	WILLIAM [6]	" Oct. 21, 1774; died 1790, ag. 16.
216.	IV.	MARY [6]	" Oct. 22, 1775.
217.	V.	ISAAC [6]	" Dec. 31, 1778.
218.	VI.	JOSEPH P. [6]	" May 8, 1780.
	VII.	SAMUEL [6]	" Sept. 24, 1782; unmar.; died at sea.
219.	VIII.	MIRIAM [6]	" March 10, 1785.
	IX.	PATIENCE [6]	" Sept. 24, 1787; mar. Philip Bump, of Pawtuxet, R. I.

Ichabod Tower[5] died in Charlton, Mass., April 23, 1826, ag. 86 y. 1 m. 25 d.

99.   **Sixth Generation.**   **Tower.**

43. LEVI[5], GIDEON[4], BENJAMIN[3], JOHN[2], JOHN[1].
Levi[5], son of Gideon[4] and Mary (Ray) Tower, b. July 19, 1742 ; mar. Mary Whipple Feb. 19, 1771. She was b. Dec. 29, 1745, and was dau. of Ensign David Whipple.

Childr. born in Cumberland, R. I.

220.	I.	EDILLA [6]	born May 27, 1771.
221.	II.	CHLOE [6]	" Sept. 7, 1773.

222.   III.   Levi[6]   born May 2, 1776.
       IV.   Nancy[6]   "   Sept. 3, 1779; died Oct. 3, 1784, ag. 5 y. 1 m.
223.   V.   Zillah[6]   "   Oct. 18, 1781.
224.   VI.   Jason[6]   "   Aug. 30, 1786.
225.   VII.   Emerson[6]   "   Jan. 31, 1789.

Mary (Whipple) Tower died, and Levi Tower [5] mar., 2d, widow
 Hannah Emerson Jan. 8, 1817.
Levi Tower [5] died about 1825, ag. 83.

100.   **Sixth Generation.**   **Tower.**

43. Reuben [5], Gideon [4], Benjamin [3], John [2], John [1].
 Reuben [5], son of Gideon [4] and Mary (Ray) Tower, b.
 Nov. 9, 1745 ; mar.

Child.

225 *a* I.   Dewey [6] born

Reuben [5] removed to Vermont during the War of the Revolution,
and his name is found on the pay-rolls of Captain Gage's company,
in Col. Ira Allen's regiment, in two alarms in October, 1780.

101.   **Sixth Generation.**   **Tower.**

43. Samuel [5], Gideon [4], Benjamin [3], John [2], John [1].
 Samuel [5], son of Gideon [4] and Mary (Ray) Tower, b.
 May 2, 1747; mar. Rebecca.

Childr.

226.   I.   Joseph [6]   born   1774.
227.   II.   Patience [6]   "
228.   III.   Hannah [6]   "
229.   IV.   Polly [6]   "

102.   Stratton.   **Sixth Generation.**   **Tower.**

43. Lydia [5], Gideon [4], Benjamin [3], John [2], John [1].
 Lydia [5], dau. of Gideon [4] and Mary (Ray) Tower, b.
 Aug. 4, 1752; mar. James Stratton, of Foxborough, Mass.,
 July 17, 1774.

Childr. born in Foxborough.

I.   John [6]   born Nov. 27, 1774.
II.   Waitstill [6]   "   March 17, 1777.
III.   Welcome [6]   "   Nov. 20, 1779.

IV. MARY [6]   born Oct. 20, 1782.
V. SALLY [6]   "   Sept. 19, 1786.
ANNA [6]   "   Sept. 18, 1789.
VI. { or
AMEY [6]

103.   **Sixth Generation.**   **Tower.**

48. JONATHAN [5], JOHN [4], BENJAMIN [3], JOHN [2], JOHN [1].
Jonathan [5], son of John [4] and Hannah (Hancock) Tower, b.
Dec. 12, 1740; mar. Sarah Whipple [5]
Feb. 17, 1763, by Elder Daniel Miller. She was b.
Aug. 27, 1743, and was dau. of John [4] and Sarah (Peck)
Whipple.

WHIPPLE.   TOWER.
Sarah [5], John [4], William [3], Hannah [2], John [1].

Childr.

230. I. ELIZABETH [6] born   1763.
II. ROBERT [6]   "   1765; died.

Jonathan Tower [5] died in the West Indies about   1765,
ag. 25.
Sarah (Whipple) Tower died in Skeneateles, N. Y., July 31,
1825, ag. 81 y. 11 m. 4 d.

Jonathan Tower [5] was one of the few members of the Tower
family who followed the sea. He died in early life at sea. His
brother John [5] was also a seafaring man, and tradition says he too
died at sea.

104. Staples.   **Sixth Generation.**   **Tower.**

48. FREELOVE [5], JOHN [4], BENJAMIN [3], JOHN [2], JOHN [1].
Freelove [5], dau. of John [4] and Hannah (Hancock) Tower, b.
Aug. 28, 1742; mar. Jonathan Staples,
Aug. 18, 1760, by Elder Nathaniel Cook.

Child.

I. COTEE, [6] born May 22, 1761.

105. Jillson.   **Sixth Generation.**   **Tower.**

48. DEBORAH [5], JOHN [4], BENJAMIN [3], JOHN [2], JOHN [1].
Deborah [5], dau. of John [4] and Hannah (Hancock) Tower, b.

Aug. 26, 1750; mar. Nathaniel Jillson, of Attleborough.
Int. pub.

Jan. 16, 1768. He was b.

Sept. 24, 1748, and was son ·of Daniel and Leah (Bucklin)
Jillson.

Childr.

I.	Otis [6]	born July 5, 1768, in Attleborough.	
II.	Isaac [6]	" Sept. 11, 1770 "	"
III.	Deidama [6]	" July 8, 1775 "	"
IV.	Rufus [6]	"	in Wrentham; mar. Dorcas Whiting, of Wrentham.
V.	James [6]	"	in Wrentham; unmar.; died 1802.
VI.	Melany [6]	"	" " mar. Alexander Balcom, of Norton, Mass.

Nathaniel Jillson died in Attleborough Feb. 8, 1817, æg. 68 y.
4 m. 15 d.

Deborah (Tower) Jillson died in Attleborough 1832,
ag. 82.

---

106.   **Sixth Generation.**   **Tower.**

48. Gideon [5], John [4], Benjamin [3], John [2], John [1].
Gideon [5], son of John [4] and Hannah (Hancock) Tower, b.
April 30, 1753; mar. Abigail Perkins
March, 1775. She was b.
Nov. 28, 1754.

Childr.

231.	I.	Hannah [6]	born Jan., 1776.	
232.	II.	Nancy [6]	" Dec., 1777.	
233.	III.	Jonathan [6]	"	
	IV.	Child [6]	"	died in infancy.
	V.	Child [6]	"	" " "
	VI.	Robert [6]	"	" Jan. 23, 1813.
234.	VII.	Abigail [6]	" June 21, 1787.	
	VIII.	John [6]	"	died 1813.
	IX.	Mary [6]	"	unmar.
235.	X.	Gideon [6]	" 1794.	
	XI.	Child [6]	"	died in infancy.
236.	XII.	Clarinda [6]	" Aug. 7, 1797.	
237.	XIII.	Alpheus P. [6]	" Jan. 21, 1800.	

Gideon Tower [5] died in Dillsborough, Dearborn County, Ind.,
1847, ag. 94.

Abigail (Perkins) Tower died in Dillsborough, Dearborn
County, Ind., 1845, ag. 91.

Gideon Tower [5] was son of John [4]. He too served in the War of the Revolution, and in an affidavit made to secure a pension under the Act of 1832 he gives a brief account of service : —

"In 1775 as a private in a company of Connecticut Militia, commanded by Captain Cleft, of Parsons' regiment; in 1776 as a private in a company of Rhode Island troops, commanded by Captain Wilcox, of Dyer's regiment; in 1778, as a substitute for Mr. Barber, in a company commanded by the same captain in the same regiment; in 1779 as a private in a company of Vermont Militia commanded by Captain Noble, in Herrick's regiment; in 1780 as an orderly-sergeant in a company of Vermont Militia commanded by Captain Hutchins, of Herrick's Regiment."

After the battle of Bunker Hill the regiment to which he belonged was called to Roxbury, Mass., where it was stationed during the siege of Boston.

It will be seen that he also removed from Cumberland to Vermont during the war, and that there he was again called into service. He afterwards removed to the State of New York, then to Kentucky, and subsequently to Indiana, where he purchased land in Dearborn County. The following account of him was written by his grandson, John Tower Lemon, and published in the Lawrenceburg " Register," March, 1843 : —

"He joined the army of the Revolution in April, 1775, and served from three to seven months every year while the war lasted. His wife was born the 28th of November, 1754, and they are both now living in Cæsar Creek Township, in this [Dearborn] county, and enjoying good health for persons of their age. They had thirteen children, fifty-nine grandchildren, seventy-nine great-grandchildren, and six great-great-grandchildren. They had two sons out in the last war, — John Tower and Gideon Tower. The former was massacred on the 23d of January, 1813, at the River Raisin. They had one grandson, Henry Millard, who had the honor of commanding the right wing of the Texan forces on the memorable 21st of April, 1836, when the Mexicans were defeated and Santa Anna made prisoner by the Texans.

"It is seldom that husband and wife live together sixty-eight years, and live to see their descendants multiply to one hundred and fifty-seven, and six of the fifth generation ; and what is yet stranger, that these generations should all be of one political opinion. All of these, so far as my knowledge extends, who were voters in 1840, voted for General Harrison."

On the 26th of April, 1833, Gideon Tower was granted a pension of $96 per annum, to commence on the 4th of March, 1831. This pension was paid to March, 1847.

In a letter written by the same grandson, April 7, 1885, he says, writing of his grandfather: —

"The old gentleman was poor when he came to my father. He was a carpenter by trade, and knew nothing about farming, and never owned any real estate that I ever heard of. He was too old to work, and was coming near to want when he agreed to come and live with father."

There are two conveyances of real estate on record in Dearborn County in which the name of Gideon Tower appears, in one of which he is grantee, and in the other he is the grantor. The former is dated Jan. 28, 1833, and the latter Feb. 20, 1833, when he was nearly eighty years old.

107.		Sixth Generation.		Tower.

50. JOSEPH [5], JOSEPH [4], BENJAMIN [3], JOHN [2], JOHN [1].
Joseph [5], son of Joseph [4] and Judith (Briggs) Tower, b. April 28, 1746; mar. Ellen Mason in Ira, Vt., May 18, 1768. She was b. Feb.   1748.

Childr. born in Ira, Vt.

238.	I.	JOSEPH [6]	born Dec. 23, 1769.
	II.	LUCY [6]	" March 28, 1771; died 1772.
239.	III.	NATHANIEL [6]	" Jan. 4, 1774.
	IV.	RUTH [6]	" Feb. 20, 1776; died, unmar., Jan. 27, 1827, ag. 58 y. 11 m. 23 d.
240.	V.	ELEANOR [6]	" Sept. 8, 1779.
241.	VI.	ELIZABETH [6]	" March 3, 1781.
242.	VII.	LYDIA [6]	" July 9, 1783.
243.	VIII.	MASON [6]	" July 25, 1785.
	IX.	DEBORAH [6]	" Sept. 23, 1789; died Aug. 6, 1790.

Ellen (Mason) Tower died in Ira, Vt., Aug. 16, 1816, ag. 68 y. 6 m.
Joseph Tower [5] mar., 2d, Zereviah (Eddy) Smith in Ira, Vt., March 2, 1818. She was the widow of Peregrine Smith and dau. of Peter Eddy, of Scituate, R. I.
Joseph Tower [5] died in Ira, Vt., Sept. 6, 1822, ag. 76 y. 4 m. 11 d.

Joseph Tower [5], son of Joseph [4], removed from Rhode Island during the Revolutionary War, and settled in Ira, Vt. He served as a soldier after his removal to Vermont. From such records of military service as have been preserved, his name is found on the roll of Capt. Tehan Noble's company, in Col. Ira Allen's regi-

ment, for services done in the alarms of October, 1780, and again
in Capt. Enoch Eastman's company, Col. Ira Allen's regiment,
for services in October, 1781.

Many of Joseph Tower's descendants now reside in Ira or in
its vicinity.

108.   **Sixth Generation.**   **Tower.**

50. NATHANIEL[5], JOSEPH[4], BENJAMIN[3], JOHN[2], JOHN[1].
     Nathaniel[5], son of Joseph[4] and Judith (Briggs) Tower, b.
     June 23, 1748; mar. Lucy Tingley
     Nov. 29, 1774. She was b. in Attleborough, Mass.,
     May 1, 1758.

Childr.

	I.	PAMELA[6]	born	Jan. 23, 1776, in Taunton, Mass.; died April 3, 1794, in Hartford, Cortland County, N. Y., ag. 18 y. 2 m. 11 d.
244.	II.	NANCY[6]	"	Dec. 15, 1777, in Attleborough, Mass.
245.	III.	OTIS[6]	"	Dec. 3, 1779, in Rupert, Vt.
	IV.	LUCY[6]	"	Nov. 17, 1783, in Rupert, Vt.; died Aug. 17, 1786, ag. 2 y. 9 m.
246.	V.	THOMAS[6]	"	May 12, 1784, in Manchester, Vt.
247.	VI.	LUCY[6]	"	Aug. 24, 1786 " " "
	VII.	CYNTHIA[6]	"	Sept. 24, 1788, in Ira, Vt.; died Nov. 19, 1805, in Lewis, Essex County, N. Y., ag. 17 y. 1 m. 26 d.
248.	VIII.	CHARLOTTE[6]	"	Jan. 20, 1791, in Ira., Vt.
249.	IX.	WELCOME[6]	"	April 23, 1793, in Hindsburg, Orleans County, N. Y.
	X.	PAMELA[6]	"	June 23, 1795, in Westfield, Chautauqua County, N. Y.; died in Westfield, July 17, 1797, ag. 2 y. 26 d.
250.	XI.	CEPHAS[6]	"	Sept. 2, 1797, in Westfield.
251.	XII.	RIAL[6]	"	Oct. 29, 1799.

Nathaniel Tower[5] died in Lenox, Susquehanna County, Pa.,
April 17, 1836, ag. 87 y. 9 m. 19 d.

Lucy (Tingley) Tower died in Lenox, Susquehanna County,
Pa., Sept. 26, 1840, ag. 82 y. 4 m. 25 d.

Nathaniel Tower[5], son of Joseph[4], also removed to Vermont
during the Revolutionary War, and served as a soldier during
that war.   In an affidavit for a pension made in 1832 he says that
he joined a company in Taunton, Mass., where he resided, in
April, 1775, on the alarm occasioned by the battle of Lexington,
and marched to Roxbury, where he remained three weeks.   He
then enlisted in the month of May in Capt. Francis Liscomb's

company, in Col. Timothy Walker's regiment, and marched to Roxbury, where he served alternately with James Stacy, each serving one month at a time, until the expiration of the period of enlistment, January, 1776.

He further says that he removed from Taunton to the town of Rupert, Vt., and that he enlisted in May, 1780, in the Vermont troops for four months, under Captain Brown, in Col. Ebenezer Allen's regiment. His name appears in Col. Ira Allen's regiment in March, 1780, and in October the same year, when the regiment was called out on alarms. He removed to Willsborough, Essex County, N. Y., where he was again called out on an alarm. He subsequently removed to Lenox, Susquehanna County, Pa., where and in the vicinity his descendants are now living, and filling positions of usefulness and responsibility in the community. Two grandsons and one great-grandson are preachers, and one grandson died while filling the office of pastor of a society. In 1836 his widow, Lucy Tower, of Lenox, applied for a pension, and one of 36\frac{76}{100}$ per annum was granted.

109.	Sixth Generation.	Tower.

52. JAMES[5], JOHN[4], JOSEPH[3], JOHN[2], JOHN[1].

James[5], son of John[4] and Rachel (Hayden) Tower, b. December, 1746; mar. Elizabeth Whitmarsh Dec. 12, 1774, by Rev. Ezra Weld.

Childr. born in Braintree, Mass.

252.	I.	ELIZABETH[6]	born	March 5, 1775.
253.	II.	JAMES[6]	"	March 4, 1777.
254.	III.	JOHN[6]	"	April 20, 1779.
	IV.	RUTH[6]	"	April 15, 1781; mar. Ralph Pope, of Quincy; *s. p.*
	V.	WILLIAM[6]	"	May 3, 1783; unmar.; died at the Sandwich Islands.
	VI.	DEBORAH[6]	"	July 25, 1785; mar. Joseph White in Boston, Oct. 22, 1807.
	VII.	CHARLES[6]	"	; died in infancy.
255.	VIII.	MARY[6]	"	Dec. 30, 1787.
	IX.	RACHEL[6]	"	March 27, 1790; mar. Charles P. L. Percival, of Providence, R. I.
256.	X.	BENJAMIN[6]	"	May 9, 1792.
257.	XI.	EBENEZER[6]	"	Jan. 26, 1795.

James Tower[5] died in Braintree, April 26, 1828, ag. 81 y. 4 m. Elizabeth (Whitmarsh) Tower died in Braintree Feb. 4, 1837, ag. 84.

James Tower [5] resided in Braintree, Mass. He served with his brother John in Captain Wild's company on the occasion of the Lexington alarm, and again in Capt. Moses French's company, in 1776, upon orders to march to Hough's Neck, in Braintree, and subsequently to Nantasket.

110.   **Sixth Generation.**   **Tower.**

52. JOHN [5], JOHN [4], JOSEPH [3], JOHN [2], JOHN [1].
     John [5], son of John [4] and Rebecca (Staples) (French) Tower, b.
          1752; mar. Mehitable Thayer in Braintree
     Feb. 23, 1776, by Rev. Ezra Weld. She was b.
          1750.

Childr.

258.	I.	MEHITABLE [6]	born Dec. 28, 1779.
	II.	NATHANIEL [6]	" ; died young.
259.	III.	CHARLOTTE [6]	"
260.	IV.	JOHN [6]	"
261.	V.	ALEXANDER [6]	" April 3, 1788.
	VI.	LUCY [6]	" mar. Jabez Shaw, of Weymouth, Mass., March 13, 1803.
262.	VII.	SAFIRA or ZERVIAH [6]	"

John Tower [5] died in Braintree, Feb. 22, 1823, ag. 71.
Mehitable (Thayer) Tower died in Weymouth, Aug. 16, 1825, ag. 75.

John Tower [5] resided in Braintree, Mass. He served as a soldier in the War of the Revolution. He is credited for nine days service in Capt. Silas Wild's company of Braintree, called out by the battle of Lexington, April 19, 1775. He served afterwards in Capt. Stephen Penniman's company in 1776 and 1777.

111. Holbrook.   **Sixth Generation.**   **Tower.**

52. SARAH [5], JOHN [4], JOSEPH [3], JOHN [2], JOHN [1].
     Sarah [5], dau. of John [4] and Rebecca (Staples) (French) Tower, b.
          , 1754; mar. Thomas Holbrook, of Braintree, Mass.
     Int. pub.
     Nov. 14, 1772. He was b. in Braintree
     Oct. 7, 1754, and was son of Ichabod and Hannah (Hayden) Holbrook.

Childr. born in Braintree.

I. THOMAS [6] born
II. JOHN [6] "
III. ABIEZER [6] "
IV. ISAAC [6] " unmar.
V. HANNAH [6] " May 10, 1783.
VI. AZUBAH [6] " Oct. , 1786.
VII. SARAH [6] " unmar.
VIII. REBECCA [6] " May 24, 1789.
IX. POLLY [6] " 1797; unmar.; died Aug. 9, 1859, ag. 62.

112. **Sixth Generation.** **Tower.**

53. GIDEON [5], GIDEON [4], JOSEPH [3], JOHN [2], JOHN [1].
Gideon [5], son of Gideon [4] and Lydia (Sylvester) Tower, b.
Feb. 29, 1752; mar. Elizabeth Cox, of Boston. She was b.
, 1755.

Childr.

	I.	ELIZABETH [6]	born March 25, 1777; died Oct. 19, 1777.
263.	II.	JOHN [6]	" March 21, 1778.
120.	III.	BETSEY [6]	" June 26, 1780.
264.	IV.	MARY [6]	" July 4, 1782.
265.	V.	SALLY [6]	" Feb. 2, 1785.
266.	VI.	LYDIA [6]	" July 26, 1787.
267.	VII.	GIDEON [6]	" Jan. 14, 1790.
268	VIII.	RUTH [6]	" April 17, 1792.
269.	IX.	CHARLOTTE [6]	" May 9, 1794.
270	X.	JOSEPH [6]	" April 27, 1796.
271.	XI.	FANNY [6]	" Jan. 23, 1798.
272.	XII.	WASHINGTON [6]	" June 20, 1800.

Gideon Tower died April, 1825, ag. 73.
Elizabeth (Cox) Tower died Jan. 13, 1836, ag. 81.

Gideon Tower [5] resided in Braintree, Mass. He is credited
by tradition with being a member of the Boston "Tea-party."
There is record of his service in the War of the Revolution in
Capt. Eliphalet Sawen's company, called out on the 4th of March,
1776, and on the 14th of June the same year.

113. Henry. **Sixth Generation.** **Tower.**

53. LYDIA [5], GIDEON [4], JOSEPH [3], JOHN [2], JOHN [1].
Lydia [5], dau. of Gideon [4] and Lydia (Sylvester) Tower, b.
; mar. Joseph Henry, of Stoughton,
Feb. 19, 1791.

Childr.

I. HANNAH[6] born
II. LYDIA[6]   "

Joseph Henry died 1825.

114. Jones.   Sixth Generation.   Tower.

53. MARGARET[5], GIDEON[4], JOSEPH[3], JOHN[2], JOHN[1].
Margaret[5], dau. of Gideon[4] and Lydia (Sylvester) Tower, b.
    ; mar. Ephraim Jones, of Randolph, Mass.

Childr.

I.	CLARISSA[6]	born	mar. Abraham Holmes, of Milton, Mass.
II.	LYDIA[6]	"	mar. Seth Turner, of Milton, Mass.
III.	POLLY[6]	"	mar. Joseph Jones, of Randolph, Mass.
IV.	SULLIVAN[6]	"	
V.	CHARLOTTE[6]	"	mar. Lemuel Wentworth, of Randolph.
VI.	GIDEON[6]	"	
VII.	EPHRAIM[6]	"	
VIII.	HANNAH[6]	"	mar. Wm. Littlefield, of Worcester County.
IX.	JEFFERSON[6]	"	

Ephraim Jones died in Randolph, 1841.

115. Hunt.   Sixth Generation.   Tower.

53. RUTH[5], GIDEON[4], JOSEPH[3], JOHN[2], JOHN[1].
Ruth[5], dau. of Gideon[4] and Lydia (Sylvester) Tower, b.
    1760; mar. Samuel Hunt, of Milton. Int. pub.
May 7, 1781. He was b.
    , 1760, and was son of Brimstead and Abigail (Matthew) Hunt.

Childr.

I.	MARY[6]	bapt. April	, 1782; mar. Horace Bowditch, of Boston, March 30, 1804.
II.	LOIS[6]	"	died young.
III.	RUTH[6]	"	mar. Alpheus T. French.
IV.	ABIGAIL[6]	" Jan. 4, 1789.	
V.	LAVINIA[6]	"	1792; mar. Ebenezer Field, of Milton, Oct. 14, 1811.

VI.	MARTIN [6]	bapt.		1794.
VII.	JOSEPH [6]	"		1796.
VIII.	BETSEY [6]	"		1800.
IX.	SAMUEL [6]	"	Nov. 4, 1802.
X.	DANIEL [6]	"	Nov. 25, 1804.
XI.	JAMES [6]	"	May 7, 1808.

Samuel Hunt died   , 1822, ag. 62.
Ruth (Tower) Hunt died Aug. 3, 1823, ag. 63 y. 8 m.

116.   **Sixth Generation.**   **Tower.**

53. BENJAMIN [5], GIDEON [4], JOSEPH [3], JOHN [2], JOHN [1].
Benjamin [5], son of Gideon [4] and Lydia (Sylvester) Tower, b.
     , 1765; mar. Eunice Liskum, of Boston. Int. pub.
Aug. 27, 1785.

Childr.

273.	I.	EUNICE [6]	born March 31, 1786, in Braintree, Mass.
274.	II.	FANNY [6]	
275.	III.	LYDIA [6] ⎫ Twins.	
276.	IV.	POLLY [6] ⎭	
277.	V.	CYNTHIA [6]	
278.	VI.	ROXANNA [6]	
279.	VII.	SARAH [6]	
280.	VIII.	BETSEY [6]	
281.	IX.	ABIGAIL [6]	
282.	X.	BENJAMIN [6]	
283.	XI.	MERIAM [6]	" Sept. 23, 1808.
284.	XII.	LUCRETIA [6]	" Jan. 4, 1812.

Eunice (Liskum) Tower died in Hinsdale, N. H., 1839.
Benjamin Tower [5] mar., 2d, widow Mary (Stearns) Barrett
     , 1841. She died in Hinsdale July 2, 1845.
Benjamin Tower [5] died in Hinsdale, April 3, 1859, ag. 94.

117. Pierce, Brown. Sixth Generation.   **Tower.**

53. ABIGAIL [5], GIDEON [4], JOSEPH [3], JOHN [2], JOHN [1].
Abigail [5], dau. of Gideon [4] and Lydia (Sylvester) Tower, b.
Sept. 12, 1772; mar.   Brown, who died; and she mar., 2d,
     Pierce, of Milton.

Child.

I.   LINDA [6] born   mar. Abiezer Thayer, of Milton, Mass.

Abigail [5] (Tower) Pierce died in Milton, Dec. 22, 1854, ag.
     82 y. 3 m. 10 d.

54. ISAAC[5], JOSEPH[4], JOSEPH[3], JOHN[2], JOHN[1].
Isaac[5], son of Joseph[4] and Rebecca ( ) Tower, b.
Feb. 22, 1767; mar. Mary Thayer in Randolph
July 1, 1798. She was b.
, 1777.

Childr. born in Randolph, Mass.

285.	I.	ORRAMELL[6]	born March 8, 1799.
286.	II.	ISAAC[6]	" Aug. 22, 1801.
287.	III.	MARY[6]	" Nov. 23, 1803.
288.	IV.	BENJAMIN F.[6]	" April 24, 1806; died on the Pacific Ocean, 1862.
289.	V.	SALLY[6]	" Dec. 29, 1807.
290.	VI.	ELMIRA[6]	" July 11, 1810.
291.	VII.	LUTHER[6]	" Feb. 22, 1813.
	VIII.	SILAS D.[6]	" Sept. 23, 1815; died Sept. 1, 1841, ag. 25 y. 11 m. 9 d.
292.	IX.	LORENZO[6]	" May 14, 1820.

Isaac Tower[5] died in Randolph, March 12, 1834, ag. 67 y. 18 d.
Mary (Thayer) Tower died in Randolph, April 11, 1831, ag. 54.

54. RUTH[5], JOSEPH[4], JOSEPH[3], JOHN[2], JOHN[1].
Ruth[5], dau. of Joseph[4] and Rebecca ( ) Tower, b.
; mar. William Kimball, of Boston,
April 21, 1791, by Rev. Jonathan Strong.
William Kimball died 1813.
Ruth (Tower) Kimball died 1814.

52. JOSEPH[5], JOSEPH[4], JOSEPH[3], JOHN[2], JOHN[1].
Joseph[5], son of Joseph[4] and Rebecca ( ) Tower, b.
1780; mar. Betsey Tower[6].
She was dau. of Gideon[5] and Elizabeth (Cox) Tower.
Betsey[6], Gideon[5], Gideon[4], Joseph[3], John[2], John[1].

Childr. born in Randolph, Mass.

293. I. JOSEPH[6] } Twins, born Aug. 31, 1804. Abram died young.
     II. ABRAM[6]
294. III. ELIZA[6]

Joseph Tower[5] died April 10, 1857, ag. about 77.
Betsey (Tower) Tower died May 19, 1848, ag. about 68.

121.   **Sixth Generation.**   **Tower.**

58. ELISHA[5], ELISHA[4], RICHARD[3], IBROOK[2], JOHN[1].
Elisha[5], son of Elisha[4] and Abigail (Joy) Tower, b.
June 30, 1728; mar. Hannah Rotch, of Boston,
May 10, 1750.

Childr. born in Cohasset.

        I. RUFUS[6]   born Nov. 30, 1751.
295. II. LURANA[6]   "   May 30, 1754.

Hannah (Rotch) Tower died in Cohasset June 26, 1755.
Elisha Tower[5] mar., 2d, Deborah Aegree in Hingham
July 30, 1759, by Rev. E. Gay. She was born
May 3, 1730, and was dau. of Duming and Rachel (Thorn)
Aegree.

Childr. born in Cohasset.

296. III. ISAIAH[6]   born March 29, 1760.
     IV. DEBORAH[6]   "   Nov. 9, 1761.
     V. LUCY[6]   "   Jan. 13, 1764.
297. VI. SYLVANUS[6]   "   Feb. 28, 1766.

Deborah (Aegree) Tower died, and Elisha Tower[5] mar., 3d,
Sarah Marble, of Boston. Int. pub. April 24, 1768.

Child.

298. VII. ELISHA[6]   born   1770.

Elisha Tower[5] died   1774, ag. 46.

122. Pritchard.   **Sixth Generation.**   **Tower.**

58. ABIGAIL[5], ELISHA[4], RICHARD[3] }
     OLIVER[5], MARTHA[4], JOHN[3] } IBROOK[2], JOHN[1].
Abigail[5], dau. of Elisha[4] and Abigail (Joy) Tower, b.
Aug. 5, 1730; mar. Oliver Pritchard in Cohasset

April 1, 1754, by Rev. John Brown. O. Pritchard b. in
  Cohasset
March 22, 1733-4, and was son of John and Martha (Tower)
  Pritchard.

Childr. born in Cohasset.

I.	JOHN [6]	born Oct. 4, 1754.
II.	RICHARD [6]	" Oct. 6, 1756; died in service during the War of the Revolution.
III.	MARY [6]	bapt. Dec. 12, 1762.
IV.	THEODORE [6]	" " " "
V.	OBADIAH [6]	" April 17, 1763.
VI.	SYLVANUS [6]	" May 28, 1764; died.
VII.	SYLVANUS [6]	" Nov. 24, 1765; "
VIII.	JETHRO [6]	" Nov. 15, 1772; unmar.; died at sea.

123.   **Sixth Generation.**   **Tower.**

58. JETHRO [5], ELISHA [4], RICHARD [3], IBROOK [2], JOHN [1].
  Jethro [5], son of Elisha [4] and Abigail (Joy) Tower, b.
  Aug. 12, 1740; mar. Margaret Gross in Cohasset
  Sept. 16, 1765, by Rev. John Brown. She was bapt. in Cohasset
  May 16, 1742, and was dau. of Isaac and Dorothy (Cobb) Gross.

Childr. none.

Jethro Tower [5] died.
Margaret (Gross) Tower died in Hingham Oct. 5, 1792, ag.
  50 y. 5 m.

124. Wheelwright. Sixth Generation.   **Tower.**

59. SILENCE [5], JOHN [4], JOHN [3], IBROOK [2], JOHN [1].
  Silence [5], dau. of John [4] and Esther (Cobb) Tower, b.
  June 9, 1728; mar. John Wheelwright,
  Sept. 27, 1759, by Rev. E. Gay. J. Wheelwright b.
    1730.

Childr. born in Cohasset.

I.	JOHN [6]	born Feb. 16, 1761.
II.	MARY [6]	" April 14, 1762.
III.	MICAH [6]	" May 30, 1764.
IV.	JOTHAM [6]	" Oct. 1767.
V.	LOT [6]	" June 7, 1770.

Silence Tower was the second wife of John Wheelwright, and
  after her death he mar., 3d, widow Ruth Cushing Oct. 25,
  1781.
John Wheelwright died in Cohasset, May 9, 1818, ag. 98.

125. **Sixth Generation.** **Tower.**

59. RICHARD [5], JOHN [4] ⎰
HANNAH [5], CORNELIUS [4] ⎱ JOHN [3], IBROOK [2], JOHN [1].

Richard [5], son of John [4] and Esther (Cobb) Tower, b.
Sept. 10, 1733; mar. Hannah Tower [5]
Nov. 24, 1762. She was b. in Cohasset
Sept. 16, 1736, and was dau. of Cornelius [4] and Hannah
(Higgins) Tower.

Childr.

299.
I.	EUNICE [6]	bapt. June 3, 1764.
II.	REBECCA [6]	" Aug. 9, 1767; mar. Philip Smith, of Whately, Mass., March 7, 1792.
III.	SUSANNA [6]	" June 17, 1770; mar. Abner Brown, of Goshen, Mass., Oct. 9, 1796.
IV.	MICAH [6]	" June 28, 1772.
V.	HANNAH [6]	" June 19, 1774; unmar.; died at Whately, March 22, 1850, ag. 76 y. 2 m.
VI.	SILENCE [6]	" April 13, 1777; mar. Gideon Reed, of Shutesbury, Mass., March 24, 1813.

Richard Tower [5] died in Goshen, Mass., 1813, ag. nearly 80.
Hannah (Tower) Tower was living in Hatfield in 1816.

Richard Tower [5] seems to have removed from Cohasset to Chesterfield, Mass., and afterwards to Hatfield, in the same State. His will, dated Oct. 8, 1812, and proved and allowed July 6, 1813, names his wife, Hannah, and five daughters; namely, Eunice Morton, Rebecca Smith, Susanna Brown, Hannah Tower, and Silence Tower. He gives " unto Richard T. Morton, of Hatfield, . . . all my real estate, lands, and tenements . . . in Hatfield," and his farm-stock and farming utensils. He gives to his wife " indoor movables, wearing apparel, and household furniture; " to his five daughters " eighty-four cents each."

The inventory of his estate gives: " The home farm, containing about fifty acres of land, with the dwelling-house, the old part of the barn, and the corn-house, in value $1,500; farm-stock $50; one pew in the Goshen meeting-house, $20; household furniture, etc., 104\frac{42}{100}$.

Richard Tower was a soldier in the old French war and in the War of the Revolution. He was in Lieut. Obadiah Beal's company of guards stationed at Hull beach from Dec. 12, 1775, to April 3, 1776. Again in the same company in Colonel Lovell's regiment, he was on duty at Hull in June, 1776. He was in Capt. Christopher Bannister's company from Chesterfield in an expedition to Stillwater and Saratoga, marching one hundred miles and having twenty-one days service. In 1778 he was in Capt. Benjamin Lapham's company, doing duty in Cambridge for three months and two days; and in 1779 he was in Capt. Abner Crane's company, on duty in Boston, three months and two days.

126. Marble.   Sixth Generation.   Tower.

59. Eunice [5], John [4]   } John [3], Ibrook [2], John [1].
     Noah [5], Esther [4] }
     Eunice [5], dau. of John [4] and Esther (Cobb) Tower, b.
     Dec. 1, 1744; mar. Noah Marble in Cohasset
     April 7, 1779, by Rev. J. Brown. N. Marble b. in Cohasset
     Sept. 4, 1730, and was son of John and Esther (Tower) Marble.

127.   Sixth Generation.   Tower.

61. Elkanah [5], Cornelius [4], John [3], Ibrook [2], John [1].
     Elkanah [5], son of Cornelius [4] and Hannah (Higgins) Tower, b.
     Sept. 3, 1734; mar. Margaret Adams, of Boston. Int. pub.
     Dec. 14, 1769.

                         No issue.

     Elkanah Tower died in Cohasset, Sept. 27, 1821, ag. 87 y.
        24 d.

128. Gross.   Sixth Generation.   Tower.

61. Silence [5], Cornelius [4], John [3], Ibrook [2], John [1].
     Silence [5], dau. of Cornelius [4] and Hannah (Higgins) Tower, b.
     Oct. 24, 1738; mar. Isaac Gross in Hingham
     May 14, 1761, by Rev. E. Gay. I. Gross, b.
        , 1738, was son of Isaac and Dorothy (Cobb) Gross.

                Childr. born in Hingham.

I.	Thomas [6]	bapt. May 17, 1762.
II.	Isaac [6]	born Aug. 19, 1763.
III.	Dorothy [6]	bapt. Aug. 25, 1765.
IV.	Richard [6]	" Oct. 12, 1766.
V.	Moses [6]	" Oct. 9, 1768.
VI.	David [6]	" Aug. 4, 1771.
VII.	Elizabeth [6]	" Oct. 10, 1773.
VIII.	Dolly [6]	" Feb. 11, 1776; died Oct. 7, 1776.

Isaac Gross died in Hingham, Feb. 16, 1777, ag. 39.
Silence (Tower) Gross died in Hingham, Dec. 26, 1776, ag. 38 y. 2 m. 2 d.

129. **Sixth Generation.** **Tower.**

61. ISAAC[5], CORNELIUS[4], JOHN[3], IBROOK[2], JOHN[1].
Isaac[5], son of Cornelius[4] and Hannah (Higgins) Tower, b. May 10, 1744; mar. Mary Sprague, of Hingham, Jan. 9, 1770, by Rev. J. Brown. She was b. in Hingham June 14, 1752, and was dau. of John and Margaret (Webb) Sprague.

Childr.

	I.	SILE[6]	born Aug. 12, 1770; died Sept. 4, 1770.
300.	II.	CORNELIUS[6]	" June 10, 1772.
301.	III.	ELKANAH[6]	" Oct. 17, 1773.
302.	IV.	ISAAC WEBB[6]	" Aug. 16, 1775.
303.	V.	MICAH[6]	" Dec. 23, 1776.
304.	VI.	JOSEPH[6]	" Oct. 13, 1778.
	VII.	JOHN[6]	" Sept. 9, 1780; mar. Muson. He lived in Portland, N. Y.
305.	VIII.	NEHEMIAH[6]	" March 8, 1782.
	IX.	ISAAC[6]	" Nov. 19, 1783.
	X.	BENJAMIN[6]	" Aug. 6, 1785.
306.	XI.	ELIJAH[6]	" May 22, 1787.
307.	XII.	OSWIN[6]	" Jan. 6, 1789.
	XIII.	Son[6]	" June 20, 1791; died June 20, 1791.
308.	XIV.	POLLY[6]	" Aug. 8, 1792.
309.	XV.	PEGGY[6]	" July 18, 1794.
310.	XVI.	SALLY[6]	" Aug. 27, 1796.

Isaac Tower[5] died in Chesterfield, Mass., March 7, 1826, ag. 81 y. 9 m. 25 d.
Mary (Sprague) Tower died in Chesterfield, Mass., April 27, 1826, ag. 73 y. 10 m. 13 d.

Isaac Tower[5], son of Cornelius[4], removed from Cohasset during the War of the Revolution. He appears to have settled in that part of Chesterfield called the " Gore," — now the town of Goshen. Tradition in the family is that Isaac's matrimonial proposals were not favorably entertained by the parents of his intended wife, and the record of publishments confirms this statement; for we find in the Hingham, records of marriage intentions the following: "Isaac Tower and Mary Sprague. . . . The BANS forbidden by John Sprague, who underwrote the publishment as the law directs." This was dated Oct. 1, 1768. Tradition further says that this impediment did not prevent continued proceedings, as we find from the same records, under date "Dec. 23, 1769," that "Isaac Tower and Mary Sprague intend marriage;" and this second intention was carried into effect. But as the marriage ceremony was performed by the Rev. John Brown instead of the minister of the parish where the bride's parents resided, according to the custom of the times, the Rev. J. Brown being the minister of Cohasset, where Isaac Tower resided, we may infer that the opposing father was not fully placated; but, like many another father, he probably found that parental guidance in matters of the affection has its limitations.

Isaac Tower [5] did service as a soldier in the War of the Revolution, and was a sergeant in Capt. Obadiah Beal's company, which marched to Dorchester on the 4th of March, 1776. He had previously served in Capt. Job Cushing's company, in Colonel Greaton's regiment. The following order is found among the military records: —

CAMBRIDGE CAMP, Dec. 18, 1775.

Please to pay Capt. Job Cushing, in Col. John Greaton's regiment, the sum of twenty-five shillings to each of us, in lieu of the coats promised to us (Inlisted Soldiers) by the Provincial Congress.

This is signed by Isaac Tower, Jesse Tower, Abraham Tower, Levi Tower, and fifty-two others.

From the Hampshire Record of Deeds, Isaac Tower is found to be the purchaser of several pieces and tracts of land in Goshen and in adjoining towns.

130.   Woodward.   Sixth Generation.   Tower.

65. HANNAH [5], DAVID [4], HEZEKIAH [3], IBROOK [2], JOHN [1].
Hannah [5], dau. of David [4] and Susannah (Tucker) Tower, b. Feb. 4, 1731–2; mar. Smith Woodward in Cohasset Jan. 18, 1749–50, by Rev. J. Brown. S. Woodward, b. in Dorchester
Sept. 10, 1725, was son of Ebenezer and Elizabeth (Bates) Woodward.

WOODWARD, BATES.   TOWER.
Smith [5], Elizabeth [4], Rachel [3], Ibrook [2], John [1].

Childr. bapt. in Cohasset.

I. EBENEZER [6]   bapt. Feb. 10, 1750–51.
II. DAVID TOWER [6]   "   Aug. 15, 1756.

131. Marble.   Sixth Generation.   Tower.

65. SUSANNAH [5], DAVID [4], HEZEKIAH [3], IBROOK [2], JOHN [1].
Susannah [5], dau. of David [4] and Susannah (Tucker) Tower, b.
May 15, 1734; mar. David Marble in Cohasset
Dec. 11, 1755, by Rev. J. Brown.   D. Marble, b.
      , was son of David and Abigail (Joy) Marble.

Childr. born in Cohasset.

   I.   THOMAS [6] born Feb. 23, 1758.
  II.   JOSEPH [6]   "   July 10, 1760.
 III.   EPHRAIM [6] "   1762.
 IV.   SUSA [6]   "   June 26, 1764.
  V.   NABBY [6]   "   Jan. 9, 1767; mar. George Merritt.
 VI.   DAVID [6]   "   Aug. 15, 1769.

David Marble died in Cohasset   1770.

132.   Sixth Generation.   Tower.

65. ROBERT [5], DAVID [4], HEZEKIAH [3], IBROOK [2], JOHN [1].
Robert [5], son of David [4] and Susannah (Tucker) Tower, b.
      1735; mar. Elizabeth Burbank
Dec. 24, 1754, by Rev. J. Brown.   She was bapt. in Cohasset
Dec. 31, 1738, and was dau. of Elizabeth (Tower) and John
      Burbank

BURBANK.   TOWER.
    Elizabeth [5], Elizabeth [4], Hezekiah [3], Ibrook [2], John [1].

Child.

311.   I.   JESSE [6] bapt. July 13, 1755.

Robert Tower died in the army Sept. 18, 1756, ag. 21.

133. Bourne.   Sixth Generation.   Tower.

65. PHEBE [5], DAVID [4], HEZEKIAH [3], IBROOK [2], JOHN [1].
Phebe [5], dau. of David [4] and Susannah (Tucker) Tower, bapt.
July 2, 1739; mar. Newcomb Bourne in Cohasset
Jan. 14, 1765, by Rev. J. Brown.   *s. p.*
Phebe (Tower) Bourne died, and N. Bourne mar., 2d,
Abigail Joy in Cohasset Nov. 4, 1766, by Rev. J. Brown.

134.   **Sixth Generation.**   **Tower.**

65. ABNER [5], DAVID [4], HEZEKIAH [3], IBROOK [2], JOHN [1].
Abner [5], son of David [4] and Susannah (Tucker) Tower, b.
April 17, 1741 ; mar. Lydia Worrick in Cohasset
April 20, 1762, by Rev. J. Brown. She was b. in Cohasset
Nov. 17, 1742, and was dau. of Chasling and Susannah (Sutton) Worrick.

Childr. born in Cohasset.

   I. EPHRAIM [6] born Jan. 11, 1763.
  II. ELIJAH [6]   "

Abner Tower [5] died in Cohasset, Nov. 2, 1765, ag. 24 y. 6 m.
13 d.
Lydia (Worrick) Tower mar., 2d, Elisha Bates.

135. Stoddard.   **Sixth Generation.**   **Tower.**

65. RACHEL [5], DAVID [4], HEZEKIAH [3], IBROOK [2], JOHN [1].
Rachel [5], dau. of David [4] and Susannah (Tucker) Tower, b.
July 31, 1746 ; mar. Matthew Stoddard
Dec. 17, 1767, by Rev. E. Gay. M. Stoddard, b. in Hingham
March 20, 1746–7, was son of Jeremiah and Sarah (McFarlin)
Stoddard.

Childr. born in Cohasset.

    I. ABNER [6]   born June 14, 1768; mar.   ; died in Boston.
   II. MARY [6]   "   July 18, 1770.
  III. JOHN [6]   "   March 27, 1772.
  IV. RACHEL [6]   "   May 16, 1778; mar. John Thomas Nov. 28, 1824.
   V. LYDIA [6]   "   Dec. 8, 1780; unmar.; died about   1826, ag. 45.
  VI. HANNAH [6]   "   March 19, 1783.
 VII. DAVID [6]   "   June 4, 1786; died in Canada, in the army, 1812.

Rachel (Tower) Stoddard died in Cohasset, Feb. 18, 1820,
ag. 73 y. 6 m. 18 d.

136.   **Sixth Generation.**   **Tower.**

68. ABRAHAM [5], DANIEL [4], DANIEL [3], IBROOK [2], JOHN [1].
Abraham [5], son of Daniel [4] and Bethiah (Nichols) Tower, b.
April 18, 1752 ; mar. Elizabeth Kent in Cohasset
Aug. 30, 1789, by Rev. J. Brown. She was bapt. in Cohasset
Feb. 4, 1759, and was dau. of Abel and Hannah (Hobart) Kent.

Childr. none.

Elizabeth (Kent) Tower died in Cohasset Dec. 26, 1797, ag.
38 y. 10 m.
Abraham Tower [5] mar., 2d, Hannah Kent in Cohasset
Oct. 18, 1800, by Rev. Jacob Flint. She was bapt. in Cohasset
Oct. 29, 1775, and was dau. of Abel and Hannah (Hobart)
Kent.

Childr. born in Cohasset.

312.	I.	ABRAHAM HOBART [6] born Oct. 20, 1801.
313.	II.	ELIZABETH [6]	"	Oct. 10, 1803.
314.	III.	HANNAH KENT [6]	"	May 8, 1806.

Abraham Tower died in Cohasset, Sept. 26, 1832, ag. 80 y.
5 m. 8 d.
Hannah (Kent) Tower died in Cohasset, May 20, 1806, ag.
30 y. 6 m.

TOWER.   IBROOK.
    Abraham [6], Daniel [5], Daniel [4], Ibrook [3], Margaret [2], Richard [1].

    KENT, HOBART.   IBROOK.
Elizabeth [6] }
Hannah [6]   } Hannah [5], Nehemiah [4], David [3], Rebecca [2], Richard [1].

Abraham Tower [5] inherited the homestead of his father, thus
continuing it in the direct line of descent from John Tower [1], to
whom the land was set off in the first division of lands made by
the proprietors of the common lands to be held in severalty. Tradition assigns him a place among the members of the "Tea-party"
in Boston in 1773. In 1775 he was a member of Capt. Job Cushing's company, at the siege of Boston, serving as a corporal.

He resided in Cohasset upon the old homestead, and in addition
to the cultivation of his lands he was quite extensively engaged in
navigation and the commercial pursuits attendant thereon.

In his will, proved Oct. 27, 1832, he gives to his son, Abraham
Hobart Tower, "all my homestead farm on which I now live, and
the buildings standing thereon; also my store and wharf at the
Cove," etc. He makes provision for his daughters, Elizabeth
Souther and Hannah Kent Lawrence, and makes his son, Abra-
ham H., the residuary legatee.

In an application for a pension, made Aug. 28, 1832, Abraham
Tower says that he was in the Continental service from about
the 1st of May, 1775, to the 1st of January, 1776.

68. ISAAC[5], DANIEL[4], DANIEL[3], IBROOK[2], JOHN[1].
     Isaac[5], son of Daniel[4] and Bethiah (Nichols) Tower, b.
     April 18, 1752; mar. Betty Stoddard in Cohasset
     June 12, 1777, by Rev. J. Brown. She was b. in Cohasset
     Dec. 31, 1759, and was dau. of Stephen and Rachel (Stoddard)
     Stoddard.

                              Childr.

315.	I.	MERCY[6] born	Jan. 31, 1779.
316.	II.	ABRAHAM[6] "	March 11, 1781.
317.	III.	ISAAC[6] "	April 20, 1783.
318.	IV.	BETSEY[6] "	June 9, 1785.
319.	V.	NANCY[6] "	Sept. 1, 1787.
320.	VI.	SALLY[6] "	May 27, 1789.
321.	VII.	STODDARD[6] "	June 7, 1791.
	VIII.	AMELIA[6] "	June 9, 1793; died March 16, 1814, ag. 20 y. 9 m. 7 d.
322.	IX.	RACHEL[6] "	Sept. 26, 1795.
	X.	THEODA[6] "	Jan. 6, 1798; mar. Daniel A. Gill, in Springfield, Vt., March 3, 1837; *s. p.*
	XI.	DANIEL[6] "	July 13, 1800; died Aug. 9, 1808, ag. 8 y. 27 d.

Betty (Stoddard) Tower died in Springfield, Vt., March 17,
1812, ag. 52 y. 2 m. 17 d.
Isaac Tower mar., 2d, Elizabeth (Bisbee) Conant in Springfield,
Vt., Oct. 29, 1819. She was the widow of Clark Conant.
Isaac Tower[5] died in Springfield, Vt., Jan. 5, 1827, ag. 74 y.
8 m. 18 d.
Elizabeth (Bisbee) (Conant) Tower died in Springfield, Vt.,
July 15, 1828, ag. 59.

Isaac Tower[5], son of Daniel[4], removed from Cohasset to Springfield, Vt., where went a number of others from Cohasset and its
vicinity. Many of these were relatives of Isaac Tower, through
a common line of descent. They went to Springfield in the early
settlement of that town. This region became known to their
fathers and to some of them as they marched through the wilderness to Ticonderoga and Crown Point in the old French war and
in the War of the Revolution. It lies directly opposite Charlestown,
N. H., across the Connecticut River. Charlestown was then Fort
No. 4, and was a station for stores and a rendezvous for the soldiers in their various expeditions to and return from the lakes.
They thus became acquainted with the country and the advantages it offered for a settlement. Mrs. Theoda (Tower) Gill, his
daughter, says: —

" My father lived on a farm about two miles east of the village, where he built a house. He was a carpenter by trade and an ingenious mechanic, and as the necessities of a new settlement required the exercise of various employments, he often made shoes. At the time of his death he was the owner of some five hundred acres of land in Springfield. . . . He was a member of the Congregational Society in Springfield, and was a constant attendant upon the services of the church."

138.   **Sixth Generation.**   **Tower.**

68. SAMUEL[5], DANIEL[4], DANIEL[3], IBROOK[2], JOHN[1].
Samuel[5], son of Daniel[4] and Bethiah (Nichols) Tower, b.
April 30, 1754; mar. Rebecca Nichols in Cohasset
Oct. 2, 1775, by Rev. D. Shute. She was b. in Cohasset
July 26, 1756, and was dau. of Jazaniah and Hannah (Cushing) Nichols.

Childr.

323.	I.	HANNAH[6]	born Feb. 29, 1776.
	II.	BETHIAH NICHOLS[6]	" May 19, 1777; died in Fitzwilliam Sept. 23, 1794, ag. 17 y. 4 m. 4 d.
	III.	SAMUEL[6]	" April 1, 1779; unmar.; died May 26, 1845, ag. 66 y. 1 m. 25 d.
324.	IV.	REBECCA N.[6]	" Oct. 11, 1780.
325.	V.	LEVI[6]	" March 14, 1782.
	VI.	BETSEY[6]	" Feb. 7, 1784; unmar.; died in Vermont.
326.	VII.	DANIEL[6]	" July 27, 1787.
	VIII.	SARAH[6]	" Nov. 15, 1789; died Dec. 9, 1789.

Samuel Tower[5] died in Fitzwilliam, N. H., April 9, 1826, ag. 71 y. 11 m. 10 d.
Rebecca (Nichols) Tower died in Fitzwilliam, N. H., Feb. 24, 1835, ag. 78 y. 6 m. 29 d.

Samuel Tower[5], another son of Daniel Tower[4], also removed from Cohasset. He went first to Winchendon, Mass., where he remained a few years, and then removed to Fitzwilliam, N. H. He was a blacksmith by trade, and is remembered as a man of great energy, and in the line of his work of untiring industry. He was the owner of considerable land in the town of Fitzwilliam.

139.   **Sixth Generation.**   **Tower.**

68. LEVI[5], DANIEL[4], DANIEL[3], IBROOK[2], JOHN[1].
Levi[5], son of Daniel[4] and Bethiah (Nichols) Tower, b.
July 25, 1756; mar. Priscilla Nichols in Cohasset

Feb. 25, 1775, by Rev. J. Brown. She was b. in Cohasset
Feb. 18, 1758, and was dau. of Thomas and Elizabeth (Lincoln) Nichols.

Childr. born in Cohasset.

327.	I.	BETSEY [6]	born Jan. 1, 1778.
328.	II.	SALLY [6]	" Oct. 11, 1780.
329.	III.	LEVI [6]	" April 9, 1783.
330.	IV.	PRISCILLA [6]	" Jan. 3, 1786.
331.	V.	NICHOLS [6]	" July 2, 1787.
	VI.	JOB [6]	bapt. June 27, 1790 ; died in infancy.
	VII.	POLLY [6]	} Twins, born Nov. 19, 1792.
332.	VIII.	PATTY [6]	}

Priscilla (Nichols) Tower died in Cohasset, May 3, 1796, ag.
38 y. 2 m. 15 d.

Levi Tower [5] mar., 2d, Ruth (Beal) Stoddard in Cohasset
May 17, 1799, by Rev. J. Flint. She was bapt. in Cohasset
Aug. 10, 1766, and was dau. of Thomas and Susannah (Lincoln) Beal, and widow of Zenas Stoddard.

Childr.

333.	IX.	ABRAHAM [6]	born Jan. 19, 1800.
334.	X.	JOB [6]	" Dec. 3, 1801.
335.	XI.	DAVID [6]	" Aug. 17, 1804.

Ruth (Beal) (Stoddard) Tower died in Cohasset, Dec. 8, 1817,
ag. 51 y. 4 m.

Levi Tower [5] mar., 3d, Rebecca Pike, widow, in Cohasset,
March 29, 1818, by Rev. J. Flint. She was bapt. in Cohasset
1767, and was dau. of Thomas and widow Rebecca (   ) (Kilby) Lincoln.

Levi Tower [5] died in Cohasset Aug. 12, 1823, ag. 67 y. 16 d.

Rebecca (Lincoln) (Pike) Tower died June 7, 1850, ag. 83 y.
10 m.

Levi Tower [5], another son of Daniel Tower [4], was a soldier in the
War of the Revolution. He was the drummer in Capt. Job Cushing's company at the siege of Boston, as appears from a roll entitled a "Muster Roll of Capt. Job Cushing's Co. in the 36 Reg't of
Foot in the Continental Army in Fort No. 2, Oct. 5, 1775." Again
he was the drummer in Capt. Obadiah Beal's company, which
marched from Cohasset to Dorchester on the 4th of March, 1776.
He was a private in Capt. Job Cushing's company in Col. Solomon
Lovell's regiment from Dec. 28, 1776, to April 1, 1777, and pre-

vious to the last-named service he was the drummer in Capt. Peter Cushing's company, called into service at Hull.

Levi Tower resided in Cohasset, where, like his brother Abraham, he not only attended to the cultivation of the soil, but he was largely engaged in navigation and commercial business. From the situation of the town and its rocky character, — the name, derived from the Indian language, being significant of this character, — navigation to and from Boston Harbor has always been imperilled by the partially submerged rocks extending from the shore into the line of passage. Many wrecks of vessels have been the consequence of this condition, valuable cargoes destroyed, and many lives have been lost. The people of Cohasset are often called upon for deeds of daring and courage in the rescue of the imperilled and in the saving of valuables, and for the exercise of kindness to those whose lives have been saved. The following account, written by the Rev. Jacob Flint, the minister of Cohasset in 1821, describes one of the many of these events. It is given here, as Levi Tower [5] received a token of esteem in recognition of his services.

"Among the many instances of distress by shipwreck in which the kindest assistance and relief have been given, one only will be here noticed; the circumstances do equal credit to those who gave, and to those who received relief. On February 12th, 1793, the ship 'Gertrude Maria,' of 400 tons, bound from Copenhagen to Boston with a cargo estimated at $40,000, and commanded by Hans Peter Clien, was wrecked on a small island among Cohasset rocks called Brush Island. . . . The ship was first thrown upon a small ledge, where she suffered but partial injury, then on the island just named, whose sides are covered with pointed ledges ; . . . and here she was broken asunder. . . . A trial was made by two men to reach the shore in a boat; but the boat was dashed to pieces, and one man was drowned, while the other recovered the wreck. At length, by extending a spar from the stern of the wreck, the survivors all got upon the island out of the reach of the waves. Here they tarried in the tempest, chilled with wet and frost, without fire or house to shelter them, till discovered early the next morning by the inhabitants of the town. . . . A boat was quickly brought to the beach, a mile over land. She was manned without delay, . . . reached the island, and brought off three of the sufferers. Another attempt was immediately made, but resulted in the destruction of the boat. Two other boats were brought from a distance, and the dauntless exertions of the boatmen were renewed till the sufferers, twenty-one in number, were all safely landed on the shore. . . . In the mean time due attention was paid to their property. . . . An account of articles of the smallest as well as of greater value was given to the master of the ship, insomuch that when all was collected that could be saved and sold at auction, the amount was $12,000.

" When leaving, the captain told his benefactors that they should hear from him again. He sailed from Boston, and touching at St. Croix, he published there an account of the hospitality he had experienced from the people of Cohasset.

" When he arrived in Denmark he gave to the king such a representation of the people here as induced his Majesty to order the College of Commerce to send in his Majesty's name four large medals of gold and ten of silver, with the likeness of himself impressed on one side, with the Danish words on the other, importing, ' Reward of Merit — Noble Deeds.'

" With the medals of gold came directions: one for Rev. Josiah C. Shaw, one for Elisha Doane, Esq., one for Capt. John Lewis, and one for Capt. Levi Tower."

Levi Tower's will is dated Sept. 2, 1819, and allowed Sept. 2, 1823. In this will he makes provision for his wife in accordance with an ante-nuptial agreement; and as a matter of curiosity and in illustration of such agreements, which were prevalent in the olden times, a copy is hereby given, namely: —

"Six cords of hard wood and two cords of pine wood cut and put down cellar, twelve bushels of corn-meal, six bushels of rye-meal, eight bushels of potatoes, three bushels of turnips, three half barrels of flour, one hundred and twelve pounds of sugar, twelve gallons of molasses, eight pounds of good Souchong tea, seven pounds of coffee, two hundred and fifty pounds of beef and tallow, one hundred and fifty pounds of pork, ten pounds of sheep's wool, twenty pounds of flax, eight pounds of cotton-wool, seventy-five dollars in cash each year. The improvement of one half of my dwelling-house as long as she shall remain my widow; also the improvement of my clock and all my household furniture, except four feather-beds, that I hereafter give to my four daughters; and the improvement of two good cows, well kept winter and summer, and the use of my horse and chaise, and two seats in my pew in the meeting-house, and the use of two feather-beds during her natural life. This includes all that she was to receive by our marriage agreement. I also give her the improvement of one half of my garden."

The widow certifies her acceptance of the provision made for her in the will, Oct. 6, 1823.

Levi Tower's estate, as appears by the appraisal, was considerable for the times, showing satisfactory results of a business life of activity and industry. The amount of the real estate was $14,187, including five thousand feet of " Salt Works," at Simon Farm Beach, $4,000, — showing a large interest in a manufacture once flourishing and profitable in the maritime towns of Massachusetts, but from changed conditions the profit from them has disappeared, and these works becoming worthless, were destroyed.

It will be noticed that nearly the whole of the service performed by Levi Tower in the War of the Revolution was that of drummer. The drum and fife at that period were all the instruments by which talent and culture in music were able to give public expression to the attainments of those gifted in this direction. And from these drummers and fifers we are not surprised to find, through inheritance, these marked qualities among their descendants at the present day, enabling them to take advanced position in culture and attainments among the most gifted in musical science and performance.

140. Hall, Lincoln. Sixth Generation. Tower.

68. PERSIS[5], DANIEL[4], DANIEL[3], IBROOK[2], JOHN[1].
Persis[5], dau. of Daniel[4] and Bethiah (Nichols) Tower, b. Aug. 1, 1759; mar. Allen Lincoln in Cohasset Nov. 23, 1775, by Rev. J. Brown. A. Lincoln, b. in Cohasset April 3, 1755, was son of Thomas and Rebecca(Kilby) Lincoln

Child born in Cohasset.

I. SALLY[6] bapt. Oct. 18, 1778.

Allen Lincoln died
Persis (Tower) Lincoln mar., 2d, James Hall, in Cohasset, Jan. 4, 1786, by Rev. J. Brown. J. Hall b. Feb. , 1750, and was son of James Hall.

Childr. born in Cohasset.

II.	GEORGE[6]	born Jan. 9, 1790.
III.	ABRAHAM TOWER[6]	bapt. Nov. 26, 1793; unmar.; died
IV.	JAMES[6]	" Aug. 24, 1802.
V.	ABRAHAM[6] } Twins	" Aug. 24, 1802. Isaac died, unmar., Feb. 18,
VI.	ISAAC[6] }	1846.
VII.	SAMUEL[6]	born Aug. 29, 1798; bapt. Aug. 24, 1802.
VIII.	MARY[6]	" " " "
IX.	HENRY KNOX[6]	" Nov. 14, 1802.

James Hall died in Cohasset, April 3, 1819, ag. 69.
Persis (Tower) (Lincoln) Hall died in Cohasset, Sept. 29, 1828, ag. 69 y. 1 m. 28 d.

141. Bates.   Sixth Generation.   Tower.

66. MARY[5], DANIEL[4], DANIEL[3], IBROOK[2] } JOHN[1].
     JOSIAH[6], ELISHA[5], JOSHUA[4], RACHEL[3], IBROOK[2] }
     Mary[5], dau. of Daniel[4] and Bethiah (Nichols) Tower, bapt.
     May 27, 1764 ; mar. Josiah Bates, of Cohasset. He was b.
     Jan. 5, 1756, and was son of Elisha[5] and Content (Hatha-
     way) Bates.

Childr.

I.	BETHIAH[6 & 7] born	1782.	
II.	POLLY[6 & 7] "	1785.	
III.	ALLEN[6 & 7] bapt. July 27, 1788.		
IV.	SOPHIA[6 & 7]		
V.	LOUISA CONTENT HATHAWAY[6 & 7]		

Josiah Bates[6] died in Springfield, Vt., Nov. 22, 1823, ag. 67 y.
     10 m. 17 d.
Mary (Tower) Bates mar., 2d, Luther Field, of Springfield, Vt.,
     Feb. 9, 1804, by S. M. Lewis, J. P.

Child.

VI. LEMIRA[6]

142. Lothrop.   Sixth Generation.   Tower.

68. BETHIAH[5], DANIEL[4], DANIEL[3], IBROOK[2], JOHN[1].
     Bethiah[5], dau. of Daniel[4] and Bethiah (Nichols) Tower, bapt.
     Jan. 24, 1768 ; mar. John J. Lothrop in Cohasset
     Aug. 10, 1788, by Rev. J. Brown. J. J. Lothrop, b. in Cohasset
     Nov. 12, 1763, was son of Thomas and Ruth (Nichols) Lothrop.

Childr.

I.	THOMAS[6]		born May 4, 1790; mar. Polly Beal in Cohasset Nov. 14, 1811.
II.	JOHN JACOB[6]	"	April 15, 1793.
III.	DANIEL T.[6]	"	Jan. 8, 1796.
IV.	WARREN[6]	"	Feb. 16, 1799.
V.	LOUISA L.[6]	"	Aug. 19, 1803.
VI.	CAROLINE[6]	"	March 29, 1806.
VII.	BETHIAH[6]	"	June 9, 1808.

John J. Lothrop died in Cohasset, April 5, 1823, ag. 59 y. 7 m.
     7 d.

143.   **Sixth Generation.**   **Tower.**

68. DANIEL [5], DANIEL [4], DANIEL [3], IBROOK [2], JOHN [1].
Daniel [5], son of Daniel [4] and Bethiah (Nichols) Tower, b.
July 29, 1771; mar. Sally Nichols. She was b. in Cohasset
July 6, 1771, and was dau. of Jazaniah and Sarah (Pratt)
Nichols.

Child.

I. DANIEL NICHOLS [6] born June 29, 1793.

Daniel Tower [5] died at sea   1794, ag. 23.
Sally (Nichols) Tower died in Cohasset, Aug. 1, 1793, ag.
22 y. 26 d.

144. Nichols.   **Sixth Generation.**   **Tower.**

69. MOLLY [5], JOB [4], DANIEL [3], IBROOK [2], JOHN [1].
Molly [5], dau. of Job [4] and Mary (Pratt) Tower, b.
Feb. 3, 1753; mar. Peter Nichols in Cohasset
Dec. 22, 1777, by Rev. J. Brown. P. Nichols, b. in Cohasset
June 4, 1754, was son of Daniel and Abigail (Beal) Nichols.

Childr. born in Cohasset.

I.	PEGGY [6]	born	April 19, 1777.
II.	OBADIAH [6]	"	March 4, 1780.
III.	ELIAS [6]	"	Nov. 14, 1782.
IV.	DAVID [6]	"	
V.	BETHIAH [6]	"	April 10, 1787.
VI.	POLLY [6]	"	Sept. 4, 1789.
VII.	RUTH [6]	bapt.	Oct. 5, 1794.
VIII.	PRISCILLA [6]	born	June 8, 1796.

Molly (Tower) Nichols [5] died in Cohasset, Oct. 6, 1839, ag.
86 y. 8 m. 3 d.

145. Nichols.   **Sixth Generation.**   **Tower.**

69. THANKFUL [5], JOB [4], DANIEL [3], IBROOK [2], JOHN [1].
Thankful [5], dau. of Job [4] and Mary (Pratt) Tower, b.
July 25, 1755; mar. Lot Nichols in Cohasset
Jan. 22, 1775, by Rev. J. Brown. L. Nichols, b. in Cohasset
Oct. 24, 1744, was son of Thomas and Elizabeth (Lincoln)
Nichols.

Childr. born in Cohasset.

I.	MARY [6]	born Aug. 1, 1776; died
II.	PATTY [6]	" Feb. 14, 1778.
III.	THOMAS [6]	" Dec. 23, 1779.
IV.	NANCY [6]	bapt. Oct. 21, 1781.
V.	JOB [6]	" June 8, 1783; died
VI.	ELEANOR [6]	born Sept. 26, 1784.
VII.	POLLY [6]	" April 27, 1788; mar. George Sampson, of Roxbury, Dec. 4, 1814.
VIII.	HARRIET [6]	" Oct. 31, 1790.
IX.	JOB [6]	" May 31, 1793.
X.	THANKFUL [6]	" March 26, 1795.

Lot Nichols [6] died in Cohasset, June 8, 1812, ag. 67 y. 7 m. 14 d.

Thankful (Tower) Nichols died in Cohasset, July 5, 1818, ag. 62 y. 11 m. 10 d.

146. Souther.   Sixth Generation.   Tower.

69. MERIEL [5], JOB [4], DANIEL [3] } IBROOK [2], JOHN [1].
    ASA [5], JOSEPH [4], CONTENT [3] }

Meriel [5], dau. of Job [4] and Mary (Pratt) Tower, bapt.
Nov. 28, 1762; mar. Asa Souther in Cohasset
Aug. 21, 1783, by Rev. J. Brown. A. Souther was b.
July 22, 1760, and was son of Joseph [4] and Abigail (Kent) Souther.

Childr. born in Cohasset.

I.	ISAIAH [6]	bapt. Jan. 23, 1785.
II.	ASA [6]	" April 13, 1795; died Dec. 20, 1814, ag. 19 y. 8 m.

Meriel [5] (Tower) Souther died   .

Asa Souther [5] mar., 2d, Sally Whiting [6] in Hingham
Nov. 29, 1795, by Rev. D. Shute. She was b. in Hanover, Mass.,
, and was dau. of Ezekiel [5] and Olive (Stoddard) Whiting.

WHITING.   **TOWER.**
Sally [6], Ezekiel [5], Benjamin [4], Sarah [3], Benjamin [2], John [1].

Childr. born in Cohasset.

III.	EZEKIEL [6]	bapt. May 6, 1798.
IV.	LABAN [6]	" Sept. 7, 1800.

Asa Souther [5] died in Cohasset, Sept.   1799, ag. 39 y. 2 m.

147. Bates. Sixth Generation. Tower.

69. SARAH[5], JOB[4], DANIEL[3]
THEOPHILUS[6], JOSHUA[5], JOSHUA[4], RACHEL[3] } IBROOK[2], JOHN[1].
Sarah[5], dau. of Job[4] and Mary (Pratt) Tower, bapt.
Oct. 21, 1770 ; mar. Theophilus Bates[6] in Cohasset
Aug. 12, 1787, by Rev. J. Brown. T. Bates, b. in Cohasset
May 4, 1763, was son of Joshua[5] and Grace (Lincoln) Bates.

Childr.

I. EMMA[6 & 7] born Sept. 2, 1788; unmar.; died in Springfield, Vt., April
9, 1876, ag. 87 y. 7 m. 7 d.
II. MERIEL[6] bapt. Oct. 3, 1790.
III. BETSEY[6] born Jan. 29, 1792.
IV. JOB[6]
V. MARTHA[6]

Sarah (Tower) Bates died in Springfield, Vt.
Theophilus Bates mar., 2d, Esther Chandler, of Chester, Vt.,
March 30, 1804, by Rev. Aaron Leland. She was b. ,
1770.
Theophilus Bates[6] died in Springfield, Vt., Jan. 28, 1847, ag.
83 y. 2 m. 24 d.
Esther (Chandler) Bates died in Springfield, Vt., March 3,
1851, ag. 81.

148. Bourn. Sixth Generation. Tower.

69. BETTY[5], JOB[4], DANIEL[3], IBROOK[2], JOHN[1].
Betty[5], dau. of Job[4] and Mary (Pratt) Tower, bapt.
Oct. 21, 1770 ; mar. Thomas Bourn in Cohasset
April 20, 1790, by Rev. John Brown. T. Bourn, b. in Cohasset
Nov. 5, 1767, was son of Thomas and Susanna (Beal) Bourn.

Childr. born in Cohasset.

I. PRISCILLA[6] born Oct. 1791; died Dec. 1792.
II. ELIZA[6] " Nov. 24, 1793.
III. PRISCILLA[6] " Jan. 1, 1797.
IV. MARY[6] " Oct. 16, 1799.
V. THOMAS[6] " Sept. 8, 1803.
VI. ELIAS[6] " Dec. 7, 1807.
VII. MARSHAL[6] " March 21, 1811.
VIII. ROBERT TOWER[6] " Dec. 9, 1814.

Betty (Tower) Bourn died in Cohasset, May 1, 1846, ag. 75 y.
6 m.

70. PETER[5], PETER[4], JEREMIAH[3], JEREMIAH[2], JOHN[1].
     Peter[5], son of Peter[4] and Patience (Garnet) Tower, bapt.
     Jan. 19, 1728–9; mar. Deborah Stowell, in Hingham, Mass.,
     Nov. 25, 1746, by Rev. E. Gay. She was b. in Hingham
     Sept. 26, 1726, and was dau. of John and Deborah (Garnet)
     Stowell.

                    Childr. born in Hingham.

166.	I.	LEAH[6]	born Nov. 14, 1747.
	II.	SARAH[6]	" April 29, 1750; mar. Abner Bates Sept. 13, 1770.
336.	III.	LYDIA[6]	" Aug. 27, 1752.
337.	IV.	STEPHEN[6]	" May 24, 1755.
338.	V.	RUFUS[6]	" Aug. 28, 1757.
339.	VI.	LUCY[6]	" April 25, 1760.
340.	VII.	ASA[6]	" July 18, 1762.
341.	VIII.	MOLLY[6]	" April 27, 1765.
342.	IX.	DEBORAH[6]	bapt. Oct. 4, 1767.
	X.	PATIENCE[6]	" April 22, 1770.

Deborah (Stowell) Tower died in Cummington, June 7, 1780,
    ag. 53 y. 8 m. 10 d.
Peter Tower[5] mar., 2d, Joanna Baker in Cummington July 11,
    1809.
Peter Tower[5] died in Cummington, Aug. 4, 1814, ag. 85 y.
    6 m. 16 d.

Peter Tower[5], though more than forty-five years old when the
War of the Revolution began, performed military service. He
was in Capt. Pyam Cushing's company, employed in guarding the
shores while the British ships were lying at the outer harbor of
Boston subsequent to its evacuation, March, 1776, and before they
sailed for Halifax. Again he served in Capt. Job Cushing's company from Dec. 18, 1776, to April 1, 1777, when he is credited
with three and one-half months' service. In 1778 he was in Capt.
Elias Whiton's company, doing guard duty in Boston.
     Peter Tower removed from Hingham to Cummington, Mass.,
near the close of the war. At this time, or soon after, his several
children went there also, and shared in the work belonging to the
early settlement of that town. His oldest child and daughter, Leah,
who had married Nathaniel Tower[5], was among the number.

150. Bicknell.   **Sixth Generation.**   **Tower.**

70. PATIENCE[5], PETER[4], JEREMIAH[3], JEREMIAH[2], JOHN[1].
Patience[5], dau. of Peter[4] and Patience (Garnet) Tower, bapt.
Dec. 10, 1730; mar. Zechariah Bicknell, of Weymouth, Mass.
Int. pub.
April 10, 1752. He was b. in Weymouth
July 25, 1728, and was son of Zechariah and Bathsheba
(Whitmarsh) Bicknell.

Childr. born in Weymouth.

I.	EZRA[6]	born March 5, 1753.	
II.	STEPHEN[6]	"	Oct. 16, 1754; died April 11, 1771, ag. 16 y. 9 m. 25 d.
III.	ZECHARIAH[6]	"	Oct. 21, 1756.
IV.	PETER[6]	"	Jan. 15, 1759.
V.	LUCY[6]	"	July 3, 1762.
VI.	PATIENCE[6]	"	May 1, 1764.
VII.	JAMES[6]	"	April 15, 1769; died July 13, 1771, ag. 2 y. 2 m. 28 d.

Zechariah Bicknell died in Weymouth, June 29, 1802, ag.
73 y. 11 m. 4 d.
Patience[5] (Tower) Bicknell died in Weymouth, April 18,
1799, ag. 68 y. 4 m. 6 d.

151. Bates.   **Sixth Generation.**   **Tower.**

70. SARAH[5], PETER[4], JEREMIAH[3], JEREMIAH[2], JOHN[1].
Sarah[5], dau. of Peter[4] and Patience (Garnet) Tower, bapt.
Oct. 22, 1732; mar. Abraham Bates, of Weymouth,
Jan. 1, 1749–50, by Rev. D. Shute. A. Bates, b. in Weymouth
Feb. 29, 1723–4, was son of John and Alice (   ) Bates.

Childr. born in Weymouth.

I.	ABRAHAM[6]	born April 28, 1751.	
II.	SUSANNA[6]	"	Dec. 9, 1752.
III.	JOSHUA[6]	"	Jan. 27, 1755.
IV.	THADDEUS[6]	"	Oct. 8, 1757.
V.	ALPHEUS[6]	"	March 12, 1759.
VI.	LEBBEUS[6]	"	Jan. 16, 1760.
VII.	ELISHA[6]	"	Sept. 27, 1763.
VIII.	JOHN[6]	"	; died in Cummington Jan. 19, 1791.
IX.	SARAH[6]	"	
X.	NABBY[6]	"	; mar. Matthew Tower[6].
XI.	JACOB ALVAN[6]	"	Nov. 3, 1777.

Abraham Bates died in Cummington, Mass., Aug. 7, 1806,
    ag. 82 y. 5 m. 9 d.

Sarah (Tower) Bates died in Cummington, April 30, 1807,
    ag. 74 y. 6 m.

152.   **Sixth Generation.**   **Tower.**

70. MALACHI [5], PETER [4], JEREMIAH [3], JEREMIAH [2], JOHN [1].
Malachi [5], son of Peter [4] and Patience (Garnet) Tower, bapt.
March 19, 1737–8 ; mar. Ruth (Hayward) Wilder in Hingham
March 15, 1760, by Rev. D. Shute. She was born in Hingham
April 19, 1733, and was dau. of Nehemiah and Bethiah Hay-
ward and widow of David Wilder.

Childr. born in Hingham.

343.   I.   MALACHI [6] born April 1, 1761.
      II. RUTH [6]   "   Oct. 23, 1764 ; mar.   Beman in Maine.
344. III. LOIS [6]   "   Jan. 20, 1769.

Ruth (Hayward) (Wilder) Tower died in Hingham, March 15,
    1769, ag. 35 y. 10 m. 24 d.

Malachi Tower [5] mar., 2d, Susannah Ward in Hingham
May 24, 1769, by Rev. D. Shute. She was born in Hingham
Nov. 1, 1733, and was dau. of Edward and Susannah (Ward)
Ward.

Child.

    IV. MOSES [6] born   died young.

Susannah (Ward) Tower died in Hingham, Aug. 24, 1802,
    ag. 64 y. 9 m. 23 d.

Malachi Tower [5] mar., 3d, widow Susannah Harris in Abington, Mass., Dec. 8, 1805, by Rev. S. Niles.

Malachi Tower [5] died in Hingham, April 21, 1806, ag. 68 y.
    1 m. 2 d.

Susannah (Harris) Tower died in Abington, April 26, 1830,
    ag. 79.

Malachi Tower [5] was a soldier in the War of the Revolution.
His name appears on the rolls in the Massachusetts Archives, and
by affidavit for pension, as follows : In June, 1776, he was in Capt.
Pyam Cushing's company, doing duty at Hull ; and during the
same year and in 1777 he was in Capt. Theophilus Wilder's company. In 1778 his name appears in Captain Ward's company,
doing guard duty in Boston, and in the same year in Capt. Joseph
Baxter's company, in General Lovell's brigade, which marched to

Rhode Island. In 1779 his name appears as " fifer " in Capt. Job Cushing's company at Tiverton, R. I., and in 1780 in Capt. Theophilus Wilder's company, in Col. Ebenezer Thayer's regiment of new levies from the county of Suffolk, raised for three months to reinforce the continental army stationed in Rhode Island.

As both Malachi Tower[5] and his son Malachi Tower[6] were, during a portion of the time embraced in the foregoing service, of the required age for military service, and the name is not distinguished by senior or junior, it may be difficult to determine by whom the several periods of service were performed.

In the statement made by Bathsheba Tower, widow of Malachi Tower[6], for obtaining a pension, Aug. 29, 1838, she claims " 6 weeks in Sullivan's expedition in R. I. in 1778. . . . 3 months in Capt. Ward's company of guards in Boston in 1778. . . . Also 3 mos. 19 days in Capt. Theophilus Wilder's company in R. I. in 1780." The statement of the widow is confirmed by the affidavits of four soldiers then residing in Hingham, who had served with him.

Malachi Tower[5] resided in Hingham at a place known as " Great Hill," nearly a mile distant from the principal villages of the town. He gave this homestead to his grandson, Moses Tower[7], who resided upon the same, and built a new house upon the site of the old one. It is now owned and occupied by Samuel C. Souther[8] — son of Rebecca[7] (Tower) and Daniel Souther — and Sarah Jane[9] (Tower), his wife. It is the retreat and home for the children of Boston who are sent here during the heated season of the year by the help of those charitably inclined. They come in relays of from fifteen to twenty, and spend a fortnight each under the care of Mr. and Mrs. Souther.

153. Robbins, White, Lovell. Sixth Generation. Tower.

70. MARY[5], PETER[4], JEREMIAH[3], JEREMIAH[2], JOHN[1].

Mary[5], dau. of Peter[4] and Patience (Garnet) Tower, bapt. Feb. 24, 1739–40 ; mar. Jacob Lovell, of Weymouth, March 6, 1760, by Rev. D. Shute. J. Lovell, b. in Weymouth Aug. 28, 1737, was son of Joshua and Betty (Pratt) Lovell.

Childr. born in Weymouth.

I.	MARY[6]	born June 12, 1760.	
II.	JOSHUA[6]	" Aug. 6, 1761.	
III.	LYDIA[6]	" April 2, 1763.	
IV.	JACOB[6]	" March 17, 1765; died March 24, 1769, ag. 4 y. 7 d.	
V.	HANNAH[6]	" April 14, 1768 ; " in infancy.	
VI.	JACOB[6]	" April 9, 1771.	
VII.	STEPHEN[6]	" Oct. 28, 1772.	
VIII.	LUCY[6]	" Oct. 6, 1776.	

Jacob Lovell died in Weymouth   1776, ag. 39.

Mary (Tower) Lovell mar., 2d, Ebenezer White, of Braintree. Int. pub.

Feb. 20, 1779. He was born in Braintree

Feb. 25, 1741–2, and was son of William and Sarah (   ) White.

Childr.

   IX. DEBORAH [6] born May 7, 1783.

   X. CHARLOTTE [6] "

Ebenezer White died May 26, 1795, ag. 53 y. 3 m. 1 d.

Mary (Tower) (Lovell) White mar., 3d, William Robbins, in Cummington, Mass., Sept. 8, 1796, by Rev. James Briggs.

William Robbins died in Cummington, Aug. 6, 1814.

Mary (Tower) (Lovell) (White) Robbins died in Weymouth Jan. 10, 1826, ag. 85 y. 10 m. 17 d.

---

154. Lane.   **Sixth Generation.**   **Tower.**

70. LUCY [5], PETER [4], JEREMIAH [3], JEREMIAH [2], JOHN [1].

Lucy [5], dau. of Peter [4] and Patience (Garnet) Tower, bapt. March 28, 1742 ; mar. Josiah Lane in Hingham

Nov. 27, 1760, by Rev. D. Shute. J. Lane, born in Hingham July 6. 1736, was son of Ebenezer and Mary (Leavitt) Lane.

Childr. born in Hingham.

   I. LEAVITT [6] born May 26, 1761.

  II. LUCY [6]   "   April 27, 1767.

  III. LYDIA [6]   "   Nov. 2, 1768.

  IV. PETER [6]   "   July 13, 1772.

  V. JOSIAH [6] bapt. May   , 1776.

Josiah Lane died in Hingham, June 13, 1813, ag. 76 y. 11 m. 7 d.

Lucy (Tower) Lane died in Hingham, Dec. 1, 1807, ag. 65 y. 9 m. 7 d.

---

155. Hersey.   **Sixth Generation.**   **Tower.**

74. MARGARET [5], JAMES [4], BENJAMIN [3], BENJAMIN [2], JOHN [1].

Margaret [5], dau. of James [4] and Mary (Day) Tower, born 1746 ; mar. Jonathan Hersey in Hingham

Oct. 23, 1766, by Rev. D. Shute. J. Hersey, born in Hingham Oct. 28, 1742, was son of Jonathan and Sarah (Whiton) Hersey.

Childr.

I.	LYDIA [6]	born Sept. 11, 1767.
II.	JONATHAN [6]	"	Aug. 4, 1769.
III.	MARGARET [6]	"	Aug. 20, 1771.
IV.	MARY [6]	"	April 2, 1773.
V.	HENRY JOHNSON [6]	"	April 15, 1775.

Margaret (Tower) Hersey died June 13, 1777, ag. 31.
Jonathan Hersey mar., 2d, Mary Berry, in Hingham,
Sept. 8, 1777, by Rev. D. Shute.

156.   **Sixth Generation.**   **Tower.**

74. LYNDE [5], JAMES [4], BENJAMIN [3], BENJAMIN [2], JOHN [1].
Lynde [5], son of James [4] and Mary (Day) Tower, b.
1749; mar. Rebecca Bowker.

Child.

345.   I.   GAD HITCHCOCK [6] born   1776.

Lynde Tower [5] mar., 2d, Lucy Gary, of Westminster, Vt.

Childr. born in Westminster.

	II.	BETSEY [6]	born Sept. 10, 1790; mar. John Sawtell. She died April 20, 1868, ag. 77 y. 7 m. 10 d., *s. p.*
346.	III.	JAMES [6]	"	May 7, 1799.
347.	IV.	REBECCA [6]	"
766.	V.	LUCY [6]	"	1803.

Lynde Tower [5] died   1805, ag. 56.
Lucy (Gary) Tower mar., 2d,   Town, of Rockingham, Vt.
She died in Westminster, Vt., April 21, 1842, ag. 74.

Lynde Tower [5], who was a soldier in the War of the Revolution, resided in Pembroke, in Plymouth County. His name appears in Capt. Eleazer Hamlen's company, in General Thomas's regiment, in Roxbury, in 1775. He subsequently enlisted for the war. In a record of service in the Continental regiments of Massachusetts, we find the name of *Lines* Tower, of Pope's company, in the fourth regiment, credited with forty-eight months service. In an account kept by Massachusetts with the United States for sums paid " to make good the depreciation of their wages for the first three years service in the Continental army," we find the name of *Lines* Tower, in Col. Wm. Shepard's regiment, credited for £97 16*s.*, of which amount there was paid by the Continent

£22 12s., and by the State £75 4s. In 1781 he is recorded as a sergeant in Capt. Isaac Pope's company in July, and is credited with service for the months of " September, October, and November;" and in February, 1782, his name appears in the same company.

At the close of the war Lynde Tower removed to Westminster, Vt., where he resided the remainder of his days, and where his descendants are now living.

His oldest son, Gad Hitchcock [6], — named for the minister of Pembroke, where he was born, — by his own energy and industry was able to obtain a college education, and was the second of the name who enjoyed this privilege. He graduated at Brown University in 1803, and was in college with Levi Tower [6], who graduated in 1800.

157. Munroe.   Sixth Generation.   Tower.

74. BETHIA [5], JAMES [4], BENJAMIN [3], BENJAMIN [2], JOHN [1].
Bethia [5], dau. of James [4] and Mary (Day) Tower, b.
     1752; mar. Thomas Munroe, of Dorchester, Mass.,
Jan. 29, 1775, by Rev. E. Gay. T. Munroe b. in Dorchester
Sept. 1, 1743.

Child.

I. THOMAS [6] born   1777.

Bethia (Tower) Munroe died in Dorchester, July 25, 1823,
     ag. 71.

158.   Sixth Generation.   Tower.

74. MATTHEW [5], JAMES [4], BENJAMIN [3], BENJAMIN [2], JOHN [1].
Matthew [5], son of James [4] and Mary (Day) Tower, b.
Dec. 1, 1755 ; mar. Jerusha Hatch, of Marshfield.

Childr.

	I.	BENJAMIN HATCH [6] born March 30, 1783; died 1807, ag. 24.		
	II.	JERUSHA [6] " Feb. 11, 1786; mar. Samuel Eells, of Hanover, Sept. 8, 1805.		
	III.	NANCY [6] " May 11, 1788.		
348.	IV.	BETSEY [6] " Aug. 3, 1790.		
	V.	HORACE [6] " Feb. 20, 1793; died at sea, 1820, ag. 27.		

Matthew Tower [5] died in Scituate, March 3, 1831, ag. 75 y.
     3 m. 2 d.

Matthew Tower[5] resided in Scituate, Mass., and was a ship-wright by trade. He was a soldier in the War of the Revolution, and his name is on the roll of Capt. Enoch Whiton's company on the 19th of April, 1775, for three days duty and for forty-two miles march. In October of the same year he was a private in Capt. Nathaniel Winslow's company, and his name appears again on the rolls of the same company in camp at Roxbury in December of the same year. In 1778, from July to September, he was in Captain Clift's company in Rhode Island.

That he performed other and more continuous service appears from an affidavit he made, May 28, 1819, in support of an application for a pension under an Act of Congress passed in 1818 for the relief of indigent soldiers. He says : —

"I enlisted in the company of artillery commanded by Captain Stevens, in Col. Henry Knox's regiment, in January, 1776, about the first day in the year. I served in Roxbury and about Boston until the 27th of March, ten days after the evacuation of the town by the British ; we having had orders on the day of the evacuation to be ready to march to Canada in ten days ; that we took up our line of march on the said 27th day of March and proceeded to Canada, I being detained on the way about four weeks by sickness; that I arrived in Canada in the month of May and joined my company in the month of May at a place called Sorel, and I continued in service until some time in the month of November of that year, about six weeks, as near as I can remember, before my year expired, and was then discharged on account of ill health."

This statement is confirmed by the affidavit of Lieut. Samuel Daggett, who served in the same company and at the same time.

A pension of eight dollars a month was granted, but in 1820 it was discontinued, as it would seem that the matter of indigence was not satisfactorily shown. It may be a matter of curiosity to learn the amount of property required to constitute a condition outside of the indigence warranting relief by a pension. Matthew Tower states that he is sixty-five years old, is a shipwright by occupation, able to perform two thirds of a man's labor. His family consisted of his wife, Jerusha, sixty-five years old, and "a small girl, named Clarissa Tower, eleven years of age."

"I have about 40 acres of land of an ordinary quality, the whole about sufficient to keep one cow, a small old dwelling-house, a small barn, half a pew, 18 old chairs, 4 tables, 2 small looking-glasses, iron, tin, glass, and wooden ware, brass kettle, skillet, 2 pair of andirons, shovel, tongs, one cow, one hog, one maple desk, a case of drawers, one old horse-cart, and loom."

The pension was not restored until 1824, with the following explanation : —

" The difficulty in this case arose from a disagreement between the certificate of the court and that of Charles Turner as to the valuation of the property in the first schedule. The court valued it at 208\frac{34}{100}$, and Turner states that it was valued at 582\frac{34}{100}$. The Hon. Mr. Hobart was informed of this on the 11th of May, 1824, and has since forwarded the certificate of J. B. Thomas, the clerk of the court, who explains the disagreement by certifying that the court, in valuing the property, deducted from the full value, $374, the amount of debts due by the claimant, which left a balance of 208\frac{34}{100}$."

The pension was restored Aug. 16, 1824.

In 1838, his widow, Jerusha Tower, at the age of eighty-two years, makes application for a pension. She mentions service of eight months in 1775, at the siege of Boston, the service in 1776, that in Rhode Island in 1778, — all of which are shown by affidavits of surviving soldiers who had served with him. The service claimed is stated as ten months in the artillery, and nine months and ten days in the infantry, for which an annual pension of 72\frac{79}{100}$ is granted, to commence on the 4th of March, 1836.

It is remembered in the family that Matthew Tower found time during the war to engage in privateering, — a method of distressing the enemy then held as honorable as any other service, — and that in his case it was unsuccessful to himself, as he was taken a prisoner. This is confirmed by his name being found in a list of forty-nine prisoners returned at New York, as seen in the Massachusetts Archives.

No son of Matthew Tower survived him; and though in humble circumstances, his oldest son graduated at Harvard College in 1806, being the third of the name who was fortunate enough to receive the privilege and honor of a collegiate education.

Matthew Tower's descendants through his daughters are still found in Plymouth County, occupying positions of honor and trust in the community.

| 159. | Sixth Generation. | Tower. |

74. BENJAMIN [5], JAMES [4], BENJAMIN [3], BENJAMIN [2], JOHN [1].
Benjamin [5], son of James [4] and Mary (Day) Tower, b. July 4, 1756; mar. Lucy Totman in Scituate. Int. pub. Aug. 30, 1778. She was b. in Scituate, Mass., 1758.

Childr.

349.	I.	BENJAMIN TURNER [6] born	Nov. 7, 1778.
350.	II.	POLLY [6]	" Sept. 17, 1780, in Westmoreland, N. H.
351.	III.	LUCY [6]	" Nov. 8, 1784, in Westminster, Vt.

	IV.	John	born	Nov. 9, 1786, in Westminster, Vt.; unmar. ; died in Bangor, N. Y., Sept. 26, 1826, ag. 39 y. 10 m. 17 d.
352.	V.	Phebe [6]	"	Aug. 13, 1788.
353.	VI.	Ephraim Dean [6]	"	Aug. 27, 1790.
	VII.	Rebecca[6]	"	Jan. 5, 1793; mar. Charles Church, of Westminster.
	VIII.	Malinda[6]	"	Jan. 29, 1796; unmar. ; died in Bangor, N. Y., May 22, 1820, ag. 24 y. 3 m. 23 d.
354.	IX.	Jacob [6]	"	Oct. 16, 1798.
355.	X.	Warren [6]	"	Feb. 15, 1801.

Benjamin Tower [5] died in Bangor, N. Y., May 10, 1829, ag. 72 y. 10 m. 6 d.

Lucy (Totman) Tower died in Malone, N. Y., April 18, 1844, ag. 85.

Benjamin Tower [5] was a soldier in the War of the Revolution. His first service began on the 19th of April, 1775, as a private in Capt. John Clapp's company, which is credited with thirteen days service and thirty-five miles march. The company was stationed at Scituate Harbor; but after the battle of Bunker Hill it was marched to Roxbury and did duty there for the remainder of the year, where the company appears to have been under the command of Capt. Nathaniel Winslow. At the expiration of this term of service, Benjamin Tower enlisted in the Continental service for a period of one year, in Capt. Joshua Jacob's company.

In 1837, Lucy Tower, of Bangor, in Franklin County, N.Y., made application for a pension, and states that she was married to Benjamin Tower in Scituate, in September, 1778, " and that in the winter following said marriage he was absent from home in the army, . . . and that early in the spring of 1779 he again enlisted in the army for the term of nine months, and immediately left home, and was gone until the month of January or February, 1780. . . . Thinks he was in Capt. Jonathan Turner's company, and that a part or the whole of said service was performed at West Point and in its vicinity. She further states that in 1780 they removed to Westmoreland in New Hampshire, where they resided three or four years, when they removed to Westminster, Vt., and resided there until they removed to Bangor, about sixteen years before the date of the application.

In an affidavit made by James Lincoln, of Scituate, Mass., July 14, 1837, he states that he was the officer who enlisted Benjamin Tower for his period of service in 1776, and that he served with him, and says, " About the 1st of April we marched to New

London, and at that place we went by water to New York;" and
he further says, "I think that the said Tower was wounded in
the wrist at the battle of Harlem Heights."

Noah Barrell, of Scituate, says that he served in the same company with Benjamin Tower, and that both were wounded at the
battle of Harlem Heights.

Benjamin Tower was an invalid pensioner at the rate of $5 a
month, and this was increased, under the Act of 1816, to $8. A
pension was granted to Lucy Tower of $80 per annum.

160.   Brooks.   Sixth Generation.   Tower.

74. POLLY[5], JAMES[4], BENJAMIN[3], BENJAMIN[2], JOHN[1].
Polly[5], dau. of James[4] and Lucy (Dunbar) Tower, b.
Oct. 11, 1783; mar. Joseph Brooks, of Hanover, Mass.,
Jan. 16, 1803. He was b. in Hanover
Jan. 1, 1781, and was son of Joseph and Lydia (Stetson)
Brooks.

Childr. born in Hanover.

I.	MARY[6]	born Feb. 1, 1804.
II.	LYDIA S.[6] "	; mar. Silas Ripley, of Abington. She died Jan. 12, 1847.
III.	LUCY[6] "	Nov. 15, 1807; died Dec. 23, 1825, ag. 18 y. 1 m. 8 d.
IV.	DEBORAH[6] "	Dec. 17, 1809; " Jan. 28, 1812, ag. 2 y. 1 m. 11d.
V.	SARAH D.[6] "	March 29, 1812.
VI.	JOSEPH[6] "	July 2, 1814.
VII.	JAMES[6] "	March 20, 1817; unmar.
VIII.	BETSEY[6] "	April 18, 1819; mar. Lucius Ford, of Abington.
IX.	GILBERT[6] "	July 18, 1821.
X.	CHARLES[6] "	Aug. 31, 1823; mar. Ames.

Polly (Tower) Brooks died in Hanover, March 21, 1847, ag.
63 y. 5 m. 10 d.

161.   Sixth Generation.   Tower.

74. SOLOMON[5], JAMES[4], BENJAMIN[3], BENJAMIN[2], JOHN[1].
Solomon[5], son of James[4] and Lucy (Dunbar) Tower, b.
Oct. 25, 1785; mar. Sarah Stoddard, of Scituate, Mass.,
Jan. 28, 1808, by Elisha Phillips, J. P.

Childr.

356.	I.	SARAH[6]	born Oct. 13, 1808.
357.	II.	HORACE S.[6]	" April 10, 1810.
358.	III.	LUCY D.[6]	" March 20, 1812.
359.	IV.	JOHN S.[6]	" March 27, 1814.
360.	V.	MARY ELIZABETH[6]	" Jan. 9, 1817.

Solomon Tower[5] died Dec. 11, 1866, ag. 80 y. 1 m. 16 d.

162.   Sixth Generation.   **Tower.**

74. DAVID[5], JAMES[4], BENJAMIN[3], BENJAMIN[2], JOHN[1].
David[5], son of James[4] and Lucy (Dunbar) Tower, b.
July 6, 1788; mar. Patience Palmer
Aug. 1811. She was b.
     1789

Childr.

	I.	PATIENCE[6] born	1812; died	**7.**
359.	II.	JANE[6] "	Aug. 29, 1813.	
361.	III.	DAVID[6] "	April 3, 1818.	
362.	IV.	PATIENCE[6] "	June 29, 1821.	
363.	V.	JOHN[6] "	July 14, 1824.	
364.	VI.	REUBEN[6] "	April 17, 1828.	
365.	VII.	MAHALA[6] "	June 29, 1831.	

David Tower[5] died Feb. 13, 1855, ag. 67 y. 4 m. 23 d.
Patience (Palmer) Tower died Feb. 6, 1865, ag. 76.

163. Damon.   Sixth Generation.   **Tower.**

74. LUCY[5], JAMES[4], BENJAMIN[3], BENJAMIN[2], JOHN[1].
Lucy[5], dau. of James[4] and Lucy (Dunbar) Tower, b.
Oct. 14, 1791; mar. Joseph Damon, of Hanover, Mass.,
Sept. 6, 1812.

Childr. born in Hanover.

I.	LUCY[6]	born July 29, 1813;	mar. Thomas Mann.	
II.	JOHN[6]	" Dec. 3, 1816;	" Martha S. Chubbuck.	
III.	ALVIRA A.[6]	" Jan. 3, 1819;	" Ezra Shaw, of Abington.	
IV.	ANNE[6]	" July 3, 1821;	" James Bates.	
V.	JOSEPH[6]	" Nov. 26, 1823;	" Mary Gerrish.	
VI.	BETSEY[6]	" Sept. 15, 1825;	" Henry Shaw, of Abington.	
VII.	DEBORAH B.[6]	" Jan. 12, 1827; died	1847, ag. 20.	
VIII.	ESTERIA[6]	" April, 1828;	" Dec. 10, 1850, ag. 22 y. 8 m.	
IX.	JAMES[6]	" July 3, 1831.		
X.	MARY A.[6]	" Feb. 3, 1835.		

164.   Sixth Generation.   **Tower.**

75. JONATHAN[5], JONATHAN[4], BENJAMIN[3], BENJAMIN[2], JOHN[1].
Jonathan[5], son of Jonathan[4] and Lydia (Hollis) Tower, bapt.
Aug. 26, 1753; mar. Basmeth Wheeler, of Acton, Mass.,
May 3, 1781. She was b. in Acton
June 24, 1761, and was dau. of Ezra and Rebecca (Davis)
Wheeler.

Childr.

366.	I.	EZRA⁶ } Twins	born April 26, 1782, in Dorchester, Mass.	
367.	II.	JAMES⁶ }		
368.	III.	JOSHUA⁶	"	Jan. 15, 1784, in Dorchester.
369.	IV.	PAMELA⁶	"	May 2, 1786.
370.	V.	JONATHAN HOLLIS⁶	"	March 5, 1788.
	VI.	BASMETH⁶	"	Sept. 20, 1790; died Oct. 1793, ag. 3 y. 1 m.
371.	VII.	GRENVILLE⁶	"	Feb. 2, 1792.
372.	VIII.	LUTHER⁶	"	Jan. 12, 1794.
373.	IX.	RUFUS⁶	"	Oct. 3, 1796.
374.	X.	ALFRED⁶	"	March 16, 1801.

Jonathan Tower⁵ died in Watertown, Mass., Aug. 23, 1806, ag. 54.

Basmeth (Wheeler) Tower mar., 2d, Foster. She died in Boxborough, Mass., Aug. 23, 1829, ag. 68 y. 1 m. 30 d.

Jonathan Tower⁵ was a soldier in the War of the Revolution, and is named on the roll of Capt. Samuel Stockbridge's company, of Scituate, called into service on the 19th of April, 1775, and credited with three weeks service and a marching distance of twenty-four miles. The company was probably employed in coast service. He was in Capt. William Turner's company, in Colonel Bailey's regiment, doing duty at the siege of Boston. His name appears again in Capt. Nathaniel Winslow's company, at Roxbury, in 1776.

165. French. **Sixth Generation.** **Tower.**

76. SARAH⁵, NATHANIEL⁴, THOMAS³, BENJAMIN², JOHN¹.
Sarah⁵, dau. of Nathaniel⁴ and Sarah (Teague) Tower, b. April 22, 1742; mar. George Lane French in Hingham Nov. 4, 1762, by Rev. E. Gay. G. L. French, b. in Hingham July 11, 1742, was son of Jonathan and Jael (Beal) French.

Childr. born in Hingham.

I.	JOSHUA⁶	born July 16, 1763; died Aug. 30, 1778, ag. 15 y. 1 m. 14 d.
II.	GEORGE⁶	"	July 2, 1765.
III.	NATHANIEL⁶	"	Jan. 19, 1767.
IV.	PHINEAS⁶	bapt.	March 12, 1769.
V.	THEODORA⁶	"	July 5, 1772.
VI.	PERES⁶	"	Jan. 7, 1776.
VII.	SARAH⁶	born	1781; died Sept. 9, 1782.

Sarah (Tower) French died in Hingham, June 11, 1782, ag. 40 y. 1 m. 19 d.

George Lane French mar., 2d, Abigail Lewis April 21, 1783.

She died in Hingham, April 17, 1790, ag. 60.   He mar., 3d,
Fanny Humphrey Nov. 17, 1791.   She died in Hingham,
Jan. 3, 1819, ag. 72.
George Lane French died in Hingham, May 12, 1814, ag.
    71 y. 10 m. 1 d.

166.   **Sixth Generation.**   **Tower.**

76. NATHANIEL[5], NATHANIEL[4], THOMAS[3], BENJAMIN[2] } JOHN[1].
     LEAH[6], PETER[5], PETER[4], JEREMIAH[3], JEREMIAH[2] }
     Nathaniel[5], son of Nathaniel[4] and Sarah (Teague) Tower, b.
     Oct. 7, 1744; mar. Leah Tower[6] in Hingham
     Oct. 18, 1770, by Rev. E. Gay.   She was b. in Hingham
     Nov. 14, 1747, and was dau. of Peter[5] and Deborah (Stowell)
     Tower.

Childr.

	I.	LEAH[6 & 7]	born	Jan. 23, 1771, in Hingham; mar. Seth Torrey Nov. 24, 1799. She died in Windsor, Mass., *s. p.*
375.	II.	NATHANIEL[6]	"	Dec. 1, 1772, in Hingham.
376.	III.	PETER[6]	"	June 12, 1775, " "
377.	IV.	AMBROSE[6]	"	Nov. 2, 1777, " "
378.	V.	SALLY[6]	"	Oct. 23, 1780.
379.	VI.	WARREN[6]	"	July 9, 1789, in Cummington, Mass.
380.	VII.	ROXY[6]	"	June 12, 1794.

Nathaniel Tower[5] died in Cummington, April 9, 1810, ag.
    65 y. 6 m. 2 d.
Leah (Tower) Tower[6] died in Cummington, Jan. 23, 1847,
    ag. 99 y. 2 m. 9 d.

Nathaniel Tower[5] was a soldier in the War of the Revolution.
His name is on the roll of Capt. James Lincoln's company, stationed at Hingham, and guarding the shores against the incursions
of the British during the siege of Boston.   This was an important
post, as the British by their fleet had complete command of all the
inner harbor of the south shore of Boston, rendering incursions
probable, as the readiest means of relief from the want of provisions and fuel so pressing during that siege.   That the British
made no successful attempts is a tribute to the activity and vigi-
lance of the soldiers intrusted with this guard duty.   His whole
period of service here was eleven months and twenty-eight days.
He afterwards served in Captain Wild's company, in Colonel
Brook's regiment of guards in 1777 and 1778, at Cambridge, when
the prisoners of Burgoyne's army were held there.   A pension of

$66\frac{66}{100}$ per annum was granted to his widow, Leah Tower, Dec. 9, 1845, with arrears to Sept. 4, 1845, of $966\frac{57}{100}$. At the date of the certificate she had entered upon the ninety-ninth year of her age. In her affidavit Leah Tower says : " We were extremely poor, and his wages would not support our family ; and he was advised to remove to the western part of the State." He seems to have removed about 1780 ; and near this time a number of his relatives of the name of Tower, and many others of other names who were relatives, removed from Hingham, Cohasset, Weymouth, and the vicinity, to the hill-towns west of the Connecticut River, then for the most part unoccupied, where they became important factors in converting this wilderness into well-cultivated and flourishing farms, rearing large families of sons and daughters, who in their turn have repeated the lessons of enterprise and industry so thoroughly learned upon these hill-tops, and have gone out through successive generations in other fields to reclaim the wilderness, until the waves of the Pacific Ocean bar any further progress.

167.   **Sixth Generation.**   **Tower.**

76. AMBROSE [5], NATHANIEL [4], THOMAS [3], BENJAMIN [2], JOHN [1].
   Ambrose [5], son of Nathaniel [4] and Sarah (Teague) Tower, b. Jan. 31, 1746–7 ; mar. Elizabeth Garnett in Hingham Nov. 19, 1767, by Rev. E. Gay. She was b. in Hingham May 14, 1743, and was dau. of Simon and Hannah (Cockril) Garnett.

Childr.

   I.   OLIVE [6] bapt. March 12, 1769.
   II. ALLEN [6] "   Aug. 18, 1771.

Ambrose Tower [5] would appear to have been a soldier of the Revolution, as we find his name on the muster-roll of Capt. Lemuel Trescott's company, dated at camp at Ticonderoga Nov. 27, 1776 : " Ambrose Tower enlisted Jany. 13, 1776 — Dead Sept. 18, 1776." No further record of the descendants of Ambrose Tower than the birth and baptism of his two children has been found.

168. **Gardner.**   **Sixth Generation.**   **Tower.**

76. BETTE [5], NATHANIEL [4], THOMAS [3], BENJAMIN [2], JOHN [1].
   Bette [5], dau. of Nathaniel [4] and Sarah (Teague) Tower, b. Feb. 18, 1760 ; mar. Ezra Gardner in Hingham March 3, 1777, by Rev. E. Gay. E. Gardner, b. in Hingham March 17, 1757, was son of David and Anna (   ) Gardner.

Childr. born in Hingham.

I. BETTE [6] born Feb. 5, 1778.
II. ANNA [6] " Aug. 16, 1779.
III. SARAH [6] " Sept. 5, 1781.
IV. EZRA [6] " June 17, 1784.

169. **Sixth Generation.** **Tower.**

77. MARTIN [5], SHADRACH [4], THOMAS [3], BENJAMIN [2], JOHN [1].
Martin [5], son of Shadrach [4], and Ruth (Cobb) Tower, b.
June 10, 1750; mar. Molly Mansfield in Hingham
Nov. 20, 1775, by Rev. E. Gay. She was b. in Hingham
June 1, 1756, and was dau. of Joseph and Sarah (Waters)
Mansfield.

Childr. born in Hingham.

381.   I. MARTIN [6] bapt. April 6, 1777.
     II. MOLLY [6] " Oct. 25, 1778.
     III. BETSEY [6] " June 1, 1783.
     IV. SALLY [6] " Jan. 9, 1785.

Martin Tower [5] died at sea   1787, ag. 37.

Martin Tower [5] was a private in Capt. Peter Cushing's third
foot company in Hingham, assembled at Dorchester March 4,
1776, and credited with four days service and thirty-six miles of
travel. In June of the same year he again did duty at Hull in
the same company, which has a credit for two days service and
twenty miles of travel. Martin Tower was a seaman by occupation, and it is quite likely that he was engaged in some of the
many privateering enterprises wherein the sailors of the seaport
towns annoyed British commerce during the war. He was lost at
sea in 1787, in the schooner "Two Friends," which sailed from
Hingham, where it was owned.

170. **Sixth Generation.** **Tower.**

77. THOMAS GROSS [5], SHADRACH [4], THOMAS [3], BENJAMIN [2], JOHN [1].
Thomas Gross [5], son of Shadrach [4] and Ruth (Cobb) Tower, b.
Aug. 12, 1754; mar. Elizabeth Fuller.

Childr.

     I. LUCY [6] born   ; died young.
382.   II. THOMAS [6] " Feb. 8, 1783.
383.   III. MARTIN [6] " April 8, 1790.

384.   IV.   WILLIAM[6] born April 25, 1793.
385.   V.   BETSEY[6]   "
386.   VI.   LUCY[6]   "
387.   VII. CHESTER[6]   "   June 15, 1798.
388.   VIII. POLLY[6]   "

Thomas Gross Tower[5] died in Florida, Mass.
Elizabeth (Fuller) Tower died in Florida, Nov. 23, 1842,
    ag. 83.

Thomas Gross Tower[5] removed from Hingham to the western
part of Massachusetts. His name does not appear upon any of
the preserved military rolls. He appears to have settled in the
town of Florida, where, and in the vicinity, his descendants are
to be found to this day among the active and energetic men of
that mountain region, some of whom have done service to town
and State in positions of responsibility and trust.

171.   **Sixth Generation.**   **Tower.**

78. SAMUEL[5], SAMUEL[4], PETER[3], BENJAMIN[2], JOHN[1].
     Samuel[5], son of Samuel[4] and Hannah (Collamore) Tower,
        bapt.
     Dec. 22, 1761; mar. Betsey Thomas in Worthington, Mass.,
     Nov. 26, 1789, by Rev. J. Spaulding.

              Childr. born in Worthington.

       I.   JOSHUA[6] bapt. Nov. 10, 1799; mar. Elizabeth Stone.
389.   II.   LYMAN[6]   "   "   "   "   born Aug. 13, 1791.
390.   III. OBADIAH[6] "   "   "   "
       IV.   BETSEY[6]   "   July 13, 1800; mar.   Bloodgood.
       V.   ORVIL[6]   "   Oct. 27, 1802; "   Peter Snyder.
       VI.   CAROLINE[6] "   Aug. 31, 1806.

Samuel Tower[5] died in Worthington   1807, ag. 46.
Betsey (Thomas) Tower mar., 2d, Thomas Hall in Worthington
Aug. 24, 1813. He died, and she mar., 3d,   Wright, of
    Catskill, N. Y.

Samuel Tower[5] went with his father's family when he was a
young man into the wilderness in Worthington, where by his
industry he wrought out for himself a productive farm and a
comfortable homestead. It was situated upon the highest part of
that hill-town. His first purchase of land appears by the record
to have been made in 1797 of a lot of fifty acres, bounded on one
side by his father's land. In 1799 he purchased adjoining land.

Here he built his house and farm-buildings, but did not live long to enjoy them. His neighbor, Ezekiel Cushing, came from the same town, and he had a farm on the other side of the street, and built his dwelling nearly opposite Samuel Tower's residence. Nothing now remains of the buildings erected here a century ago by these pioneers and many others in the vicinity, save the cellars and the fallen stone chimneys with the remains of which the cellars are filled. A few decaying apple-trees alone bear testimony to the labors of a former generation, and the land is slowly passing through the intermediate stages of grazing-land, with encroaching bushes, preparatory to its former condition of wood and forest, from which it has had a century's reclaim. None of Samuel Tower's descendants are now living in Worthington, and very little is known of them. His son Lyman [6] removed to Franklin, Delaware County, N. Y., where at his death he left an only daughter, whose descendants now live there.

172. Alford. Sixth Generation. Tower.

79. ANN [5], SAMUEL [4], PETER [3], BENJAMIN [2], JOHN [1].
Ann [5], dau. of Samuel [4] and Hannah (Collamore) Tower, b. Sept. 10, 1763; mar. Daniel Alford, of Deruyter, N. Y.

Child.

I. JOB [6] born

173. Sixth Generation. Tower.

79. SHUBAEL [5], SAMUEL [4], PETER [3], BENJAMIN [2], JOHN [1].
Shubael [5], son of Samuel [4] and Hannah (Collamore) Tower, b. Sept. 28, 1767; mar. Abigail Bates, of Cohasset, Nov. 13, 1794. She was b. in Cohasset Dec. 8, 1774, and was dau. of James and Abigail (Litchfield) Bates.

BATES. TOWER.

Abigail [6], James [5], Solomon [4], Rachel [8], Ibrook [2], John [1].

Childr.

391.	I.	HANNAH [6 & 7]	born Feb. 20, 1795.
392.	II.	SALMA [6]	" Dec. 13, 1797.
	III.	LAURA [6]	" Feb. 14, 1800; died Dec. 17, 1801, ag. 1 y. 10 m. 3 d.
393.	IV.	WILLIAM [6]	" May 20, 1802.
394.	V.	ALMON [6]	" Dec. 7, 1804.
395.	VI.	OBADIAH [6]	" Jan. 21, 1807.

VII.   URIAH[6]   born March 27, 1809; died April 27, 1809.
396. VIII.   RODNEY[6]   "   May 29, 1810.
397.   IX.   JAMES BATES[6]   "   Jan. 20, 1815.
398.   X.   SAMUEL NELSON[6]   "   July 12, 1818.

Shubael Tower[5] died in Plymouth, N. Y., March, 1858, ag.
90 y. 6 m.
Abigail (Bates) Tower died in Plymouth, N. Y.,   1858,
ag. 83.

Shubael Tower[6] removed quite early in life to Plymouth, Chenango County, N. Y., where, in the beautiful valley of the Chenango, and in rural pursuits, he passed the uneventful years of
his long life, and in such condition of health that "he was not
confined to his house a single day on account of sickness until he
was eighty years old." Some of his descendants are living in
Chenango County, but the greater part of them have found homes
in the many Western States.

174. Hall.   Sixth Generation.   Tower.

79. HANNAH[5], SAMUEL[4], PETER[3], BENJAMIN[2], JOHN[1].
Hannah[5], dau. of Samuel[4] and Hannah (Collamore) Tower, b.
Feb. 3, 1770; m. Thomas Hall, of Worthington, Mass.

Childr.

  I.   ANSEL[6]   bapt. July 24, 1808, in Worthington.
 II.   SAMUEL[6]   "   "   "   "   "   "
III.   LUCY[6]   "   "   "   "   "   "   ; mar.   Goodell.
 IV.   ALMEDA[6]   ; mar.   Wilder.

175.   Sixth Generation.   Tower.

79. PETER[5], SAMUEL[4], PETER[3], BENJAMIN[2], JOHN[1].
Peter[5], son of Samuel[4] and Hannah (Collamore) Tower, b.
Sept. 26, 1776; mar. Rene Abby.

Childr.

399.   I.   SABIAH[6] born Oct. 19, 1798.
400.   II.   LABAN[6]   "   Jan. 17, 1800.
401. III.   LAURA[6]   "
402.   IV.   ANN[6]   "
       V.   THEDA[6]   "   ; mar. William Furgeson.
403.   VI.   EUNICE[6]   "
404. VII.   ASENATH[6]   "
405. VIII.   SALLY[6]   "
       IX.   RENE[6]   "

Peter Tower[5] died in Cheshire, Mass.

Peter Tower[5] lived some seven or eight years in Chenango County, N. Y., whence he removed to Cheshire, Berkshire County, Mass., where, and in the vicinity, many of his descendants are now living.

176. Beal.   **Sixth Generation.**   **Tower.**

80. LYDIA[5], ISAIAH[4], PETER[3], BENJAMIN[2], JOHN[1],
   Lydia[5], dau. of Isaiah[4] and Lydia (Gill) Tower, b.
   May 26, 1761; mar. Elisha Beal in Hingham
   Oct. 29, 1780, by Rev. D. Shute. E. Beal b. in Hingham
   May 11, 1762, and was son of Isaac and Hannah ( ) Beal.

Childr. born in Hingham.

I. CELIA[6] born Jan. 7, 1785.
II. LEVI[6] " March 31, 1786.
III. ELIAS[6] " July 27, 1790; mar. Eliza Gilbert, May 19, 1811.
IV. LYDIA[6] " June 13, 1796; unm.; died

Lydia (Tower) Beal died in Hingham   1837, ag. 76.

177.   **Sixth Generation.**   **Tower.**

80. ISAIAH[5], ISAIAH[4], PETER[3], BENJAMIN[2], JOHN[1].
   Isaiah[5], son of Isaiah[4] and Lydia (Gill) Tower, b.
   April 12, 1766; mar. Hannah Jacob in Hingham
   April 19, 1789, by Rev. D. Shute. She was b. in Hingham
   Feb. 5, 1771, and was daughter of John and Lydia (Beal)
   Jacob.

Childr. born in Hingham.

406. I. ISAIAH[6] born July 31, 1789.
407. II. JOSHUA[6] " Oct. 7, 1790.
408. III. LEAVITT[6] " Jan. 1, 1793.
409. IV. REUBEN[6] " July 3, 1795.

Isaiah Tower[5] died in Hingham, July 14, 1807, ag. 41 y. 3 m. 2 d.
Hannah (Jacob) Tower died Feb. 23, 1844, ag. 73 y. 18 d.

Isaiah Tower[5] lived in Hingham, and to him the real estate of his father was devised; but dying before his father, it passed by inheritance to the sons of Isaiah[5]. The homestead is on the corner of Main and High Streets in Hingham, and by the division of the real estate this homestead came into the possession of three of Isaiah's sons, Isaiah, Leavitt, and Reuben, upon which they lived and died. This old homestead has been subdi-

vided, and much of it has been built upon and is now occupied by
dwelling-houses. The dwelling-house built by Isaiah Tower[6] has
been removed, and the land is now a part of the High Street Cemetery, affording an entrance thereto from the Main Street. The
grounds have been graded, and enclosed by a substantial wall and
gateway, adding much to the beauty of the cemetery and of the
adjoining estates. The portion of the original estate which fell to
Reuben Tower[6] is now occupied by his descendants, while the
portion which fell to Leavitt Tower[6], containing the ancient dwelling-house, has passed by devise under his will to the widow of
his nephew, Charles F. Tower[7], late of Ohio, deceased.

178. Jacobs.   Sixth Generation.   Tower.

82. GRACE[5], LABAN[4], PETER[3], BENJAMIN[2], JOHN[1].
Grace[5], dau. of Laban[4] and Esther (Cushing) Tower, b.
March 23, 1777 ; m. Jotham Jacobs in Hingham
July 3, 1796, by Rev. D. Shute. J. Jacobs, b. in Hingham
April 27, 1775, was son of John and Lydia (Beal) Jacobs.

Childr. born in Hingham.

I.	LUCY[6]	born	April 9, 1798.
II.	LABAN[6]	"	March 10, 1800.
III.	DEBORAH[6]	"	July 19, 1804.
IV.	BETSEY[6]	"	Sept. 7, 1809.
V.	ESTHER C.[6]	"	May 17, 1811.
VI.	CYNTHIA C.[6]	"	Feb. 12, 1815.
VII.	MARY[6]		
VIII.	JOSHUA[6]	"	March 26, 1820.

Jotham Jacobs died in Hingham, Oct. 10, 1852, ag. 77y. 5 m. 13 d.
Grace (Tower) Jacobs died in Hingham, Jan. 25, 1852, ag.
74 y. 10 m. 2 d.

179.   Sixth Generation.   Tower.

82. LUCY[5], LABAN[4], PETER[3], BENJAMIN[2], JOHN[1].
Lucy[5], dau. of Laban[4] and Esther (Cushing) Tower, b.
May 19, 1780.

Child born in Hingham.

410. I. WILLIAM[6] born April 18, 1808.

Lucy Tower[5] died in Hingham, April 20, 1855, ag. 74 y.
11 m. 1 d.

180.   Sixth Generation.   Tower.

83. ISAAC⁵, JOSEPH⁴, AMBROSE³, BENJAMIN², JOHN¹.
     Isaac⁵, son of Joseph⁴ and Hepzibah (Gibbs) Tower, b.
     Feb. 2, 1752; mar. Elizabeth Wheeler in Rutland, Mass.,
     Jan. 24, 1781, by Rev. Joseph Buckminster. She was b. in
     Rutland
     Oct. 9, 1764, and was dau. of James and Abigail (Ball)
     Wheeler.

Childr.

	I.	JOSEPH⁶	born Sept. 1781; died in Paxton, Mass., 1797, ag. 16.
411.	II.	BETSEY⁶	" June 1, 1783.
412.	III.	ISAAC⁶	" April 13, 1785.
413.	IV.	LURANA⁶	" June 17, 1787.
414.	V.	JOB⁶	" June 24, 1789.
415.	VI.	JOHN⁶	" Sept. 8, 1791.
416.	VII.	SIBYL⁶	" April 15, 1794.
417.	VIII.	SAMUEL⁶	" Nov. 26, 1796.
	IX.	DAVID⁶	" June 12, 1799; unmar.; died in Ogden, N. Y., Feb. 1830, ag. 31.
	X.	HEPZIBAH⁶	" June 29, 1802; died 1806, ag. 4.

Isaac Tower⁵ died in Bristol, N. Y., Feb. 13, 1823, ag. 71 y.
11 d.
Elizabeth (Wheeler) Tower died in Bristol, N. Y., March 8,
1841, ag. 76 y. 4 m. 27 d.

Isaac Tower⁵ was a soldier in the War of the Revolution. His
name appears in Capt. Samuel Sawyer's company of Lancaster on
the 19th of April, 1775, with a credit for seven days service. In
August, 1777, he was a member of Capt. Christopher Banister's
company in Col. John Dickinson's regiment, which marched to
Bennington on an alarm, with a credit of one hundred and eight
miles travel. He was a sergeant in Capt. Ebenezer Belknap's
company in Colonel Wade's regiment of Massachusetts, serving
from Jan. 1, 1778, to Dec. 1 of the same year, his name appearing
upon several pay-rolls during that period.
     His daughter, Mrs. "Sibbel Pomroy," in an affidavit for a pen-
sion, states that her father was a soldier in the War of the Revolution, having the rank of a sergeant. "I often heard my father
say he was at the battle of Bunker Hill, and served all through
the State of New Jersey."
     In the latter part of his life he removed to Bristol, Ontario
County, N. Y., where some of his children had gone in the
early settlement of that county, and where in Canandaigua, the

adjoining town, his son-in-law, Eli Haskell, was for many years a Baptist preacher.

Samuel Tower[6], of Hadley, Mass., remembers the migration of the family to the State of New York. He was a young man, and went with Eli Haskell to Bristol, and says " that the journey was made in a large covered wagon drawn by two yoke of oxen. The wagon contained the household goods and the farming tools. The women and children rode in the wagon, while the men made the journey on foot. On reaching the destination the wagon continued to be the household shelter until the log-house was constructed. Among the stumps of the clearing, grain and grass-seed were sown, and in a year or two all the essentials for living were in abundance."

181. Wheeler.　　　　Sixth Generation.　　　　Tower.

83. THANKFUL[5], JOSEPH[4], AMBROSE[3], BENJAMIN[2], JOHN[1].
Thankful[5], dau. of Joseph[4] and Hepzibah (Gibbs) Tower, b.
Feb. 9, 1754; mar. James Wheeler, of Rutland, Mass.,
March 20, 1781, by John Frink, J. P. J. Wheeler, b.
June 22, 1759, was son of James and Abigail (Ball) Wheeler.

Childr.

I.	POLLY[6]	born June 1, 1782; mar.	Webber; 2 childr.
II.	HEPZIBAH[6]	" May 11, 1784.	
III.	BETSEY[6]	" Sept. 3, 1786.	
IV.	JOSEPH[6]	" Aug. 23, 1788.	
V.	JONATHAN[6]	" April 1, 1790.	
VI.	SALLY[6]	" Aug. 8, 1792.	
VII.	PATTY[6]	" Nov. 27, 1794.	
VIII.	DIODAMA[6]	" April, 1797.	

182.　　　　Sixth Generation.　　　　Tower.

83. JEDUTHUN[5], JOSEPH[4], AMBROSE[3], BENJAMIN[2], JOHN[1].
Jeduthun[5], son of Joseph[4] and Hepzibah (Gibbs) Tower, b.
May 17, 1756; mar. Mary Smith in Rutland, Mass.,
March 16, 1786, by Rev. J. Buckminster. She was b. in Worcester, Mass.,
Oct. 13, 1763, and was dau. of John and Elizabeth (　) Smith.

Childr.

418.	I.	REUBEN[6] born Feb. 15, 1787, in Rutland, Mass.		
419.	II.	DANIEL[6]	" March 11, 1789,	" "
420.	III.	PATTY[6]	" May 20, 1791,	" "
421.	IV.	ACHSAH[6]	" July 19, 1793.	

422.　V.　Jonas[6]　born April 30, 1796, in Paris, Oneida Co., N. Y.
423.　VI.　Polly[6]　"　July 13, 1798　"　"　"
424.　VII.　Ursula[6] "　June 26, 1803　"　"　"

Jeduthun Tower[5] died in Paris, N. Y., Aug. 27, 1817, ag. 61 y.
　　3 m. 10 d.
Mary (Smith) Tower died in Pomfret, N. Y., Dec. 30, 1835, ag.
　　72 y. 2 m. 17 d.

Jeduthun Tower[5] resided during the early part of his manhood
in Rutland, Mass., where he succeeded to his father's homestead,
as appears by a deed from his brothers and sisters dated Jan. 29,
1795, and recorded with Worcester County Record of Deeds.
He was a soldier in the War of the Revolution, and so much of
the record of his service is preserved as shows a term of duty from
Jan. 1, 1778, to Jan. 1, 1779, his name appearing on several pay-
rolls during the year.

The work of his life seems to have been passed in the quiet
pursuits of agriculture as these pursuits were then conducted in
the New England towns. The better lands had been brought
from a wilderness to as high a condition of cultivation as they
were capable, and successive years of cropping had tended to
reduce the capacity of these lands for the production of remune-
rative crops without fertilizing aid, which could not be readily
obtained. The combined labor of all the members of the family
in a constant round of industry was required to furnish shelter,
food, and raiment, with small margin for accumulation. Out of
these conditions the prospect was not very encouraging for a
young man, on attaining his majority, to secure the necessary
means for buying a farm by the product of his labor. The various trades and handicrafts called for only a limited number of
hands, and those hives of manufacturing industry which have
caught all the waterfalls in the State, subjecting them to the
various purposes of ingenuity and skill, were as yet unknown.

The enticing field for enterprise lay in the unbroken wilderness
in the farther west. This was the condition of the greater part of
the State of New York; and to this wilderness of fertile lands the
people of these older towns turned as a source and means of better-
ing their condition. The subduing of the wilderness was a tempt-
ing field for enterprise and ability which had confidence in the power
to produce all the means of living from it, and could see in the
result of years of labor a suitable accumulation in well-ordered
farms, in whose increased value they might have competence.

To these new lands came Jeduthun Tower, with his younger
brothers, Justus and Jotham, and with his family of sons and

daughters, and found a habitation in the township of Sangerfield, in the southern part of Oneida County. From the records of the county we find that he bought lands there in the years 1804 and 1807.

183.   **Sixth Generation.**   **Tower.**

83. JONATHAN[5], JOSEPH[4], AMBROSE[3], BENJAMIN[2], JOHN[1].
Jonathan[5], son of Joseph[4] and Hepzibah (Gibbs) Tower, b.
Aug. 7, 1758; mar. Tirzah Dimmock, of Brimfield, Mass.
Int. pub.
Nov. 17, 1796. She was b. in Brimfield
Oct. 1770, and was dau. of James Dimmock.

Child born in Rutland.

425. I. LUKE[6] born Oct. 22, 1797.

Jonathan Tower[5] died in Rutland, April 20, 1846, ag. 87 y. 8 m. 13 d.
Tirzah (Dimmock) Tower died in Rutland, Aug. 14, 1845, ag. 74 y. 10 m.

Jonathan Tower[5] passed the greater part of his life in Rutland, Mass., and lived near his father's place in that town. His business was the making of carpenters' and cabinet-makers' tools. He was a worthy and exemplary man, and is remembered for some eccentric habits and traits of character. He kept a horse, but had no wheeled vehicle, and was accustomed in harvesting his crop of grass to draw the hay from the field on a sled. He was very tender and considerate in the treatment of his horse, keeping one until it was thirty years old; and in his business visits to the village he would be seen trudging along the highway leading the horse by the bridle, instead of riding upon its back.

The part of the town where he resided gained the unenviable name of "Deathville," and it was a common saying that the judgment of Heaven was only averted from it by the fact that one righteous man lived there, — namely, Jonathan Tower. He was accustomed to read his Bible through in course at stated intervals.

His son Luke[6] says that his father cut his foot with an adze in early life, and that the wound was so severe as to prevent him from doing military duty of any great amount; though when the prisoners of war, on Burgoyne's surrender, were quartered in Rutland, he did guard duty. His great-grandson, Henry M. Tower[8], says that his great-grandfather was fond of books, and had collected during his life quite a library, which after his death was destroyed.

184. Packard. Sixth Generation. **Tower.**

83. LURANY[5], JOSEPH[4], AMBROSE[3], BENJAMIN[2], JOHN[1].
Lurany[5], dau. of Joseph[4] and Hepzibah (Gibbs) Tower, b.
Jan. 4, 1763; mar. Ichabod Packard, of Oakland, Mass. Int.
pub.
Dec. 27, 1786. He was b.
Mar. 29, 1763.

Childr.

I.	ISAAC[6]	born April 14, 1788.	
II.	JONATHAN[6]	"	Aug. 31, 1789.
III.	ORRICK[6]	"	May 26, 1791.
IV.	SYLVESTER[6]	"	March 28, 1793; died Nov. 3, 1793.
V.	SYLVESTER[6]	"	Sept. 30, 1794.
VI.	HART[6]	"	Feb. 9, 1797; died Jan. 27, 1798.
VII.	EMILY[6]	"	July 25, 1798.
VIII.	EMORY H.[6]	"	June 16, 1800.

Ichabod Packard died Nov. 23, 1813, ag 50 y. 7 m. 25 d.
Lurany (Tower) Packard mar., 2d., Gershom Hawkes, Jan.
30, 1816, and, 3d, Oliver Edgerton in Ohio.

---

185. Sixth Generation. **Tower.**

83. JUSTUS[5], JOSEPH[4], AMBROSE[3], BENJAMIN[2], JOHN[1].
Justus[5], son of Joseph[4] and Hepzibah (Gibbs) Tower, b.
Oct. 16, 1765; mar. Dilla Desmond, of Rutland, Mass.,
Nov. 15, 1789. She was b. in Rutland, Mass.,
1769, and was dau. of Elijah Desmond.

Childr.

	I.	LUCY[6]	born	1790, in Rutland; died in infancy.
426.	II.	BETSEY[6]	"	Jan. 20, 1792, "
427.	III.	HORACE D.[6]	"	Nov. 20, 1793, "
428.	IV.	HENRY[6]	"	Nov. 20, 1796, in Paris, N Y.
	V.	ORRIN[6]	"	May 14, 1798 " " died April 16, 1805, ag. 6 y. 11 m. 2 d.
429.	VI.	CLARISSA[6]	"	March 2, 1802, in Paris, N. Y.
430.	VII.	JUSTUS[6]	"	July 23, 1804, in Sangerfield, N. Y.

Justus Tower[5] died in Sangerfield, April 17, 1804, ag. 38 y.
6 m. 1 d.
Dilla (Desmond) Tower mar., 2d, Haven, and died in
Sangerfield, Oct. 27, 1849, ag. 80.

Justus Tower[5] purchased lands in Sangerfield in the years 1801, 1804, and 1805. He afterwards came into the village, where he built a mill, and became the owner of a considerable tract of land near it, where the Bacon's Mill now is.

In a heavy freshet the dam was threatened with destruction, and while he was upon it, trying to prevent the disaster, it was carried away, and he was drowned. Two of his sons became prominent business men in Waterville, one of whom, Horace D.[6], died at the advanced age of nearly ninety-two years, with the remarkable record of not having been confined to his bed by sickness during the whole period of his life.

186.   **Sixth Generation.**   **Tower.**

83. JONAS[5], JOSEPH[4], AMBROSE[3], BENJAMIN[2], JOHN[1].
   Jonas[5], son of Joseph[4] and Hepzibah (Gibbs) Tower, b. March 8, 1768; mar. Fanny Parmenter, of Petersham, Mass., Feb. 16, 1792, by Rev. Solomon Reed. She was b.
   1772, and was dau. of John Parmenter.

Childr. born in Petersham.

431.	I.	CHARLES[6]	born July 2, 1793.
432.	II.	OREN[6]	" Sept. 25, 1794.
433.	III.	LOUISA[6]	" Jan. 2, 1797.
434.	IV.	FANNY[6]	" Nov. 5, 1800.
	V.	HORATIO[6]	" 1803; died young.
435.	VI.	HORATIO N.[6]	" 1806; bapt. Nov. 9, 1817.
	VII.	HARRIET[6]	bapt. Nov. 9, 1817; unm.; died March 11, 1827, ag. 19.
	VIII.	JOHN PARMENTER[6]	" Nov. 9, 1817; unm.; died in Wisconsin, 1843, ag. 33.
436.	IX.	MARY ANN[6]	born Aug. 11, 1812.

Fanny (Parmenter) Tower died in Petersham, Oct. 25, 1815, ag. 43.
Jonas Tower[5] mar., 2d, Nancy Stone, Nov. 24, 1816.

Childr.

437.	X.	SAMUEL S.[6]	born July 17, 1817.
438.	XI.	NANCY[6]	" Dec. 23, 1818.
	XII.	MARIA[6]	" 1821; died 1828, ag. 7.

Nancy (Stone) Tower died   1822.
Jonas Tower[5] died in Petersham, April 12, 1827, ag. 59 y. 1 m. 4 y.

Jonas Tower[5] resided in Petersham,. Mass. His son, Oren Tower[6], of Petersham, says that his father was for many years a mail-carrier. His route extended from Providence, R. I., to Brattleboro', Vt. He conveyed the mail on horseback, distributing and collecting at the several towns and villages through which he passed. His residence was sufficiently central between the extreme points of his route. This was a most exacting occupation, taxing alike his fidelity and powers of endurance.

187. **Sixth Generation.** **Tower.**

83. JOHN[5], JOSEPH[4], AMBROSE[3], BENJAMIN[2], JOHN[1].
John[5], son of Joseph[4] and Hepzibah (Gibbs) Tower, b. May 13, 1770; mar. Catherine Haynes in Rutland, Mass., Nov. 19, 1794, by Rev. Hezekiah Goodrich. She was b. Sept. 13, 1770, and was dau. of Thaddeus Haynes, of Rutland.

Childr. born in Rutland.

439.	I.	RUSSELL[6]	born Feb. 8, 1796.
	II.	LURANA[6]	" Sept. 9, 1798; unmar.; died Sept. 8, 1827, ag. 28 y. 11 m. 30 d.
	III.	IRA[6]	" Nov. 12, 1800; unmar.; died Aug. 1, 1823; ag. 22 y. 8 m. 20 d.
440.	IV.	WILLIAM[6]	" Feb. 5, 1802.
	V.	LAVINA[6]	" Nov. 16, 1804; unmar.
441.	VI.	JOHN H.[6]	" Feb. 22, 1807.
	VII.	MARIA[6]	" May 10, 1809; mar. John Walker; died Jan. 30, 1841, ag. 31 y. 8 m. 20 d., *s. p.*
	VIII.	FANNY[6]	" ; mar. George Munger.
442.	IX.	CHARLOTTE H.[6]	" Oct. 8, 1813.

John Tower[5] died May 4, 1838, ag. 66 y. 11 m. 21 d.
Catherine (Haynes) Tower died March 26, 1852, ag. 81 y. 6 m. 13 d.

John Tower[5] also removed from Rutland, Mass., to Oneida County, N. Y. He was a carriage-maker by trade. He has left but few descendants bearing the name of Tower. His son, Col. John H. Tower[6], who recently died in Clinton, N. Y., was a man of much energy of character, and is remembered for the many enterprises in which he was engaged during his life.

188. **Sixth Generation.** **Tower.**

83. JOTHAM[5], JOSEPH[4], AMBROSE[3], BENJAMIN[2], JOHN[1].
Jotham[5], son of Joseph[4] and Hepzibah (Gibbs) Tower, b. Jan. 28, 1774; married Ursula Hawley, of Paris, N. Y., 1798.

Childr. born in Waterville, N. Y.

I.   LOUISA [6] born Jan. 15, 1800; unmar.; died Dec. 8,1828, ag. 28 y.
10 m. 23 d.

II. Infant   "   ; died

III.   "   "   "

IV. Daughter " Oct. 8, 1805; died Oct. 9, 1805.

V.   Son   " Nov. 10, 1806; died Nov. 10, 1806.

Ursula (Hawley) Tower died in Sangerfield, N. Y., and
Jotham Tower mar., 2d, Polly Barrett. She was born in
Winchendon, Mass.,
1784, and was dau. of Stephen Barrett.

Childr.

443.	VI.	MARY ANN [6]	born Nov. 2, 1808.
444.	VII.	URSULA CALISTA [6]	" Jan. 8, 1811.
	VIII.	FIDELIA AUGUSTA [6]	" July 4, 1813; unmar.; died April 26, 1828, ag. 14 y. 9 m. 22 d.
	IX.	SHERMAN BARTHOLOMEW [6]	" Aug. 30, 1815; died in Houston, Tex., Oct. 25, 1838, ag. 23 y. 1 m. 26 d.
	X.	MILTON [6]	" Aug. 30,1817; died May 17,1818.
	XI.	MARCUS BENNET [6]	" March 30,1819; died April 19, 1847, ag. 28 y. 20 d.
445.	XII.	JULIUS CANDEE [6]	" Nov. 23, 1821.
446.	XIII.	ALONZO BACON [6]	" May 6, 1824.
447.	XIV.	HARRIET ELIZABETH [6]	" Dec. 14, 1826.
	XV.	GEORGE CLEAVELAND [6]	" Feb. 24, 1829; died July 26, 1831, ag. 2 y. 5 m. 2 d.

Jotham Tower [5] died in Waterville, N. Y., Sept. 14, 1845, ag.
71 y. 7 m. 17 d.

Polly (Barrett) Tower died in Waterville, N. Y., March 31,
1847, ag. 63.

Jotham Tower [5], the youngest surviving son of his father's large
family of sons, emigrated with his brothers in early life to Oneida
County, N. Y. He purchased several tracts of land, as may be
seen in several recorded deeds where his name appears as grantee.
Many of his descendants yet remain in Waterville, filling positions
of honor and usefulness in the community.

189. Goodenow, Ingersol.   Sixth Generation.   Tower.

84. SILENCE [5], AMBROSE [4], AMBROSE [3], BENJAMIN [2], JOHN [1].
Silence [5], dau. of Ambrose [4] and Jerusha (Clapp) Tower, b.
Aug. 31, 1754; mar. Simeon Ingersol
Jan. 20, 1774.

Child.

I.   POLLY [6] born June 1774.

Simeon Ingersol died, and Silence (Tower) Ingersol mar.,
2d, Abraham Goodenow, of Nelson, N. H.,
May 14, 1780. He was born
April 27, 1749.

Childr.

II.	CALEB [6]	born	Jan. 2, 1781; died July 6, 1800, ag. 19 y. 6 m. 4 d.
III.	LUCY [6]	"	Jan. 9, 1783.
IV.	SILENCE [6]	"	June 17, 1785.
V.	SIMEON [6]	"	May 6, 1788.
VI.	BETSEY [6]	"	Sept. 1, 1790; unmar.; died July 13, 1822, ag. 31 y. 10 m. 12 d.
VII.	DANIEL [6]	"	April 24, 1793.
VIII.	RUTH [6]	"	March 16, 1797; died Oct. 4, 1798, ag. 1 y. 6 m. 18 d.
IX.	LUCRETIA [6]	"	Nov. 11, 1799.

Abraham Goodenow died in Nelson, N. H., Sept. 15, 1804,
ag. 55 y. 4 m. 19 d.
Silence (Tower) Goodenow died in Nelson, N. H., July 28,
1800, ag. 45 y. 10 m. 28 d.

190.   **Sixth Generation.**   **Tower.**

84. SILAS [5], AMBROSE [4], AMBROSE [3], BENJAMIN [2], JOHN [1].
Silas [5], son of Ambrose [4] and Jerusha (Clapp) Tower, b.
Aug. 15, 1756 ; mar. Ruth Smith in Sudbury, Mass.,
Jan. 11, 1781, by Rev. Jacob Bigelow. She was b. in Sudbury,
June 16, 1763, and was dau. of Henry and Lucretia (   )
Smith.

Childr. born in Sudbury.

448.	I.	POLLY [6]	born July 29, 1781.	
449.	II.	SUKEY [6]	"	March 18, 1783.
450.	III.	JERUSHA [6]	"	March 27, 1785.
451.	IV.	THADDEUS [6]	"	July 27, 1787.
452.	V.	RUTH [6]	"	Sept. 17, 1789.
	VI.	LUCRETIA [6]	"	Oct. 10, 1791; mar. Ellenwood, of Bolton, Mass., *s. p.*
453.	VII.	JONAS [6]	"	Nov. 28, 1793.
454.	VIII.	SALLY [6]	"	Feb. 28, 1796.
	IX.	HENRY [6]	"	April 7, 1798; unmar.; died in Sudbury, 1869; ag. 71.
455.	X.	ELIZABETH [6]	"	April 10, 1800.
456.	XI.	RELIEF [6]	"	July 11, 1802.

Silas Tower [5] died in Sudbury,   1816, ag. 70.
Ruth (Smith) Tower mar., 2d, Jazaniah Houghton, of Bolton,
Mass. She died June 8, 1843, ag. 79 y. 11 m. 23 d.

Silas Tower [5] was a soldier in the War of the Revolution. He
was in Capt. Aaron Haynes's company, of Sudbury, April 19,
1775, when he is credited with four days service and forty miles
travel; and in 1779 he appears as a private in Capt. Nathaniel
Laken's company in Col. John Jacob's regiment of Light Infantry.

191.   **Sixth Generation.**   **Tower.**

84. ABEL [5], AMBROSE [4], AMBROSE [3], BENJAMIN [2], JOHN [1].
Abel [5], son of Ambrose [4] and Jerusha (Clapp) Tower, b.
June 16, 1758; mar. Eleanor Parmenter, in Sudbury, Mass.,
May 14, 1780, by Rev. Jacob Bigelow. She was b.
Aug. 25, 1766, and was dau. of James and Mary (Carter)
Parmenter.

Childr. born in Sudbury.

457.	I.	ABEL [6]	born Dec. 7, 1780.
458.	II.	POLLY [6]	" Sept. 10, 1782.
459.	III.	DAVID [6]	" May 5, 1787.
	IV.	NABBY [6]	" July 11, 1789.
460.	V.	ELEANOR [6]	" July 16, 1791.
461.	VI.	NANCY [6]	" Nov. 12, 1793.
462.	VII.	CALEB [6]	" Aug. 17, 1796.

Abel Tower [5] died in Sudbury, April 25, 1809, ag. 50 y. 10 m. 9 d.
Eleanor (Parmenter) Tower died Feb. 22, 1837, ag. 80 y.
5 m. 28 d.

Abel Tower [5] was a soldier in the War of the Revolution. He
was in Capt. Aaron Haynes's company, of Sudbury, April 19,
1775, when he is credited with four days service and forty
miles travel.

192.   **Sixth Generation.**   **Tower.**

84. ASAHEL [5], AMBROSE [4], AMBROSE [3], BENJAMIN [2], JOHN [1].
Asahel [5], son of Ambrose [4] and Jerusha (Clapp) Tower, b.
Oct. 9, 1760; mar. Milicent Wyman in Sudbury, Mass.,
May 30, 1784, by Rev. Jacob Bigelow. She was born in
Woburn, Mass.,
May 2, 1761.

Childr. The first-named born in Leominster, Mass., and all the others in Lancaster, Mass.

		I. SALLY[6]	born March 25, 1785; unmar.; died in Dracut, Mass., March 23, 1845, ag. 59 y. 11 m. 26 d.
463.	II.	ASAHEL[6]	" Aug. 11, 1787.
	III.	MILICENT[6]	" July 7, 1790; unmar.; died in Lowell, Mass., April 14, 1862, ag. 71 y. 9 m. 7 d.
	IV.	WILLIAM[6]	" Aug. 24, 1792; unmar.; died in Sparta, Ga., Dec. 15, 1825, ag. 33 y. 3 m. 2 d.
	V.	JAMES[6]	" Sept. 24, 1794; died in Lancaster July 22, 1795, ag. 9 m. 28 d.
464.	VI.	JAMES[6]	" May 16, 1796.
	VII.	LUCINDA[6]	" Sept. 28, 1798; unmar.; died in Lowell Oct. 2, 1856, ag. 58 y. 4 d.
	VIII.	DANIEL CLAPP[6]	" Nov. 20, 1800; unmar.; died in Dracut Nov. 30, 1844, ag. 44 y. 10 d.
465.	IX.	HENRY[6]	" March 13, 1803.
	X.	CHRISTOPHER[6]	" Sept. 10, 1805; unmar.; died in New Orleans Nov., 1832, ag. 27.

Asahel Tower[5] died in Lancaster, Aug. 3, 1833, ag. 72 y. 9 m. 24 d.

Milicent (Wyman) Tower died in Lancaster, Sept. 20, 1820, ag. 59 y. 5 m. 18 d.

193. Warren.   Sixth Generation.   Tower.

84. JERUSHA[5], AMBROSE[4], AMBROSE[3], BENJAMIN[2], JOHN[1].
Jerusha[5], dau. of Ambrose[4] and Jerusha (Clapp) Tower, b.
July 16, 1769; mar. Bernard M. Warren
June 13, 1794, by Samuel Griffin, J. P.

Childr. born in Nelson, N. H.

I.	HENRY[6]	born Aug. 23, 1794.
II.	FANNY[6]	" Oct. 16, 1796.
III.	DANIEL CLAPP[6]	" Feb. 26, 1798.
IV.	CHAUNCEY[6]	" Jan. 29, 1799; died Aug. 11, 1800, ag. 1 y. 6 m. 13 d.
V.	ELIZA[6]	" Feb. 25, 1802.

194.   Sixth Generation.   Tower.

84. DANIEL[5], AMBROSE[4], AMBROSE[3], BENJAMIN[2], JOHN[1].
Daniel[5], son of Ambrose[4] and Jerusha (Clapp) Tower, b.
Feb. 3, 1772; mar. Mary Leeds in Dorchester, Mass.,
Sept. 13, 1804, by Rev. T. Harris. She was b. in Dorchester
Nov. 12, 1779, and was dau. of Daniel and Abigail (Gore)
Leeds.

Childr.

466. I.   Samuel Gore[6] born March 27, 1806, in Boston.
      II. Mary Leeds[6]   "   Sept. 20, 1807,   "   "   ; died Oct. 1,
                            1808, ag. 1 y. 11 d.
467. III. Mary Leeds[6]   "   March 10, 1809.
      IV. Abigail Gore[6] "   Aug. 17, 1811; died Aug. 27, 1811.

Mary (Leeds) Tower died Aug. 27, 1811, ag. 31 y. 9 m. 15 d.
Daniel Tower[5] mar., 2d, Lucy Cushing, in Walpole, Mass.,
Feb. 22, 1816. She was b. in Waltham, Mass.,
Oct. 25, 1782, and was dau. of Wareham and Lucy (Harring-
ton) Cushing.

Child.

468. V. Lucy A.[6] born March 7, 1818.

Daniel Tower[5] died in Waltham, Aug. 2, 1822, ag. 50 y. 5 m.
30 d.
Lucy (Cushing) Tower died in Waltham, Nov. 15, 1861, ag.
79 y. 20 d.

195. Park.   Sixth Generation.   Tower.

85. Beulah[5], Jonathan[4], Ambrose[3], Benjamin[2], John[1].
    Beulah[5], dau. of Jonathan[4] and Eunice (Allen) Tower, b.
    Aug. 27, 1760 ; mar. Josiah Park, of Lincoln, Mass. Int. pub.
    June 19, 1780. He was b. in Lincoln
    Aug. 5, 1757, and was son of Ephraim and Mary (   ) Park.

Childr. born in Lincoln.

      I.   Josiah[6]   born   1781.
      II. Elijah[6]   "   1783.
      III. Sarah[6]   "   1785; unmar.; died   1800, ag. 15.
      IV. Cyrus[6]   "   1787.
      V.   Eunice[6]   "   Feb. 15, 1789.
      VI. Emerson[6]   "   1792.
      VII. Priscilla[6]   "   April 9, 1796.
      VIII. William[6]   "   1798.
      IX. Sally[6]   "   1801.

Josiah Park died in Lincoln, June 14, 1841, ag. 83 y. 10 m.
9 d.
Beulah (Tower) Park died in Lincoln, Oct. 24, 1844, ag. 84 y.
1 m. 27 d.

196. Park. Sixth Generation. **Tower.**

85. EUNICE[5], JONATHAN[4], AMBROSE[3], BENJAMIN[2], JOHN[1].
Eunice[5], dau. of Jonathan[4] and Eunice (Allen) Tower, b.
Oct. 16, 1762; mar. Jonas Park in Lincoln, Mass.,
Jan. 30, 1783, by Rev. Charles Stearns. J. Park, b. in Lincoln
Oct. 10, 1755, was son of David and Sarah (   ) Park.

Child.

I.   JONAS[6] born   1807.

Eunice (Tower) Park[6] died in Lincoln,   , 1846, ag. 84.

197. Sixth Generation. **Tower.**

85. JONATHAN[5], JONATHAN[4], AMBROSE[3], BENJAMIN[2], JOHN[1].
Jonathan[5], son of Jonathan[4] and Eunice (Allen) Tower, b.
Oct. 16, 1764; mar. Anna Park in Lincoln, Mass. Int. pub.
June 10, 1787.

Childr. born in Concord, Mass.

469.   I.   JONATHAN[6] born   1794.
470.   II. DANIEL[6]   "   1796.
471.   III. CALVIN[6]   " July 4, 1798.
472.   IV. ANNA P.[6]   " Sept. 12, 1800.

Anna (Park) Tower died, and Jonathan Tower[5] mar., 2d,
Abigail Dudley in Lincoln, Aug. 28, 1802.

Childr. born in Lincoln.

473.   V.   MARY ANN[6] born Dec. 7, 1802.
474.   VI. CYNTHIA[6]   "   Sept. 29, 1805.

Jonathan Tower[5] died in Lincoln, Jan. 26, 1835, ag. 70 y. 2 m.
10 d.

Jonathan Tower[5] was a soldier in the War of the Revolution.
When hostilities commenced in the engagement at Lexington and
Concord he resided in Lincoln, formerly a part of Concord, and
was a lad eleven years of age. In February, 1781, when only
sixteen years old, he enlisted in the Continental service for three
years, in Capt. Jonathan Maynard's company, in the Seventh Massachusetts Regiment, under the command of Colonel Brooks, and
served until he was discharged at the close of the war. He is

described as five feet four inches in height, with dark complexion, hair, and eyes. He made application for a pension in 1818, under the law then recently passed. He states that he is in indigent circumstances, and that he is suffering from the effects of sickness and wounds. A pension of eight dollars per month was granted him.

198.   **Sixth Generation.**   **Tower.**

85. DANIEL [5], JONATHAN [4], AMBROSE [3], BENJAMIN [2], JOHN [1].
Daniel [5], son of Jonathan [4] and Eunice (Allen) Tower, b. Oct. 18, 1771 ; mar. Mary Childs, of Waltham, Mass.

Childr.

475. I. LYDIA [6]   born
476. II. VARAZINA [6] bapt. Feb. 4, 1798, in Concord, Mass.

Mary (Childs) Tower died, and Daniel Tower [5] mar., 2d, Rebecca Farrar in Lincoln, Mass.,
Aug. 16, 1802. She was b.
Dec.   , 1777, and was dau. of Thomas and Rebecca (   ) Farrar.

Childr.

477. III. MARY [6]   born May 28, 1803, in Sharon, Mass.
      IV. ALEXANDER [6] "   Nov. 28, 1804, in Littleton, Mass., unmar.; died Dec. 25, 1841, ag. 37 y. 27 d.
478. V. ELI [6]   "   Jan. 15, 1807, in Townsend, Mass.
      VI. ELEANOR [6]   "   Jan. 28, 1809, "   "   " ; unmar.; d. April 23, 1860, ag. 51 y. 2 m. 26 d.
      VII. GEORGE W. [6] " Oct. 10, 1810, in Townsend; died Feb. 7, 1867, ag. 56 y. 3 m. 28 d.
      VIII. DANIEL [6]   "   Aug. 2, 1812, in Townsend.
      IX. SAMUEL [6]   "   April 1, 1815, "   " ; died young.
      X. JOHN [6]   "   March 31, 1817, "   " ; unmar.
      XI. SAMUEL [6]   "   "   " ; died young.
479. XII. MELZAR T. [6] " June 15, 1821.

Daniel Tower [5] died in Lunenburg, Mass., July 26, 1859, ag. 87 y. 9 m. 8 d.
Rebecca (Farrar) Tower died in Lunenburg, Mass., March 6, 1866, ag. 88 y. 3 m.

At the funeral services of Daniel Tower [5] it is remembered that the minister who officiated said that Mr. Tower was of such a quiet and peaceable disposition, and had so lived among his fellow-citizens as to secure their affection and esteem, and that he had not made a single enemy in the whole course of his life.

199. **Sixth Generation.** Tower.

85. NATHAN[5], JONATHAN[4], AMBROSE[3], BENJAMIN[2], JOHN[1].
Nathan[5], son of Jonathan[4] and Eunice (Allen) Tower, b.
April 26, 1775 ; mar. Sevia Warren
March 27, 1805.

Childr. born in Lincoln, Mass.

480.   I.   LEWIS[6] born May 6, 1806.
     II.   GEORGE[6] bapt. July 17, 1808.
    III.   SEVIA[6]   "   July 5, 1810; died in Lincoln, April 27, 1878, ag. 68.

Nathan Tower[5] died in Lincoln, March 19, 1817, ag. 41 y.
10 m. 7 d.
Sevia (Warren) Tower mar., 2d, William Greenwood in Lincoln, Aug. 24, 1817 ; and 3d,   Wyman.

200. **Sixth Generation.** Tower.

87. PETER[5], BENJAMIN[4], AMBROSE[3], BENJAMIN[2], JOHN[1].
Peter[5], son of Benjamin[4] and Anne (Vorce) Tower, b.
June 1, 1761 ; mar. Sarah Putnam in Sudbury, Mass.,
Feb. 8, 1784, by Rev. Jacob Bigelow. She was b.
, 1762.

Childr.

     I.   ENOS[6]   born Oct. 14, 1784, in Sudbury; died in New Orleans.
     II.   LEWIS[6]   "   ; died in infancy.
481.   III.   SALLY[6]   "   Aug. 16, 1790, in Westford, Mass.
482.   IV.   RUEL[6]   "   May 30, 1792, "   "
     V.   ELI[6]   "   April 26, 1794, "   "   ; died in the army,
              at Plattsburg, N. Y., 1814.
483.   VI.   NANCY[6]   "   Aug. 17, 1797, in Carlisle, Mass.

Peter Tower[5] died   , 1799, ag. 38.
Sarah (Putnam) Tower mar., 2d,   Wright, of Waterford,
Me.
She died Feb. 13, 1811, ag. 49.

Peter Tower[5] was a soldier in the War of the Revolution. His
name is found among the new levies raised for six months, but
without date. In July 3, 1780, a descriptive list of six months'
men under the care of Daniel Frye, of the artificers, is given.
Among them is Peter Tower, of Sudbury, five feet nine inches in
height, of a ruddy complexion, and nineteen years of age. His
name appears in Captain Holden's company, credited with a ser-

vice of thirty-six months, under an enlistment for three years. In his enlistment for six months, in 1780, he is credited for five months and twenty days service, with one hundred and eighty miles travel. He was in Capt. John Holmes's company, in Col. Jonathan Reed's regiment of guards, at Cambridge from April 2 to July 4, 1778.

In an account of the State of Massachusetts with the United States, the latter is charged with the amount paid by the former for making good the depreciation of wages. Peter Tower's wages are £66 14s. 8d. Paid by the Continent, £13 2s. Paid by the State, £53 12s. 8d.

In an account of the balance drawn between the United States and the Sixth Massachusetts Regiment, in a settlement of a clothing account from Jan. 1, 1778, to Dec. 31, 1782, Peter Tower is entitled to £13 10s.

In vol. liv. page 204 of the Massachusetts Records is found the following : —

To Caleb B. Hayward, Agent of the late 6th Mass. Regt.

Sir, — Please to pay Mr. Benj? Tower all the wages and balance of clothing that may be found due to me for my service as a soldier in the 6th company, 6 Mass. Reg't for the years 1781 & 1782, and this shall be your sufficient voucher for the same.

PETER TOWER.

Attest : GIDEON RICHARDSON,
    JOHN NIXON.

February 22, 1784.

201. Parmenter. Sixth Generation.   Tower.

87. RUTH[5], BENJAMIN[4], AMBROSE[3], BENJAMIN[2], JOHN[1].
 Ruth[5], dau. of Benjamin[4] and Anne (Vorce) Tower, b. Oct. 27, 1762 ; mar. Thaddeus Parmenter in Sudbury, Mass., Dec. 3, 1789, by Rev. Jacob Bigelow. T. Parmenter b. March 15, 1767, and was son of Deliverance and Mary (Osborn) Parmenter.

Childr. born in Marlborough, N. H.

I.	SALLY[6]	born Aug.	1, 1790.
II.	ETHEL[6]	" June	4, 1793.
III.	ZILPAH[6]	"	1794; died in infancy.
IV.	PHEBE[6]	" May	4, 1795.
V.	OLIVE[6]	" Nov.	22, 1796.
VI	EDWARD[6]	" Sept.	12, 1799.
VII.	LUCAS[6]	"	1802; died Aug. 22, 1813, ag. 11.

Thaddeus Parmenter died in Marlborough, June 12, 1844, ag.
77 y. 2 m. 28 d.

Ruth (Tower) Parmenter died in Marlborough, June 7, 1851,
ag. 88 y. 7 m. 11 d.

202.	Sixth Generation.	Tower.

87. Augustus [5], Benjamin [4], Ambrose [3], Benjamin [2], John [1].
Augustus [5], son of Benjamin [4] and Anne (Vorce) Tower, b.
June 23, 1767; mar. Polly Leathe
Dec. 31, 1792. She was born
1767.

Childr. born in Stow, Mass.

484.	I.	Charles [6]	born May 19, 1794.
	II.	Mary [6]	" April 6, 1796; died Jan. 20, 1862, ag. 65 y. 9 m. 14 d.
485.	III.	Harriet [6]	" Sept. 28, 1799.
486.	IV.	Augustus [6]	" Aug. 16, 1801.
487.	V.	Lucy [6]	" June 14, 1803.
488.	VI.	Jedediah Leathe [6]	" April 25, 1805.
489.	VII.	Eliza [6]	" Dec. 30, 1807.
	VIII.	Francis [6]	" Feb. 8, 1811.

Augustus Tower [5] died in Stow, July 4, 1838, ag. 71 y. 11 d.

Augustus Tower [5] was not quite eight years old when the fight
at Lexington and Concord commenced the War of the Revolution,
yet he did service as a soldier before the close of the war. In his
application for a pension in 1832 he gives the following account
of his service : —

"In the month of March, 1782, I enlisted as a private for three years,
was mustered in Boston by Colonel Badlam, and joined the army the last
of April or the forepart of the May following. I was put into the Seventh
Massachusetts Regiment, commanded by Col. John Brooks, and into the
light infantry company commanded by Captain Coburn, Lieutenant Given,
and Ensign Seaver. The regiment lay in the York Huts above West
Point. Our company remained with regiment until July. We then went
down to the lines near Kingsbridge for the purpose of catching the 'Cow
Boys,' as then called.

"We stayed about there and at Fishkill till late in the fall, when we
joined our regiment, which lay in the huts back of Newberg, or New
Windsor. Here we remained until the next June, when the 'new arrangement' took place; then our company was commanded by Captain
Mills.

"Our company then went down to New Rochelle, and was there and at West Chester, near Kingsbridge, until the fall of the year. We then joined a regiment commanded by Col. William Hull, and marched into the city of New York at the time the British troops left. We stayed in the city till the last of December or first of January, when our company went to West Point. Our company was then commanded by Captain Frye. We stayed at West Point until some time in June, when I received my discharge, which I have lost."

A pension was granted Jan. 5, 1833, and was continued to his widow, Polly Tower, after his death.

Augustus Tower[5] resided in Stow, Middlesex County, Mass., and was for many years a magistrate for the county, and filled many offices of trust and responsibility, to which he was repeatedly elected by his townsmen.

In 1799 he was one of the selectmen and one of the assessors of the town, to which offices he was repeatedly chosen.

In 1804 he was chosen town clerk and treasurer, and seems to have filled these offices uninterruptedly until the year 1826, when his son, Charles Tower[6], succeeded him.

In 1809 he was elected a representative to the General Court of Massachusetts, and by continuous elections he held that office until 1816. He was again chosen to that office in 1819, and continued therein until 1824, and was again chosen to the same office in 1826. To his occupation of a carpenter he added that of land surveyor.

203.   **Sixth Generation.**   **Tower.**

87. REUBEN[5], BENJAMIN[4], AMBROSE[3], BENJAMIN[2], JOHN[1].
   Reuben[5], son of Benjamin[4] and Anne (Vorce) Tower, b.
   June 3, 1774; mar. Susannah Carr in Sudbury, Mass.,
   Jan. 15, 1795, by Rev. Jacob Bigelow.

Childr.

I.	REUBEN[6]	born Oct. 28, 1795, in Sudbury.
II.	AMASA[6]	"
III.	THOMAS[6]	bapt. Jan. 10, 1800.
IV.	NAHUM[6]	
V.	JONAS[6]	
VI.	CATHERINE[6]	
VII.	ANNA[6]	
VIII.	ABIGAIL[6]	

Reuben Tower[5] removed from Sudbury, Mass., and seems to have resided for a time in Chenango County, in the State of New

York, though his name does not appear upon any of the records of the county. In the Record of Deeds for the county the names of his sons Amasa and Thomas appear. It is said that the family removed to Ohio; but no trace of the sons of Reuben[5] or of their descendants has yet been found.

204. Sweet. **Sixth Generation.** **Tower.**

87. ABIGAIL W.[5], BENJAMIN[4], AMBROSE[3], BENJAMIN[2], JOHN[1].
Abigail W.[5], dau. of Benjamin[4] and Anne (Vorce) Tower, b. Feb. 3, 1780; mar.   Sweet, of Roxbury, Mass.

Child.

I. THATCHER[6] born   , 1804.

Abigail W. (Tower) Sweet died in Roxbury, Nov. 11, 1828, ag. 48 y. 9 m. 8 d.

205. **Sixth Generation.** **Tower.**

88. MATTHEW[5], MATTHEW[4], SAMUEL[3], SAMUEL[2], JOHN[1].
Matthew[5], son of Matthew[4] and Lydia (Wilder) Tower, b. Jan. 15, 1746–7; mar. Lydia Beal in Abington, Mass., Nov. 27, 1766, by Rev. Mr. Dodge.

Childr.

490. I. MATTHEW[6] born   , 1769.
II. JEREMIAH[6] "   ; mar., and died at the age of 36 ?

Matthew Tower[5] died in Cummington, Mass.,   1782, ag. 35.

206. **Sixth Generation.** **Tower.**

91. BELA TOWER[5], ALICE[4], DANIEL[3], SAMUEL[2], JOHN[1].
Bela Tower[5], son of Alice Tower[4], b. in Hingham May 28, 1760; mar. Emma Cushing in Hingham March 20, 1793, by Rev. D. Shute. She was b. in Hingham Jan. 17, 1772, and was dau. of Theophilus and Patience (Dunbar) Cushing.

Childr. none.

Bela Tower[5] died in Hingham, Nov. 16, 1836, ag. 76 y. 5 m. 18 d.
Emma (Cushing) Tower died in Hingham, June 3, 1852, ag. 80 y. 4 m. 17 d.

Bela Tower [5] was a soldier in the War of the Revolution. His name is on the roll of Capt. Jotham Loring's company, doing thirteen days duty, called out on the 19th of April, 1775, though he was not quite fifteen years old. He was a fifer in Capt. Pyam Cushing's company, called out on the occasion of taking possession of Dorchester Heights, March 4, 1776, and credited with four days service and thirty-six miles of travel. From the 22d of May to the 1st of August of the same year he was a private in Capt. Seth Stower's company, doing duty at Hull. In the same year his name appears on the roll of Captain Penniman's company of Braintree as a fifer, and also from March 11 to the 29th he was a fifer in Capt. Pyam Cushing's company, doing guard duty at the shores. In 1778 he is credited with two months and twenty-eight days service in guarding and fortifying the posts around Boston, as a private. In 1780, from July 22 to October 29, he performed three months and eleven days duty as a fifer in Capt. Theophilus Wilder's company of three-months men to reinforce the army stationed at Rhode Island.

He was a pensioner under the Act of 1832. In his application he states that in August, 1776, he enlisted in Captain Penniman's company as a fifer for four months, and at the expiration of that time he enlisted for three months additional service. This service was performed at Dorchester Heights. A pension of 45\frac{58}{100}$ per annum was granted, and this was continued to his widow until the time of her death.

Bela Tower was a trader, and kept a store in Hingham. By his will he gave his homestead, which included his store, to his nephew, Bela Tower Sprague, the same being subject to the use of the testator's wife during her life. Mr. Sprague continued the store for many years, and it is still kept for the same purpose.

207.   Sixth Generation.   Tower.

94. ABNER [5], JOSEPH [4], JOSEPH [3], SAMUEL [2], JOHN [1].
Abner [5], son of Joseph [4] and Sarah (Hersey) Tower, b. Nov. 28, 1767; mar. Lucina Spencer, of Suffield, Conn., Dec. 28, 1791. She was b. in Suffield Oct. 28, 1771.

Childr. born in Worthington, Mass.

491.	I.	LUTHER [6]	born May 15, 1793.
492.	II.	SALLY A. [6]	" Nov. 13, 1795.
493.	III.	MARY [6]	" July 10, 1798.

IV. DEBORAH P.[6] born July 11, 1801; unmar.; died May 24, 1867,
                  ag. 65 y. 10 m. 13 d.

494. V. ABNER [6]   " Feb. 5, 1804.
495. VI. ELVIRA J.[6] " Aug. 15, 1806.
496. VII. SPENCER [6]   " Aug. 17, 1813.

Abner Tower [5] died in Chesterfield, Mass., May 21, 1846, ag.
78 y. 5 m. 23 d.

Lucina (Spencer) Tower d. in Chesterfield, Mass., July 23,
1846, ag. 74 y. 8 m. 25 d.

208. Lovell.   Sixth Generation.   Tower.

94. SARAH [5], JOSEPH [4], JOSEPH [3], SAMUEL [2], JOHN [1].
Sarah [5], dau. of Joseph [4] and Sarah (Hersey) Tower, b.
      mar. Joshua Lovell
May 25, 1807, by Rev. Jonathan Pomeroy. J. Lovell was b.
Aug. 6, 1761, and was son of Mary [5] (Tower) and Jacob Lovell.

Childr. born in Cummington.

I. PYAM [6] born Dec. 12, 1812; died Dec. 12, 1812.
II. PYAM [6] " Aug. 28, 1815.

Sarah (Tower) Lovell died, and Joshua Lovell mar. widow
Annah Brewster, June 10, 1819.

He died in Cummington, Sept. 1843, ag. 82 y. 1 m.

209.   Sixth Generation.   Tower.

94. PYAM [5], JOSEPH [4], JOSEPH [3], SAMUEL [2], JOHN [1].
Pyam [5], son of Joseph [4] and Sarah (Hersey) Tower, b.
      mar. Rachel Cowing, of Chesterfield, Mass. Int. pub.
Jan. 10, 1801.

Childr.

497. I. LYDIA [6]   born Oct. 1, 1801.
     II. RELIEF [6]   "   ; died at the age of 7 years.
     III. WEALTHY [6] "   ; mar.
     IV. EMILY [6]   "   ; mar. Jacob Snyder.
498. V. SALMON PYAM [6] "
499. VI. SUSAN [6]   " Aug. 23, 1816.
     VII. LUCY ANN [6] "   ; mar. William Edgar Gilmore.

Pyam Tower [5] died in Munsville, Madison County, N. Y.

Rachel (Cowing) Tower died in Munsville, Madison County,
N. Y.

210.   **Sixth Generation.**   **Tower.**

94. EZEKIEL[5], JOSEPH[4], JOSEPH[3], SAMUEL[2], JOHN[1].
     Ezekiel[5], son of Joseph[4] and Sarah (Hersey) Tower, b.
     Dec.   1781; mar. Betsey E. Josselyn. Int. pub.
     June 25, 1803. She was b.
     June   1783, and was dau. of Abraham and Eunice (   )
        Josselyn.

                 Childr. born in Worthington, Mass.

	I.	ELISHA[6]	born	; died at the West.
500.	II.	JOSEPH P.[6]	"	1805.
501.	III.	LYMAN J.[6]	"	May 29, 1809.
502.	IV.	WILLIAM E.[6]	"	1812.
	V.	WEALTHY[6]	"	1813; died Sept. 13, 1828, ag. 15.
503.	VI.	ELIZABETH[6]	"	1818.

Ezekiel Tower[5] died in Worthington, Mass., March 6, 1855,
    ag. 73 y. 3 m.
Betsey E. (Josselyn) Tower died in Worthington, Mass., Oct.
    14, 1867, ag. 84 y. 4 m.

211.   **Seventh Generation.**   **Tower.**

97. WANTON[6], ENOCH[5], GIDEON[4], BENJAMIN[3], JOHN[2], JOHN[1].
     Wanton[6], son of Enoch[5] and Lucy (Lovett) Tower, b.
     Jan. 4, 1768 ; mar. Finis Cook in Cumberland, R. I.,
     May 26, 1793, by Elder Abner Ballou.

                 Childr. born in Cumberland, R. I.

	I.	LUCY[7]	born	
	II.	MANNING[7]	"	1796; died, unmar., Nov. 12, 1818, ag. 22.
	III.	ARIEL[7]	"	; died in Cumberland.
505.	IV.	MARY[7]	"	May 6, 1801.

504. appears before Lucy.

Wanton Tower[6] died in Cumberland,   , 1805, ag. 37.
Finis (Cook) Tower died in Cumberland,   , 1803.

212. Follett.   **Seventh Generation.**   **Tower.**

97. LOIS[6], ENOCH[5], GIDEON[4], BENJAMIN[3], JOHN[2], JOHN[1].
     Lois[6], dau. of Enoch[5] and Lucy (Lovett) Tower, b.
     Dec. 15, 1773; mar. Comfort Follett in Cumberland, R. I.,
     May 27, 1792, by Elder Abner Ballou. C. Follett b. in
        Cumberland
     April 4, 1768, and was son of Abraham and Patience (   )
        Follett.

Childr. born in Cumberland, R. I.

I.	AMOROUS[7]	born	Sept. 18, 1792.
II.	ELLIS[7]	"	April 7, 1795.
III.	RUTH[7]	"	April 13, 1797.
IV.	NATHAN[7]	"	April 30, 1800; died Feb. 11, 1816, ag. 15 y. 9 m. 12 d.
V.	LYNDA[7]	"	June 8, 1802.
VI.	WILLARD[7]	"	May 26, 1807.
VII.	ADALINE[7]	"	July 20, 1809.
VIII.	ALBERT[7]	"	Feb. 10, 1811.
IX.	LAURA ANN[7]	"	May 3, 1813.
X.	HORACE[7]	"	Aug. 8, 1815; died Feb. 5, 1816.

213. Luther   **Seventh Generation.**   **Tower.**

97. CYNTHIA[6], ENOCH[5], GIDEON[4], BENJAMIN[3], JOHN[2], JOHN[1].
Cynthia[6], dau. of Enoch[5] and Lucy (Lovett) Tower, b.
    ; mar. Elisha Luther, of Swansey, Mass.,
July 3, 1791, by Levi Ballou, J. P. E. Luther, b. in Swansey
July 9, 1767, was son of Eleazer and Mary (   ) Luther.

214. Lapham.   **Seventh Generation.**   **Tower.**

98. AMY[6], ICHABOD[5], GIDEON[4], BENJAMIN[3], JOHN[2], JOHN[1].
Amy[6], dau. of Ichabod[5] and Mary (Pullen) Tower, b.
Oct. 29, 1769; mar. Abner Lapham in Cumberland, R. I.,
June 29, 1797, by Rev. Stephen Place. A. Lapham was son
of Abner and Mary (Mowry) Lapham.

Childr. born in Cumberland, R. I.

I.	ELIZA[7]	born	Feb. 5, 1798.
II.	MOLLY[7]	"	March 1, 1800.
III.	OLIVE MOWRY	"	April 14, 1802.
IV.	MARY[7]	"	May 12, 1804.
V.	DORCAS[7]	"	Aug. 10, 1806.

215.   **Seventh Generation.**   **Tower.**

98. DAVID[6], ICHABOD[5], GIDEON[4], BENJAMIN[3], JOHN[2], JOHN[1].
David[6], son of Ichabod[5] and Mary (Pullen) Tower, b.
May 27, 1771; mar. Pamelia Darrow.

Childr.

	I.	SAMUEL[7]	born	1804; died 1806, ag. 2.
	II.	JOHN WILSON[7]	"	1806; unmar.
506.	III.	JANE GLASBY[7]	"	1809.

507.	IV.	MARY REMINGTON [7]	born		1811.
508.	V.	LORA ANDERSON [7]	"		1813.
509.	VI.	CYNTHIA [7]	"		1815.
510.	VII.	DAVID [7]	"		1817.
511.	VIII.	PAMELIA ELIZABETH [7]	"		1820.
512.	IX.	GEORGE WASHINGTON [7]	"	June 7,	1822.
513.	X.	JAMES MUNROE [7]	"	June 6,	1824.

David Tower [6] died on a farm on the Maumee River, Ohio, 1836, ag. 65.

Pamelia (Darrow) Tower died in Beloit, Wisconsin, 1853.

216. Remington. Seventh Generation. Tower.

98. MARY [6], ICHABOD [5], GIDEON [4], BENJAMIN [3], JOHN [2], JOHN [1].
Mary [6], dau. of Ichabod [5] and Mary (Pullen) Tower, b.
Oct. 22, 1775 ; mar. Peleg Remington, of Pawtuxet, R. I.,
Sept. 9, 1799. He was b.
April 22, 1764, and was son of Peleg and Waitey (   )
Remington.

Childr. born in Pawtuxet.

	I.	SALLY [7]	born Feb. 20, 1801.
	II.	SAMUEL TOWER [7]	" March 10, 1806.
	III.	MARY TOWER [7]	" Sept. 10, 1808.
	IV.	WAITEY RHODES [7]	" Jan. 1, 1810.

Peleg Remington died in Pawtuxet, Jan. 17, 1838, ag. 73 y. 8 m. 26 d.

Mary (Tower) Remington died in Pawtuxet, April 25, 1872, ag. 96 y. 6 m. 3 d.

217. Seventh Generation. Tower.

98. ISAAC [6], ICHABOD [5], GIDEON [4], BENJAMIN [3], JOHN [2], JOHN [1].
Isaac [6], son of Ichabod [5] and Mary (Pullen) Tower, b.
Dec. 31, 1778 ; mar. Rebecca Dexter, of Smithfield, R. I.,
Feb. 4, 1802. She was b. in Smithfield
Sept. 27, 1783, and was dau. of Nathan and Elsey (Warren)
Dexter.

Childr.

514.	I.	ANN ELIZA [7]	born Nov. 28, 1802, in Smithfield, R. I.
	II.	SALLY REBECCA [7]	" July 2, 1804, " Attleborough, Mass.
515.	III.	WILLIAM [7]	" Feb. 6, 1806, " " "
516.	IV.	ELSEY [7]	" Sept. 27, 1807, " Lanesborough, "

517.   V.   ISAAC[7]   born Mar. 27, 1810, in Charlton, Mass.
518.   VI.   ALANSON PORTER[7] " May 30, 1814, "   "   "
524.   VII.   MARY DEXTER[7]   " Sept. 20, 1817, "   "   "
519.   VIII.   JOHN[7]   " July 27, 1820, "   "   "
       IX.   GEORGE[7]   " Dec. 23, 1822, "   "   "

Isaac Tower[6] died in Charlton, Mass., June 23, 1863, ag.
84 y. 5 m. 23 d.

Rebecca (Dexter) Tower died in Charlton, Mass., Nov. 12.
1863, ag. 80 y. 1 m. 16 d.

218.   **Seventh Generation.**   **Tower.**

98. JOSEPH P.[6], ICHABOD[5], GIDEON[4], BENJAMIN[3], JOHN[2], JOHN[1].
Joseph P.[6], son of Ichabod[5] and Mary (Pullen) Tower, b.
May 8, 1780; mar. Cynthia Pullen
    , 1805, by P. Swift, J. P. She was b.
    1787.

Childr.

520.   I.   PAMELIA[7]   born Jan. 23, 1806.
     II.   POLLY[7]   " April 9, 1808; died Sept. 13, 1808.
521.   III.   SALLY[7]   " May 15, 1809.
522.   IV.   LUCINDA[7]   " Sept. 11, 1810.
523.   V.   JOSEPH H.[7]   " Feb. 1, 1812.
524.   VI.   ISAAC WILSON[7] " Aug. 1, 1813.
525.   VII.   WILLIAM P.[7]   " Sept. 12, 1815.
526.   VIII.   JAMES P.[7]   " May 31, 1817.
     IX.   JOHN S.[7]   " Jan. 28, 1820, unmar.; died June 23, 1842,
                         ag. 22 y. 4 m. 25 d.
     X.   ICHABOD RAY[7] " Jan. 6, 1822; died Sept. 11, 1829, ag. 7 y.
                         8 m. 5 d.
527.   XI.   SAMUEL R.[7]   " Dec.   , 1823.
528.   XII.   HARRIET D.[7]   " May 15, 1825.
     XIII.   ELIZABETH B.[7] " Sept. , 1826; died Jan.   , 1828, ag. 1 y.
                         4 m.
529.   XIV.   ELIZABETH B.[7] " Feb. 22, 1828.
530.   XV.   CORNELIA N.[7]   " Sept. 16, 1829.
531.   XVI.   EMMA[7]   " March 18, 1831.

Joseph P. Tower[6] died in Addison, Mich., Sept.   , 1846, ag.
66 y. 4 m.

Cynthia (Pullen) Tower died in Addison, Oct. 9, 1857, ag. 70.

219.   **Jillson.**   **Seventh Generation.**   **Tower.**

98. MIRIAM[6], ICHABOD[5], GIDEON[4], BENJAMIN[3], JOHN[2], JOHN[1].
Miriam[6], dau. of Ichabod[5] and Mary (Pullen) Tower, b.
March 10, 1785; mar. Olney Jillson
Dec. 15, 1803. He was b.
April 15, 1777.

Childr.

I. SAMUEL TOWER[7] born Jan. 16, 1806, in Cumberland, R. I.
II. MARY S.[7]   " Dec.   6, 1806, "   "   "
III. AMY[7]   " Sept. 19, 1809, "   "   "
IV. WELCOME[7]   " Sept. 11, 1812, in Mendon, Mass.
V. LAWSON[7]   "   in Burrillville, R. I.; died young.
VI. LEWIS[7]   "   "   "   "

Olney Jillson died in Cumberland, Mass., May 22, 1823, ag.
46 y. 1 m. 7 d.
Miriam (Tower) Jillson died in Webster, Mass., July 25, 1847,
ag. 62 y. 4 m. 15 d.

220. Ballou.   Seventh Generation.   Tower.

99. EDILLA[6], LEVI[5], GIDEON[4], BENJAMIN[3], JOHN[2], JOHN[1].
Edilla[6], dau. of Levi[5] and Mary (Whipple) Tower, b.
May 27, 1771; mar. Ariel Ballou in Cumberland, R. I.,
July 2, 1802. He was b.
Feb. 21, 1758, and was son of Ariel and Jerusha (Slack)
Ballou.

Childr. born in Cumberland.

I. ADIN[7] born April 23, 1803.
II. ARIEL[7] " Oct. 25, 1805.

Ariel Ballou died in Cumberland, Sept. 26, 1839, ag. 81 y.
7 m. 5 d.
Edilla (Tower) Ballou died in Cumberland, Dec. 27, 1834, ag.
63 y. 7 m.

221. Mason.   Seventh Generation.   Tower.

99. CHLOE[6], LEVI[5], GIDEON[4], BENJAMIN[3], JOHN[2], JOHN[1].
Chloe[6], dau. of Levi[5] and Mary (Whipple) Tower, b.
Sept. 7, 1773; mar. Chad Mason, son of Jonathan Mason.

Childr. born in Cumberland, R. I.

I. OTIS[7]   born June 5, 1791.
II. OLNEY[7]   " Dec. 1, 1793.
III. NANCY[7] " Aug. 23, 1796; unmar.
IV. JESSE[7]   " Dec. 17, 1799.
V. LUCINA[7] " Nov. 9, 1801; unmar.

222. Seventh Generation. Tower.

99. LEVI [6], LEVI [5], GIDEON [4], BENJAMIN [3], JOHN [2], JOHN [1].
Levi [6], son of Levi [5] and Mary (Whipple) Tower, b.
May 2, 1776 ; mar. widow Elizabeth W. (Cooke) Wood in
Newport, R. I.,
Jan. 29, 1807. She was dau. of John and Margaret Cooke,
and widow of Godfrey Wood, an officer in the U. S. Navy.

Childr.

	I.	MARY W.[7] born	; died at the age of 16 years.
532.	II.	JOHN C.[7] " Feb. 7, 1809.	
	III.	ELIZABETH [7] "	; mar. B. J. Totten, U. S. N.; *s. p.*
	IV.	MARGARET [7] "	; mar. James Dana, of Boston.
	V.	RUTH M.[7] "	; died at the age of 16 years.
	VI.	FRANCES [7] "	; " in infancy.
	VII.	SARAH [7] "	; " " "
	VIII.	AUGUSTUS [7] "	; unmar.; died in Newport, R. I.
	IX.	LEVI [7] "	; died in infancy.
533.	X.	AMELIA C.[7] "	

Levi Tower [6] died in Newport, R. I., June 4, 1854, ag. 78 y.
1 m. 2 d.

223. Sayles. Seventh Generation. Tower.

99. ZILLAH [6], LEVI [5], GIDEON [4], BENJAMIN [3], JOHN [2], JOHN [1].
Zillah [6], dau. of Levi [5] and Mary (Whipple) Tower, b.
Oct. 18, 1781 ; mar. Pardon Sayles
Jan. 8, 1807, by Isaac Raze, J. P.   P. Sayles b. in Smith-
field, R. I.,
Dec. 11, 1784.

Childr. born in Cumberland, R. I.

I.	JULIANA [7]	born Oct. 31, 1807.
II.	STEPHEN WHIPPLE [7]	" Dec. 7, 1809.
III.	MARY [7]	" Dec. 10, 1811; died Sept. 13, 1813, ag. 1 y. 9 m. 3 d.
IV.	MARY ANN [7]	" June 18, 1813; " April 16, 1815, ag. 1 y. 9 m. 29 d.
V.	HENRY WARD [7]	" Feb. 7, 1816.
VI.	HARRIET [7]	" Dec. 15, 1818, died March 5, 1834, ag. 15 y. 2 m. 18 d.

Zillah (Tower) Sayles died Oct. 31, 1834.

14

99. JASON [6], LEVI [5], GIDEON [4], BENJAMIN [3], JOHN [2], JOHN [1].
Jason [6], son of Levi [5] and Mary (Whipple) Tower, b.
Aug. 30, 1786; mar. Philena Howard in Wrentham, Mass.,
Jan. 10, 1810. She was b.
June 8, 1787, and was dau. of John and Lydia (Rhodes)
Howard.

Childr.

534.	I.	WILLIAM EMERSON [7] born May 13, 1811.
535.	II.	MARY [7]	" Jan. 10, 1813.
536.	III.	JOHN HOWARD [7]	" Dec. 6, 1814.
537.	IV.	LYDIA [7]	" July 13, 1816.
538.	V.	NANCY RAY [7]	" Aug. 19, 1818.
539.	VI.	LEVI [7]	" Sept. 10, 1820.
540.	VII.	PHILENA [7]	" Sept. 27, 1822.
541.	VIII.	JASON [7]	" Nov. 16, 1824.

Jason Tower [6] died in Cumberland, R. I., Aug. 17, 1844, ag.
57 y. 11 m. 17 d.
Philena (Howard) Tower died in Cumberland, May 21, 1861,
ag. 73 y. 11 m. 13 d.

99. EMERSON [6], LEVI [5], GIDEON [4], BENJAMIN [3], JOHN [2], JOHN [1].
Emerson [6], son of Levi [5] and Mary (Whipple) Tower, b.
Jan. 31, 1789; mar. Sally Thurston, of Franklin, Mass.,
May 4, 1810, by Isaac Raize, J. P. She was dau. of James
Thurston.

Childr. born in Cumberland, R. I.

542.	I.	POLLY T. [7]	born March 31, 1811.
543.	II.	DELIA [7]	" Dec. 2, 1812.
544.	III.	CALISTA [7]	" Sept. 25, 1814.
545.	IV.	LYDIA [7]	" Sept. 19, 1816.
546.	V.	EMERSON [7]	" June 29, 1818.
	VI.	SEREPHINA [7]	" July 13, 1827; died Nov. 18, 1827.

Sally (Thurston) Tower died in Cumberland Aug. 8, 1827.
Emerson Tower [6] mar., 2d, Sally Whipple
May 4, 1828. She was b.
April 13, 1792, and was dau. of Eleazer and Betty (Bate)
Whipple.

Childr.

547.	VII.	DELILA[7]	born Nov. 14, 1828.
548.	VIII.	CHLOE[7]	" Nov. 19, 1830.
	IX.	RUTH ANN[7]	" May 15, 1832; died Jan. 21, 1835, ag. 2 y. 8 m. 6 d.
549.	X.	ZILLA[7]	" Sept. 27, 1834.

Emerson Tower[6] died in Cumberland, R. I., Oct. 23, 1862, ag. 73 y. 8 m. 27 d.

Sally (Whipple) Tower died in Cumberland, March 11, 1879, ag. 86 y. 10 m. 26 d.

225 a.   **Seventh Generation.**   **Tower.**

100. DEWEY[6], REUBEN[5], GIDEON[4], BENJAMIN[3], JOHN[2], JOHN[1].
Dewey[6], son of Reuben[5] and   , b.
    ; mar.   Wiggins (?)

Childr.

I.	REUBEN[7]	born July 6, 1808, near Saratoga, N. Y.
II.	GEORGE[7]	" ; died in Marshall Co., Iowa, 1882.
III.	MARY[7]	" April 12, 1813; died in Dacota Co., Minn., Dec. 29, 1881.
IV.	HIRAM[7]	" ; " " Clyde, Ohio, 1853.
V.	JOHN[7]	" ; " " Shermansville, Pa., 1875.

Dewey Tower[6] died in Ashtabula, Ashtabula County, Ohio., 1871 or 1872.

226.   **Seventh Generation.**   **Tower.**

101. JOSEPH[6], SAMUEL[5], GIDEON[4], BENJAMIN[3], JOHN[2], JOHN[1].
Joseph[6], son of Samuel[5] and Rebecca (   ) Tower, b.
    1774; mar. widow Polly (Steward) Hurlburt
    1808. She was b.
    1778, and was dau. of Abraham Steward.

Childr.

550.	I.	OMYRA[7]	born 1809, in Shoreham, Vt.
551.	II.	SAMUEL[7]	" Aug. 11, 1811, " " "
	III.	MARTHA[7]	" 1815, " Sudbury, Vt.; died 1820, ag. 5 years.
552.	IV.	HARVEY[7]	" March 3, 1817, " " "
553.	V.	HARRIET[7]	" " " "

Joseph Tower[6] died in Addison, Vt.,   1846, ag. 72.
Polly (Steward) (Hurlburt) Tower died in Pentwater, Mich., 1862, ag. 84.

227. Warner.   Seventh Generation.   Tower.

101. PATIENCE [6], SAMUEL [5], GIDEON [4], BENJAMIN [3], JOHN [2], JOHN [1].
Patience [6], dau. of Samuel [5] and Rebecca Tower, b.
          ; mar. Nathaniel Warner, of Addison, Vt.

Childr.

    I. NATHANIEL [7].
   II. SAMUEL [7].
  III. IRA [7].
  IV. REBECCA [7].
    V. EZRA [7].

228. Clark.   Seventh Generation.   Tower.

101. HANNAH [6], SAMUEL [5], GIDEON [4], BENJAMIN [3], JOHN [2], JOHN [1].
Hannah [6], dau. of Samuel [5] and Rebecca Tower, b.
          ; mar. Asahel Clark, of Addison, Vt.

Childr.

    I. DEMYRA [7].
   II. ALVIN [7].
  III. ALVIRA [7].
  IV. DELIA [7].
    V. ELLIOT [7].

229. Olin.   Seventh Generation.   Tower.

101. POLLY [6], SAMUEL [5], GIDEON [4], BENJAMIN [3], JOHN [2], JOHN [1].
Polly [6], dau. of Samuel [5] and Rebecca Tower, b.
          ; mar. Justin Olin.

Child.

    I. JUSTIN [7].

230. Wilkinson.   Seventh Generation.   Tower.

103. ELIZABETH [6], JONATHAN [5], JOHN [4], BENJAMIN [3], JOHN [2], JOHN [1].
Elizabeth [6], dau. of Jonathan [5] and Sarah (Whipple) Tower, b.
          1763 ; mar. John Wilkinson.   He was b. in Cum-
berland, R. I.,
Nov. 13, 1758, and was son of Daniel and Abigail (Inman)
Wilkinson.

Childr.

I. ELPHA[7] born Oct. 17, 1783.
II. ALFRED[7] " July 6, 1786.
III. JOHN[7] " Sept. 30, 1798.
IV. DIANA[7] " Nov. , 1801.

John Wilkinson died in Skaneateles, N. Y., 1801, ag. 43.

231. Pease. Seventh Generation. Tower.

106. HANNAH[6], GIDEON[5], JOHN[4], BENJAMIN[3], JOHN[2], JOHN[1].
Hannah[6], dau. of Gideon[5] and Abigail (Perkins) Tower, b.
Jan. , 1776; mar. Pease.

Childr.

I. HARVEY[7] born
II. Daughter[7] "

Hannah (Tower) Pease died in Indiana 1866, ag. 90.

232. Millard. Seventh Generation. Tower.

106. NANCY[6], GIDEON[5], JOHN[4], BENJAMIN[3], JOHN[2], JOHN[1].
Nancy[6], dau. of Gideon[5] and Abigail (Perkins) Tower, b.
Dec. , 1777; mar. Millard.

Childr.

I. HENRY[7]
II. SIDNEY ; mar.
III. DARCOURT J. OTHO[7]
IV. NANCY[7] ; " George O. Brien. She died in Chambers
Co., Texas.
V. ALFRED[7]
VI. JEDEDIAH[7] ; " He died in Sabine Pass, Texas.

Nancy (Tower) Millard died 1867 ag. 90.

233. Seventh Generation. Tower.

106. JONATHAN[6], GIDEON[5], JOHN[4], BENJAMIN[3], JOHN[2], JOHN[1].
Jonathan[6], son of Gideon[5] and Abigail (Perkins) Tower, b.
; mar.

Childr.

554.	I.	ROBERT [7]		
555.	II.	JOHN [7]		
556.	III.	AMANDA [7]		
557.	IV.	ALFRED [7]		
558.	V.	LEWIS [7]	born	1824.
	VI.	CLARISSA [7]		; died young.
	VII.	BETTY [7]		; died at about the age of 20.
	VIII.	JONATHAN [7]		

234. Lemon.   Seventh Generation.   Tower.

106. ABIGAIL [6], GIDEON [5], JOHN [4], BENJAMIN [3], JOHN [2], JOHN [1].
    Abigail [6], dau. of Gideon [5] and Abigail (Perkins) Tower, b.
    June 21, 1787; mar. William Lemon in Cincinnati, Ohio,
        1804. He was b.
    Feb. 23, 1782, and was son of William and Martha (Liv-
        ingston) Lemon.

Childr.

I.	SAMUEL [7]	born April 10, 1805.
II.	JOHN T. [7]	"	1807; died in Kentucky Aug. 15, 1808.
III.	JOHN TOWER [7]	" Dec. 20, 1808.
IV.	JAMES [7]	" April 2, 1810; died in Kentucky Aug. 26, 1811,
		ag. 1 y. 4 m. 24 d.
V.	WILLIAM [7]	" Oct. 28, 1811.
VI.	ELIZA L. [7]	" July 15, 1813.
VII.	MARTHA J. [7]	" July 9, 1815.
VIII.	HARRIET D. [7]	" March 28, 1817.
IX.	WILLIS [7]	" Jan. 30, 1819.
X.	OMER [7]	" Feb. 7, 1821.
XI.	ABIGAIL [7]	" March 27, 1823.
XII.	ALECTA ANN [7]	" July 11, 1825.
XIII.	JAMES [7]	" Nov. 15, 1827.
XIV.	CAROLINE [7]	" Jan 14, 1830; died June 21, 1830.

William Lemon died near Oleon, Ind., Nov.   , 1861, ag. 79 y.
    9 m.
Abigail (Tower) Lemon died in Dillsborough Nov.   , 1844,
    ag. 57 y. 5 m.

235.   Seventh Generation.   Tower.

106. GIDEON [6], GIDEON [5], JOHN [4], BENJAMIN [3], JOHN [2], JOHN [1].
    Gideon [6], son of Gideon [5] and Abigail (Perkins) Tower, b.
        1794; mar. Roxana Scranton.

Childr.

559.	I.	ALMA [7]	born Dec. 3, 1822.		
	II.	LOVINIA [7]	"		; unmar.; died young.
560.	III.	WILLIAM SCRANTON [7]	"	June 10, 1826.	
561.	IV.	GIDEON [7]	"	June 2, 1830.	
	V.	CLARISSA [7]	"		; died young.
	VI.	ROWENA [7]	"		; " "
	VII.	NANCY [7]	"		; mar. Joseph Brinson,

and died in Switzerland Co., Ind., ag. 24.

Gideon Tower [6] died in Switzerland County, Ind., 1838–1841.
Roxana (Scranton) Tower died in Switzerland County, Ind.,
June 2, 1830.

236. Lareu. Seventh Generation. Tower.

106. CLARINDA [6], GIDEON [5], JOHN [4], BENJAMIN [3], JOHN [2], JOHN [1].
Clarinda [6], dau. of Gideon [5] and Abigail (Perkins) Tower, b.
Aug. 7, 1797 ; mar. Benjamin Lareu
Dec. 9, 1819. He was b. in Pennsylvania
July 1, 1791, and was son of Abraham and Abigail (Ritten-
house) Lareu.

Childr.

I.	NELSON [7]	born Sept. 11, 1820; died Feb. 5, 1822, ag. 1 y 4 m. 25 d.	
II.	WILLIAM [7]	"	Sept. 17, 1822.
III.	JOHN T. [7]	"	Dec. 7, 1823.
IV.	BENJAMIN [7]	"	Sept. 21, 1825; died Dec. 7, 1826, ag. 1 y. 2 m. 16 d.
V.	ELIAS HUTCHINS [7]	"	Nov. 28, 1827.
VI.	ELIZA [7]	"	Nov. 2, 1829.

Benjamin Lareu died in Switzerland County, Ind., Feb. 8,
1845, ag. 53 y. 7 m. 7 d.
Clarinda (Tower) Lareu died in Switzerland County, Ind.,
Sept. 16, 1839, ag. 42 y. 1 m. 9 d.

237. Seventh Generation. Tower.

106. ALPHEUS P. [6], GIDEON [5], JOHN [4], BENJAMIN [3], JOHN [2], JOHN [1].
Alpheus P. [6], son of Gideon [5] and Abigail (Perkins) Tower, b.
Jan. 21, 1800 ; mar. Orpah Hunter in Dearborn County, Ind,.
Jan.   1819.

Childr. born in Dearborn County, Ind.

562. I. ROXSENA [7]   born May 20, 1820.
      II. SAMANTHA J. [7]   " Jan. 18, 1823; died Aug. , 1831, ag. 8 y.
                                                        7 m.
563. III. JOSEPH HUNTER [7] " Feb. 24, 1825.
564. IV. CINDERILLA L. [7]   " Nov. 14, 1827.

Alpheus P. Tower [6] died, and Orpah (Hunter) Tower mar.,
    2d, Adolphus Higgins, of Ripley County, Ind. She died
    at Dowds Station, Iowa, Nov. 14, 1870, ag. 69 y. 1 m. 15 d.

238.   **Seventh Generation.**   **Tower.**

107. JOSEPH [6], JOSEPH [5], JOSEPH [4], BENJAMIN [3], JOHN [2], JOHN [1].
      Joseph [6], son of Joseph [5] and Ellen (Mason) Tower, b.
      Dec. 23, 1769 ; mar. Priscilla Edmonds
      Dec. 18, 1796. She was b.
           , 1777.

                  Childr. born in Ira, Vt.

565. I. LUCY [7]   born Sept. 21, 1797.
566. II. AMOS [7]   " Feb. 21, 1799.
      III. EDMONDS [7]   " Dec. 15, 1800, unmar.; died June 9,
                                   1822, ag. 21 y. 5 m 25 d.
      IV. ALTHEDA [7]   " Jan. 17, 1803; died March 2, 1804,
                                   ag. 1 y. 1 m. 15 d.
      V. ITHAMER [7]   " Nov. 15, 1804; died March 6, 1805.
567. VI. HENRY [7]   " Nov. 26, 1805.
568. VII. ABIGAIL [7]   " April 1, 1808.
      VIII. ELEANOR [7]   " July 9, 1810 ; died Feb. 26, 1811.
569. IX. JOSEPH [7]   " Dec. 20, 1811.
      X. GEORGE WASHINGTON [7] " Feb. 3, 1814; died Oct. 9, 1822, ag.
                                   8 y. 8 m. 6 d.
570. XI. ALPHA L. [7]   " Oct. 21, 1816.
      XII. JAMES ORSON [7]   " March 6, 1819.

Joseph Tower [6] died in Ira, Vt., Jan. 31, 1840, ag. 70 y. 1 m.
    7 d.
Priscilla (Edmonds) Tower died in Ira, Sept. 2, 1851, ag. 74.

239.   **Seventh Generation.**   **Tower.**

107. NATHANIEL [6], JOSEPH [5], JOSEPH [4], BENJAMIN [3], JOHN [2], JOHN [1].
      Nathaniel [6], son of Joseph [5] and Ellen (Mason) Tower, b.
      Jan. 4, 1774 ; mar. Amanda Johnson.

Childr.

    I. William[7] born   , 1807.
   II. Hiram[7]   "   , 1810.

Nathaniel Tower[6] died in Ira, Vt., Jan. 6, 1810, ag. 36 y.
   2 d.

240. Fish.   Seventh Generation.   Tower.

107. Eleanor[6], Joseph[5], Joseph[4], Benjamin[3], John[2], John[1].
Eleanor[6], dau. of Joseph[5] and Ellen (Mason) Tower, b.
Sept. 8, 1779; mar. Robert Fish, of Ira, Vt. He was b.
   , 1778.

Childr.

     I. Malany[7]   ; died young.
    II. Infant[7]   ;   "   "
  III. David[7]   born Feb. 17, 1806.
  IV. Phebe[7]   "   May 27, 1808; died in Union Township, Clark Co.
                    Ia., April   , 1867, ag. 54 y. 11 m.
   V. John[7]   "   April 14, 1810.
  VI. George[7]   "   Jan. 2, 1813, unmar.; died in Stockton, N. Y.
 VII. Infant[7]   "   "   "   "   "

Robert Fish died in Ira, Vt., March 4, 1829, ag. 51.
Eleanor (Tower) Fish died in Stockton,   , 1845, ag. 66.

241. McCarey.   Seventh Generation.   Tower.

107. Elizabeth[6], Joseph[5], Joseph[4], Benjamin[3], John[2], John[1].
Elizabeth[6], dau. of Joseph[5] and Ellen (Mason) Tower, b.
March 3, 1781; mar. John McCarey, of Ira, Vt.

Childr.

    I. Russell[7] born
   II. Tower[7]   "

Elizabeth (Tower) McCarey died in Ira, Vt.
John McCarey mar., 2d, Amanda (Johnson) Tower, widow
   of Nathaniel Tower[6], deceased.

242. Fish.   Seventh Generation.   Tower.

107. Lydia[6], Joseph[5], Joseph[4], Benjamin[3], John[2], John[1].
Lydia[6], dau. of Joseph[5] and Ellen (Mason) Tower, b.
July 9, 1783; mar. Daniel Fish, of Moriah, N. Y.

Childr.

I.   ORRIN [7]
II. LAURA [7]   ; mar.   Waldron, and died in Stockton,
                              N. Y., *s. p.*
III. JOSEPH [7]   ; " Abigail Sheldon, of N. Adams, Mass.,
                              and died in Wisconsin,   , 1843.
IV. GEORGE [7]

Daniel Fish died in Castleton, Vt.
Lydia (Tower) Fish died in Moriah, N. Y.

243.   **Seventh Generation.**   **Tower.**

107. MASON [6], JOSEPH [5], JOSEPH [4], BENJAMIN [3], JOHN [2], JOHN [1].
Mason [6], son of Joseph [5] and Ellen (Mason) Tower, b.
July 25, 1785 ; mar. Mabel

Child.

571.   I. GALUSHA A. [7] born   ; mar.   Mabbitt, of Fre-
                              donia, N. Y.

Mabel (   ) Tower died in Ira, Vt., March 7, 1813, ag. 28.
Mason Tower mar., 2d, Phebe

Childr.

II. PHEBE [7] born   ; died in Stockton, N. Y.

Phebe (   ) Tower died in Ira, Vt., April 27, 1815.
Mason Tower died in Sheffield, Ashtabula County, Ohio,
, 1868.

244. **Lindley.**   **Seventh Generation.**   **Tower.**

108. NANCY [6], NATHANIEL [5], JOSEPH [4], BENJAMIN [3], JOHN [2], JOHN [1].
Nancy [6], dau. of Nathaniel [5] and Lucy (Tingley) Tower, b.
Dec. 15, 1777 ; mar. Abiah Lindley in Kingsbury, N. Y.,
June 1, 1794. He was b. in Bristol, Conn.

Childr.

I.   EPHRAIM [7] born Sept. 16, 1796.
II. JACOB [7]   " July 25, 1798.
III. ARVIN [7]   "   ; died, ag. 6 years.
IV. POLLY [7]   "   ; "   " 4 "

Nancy (Tower) Lindley died in Bristol, Conn., Dec. 20,
1803, ag. 26 y. 6 m. 5 d.

245. Seventh Generation. **Tower.**

108. OTIS[6], NATHANIEL[5], JOSEPH[4], BENJAMIN[3], JOHN[2], JOHN[1].
Otis[6], son of Nathaniel[5] and Lucy (Tingley) Tower, b.
Dec. 3, 1779; mar. Sarah Edmonds in Danby, Vt.,
Sept. 11, 1803. She was b.
Oct. 1, 1782, and was dau. of Obadiah Edmonds.

Childr.

	I.	Infant[7]	born	; died.
572.	II.	ALANSON[7]	"	April 22, 1805.
	III.	ALTHEDA[7]	"	July 12, 1808; unmar.; died.
573.	IV.	LYMAN[7]	"	July 10, 1810.
574.	V.	ALMIRA[7]	"	June 7, 1812.
575.	VI.	LOAMI[7]	"	Aug. 4, 1814.
	VII.	SAMUEL DEXTER[7]	"	July 19, 1817; died Oct. 19, 1833, ag. 16 y. 3 m.
	VIII.	SARAH[7]	"	Nov. 3, 1818; unmar.
	IX.	NATHANIEL[7]	"	Dec. 11, 1820; died Nov. 11, 1822, ag. 1 y. 11 m.
	X.	ZERUAH[7]	"	Nov. 27, 1822; " Aug. 3, 1836, ag. 13 y. 8 m. 7 d.
576.	XI.	RIAL[7]	"	

Otis Tower[6] died in Hanover, N. Y., Aug. 16, 1854, ag. 74 y.
8 m. 13 d.
Sarah (Edmonds) Tower died in Hanover, N. Y., Nov. 22,
1859, ag. 77 y. 1 m. 21 d.

246. Seventh Generation. **Tower.**

108. THOMAS[6], NATHANIEL[5], JOSEPH[4], BENJAMIN[3], JOHN[2], JOHN[1].
Thomas[6], son of Nathaniel[5] and Lucy (Tingley) Tower, b.
May 12, 1784; mar. Polly McCoy in Clarendon, Vt.,
Aug. 29, 1802. She was b. in Lewis, N. Y.,
May 6, 1780.

Childr.

577.	I.	CHARLOTTE[7]	born	Feb. 15, 1803.
578.	II.	DAVID[7]	"	July 31, 1804.
579.	III.	CYNTHIA[7]	"	March 26, 1806.
580.	IV.	ELECTA[7]	"	Dec. 8, 1807.
	V.	THOMAS[7]	"	Feb. 10, 1810; died , 1822, ag. 12 years.
581.	VI.	LYMAN[7]	"	Jan. 4, 1812.
	VII.	MARY[7]	"	Feb. 27, 1814; mar. Philip Worcester, of Kankakee, Ill., *s. p.* She died in Ill.
566.	VIII.	EMELINE[7]	"	Feb. 13, 1816.
582.	IX.	LAURA[7]	"	June 13, 1818.
583.	X.	BRADLEY CHAPMAN[7]	"	Oct. 2, 1820.

Thomas Tower[6] died in Ira, Vt., July 14, 1863, ag. 79 y.
2 m. 2 d.
Polly (McCoy) Tower died in Ira, Vt., Nov. 30, 1872, ag. 92 y.
6 m. 24 d.

247. Brown.   Seventh Generation.   Tower.

108. LUCY[6], NATHANIEL[5], JOSEPH[4], BENJAMIN[3], JOHN[2], JOHN[1].
Lucy[6], dau. of Nathaniel[5] and Lucy (Tingley) Tower, b.
Aug. 24, 1786; mar. Marshal Brown in Lewis, N. Y.,
Oct. 17, 1808. He was b.
        , 1782.

Childr.

I.	GEORGE DOUGHARTHY[7] born	, 1806.	
II.	SIDNEY[7]	" Sept. 10, 1809, in Brookfield, N. Y.	
III.	PAMELIA[7]	" Jan. 20, 1812, " " ; died Oct. , 1813, ag. 1 y. 9 m.	
IV.	FIDELIA C.[7]	" Feb. 26, 1815, in Hanover, N. Y.	
V.	ASENATH B.[7]	" Jan. 20, 1817, " "	
VI.	LUCY ADELINE[7]	" May 10, 1818, " "	
VII.	CLARISSA[7]	" July 10, 1820, " " ; died Jan. 13, 1822, ag. 1 y. 6 m. 3 d.	
VIII.	MARIA[7]	" Nov. 17, 1827.	
IX.	MARSHAL[7]	" Jan. 5, 1830.	

Marshal Brown died in Hanover, N. Y., Feb. 17, 1846, ag. 74.
Lucy (Tower) Brown died in Hanover, N. Y., Sept. 26, 1883,
ag. 97 y. 1 m. 2 d.

248. { Rich, Whiteman, Otis, Darling. } Seventh Generation.   Tower.

108. CHARLOTTE[6], NATHANIEL[5], JOSEPH[4], BENJAMIN[3], JOHN[2],
JOHN[1].
Charlotte[6], dau. of Nathaniel[5] and Lucy (Tingley) Tower, b.
Jan. 20, 1791; mar. Elijah Darling in Lewis, N. Y.,
Oct. 17, 1808. He was son of Jacob and Sarah (Cutler)
Darling.

Childr.

I.	ALFRED W.[7] born Oct. 6, 1810, in Jay, N. Y.	
II.	MELISSA[7]	" March 29, 1814; died July 28, 1815, ag. 1 y. 3 m. 30 d.

Elijah Darling died in Kentucky Sept. 24, 1814.
Charlotte (Tower) Darling mar., 2d, William Otis
Dec. 17, 1817. He was b.
Dec. 3, 1786, and was son of James and Isabella (Moore) Otis.

Child.

III. ISABELLA M.[7] born Oct. 3, 1818, in Hanover, N. Y.

William Otis died in Manchester, Ind., June 17, 1821.
Charlotte (Tower) (Darling) Otis mar., 3d, Titus Whiteman
Aug. 22, 1822.   He was son of Titus and —— (Vaughn)
Whiteman.

Childr. none.

Titus Whiteman died in Manchester, Ind., June 24, 1823.
Charlotte (Tower) (Darling) (Otis) Whiteman mar., 4th,
Elijah Rich
April 4, 1824.   He was b. in Taunton, Mass.,
Jan. 29, 1792, and was son of Elijah and Sarah (Spaulding)
Rich.

Childr.

IV. LUCY T. T.[7] born Jan. 24, 1825.
V. NANCY[7] " Feb. 25, 1829.
VI. CELESTIA[7] " ; mar. Herman Helmuth.

Elijah Rich died in Bloomington, Minn., April 16, 1862,
ag. 70 y. 2 m. 18 d.
Charlotte (Tower) (Darling) (Otis) (Whiteman) Rich died
April 29, 1875, ag. 84 y. 3 m. 9 d.

---

249.   Seventh Generation.   **Tower.**

108. WELCOME[6], NATHANIEL[5], JOSEPH[4], BENJAMIN[3], JOHN[2], JOHN[1].
Welcome[6], son of Nathaniel[5] and Lucy (Tingley) Tower, b.
April 23, 1793; mar. Betsey Rowe in Tinmouth, Vt.,
Oct. 2, 1814.   She was b.
Aug. , 1789.

Childr.

584. I. FRANKLIN[7] born July 26, 1815.
585. II. MELISSA[7] " May 7, 1819.
586. III. WILLIAM OTIS[7] " June 30, 1823.
587. IV. ROLLIN C.[7] " June 7, 1828.

Welcome Tower[6] died in Middleton, Vt., May 9, 1830,
ag. 37 y. 16 d.
Betsey (Rowe) Tower died in Benson, Vt., July 27, 1834,
ag. 44 y. 11 m.

250.   Seventh Generation.   Tower.

108. CEPHAS [6], NATHANIEL [5], JOSEPH [4], BENJAMIN [3], JOHN [2], JOHN [1].
Cephas [6], son of Nathaniel [5] and Lucy (Tingley) Tower, b.
Sept. 2, 1797 ; mar. Sophia Comstock in Hanover, N. Y.
                              She was b.
March 3, 1792.
                         Childr.
        588.   I. MARYETTE D. [7] born Dec. 3, 1818.
        589.   II. NATHANIEL F. [7] " Feb. 10, 1821.

Cephas Tower [6] died in Manchester, Ind., June 17, 1827,
ag. 29 y. 9 m. 15 d.
Sophia (Comstock) Tower mar., 2d, John L. Mason
Aug. 10, 1837, and died in Milan, Ind., Dec.   , 1843,
ag. 51 y. 9 m.

251.   Seventh Generation.   Tower.

108. RIAL [6], NATHANIEL [5], JOSEPH [4], BENJAMIN [3], JOHN [2], JOHN [1].
Rial [6], son of Nathaniel [5] and Lucy (Tingley) Tower, b.
Oct. 29, 1799 ; mar. Betsey Pierce Car in Clarendon, Vt.,
Jan. 30, 1823. She was b.
Oct.   , 1802.
                         Childr.
590.   I.   SALLY ELIZABETH [7]   born Oct. 28, 1823, in Harford, Pa.
591.   II. POLLY MARIA [7]   " Nov. 16, 1825.
592.   III. EMILY FULLER [7]   " Sept. 9, 1827.
593.   IV. WARNER CAR [7]   " Sept. 17, 1829.
594.   V.   DIANTHA E. [7]   " Dec. 10, 1831.
595.   VI. PURRINGTON RIAL [7]   " March 22, 1834.
596.   VII. WILLIAM NATHANIEL [7]   " Oct. 24, 1836.
597.   VIII. LUCY ZERUAH [7]   " April 8, 1839.
        IX. PHILENA MELINA [7]   "   ; died in infancy.
598.   X.   CHARLES MILLER [7]   " June 19, 1844.

Rial Tower [6] died July 29, 1878, ag. 78 y. 9 m.
Betsey P. (Car) Tower died March 2, 1875, ag. 72 y. 5 m.

252. Pope.   Seventh Generation.   Tower.

109. ELIZABETH [6], JAMES [5], JOHN [4], JOSEPH [3], JOHN [2], JOHN [1].
Elizabeth [6], dau. of James [5] and Elizabeth (Whitmarsh)
    Tower, b.
March 5, 1775 ; mar. Joseph Pope, of Stoughton, Mass.,
Dec. 3, 1796, by Rev. T. Harris, of Dorchester.

Childr.

I. NANCY[7]   mar.   Bisbee, of Stoughton.
II. JOSEPH[7]

---

253.   Seventh Generation.   Tower.

109. JAMES[6], JAMES[5], JOHN[4], JOSEPH[3], JOHN[2], JOHN[1].
James[6], son of James[5] and Elizabeth (Whitmarsh) Tower, b.
March 4, 1777; mar. Elizabeth Thayer, of Randolph,
Nov. 23, 1799.
James Tower[6] died   1800, ag. 23.

---

254.   Seventh Generation.   Tower.

109. JOHN[6], JAMES[5], JOHN[4], JOSEPH[3], JOHN[2], JOHN[1].
John[6], son of James[5] and Elizabeth (Whitmarsh) Tower, b.
April 20, 1779; mar. Betsey Parker, of Newburyport, Mass.
     She was b.
         1783, and was dau of Silas and Elizabeth (   )
Parker.

Childr.

I. JOHN[7]   born   1813; unm.; died June 10, 1867, ag. 54.
II. ELIZABETH A.[7]   "   1821; mar. John L. Varina, of New-
                           buryport, Mass., June 8, 1853.
599. III. CHARLES[7]   "

Betsey (Parker) Tower died Jan. 9, 1865, ag. 82.

---

255. Upham, Bussey.   Seventh Generation.   Tower.

109. MARY[6], JAMES[5], JOHN[4], JOSEPH[3], JOHN[2], JOHN[1].
Mary[6], dau. of James[5] and Elizabeth (Whitmarsh) Tower, b.
Dec. 30, 1787; mar. William Bussey; 2d, Joel Upham, of
Canton, Mass.
Mary (Tower) (Bussey) Upham died Feb. 1, 1878, ag. 90 y.
1 m. 2 d.

---

256.   Seventh Generation.   Tower.

109. BENJAMIN[6], JAMES[5], JOHN[4], JOSEPH[3], JOHN[2], JOHN[1].
Benjamin[6], son of James[5] and Elizabeth (Whitmarsh)
Tower, b.

May 9, 1792; mar. Alice Baker Hunter, of Enfield, Mass.,
May 25, 1824. She was b.
Feb. 13, 1803, and was dau. of Isaac Cowan and Alice Wilson Hunter.
They adopted a daughter, and gave her the name of

Mary A. Tower born   1834; died, unmar., Nov. 17, 1866, ag. 32.

Benjamin Tower[6] died in Boston, Feb. 16, 1876, ag. 83 y.
9 m. 7 d.
Alice B. (Hunter) Tower died in Somerville, Mass., July 4,
1881, ag. 78 y. 4 m. 21 d.

257.   **Seventh Generation.**   **Tower.**

109. EBENEZER[6], JAMES[5], JOHN[4], JOSEPH[3], JOHN[2], JOHN[1].
Ebenezer[6], son of James[5] and Elizabeth (Whitmarsh)
Tower, b.
Jan. 26, 1795; mar. Roxana Blackman, of Canton, Mass.,
Dec. 5, 1822. She was b.
July 2, 1798, and was dau of Samuel and Abigail (Wentworth) Blackman.

Childr.

I.   JULIA B.[7] born Jan. 15, 1824; died May 15, 1826, ag. 2 y. 4 m.
II. LUCIUS[7]   "   Jan. 23, 1827.
III. CLARIS[7]   "   ;   "
IV. JULIA B.[7]   "   Oct. 26, 1830;   "   Jan. 26, 1832, ag. 1 y. 3 m.
600. V. ANNIE E.[7]   "   Oct. 20, 1836.

Ebenezer Tower[6] died in Worcester, Mass., July 30, 1845,
ag. 50 y. 6 m. 4 d.
Roxana (Blackman) Tower d. in Canton, Mass., Aug. 26,
1869, ag. 71 y. 1 m. 24 d.

258. Orcutt.   **Seventh Generation.**   **Tower.**

110. MEHITABLE[6], JOHN[5], JOHN[4], JOSEPH[3], JOHN[2], JOHN[1].
Mehitable[6], dau. of John[5] and Mehitable (Thayer) Tower, b.
Dec. 28, 1779; mar. Benjamin Orcutt, of Weymouth,
Oct. 30, 1806. He was b. in Weymouth
Jan. 20, 1783, and was son of Moses and Silence (Kingman) Orcutt.

Childr.

600 *a*
I. JAMES TOWER [7] born   **1798.**
II. MEHITABLE [7]   "   May 7, 1807.
III. BENJAMIN [7]   "   July 4, 1808.
IV. LUCY [7]   "   Jan. 5, 1810.
V. MARY ANN [7]   "   Jan. 11, 1812.
VI. WASHINGTON [7]   "   Aug. 26, 1814.
VII. CHARLOTTE [7]   "   March 18, 1818.

Mehitable (Tower) Orcutt died in Abington, Jan. 17, 1873, ag. 93 y. 20 d.

---

259. Willis. Seventh Generation. Tower.

110. CHARLOTTE [6], JOHN [5], JOHN [4], JOSEPH [3], JOHN [2], JOHN [1].
Charlotte [6], dau. of John [5] and Mehitable (Thayer) Tower, b.
         ; mar. Ephraim Willis, of Bridgewater, Mass.
Int. pub.
     1811.

Childr.

I. EDWIN [7]   born
II. GEORGE W. [7]   "   April 15, 1814.
III. JAMES M. [7]   "
IV. FRANCES L. [7]   "   ; mar. James Capen 2d.   Int. pub.
                               Oct. 21, 1843.

---

260. Seventh Generation. Tower.

110. JOHN [6], JOHN [5], JOHN [4], JOSEPH [3], JOHN [2], JOHN [1].
John [6], son of John [5] and Mehitable (Thayer) Tower, b.
         ; mar. widow Mary (Bates) Thompson, of
Bridgewater, Mass. Int. pub.
April 12, 1816. She was b.
Nov. 12, 1788.

Child.

I. MARY [7] born   ; mar. Austin Wales, of Abington, Mass. Int.
                    pub. July 27, 1838.

John Tower [6] died
Mary (Bates) Tower died in Weymouth, June 12, 1855, ag.
66 y. 7 m.

261.   Seventh Generation.   Tower.

110. ALEXANDER[6], JOHN[5], JOHN[4], JOSEPH[3], JOHN[2], JOHN[1].
Alexander[6], son of John[5] and Mehitable (Thayer) Tower, b.
April 3, 1788; mar. Celia Pratt in Weymouth
May 11, 1808. She was b.
June 29, 1787, and was dau. of Joseph and Mercy (Shaw)
Pratt.

Childr. born in Braintree, Mass.

601.   I. ISAAC P.[7]   born Jan. 25, 1809.
602.   II. MARY[7]   " June 17, 1811.
603.   III. EMELINE K.[7] " Feb. 13, 1813.
604.   IV. LUCY A.[7]   " March 27, 1816.
605.   V. SELAH[7]   " March 23, 1819.
       VI. ALEXANDER[7]   " Oct. 22, 1822; died about   1839.

Alexander Tower[6] died in Braintree, Dec. 1, 1839, ag. 51 y.
7 m. 28 d.
Celia (Pratt) Tower died in Braintree, June 10, 1847, ag.
59 y. 11 m. 12 d.

262. Thomas, Ager.   Seventh Generation.   Tower.

110. ZERVIAH[6], JOHN[5], JOHN[4], JOSEPH[3], JOHN[2], JOHN[1].
Zerviah[6], dau. of John[5] and Mehitable (Thayer) Tower, b.
                    ; mar. Jonathan Ager, of Weymouth, Mass.
Int. pub.
Oct. 23, 1807.   He was b.
May 23, 1788.

Childr.

I. CHARLES[7]   born March 11, 1810.
II. RELIEF[7] } Twins " March 27, 1812.
III. CHARLOTTE[7] }
IV. SARAH[7]   " May 20, 1814.

Jonathan Ager died   1842.
Zerviah (Tower) Ager mar., 2d, Andrew Thomas, of Wey-
mouth.
Andrew Thomas died in Weymouth   1857.

263.   Seventh Generation.   Tower.

112. JOHN[6], GIDEON[5], GIDEON[4], JOSEPH[3], JOHN[2], JOHN[1].
John[6], son of Gideon[5] and Elizabeth (Cox) Tower, b.

March 21, 1778; mar. Polly Holbrook.
She was b.
March 23, 1779, and was dau. of Nehemiah and Elizabeth (Hobart) Holbrook.

Childr. born in Braintree, Mass.

I. MARY[7] born Sept. 28, 1800; mar. Hervey Drake. She died in New York city, 1839.

606. II. JULIA[7] " July 18, 1802.
607. III. JOHN[7] " June 27, 1804.

Polly (Holbrook) Tower died in Braintree, Jan. 10, 1861, ag. 81 y. 9 m. 18 d.

---

264. Stetson. Seventh Generation. Tower.

112. MARY[6], GIDEON[5], GIDEON[4], JOSEPH[3], JOHN[2], JOHN[1].
Mary[6], dau. of Gideon[5] and Elizabeth (Cox) Tower, b. July 4, 1782; mar. Josiah Stetson.

Childr.

I.	MARY[7].	VIII.	AMASA[7].
II.	SARAH[7].	IX.	BENJAMIN[7].
III.	JOSIAH[7].	X.	DANIEL[7].
IV.	ISANNA[7].	XI.	Child.
V.	ELIZABETH[7].	XII.	"
VI.	JULIA ANN[7].	XIII.	"
VII.	HARRIET[7].		

---

265. Dickey. Seventh Generation. Tower.

112. SALLY[6], GIDEON[5], GIDEON[4], JOSEPH[3], JOHN[2], JOHN[1].
Sally[6], dau. of Gideon[5] and Elizabeth (Cox) Tower, b. Feb. 2, 1785; mar. William Dickey, of Lincolnville, Me.

Childr.

I. MADISON[7].   II. LOUISA[7].   III. ELBRIDGE[7].

---

266. George. Seventh Generation. Tower.

112. LYDIA[6], GIDEON[5], GIDEON[4], JOSEPH[3], JOHN[2], JOHN[1].
Lydia[6], dau. of Gideon[5] and Elizabeth (Cox) Tower, b. July 26, 1787; mar. William George in Boston July 31, 1810, by Rev. Charles Lowell. W. George b. in Haverhill, Mass., July 6, 1776, and was son of Timothy and Sarah (Emerson) George.

Childr.

I. ELIZABETH E.[7] born Aug. 14, 1811, in Medford, Mass.
II. SARAH A.[7] " Oct. 25, 1814, " Randolph, "
III. CHARLOTTE [7] " Jan. 31, 1817, " Boston, "
IV. WILLIAM W.[7] " Sept. 25, 1821, " Randolph, " , unmar., 1880.
V. LYDIA [7] " Jan. 13, 1824, " " "

William George died in Stoughton, Sept. 8, 1852, ag. 76 y.
1 m. 18 d.
Lydia (Tower) George died in Stoughton, Aug. 24, 1872,
ag. 85 y. 29 d.

267. **Seventh Generation.** **Tower.**

112. GIDEON [6], GIDEON [5], GIDEON [4], JOSEPH [3], JOHN [2], JOHN [1].
Gideon [6], son of Gideon [5] and Elizabeth (Cox) Tower, b.
Jan. 14, 1790; mar. Fanny .
Gideon Tower [6] died in Lincolnville, Me., Oct. 29, 1864,
ag. 74 y. 9 m. 15 d.

268. Carter. **Seventh Generation.** **Tower.**

112. RUTH [6], GIDEON [5], GIDEON [4], JOSEPH [3] JOHN [2], JOHN [1].
Ruth [6], dau. of Gideon [5] and Elizabeth (Cox) Tower, b.
April 17, 1792; mar. John Carter in Randolph, Mass.,
Jan. 1, 1815. He was b. in Stockport, Chester Co., England,
Aug. 18, 1785.

Childr.

I. ANN [7] born Jan. 3, 1816.
II. GEORGE TOMILSON [7] " March 5, 1819.
III. ELIZABETH RYDER [7] " July 16, 1825.
IV. THOMAS [7] " Jan. 29, 1828; died April 19, 1842, ag. 14 y.
2 m. 21 d.
V. JOHN [7] " Oct. 26, 1830; " Feb. 27, 1854, " 23 y.
4 m. 4 d.
VI. WILLIAM HENRY [7] " May 20, 1833.

John Carter died Sept. 13, 1877, ag. 92 y. 26 d.
Ruth (Tower) Carter died Feb. 14, 1872, ag. 79 y. 9 m. 28 d.

269. White. **Seventh Generation.** **Tower.**

112. CHARLOTTE [6], GIDEON [5], GIDEON [4], JOSEPH [3], JOHN [2], JOHN [1].
Charlotte [6], dau. of Gideon [5] and Elizabeth (Cox) Tower, b.
May 9, 1794; mar. Azel White in Dorchester, Mass.,
Dec. 3, 1818, by Rev. T. Harris.

Childr.

I. JAMES MUNROE [7] born Jan. , 1820.	VI. ELIZABETH [7].
II. MATILDA [7].	VII. CHARLOTTE [7].
III. MARIA [7].	VIII. VESTA [7].
IV. ISANNA [7].	IX. GEORGIANNA [7].
V. MARY JANE [7].	

270.   **Seventh Generation.**   **Tower.**

112. JOSEPH [6], GIDEON [5], GIDEON [4], JOSEPH [3], JOHN [2], JOHN [1].
Joseph [6], son of Gideon [5] and Elizabeth (Cox) Tower, b.
April 27, 1796 ; mar. Polly Hayden.

Childr.

608.	I. GEORGE [7].	III.	MADISON [7].
	II. FANNY [7].	IV.	MARY [7].

Joseph Tower [6] died in Maine.
Polly (Hayden) Tower died in Maine.

271. Wales.   **Seventh Generation.**   **Tower.**

112. FANNY [6], GIDEON [5], GIDEON [4], JOSEPH [3], JOHN [2], JOHN [1].
Fanny [6], dau. of Gideon [5] and Elizabeth (Cox) Tower, b.
Jan. 23, 1798; mar. John Wales, of Stoughton, Mass.

Child.

Daughter born   ; mar. Samuel W. Hodges.

272.   **Seventh Generation.**   **Tower.**

112. WASHINGTON [6], GIDEON [5], GIDEON [4], JOSEPH [3], JOHN [2], JOHN [1].
Washington [6], son of Gideon [5] and Elizabeth (Cox) Tower, b.
June 20, 1800 ; mar. Rebecca Thayer French, of Milton,
Nov. 14, 1821, by Rev. Mr. Gill. She was b.
Nov. 14, 1801, and was dau. of Alexander and Charlotte
(Clark) French.

Childr.

609.	I. ELIZA ANN [7]	born Oct. 16, 1822.
610.	II. WASHINGTON [7]	" Dec. 13, 1824.
611.	III. IRA F. [7]	" Oct. 2, 1826.
612.	IV. FRANCIS W. D. [7]	" Jan. 19, 1828.
	V. EDWIN [7]	" Dec. 25, 1830; died Feb. 20, 1831.
613.	VI. GEORGE EDWIN [7]	" March 16, 1832.
	VII. JAMES [7]	" June 21, 1834; died Feb. 7, 1843, ag. 8 y. 7 m. 16 d.
614.	VIII. REBECCA FRENCH [7]	" July 6, 1836.
615.	IX. MARY ELIZABETH [7]	" Aug. 3, 1840.
	X. JAMES ELMER [7]	" Oct. 22, 1844; died Jan. 20, 1846, ag. 1 y. 2 m. 29 d.

Washington Tower[6] died in Stoughton, March 4, 1873, ag. 72 y. 8 m. 13 d.

Rebecca T. (French) Tower died in Stoughton, May 27, 1855, ag. 53 y. 6 m. 13 d.

273. Howard, Baldwin, Shattuck. Seventh Generation. Tower.

116. EUNICE[6], BENJAMIN[5], GIDEON[4], JOSEPH[3], JOHN[2], JOHN[1].
Eunice[6], dau. of Benjamin[5] and Eunice (Liskum)Tower, b. March 31, 1786; mar. Gideon Shattuck, of Hinsdale, N. H., April 8, 1804, by S. Hooker, J. P.

Childr.

I.	SAMUEL[7]	born March 20, 1805.
II.	ASA[7]	" April 28, 1806.
III.	GIDEON[7]	" Nov. 5, 1808.
IV.	EUNICE M.[7]	" June 28, 1810.
V.	MARTHA[7]	" June 14, 1812.
VI.	BENJAMIN[7]	"
VII.	MARY E.[7]	"

Gideon Shattuck died June 9, 1818, and Eunice (Tower) Shattuck mar., 2d,   Baldwin; and 3d,   Howard.

Childr.

VIII.	ABIAH[7]	born	; died young.
IX.	EDMUND[7]	"	May 15, 1823.
X.	EDNA[7]	"	June 10, 1824.
XI.	DOLLY[7]	"	Sept. 25, 1825.
XII.	HORACE[7]	"	
XIII.	FOSTER[7]	"	1828.
XIV.	PHILENA[7]	"	Feb. 5, 1829.

Eunice (Tower) (Shattuck) (Baldwin) Howard died in Lansing, Mich.,   1873, ag. 87.

274. Cutler, Butler. Seventh Generation.   Tower.

116. FANNY[6], BENJAMIN[5], GIDEON[4], JOSEPH[3], JOHN[2], JOHN[1].
Fanny[6], dau. of Benjamin[5] and Eunice (Liskum) Tower, b.   1788; mar. Josiah Butler, of Hempstead, Vt., March 26, 1807, by Seth Hooker, J. P.

Childr.

I.	Daughter	; died young.
II.	CHARLES[7]	
III.	ELMIRA[7]	} Twins, born Oct. 8, 1811.
IV.	ELVIRA[7]	
V.	MARY[7]	"
VI.	BELINDA[7]	" Aug. 19, 1817.

Josiah Butler died, and Fanny (Tower) Butler mar., 2d, Jonathan Cutler, of Brookline, Vt.,
  , 1821.

Childr.

VII.	LAURINDA[7] born	; mar.	White, of Waterbury, Conn.
VIII.	CALISTA[7] "		
IX.	FANNY[7] "	; mar.	Joseph Bennet, of Thompsonville, Conn.

Fanny (Tower) (Butler) Cutler died 1859, ag. 71.

---

275. Fitch. **Seventh Generation.** **Tower.**

116. LYDIA[6], BENJAMIN[5], GIDEON[4], JOSEPH[3], JOHN[2], JOHN[1].
Lydia[6], dau. of Benjamin[5] and Eunice (Liskum) Tower, b.
 ; mar. John Fitch, of Keene, N. H.

Child.

| I. | MARY ANN[7] | ; mar. | Miller, of Keene, N. H. |

---

276. Thomas. **Seventh Generation.** **Tower.**

116. POLLY[6], BENJAMIN[5], GIDEON[4], JOSEPH[3], JOHN[2], JOHN[1].
Polly[6], dau. of Benjamin[5] and Eunice (Liskum) Tower, b.
 ; mar. John Thomas, of Halifax, Vt.

Childr.

| I. | ALBERT[7]. | III. | MERIAM[7]. |
| II. | ELBRIDGE[7]. | IV. | POLLY[7]. |

---

277. Cole. **Seventh Generation.** **Tower.**

116. CYNTHIA[6], BENJAMIN[5], GIDEON[4], JOSEPH[3], JOHN[2], JOHN[1].
Cynthia[6], dau. of Benjamin[5] and Eunice (Liskum) Tower, b.
 ; mar. Cole, of New Jersey.

Childr.

| I. | CYNTHIA[7] | ; mar. | Conant, of New York. |
| II. | PAMELIA[7] | ; " | Willis, of Ellisburg, N. Y. |

---

278. Newcomb. **Seventh Generation.** **Tower.**

116. ROXANNA[6], BENJAMIN[5], GIDEON[4], JOSEPH[3], JOHN[2], JOHN[1].
Roxanna[6], dau. of Benjamin[5] and Eunice(Liskum)Tower, b.
 ; mar. Hartwell Newcomb, of Bernardston, Mass.

s. p.

Hartwell Newcomb died in Bernardston, Mass.,   1860 ?
Roxanna (Tower) Newcomb died in Northfield, Mass.,
1867 ?

279. Howard, Masters. Seventh Generation.   Tower.

116. SARAH [6], BENJAMIN [5], GIDEON [4], JOSEPH [3], JOHN [2], JOHN [1].
Sarah [6], dau. of Benjamin [5] and Eunice (Liskum) Tower, b.
; mar. James Masters, of Putney, Vt.
March 9, 1818, by Rev. Elisha Andrews. J. Masters b. in
Middletown, Ct.

Childr.

I. MERRILL [7]   ; mar. and died in Winchester, N. H., 1844?
II. HENRY HOWARD [7].
III. HARRIET [7].   VI. HORACE [7].
IV. MARY [7].   VII. LYDIA [7].
V. BENJAMIN [7].   VIII. GEORGE [7].

James Masters died, and Sarah (Tower) Masters mar., 2d,
Jotham Howard.

280. Taylor, Barrett. Seventh Generation.   Tower.

116. BETSEY [6], BENJAMIN [5], GIDEON [4], JOSEPH [3], JOHN [2], JOHN [1].
Betsey [6], dau. of Benjamin [5] and Eunice (Liskum) Tower, b.
; mar. Elisha Barrett, of Hinsdale, N. H.

Childr.

I. BAXTER [7]
II. WILLIAM [7]
III. ALEXANDER [7]
IV. JOSEPH [7]   ; unmar.; died
V. ELIZABETH [7]   ; mar. William Welsh, of Hinsdale, N. H.
VI. JONATHAN [7]
VII. LYDIA [7]   ; unmar.

Elisha Barrett died, and Betsey (Tower) Barrett mar.,
2d, Ezra Taylor, of Winchendon, Mass. She died in
Winchendon.

281. Millings. Seventh Generation.   Tower.

116. ABIGAIL [6], BENJAMIN [5], GIDEON [4], JOSEPH [3], JOHN [2], JOHN [1].
Abigail [6], dau. of Benjamin [5] and Eunice (Liskum) Tower, b.
; mar. Emory Millings, of Ellisburg, N. Y.

Childr.

I. EMORY [7].   II. MARY JANE [7].

282. Seventh Generation. Tower.

116. BENJAMIN [6], BENJAMIN [5], GIDEON [4], JOSEPH [3], JOHN [2], JOHN [1].
Benjamin [6], son of Benjamin [5] and Eunice (Liskum) Tower, b.
     ; mar. Martha Elmore. She was dau. of Elijah
and Patty (Orvis) Elmore.

Childr.

I.	EMELINE [7]	; mar. Howe.	III.	MARIETTA [7]
II.	MARTHA [7]	; "	IV.	BENJAMIN F.[7]

Benjamin Tower [6] died   1853 (?), in Winchester, N. H.
Martha (Elmore) Tower mar., 2d,   Whitney, of Warwick,
Mass.

283. Battles, Barrett. Seventh Generation. Tower.

116. MERIAM [6], BENJAMIN [5], GIDEON [4], JOSEPH [3], JOHN [2], JOHN [1].
Meriam [6], dau. of Benjamin [5] and Eunice (Liskum) Tower, b.
Sept. 23, 1808; mar. Gardner Barrett, of Hinsdale, N. H.
     Int. pub.
March 26, 1827. He was b.
May   , 1801.

Childr.

I.	MARY JANE [7]	born Dec. 28, 1828.
II.	LUCRETIA [7]	" Dec. 28, 1831; died Dec. 1839, aged 8 years.
III.	ALMIRA [7]	" Aug. 13, 1841.
IV.	CHARLES RODNEY [7]	" June 18, 1843.
V.	WILLIAM WILSON [7]	" March 11, 1845; unmar.

Gardner Barrett died May 4, 1857, ag. 56.
Meriam (Tower) Barrett mar., 2d, Ichabod Dexter Battles,
     of Northfield, Mass., Dec. 29, 1861. He was b.
March 5, 1801.

284. Thomas. Seventh Generation. Tower.

116. LUCRETIA [6], BENJAMIN [5], GIDEON [4], JOSEPH [3], JOHN [2], JOHN [1].
Lucretia [6], dau. of Benjamin [5] and Eunice (Liskum) Tower, b.
Jan. 4, 1812; mar. Nathan Thomas, of Hinsdale, N. H.,
     He was b.
Dec. 21, 1812, and was son of Charles and Sarah (Barrett)
     Thomas.

Childr.

I.	MERIAM[7]	; mar. Maynard, of Winchendon, Mass.
II.	CHARLES N.[7]	; " ; resides in Leominster, Mass.
III.	HENRY[7]	; resides in Springfield, Mass.
IV.	ABIGAIL[7]	; mar. Cutting, of Lowell, Mass.
V.	JEROME[7]	; resides in Keene, N. H.

Lucretia (Tower) Thomas died in Keene, N. H., Aug. 15, 1877, ag. 65 y. 7 m. 11 d.

285.   **Seventh Generation.**   **Tower.**

118. ORRAMELL[6], ISAAC[5], JOSEPH[4], JOSEPH[3], JOHN[2], JOHN[1].
Orramell[6], son of Isaac[5] and Mary (Thayer) Tower, b.
March 8, 1799; mar. Phebe Thayer, of Randolph, Mass.,
Sept. 17, 1820. She was b.
July 13, 1800, and was dau. of Micah and Phebe (Stetson)
 Thayer.

Child.

616.   I. ELIZA ANN[7] born Aug. 9, 1821.

Phebe (Thayer) Tower died Jan.   , 1834, ag. 33 y. 6 m.
Orramell Tower[6] mar., 2d, Sarah A. Doran in Baltimore, Md.,
April 14, 1836. She was b. in Newark, Del.,
Sept. 30, 1806.

Childr.

617.   II. GEORGIANA[7] born Jan. 15, 1837, in Baltimore.
618.   III. DANIEL W.[7] " Jan. 26, 1841, in Farmington, Iowa.

Sarah (Doran) Tower died in Ottumwa, Iowa, April 24, 1879,
 ag. 72 y. 6 m. 24 d.
Orramell Tower[6] lives in Ottumwa (1883).

286.   **Seventh Generation.**   **Tower.**

118. ISAAC[6], ISAAC[5], JOSEPH[4], JOSEPH[3], JOHN[2], JOHN[1].
Isaac[6], son of Isaac[5] and Mary (Thayer) Tower, b.
Aug. 22, 1801; mar. Minora A. Bracket, of Braintree, Vt.,
 She was b.
Sept. 16, 1806, and was dau. of Henry and Elephol (Bur-
 gess) Bracket.

Childr.

619.	I.	ISAAC H.[7]	born	1829.
620.	II.	MINORA E.[7]	"	1830.
621.	III.	JAMES A.[7]	"	1833.

IV. ELEPHOL O.[7] born   1838; mar. Stillman Mann, of Empire City, Oregon.

622.   V. MORTON [7]   "   1840.

VI. CHARLES W.[7]   "   1842.

623.   VII. MARY EMMA [7]   "   1847.

Isaac Tower[6] died in Randolph, Mass., March 18, 1865, ag. 63 y. 6 m. 24 d.

Minora A. (Bracket) Tower died in Randolph, Mass., July 24, 1865, ag. 58 y. 10 m. 8 d.

287.   Alden.   Seventh Generation.   Tower.

118. MARY [6], ISAAC [5], JOSEPH [4], JOSEPH [3], JOHN [2], JOHN [1].

Mary [6], daughter of Isaac [5] and Mary (Thayer) Tower, b. Nov. 23, 1803 ; mar. Hiram Alden Feb. 26, 1824, by Rev. Benjamin Putnam. H. Alden b. Nov. 14, 1804, and was son of Simeon and Rachel (French) Alden.

Childr. born in Randolph, Mass.

I.   JULIA ANN [7]   born July 14, 1824.

II.   HIRAM CARROLL [7]   "   July 21, 1826.

III.   CHARLOTTE AUGUSTA [7]   "   March 13, 1829.

IV.   MARGARET [7]   "   Aug. 18, 1831.

V.   CAROLINE FRANCIS [7]   "   June 5, 1834; died Feb. 23, 1856, ag. 21 y. 8 m. 18 d.

VI.   MARY CELESTIA [7]   "   June 29, 1836; " Nov. 21, 1840, ag. 4 y. 4 m. 22 d.

VII.   WILLIAM HART [7]   "   April 26, 1839.

VIII.   CELESTIA JUSTINA [7]   "   Aug. 16, 1842; died May 6, 1843, ag. 8 m. 21 d.

IX.   MARY JUSTINA [7]   "   June 16, 1846.

288.   Seventh Generation.   Tower.

118. BENJAMIN F.[6], ISAAC [5], JOSEPH [4], JOSEPH [3], JOHN [2], JOHN [1].

Benjamin F.[6], son of Isaac [5] and Mary (Thayer) Tower, b. April 24, 1806 ; mar. Esther Hollis, of Randolph, Mass., Dec. 10, 1826. She was b. Dec. 9, 1809, and was dau. of Ebenezer and Ruth (Holbrook) Hollis.

Childr.

I.   MARION [7] born May 9, 1828, in Randolph; died away from home.

624.   II.   ANN [7]   "   Jan. 16, 1831,   "

III.   EVANDER [7]   "   May 9, 1837,   "   " March 1, 1864.

IV.   JULIAN [7]   "   Aug. 21, 1840, in Farmington, Iowa; died June 6, 1856, ag. 15 y. 9 m. 16 d.

Benjamin F. Tower [6] died at sea, Jan. 1, 1862, ag. 55 y. 8 m. 7 d.

289. Orr.   Seventh Generation.   Tower.

118. SALLY [6], ISAAC [5], JOSEPH [4], JOSEPH [3], JOHN [2], JOHN [1].
Sally [6], dau. of Isaac [5] and Mary (Thayer) Tower, b.
Dec. 29, 1807; mar. Mellville Orr, of Brockton, Mass.

Child.

I. LUCIA R. [7] born May 15, 1846; died Feb. 4, 1851, ag. 4 y. 8 m. 20 d.

Sally (Tower) Orr died in Brockton, July 22, 1872, ag. 64 y. 6 m. 24 d.

290. Cushman.   Seventh Generation.   Tower,

118. ELMIRA [6], ISAAC [5], JOSEPH [4], JOSEPH [3], JOHN [2], JOHN [1].
Elmira [6], dau. of Isaac [5] and Mary (Thayer) Tower, b.
July 11, 1810; mar. Winslow B. Cushman in Brockton, Mass.,
Oct. 5, 1828, by Rev. Daniel Huntington. W. B. Cushman, b. in Plympton, Mass.,
May 1, 1805, was son of Jacob and Sylvia (Sampson) Cushman.

Childr.

I.	ANN MATILDA [7]	born July 8, 1829.
II.	MARY ELIZA [7]	" Jan. 2, 1834.
III.	HARRIET ALDRICH [7]	" May 8, 1836.
IV.	ORRAMELL BRADFORD [7]	" Aug. 18, 1837.
V.	WILLIAM HARRISON [7]	" Oct. 4, 1840.
VI.	JULIA MINORA [7]	" Jan. 14, 1843; unmar.
VII.	ELISENA CARLL [7]	" May 24, 1848; died Sept. 4, 1849, ag. 1 y. 3 m. 11 d.

291.   Seventh Generation.   Tower.

118. LUTHER [6], ISAAC [5], JOSEPH [4], JOSEPH [3], JOHN [2], JOHN [1].
Luther [6], son of Isaac [5] and Mary (Thayer) Tower, b.
July 22, 1813; mar. Adah Warren, of Bridgewater, Mass.,
Sept. 8, 1833. She was b.
June 29, 1815, and was dau. of Cyrus and Olive (Bisbee) Warren.

Childr.

625.	I.	SILAS FRANKLIN [7]	born Sept. 3, 1837.
	II.	LUCY JANE [7]	" Sept. 28, 1840; died Jan. 14, 1843, ag. 2 y. 3 m. 17 d.
	III.	ROSA J. [7]	" May 16, 1843.
626.	IV.	L. ADDIE [7]	" Dec. 30, 1845.
627.	V.	GEORGE MARIUS [7]	" June 6, 1848.
	VI.	MARY ELLEN [7]	" Nov. 18, 1851; " Dec. 22, 1854, ag. 3 y. 1 m. 4 d.

| 292. | Seventh Generation. | Tower. |

118. LORENZO [6], ISAAC [5], JOSEPH [4], JOSEPH [3], JOHN [2], JOHN [1].
Lorenzo [6], son of Isaac [5] and Mary (Thayer) Tower, b.
May 14, 1820 ; mar. Hannah L. Perry, of Halifax, Mass.,
Jan. 4, 1844, by Rev. Flavel Shurtleaf. She was b. in
Pembroke, Mass.,
June 7, 1827, and was dau. of C. B. and Sally (Thomas)
Perry.

Childr. born in Halifax.

	I.	MARY ALDEN [7]	born	Sept. 4, 1844; died Sept. 27, 1847, ag. 3 y. 23 d.
628.	II.	L. AUGUSTUS [7]	"	July 11, 1846.
	III.	ABBY FRANCES [7]	"	Aug. 5, 1848; died Dec. 22, 1851, ag. 3 y. 4 m. 17 d.
629.	IV.	HELEN ADELAIDE [7]	"	Nov. 15, 1852.
	V.	CARRIE ALDEN [7]	"	May 9, 1856; died May 17, 1863, ag. 7 y. 8 d.

Lorenzo Tower [6] died in Berwick City, La., May 15, 1863,
ag. 43 y. 1 d.
Hannah L. (Perry) Tower mar., 2d, Josiah Bourne, of
Halifax, May 17, 1865. She died Sept. 3, 1867, ag. 40 y.
2 m. 27 d.

| 293. | Seventh Generation. | Tower. |

120. JOSEPH [6], JOSEPH [5], JOSEPH [4], JOSEPH [3], JOHN [2], JOHN [1].
Joseph [6], son of Joseph [5] and Betsey [6] (Tower) Tower, b.
Aug. 31, 1804 ; mar. Eliza A. Thayer in Randolph
She was b.
Sept. 20, 1806, and was dau. of Shadrach and Hepzibah
(Howard) Thayer.

Childr. born in Randolph, Mass.

	I.	ELIZA ANN [7]	born	Sept. 29, 1828 ; died Oct. 3, 1828.
630.	II.	ABRAHAM W. [7]	"	Sept. 10, 1829.

Eliza A. (Thayer) Tower died Jan. 4, 1830, ag. 23 y. 3 m.
15 d.
Joseph Tower [6] mar., 2d, Fanny Wales Porter, of Stoughton,
Mass.,
Aug. 15, 1832, by Rev. Calvin Hitchcock. She was b.
Oct. 2, 1808, and was dau. of Robert and Elizabeth (Gay)
Porter.

Childr.

	III.	JOSEPH PORTER [7]	born Nov. 17, 1833; died Nov. 25, 1833.
631.	IV.	ELIZA ANN [7]	" March 14, 1835.
	V.	ELLEN FRANCES [7]	" Feb. 22, 1837; unmar.
	VI.	RUTH CARTER [7]	" Oct. 29, 1840; died Oct. 11, 1841.
	VII.	JOSEPH EDWARDS CARTER [7]	" Aug. 3, 1844.

Joseph Tower [6] died in Worcester, Mass., Dec. 20, 1851, ag. 47 y. 3 m. 20 d.

Fanny W. (Porter) Tower died in Natick, Mass., Aug. 13, 1872, ag. 63 y. 10 m. 11 d.

---

294. Niles. **Seventh Generation.** **Tower.**

120. ELIZA [6], JOSEPH [5], JOSEPH [4], JOSEPH [3], JOHN [2], JOHN [1].
Eliza [6], dau. of Joseph [5] and Betsey [6] (Tower) Tower, b.
; mar. Jacob Niles.

Childr.

I.	ELIZA [7]	born	; mar. Prescott, in Maine.
II.	ANN MARIA [7]	"	; " Horatio Thayer, of Randolph, Mass.

---

295. Proud. **Seventh Generation.** **Tower.**

121. LURANA [6], ELISHA [5], ELISHA [4], RICHARD [3], IBROOK [2], JOHN [1].
Lurana [6], dau. of Elisha [5] and Hannah (Rotch) Tower, b.
May 30, 1754; mar. John Proud, of New Bedford, Mass.

Childr. born in New Bedford, except the last.

I.	JOHN G. [7]	born Nov. 26, 1776.
II.	NANCY [7]	"	Sept. 11, 1778; mar. Nathaniel Green Maxwell, of Washington, D. C. Int. pub. Sept. 7, 1811.
III.	LURANA [7]	"	July 14, 1780, unmar.; died May 9, 1814, ag. 33 y. 9 m. 25 d.
IV.	ELIZABETH [7]	"	Sept. 1, 1782, " ; died in Baltimore, July 11, 1808, ag. 25 y. 10 m. 11 d.
V.	REBECCA [7]	"	Aug. 22, 1784, unmar.; died June 12, 1806, ag. 21 y. 9 m. 21 d.
VI.	SARAH [7]	"	Sept. 20, 1786.
VII.	WILLIAM [7]	"	July 14, 1788.
VIII.	HANNAH [7]	"	May 25, 1790.
IX.	JOSEPH [7]	"	Aug. 13, 1792, in Troy, N. Y.

John Proud died in New Bedford, Nov. 28, 1815, ag. 68.

296.   Seventh Generation.   **Tower.**

121. Isaiah [6], Elisha [5], Elisha [4], Richard [3], Ibrook [2], John [1].
Isaiah [6], son of Elisha [5] and Deborah (Aegree) Tower, b.
May 29, 1760; mar. Silvia Tobey in New Bedford, Mass.,
April 22, 1787. She was b. in New Bedford, Mass.,
Sept. 20, 1767, and was dau. of Zacheus Tobey.

     Childr.   The first-named born in New Bedford, and
           all the rest in Duanesburg, N. Y.

632.	I.	Elisha [7]	born May 10, 1788.
633.	II.	Rhuamy [7]	" Sept. 9, 1790.
	III.	Benjamin [7]	" March 22, 1793; died 1805, ag. 22.
634.	IV.	Isaiah [7]	" March 7, 1795.
	V.	Silvanus [7]	" March 12, 1797.
635.	VI.	John Aegree [7]	" Aug. 17, 1799.
636.	VII.	Jeremiah B. [7] } Twins	" Dec. 8, 1801. Deborah died, unmar.,
	VIII.	Deborah [7] }	1822, ag. 21.
637.	IX.	Joseph [7]	" Nov. 16, 1803.
638.	X.	Silvia [7]	" March 7, 1806.
639.	XI.	Stephen G. [7]	" March 8, 1808.
	XII.	Zacheus [7]	" Feb. 7, 1811; unmar.; died in Utica, N. Y.

Isaiah Tower [6] died in Duanesburg, N. Y., Jan. 27, 1846,
     ag. 85 y. 9 m. 28 d.
Silvia (Tobey) Tower died in Rome, N. Y.
She is buried in Duanesburg.

297.   Seventh Generation.   **Tower.**

121. Sylvanus [6], Elisha [5], Elisha [4], Richard [3], Ibrook [2], John [1].
Sylvanus [6], son of Elisha [5] and Deborah (Aegree) Tower, b.
Feb. 18, 1766; mar.

Childr.

640.	I.	Elizabeth [7] born Feb. , 1792.
641.	II.	Daniel [7] " Oct. 22, 1794.

298.   Seventh Generation.   **Tower.**

121. Elisha [6], Elisha [5], Elisha [4], Richard [3], Ibrook [2], John [1].
Elisha [6], son of Elisha [5] and Sarah (Marble) Tower, b.
      ; 1770; mar. Hannah Baxter, of Boston.   Int. pub.
Aug. 5, 1795.

Childr. born in Boston.

642. I.   ELISHA[7] born Jan. 25, 1802.
      II. SARAH[7]   "   ; mar. Samuel Harris, of Boston.
      III. HANNAH[7]   "   ; died, ag. 18.

Elisha Tower[6] died in the service of the country in the War of 1812–15.

299. Morton.   Seventh Generation.   Tower.

125. EUNICE[6], RICHARD[5], JOHN[4], JOHN[3], IBROOK[2], JOHN[1].
      Eunice[6], dau. of Richard[5] and Hannah (Tower) Tower, bapt.
      June 3, 1764; mar. Solomon Morton, of Williamsburg, Mass.
      Int. pub.
      Nov. 17, 1784.

Childr. born in Hatfield or in Whateley, Mass.

I.	SARAH[7]	born Aug. 13, 1785.
II.	Son[7]	" June 8, 1787; died June 8, 1787.
III.	ELECTA[7]	" July 5, 1788.
IV.	SOPHIA[7]	" Aug. 22, 1790.
V.	RICHARD TOWER[7]	" Aug. 1, 1791.
VI.	SOLOMON[7]	" July 11, 1793; died.
VII.	SOLOMON[7]	" June 1, 1794; mar., and removed to Ohio.
VIII.	SUSANNA[7]	" Sept. , 1795.
IX.	THEODOSIA[7]	" May 7, 1798.
X.	DAVID[7]	" July 5, 1801?
XI.	WILLIAM[7]	" Nov. 28, 1803? unmar.; died.
XII.	Son[7]	" Aug. 17, 1807?

Solomon Morton died in Painesville, Ohio.

300.   Seventh Generation.   Tower.

129. CORNELIUS[6], ISAAC[5], CORNELIUS[4], JOHN[3], IBROOK[2], JOHN[1].
      Cornelius[6], son of Isaac[5] and Mary (Sprague) Tower, b.
      June 10, 1772; mar. Abby Potter, of Paris, N. Y.

Childr.

	I.	MARY[7]	; mar. Collins.
	II.	RODNEY[7] born 1795;	" He died in the State of New York.
643.	III.	DANIEL WOODRUFF P.[7] born June 7, 1803.	
	IV.	SPRAGUE[7]	
	V.	LEMUEL[7]	; mar. He lived in Warsaw, N. Y.
	VI.	WILLIAM[7]	; " He was killed at a mill by a log rolling upon him.
	VII.	HENRY[7]	; died ag. 18 years. He was killed by a tree falling upon him.

VIII. MARIA [7]
IX. LAURA [7]   ; mar. She is living in Oakland, Mich., 1883.
X. LYDIA [7]   ; " Henry Hemingway, of Flint Co., Mich.

Cornelius Tower [6] died near Warsaw, N. Y.
Abigail (Potter) Tower died near Warsaw, N. Y.

301.   **Seventh Generation.**   **Tower.**

129. ELKANAH [6], ISAAC [5], CORNELIUS [4], JOHN [3], IBROOK [2], JOHN [1].
Elkanah [6], son of Isaac [5] and Mary (Sprague) Tower, b.
Oct. 17, 1773 ; mar. Elizabeth Frissell, of Woodstock, Conn.,
Jan. 10, 1800. She was b. in Petersham, Mass.,
1777, and was dau. of Joseph and   (Johnson)
Frissell.

Childr.

    I. FRANCES [7] born Jan. 15, 1802; died Aug. 21, 1803, ag. 1 y.
                                        7 m. 6 d.
644.   II. JOSEPH F. [7]   "   Aug. 14, 1805.
645.   III. MARIA [7]   "   March 3, 1807.

Elizabeth (Frissell) Tower died March 10, 1811, ag. 34.
Elkanah Tower [6] mar., 2d, Elizabeth Stone in Windsor, Vt.,
Dec. 25, 1814. She was b. in Petersham, Mass.

Childr.

646.   IV.   EDWARD [7]   born Oct. 5, 1815.
647.   V.   ELIZABETH F. [7]   "   Aug. 5, 1817.
       VI.   GEORGE [7]   "   Nov. 19, 1819; died Sept. 26, 1820.
648.   VII.   GEORGE A. [7]   "   Oct. 29, 1821.
649.   VIII.   ELI [7]   "   March 10, 1823.
       IX.   MARTHA [7]   "   Feb. 10, 1825.
650.   X.   FRANCES A. [7]   "   Jan. 6, 1828.

Elkanah Tower [6] died Sept. 21, 1827, ag 53 y. 11 m. 4 d.
Elizabeth (Stone) Tower died May 30, 1839, ag. 53.

302.   **Seventh Generation.**   **Tower.**

129. ISAAC WEBB [6], ISAAC [5], CORNELIUS [4], JOHN [3], IBROOK [2], JOHN [1].
Isaac Webb [6], son of Isaac [5] and Mary (Sprague) Tower, b.
Aug. 16, 1775 ; mar. Zeruah Hitchcock in Northampton,
Mass.,
Dec. 27, 1799, by Rev. Solomon Williams. She was b.
1780.

Childr.

651.	I.	Lucinda [7]	born Sept. 25, 1800.
	II.	William [7]	" ; mar.; died. His widow died in Northampton, July 26, 1843, ag. 40.
	III.	James [7]	" 1802; died young.
	IV.	Thomas [7]	" 1804. He went to the State of New York in early life.
	V.	Mary [7]	" 1806; mar. Rufus Brown, of Flushing, N. Y.; *s. p.*
652.	VI.	Sophia [7]	" 1808.
653.	VII.	Elizabeth Frissell [7]	" 1810.
	VIII.	Henry [7]	" 1812. He went from Northampton in early life.
654.	IX.	Sally [7]	" 1814.
	X.	Isaac W. [7]	" ; mar. He had one son.
655.	XI.	Nancy [7]	" 1820.

Isaac Webb Tower [6] died in Northampton, Mass., Aug. 19, 1821, ag. 46 y. 3 d.

Zeruah (Hitchcock) Tower died in Northampton, Mass., March 27, 1846, ag. 66.

303.   **Seventh Generation.**   **Tower.**

129. Micah [6], Isaac [5], Cornelius [4], John [3], Ibrook [2], John [1].
Micah [6], son of Isaac [5] and Mary (Sprague) Tower, b.
Dec. 23, 1776 ; mar. Pamela Clark in Northampton, Mass.,
Feb. 6, 1803, by Rev. Solomon Williams. She was b. in
Northampton,
June 28, 1786, and was dau. of Job and Esther (Bird) Clark.

Childr. born in Northampton, Mass.

656.	I.	Lewis C. [7]	born May 17, 1803.
657.	II.	Delia [7]	" Aug. 29, 1805.
	III.	Charles [7]	" Sept. 13, 1807; died Jan. 26, 1808.
	IV.	Charles [7]	" Dec. 25, 1808; " Dec. 23, 1826, ag. 17 y. 11 m. 28 d.
	V.	Esther Maria [7]	" July 22, 1817; died July 8, 1835, ag. 17 y. 11 m. 17 d.
	VI.	Ezra [7]	" Sept. 10, 1820; died July 14, 1822, ag. 1 y. 10 m. 4 d.

Micah Tower [6] died in Northampton, Dec. 8, 1822, ag. 45 y. 11 m. 15 d.

Pamela (Clark) Tower died in Northampton, Feb. 24, 1882, ag. 95 y. 7 m. 27 d.

304.   Seventh Generation.   Tower.

129. JOSEPH [6], ISAAC [5], CORNELIUS [4], JOHN [3], IBROOK [2], JOHN [1].
Joseph [6], son of Isaac [5] and Mary (Sprague) Tower, b.
Oct. 13, 1778; mar. Naomi Strong in Northampton, Mass.,
May 22, 1800, by Rev. Solomon Williams. She was dau. of
Daniel and Tryhosa (   ) Strong.

Childr.

	I.	ELIZA [7]	born March 4, 1801, in Northampton.
658.	II.	SOLOMON [7]	"
659.	III.	SAMUEL STEBBENS [7]	"
660.	IV.	DAVID J. [7]	" July 6, 1807, in Windsor, Vt.
	V.	MARY S. [7]	"
661.	VI.	JOSEPH [7]	" Aug. 20, 1812, in New York State.
	VII.	NANCY [7]	"

Joseph Tower [6] died in Wayne County, N. Y., 1819, ag. 41.

305.   Seventh Generation.   Tower.

129. NEHEMIAH [6], ISAAC [5], CORNELIUS [4], JOHN [3], IBROOK [2], JOHN [1].
Nehemiah [6], son of Isaac [5] and Mary (Sprague) Tower, b.
March 8, 1782; mar. Mary Hamilton
Dec. 23, 1808, by Rev. Philip Wager. She was b.
1786.

Childr.

I.	LUTHER JACKSON [7]	born Oct. 2, 1809.
II.	ISAAC SPRAGUE [7]	" Nov. 17, 1810.
III.	NEHEMIAH JOHNSON [7]	" March 11, 1812.
IV.	WILLIAM H. [7]	" July 15, 1813; died Arg. 27, 1813.
V.	MANLEY [7]	" Aug. 10, 1814.
VI.	BENJAMIN H. [7]	" May 10, 1816.
VII.	MARY [7]	" April 5, 1817.
VIII.	ANN [7]	" Sept. 5, 1820.

Nehemiah Tower [6] died Oct. 19, 1852, ag. 70 y. 7 m. 11 d.

306.   Seventh Generation.   Tower.

129. ELIJAH [6], ISAAC [5], CORNELIUS [4], JOHN [3], IBROOK [2], JOHN [1].
Elijah [6], son of Isaac [5] and Mary (Sprague) Tower, b.
May 22, 1787; mar. Elvira Russell
Feb. 14, 1827. She was b.
Nov. 30, 1792, and was dau. of Solomon and Sarah (Brown)
Russell.

Childr.

	I.	LUCY SPRAGUE[7]	born Nov. 8, 1827; died July 20, 1833, ag. 5 y. 8 m. 12 d.
662.	II.	CHARLES HENRY[7]	"	Aug. 23, 1829.
663.	III.	HARVEY RUSSELL[7]	"	Oct. 19, 1831.
664.	IV.	LUCY ELVIRA[7]	"	Dec. 21, 1833.

Elijah Tower[6] died Dec. 12, 1859, ag. 72 y. 6 m. 20 d.

Elvira (Russell) Tower died May 13, 1873, ag. 80 y. 5 m. 13 d.

307.　　　　Seventh Generation.　　　　Tower.

129. OSWIN[6], ISAAC[5], CORNELIUS[4], JOHN[3], IBROOK[2], JOHN[1].
Oswin[6], son of Isaac[5] and Mary (Sprague) Tower, b.
Jan. 6, 1789; mar. Clarissa Ludden. Int. pub.
Oct. 30, 1812. She was b.
July 27, 1793.

Childr.

665.	I.	BENJAMIN[7]	born	June 6, 1814.
666.	II.	LEVI[7]	"	Sept. 19, 1816.
667.	III.	FRANCES JENETTE[7]	"	March 9, 1818.
668.	IV.	ANISE[7]	"	June 21, 1820.
669.	V.	QUARTUS[7]	"	Aug. 27, 1822.
670.	VI.	ASA DWIGHT[7]	"	Oct. 4, 1825.
	VII.	MARY[7]	"	March 26, 1827; died July 14, 1833, ag. 6 y. 3 m. 19 d.
	VIII.	ISAAC[7]	"	Feb. 9, 1829; died Sept. 15, 1829.
671.	IX.	GEORGE[7]	"	March 24, 1830.
	X.	CLARISSA MARI[7]	"	Dec. 25, 1831; died July 14, 1844, ag. 12 y. 6 m. 20 d.
	XI.	HORATIO OSWIN[7]	"	May 28, 1837; died in Newbern, N. C., June 8, 1862, ag. 25 y. 19 d.

Oswin Tower[6] died in Chesterfield, Mass., July 9, 1857, ag. 68 y. 6 m. 3 d.

Clarissa (Ludden) Tower died in Williamsburg, Mass., March 6, 1865, ag. 71 y. 7 m. 9 d.

308. Warner.　Seventh Generation.　　　　Tower.

129. POLLY[6], ISAAC[5], CORNELIUS[4], JOHN[3], IBROOK[2], JOHN[1].
Polly[6], dau. of Isaac[5] and Mary (Sprague) Tower, b.
Aug. 8, 1792; mar. Silas Warner, of Chesterfield, Mass.
Int. pub.
Dec. 18, 1830; *s. p.*
Polly (Tower) Warner died in Chesterfield, Aug. 28, 1860, ag. 68 y. 20 d.

309. Hannum. Seventh Generation. Tower.

129. PEGGY [6], ISAAC [5], CORNELIUS [4], JOHN [3], IBROOK [2], JOHN [1].
Peggy [6], dau. of Isaac [5] and Mary (Sprague) Tower, b.
July 18, 1794; mar. Gaius Hannum
Sept. 20, 1834. He was b.
July 25, 1783; *s. p.*
Gaius Hannum died in West Springfield, Mass., Feb. 7, 1854,
ag. 70 y. 6 m. 12 d.
Peggy (Tower) Hannum died in West Springfield, Mass.,
April 11, 1862, ag. 67 y. 8 m. 24 d.

310. Graves. Seventh Generation. Tower.

129. SALLY [6], ISAAC [5], CORNELIUS [4], JOHN [3], IBROOK [2], JOHN [1].
Sally [6], dau. of Isaac [5] and Mary (Sprague) Tower, b.
Aug. 27, 1796; mar. Henry Graves, of West Springfield,
Mass.,
Oct. 12, 1824. He was b.
April 4, 1799, and was son of Seth Graves.

Childr.

I.	HENRY FRANKLIN [7]	born July 4, 1825.
II.	SETH [7]	" Nov. , 1826.
III.	MARGARET TOWER [7]	" Jan. 18, 1828.
IV.	MARIA [7]	" Nov. 27, 1830; mar. Orion A. Mason, Dec. 31, 1857.
V.	HELEN M. [7]	" April 14, 1833.
VI.	GEORGE BRONSON [7]	" Jan. 21, 1836; mar. Charlotte Stoddard, March 31, 1856.

Henry Graves died March 18, 1847, ag. 47 y. 11 m. 14 d.
Sally (Tower) Graves died Nov. 25, 1845, ag. 49 y. 2 m. 28 d.

311. Seventh Generation. Tower.

132. JESSE [6], ROBERT [5], DAVID [4], HEZEKIAH [3], IBROOK [2], JOHN [1].
Jesse [6], son of Robert [5] and Elizabeth (Burbank) Tower, bapt.
July 13, 1755; mar. Rebecca Cushing in Cohasset, Mass.,
May 1, 1786, by Rev. J. Brown. She was bapt. in Cohasset
Dec. 30, 1759, and was dau. of Samuel Cushing, Jr.

Childr. born in Cohasset.

672.	I.	ASA CUSHING [7]	bapt. March 25, 1787.
	II.	RUTH [7]	" Aug. 24, 1788; died.
673.	III.	ELIZABETH BURBANK [7]	born June 28, 1790.

674.	IV.	JESSE [7]	born June　, 1792.
675.	V.	REBECCA [7]	"　June 12, 1794.
	VI.	SARAH D. [7]	bapt.　　　　; mar. John Despage, Nov. 2, 1817.
676.	VII.	RUTH LOW [7]	"　Oct. 28, 1798.

Jesse Tower [6] died in Cohasset, Dec. 20, 1812, ag. 57 y. 5 m.
7 d. ?

312.　　　　　　**Seventh Generation.**　　　　　**Tower.**

136. ABRAHAM HOBART [6], ABRAHAM [5], DANIEL [4], DANIEL [3], IBROOK [2],
JOHN [1].

Abraham H. [6], son of Abraham [5] and Hannah (Kent) Tower, b.
Oct. 20, 1801 ; mar. Charlotte Bates [3] in Cohasset, Mass.,
April 30, 1826, by Rev. J. Flint. She was b. in Cohasset
Oct. 4, 1806, and was dau. of Newcomb and Lydia (Nichols)
Bates.

BATES, NICHOLS, BATES.　　　　　　　　TOWER.
Charlotte [8], Lydia [7], Zibiah [6], Joshua [5], Joshua [4], Rachel [3], Ibrook [2],
John [1].

Childr.

	I.	MARY NASH [7]	born Aug. 25, 1827; died April 3, 1829.
677.	II.	ABRAHAM H. [7]	"　April 1, 1829.
678.	III.	HENRY CLAY [7]	"　April 16, 1831.
679.	IV.	CHARLES CARROLL [7]	"　Sept. 26, 1833.
1185.	V.	CHARLOTTE M. B. [7]	"　Feb. 28, 1836.
680.	VI.	NEWCOMB B. [7]	"　Feb. 20, 1840.
681.	VII.	DANIEL N. [7]	"　Feb. 28, 1846.

Abraham H. Tower [6] died in Cohasset, June 19, 1881,
ag. 79 y. 7 m. 30 d.
Charlotte (Bates) Tower died in Cohasset, June 11, 1869,
ag. 62 y. 8 m. 7 d.

313. Souther.　　　**Seventh Generation.**　　　　**Tower.**

136. ELIZABETH [6], ABRAHAM [5], DANIEL [4], DANIEL [3], IBROOK [2], JOHN [1].
Elizabeth [6], dau. of Abraham [5] and Hannah (Kent) Tower, b.
Oct. 10, 1803 ; mar. Laban Souther [6] in Cohasset
Jan.　, 1821, by Rev. Jacob Flint. He was bapt. in Cohasset
Sept. 7, 1800, and was son of Asa [5] and Sally [6] (Whiting)
Souther.

Laban [6], Asa [5], Joseph [4], Content [3], Ibrook [2]　　} John [1].
Sally [6], Ezekiel [5], Benjamin [4], Sarah [3], Benjamin [2]　}

Childr. born in Cohasset.

I. EDWIN[7]   born Dec. 1, 1822.
II. SARAH E.[7]   "   1825?
III. ABIGAIL T.[7]   "   Sept. 15, 1827; died May 16, 1859, ag. 31 y. 8 m. 1 d.
IV. ANDREW JACKSON[7]   "   Oct. 1, 1830.
V. ABRAHAM T.[7]   "   May 25, 1833; died May 22, 1850, ag. 16 y. 11 m. 28 d.
VI. MARY L.[7]   "   Jan. 25, 1836; died July 30, 1838, ag. 2 y. 5 d.
VII. ANNA[7]   "   Aug. 22, 1842.
VIII. HANNAH HOBART[7]   "   Aug. 5, 1846.

Laban Souther[6] died in Cohasset, Aug. 5, 1860, ag. 60 y. 7 m.
Elizabeth[6] (Tower) Souther died in Cohasset, Nov. 10, 1888, ag. 85 y. 1 m.

314. Laurence.   **Seventh Generation.**   **Tower.**

136. HANNAH KENT[6], ABRAHAM[5], DANIEL[4], DANIEL[3], IBROOK[2], JOHN[1].

Hannah Kent[6], dau. of Abraham[5] and Hannah (Kent) Tower, b.

May 8, 1806; mar. Josiah O. Laurence in Cohasset, Mass.

Nov. 12, 1826, by Rev. Jacob Flint. J. O. Laurence, b. in Cohasset

May 1, 1797, was son of Thaddeus and Joa ( ) Laurence.

Childr. born in Cohasset.

I. LYSANDER T.[7]   born Aug. 21, 1827; died Oct. 6, 1828, ag. 1 y. 1 m. 15 d.
II. MARIA S.[7]   "   Dec. 23, 1828.
III. GEORGE W.[7]   "   Feb. 29, 1832; died Oct. 3, 1860, ag. 28 y. 7 m. 4 d.
IV. ELLEN AUGUSTA[7]   "   Sept. 6, 1834; "   April 21, 1838, ag. 3 y. 7 m. 15 d.
V. LYMAN[7]   "   Sept. 2, 1837; "   May 3, 1838.
VI. LYMAN[7]   "   June 16, 1839.
VII. WILLIAM EDWARD[7]   "   March 31, 1842; "   May 17, 1842.
VIII. HANNAH K.[7]   "   June 16, 1843.

Hannah K. (Tower) Laurence died in Cohasset, Dec. 14, 1843, ag. 37 y. 7 m. 6 d.
Josiah O. Laurence died in Cohasset, April 26, 1865, ag. 67 y. 11 m. 25 d.

315.   Spencer, Shattuck.   Seventh Generation.   Tower.

137. MERCY [6], ISAAC [5], DANIEL [4], DANIEL [3], IBROOK [2], JOHN [1].
Mercy [6], dau. of Isaac [5] and Betsey (Stoddard) Tower, b.
Jan. 31, 1779 ; mar. Lemuel Shattuck in Springfield, Vt.,
Sept. 23, 1804, by Rev. R. Smiley ; *s. p.*
Mercy(Shattuck)Tower mar., 2d, Jonas Spencer in Springfield
Sept. 26, 1822, by Rev. R. Smiley.   J. Spencer, b.
March 2, 1773.

Child.

I.   MARCIA [7] born

Jonas Spencer died in Springfield, Oct. 2, 1839, ag. 66 y. 7 m.
Mercy (Tower) Spencer died in Springfield, Dec. 4, 1856,
ag. 77 y. 10 m. 4 d.

316.   **Seventh Generation.**   **Tower.**

137. ABRAHAM [6], ISAAC [5], DANIEL [4], DANIEL [3], IBROOK [2], JOHN [1].
Abraham [6], son of Isaac [5] and Betsey (Stoddard) Tower, b.
March 11, 1781 ; mar. Bethia Field in Springfield, Vt.,
Jan. 8, 1807, by Rev. R. Smiley.   She was b. in Sharon, Ct.,
Dec. 4, 1786, and was dau. of Luther and Hannah (Williams)
Field.

Childr. born in Springfield.

682.	I.	LUTHER F. [7]	born Nov. 5, 1808.
683.	II.	IBROOK [7]	" Sept. 10, 1810.
	III.	PLINY [7]	" Dec. 11, 1812; died in Woodville, Miss., July 14, 1838, ag. 25 y. 7 m. 3 d.
684.	IV.	ABRAHAM [7]	" Jan. 12, 1815.
	V.	SARAH [7]	" April 20, 1817; unmar.; lives in Daphne, Ala.
685.	VI.	JOHN [7]	" Nov. 14, 1819.
686.	VII.	ISAAC [7]	" June 13, 1822.
	VIII.	AMANTHA [7]	" Oct. 13, 1825; mar. Henry L. Bisbee, of Athens, Mich.
	IX.	JACOB STODDARD [7]	" Nov. 8, 1828.
687.	X.	JANE M. [7]	" May 10, 1832.

Bethia (Field) Tower died in Springfield, Sept. 11, 1839,
ag. 52 y. 9 m. 7 d.
Abraham Tower [6] mar., 2d, widow Almira Holt in Springfield, Vt.,
April 30, 1840, by Rev. A. C. Howard.   She was b.

April 4, 1790, and was dau. of Asa and Margaret (Hammond) Hall.

Abraham Tower [6] died in Springfield, June 15, 1857, ag. 76 y. 3 m. 4 d.

Almira (Holt) Tower died in Springfield, Oct. 7, 1874, ag. 84 y. 6 m. 3 d.

317.　　　　　Seventh Generation.　　　　　Tower.

137. ISAAC [6], ISAAC [5], DANIEL [4], DANIEL [3], IBROOK [2], JOHN [1].
Isaac [6], son of Isaac [5] and Betsey (Stoddard) Tower, b.
April 20, 1783; mar. Susanna Field in Springfield, Vt.,
Jan. 20, 1805, by S. M. Lewis, J. P.　She was b.
May 7, 1785, and was dau. of Daniel and Hannah (Whitman) Field.

Childr. born in Springfield.

688.	I.	ELIZABETH S. [7]	born	Nov. 10, 1805.
689.	II.	DANIEL F. [7]	"	Aug. 29, 1807.
	III.	CAROLINE [7]	"	Feb. 2, 1809; died Feb. 12, 1811, ag. 2 y. 10 d.
690.	IV.	LEVI [7]	"	Oct. 18, 1810.
691.	V.	STEPHEN S. [7]	"	Aug. 16, 1812.
692.	VI.	LEWIS [7]	"	Jan. 10, 1814.
693.	VII.	ISAAC NICHOLS [7]	"	May 11, 1816.
694.	VIII.	WINSLOW [7]	"	Sept. 1, 1817.
695.	IX.	SAMUEL [7]	"	July 20, 1819.
696.	X.	SUSAN M. [7]	"	May 18, 1821.
	XI.	JOB [7]	"	Jan. 27, 1823; unmar.; lives in California.
697.	XII.	HANNAH [7]	"	May 27, 1824.
698.	XIII.	DAVID [7]	"	Dec. 23, 1825.
699.	XIV.	THEODA [7]	"	Sept. 21, 1827.
	XV.	RACHEL [7]	"	Dec. 26, 1831; unmar.; died July 16, 1861, ag. 29 y. 6 m. 20 d.

Isaac Tower [6] died in Michigan, April 19, 1858, ag. 74 y. 11 m. 30 d.

Susanna (Field) Tower died in Michigan, 1859? ag. 74?

318. Smith.　　Seventh Generation.　　　　　Tower.

137. BETSEY [6], ISAAC [5], DANIEL [4], DANIEL [3], IBROOK [2], JOHN [1].
Betsey [6], dau. of Isaac [5] and Betsey (Stoddard) Tower, b.
June 9, 1785; mar. Hugh Smith, of Springfield, Vt.,
Dec. 10, 1803, by Rev. R. Smiley.　H. Smith b.
July 30, 1769.

Childr. born in Springfield.

I.	SILVANUS[7]	born	Dec. 22, 1804.
II.	ISAAC TOWER[7]	"	Nov. 11, 1806; died in Richmond, Va., 1832 ? ag. 26 ?
III.	HIRAM M.[7]	"	Sept. 22, 1809.
IV.	ELIZABETH STODDARD[7]	"	June 9, 1812; died July 13, 1829, ag. 17 y. 1 m. 4 d.
V.	AMELIA[7]	"	July 11, 1814 ; mar. Peter T. Spencer, of Springfield.
VI.	HUGH[7]	"	March 10, 1817 ; died in Richmond, Va., Sept. , 1879, ag. 62 y. 6 m.
VII.	JERUSHA[7]	"	April 19, 1819; died Dec. 9, 1839, ag. 20 y. 7 m. 20 d.
VIII.	MARCIA[7]	"	July 20, 1821; mar. Langdon Sawyer, of Springfield. She died in Springfield.
IX.	DANIEL[7]	"	Jan. 7, 1824.

Hugh Smith died in Springfield, May 30, 1862, ag. 92 y. 10 m.
Betsey (Tower) Smith died in Springfield, June 19, 1858,
ag. 73 y. 10 d.

319. Safford.   Seventh Generation.   Tower.

137. NANCY[6], ISAAC[5], DANIEL[4], DANIEL[3], IBROOK[2], JOHN[1].
Nancy[6], dau. of Isaac[5] and Betsey (Stoddard) Tower, b.
Sept. 1, 1787; mar. Noah Safford, of Springfield, Vt.,
Dec.   , 1812. He was b.
Oct. 12, 1789, and was son of Philip and Elizabeth (   )
Safford.

Childr. born in Springfield.

I.	NOAH BIGELOW[7]	born	Jan. 1, 1818.
II.	HENRY[7]	"	Oct. 17, 1819.
III.	CHARLES HERBERT[7]	"	Feb. 10, 1822.
IV.	ISAAC TOWER[7]	"	June 27, 1825.
V.	REBECCA[7]	"	March 28, 1828; mar. John C. Holmes, of Springfield, March 9, 1859.

Noah Safford died in Springfield, Nov. 28, 1863, ag. 74 y.
1 m. 16 d.
Nancy (Tower) Safford died in Springfield, Aug. 10, 1854,
ag. 66 y. 11 m. 9 d.

320. Cook.   Seventh Generation.   Tower.

137. SALLY[6], ISAAC[5], DANIEL[4], DANIEL[3], IBROOK[2], JOHN[1].
Sally[6], dau. of Isaac[5] and Betsey (Stoddard) Tower, b.
May 27, 1789; mar. Philip Cook in Springfield, Vt.,
Oct. 26, 1817, by Rev. R. Smiley.

Childr. born in Springfield.

I. Philip[7] born Nov. 30, 1819; died July 17, 1844, ag. 24 y. 7 m. 17 d.
II. Sarah[7] "
III. Thomas[7] "   ; died young.
IV. Abraham[7] "

321.   Seventh Generation.   Tower.

137. Stoddard[6], Isaac[5], Daniel[4], Daniel[3], Ibrook[2], John[1].
Stoddard[6], son of Isaac[5] and Betty (Stoddard) Tower, b.
June 7, 1791; mar. Sally Bates[7] in Springfield, Vt.,
May 20, 1819, by Rev. R. Smiley. She was b.
Dec. 16, 1794, and was dau. of Phineas[6] and Abigail (Lincoln) Bates.

Sally[7], Phineas[6], Joshua[5], Joshua[4], Rachel[3], Ibrook[2], John[1].

Childr. born in Springfield, Vt.

I. Sarah[7]   born   ; mar. John G. Crombie.
                                She died in Pontiac, Mich.
II. Elizabeth[7]   "   ; mar. Samuel T. Manson, of
                                Boston.
III. Grace[7]   "   ; "   Charles Bennett, of
                                Richmond, Va.
700. IV. Isaac Stoddard[7] " Feb. 5, 1830.
     V. Abby[7]   "   1832; unmar. She is a teacher in
                                St. Louis.
    VI. Jennie[7]   "   1834; "   She is a teacher in
                                Boston.
   VII. Henrietta[7]   "   1837; died   1867.

Sally (Bates) Tower died in Springfield, Vt., Oct. 28, 1839,
ag. 44 y. 10 m. 12 d.
Stoddard Tower[6] mar., 2d, Esther Bates in Springfield
Oct. 6, 1840. She was born in Springfield
Sept. 24, 1812, and was dau. of Phineas and Abigail (Lincoln) Bates.

Childr.

VIII. Ellen B.[7] born Dec. 4, 1842; mar. Charles B. Caldwell, Jan. 17,
                1861.
 IX. Mary N.[7]   " April 7, 1847; " F. R. Arnold, of Portland, Or.

Esther (Bates) Tower died in Springfield, Oct. 3, 1851,
ag. 39 y. 9 d.
Stoddard Tower[6] mar., 3d, Laura (Sawyer) Heard in
Springfield
Sept. 1, 1853, by Rev. S. P. Giddings.
Stoddard Tower[6] died in Springfield, March 1, 1868, ag. 76 y.
9 m. 14 d.

322. Bates. **Seventh Generation.** **Tower.**

137. RACHEL[6], ISAAC[5], DANIEL[4], DANIEL[3], IBROOK[2], JOHN[1].
Rachel[6], dau. of Isaac[5] and Betty (Stoddard) Tower, b.
Sept. 26, 1795; mar. Davis Bates, of Springfield, Vt.
He was b. in Springfield
Sept. 5, 1792, and was son of Phineas and Abigail (Lincoln)
Bates.

Childr. born in Springfield.

I.	THOMAS LINCOLN[7] born Dec.	, 1819; died March 6, 1822, ag. 2 y. 6 m.
II.	ABBY DELIA[7]	"	1824.
III.	THOMAS LINCOLN[7]	"	1827; died Oct. 11, 1847, ag. 20 ?
IV.	NICHOLS TOWER[7]	"	1830; " April 20, 1850, ag. 20 ?
V.	SAMUEL[7]	"	

Davis Bates died in Springfield, Feb. 17, 1865, ag. 72 y. 5 m.
12 d.
Rachel (Tower) Bates died in Springfield, Nov. 15, 1868,
ag. 73 y. 1 m. 20 d.

323. Harris. **Seventh Generation.** **Tower.**

138. HANNAH[6], SAMUEL[5], DANIEL[4], DANIEL[3], IBROOK[2], JOHN[1].
Hannah[6], dau. of Samuel[5] and Rebecca (Nichols) Tower, b.
Feb. 29, 1776; mar. Stephen Harris, of Fitzwilliam, N. H.,
July 11, 1795, by Rev. Benjamin Brigham. S. Harris, b.
, 1771, was son of Stephen and Mary ( ) Harris.

Childr.

I.	JOSEPH[7]	born Aug. 21, 1796.
II.	LEVI[7]	" Sept. 15, 1797.
III.	REBECCA[7]	" April 27, 1799; died April 9, 1800.
IV.	BENJAMIN[7]	" Dec. 14, 1800; " in N. Y., 1821, ag. 21.
V.	REBECCA[7]	" Feb. 11, 1802; " Feb. , 1803.
VI.	SAMUEL[7]	" Feb. 11, 1804.
VII.	MALINDA[7]	" Nov. 29, 1805; mar. died.
VIII.	BETHIAH[7]	" March 1, 1808; " John Kimball.
IX.	STEPHEN[7]	" Jan. 21, 1810.
X.	DANIEL[7]	" Feb. 9, 1812; " ; 2 ch., died in N. Y., ag. 29?

Stephen Harris died in Volney, N. Y., Jan. 2, 1836, ag. 65 ?
Hannah (Tower) Harris died at Saratoga Springs, N. Y.,
, 1815, ag. 39 ?

324. Hayden.   Seventh Generation.   Tower.

138. REBECCA N.[6], SAMUEL[5], DANIEL[4], DANIEL[3], IBROOK[2], JOHN[1].
Rebecca N.[6], dau. of Samuel[5] and Rebecca (Nichols) Tower, b.
Oct. 11, 1780 ; mar. Joel Hayden, of Fitzwilliam, N. H.

Childr.

I.	DANIEL T.[7] born	1808 ; mar. Sarah Reed. He died Aug. 18, 1838, ag. 30 ?
II.	JOEL[7] "	1816; died Nov. 28, 1817, ag. 1 year.
III.	JOEL[7] bapt.	Sept. 27, 1818; mar. Harriet Wilson; *s. p.* He died in Boston.
IV.	HARRIET[7] "	; " John Perkins.
V.	REBECCA[7] "	; " Charles Richardson; *s. p.*
VI.	ELIZABETH[7] "	; " Lucius N. Briggs, of Keene, N. H., April 2, 1836.
VII.	MILTON M.[7] "	; unmar. He resides in New York.

Joel Hayden died in Fitzwilliam, Dec. 2, 1856, ag. 76.
Rebecca N. (Tower) Hayden died in Fitzwilliam, July 18,
1855, ag. 74 y. 9 m. 7 d.

---

325.   Seventh Generation.   Tower.

138. LEVI[6], SAMUEL[5], DANIEL[4], DANIEL[3], IBROOK[2], JOHN[1].
Levi[6], son of Samuel[5] and Rebecca (Nichols) Tower, b.
March 14, 1782 ; mar. Anstis Stratton, of Athol, Mass.,
July 31, 1803, by Nahum Parker, J. P. She was b.
Dec. 14, 1784, and was dau. of Thomas and Thankful (Rich)
Stratton.

Childr.

	I.	LYSANDER[7]	born Aug. 22, 1803; unmar. ; died Nov. 7, 1826, ag. 23 y. 2 m. 16 d.
	II.	Child "	; died May 18, 1805.
	III.	Child "	; " Aug. 14, 1806.
701.	IV.	ABIGAIL[7] "	Aug. 11, 1807.
	V.	ANSTIS[7] "	June 3, 1810 ; died Jan. 3, 1825, ag. 14 y. 7 m.
702.	VI.	AMBRA[7] "	May 26, 1813.
	VII.	HANNAH[7] "	Feb. 27, 1816; died Sept. 5, 1837, ag. 21 y. 6 m. 9 d.
	VIII.	REBECCA NICHOLS[7] "	Sept. 10, 1819; mar. Franklin Lufkin. She died July 27, 1844, ag. 24 y. 10 m. 17 d., *s. p.*

Levi Tower[6] died in Fitzwilliam, N. H., Nov. 8, 1869,
ag. 87 y. 7 m. 25 d.
Anstis (Stratton) Tower died in Fitzwilliam, N. H., Nov.
14, 1872, ag. 87 y. 11 m.

138. DANIEL [6], SAMUEL [5], DANIEL [4], DANIEL [3], IBROOK [2], JOHN [1].
Daniel [6], son of Samuel [5] and Rebecca (Nichols) Tower, b.
July 27, 1787 ; mar. Mary Buswell, of Peacham, Vt.,
Feb. 4, 1816. She was b. in Peacham,
July 5, 1795, and was dau. of Nicholas Colby Buswell.

Childr.

	I.	SILAS BUSWELL [7]	born Dec. 22, 1816.
	II.	ELIZABETH CHAMBERLAIN [7]	" July 26, 1818; mar. Charles H B. Woodbury, of Dover, Me. ; died in Dover, Me.
703.	III.	MARIA [7]	" July 30, 1820.
	IV.	MILTON HAYDEN [7]	" July 8, 1822; died Sept. 16, 1824, ag. 2 y. 2 m. 8 d.
704.	V.	REBECCA BUSWELL [7]	" May 14, 1825.
705.	VI.	MARY [7]	" Aug. 10, 1827.
706.	VII.	LUCINDA BUSWELL [7]	" June 28, 1829.
	VIII.	ABIGAIL COCHRANE [7]	" Aug. 11, 1832; died Sept. 10, 1832.
707.	IX.	LEVI NICHOLAS COLBY [7]	" March 6, 1834.
708.	X.	ABBY FRANCES [7]	" Jan 1, 1837.

Daniel Tower [6] died in Peoria, Ill., March 13, 1865, ag. 77 y.
8 m. 19 d.
Mary (Buswell) Tower died in Dover, Me., May 17, 1873,
ag. 77 y. 10 m. 12 d.

139. BETSEY [6], LEVI [5], DANIEL [4], DANIEL [3], IBROOK [2], JOHN [1].
Betsey [6], dau. of Levi [5] and Priscilla (Nichols) Tower b.
Jan. 1, 1778; mar. Peter Lothrop, of Cohasset,
He was b. in Cohasset
July 28, 1776, and was son of Thomas and Ruth (Nichols)
Lothrop.

Childr. born in Cohasset.

I.	CALEB [7]	born May 8, 1799.
II.	PRISCILLA NICHOLS [7]	" July 26, 1801.
III.	PATTY TOWER [7]	" April 26, 1803.
IV.	SARAH YOUNG [7]	" June 16, 1805.
V.	MARY [7]	" June 19, 1807.
VI.	LORING [7]	" Aug. 5, 1809; died March 21, 1814, ag. 4 y. 7 m. 16 d.
VII.	WILLIAM [7]	" Dec. 15, 1811; " April 11, 1815, ag. 3 y. 3 m. 27 d.

VIII. ELIZABETH[7]   born Nov. 4, 1813.
  IX. LORING[7]   "   Nov. 5, 1816.
   X. REBECCA ALLEN[7] "   June 16, 1822.

Peter Lothrop died in Cohasset, Dec. 27, 1848, ag. 72 y. 4 m. 29 d.

Betsey (Tower) Lothrop died Aug. 2, 1859, ag 81 y. 7 m. 1 d.

---

328. Bates.   Seventh Generation.   Tower.

139. SALLY[6], LEVI[5], DANIEL[4], DANIEL[3]   } IBROOK[2],
DANIEL[7], ZEALOUS[6], JOSHUA[5], JOSHUA[4], RACHEL[3] } JOHN[1].

Sally[6], dau. of Levi[5] and Priscilla (Nichols) Tower, b. Oct. 11, 1780; mar. Daniel Bates[7], of Cohasset,
          He was b. in Cohasset
Jan. 21, 1778, and was son of Zealous[6] and Abigail (Nichols) Bates.

Childr. born in Cohasset.

	I.	JOB TOWER[7&8]	born	May 26, 1797.
709.	II.	ZEALOUS[7]	"	Nov. 19, 1799.
	III.	SALOME[7]	"	Nov. 1, 1801; died June 16, 1841, ag. 39 y. 7 m. 15 d.
	IV.	LEVI[7]	"	June 9, 1805.
	V.	ABIGAIL[7]	"	Dec. 2, 1807.
	VI.	SARAH[7]	"	Dec. 18, 1809.
	VII.	DANIEL[7]	"	Dec. 3, 1811.
	VIII.	JAMES[7]	"	Feb. 10, 1814.
	IX.	CALEB N.[7]	"	June 5, 1816.
	X.	ANNA G.[7]	"	Sept. 8, 1818; mar. Henry Lincoln, of Boston, Jan. 12, 1841; 2d, James Bates, of Malden, Mass., 1885.
729.	XI.	LORENZO[7]	"	Feb. 11, 1824.

Daniel Bates[7] died in Cohasset, Dec. 4, 1860, ag. 82 y. 10 m. 14 d.

Sally[6] (Tower) Bates died in Cohasset, April 25, 1857, ag. 76 y. 6 m. 16 d.

---

329.   Seventh Generation.   Tower.

139. LEVI[6], LEVI[5], DANIEL[4], DANIEL[3], IBROOK[2], JOHN[1].
Levi[6], son of Levi[5] and Priscilla (Nichols) Tower, b. April 9, 1783; mar. Abigail Nichols in Cohasset May 23, 1802, by Rev. J. Flint. She was bapt. in Cohasset Oct. 20, 1782, and was dau. of Israel and Anne (   ) Nichols.

Childr. born in Cohasset.

	I.	MARY[7]	born Sept.	, 1802; died Oct. , 1802.
709.	II.	ANNE HUMPHREY[7]	"	Dec. 15, 1803.
710.	III.	NICHOLS[7]	"	Feb. 10, 1805.
711.	IV.	EDWARD[7]	"	Dec, 3, 1807.
712.	V.	LEVI[7]	"	Jan. 1, 1810.
	VI.	ISRAEL NICHOLS[7]	"	Aug. 17, 1812; died Sept. 4, 1814. ag. 2 y. 18 d.
	VII.	LEWIS[7]	"	March 24, 1815; " May 7, 1818, ag. 3 y. 1 m. 13 d.
713.	VIII.	WILLIAM BOARDMAN[7]	"	Aug. 11, 1817.
	IX.	ABIGAIL N.[7]	"	March 17, 1820; mar. Francis G. Allen Jan. 1, 1851.
714.	X.	LEWIS[7]	"	April 17, 1822.
715.	XI.	PRISCILLA NICHOLS[7]	"	Dec. 19, 1824.

Levi Tower[6] died in Cohasset, June 15, 1835, ag. 52 y. 2 m. 6 d.

Abigail (Nichols) Tower died in Cohasset, Feb. 3, 1844, ag. 61 y. 3 m. 14 d. ?

330. Bates.   Seventh Generation.   Tower.

139. PRISCILLA[6], LEVI[5], DANIEL[4], DANIEL[3] ⎱ IBROOK[2],
PAUL[7], ZEALOUS[6], JOSHUA[5], JOSHUA[4], RACHEL[3] ⎰ JOHN[1].
Priscilla[6], dau. of Levi[5] and Priscilla (Nichols) Tower, b.
Jan. 3, 1786 ; mar. Paul Bates[7] in Cohasset
Nov. 29, 1805, by Rev. J. Flint.   P. Bates, born in Cohasset
Aug. 10, 1781, was son of Zealous[6] and Abigail (Nichols)
Bates.

Childr. born in Cohasset.

	I.	RUTH[7 & 8]	born April 21, 1806.	
	II.	PAUL[7]	"	Nov. 27, 1807.
	III.	CHARLES[7]	"	July 19, 1809.
	IV.	MARTHA N.[7]	"	April 11, 1811.
718.	V.	JANE B.[7]	"	Jan. 3, 1813.
	VI.	GEORGE[7]	"	June 25, 1815.
	VII.	PRISCILLA[7]	"	April 9, 1817.
	VIII.	DAVID[7]	"	April 9, 1819; unmar; died Oct. 6, 1843, ag. 24 y. 5 m. 27 d.
	IX.	ADELINE[7]	"	April 9, 1821; mar. Lincoln L. Jenkins, Oct. 14, 1840.
720.	X	ELIZABETH[7]	"	April 12, 1823.
	XI.	GORHAM[7]	"	Feb. 11, 1825.
	XII.	ABIGAIL[7]	"	Dec. 5, 1829; unmar.
	XIII.	ZEALOUS[7]	"	Dec. 13, 1830; resides in California.

Paul Bates[7] died in Cohasset, July 7, 1839, ag. 57 y. 10 m. 28 d.

Priscilla[6] (Tower) Bates died in Cohasset, April 23, 1855, ag. 69 y. 3 m. 20 d.

331.   **Seventh Generation.**   **Tower.**

139. NICHOLS[6], LEVI[5], DANIEL[4], DANIEL[3]   } IBROOK[2], ANNE[7], ZEALOUS[6], JOSHUA[5], JOSHUA[4], RACHEL[3] { JOHN[1].
Nichols[6], son of Levi[5] and Priscilla (Nichols) Tower, b. July 2, 1787; mar. Ann Bates[7], of Cohasset, Aug. 5, 1807. She was b. in Cohasset March 22, 1787, and was dau. of Zealous[6] and Abigail (Nichols) Bates.

Childr. born in Cohasset.

716.	I.	DAVID B.[7 & 8]	born	May 7, 1808.
717.	II.	GEORGE[7]	"	April 9, 1811.
718.	III.	THOMAS NICHOLS[7]	"	June 18, 1813.
719.	IV.	DANIEL[7]	"	Jan. 25, 1815.
	V.	NICHOLS[7]	"	May 22, 1817; unmar.
	VI.	ZEALOUS B.[7]	"	Jan. 12, 1819; "
720.	VII.	FREDERIC[7]	"	Oct. 21, 1820.
	VIII.	LEVI[7]	"	Nov. 15, 1823; mar. Helen Smith June 9, 1860; *s. p.*
721.	IX.	ABIGAIL[7]	"	Sept. 7, 1826.
722.	X.	ADELINE[7]	"	Feb. 9, 1828.
723.	XI.	SARAH PRISCILLA N.[7]	"	March 20, 1830.

Nichols Tower[6] died in Cohasset, Dec. 28, 1866, ag. 79 y. 5 m. 26 d.

Anne (Bates) Tower died in Cohasset, Dec. 6, 1858, ag. 71 y. 8 m. 14 d.

332. Stoddard.   **Seventh Generation.**   **Tower.**

139. PATTY[6], LEVI[5], DANIEL[4], DANIEL[3], IBBOOK[2], JOHN[1].
Patty[6], dau. of Levi[5] and Priscilla (Nichols) Tower, b. Nov. 19, 1792; mar. Thomas Stoddard in Cohasset Sept. 1, 1815, by Rev. J. Flint. T. Stoddard, bapt. in Cohasset Aug. 17, 1788, was son of Zenas and Ruth (Beal) Stoddard.

Childr. born in Cohasset.

     I.   MARY B.[7] born June 11, 1816.
     II.   RUTH[7]   "   Dec. 11, 1817.
     III.   ANNA[7]   "   Aug. 9, 1819.

IV. GEORGE[7] born Dec. 28, 1822; unmar.; died in California.
V. MARTHA[7] " Nov. 28, 1826.
VI. SARAH[7] " July 7, 1836; unmar.

Thomas Stoddard died March 30, 1854, ag. 66 y. 11 m.
Patty (Tower) Stoddard died July 24, 1859, ag. 66 y. 8 m.
5 d.

333. **Seventh Generation.** **Tower.**

139. ABRAHAM[6], LEVI[5], DANIEL[4], DANIEL[3], IBROOK[2], JOHN[1].
Abraham[6], son of Levi[5] and Ruth (Beal) Tower, b.
Jan. 19, 1800; mar. Marcia Dunlap Lothrop, of Cohasset,
Mass.,
Jan. 2, 1842. She was bapt. in Cohasset,
Aug. 6, 1821, and was dau. of Anselm and Priscilla (Lin-
coln) Lothrop.

Childr. born in Cohasset.

724. I. MARCIA DUNLAP[7] born Feb. 19, 1843.
II. SARAH CUMMINGS[7] " Oct. 1, 1844; died Oct. 6, 1859, ag.
15 y. 5 d.
III. Infant[7] " Oct. 19, 1846; " Nov. 20, 1846.
725. IV. ABRAHAM[7] " March 6, 1851.
V. Infant[7] " Aug. 14, 1853; died Sept. 14, 1853.

Abraham Tower[6] died June 7, 1854, ag. 54 y. 4 m. 19 d.

334. **Seventh Generation.** **Tower.**

139. JOB[6], LEVI[5], DANIEL[4], DANIEL[3], IBROOK[2], JOHN[1].
Job[6], son of Levi[5] and Ruth (Beal) Tower, b.
Dec. 3, 1801; mar. Louisa L. Lothrop[6], of Cohasset, Mass.,
May 15, 1825. She was b. in Cohasset
Aug. 19, 1803, and was dau. of John J. and Bethia[5] (Tower)
Lothrop.
Louisa L.[6], Bethia[5], Daniel[4], Daniel[3], Ibrook[2], John[1].

Childr. born in Cohasset.

726. I. JOB[7] born Aug. 15, 1826.
727. II. WARREN L.[7] " Jan. 14, 1831.
III. LOUISA CAROLINE[7] " March 24, 1834; died March 27, 1836,
ag. 2 y. 3 d.
728. IV. JOHN JACOB[7] " April 6, 1837.
V. LOUISA C.[7] " July 3, 1842.

Job Tower [6] died in Boston, Feb. 25, 1881, ag. 79 y. 2 m. 22 d.
Louisa L. (Lothrop) Tower died in Boston, May 14, 1880,
ag. 76 y. 8 m. 26 d.

335. **Seventh Generation.** **Tower.**

139. DAVID [6], LEVI [5], DANIEL [4], DANIEL [3], IBROOK [2], JOHN [1].
David [6], son of Levi [5] and Ruth (Beal) Tower, b.
Aug. 17, 1804; mar. Jane Laurence, of Cohasset, Mass.,
Nov. 17, 1823. She was b. in Cohasset
Dec. 15, 1806, and was dau. of Jonathan and Mary Laurence.

Childr.

729.	I.	MARY JANE [7]	born Dec. 31, 1825.
	II.	JOSEPH WINCHESTER [7]	" Sept. 10, 1827; died May 27, 1833, ag. 5 y. 8 m. 16 d.
	III.	DAVID [7]	" Dec. 31, 1829; died in New Orleans, Oct. 20, 1852, ag. 22 y. 9 m. 20 d.
730.	IV.	JAMES J. [7]	" May 25, 1832.
	V.	SARAH ANN [7]	" May 10, 1836; died Aug. 27, 1844, ag. 8 y. 3 m. 17 d.
	VI.	ABRAHAM [7]	" Sept. 21, 1839; died June 14, 1841, ag. 1 y. 8 m. 23 d.
731.	VII.	JOHN WILSON [7]	" Nov. 13, 1842.
732.	VIII.	FRANCIS CARY [7]	" Feb. 17, 1845.

David Tower [6] died Oct. 8, 1844, ag. 40 y. 1 m. 22 d.

336. Cushing. **Seventh Generation.** **Tower.**

149. LYDIA [6], PETER [5], PETER [4], JEREMIAH [3], JEREMIAH [2], JOHN [1].
Lydia [6], dau. of Peter [5] and Deborah (Stowell) Tower, b.
Aug. 27, 1752; mar. Bela Cushing in Hingham, Mass.,
Jan. 6, 1772, by Rev. D. Shute. B. Cushing, b. in Weymouth
May 3, 1748, was son of Hezekiah and Lydia (   ) Cushing.

Childr.

I.	LYDIA [7]	born	; mar. Edward Convis, of Windsor, Mass.
II.	DEBORAH [7]	" Aug.	3, 1786, in Cummington, Mass.
III.	HANNAH [7]	" Oct.	15, 1790, " " "
IV.	BETSEY [7]	" March	11, 1793, " " "

337. **Seventh Generation.** **Tower.**

149. STEPHEN [6], PETER [5], PETER [4], JEREMIAH [3], JEREMIAH [2], JOHN [1].
Stephen [6], son of Peter [5] and Deborah (Stowell) Tower, b.
May 24, 1755 ; mar. Anna Bowker, of Scituate,
April 21, 1776.

Childr. born in Hingham and Cummington, Mass.

733.	I.	ANNA[7]	born Sept. 15, 1776.
734.	II.	STEPHEN[7]	" March 8, 1778.
	III.	LUKE[7]	" May 7, 1780; died Sept. 11, 1804, ag. 24 y. 4 m. 4 d.
735.	IV.	JOHN[7]	" July 8, 1781.
736.	V.	DAVID[7]	" Dec. 11, 1782.
737.	VI.	JOANNA[7]	" Sept. 27, 1784.
738.	VII.	DEBORAH[7]	" July 16, 1786.
739.	VIII.	CLARISSA[7]	" May 3, 1788.
740.	IX.	PETER[7]	" July 10, 1790.
741.	X.	OTIS[7]	" Oct. 28, 1791.
	XI.	SALOME[7]	" Jan. 27, 1793.
	XII.	GALEN[7]	" March 1, 1794.
379.	XIII.	RHODA[7]	" Nov. 26, 1795.

Anna (Bowker) Tower died in Cummington, Jan. 2, 1821, ag. 69 ?

Stephen Tower[6] mar., 2d, Mary

He died in Cummington, April 25, 1826, ag. 70 y. 11 m. 1 d.

Mary (   ) Tower died in Cummington, Sept.   , 1826, ag. 56 ?

338.   **Seventh Generation.**   **Tower.**

149. RUFUS[6], PETER[5], PETER[4], JEREMIAH[3], JEREMIAH[2], JOHN[1].
Rufus[6], son of Peter[5] and Deborah (Stowell) Tower, b. Aug. 28, 1757 ; mar. Sally

Childr.

742.	I.	RUFUS[7]	born 1783.
	II.	ESTHER[7]	" ; mar. Richard Leach, of Marble-head, Mass., Oct. 2, 1805.
	III.	FREDERICK[7]	"

Rufus Tower[6] died in Boston   1819 ?

Sally (   ) Tower mar., 2d, Thomas Waite, of Boston, July 20, 1820.

339. Bailey, Farrar. Seventh Generation.   Tower.

149. LUCY[6], PETER[5], PETER[4], JEREMIAH[3], JEREMIAH[2], JOHN[1].
Lucy[6], dau. of Peter[5] and Deborah (Stowell) Tower, b. April 25, 1760 ; mar. Jonathan Farrar[5] in Hingham, Mass., Jan. 31, 1780, by Rev. D. Shute. J. Farrar, b. in Hingham June 19, 1756, was son of David and Sarah (Pratt) Farrar.

FARRAR, PRATT.   TOWER.
Jonathan[5], Sarah[4], Christian[3], Benjamin[2], John[1].

Childr.

I. Lucy[6 & 7] bapt. March   , 1781.
II. Peter[7]   born Sept. 10, 1781.
III. Calvin[7]   "   June   , 1788; died young.
IV. Sally[7]   "
V. Jonathan[7] "   1793.
VI. Susanna[7] "   July   , 1794; died young.

Jonathan Farrar[5] died, and Lucy (Tower) Farrar mar., 2d,
  John Bailey, of Worthington, Mass.,
June 16, 1796, by Rev. James Briggs in Cummington.

Childr.

VII. Hannah[7] born   1797.
VIII. Joanna[7]   "   Feb. 9, 1799.
IX. Polly T.[7]   "   July 1, 1801.
X. Nelson[7]   "

John Bailey died in Cummington, Oct. 27, 1826, ag. 67 ?
Lucy (Tower) (Farrar) Bailey died in Porter, N. Y., March
  17, 1831, ag. 70 y. 10 m. 20 d.

340.   Seventh Generation.   Tower.

149. Asa[6], Peter[5], Peter[4], Jeremiah[3], Jeremiah[2], John[1].
Asa[6], son of Peter[5] and Deborah (Stowell) Tower, b.
July 18, 1762; mar. Deborah Dyer in Weymouth, Mass.,
Dec. 25, 1783, by Rev. S. Williams. She was b. in Weymouth
Aug. 14, 1766, and was dau. of Stephen and Leah (Bates)
Dyer.

Childr. born in Weymouth and Cummington.

743.   I. Asa[7]   born Oct. 15, 1784.
744.   II. Polly[7]   "   Jan. 19, 1787.
745.   III. Hannah W.[7] "   Sept. 23, 1789.
746.   IV. Jane[7]   "   May 5, 1792.
        V. Deborah[7]   "   April 20, 1794; mar. Ithiel Smith, and lived in
                 Vermont.
        VI. Leah[7]   "   June 28, 1796; died
        VII. William[7]   "   Oct. 6, 1798;   "   1817, ag. 19.
747. VIII. Leah[7]   "   Sept. 24, 1801.
748.   IX. Dyer[7]   "   Aug. 24, 1804.
749.   X. Stephen D.[7] "   Dec. 9, 1807.

Asa Tower[6] died in Cummington, Oct. 31, 1843, ag. 81 y.
  3 m. 13 d.
Deborah (Dyer) Tower died in Cummington, June 30, 1851,
  ag. 84 y. 10 m. 16 d.

341. Johnson.   Seventh Generation.   Tower.

149. MOLLY[6], PETER[5], PETER[4], JEREMIAH[3], JEREMIAH[2], JOHN[1].
Molly [6], dau. of Peter[5] and Deborah (Stowell) Tower, b.
April 27, 1765 ; mar. Moses Johnson, of Coleraine, Mass.,
July 7, 1807, by Rev. James Briggs.

Child.

I. PURLEY[7] born March 21, 1809.

342. Pratt.   Seventh Generation.   Tower.

149. DEBORAH[6], PETER[5], PETER[4], JEREMIAH[3], JEREMIAH[2], JOHN[1].
Deborah [6], dau. of Peter[5] and Deborah (Stowell) Tower, bapt.
Oct. 4, 1767 ; mar. Josiah Pratt, of Weymouth, Mass.   Int.
pub.
Jan. 14, 1789.   He was b. in Weymouth
Jan. 21, 1768, and was son of Jonathan and Sarah (Dyer)
Pratt.

Childr.

I.	DEBORAH[7]	born Aug. 3, 1792.
II.	JOSIAH[7]	"	Aug. 5, 1794.
III.	DORRANCE GORDON[7]	"	May 21, 1797 ; mar. Maria Boyd.
IV.	ALONZO[7]	"	1803, died in Windsor, Mass., March 9, 1806, ag. 3 ?
V.	PHILENA[7]	"	Oct. 9, 1805; died in Windsor, Oct. 24, 1831, ag. 26 y. 15 d.
VI.	MARY A.[7]	"	May 4, 1809.
VII.	CAROLINE[7]	"	May 30, 1812; mar. Emery Bruce; *s. p.*

Josiah Pratt died in Windsor, May 14, 1845, ag. 77 y. 3 m.
23 d.
Deborah (Tower) Pratt died in Windsor, May 3, 1853, ag.
85 y. 6 m. 29 d.

343.   Seventh Generation.   Tower.

152. MALACHI[6], MALACHI[5], PETER[4], JEREMIAH[3], JEREMIAH[2], JOHN[1].
Malachi[6], son of Malachi[5] and Ruth (Hayward) Tower, b.
April 1, 1761 ; mar. Bathsheba Weatherbee in Milton, Mass.,
Aug. 6, 1783, by Rev. Mr. Thatcher.

Childr.

750.	I.	MOSES[7]	born April 5, 1785, in Dedham.
751.	II.	PETER[7]	"	April 14, 1787.
	III.	SALLY[7]	"	Jan. 29, 1789 ; unmar.; died in Hanover, Mass., Nov. 30, 1821, ag. 32 y. 10 m. 2 d.
752.	IV.	COMFORT[7]	"	Aug. 26, 1790.
753.	V.	JOHN HANCOCK[7]	"	Oct. 6, 1794.

Malachi Tower[6] died in Lincolnville, Me., Dec. 1, 1833, ag. 72 y. 8 m. 14 d.

344. Burrell.   **Seventh Generation.**   **Tower.**

152. LOIS[6], MALACHI[5], PETER[4], JEREMIAH[3], JEREMIAH[2], JOHN[1].
Lois[6], dau. of Malachi[5] and Ruth (Hayward) Tower, b.
Jan. 20, 1769; mar. Benjamin Burrell, of Hingham, Mass.,
June 19, 1788, by Rev. D. Shute. Benjamin Burrell, b. in
Weymouth,
July 29, 1764, was son of Joseph and Hannah (Bicknell)
Burrell.

Childr. born in Hingham.

I. BENJAMIN[7] born Jan. 29, 1789.	VII. ASA[7] born April 11, 1801.
II. MARTIN[7] " Nov. 4, 1790.	VIII. MARY[7] " May 25, 1803.
III. JOHN[7] " Nov. 14, 1792.	IX. WARREN[7] " June 5, 1805.
IV. SUSANNA[7] " March 3, 1795.	X. LOUISA[7] " July 4, 1807.
V. MALACHI[7] " Feb. 9, 1797.	XI. JOSEPH[7] " Dec. 22, 1809.
VI. RUTH[7] " April 17, 1799.	XII. SOPHIA[7] "

Benjamin Burrell died in Hingham, Aug. 27, 1846, ag. 82 y. 30 d.

Lois (Tower) Burrell died in Hingham, March 10, 1844, ag. 75 y. 1 m. 21 d.

345.   **Seventh Generation.**   **Tower.**

156. GAD HITCHCOCK[6], LYNDE[5], JAMES[4], BENJAMIN[3], BENJAMIN[2], JOHN[1].
Gad H.[6], son of Lynde[5] and Rebecca (Bowker) Tower, b.
1776; mar. Martha Cook in Pennsylvania
Feb. 27, 1806, by Rev. Mr. Wyley. She was b. in Penn.
1789, and was dau. of Edward and Rebecca (Wilson) Cook.

Childr.

754.	I.	REBECCA PRATT[7] born Dec. 27, 1806.
755.	II.	ANGELINE WHITMAN[7] " June 27, 1808.
756.	III.	EDWIN WHITMAN[7] " Feb. 3, 1810.
757.	IV.	EDWARD COOK[7] " June 1, 1814.
758.	V.	MARTHA[7] "
	VI.	MARY L.[7] " ; mar. M. Lyttleton, 1844.
759.	VII.	G. H.[7] " April 14, 1820.
760.	VIII.	ORELLA[7] "
	IX.	VIRGIL MARCY[7] "
761.	X.	THEODORE SEDWICK[7] " 1824.
	XI.	ALFRIDA[7] " ; died, ag. 12.

Gad Hitchcock Tower [6] died   1839 ? ag. 63 ?

Martha (Cook) Tower died in Pittsburg, Pa., June 26, 1865, ag. 76.

346.   **Seventh Generation.**   **Tower.**

156. JAMES [6], LYNDE [5], JAMES [4], BENJAMIN [3], BENJAMIN [2], JOHN [1].
James [6], son of Lynde [5] and Lucy (Gary) Tower, b.
May 7, 1799 ; mar. Persis Averill in Westminster, Vt.,
March 17, 1823, by Rev. S. Sage. She was b.
July 19, 1795, and was dau. of Obed and Susan (   )
Averill.

Childr. born in Westminster, Vt.

762.	I.	LYNDE [7]	born April 22, 1824.
763.	II.	BETSEY ANN [7] "	Feb. 18, 1827.
764.	III.	ANGELINE P. [7] "	Nov. 25, 1828.
765.	IV.	CYNTHIA H. [7] "	Nov. 21, 1832.
	V.	FRANCES D. [7] "	April 13, 1835; unmar.

James Tower [6] died in Westminster, Oct. 25, 1872, ag. 73 y. 5 m. 18 d.

Persis (Averill) Tower died in Westminster, Oct. 24, 1876, ag. 81 y. 3 m. 5 d.

347. Holton.   **Seventh Generation.**   **Tower.**

156. REBECCA [6], LYNDE [5], JAMES [4], BENJAMIN [3], BENJAMIN [2], JOHN [1].
Rebecca [6], dau. of Lynde [5] and Lucy (Gary) Tower, b.
   ; mar. Reuben Holton.

Childr.

I.	LYNDE [7],	; died in Illinois.	III. SABRA [7].
II.	NELSON [7].		IV. HARRIET [7].

348. Fogg, Whittemore. Seventh Generation.   **Tower.**

158. BETSEY [6], MATTHEW [5], JAMES [4], BENJAMIN [3], BENJAMIN [2], JOHN [1].
Betsey [6], dau. of Matthew [5] and Jerusha (Hatch) Tower, b.
Aug. 3, 1790 ; mar. Isaac Whittemore in Scituate, Mass.,
June 27, 1811.

Child born in Scituate.

I. JOSEPH JAMES LLOYD [7] born Oct. 15, 1811; mar.

Isaac Whittemore died
Betsey (Tower) Whittemore mar., 2d, Ebenezer T. Fogg, of Scituate,
July 20, 1820. He was born in Braintree, Mass., March 28, 1795.

Childr. born in Scituate.

II.   GEORGE PARSONS[7] born June 27, 1821.
III. HORACE TOWER[7]   "   Sept. 27, 1823; died in St. Paul, Brazil, Nov.
                             , 1877, ag. 54 y. 2 m.
IV.   CHARLES EDWARD[7] "   Feb. 18, 1825.
V.   EBENEZER THAYER[7] " Oct. 30, 1826.
VI.   ELIZABETH ANN[7]   " May 8, 1829.
VII. ISABELLA THAYER[7] " Sept. 15, 1831.

Ebenezer T. Fogg died in South Scituate, May 12, 1861,
  ag. 66 y. 1 m. 15 d.
Betsey (Tower) Fogg died in South Scituate, Jan. 3, 1876,
  ag. 85 y. 5 m.

349.   **Seventh Generation.**   **Tower.**

159. BENJAMIN T.[6], BENJAMIN[5], JAMES[4], BENJAMIN[3], BENJAMIN[2],
     JOHN[1].
     Benjamin T.[6] son of Benjamin[5] and Lucy (Totman) Tower, b.
     Nov. 7, 1778 ; mar. Chloe Bates, of Attleborough, Mass.,
     April 25, 1799.

Childr.

766. I.   BENJAMIN[7] born July 17, 1799.
767. II. WASHINGTON[7] " Aug. 11, 1801.
768. III. AMASA[7]   "   1804.
      IV. SYLVESTER[7] "   1805; unmar. ; died in Westminster,
                                   Oct. 23, 1870, ag. 65.
769. V.   GARDNER[7]   " Jan. 26, 1811.

Chloe (Bates) Tower died in Rochester, Vt., Nov.   , 1846.
Benjamin T. Tower[6] mar., 2d, Phebe Porter, of Westminster,
  Vt.,
Oct. 28, 1847. She died in Rochester, Jan. 28, 1863, ag.
  75 y. 6 m. 20 d.
Benjamin T. Tower[6] died in Rochester, Nov. 18, 1863, ag.
  85 y. 11 d.

350. Clough.   **Seventh Generation.**   **Tower.**

159. POLLY[6], BENJAMIN[5], JAMES[4], BENJAMIN[3], BENJAMIN[2], JOHN[1].
     Polly[6], dau. of Benjamin[5] and Lucy (Totman) Tower, b.
     Sept. 17, 1780 ; mar. Peter Clough, of Westminster, Vt.,
     Sept. 11, 1808. He was b. in Sandwich, N. H.

Childr.

I.	ELIZA [7]	born	Aug. 11, 1804.
II.	FANNY [7]	"	June 19, 1809.
III.	NANCY ADELINE [7]	"	May 8, 1811; mar. Lucius Oakes, of Moriah, N. Y.; *s. p.* She died soon after marriage.
IV.	WILLIAM [7]	"	Feb. 11, 1813.
V.	CHARLES [7]	"	Dec. 26, 1814; died in Michigan.
VI.	JOHN [7]	"	June 17, 1817.
VII.	HENRY [7]	"	Aug. 8, 1819.
VIII.	DAVID [7]	"	April 10, 1821; unmar.

Polly (Tower) Clough died in Westminster, Vt., April 15, 1821, ag. 40 y. 4 m. 29 d.

Peter Clough mar., 2d, Hannah Perham Aug. 12, 1821.

Peter Clough died in Bangor, N. Y., Feb.   , 1845.

351. McLaughlin.   Seventh Generation.   Tower.

159. LUCY [6], BENJAMIN [5], JAMES [4], BENJAMIN [3], BENJAMIN [2], JOHN [1].
Lucy [6], dau. of Benjamin [5] and Lucy (Totman) Tower, b. Nov. 8, 1784; mar. John McLaughlin in Westminster, Vt., April   , 1815.

Childr.

I.	WILLIAM [7]	; died	
II.	LYMAN [7]	; "	
III.	JOHN [7]	; "	
IV.	BENJAMIN [7]		
V.	WARREN [7]	; "	
VI.	REBECCA [7]	; mar.	Rafferty, of Walpole, N. H.
VII.	LUCY [7]	; "	

John McLaughlin died in Moriah, N. Y., Feb. 12, 1866.
Lucy (Tower) McLaughlin died in Moriah, N. Y., Oct. 30, 1863, ag. 78 y. 11 m. 22 d.

352. Paine.   Seventh Generation.   Tower.

159. PHEBE [6], BENJAMIN [5], JAMES [4], BENJAMIN [3], BENJAMIN [2], JOHN [1].
Phebe [6], dau. of Benjamin [5] and Lucy (Totman) Tower, b. Aug. 13, 1788; mar. Daniel Paine.
He was b.
Feb. 29, 1780, and was son of Miller Paine.

Child.

I.	ESTHER G. [7]	born Oct.	, 1812.	
II.	DANIEL [7]	"	; died at the age of 4 or 5 years.	
III.	DANIEL [7]	" Dec.	, 1818; died Dec. 29, 1836, ag. 18.	
IV.	PHEBE [7]	" Jan.	16, 1822.	
V.	CHARLES H. [7]	" Jan.	24, 1824.	

Daniel Paine died in Bangor, N.Y., March 21, 1861, ag. 81 y. 21 d.

Phebe (Tower) Paine died in Malone, N. Y., May 15, 1864, ag. 75 y. 9 m. 2 d.

353. **Seventh Generation.** **Tower.**

159. EPHRAIM DEAN [6], BENJAMIN [5], JAMES [4], BENJAMIN [3], BENJAMIN [2], JOHN [1].

Ephraim D.[6], son of Benjamin [5] and Lucy (Totman) Tower, b. Aug. 27, 1790; mar. Betsey Emery, of Rockingham, Vt., Sept. , 1811. She was b.

April 7, 1793, and was dau. of Samuel and Mary (Green) Emery.

Childr.

770.	I.	LUCY [7]	born March , 1812.	
	II.	EPHRAIM [7]	" 1813; died in Rockingham, Vt., 1815, ag. 1 y. 6 m.?	
	III.	ELEAZER E.[7]	" Feb. , 1815; died Nov. , 1868, ag. 53 y. 9 m. ?	
	IV.	MARY [7] }	Twins " Oct. 12, 1817 { unmar.	
	V.	JOHN [7] }		died Nov. 9, 1817.
771.	VI.	LYNDE [7]	" May 14, 1820.	

Betsey (Emery) Tower died in Northfield, Vt., Oct. 23, 1832, ag. 39 y. 6 m. 16 d.

Ephraim D. Tower [6] mar., 2d, Phebe .

She died in Malone, N. Y., 1866 ?

Ephraim D. Tower [6] died in Northfield, Vt., Dec. 29, 1875, ag. 85 y. 4 m. 2 d.

354. **Seventh Generation.** **Tower.**

159. JACOB [6], BENJAMIN [5], JAMES [4], BENJAMIN [3], BENJAMIN [2], JOHN [1].

Jacob [6], son of Benjamin [5] and Lucy (Totman) Tower, b. Oct. 16, 1798; mar. Lucia Prentiss in Brandon, N. Y., 1825. She was b. in Townsend, Vt.,

Nov. 30, 1805, and was dau. of Elijah and Abby (Ewings) Prentiss.

Child. born in Bangor, N. Y.

772. I. AMBROSE [7] born Dec. 17, 1825.

Lucia (Prentiss) Tower died in Bangor, N. Y., April , 1827, ag. 21 y. 5 m.

Jacob Tower [6] mar., 2d, Sevona Kingsbury in Bangor Jan. 4, 1828. She was b.

July 15, 1806, and was dau. of Benjamin and Sarah (Smith) Kingsbury.

Childr.

773.	II.	WARREN J.[7]	born Feb. 4, 1829.		
	III.	LUCIA [7]	" May 30, 1830; died	1849, ag. 19.	
774.	IV.	ROXANA [7]	" Sept. 15, 1831.		
775.	V.	RANSOM J.[7]	" March 31, 1833.		
776.	VI.	ALBERT [7]	" Aug. 29, 1835.		
	VII.	DANIEL E.[7]	" March 30, 1837; mar.	Farr; died in the	
			army in Yorktown, Va.		
	VIII.	HORACE B.[7]	" Feb. 9, 1839; mar.	Hall.	
	IX.	AUSTIN W.[7]	" Sept. 16, 1840; unmar.		
777.	X.	ALMON N.[7]	" Aug. 24, 1842.		
778.	XI.	ADELINE P.[7]	" April 11, 1845.		
779.	XII.	EDWIN R.[7]	" April 5, 1848.		

Jacob Tower [6] died in Malone, N. Y., Jan. 31, 1877, ag. 78 y. 3 m. 15 d.

355.   **Seventh Generation.**   **Tower.**

159. WARREN [6], BENJAMIN [5], JAMES [4], BENJAMIN [3], BENJAMIN [2], JOHN [1].

Warren [6], son of Benjamin [5] and Lucy (Totman) Tower, b. Feb. 15, 1801; mar. Laurinda Holbrook; *s. p.*
She died in Bangor, N. Y., July 13, 1864, ag. 65.
Warren Tower [6] mar., 2d, Naomi Conger; *s. p.*
Warren [6] and Naomi (Conger) Tower adopted a dau. named

LUCIA P., who died in Bangor, March 29, 1871, ag. 14.

Warren Tower [6] died in Bangor, July 1, 1876, ag. 75 y. 4 m. 16 d.

356. Brown.   **Seventh Generation.**   **Tower.**

161. SARAH [6], SOLOMON [5], JAMES [4], BENJAMIN [3], BENJAMIN [2], JOHN [1].
Sarah [6], dau. of Solomon [5] and Sarah (Stoddard) Tower, b. Oct. 13, 1808; mar. William Brown in Weymouth, Mass.

Child born in Scituate, Mass.

I. PRISCILLA BEALS [7] born Oct. 6, 1842.

William Brown died   .
Sarah (Tower) Brown mar., 2d, Charles Brown, of East Bridgewater,
Dec. 20, 1855. He was brother of William, deceased.

357.   Seventh Generation.   **Tower.**

161. HORACE STUDLEY[6], SOLOMON[5], JAMES[4], BENJAMIN[3], BENJA-
MIN[2], JOHN[1].

    Horace S.[6], son of Solomon[5] and Sarah (Stoddard) Tower, b.
April 10, 1810; mar. Malinda H. Hammond, of New Bedford.
Int. pub.
Nov. 4, 1837.

Childr. born in New Bedford, Mass.

780.	I.	ABBY JANE[7]	born	1839
	II.	LUCY ANNA[7]	"	Sept. , 1840; unmar.; died July 17, 1862; ag. 21 y. 10 m. ?
781.	III. IV.	CHARLES E.[7] } LEWIS F.[7] } Twins	"	Nov. 2, 1842; Charles E. died Dec. 2, 1868, ag. 26 y. 1 m.
	V.	HORACE F.[7]	"	Dec. 30, 1844; unmar.
	VI.	MALINDA[7]	"	Sept. , 1846; died Jan. 12, 1847.
	VII.	GEORGE A.[7]	"	April 10, 1848; " July 10, 1848.
782.	VIII.	MALINDA F.[7]	"	May 10, 1849.
	IX.	WILLIAM H.[7]	"	July , 1851; " Nov. 27, 1851.
	X.	WILLIE B.[7]	"	Dec. 7. 1853; " July 7, 1871, ag. 17 y. 7 m.

Malinda (Hammond) Tower died June 12, 1875, ag. 57.

358. Leavitt.   Seventh Generation.   **Tower.**

161. LUCY D.[6], SOLOMON[5], JAMES[4], BENJAMIN[3], BENJAMIN[2], JOHN[1].
Lucy D.[6], dau. of Solomon[5] and Sarah (Stoddard) Tower, b.
March 20, 1812; mar. Jairus Leavitt, of Scituate,
April 22, 1832.

Childr.

I. JAIRUS W.[7]	born	1836.	V. GEORGE H.[7]	born		1850.
II. LUCY D.[7]	"	1839.	VI. ALBION T.[7]	"	June 2, 1854,
III. EMMA J.[7]	" July 13, 1845.		in Scituate.		
IV. ELIZA D.[7]	" Nov. , 1846.				

359.   Seventh Generation.   **Tower.**

161. JOHN S.[6], SOLOMON[5], JAMES[4], BENJAMIN[3], BENJAMIN[2], JOHN[1].
John S.[6], son of Solomon[5] and Sarah (Stoddard) Tower, b.
March 27, 1814; mar. Jane Tower[6]. She was b. in Scitu-
ate, Mass.,
Aug. 29, 1813, and was dau. of David and Patience (Palmer)
Tower.
Jane[6], David[5], James[4], Benjamin[3], Benjamin[2], John[1].

Child.

783.   I.   JAMES A.[7] born   1838.

Jane (Tower [6]) Tower died Aug. 22, 1849, ag. 35 y. 11 m. 23 d.
John S. Tower [6] mar., 2d, Harriet A. Foster
June 19, 1851.   She was dau. of Joseph Foster.

Childr.

II.   JOHN H.[7]   born July 18, 1854.
III. ARTHUR WILBUR [7] " April 22, 1858.
IV.   MARY ELLEN [7]   " Aug. 13, 1862.

John S. Tower [6] died in Abington, Aug. 19, 1873, ag. 59 y.
    4 m. 22 d.

360.   Sylvester.   Seventh Generation.   Tower.

161.   MARY ELIZABETH [6], SOLOMON [5], JAMES [4], BENJAMIN [3], BENJA-
       MIN [2], JOHN [1].
       Mary E.[6], dau. of Solomon [5] and Sarah (Stoddard) Tower, b.
       Jan. 9, 1817; mar. Henry Sylvester, of Scituate, Mass.

Childr.

I.   WILLIAM HENRY [7] born   1841.
II. MARY ELIZABETH [7] " Oct.   , 1845; died in Hull, Dec. 10, 1872, ag.
                                    27 y. 2 m.

361.   Seventh Generation.   Tower.

162   DAVID [6], DAVID [5], JAMES [4], BENJAMIN [3], BENJAMIN [2], JOHN [1].
      David [6], son of David [5] and Patience (Palmer) Tower, b.
      April 3, 1818; mar. Lydia McFarland, of Pembroke, Mass.
      She died Oct. 26, 1843, ag. 27 ; s. p.
      David Tower [6] mar., 2d, Ruth McFarland, of Pembroke.

Child.

I.   DAVID [7] born March 2, 1847.

Ruth (McFarland) Tower died Jan. 12, 1851, ag. 29.
David Tower [6] mar., 3d, widow Lucy D. Hayden in Wey-
    mouth, Mass.,
May 12, 1853.   She was b. in Weymouth
June 1, 1822, and was dau. of Joseph and Nancy (Dyer)
    Pratt.
PRATT.   TOWER.
Lucy D.[7], Joseph [6], Lydia [5], Joseph [4], Christian [3], Benjamin [2], John [1].

Child.

II. RUTH ESTELLA[7] born Jan. 17, 1858.

362. Hollis.   Seventh Generation.   Tower.

162. PATIENCE[6], DAVID[5], JAMES[4], BENJAMIN[3], BENJAMIN[2], JOHN[1].
Patience[6], dau. of David[5] and Patience (Palmer) Tower, b.
Jan. 29, 1821; mar. Henry F. Hollis in Weymouth, Mass.,
Feb. 2, 1848.   He was b.
         , 1822, and was son of Enoch and Hannah (   ) Hollis.

Childr.

I. MAHALA[7].
II. JANE[7].
III. ALICE[7] born   1859.

Henry F. Hollis died in the War of the Rebellion.

363.   Seventh Generation.   Tower.

162. JOHN[6], DAVID[5], JAMES[4], BENJAMIN[3], BENJAMIN[2], JOHN[1].
John[6], son of David[5] and Patience (Palmer) Tower, b.
July 14, 1824; mar. Nancy Sylvester
April 26, 1846.   She was b.
June 18, 1827, and was dau. of Anthony and Nancy (Tay-
lor) Sylvester.

Childr.

784.	I. HORACE S.[7]	born May 11, 1847.
	II. JOHN F.[7]	" Nov. 10, 1849.
	III. MARY P.[7]	" Sept. 25, 1853.
	IV. FRANK A.[7]	" March 2, 1856.
	V. ELIZABETH[7]	" Feb. 2, 1858; died Feb. 28, 1859, ag. 1 y. 26 d.
	VI. CLARENCE[7]	" Jan. 2, 1861.
	VII. CHARLES C.[7]	" May 9, 1863.
	VIII. WILLIE COBB[7]	" July 6, 1865.
	IX. NELLIE ELLSWORTH[7]	" May 24, 1868.
	X. JENNIE M.[7]	" Jan. 8, 1870.

364.   Seventh Generation.   Tower.

162. REUBEN[6], DAVID[5], JAMES[4], BENJAMIN[3], BENJAMIN[2], JOHN[1].
Reuben[6], son of David[5] and Patience (Palmer) Tower, b.
April 17, 1828; mar. Hannah Hollis in Hanover, Mass.,
March 6, 1865, by Rev. C. C. Clark.   She was b. in Hanover
         1838, and was dau. of Silas and Hannah (Dwelley)
Hollis.   *S. p.*

162. MAHALA [6], DAVID [5], JAMES [4], BENJAMIN [3], BENJAMIN [2], JOHN [1].
Mahala [6], dau. of David [5] and Patience (Palmer) Tower, b.
July 29, 1831; mar. Francis Corbin, of Weymouth, Mass.,
Nov. 23, 1851. He was b.
1829, and was son of Roswell and Mehitable (   )
Corbin.

Childr.

I.   ROSA [7].   IV.   LEONA [7].
II.   FRANK [7].   V.   Son [7].
III.   MARY [7].

164. EZRA [6], JONATHAN [5], JONATHAN [4], BENJAMIN [3], BENJAMIN [2],
JOHN [1].
Ezra [6], son of Jonathan [5] and Basmeth (Wheeler) Tower, b.
April 26, 1782; mar. Sally Fuller, of Wrentham, Mass.,
May 18, 1806, by Rev. Mr. Gardner. She was born in
Wrentham
July 13, 1783.

Childr.

	I.	SALLY [7]	born March 10, 1807, in Newton, Mass.
	II.	GEORGE WASHINGTON [7]	" Aug. 11, 1809, in Patchouge, N. Y.
	III.	LEWIS NORCROSS [7]	" Nov. 23, 1811, " " ; died Oct. 30, 1813, ag. 1 y. 11 m. 7 d.
785.	IV.	LUTHER WHEELER [7]	" Dec. 23, 1813, in Patchouge.
786.	V.	BELINDA B. B. [7]	" May 16, 1816.
	VI.	PAMELA LAWTON [7]	" Aug. 31, 1818; unmar.
787.	VII.	JERUSHA EMERY EARL [7]	" Feb. 8, 1821.
	VIII.	SYLVIA NEWMAN [7]	" April 15, 1823; unmar.
788.	IX.	EMILY HARADON [7]	" Dec. 11, 1825.

Ezra Tower [6] died in Wallingford, Vt., May 20, 1867, ag.
85 y. 24 d.
Sally (Fuller) Tower died in Wallingford, Vt., Sept. 17,
1855, ag. 72 y. 2 m. 4 d.

164. JAMES [6], JONATHAN [5], JONATHAN [4], BENJAMIN [3], BENJAMIN [2],
JOHN [1].
James [6], son of Jonathan [5] and Basmeth (Wheeler) Tower, b.
April 26, 1782; mar. Eliza Avery.

Childr.

I. Daughter.   II. Daughter.

Eliza (Avery) Tower died, and James Tower[6] mar., 2d,
   Sarah
He died in Scituate, Mass., July 28, 1842, ag. 60 y. 3 m.
   2 d.

368.   **Seventh Generation.**   **Tower.**

164. JOSHUA[6], JONATHAN[5], JONATHAN[4], BENJAMIN[3], BENJAMIN[2],
   JOHN[1].
Joshua[6], son of Jonathan[5] and Basmeth (Wheeler) Tower, b.
   Jan. 15, 1784; mar. Eliza Crouch
June 30, 1805. She was b.
Aug. 12, 1780.

Childr.

789.	I.	ALMIRA[7]	born Nov. 13, 1805.	
	II.	Infant[7]	" March 12, 1808; died March 12, 1808.	
	III.	PAMELA[7]	" Dec. 23, 1812; " Oct. 10, 1818, ag. 5 y. 9 m.	
			17 d.	
	IV.	SYLVIA S.W.[7]	" Oct. 25, 1816; " Oct. 5, 1818, ag. 1 y. 11 m.	
			10 d.	

Eliza (Crouch) Tower died Nov. 29, 1818, ag. 38 y. 3 m. 17 d.
Joshua Tower[6] mar., 2d, Elizabeth Woodcock in Needham,
   Mass.,
Sept. 22, 1825, by Rev. Mr. Richie. She was b. in Needham
Oct. 16, 1797, and was dau. of Samuel and Mary (Washburn)
   Woodcock.

Childr.

	V.	MARY BASMETH[7]	born Sept. 6, 1826, in Milford, Mass.; unmar.
790.	VI.	JOSHUA HOLLIS[7]	" Jan. 31, 1828, " "
791.	VII.	SAMUEL WILLIAM[7]	" Oct. 29, 1829, " "
792.	VIII.	SARAH PERMELIA[7]	" May 17, 1832, " Hopkinton, Mass.
793.	IX.	CAROLINE EDE[7]	" March 16, 1835.
794.	X.	WILBER ISAIAH[7]	" Feb. 24, 1839.

Joshua Tower[6] died in Holliston, Mass., Aug. 3, 1868, ag.
   84 y. 6 m. 19 d.
Elizabeth (Woodcock) Tower died in Holliston, July 8, 1849,
   ag. 51 y. 8 m. 23 d.

369.   Lawton.   Seventh Generation.   Tower.

164. PAMELA[6], JONATHAN[5], JONATHAN[4], BENJAMIN[3], BENJAMIN[2], JOHN[1],

Pamela[6], dau. of Jonathan[5] and Basmeth (Wheeler) Tower, b.

May 2, 1786 ; mar. Hague Lawton, who was b. in Yorkshire, England.

Childr.

I.   BASMETH[7]   born   in Boston.
II.   MARY[7]   "   "   "   ; mar.; ch. 6. She died in Bordeaux, S. C.,   1879.
III. JOSIAH[7]   "   in Boston; mar.; died in Abbeville Co., S. C.,   1865.
IV. ELIZA[7]   " Feb. 19, 1814.
V.   BARUCH[7]   "   in South Carolina ; *s. p.* ; died in Abbeville Co., S. C.,   1869.
VI. FELIX[7]   "   died in infancy.

Hague Lawton died near Fort Hannah, Mt. Carmel, Abbeville Co., S. C., Dec. 26, 1864.

Pamela (Tower) Lawton died in Bordeaux, S. C., March 15, 1845, ag. 58 y. 10 m. 13 d.

370.   Seventh Generation.   Tower.

164. JONATHAN HOLLIS[6], JONATHAN[5], JONATHAN[4], BENJAMIN[3], BENJAMIN[2], JOHN[1].

Jonathan H.[6], son of Jonathan[5] and Basmeth (Wheeler) Tower, b.

March 5, 1788 ; mar. Hannah Ross Oct. 30, 1808.   She was b. in Patchouge, N. Y., May 24, 1792.

Childr.

795.	I.	SANFORD MERTON[7] born Sept.	1, 1809.
796.	II.	HARRIET HETTY[7] " Oct.	19, 1811.
797.	III.	JAMES LAURENCE[7] " June	4, 1817.
798.	IV.	LUCY ANN[7] " April	8, 1819.
799.	V.	WILLIAM WARREN[7] " Sept.	10, 1821.
800.	VI.	MARY JANE[7] " March	28, 1824.
801.	VII.	MARIAH LOIZA[7] " Dec.	4, 1827.
802.	VIII.	PAMELA LAWTON[7] " April	19, 1830.

Jonathan H. Tower[6] died in Watertown, Mass., March 14, 1831, ag. 43 y. 9 d.

Hannah (Ross) Tower died in Yonkers, N. Y., July 25, 1881, ag. 89 y. 2 m. 1 d.

371.   Seventh Generation.   **Tower.**

164. GRENVILLE⁶, JONATHAN⁵, JONATHAN⁴, BENJAMIN³, BENJA-
      MIN², JOHN¹.
      Grenville⁶, son of Jonathan⁵ and Basmeth (Wheeler)
         Tower, b.
      Feb. 2, 1792; mar. Mary Saye
      July 5, 1816, by Rev. Mr. Gildersleve. She was b.
      July 20, 1797.

                            Childr.

803.	I. HANNAH⁷	born June 29, 1817, in Elizabeth, N. J.
804.	II. EZRA⁷	" Jan. 24, 1819, " " "
805.	III. JOB S.⁷	" Jan. 9, 1821, " " "
	IV. GEORGE WASHINGTON⁷	" Feb. 15, 1823, " Newark, "
		died Sept. , 1824, ag. 1 y. 7 m.
		0 d. (?)

Grenville Tower⁶ died Aug.   , 1824, ag. 32 y. 6 m. 0 d.(?)

372.   Seventh Generation.   **Tower.**

164. LUTHER⁶, JONATHAN⁵, JONATHAN⁴, BENJAMIN³, BENJAMIN²,
      JOHN¹.
      Luther⁶, son of Jonathan⁵ and Basmeth (Wheeler) Tower, b.
      Jan. 12, 1794 ; mar. Mary Ware
      July 1, 1817. She was b. in Needham, Mass.,
      Nov. 21, 1798, and was dau. of Nathaniel and Mary (   )
         Ware.

                            Childr.

806.	I. MARY P.⁷	born Feb. 17, 1818.
807.	II. LUTHER W.⁷	" Sept. 24, 1823.
808	III. ADELINE R.⁷	" Aug. 2, 1831; mar. ; died .
	IV. MARTHA M.⁷	" Aug. 8, 1833; died Oct. 7, 1834, ag. 1 y. 1 m
		29 d.
809.	V. CHARLES E.⁷	" March 4, 1839.

Mary (Ware) Tower died in Dedham, Nov. 20, 1865, ag.
   66 y. 11 m. 30 d.
Luther Tower mar., 2d, Polly Cunningham
         1868, by Rev. W. C. Richards. She was born
         1807, and was dau. of Jonathan and Abigail

164. RUFUS[6], JONATHAN[5], JONATHAN[4], BENJAMIN[3], BENJAMIN[2],
JOHN[1].
Rufus[6], son of Jonathan[5] and Basmeth (Wheeler) Tower, b.
Oct. 3, 1796 ; mar. Elizabeth Willis, of Sudbury, Mass.,
March 4, 1821, by Rev. Rufus Hurlburt.

Childr.

810.	I.	ELIZABETH[7] born		1828.
811.	II.	FRANK[7]	" Jan. 25, 1834.	
812.	III.	JOHN H.[7]	"	
813.	IV.	FREEMAN G.[7] "		1840.

164. ALFRED[6], JONATHAN[5], JONATHAN[4], BENJAMIN[3], BENJAMIN[2],
JOHN[1].
Alfred[6], son of Jonathan[5] and Basmeth (Wheeler) Tower, b.
March 16, 1801 ; mar.

Childr.

    I. MARTIN LUTHER[7].
    II. ANGELINE[7].

Alfred Tower[6] died March 26, 1869, ag. 68 y. 10 d.
(   ) Tower died Sept. 13, 1870.

166. NATHANIEL[6], NATHANIEL[5], NATHANIEL[4], THOMAS[3], BENJA-
MIN[2], JOHN[1].
Nathaniel[6], son of Nathaniel[5] and Leah[6] (Tower) Tower, b.
Dec. 1, 1772 ; mar. Hannah Reed, of Cummington, Mass.
She was b.
Feb. 20, 1774, and was dau. of Silas and Patty (Russell)
Reed.

Childr. born in Cummington.

814.	I.	AMANDA[7]	born July 25, 1800.	
815.	II.	AMELIA[7]	" July 28, 1804.	
816.	III.	ALDEN[7]	" March 2, 1808.	
	IV.	OSMOND[7]	" Sept. 20, 1809; died April 2, 1810.	
817.	V.	OSMOND[7]	" Feb. 16, 1811.	
818.	VI.	AMBROSE[7]	" March 9, 1813.	
	VII.	NATHANIEL[7] "	1816; unmar.	

Hannah (Reed) Tower died in Cummington, March 12, 1815, ag. 41 y. 22 d.

Nathaniel Tower[6] mar., 2d, Hannah (Williams) Porter, of Goshen, Mass.,

Jan. 28, 1819. She was born

Dec. 16, 1780, and was dau. of John and Mercy (Weeks) Williams.

Childr.

818. VIII. Louisa H.[7]   born Oct. 22, 1820.
820.   IX. Almira Cordelia[7] " March 24, 1823.

Nathaniel Tower[6] died in Goshen, Jan. 12, 1850, ag. 77 y. 1 m. 11 d.

Hannah (Williams) Tower died in Goshen,   1854 (?).

---

376.   Seventh Generation.   Tower.

166. Peter[6], Nathaniel[5], Nathaniel[4], Thomas[3], Benjamin[2], John[1].

Peter[6], son of Nathaniel[5] and Leah[6] (Tower) Tower, b. June 12, 1775; mar. Polly Bartlett in Cummington, Mass., Sept. 23, 1800, by Rev. James Briggs. She was b. Dec. 23, 1777, and was dau. of Edward and Zilpah (Cole) Bartlett; *s. p.*

Peter Tower[6] died in Catskill, N. Y., March 9, 1825, ag. 49 y. 8 m. 25 d.

Polly (Bartlett) Tower mar., 2d,   Morse.

---

377.   Seventh Generation.   Tower.

166. Ambrose[6], Nathaniel[5], Nathaniel[4], Thomas[3], Benjamin[2], John[1].

Ambrose[6], son of Nathaniel[5] and Leah[6] (Tower) Tower, b. Nov. 2, 1777; mar. Rachel Bartlett in Cummington, Mass., June 20, 1802, by Rev. James Briggs. She was b. Jan. 14, 1780, and was dau. of Edward and Zilpah (Cole) Bartlett.

Childr. born in Cummington.

821.   I. Leah[7]   born Dec. 5, 1802.
      II. Elmina[7]   " Sept. 11, 1804; died May 5, 1807, ag. 2 y. 7 m. 24 d.
      III. Sabrina[7] " Aug. 4, 1806; " March 9,1813, ag. 6 y. 7 m. 5 d.
      IV. Holliston[7"] July 14, 1808; " March 7, 1810, ag. 1 y. 7m. 2 d.
822.   V. Holliston[7"] Oct. 20, 1810.

Ambrose Tower[6] died in Cummington, March 6, 1813, ag. 35 y. 4 m. 4 d.

Rachel (Bartlett) Tower died in Cummington, Dec. 31,1814, ag. 34 y. 11 m. 21 d.

378. Miner.   Seventh Generation.   Tower.

166. SALLY[6], NATHANIEL[5], NATHANIEL[4], THOMAS[3], BENJAMIN[2], JOHN[1].

Sally[6], dau. of Nathaniel[5] and Leah[6] (Tower) Tower, b. Oct. 23, 1780; mar. Jonathan Miner, of Windsor, Mass., Oct. 24, 1803. He was b. June 24, 1780.

Childr. born in Windsor.

I.	NORMAN[7]	born June 19, 1804.	
II.	MARSHAL[7]	" May 3, 1806.	
III.	SALLY[7]	" Feb. 10, 1808; died Feb. 18, 1808.	
IV.	Infant[7]	" ; " Aug. 20, 1809.	
V.	AUSTIN[7]	" Aug. 20, 1809; " Feb. 20, 1810.	
VI.	SALLY GOODELL[7]	" July 9, 1811.	
VII.	JONATHAN GARDNER[7]	" April 9, 1814.	
VIII.	ELIZABETH[7]	" Nov. 25, 1819.	

Jonathan Miner died in Windsor, April 13, 1842, ag. 61 y. 9 m. 20 d.

Sally (Tower) Miner died in Windsor, Aug. 19, 1849, ag. 68 y. 9 m. 27 d.

379.   Seventh Generation.   Tower.

166. WARREN[6], NATHANIEL[5], NATHANIEL[4], THOMAS[3], BENJAMIN[2]

RHODA[7], STEPHEN[6], PETER[5], PETER[4], JEREMIAH[3], JEREMIAH[2]

} JOHN[1].

Warren[6], son of Nathaniel[5] and Leah[6] (Tower) Tower, b. July 9, 1789; mar. Rhoda Tower[7] in Cummington, Mass., April 1, 1817, by Rev. James Briggs. She was b. in Cummington Nov. 26, 1795, and was dau. of Stephen[6] and Anna (Bowker) Tower.

Childr. born in Cummington.

823.	I.	SALOME[7 & 8] born Oct. 9, 1817.	
	II.	NAAMAN[7] " Jan. 25, 1819; died Jan. 29, 1819.	
1195.	III.	SABRINA[7] " May 29, 1820.	
823 a.	IV.	ELMINA[7] " Oct. 6, 1822.	
824.	V.	WARREN E.[7] " April 5, 1824.	
825.	VI.	LORENZO H.[7] " Aug. 14, 1830.	

Warren Tower[6] died in Cummington, May 26, 1834, ag. 44 y. 10 m. 17 d.

Rhoda[7] (Tower) Tower died in Cummington, Aug. 2, 1833, ag. 37 y. 8 m. 7 d.

380. Bartlett. Seventh Generation. Tower.

166. ROXY[6] { NATHANIEL[5], NATHANIEL[4], THOMAS[3], BENJAMIN[2] LEAH[6], PETER[5], PETER[4], JEREMIAH[3], JEREMIAH[2] } JOHN[1].

Roxy[6], dau. of Nathaniel[5] and Leah[6] (Tower) Tower, b. June 12, 1794; mar. Stephen Bartlett, of Worthington, Mass.,

Oct. 10, 1811, by. Rev. James Briggs. S. Bartlett, b.
1789, was son of Edward and Zilpah (Cole) Bartlett.

Childr. born in Worthington.

I.	MARY[7]	born	Dec. 14, 1811.
II.	NATHANIEL LLOYD[7]	"	July 12, 1814.
III.	EDWARD STEPHEN[7]	"	Feb. 22, 1816
IV.	ROXANA[7]	"	Oct. 25, 1818.
V.	LUTHER A.[7]	"	Oct. 3, 1824, died Jan. 3, 1830, ag. 5 y. 3 m.
VI.	AUGUSTINE[7] } Twins	"	Jan. 20, 1830; Augustine mar.; Austin died
VII.	AUSTIN[7]		Jan. 20, 1834, ag. 4 y.
VIII.	AUSTIN[7]	"	; mar.; d. 1879.
IX.	FRANKLIN[7]	"	
X.	SYLVESTER[7]	"	

Roxy (Tower) Bartlett died in Worthington, July 18, 1842, ag. 48 y. 1 m. 6 d.

Stephen Bartlett mar., 2d, widow Abby Dyas Feb. 11, 1845. He died in Worthington, Jan. 17, 1861, ag. 72.

381. Seventh Generation. Tower.

169. MARTIN[6], MARTIN[5], SHADRACH[4], THOMAS[3], BENJAMIN[2], JOHN[1].

Martin[6], son of Martin[5] and Molly (Mansfield) Tower, b. April 6, 1777; mar. Nancy Christy
Sept. 8, 1799.

Childr.

	I.	MARTIN[7]	born	Sept. 27, 1800; unmar.; died.
	II.	FREDERICK[7]	"	Feb. 22, 1802; " " 1845, ag. 43 (?).
826.	III.	MARY ANN[7]	"	June 11, 1803.
	IV.	NATHANIEL CHADWICK[7]	"	March 14, 1806; unmar.; died.
	V.	HANNAH CHRISTY[7]	"	March 20, 1809.

Martin Tower[6] died in Hingham, Aug. 11, 1819, ag. 42 y.
4 m. 5 d.

Nancy (Christy) Tower died in Hingham Oct. 14, 1818.

382.   **Seventh Generation.**   **Tower.**

170. THOMAS[6], THOMAS GROSS[5], SHADRACH[4], THOMAS[3], BENJA-
MIN[2], JOHN[1].

Thomas[6], son of Thomas Gross[5] and Elizabeth (Fuller)
Tower, b.
Feb. 8, 1783; mar. Sarah Man, of Savoy, Mass.,
Jan. 4, 1807. She was b. in Boston
Feb. 6, 1785.

Childr.

827.	I.	SALLY[7]	born Oct. 19, 1807.
828.	II.	HORACE[7]	" Jan. 18, 1809.
829.	III.	EPHRAIM[7]	" March 28, 1811.
830.	IV.	CLARISSA T.[7]	" Dec. 9, 1813.
	V.	JERUSHA[7]	" Aug. 25, 1816; died Nov. 29, 1816.
	VI.	ALFRED LYMAN[7]	" March 10, 1820; " Sept. 12, 1820.

Thomas Tower[6] died in Florida, Mass., July 4, 1859, ag.
76 y. 4 m. 26 d.

Sarah (Man) Tower died in Florida, Nov. 19, 1870, ag. 85 y.
9 m. 13 d.

383.   **Seventh Generation.**   **Tower.**

170. MARTIN[6], THOMAS G.[5], SHADRACH[4], THOMAS[3], BENJAMIN[2],
JOHN[1].

Martin[6], son of Thomas G.[5] and Elizabeth (Fuller) Tower, b.
April 8, 1790; mar. Fanny Clark, of Florida, Mass.,
March 20, 1817. She was b. in Florida
1800, and was dau. of Sylvanus and Content
(   ) Clark.

Childr. born in Florida.

831.	I.	ALVIN[7]	born Dec. 9, 1817.
832.	II.	CALVIN[7]	" Jan. 8, 1819.
833.	III.	ORRIN[7]	" April 1, 1820.
834.	IV.	FANNY[7]	} Twins " Dec. 14, 1822.
835.	V.	PHILA DIANA[7]	
	VI.	LUCY[7]	" Nov. 11, 1823; died Aug. 29, 1850, ag. 26 y. 9 m. 18 d.
	VII.	HARRY[7]	" Jan. 2, 1825; died Dec. 25, 1853, ag. 28 y. 11 m. 23 d.

	VIII.	WILLIAM J.[7]	born June 6, 1826; died Sept. 17, 1829.
836.	IX.	WARREN FULLER [7]	" April 23, 1828.
837.	X.	CALISTA [7]	" May 16, 1831.
	XI.	WILLIAM [7]	" Nov. 4, 1833; unmar.; died in Virginia 1864, ag. 30.
838.	XII.	HOUGHTON [7]	" Aug. 2, 1835.
839.	XIII.	ELI [7]	" Nov. 15, 1836.
840.	XIV.	SIDNEY [7]	" June 15, 1839.
841.	XV.	MILES [7] } Twins	" Aug. 29, 1844.
842.	XVI.	MINOR [7] }	

Fanny (Clark) Tower died in Florida, April 22, 1857, ag. 57.

Martin Tower [6] mar., 2d, Mary Jane Pike
Aug. 1, 1857. She was b.
1812.

Martin Tower [6] died in Florida, June 19, 1864, ag. 74 y. 2 m.
11 d.

384.   **Seventh Generation.**   **Tower.**

170. WILLIAM [6], THOMAS G. [5], SHADRACH [4], THOMAS [3], BENJAMIN [2], JOHN [1].

William [6], son of Thomas G. [5] and Elizabeth (Fuller) Tower, b.
April 25, 1793; mar. Anna Thatcher in Florida, Mass.,
Oct. 22, 1816. She was b. in Florida
Jan. 5, 1801, and was dau. of Ebenezer and Hannah (Burnett) Thatcher.

Childr. b. in Florida.

843.	I.	DENNIS [7]	born July 28, 1817.
	II.	LUCINDA P.[7]	" Nov. 24, 1818; mar. Sylvanus Clark, of Wilmington, Vt., May 22, 1836; *s. p.*
844.	III.	RIZPAH [7]	" Aug. 4, 1820.
845.	IV.	SARAH [7]	" Jan. 27, 1822.
846.	V.	NANCY [7]	" Jan. 29, 1827.
847.	VI.	SEDATE THATCHER [7]	" Sept. 10, 1838.
848.	VII.	MARSHAL W.[7]	" Aug. 26, 1840.

Anna (Thatcher) Tower died in Florida, May 9, 1854, ag.
53 y. 4 m. 4 d.

William Tower [6] mar., 2d, Candace (Cross) Goodnow
Aug. 6, 1854.

William Tower [6] died in Florida, Sept. 14, 1858, ag. 65 y.
4 m. 20 d.

Candace (Cross) Tower died in Charlemont, Mass.

385. Manning.   Seventh Generation.   Tower.

170. BETSEY[6], THOMAS G.[5], SHADRACH[4], THOMAS[3], BENJAMIN[2],
JOHN[1].
Betsey[6], dau. of Thomas G.[5] and Elizabeth (Fuller) Tower, b.
; mar. John Manning.

Childr.

I.	ALBERTUS[7]	born Feb. 1, 1819.
II.	ADELINE[7]	"	March 24, 1821.
III.	EMELINE[7]	"	Oct. 14, 1823.
IV.	ELIZA[7]	"	Sept. 10, 1827; mar. Levi Porter. He died.
V.	CHLOE[7]	"	Nov. 4, 1834; " Joel Whitcomb.

Betsey (Tower) Manning died   1838 (?).
John Manning mar., 2d, Rispah (Thatcher) Brown.
He died in Florida, Aug. 27, 1879, ag. 82 y. 4 m. 11 d.

386. Putney.   Seventh Generation.   Tower.

170. LUCY[6], THOMAS G.[5], SHADRACH[4], THOMAS[3], BENJAMIN[2],
JOHN[1].
Lucy[6], dau. of Thomas G.[5] and Elizabeth (Fuller) Tower, b.
; mar. Samuel Putney.

Child.

I. MARY[7] born   ; mar.   Sibly.

Lucy (Tower) Putney died   .

387.   Seventh Generation.   Tower.

170. CHESTER[6], THOMAS G.[5], SHADRACH[4], THOMAS[3], BENJAMIN[2],
JOHN[1].
Chester[6], son of Thomas G.[5] and Elizabeth (Fuller) Tower, b.
June 15, 1798; mar. Grateful Thatcher
Sept. 6, 1822.   She was b.
Sept. 9, 1803, and was dau. of Ebenezer and Hannah (   )
Thatcher.

Childr. born in Florida, Mass.

I.	GRATA LOUISA[7]	born April 25, 1823; mar. Asa Harkness March 14, 1842.
II.	HANNAH[7]	" Oct. 22, 1824; unmar.; died May 24, 1852, ag. 27 y. 7 m. 2 d.

849.	III.	CHESTER L.[7]	born Oct. 16, 1826.
850.	IV.	FRANCIS O.[7]	" Jan. 1, 1834.
851.	V.	MATILDA R.[7]	" April 28, 1835.
852.	VI.	HARVEY B.[7]	" Nov. 22, 1838.

Chester Tower[6] died in Florida, Feb. 22, 1871, ag. 72 y. 8 m. 7 d.

Grateful (Thatcher) Tower died in Florida, March 1, 1880, ag. 76 y. 5 m. 21 d.

388. Putney. Seventh Generation. Tower.

170. POLLY[6], THOMAS G.[5], SHADRACH[4], THOMAS[3], BENJAMIN[2], JOHN[1].

Polly[6], dau. of Thomas G.[5] and Elizabeth (Fuller) Tower, b. ; mar. Samuel Putney.

Childr.

I.	JOSEPH[7]	born	
II.	LUCINDA[7]	"	; mar. Gardner Burdeck.
III.	SARAH[7]	"	

389. Seventh Generation. Tower.

171. LYMAN[6], SAMUEL[5], SAMUEL[4], PETER[3], BENJAMIN[2], JOHN[1].

Lyman[6], son of Samuel[5] and Betsey (Thomas) Tower, b. Aug. 13, 1791; mar. Julia Welton Dec. 9, 1821. She was b. Aug. 21, 1802, and was dau. of Jesse Welton.

Childr. born in Franklin, N. Y.

853. I. BETSEY SOPHIA[7] born May 15, 1823.
II. ERASTUS LYMAN[7] " Jan. 15, 1828; died June 6, 1834, ag. 6 y. 4 m. 22 d.

Lyman Tower[6] died in Franklin, Nov. 23, 1873, ag. 82 y. 3 m. 10 d.

Julia (Welton) Tower died in Franklin, Dec. 12, 1870, ag. 68 y. 3 m. 21 d.

390. Seventh Generation. Tower.

170. OBADIAH[6], SAMUEL[5], SAMUEL[4], PETER[3], BENJAMIN[2], JOHN[1].

Obadiah[6], son of Samuel[5] and Betsey (Thomas) Tower, bapt. Nov. 10, 1799; mar. Hannah Phillips Oct. 30, 1817, by Rev. J. L. Pomeroy.

Childr.

I. LYMAN [7] born   ; died young.
II. ELIZABETH [7] "   ; mar. Thomas Gagan. She died near Rochester, N. Y.
III. SARAH [7]   "   ; unmar.; died   ag. 25 (?)

Obadiah Tower [6] died in Wilson, Niagara Co., N. Y.

391. Ferguson.   Seventh Generation.   Tower.

173. HANNAH [6], SHUBAEL [5], SAMUEL [4], PETER [3], BENJAMIN [2], JOHN [1].
Hannah [6], dau. of Shubael [5] and Abigail (Bates) Tower, b.
Feb. 20, 1795 ; mar. Lemuel Ferguson.

Childr.

I. RODNEY G. [7]   born
II. MARIA [7]   "
III. SALMA URIAH [7] "   ; unmar.; died.
IV. ORIN KNOX [7]   "   ; mar.; died June   , 1876.
V. HENRY G. [7]   "
VI. HARVEY B. [7]   "

Hannah (Tower) Ferguson died in Smyrna, N. Y., Dec. 25, 1829, ag. 34 y. 10 m. 5 d.

392.   Seventh Generation.   Tower.

173. SALMA [6], SHUBAEL [5], SAMUEL [4], PETER [3], BENJAMIN [2], JOHN [1].
Salma [6], son of Shubael [5] and Abigail (Bates) Tower, b.
Dec. 13, 1797 ; mar. Sally Carpenter in Lisle, Broome Co., N. Y.,
March 19, 1841, by Rev. Mr. Sargeant. She was b. in Oneonta, N. Y.,
June 19, 1805, and was dau. of Samuel and Irena (Philips) Carpenter.

Child.

I. ROSELLA [7] born April 30, 1842; unmar.

Salma Tower [6] died in Smyrna, N. Y., June 20, 1844, ag. 46 y. 6 m. 7 d.

393.   Seventh Generation.   Tower.

173. WILLIAM [6], SHUBAEL [5], SAMUEL [4], PETER [3], BENJAMIN [2], JOHN [1].
William [6], son of Shubael [5] and Abigail (Bates) Tower, b.
May 20, 1802 ; mar. Diana Sacket, of Plymouth, N. Y.,
Sept. 7, 1831, by Rev. Luther Clark. She was b.
May 28, 1801, and was dau. of Martin and Miriam (Bancroft) Sacket.

Childr.

854. I. MARY AMELIA[7]   born May 21, 1835.
II. LUCINDA ARMENIA[7]   "   Oct. 18, 1838 ; died Oct. 6, 1843, ag. 4 y.
11 m. 18 d.

Diana (Sacket) Tower died May 10, 1879, ag. 77 y. 11 m. 12 d.

394.   **Seventh Generation.**   **Tower.**

173. ALMON[6], SHUBAEL[5], SAMUEL[4], PETER[3], BENJAMIN[2], JOHN[1].
Almon[6], son of Shubael[5] and Abigail (Bates) Tower, b.
Dec. 7, 1804 ; mar. Mary Sexton
Sept. 7, 1831, by Rev. Luther Clark. She was b. in Plymouth,
N. Y.,
Dec. 17, 1809, and was dau. of Seth and Nancy (Bisbee)
Sexton.

Childr.

       I. JAMES OTIS[7] born March   4, 1833; died March 23, 1833.
855. II. MIRON[7]   "   March 20, 1834.
856. III. ADDISON[7]   "   Nov. 15, 1836.
857. IV. AMASA[7]   "   March 24, 1839.
858.   V. NANCY A.[7]   "   April 14, 1841.
859. VI. WARREN[7]   "   Aug. 17, 1843.
860. VII. MARY A.[7]   "   Nov. 23, 1846.
     VIII. ALMON[7]   "   Aug. 24, 1849; died March 9, 1850.
861. IX. FLORA ELIZA[7] "   Sept. 12, 1854.

Almon Tower[6] died May 1, 1878, ag. 73 y. 4 m. 24 d.

395.   **Seventh Generation.**   **Tower.**

173. OBADIAH[6], SHUBAEL[5], SAMUEL[4], PETER[3], BENJAMIN[2], JOHN[1].
Obadiah[6], son of Shubael[5] and Abigail (Bates) Tower, b.
Jan. 21, 1807 ; mar. Fidelia Munroe of Sandisfield, Mass.,
April 22, 1830. She was b.
Dec. 5, 1806, and was dau. of Dan and Deborah (Sexton)
Munroe.

Childr.

       I. ALLEN F.[7]   born March 18, 1832; died April 20, 1832.
862. II. MARIA H.[7]   "   April 21, 1833.
863. III. EDWIN MURRAY[7]   "   March 24, 1835.
      IV. MILTON NELSON[7]   "   March 4, 1838; died Oct. 10, 1842, ag. 4 y.
7 m. 6 d.
864.   V. CYRUS OBADIAH[7]   "   July 19, 1845.

Fidelia (Munroe) Tower died July 16, 1867, ag. 60 y. 2 m.
11 d.
Obadiah Tower[6] mar., 2d, widow Maria (Gibson) Curtis
June 26, 1873. She was born in Greene, N. Y.,
Aug. 28, 1832.

396.   Seventh Generation.   **Tower.**

173. RODNEY [6], SHUBAEL [5], SAMUEL [4], PETER [3], BENJAMIN [2], JOHN [1].
      Rodney [6], son of Shubael [5] and Abigail (Bates) Tower, b.
      May 29, 1810 ; mar. Fidelia Robinson [8], of Sherburne, N.Y.,
      March 14, 1833, by Rev. Mr. Sprague. She was b. in Ham-
      ilton, N. Y.,
      Dec. 24, 1817, and was dau. of Samuel and Anna (Tower)
      Robinson.

  ROBINSON.   TOWER.
Fidelia [8], Anna [7], Stephen [6], Peter [5], Peter [4], Jeremiah [3], Jeremiah [2], John [1].

Childr.

865.	I.	LAURA DELANO [7 & 9] born Feb. 28, 1834, in Smyrna, N. Y.
866.	II.	HELEN SELANA [7]	" Feb. 7, 1840, " " "
867.	III.	ADELINE F.[7]	" April 8, 1846, " Lynn, Wis.
868.	IV.	ORVILLE R.[7]	" March 3, 1849, " " "
869.	V.	EDGAR ALPHONSO [7]	" Nov. 13, 1851, " " "

Rodney Tower [6] died in Mindora, Wis., June 12, 1884, ag. 74 y.
14 d.

397.   Seventh Generation.   **Tower.**

173. JAMES BATES [6], SHUBAEL [5], SAMUEL [4], PETER [3], BENJAMIN [2],
      JOHN [1].
      James Bates [6], son of Shubael [5] and Abigail (Bates) Tower, b.
      Jan. 20, 1815 ; mar. Amanda F. Powell, of Pharsalia, N.Y.,
      May 27, 1836, by Rev. Mr. Hamilton. She was b.
      Dec. 5, 1813, and was dau. of Elijah and Jane (Temple) Powell.

Childr.

870.	I.	JAMES BENSON [7]	born Aug. 24, 1840, in Pitcher, N. Y.
	II.	MARTIN CARROLL [7]	" Oct. 3, 1844, in Geneva, Wis. ; died Jan. 26, 1849, ag. 4 y. 3 m. 23 d.
871.	III.	FRANKLIN HENRY [7]	" Jan. 6, 1847, in Lynn, Wis.

Amanda F. (Powell) Tower died Jan. 23, 1854, ag. 40 y. 1 m.
18 d.
James B. Tower [6] mar., 2d, Lorina J. Furness,
Oct. 8, 1854. She was born in Westport, N. Y.,
Feb. 23, 1815, and was dau. of Jacob and Mary (Fish)
Matthews, and widow of Daniel H. Furness.

Child.

  IV. FREDDIE [7] born May 12, 1857 ; died Nov. 15, 1857.

398.   **Seventh Generation.**   **Tower.**

173. SAMUEL NELSON[6], SHUBAEL[5], SAMUEL[4], PETER[3], BENJAMIN[2],
JOHN[1].

Samuel N.[6], son of Shubael[5] and Abigail (Bates) Tower, b.
July 12, 1818; mar. Hannah Lewis
Oct. 9, 1839. She was b.
June 18, 1818, and was dau. of William and Rhoda (Breed)
Lewis.

Childr.

872.   I. HANNAH ADELAIDE[7] born March 2, 1843.
873.   II   LEWIS NELSON[7]   "   Aug. 19, 1848.

399. Smith.   **Seventh Generation.**   **Tower.**

175. SABIAH[6], PETER[5], SAMUEL[4], PETER[3], BENJAMIN[2], JOHN[1].
Sabiah[6], dau. of Peter[5] and Rene (Abby) Tower, b.
Oct. 19, 1798; mar. Obadiah Smith, of Middlefield, Mass.

Childr.

I.	LORINDA[7]	; mar. 1st,	King.
		" 2d,	Fisher, of Huntington, Mass.
II.	CLARINDA[7]		
III.	MATILDA[7]		
IV.	AMANDA[7]	; mar. John Fay, of Otis, Mass.	
V.	SABIAH[7]	; died in Huntington, 187?.	

400.   **Seventh Generation.**   **Tower.**

175. LABAN[6], PETER[5], SAMUEL[4], PETER[3], BENJAMIN[2], JOHN[1].
Laban[6], son of Peter[5] and Rene (Abby) Tower, b.
Jan. 17, 1800; mar. Patty Johnson, of Becket, Mass.,
April 19, 1825, by Rev. Joseph Mills. She was b.
Oct. 1, 1798, and was dau. of Moody and Hannah (Barnes)
Johnson.

Childr.

874.	I.	LUCINA A.[7]	born April 14, 1826.
	II.	MILO BRIGGS[7]	" Dec. 11, 1827; died April 14, 1828.
875.	III.	AURELIA M.[7]	" July 22, 1829.
	IV.	HARMONY[7]	" ` July 14, 1831; died Aug. 22, 1838, ag. 7 y. 1 m. 8 d.
	V.	NANCY A.[7]	" July 13, 1833; " Sept. 20, 1846, ag. 13 y. 2 m. 7 d.
876.	VI.	JOHN WESLEY[7]	" May 16, 1839
877.	VII.	SAMUEL D.[7]	" Jan. 5, 1842.

Laban Tower[6] died Sept. 20, 1850, ag. 50 y. 8 m. 3 d.
Patty (Johnson) Tower mar., 2d, Ira Clark, of Hoosac, N. Y.,
Dec. 31, 1856.

401. Johnson.   Seventh Generation.   Tower.

175. LAURA [6], PETER [5], SAMUEL [4], PETER [3], BENJAMIN [2], JOHN [1].
Laura [6], dau. of Peter [5] and Rene (Abby) Tower, b.
                ; mar. John J. Johnson, of Worthington, Mass.
     Int. pub.
May 15, 1822.
                        Childr.
        I. LUCY [7].   II. RENE [7].

402. Olmstead.   Seventh Generation.   Tower.

175. ANN [6], PETER [5], SAMUEL [4], PETER [3], BENJAMIN [2], JOHN [1].
Ann [6], dau. of Peter [5] and Rene (Abby) Tower, b.
                ; mar. Rowland Olmstead.

                        Childr.

    I. CHLOE [7].   II. MINERVA [7].   III. LABAN F. [7]

403. Wells, Mason.   Seventh Generation.   Tower.

175. EUNICE [6], PETER [5], SAMUEL [4], PETER [3], BENJAMIN [2], JOHN [1].
Eunice [6], dau. of Peter [5] and Rene (Abby) Tower, b.
                ; mar. John Mason, of Cheshire, Mass.

                        Childr.
I. GEORGE [7] born May 28, 1831.   II. LUCY [7].   III. SABIAH [7].

    John Mason died in Cheshire   1833 ?
    Eunice (Tower) Mason mar., 2d, Shubael Wells, of Cheshire.
                        Childr.
        IV. NORMAN [7].   V. SHUBAEL [7].

    Shubael Wells died in Adams, Mass.,   1875 ?
    Eunice (Tower) Wells died in Holyoke Feb. 28, 1873.

404. Hoxie.   Seventh Generation.   Tower.

175. ASENATH [6], PETER [5], SAMUEL [4], PETER [3], BENJAMIN [2], JOHN [1].
Asenath [6], dau. of Peter [5] and Rene (Abby) Tower, b.
                ; mar. Cyrus Hoxie, of Cheshire, Mass.

                        Childr.
        I. LUCY [7].   II. MINERVA [7].

405. Collins.   Seventh Generation.   Tower.

175. SALLY [6], PETER [5], SAMUEL [4], PETER [3], BENJAMIN [2], JOHN [1].
Sally [6], dau. of Peter [5] and Rene (Abby) Tower, b.
                ; mar. Squire Collins, of Tyringham, Mass.

Child.

878. Edwin O. Tower [7] b. Dec.   , 1832, in Cheshire, Mass.

406.   **Seventh Generation.**   **Tower.**

177. Isaiah [6], Isaiah [5], Isaiah [4], Peter [3], Benjamin [2], John [1].
Isaiah [6], son of Isaiah [5] and Hannah (Jacob) Tower, b.
July 31, 1789 ; mar. Polly Wilder in Hingham, Mass.,
June 9, 1811, by Rev. N. B. Whitney. She was bapt. in
Hingham
Oct.   , 1791, and was dau. of Samuel and Hannah (Lazell)
Wilder.

> Childr. born in Hingham.
>
> 879.   I. Hannah Jacob [7] born Sept. 4, 1811.
> 880. II. Isaiah Gill [7]   " Aug. 26, 1813.

Polly (Wilder) Tower died in Hingham, July 4, 1815, ag.
23 y. 9 m.
Isaiah Tower [6] mar., 2d, Chloe Gardner in Hingham
March 24, 1816, by Rev. N. B. Whitney. She was b. in
Hingham
Nov. 8, 1796, and was dau. of Samuel and Chloe (Whiton)
Gardner.

> Childr. born in Hingham.
>
> 881. III. George Augustus [7] born July 6, 1818.
> 882. IV. Charles F. [7]   " April 19, 1823.

Chloe (Gardner) Tower died in Hingham, Jan. 6, 1824, ag.
27 y. 1 m. 29 d.
Isaiah Tower [6] mar., 3d, Martha C. Wilder in Hingham
Oct. 1, 1826, by Rev. N. B. Whitney. She was b. in
Hingham
Oct. 30, 1797, and was dau. of Crocker and Deborah (Jacob)
Wilder ; *s. p.*
Isaiah Tower [6] died in Hingham, May 13, 1842, ag. 52 y. 9 m.
12 d.
Martha C. (Wilder) Tower died in Hingham, Aug. 16, 1875,
ag. 77 y. 9 m. 17 d.

407.   **Seventh Generation.**   **Tower.**

177. Joshua [6], Isaiah [5], Isaiah [4], Peter [3], Benjamin [2], John [1].
Joshua [6], son of Isaiah [5] and Hannah (Jacob) Tower, b.
Oct. 7, 1790 ; mar. Anna Hersey in Hingham, Mass.,

Nov. 21, 1811, by Rev. N. B. Whitney. She was b. in
Hingham

June 14, 1788, and was dau. of John and Anna (Cushing)
Hersey.

Childr. born in Hingham.

883.	I.	JOSHUA [7]	born Aug. 27, 1812.
	II.	ANNA CUSHING [7]	" Oct. 2, 1815; died Dec. 6, 1818, ag. 3 y. 2 m. 4 d.
884.	III.	ANGELINA H. [7]	" Feb. 9, 1818.
885.	IV.	EDWIN [7]	" Dec. 11, 1821.
886.	V.	MARY J. [7]	" July 16, 1824.
	VI.	ANNA HERSEY [7]	" Oct. 27, 1827; unmar.
	VII.	SIDNEY JOHN [7]	" Aug. 28, 1832; died April 13, 1837, ag. 4 y. 7 m. 16 d.

Joshua Tower[6] died in Hingham, June 15, 1845, ag. 54 y.
8 m. 8 d.

Anna (Hersey) Tower died in Hingham, May 25, 1876, ag.
87 y. 11 m. 11 d.

408.   **Seventh Generation.**   **Tower.**

177. LEAVITT[6], ISAIAH[5], ISAIAH[4], PETER[3], BENJAMIN[2], JOHN[1].
Leavitt[6], son of Isaiah[5] and Hannah (Jacob) Tower, b.
Jan. 1, 1793; mar. Mary J. Jacob in Hingham
Dec. 28, 1815. She was b.
June 30, 1798, and was dau. of Daniel and Mary (Jones)
Jacob.

Childr. born in Hingham.

	I.	DANIEL JACOB [7]	born June 11, 1817; unmar.; died March 26, 1861, ag. 43 y. 9 m. 17 d.
	II.	LEAVITT B. [7]	" May 19, 1821; died Jan. 3, 1839, ag. 17 y. 7 m. 14 d.
887.	III.	MARY RICHMOND [7]	" Nov. 26, 1824.

Mary (Jacob) Tower died in Hingham, July 7, 1845, ag.
47 y. 7 d.

Leavitt Tower[6] mar., 2d, Mary E. Bisbee, of Dayton, Ohio,
April 26, 1862. She was b. in Belgrade, Me.,

March 11, 1818, and was dau. of Thomas H. and Betsey
(Philbrook) Bisbee; *s. p.*

Leavitt Tower[6] died in Hingham, Sept. 24, 1882, ag. 89 y.
8 m. 23 d.

Mary E. (Bisbee) Tower died in Hingham, Nov. 22, 1880,
ag. 62 y. 8 m. 11 d.

177. REUBEN[6], ISAIAH[5], ISAIAH[4], PETER[3], BENJAMIN[2], JOHN[1].
Reuben[6], son of Isaiah[5] and Hannah (Jacob) Tower, b.
July 3, 1795; mar. Rebecca Hathaway, of Plymouth, Mass.,
Dec. 2, 1819. She was b.
Aug. 1, 1795, and was dau. of Alanson and Rebecca (Brattles) Hathaway.

Childr.

888.	I.	REUBEN[7]	born Dec.	30, 1820.
889.	II.	REBECCA[7]	" Feb.	18, 1822.
889 a.	III.	BETSEY ANN[7]	" Sept.	3, 1823.
890.	IV.	CAROLINE[7]	" March	17, 1825.
891.	V.	WILLIAM SEWALL[7]	" July	7, 1826.
892.	VI.	JOHN BROOKS[7]	" Jan.	3, 1828.
893.	VII.	ANDREW[7]	" May	26, 1829.
894.	VIII.	JAMES G.[7]	" March	26, 1831.
895.	IX.	HENRY T.[7]	" April	9, 1833.
	X.	GEORGE F.[7]	" April	13, 1834; unmar.
	XI.	CHARLES S.[7]	" May	9, 1836; died Sept. 9, 1836.
896.	XII.	CHARLES S.[7]	" Dec.	27, 1838.
	XIII.	ADELINE E.[7]	" Sept.	, 1840; unmar.
	XIV.	HANNAH J.[7]	"	1842; unmar.

Reuben Tower[6] died in Hingham, Oct. 27, 1881, ag. 86 y.
3 m. 24 d.
Rebecca (Hathaway) Tower died in Hingham, Aug. 22,
1876, ag. 81 y. 21 d.

179. WILLIAM[6], LUCY[5], LABAN[4], PETER[3], BENJAMIN[2], JOHN[1].
William[6], son of Lucy Tower[5], b.
April 18, 1808; mar. Lucy A. Young, of Bath, Me.,
Sept. 13, 1840. She was b. in Bath
May 4, 1820, and was dau. of John and Lucy (Chubbuck)
Young.

Childr. born in Hingham.

897.	I.	LUCY ANN[7]	born Oct.	17, 1853.
898.	II.	WILLIAM ARTHUR[7]	" July	16, 1855.
899.	III.	CHARLES SUMNER[7]	" June	18, 1856.
	IV.	JOHN HENRY[7]	" June 16, 1858; mar. Georgie E. Batchelder, of Weymouth, Aug. 3, 1879.
900.	V.	ELIZABETH MARIA[7]	" Dec.	31, 1861.

William Tower[6] died in Hingham, April 12, 1879, ag. 70 y.
11 m. 25 d.

411. Haskell.   Seventh Generation.   Tower.

180. BETSEY[6], ISAAC[5], JOSEPH[4], AMBROSE[3], BENJAMIN[2], JOHN[1].
Betsey[6], dau. of Isaac[5] and Elizabeth (Wheeler) Tower, b.
June 1, 1783; mar. Eli Haskell in Belchertown, Mass.,
March 24, 1808. He was b.
          , 1783.

                        Childr.

I.	ABEL[7]	born May 7, 1809, in Belchertown.
II.	LEVI[7]	" Jan.18, 1811, " "
III.	ELIZABETH[7]	" Oct. 8, 1813; died Sept. 8, 1814.
IV.	ELI[7]	" Aug. 7, 1815.
V.	ISAAC[7]	
VI.	WILLIAM[7]	} Twins " Dec. 15, 1817, in Bristol, N. Y.
VII.	JEREMIAH[7]	" Oct. 14, 1820, " " "
VIII.	ACHSAH[7]	" Jan. 23, 1824; mar. Samuel Shah, of Canandaigua, N. Y., 1856; *s. p.*
IX.	NANCY[7]	" March 13, 1826; died April 9, 1844, ag. 18 y. 27 d.

Eli Haskell died in Canandaigua, N.Y., Oct. 7, 1855, ag. 72 ?
Betsey (Tower) Haskell died in Canandaigua, N. Y., Feb. 9,
1863, ag. 79 y. 8 m. 6 d.

412.   Seventh Generation.   Tower.

180. ISAAC[6], ISAAC[5], JOSEPH[4], AMBROSE[3], BENJAMIN[2], JOHN[1].
Isaac[6], son of Isaac[5] and Elizabeth (Wheeler) Tower, b.
April 13, 1785; mar. Polly Haskell in Belchertown, Mass.,
March 22, 1809.

                        Childr.

	I.	MARY[7]	born April 22, 1810; died in Bristol, N.Y., May 24, 1827, ag. 17 y. 1 m. 2 d.
901.	II.	PHILO[7]	" Jan. 1, 1812, in Belchertown.
902.	III.	LOUISA[7]	" June 23, 1813, " "
903.	IV.	ANDREW JACKSON[7]	" July 4, 1815, " "
904.	V.	HANNAH[7]	" April 25, 1819, in Bristol, N. Y.
	VI.	LUTHER[7]	" Oct. 9, 1821, " " " ; died 1840, ag. 19 ?
905.	VII.	CHARLES H.[7]	" Jan. 28, 1825.

Isaac Tower[6] died in Rochester, N. Y., July   , 1825, ag.
40 y. 3 m. 0 d. ?

413. Pettingill. Seventh Generation.   Tower.

180. LURANA[6], ISAAC[5], JOSEPH[4], AMBROSE[3], BENJAMIN[2], JOHN[1].
Lurana[6], dau. of Isaac[5] and Elizabeth (Wheeler) Tower, b.
June 17, 1787; mar. Nathan Pettingill, of Belchertown, Mass.,
Dec. 17, 1808. He was b.
April 14, 1787.

Childr.

I.	RHODA SYBELLA [7]	born Nov. 23, 1809, in Cincinnati, Ohio.
II.	LURANA [7]	" April 14, 1811, " " "
III.	NATHAN [7]	" March , 1813, in Pelham, Mass.; died , 1813.
IV.	HEPZIBAH [7]	" April , 1815, " " "
V.	CYRUS [7]	" Feb. 27, 1817, " Bristol, N. Y.; mar. Mirinda Beach.
VI.	JOB WHEELER [7]	" Aug. 22, 1819.
VII.	ADONIRAM JUDSON [7]	" Oct. 3, 1821.
VIII.	ELIZABETH [7]	" Aug. 14, 1823.
IX.	HENRY ORMAN [7]	" April , 1825; died 1829, ag. 4 ?
X.	HENRY NATHAN [7]	" April , 1827.
XI.	JONATHAN LEECH [7]	" , 1829 ; died 1835, ag. 6 ?

Nathan Pettingill died in St. Joseph, Mich., Dec. , 1842, ag. 55 y. 8 m. 0 d. ?

Lurana (Tower) Pettingill died in St. Joseph, Mich., May 1851, ag. 63 y. 11 m. 0 d. ?

414. Seventh Generation. **Tower.**

180. JOB [6], ISAAC [5], JOSEPH [4], AMBROSE [3], BENJAMIN [2], JOHN [1].
Job [6], son of Isaac [5] and Elizabeth (Wheeler) Tower, b. June 24, 1789 ; mar. Nancy Sanger in Boston Jan. ? , 1818. She was b.
1793, and was dau. of Zedekiah and Mary (Dench) Sanger.

Childr.

	I.	JAMES MUNROE [7]	born June 1, 1819; died at sea, 1846 ?
	II.	SUSAN ANN [7]	" Sept. 30, 1821; " June , 1830, ag. 8 y. 9 m.
906.	III.	ISAAC [7]	" Nov. 24, 1823.
907.	IV.	ALICE MARIA [7]	" Aug. 14, 1825.
908.	V.	MARY [7]	" Feb. 24, 1828.
	VI.	SUSAN [7]	" March 28, 1831; died Feb. 20, 1848, ag. 16 y. 23 d.
	VII.	LURANA [7]	Twins " May 19, 1833 ; died Dec. 2, 1853, ag. 20 y. 6 m. 13 d.
	VIII.	AMANDA [7]	May 19, 1833; died April 2, 1835, ag. 1 y. 10 m. 14 d.
909.	IX.	CHARLES [7]	" July 24, 1836.

Job Tower [6] died in Boston, Jan. 10, 1846, ag. 56 y. 6 m. 17 d.
Nancy (Sanger) Tower died in Boston, Nov. 2, 1836, ag. 43 ?

415. Seventh Generation. **Tower.**

180. JOHN [6], ISAAC [5], JOSEPH [4], AMBROSE [3], BENJAMIN [2], JOHN [1].
John [6], son of Isaac [5] and Elizabeth (Wheeler) Tower, b. Sept. 8, 1791 ; mar. Lucretia Ryder, of Enfield, Mass.

Childr.

I.   NANCY[7] born Nov. 4, 1818, in Belchertown; mar. Charles Dudley.
II. OLIVIA[7]   " Aug. 25, 1820, "   "   ; unmar.; died

John Tower[6] died   1821, ag. 30 ?
Lucretia (Ryder) Tower mar., 2d, Horace Rice, of Ware,
     Mass.,
Int. pub. Sept. 27, 1823.

416.   Pomeroy.   Seventh Generation.   Tower.

180. SIBYL[6], ISAAC[5], JOSEPH[4], AMBROSE[3], BENJAMIN[2], JOHN[1].
      Sibyl[6], dau. of Isaac[5] and Elizabeth (Wheeler) Tower, b.
      April 15, 1794; mar. Luther Pomeroy, of Amherst, Mass.
         Int. pub.
      July 20, 1812. He was b.
      Sept. 19, 1788, and was son of Simeon and Mary (Hastings)
         Pomeroy.

Childr.

I.   MARY ANN[7]   born March 18, 1813.
II.   LUCY[7]   " Aug. 8, 1814; died Oct.   , 1832, ag. 18 y. 2 m.
                         0 d. ?
III. ELIZABETH W.[7] " Sept. 16, 1816; mar. Seymour Ganicard; *s. p.*
IV.   EMELINE[7]   " March 22, 1819.
V.   LUTHER[7]   " July 21, 1822.
VI.   CHLOE[7]   " March 17, 1826.
VII. NAOMI[7]   " April 6, 1832; unmar.; died May 7, 1852, ag.
                         20 y. 1 m. 1 d.
VIII. LUCY ANN[7]   " Dec. 25, 1837; died April   , 1841, ag. 4 y. 4 m.
                         0 d. ?

Luther Pomeroy died in Ghent, Ohio, Dec. 20, 1883, ag. 95 y.
     3 m. 1 d.
Sibyl (Tower) Pomeroy died   March 17, 1852, ag.
     57 y. 11 m. 2 d.

417.   Seventh Generation.   Tower.

180. SAMUEL[6], ISAAC[5], JOSEPH[4], AMBROSE[3], BENJAMIN[2], JOHN[1].
      Samuel[6], son of Isaac[5] and Elizabeth (Wheeler) Tower, b.
      Nov. 26, 1796; mar. Asenath Dickenson, of Ludlow, Mass.,
      May 4, 1820, by Ethamer McConcky, J. P. She was b.
               and was dau. of Erastus and Flavia (Root)
      Dickenson.

Childr.

I. MIRIAM C.[7]   born Oct. 21, 1821; died Sept. 8, 1823, ag. 1 y. 10 m. 18 d.

910.   II. JOSHUA CLARK[7] "   July 19, 1823.

III. SAMUEL DAVIS[7] "   Sept. 22, 1825; died Jan. 3, 1826.

IV. MIRIAM E.[7]   "   March , 1828; unmar.; died Dec. 30, 1851. ag. 23 y. 9 m. 0 d. ?

Asenath (Dickenson) Tower died Sept. 1, 1829.

Samuel Tower[6] mar., 2d, Mary Clark

April 7, 1830. She was b.

Jan. 9, 1805, and was dau. of Noah and Mary (Butterfield) Clark.

Childr.

V. EMERSON ADRIAN[7] born Jan. 10, 1831; unmar.

911.   VI SAMUEL M.[7]   "   Aug. 14, 1832.

912. VII. J. EDWIN[7]   "   June 9, 1834.

913. VIII. MARY ANN[7]   "   May 23, 1837.

IX. ELLEN M.[7]   "   June 17, 1844; died May 21, 1864, ag. 19 y. 11 m. 4 d.

Samuel Tower[6] died in Hadley, April 27, 1877, ag. 80 y. 5 m. 1 d.

Mary (Clark) Tower died in Hadley, June 15, 1882, ag. 77 y. 5 m. 6 d.

418.   **Seventh Generation.**   **Tower.**

182. REUBEN[6], JEDUTHUN[5], JOSEPH[4], AMBROSE[3], BENJAMIN[2], JOHN[1].

Reuben[6], son of Jeduthun[5] and Mary (Smith) Tower, b.

Feb. 15, 1787 ; mar. Deborah Taylor Pierce in Paris, N. Y.,

Feb. 15, 1808. She was b. in Little Compton, R. I.,

July 6, 1785, and was dau. of Stephen and Abigail (Taylor) Pierce.

Childr.

914.   I. CHARLEMAGNE[7]   born April 18, 1809, in Paris, N. Y.

915.   II. JULIUS[7]   "   April 17, 1811, " Waterville, N. Y.

916. III. HENRIETTA[7]   "   Aug. 30, 1814, "   "

917. IV. FAYETTE BARTHOLOMEW[7] "   Jan. 29, 1817, "   "

918.   V. DEWITT CLINTON[7]   "   Jan. 20, 1821, "   "

919. VI. JAMES MONROE[7]   "   March 21, 1823, " Marshall, N.Y.

920. VII. FRANCIS MARION[7]   "   July 31, 1825, "   "   "

VIII. REUBEN[7]   "   June 17, 1829, " Waterville; unmar.

Reuben Tower[6] died in St. Augustine, Fla., March 14, 1832, ag. 45 y. 28 d.

Deborah T. (Pierce) Tower died in Waterville, N. Y., Dec. 30, 1864, ag. 79 y. 5 m. 24 d.

182. DANIEL[6], JEDUTHUN[5], JOSEPH[4], AMBROSE[3], BENJAMIN[2], JOHN[1].

Daniel[6], son of Jeduthun[5] and Mary (Smith) Tower, b.
March 11, 1789; mar. Thirza Whitmarsh in Paris, N. Y.,
April 12, 1813. She was b. in Westerlo, N. Y.,
June 30, 1795, and was dau. of Abiathar and Margaret
(Stanton) Whitmarsh.

Childr. born in Waterville, N. Y.

921.	I.	HARRIET AMELIA[7]	born Oct. 30, 1815.
922.	II.	MARY JANE[7]	"	Sept. 3, 1817.
923.	III.	CHARLES[7]	"	Jan. 18, 1819.
924.	IV.	LENTHEL[7]	"	Dec. 23, 1820.

Daniel Tower[6] died in Paris, N. Y., Jan. 9, 1837, ag. 47 y.
9 m. 29 d.

Thirza (Whitmarsh) Tower died in Chenango, N. Y., June
21, 1858, ag. 62 y. 11 m. 21 d.

182. PATTY[6], JEDUTHUN[5], JOSEPH[4], AMBROSE[3], BENJAMIN[2], JOHN[1].

Patty[6], dau. of Jeduthun[5] and Mary (Smith) Tower, b.
May 20, 1791; mar. Lewis Keith, of Easton, Mass.,
Dec. 16, 1814.

Childr.

I.	HARRIET MARIA[7]	born Nov. 6, 1815.
II.	URSULA[7]	"
III.	LOTHROP[7]	"	Feb. 25, 1822.
IV.	RHODA[7]	"	Feb. 29, 1824.
V.	DELOS[7]	"	; died, ag. 20?

Lewis Keith died in Stockton, N. Y., Oct. 15, 1871.

Patty (Tower) Keith died in Pomfret, N. Y., Oct. 13, 1827,
ag. 36 y. 4 m. 23 d.

182. ACHSAH[6], JEDUTHUN[5], JOSEPH[4], AMBROSE[3], BENJAMIN[2], JOHN[1].

Achsah[6], dau. of Jeduthun[5] and Mary (Smith) Tower, b.
July 19, 1793; mar. Sylvester Munger, of Ludlow, Mass.,
Feb. 21, 1816. He was son of Joseph Munger.

Childr.

I. Son.		II. Son.
III. HELEN[7]	; mar. Julius Hatch, of Syracuse, N. Y.; ch. daughter. Helen (Munger) Hatch died	

Achsah (Tower) Munger died in Paris, N. Y., April 2, 1821, ag. 27 y. 8 m. 14 d.

422. **Seventh Generation.** **Tower.**

182. JONAS [6], JEDUTHUN [5], JOSEPH [4], AMBROSE [3], BENJAMIN [2], JOHN [1].

Jonas [6], son of Jeduthun [5] and Mary (Smith) Tower, b. April 30, 1796 ; mar. Almira Stone, of Bethlehem, Conn., Feb. 8, 1817. She was b. in Bethlehem June 18, 1796, and was dau. of Norman Stone.

Childr.

925.	I.	ALBERT [7]	born Nov. 8, 1817, in Paris, N. Y.
	II.	MARIA [7]	" July 14, 1821, in Middleburg, Ohio; died in Madison, Ohio, Nov. 25, 1840, ag. 19 y. 4 m. 11 d.
926.	III.	SARAH JANE [7]	" Feb. 13, 1824, in Middleburg.
	IV.	MARY [7]	" July 5, 1827, in Painsville, Ohio; unmar.
	V.	ADA [7]	" Oct. 8, 1832, in Madison, Ohio; mar. Walter Shriver, of Cumberland, Ind.

Almira (Stone) Tower died in Madison, Ohio, Nov. 20, 1846, ag. 50 y. 5 m. 2 d.

Jonas Tower [6] mar., 2d, Martha (Dickinson) Frost in Constantia, N. Y.,

Oct.   , 1848. She was widow of Charles M. Frost.

Jonas Tower [6] died in Ironton, Wis., Oct. 20, 1864, ag. 68 y. 7 m. 20 d.

Martha (Dickinson) Tower died in Kansas City, Mo., Jan. 29, 1879.

423. **Munger.** **Seventh Generation.** **Tower.**

182. POLLY [6], JEDUTHUN [5], JOSEPH [4], AMBROSE [3], BENJAMIN [2], JOHN [1].

Polly [6], dau. of Jeduthun [5] and Mary (Smith) Tower, b. July 13, 1798 ; mar. Parley Munger, Jan. 13, 1819. He was b.

June 6, 1797, and was son of Reuben and Laurinda (Chapin) Munger.

Childr.

I.	JEDUTHUN [7]	born Sept. 10, 1820; died in Pomfret, N. Y., July 8, 1847, ag. 26 y. 9 m. 28 d.
II.	MARITTA [7]	" Aug. 2, 1822 ; died in Pomfret, Oct. 29, 1845, ag. 23 y. 2 m. 27 d.
III.	ACHSAH [7]	" Feb. 12, 1824.
IV.	NAOMI [7]	" April 4, 1826 ; died in Pomfret, Oct. 8, 1844, ag. 18 y. 6 m. 4 d.

Parley Munger died in Pomfret, March 24, 1864, ag. 66 y. 9 m. 18 d.

Polly (Tower) Munger died in Pomfret, Nov. 17, 1849, ag. 51 y. 4 m. 4 d.

424. Keith.　　**Seventh Generation.**　　**Tower.**

182. URSULA[6], JEDUTHUN[5], JOSEPH[4], AMBROSE[3], BENJAMIN[2], JOHN[1].

Ursula[6], dau. of Jeduthun[5] and Mary (Smith) Tower, b. June 26, 1803 ; mar. Ruel L. Keith, Jan. 11, 1820. He was b. in Easton, Mass., March 7, 1794.

Childr.

I.	MARY[7]	born Dec. 12, 1820.
II.	FREEMAN[7]	" May 15, 1822.
III.	GEORGE[7]	" March 3, 1824.
IV.	SHEPARD[7]	" Dec. 29, 1825.
V.	CHARLES[7]	" March 27, 1828.
VI.	JAMES[7]	" Oct. 6, 1830 ; died in Ironton, Wis., May 19, 1862, ag. 31 y. 7 m. 13 d.
VII.	REUBEN[7]	" April 24, 1833.
VIII.	MARTHA[7]	" Feb. 3, 1835 ; died March 22, 1835.
IX.	WALTER[7]	" Jan. 26, 1836 ; died in Manatee, Fla., Feb. 18, 1859, ag. 23 y. 23 d.
X.	EDWARD[7]	" Feb. 26, 1842 ; died in Pomfret, N. Y., Sept. 16, 1849, ag. 7 y. 6 m. 18 d.
XI.	ACHSAH ELLEN[7]	" May 8, 1845.

Ruel L. Keith died in Pomfret, N. Y., Jan. 16, 1871, ag. 76 y. 10 m. 9 d.

Ursula (Tower) Keith died in Pomfret, N. Y., April 15, 1847, ag. 43 y. 9 m. 20 d.

425.　　**Seventh Generation.**　　**Tower.**

183. LUKE[6], JONATHAN[5], JOSEPH[4], AMBROSE[3], BENJAMIN[2], JOHN[1].

Luke[6], son of Jonathan[5] and Tirzah (Dimmock) Tower, b. Oct. 22, 1797 ; mar. Mary May, of Spencer, Mass., March 19, 1817, by Benjamin Dewey, Esq. She was b. Dec. 20, 1789, and was dau. of William and Polly (Snow) May.

Childr.

927.	I.	LOUISA[7]	born April 21, 1817, in Rutland, Mass.
928.	II.	LURANA[7]	" Nov. 24, 1818, " " "
929.	III.	AMBROSE MENDELL[7]	" March 27, 1821, " " "
930.	IV.	LORENZO[7]	" Nov. 24, 1824, " " "
931.	V.	MARVIN[7]	" Oct. 5, 1831, " Oakham, "

Mary (May) Tower died in Spencer, Sept. 8, 1865, ag. 75 y. 8 m. 19 d.

Luke Tower[6] mar., 2d, Eliza (Snell) Lothrop,

Oct. 21, 1866. She was born

June 4, 1836, and was dau. of Amos and Phebe (Howlett) Snell.

Luke Tower[6] died in Windsor, Mass., May 11, 1881, ag. 83 y. 6 m. 19 d.

Eliza (Snell) (Lothrop) Tower died in Westford, Conn., April 9, 1881, ag. 44 y. 10 m. 5 d.

426. Clark.   **Seventh Generation.**   **Tower.**

185. BETSEY[6], JUSTUS[5], JOSEPH[4], AMBROSE[3], BENJAMIN[2], JOHN[1].
Betsey[6], dau. of Justus[5] and Dilla (Desmond) Tower, b.
Jan. 20, 1792; mar. Jeremiah Clark in Paris, N. Y.,
He was b. in Adams, Mass.,
Jan. 7, 1790, and was son of J. and Susanna (Miller) Clark.

Childr.

I.	CHARLES AUGUSTUS[7]	born	Sept. 19, 1815, in Waterville, N. Y.
II.	WILLIAM TOWER[7]	"	July 12, 1817, " " "
III.	SUSAN W.[7]	"	Sept. 9, 1819.
IV.	HENRY CLAY[7]	"	Oct. 4, 1821; died in New Orleans or in the Confederate army.
V.	JAMES STEWART[7]	"	Jan. 23, 1824.
VI.	JANE PORTER[7]	"	Dec. 17, 1826.
VII.	ELIZA HAVEN[7]	"	March 25, 1829.
VIII.	SARAH BRUCE[7]	"	Dec. 8, 1831.
IX.	JUSTUS TOWER[7]	"	June 9, 1834; died Aug. 26, 1843, ag. 9 y. 2 m. 17 d.

Jeremiah Clark died in Waterville, N. Y., Dec. 15, 1839, ag. 49 y. 11 m. 8 d.

Betsey (Tower) Clark died in Waterville, N. Y., June 5, 1839, ag. 47 y. 4 m. 16 d.

427.   **Seventh Generation.**   **Tower.**

185. HORACE D.[6], JUSTUS[5], JOSEPH[4], AMBROSE[3], BENJAMIN[2],
JOHN[1].
Horace D.[6], son of Justus[5] and Dilla (Desmond) Tower, b.
Nov. 20, 1793; mar. Susan Wolcott, of Cheshire, Mass.,
June 20, 1817. She was b.
Feb. 19, 1795.

Childr.

I.	HARRIET[7]	born	April 24, 1819, in Ashtabula, Ohio; unmar.; died in Sangerfield, N. Y., Feb. 19, 1840, ag. 20 y. 8 mo. 26 d.

932. II. JULIA S.[7] born July 16, 1821, in Lanesborough, Mass.
933. III. HORACE W.[7] " July 19, 1824, " " "
934. IV. HENRY N.[7] " Sept. 17, 1830, " Sangerfield, N. Y.

Horace D. Tower died in Waterville, N. Y., Aug. 22, 1885, ag. 91 y. 9 m. 2 d.

Susan (Wolcott) Tower died in Sangerfield, N. Y., Oct. 19, 1867, ag. 72 y. 8 m.

428. **Seventh Generation.** **Tower.**

185. HENRY [6], JUSTUS [5], JOSEPH [4], AMBROSE [3], BENJAMIN [2], JOHN [1].
Henry [6], son of Justus [5] and Dilla (Desmond) Tower, b. Nov. 20, 1796; mar. Eliza Haynes, of Grand Island, Vt., May 1, 1818. She was b. in Grand Island July 12, 1798, and was dau. of Samuel and Rachel (Stanton) Haynes.

Childr.

935. I. LAURA H.[7] born Aug. 15, 1820, in Ashtabula, Ohio.
936. II. MARY W.[7] " April 30, 1822, " " "
937. III. ELIZABETH H.[7] " July 30, 1825, " " "
IV. JULIA S.[7] " June 9, 1828, " Sangerfield, N. Y.; unmar.; died May 8, 1864, ag. 35 y. 10 m. 29 d.
V. SAMUEL HENRY [7] " June 3, 1831, in Sangerfield; died March 11, 1832.

Henry Tower [6] died in Sangerfield, June 27, 1872, ag. 75 y. 7 m. 7 d.

429. Whitney. **Seventh Generation.** **Tower.**

185. CLARISSA [6], JUSTUS [5], JOSEPH [4], AMBROSE [3], BENJAMIN [2], JOHN [1].
Clarissa [6], dau. of Justus [5] and Dilla (Desmond) Tower, b. March 2, 1802; mar. Richard Whitney, of Lanesborough, Mass.,
He was b. in Lanesborough Aug. 2, 1800, and was son of Timothy and Lois (Baker) Whitney.

Childr. born in Lanesborough.

I. CHARLES B.[7] born Oct. 6, 1827.
II. SILAS F.[7] " Sept. 29, 1830; died Nov. 20, 1853, ag. 23 y. 1 m. 22 d.
III. ELIZA A.[7] " Oct. 6, 1835.
IV. HENRY F.[7] " July 24, 1841; " Dec. 31, 1853, ag. 12 y. 5 m. 7 d.

Richard Whitney died in Lanesborough, March 24, 1869, ag. 68 y. 7 m. 22 d.

Clarissa (Tower) Whitney died in Pittsfield, Mass., Sept. 8, 1887, ag. 85 y. 6 m. 6 d.

430. Seventh Generation. **Tower.**

185. JUSTUS [6], JUSTUS [5], JOSEPH [4], AMBROSE [3], BENJAMIN [2], JOHN [1].
Justus [6], son of Justus [5] and Dilla (Desmond) Tower, b.
July 23, 1804; mar. Emeline A. Talcott, of Lanesborough,
June 14, 1827. She was dau. of Nehemiah Talcott.

Childr.

	I.	FRANCES E. [7]	born July 30, 1828, in Lanesborough; mar. John A. Stevens, of Ogdensburg, N. Y. He died .
938.	II.	JANE A. [7]	" March 11, 1830, in Lanesborough.
939.	III.	EDWARD J. [7]	" Oct. 4, 1832, in Williamstown, Mass.
940.	IV.	HARRIET N. [7]	" Sept. 2, 1834, " "
941.	V.	MARTHA L. [7]	" May 8, 1838, " "
	VI.	CARLTON T. [7]	" March 2, 1844; died April 24, 1846, ag. 2 y. 1 m. 22 d.
	VII.	JULIAN TALCOTT [7]	" May 25, 1846; died Dec. 6, 1862, ag. 16 y. 6 m. 12 d.
942.	VIII.	MARY [7]	" April 6, 1853, in Lanesborough.

Justus Tower [6] died in Lanesborough, Nov. 20, 1880, ag. 76 y.
3 m. 28 d.

431. Seventh Generation. **Tower.**

186. CHARLES [6], JONAS [5], JOSEPH [4], AMBROSE [3], BENJAMIN [2], JOHN [1].
Charles [6], son of Jonas [5] and Fanny (Parmenter) Tower, b.
July 2, 1793; mar. Sarah Pratt
Nov. 20, 1821. She was b. in Southbridge, Mass.,
Aug. 11, 1800, and was dau. of Freeman Pratt.

Childr.

943.	I.	MARIA E. [7]	born July 17, 1823.
	II.	JONAS F. [7]	" Oct. 6, 1824; died Feb. 4, 1825.
944.	III.	SARAH A. [7]	" Nov. 17, 1826.
	IV.	ABIAL F. [7]	" July 15, 1828; " Sept. 5, 1829, ag. 1 y. 1 m. 21 d.
945.	V.	FRANCES E. [7]	" Feb. 14, 1831.
946.	VI.	LENDALL P. [7]	" Jan. 13, 1833.
947.	VII.	CHARLES H. [7]	" May 12, 1835.
948.	VIII.	FREEMAN P. [7]	" Feb. 13, 1838.
	IX.	MARY L. [7]	" May 13, 1840; died May 8, 1848, ag. 7 y. 11 m. 25 d.
949.	X.	SUSAN N. [7]	" Jan. 23, 1842.
950.	XI.	ELLEN R. [7]	" March 17, 1843.

Charles Tower [6] died in Southbridge, Feb. 12, 1882, ag. 88 y.
6 m. 19 d.
Sarah (Pratt) Tower died in Southbridge, Aug. 11, 1880,
ag. 80.

186. OREN⁶, JONAS⁵, JOSEPH⁴, AMBROSE³, BENJAMIN², JOHN¹.
Oren⁶, son of Jonas⁵ and Fanny (Parmenter) Tower, b.
Sept. 25, 1794; mar. Harriet Gleason
June 1, 1823, by Rev. Luther Willson. She was bapt.
May 3,,1808, and was dau. of Joseph and Sukey (Whitney)
Gleason.

Childr. born in Petersham, Mass.

951.	I.	WILLIAM AUGUSTUS⁷ born Feb. 26, 1824.	
	II.	HARRIET ELLEN⁷	" Aug. 29, 1826; unmar.; died May 28, 1855, ag. 28 y. 8 m. 29 d.
952.	III.	SUSAN WHITNEY⁷	" July 22, 1828.
	IV.	LOUISA GLEASON⁷	" Jan. 3, 1831; unmar.; died July 2, 1854, ag. 23 y. 5 m. 29 d.

Harriet (Gleason) Tower died in Petersham April 13, 1832.
Oren Tower⁶ mar., 2d, Lucy L. Foster
Feb. 5, 1836, by Rev. Caleb Tracy. She was b.
March 4, 1814, and was dau. of John and Hannah (Lincoln)
Foster.

Childr.

953.	V.	FRANCIS EMERY⁷	born Nov. 30, 1836.
954.	VI.	GEORGE HAMMOND⁷	" Sept. 1, 1839.
	VII.	HARRIET AUGUSTA⁷	" April 11, 1843.
	VIII.	JOHN FOSTER⁷	" Aug. 1, 1845; died Nov. 18, 1849, ag. 4 y. 3 m. 17 d.
	IX.	CATHERINE LUCY⁷	" Sept. 29, 1847.
	X.	HORATIO NELSON⁷	" Nov. 1, 1850.
	XI.	ALFRED OREN⁷	" Feb. 25, 1855.

Oren Tower⁶ died in Petersham, Dec. 3, 1878, ag. 84. y.
2 m. 8 d.

433. Packard.   Seventh Generation.   Tower.

186. LOUISA⁶, JONAS⁵, JOSEPH⁴, AMBROSE³, BENJAMIN², JOHN¹.
Louisa⁶, dau. of Jonas⁵ and Fanny (Parmenter) Tower, b.
Jan. 2, 1797; mar. Hubbard Packard, of Petersham, Mass.,
, 1835; *s. p.*
Louisa (Tower) Packard died in Petersham, Aug. 8, 1864, ag.
67 y. 7 m. 6 d.

434. Hildreth.   Seventh Generation.   Tower.

186. FANNY⁶, JONAS⁵, JOSEPH⁴, AMBROSE³, BENJAMIN², JOHN¹.
Fanny⁶, dau. of Jonas⁵ and Fanny (Parmenter) Tower, b.

Nov. 5, 1800; mar. Paul Hildreth, of Petersham, Mass. Int. pub.
Oct. 10, 1824.

Child.

I. COLLINS[7] born   1825 ? mar.

Fanny (Tower) Hildreth died in Petersham, March 18, 1827, ag. 26 y. 4 m. 13 d.

435.   **Seventh Generation.**   **Tower.**

186. HORATIO N.[6], JONAS[5], JOSEPH[4], AMBROSE[3], BENJAMIN[2], JOHN[1].

Horatio N.[6], son of Jonas and Fanny (Parmenter) Tower b. 1806; mar. Rebecca Patch, of Worcester, Mass.

Childr.

I. GEORGE B.[7] born Feb. , 1832; died May 22, 1848, ag. 16 y.
3 m. 0 d.?
II. CHARLES H.[7] "   1834.

Rebecca (Patch) Tower died
Horatio N. Tower[6] mar., 2d, Emeline Goodnow
Feb. 12, 1845. She was b.
, 1823, and was dau. of Jotham Goodnow.

. Childr.

III. NELSON[7]   born Oct. 4, 1847; died   1850?
955. IV. GEORGE N.[7] " March 6, 1850.
956. V. FRANK G.[7] " Oct. 28, 1853.

Horatio N. Tower[6] died in Bloomfield, N. J., Oct. 9, 1884, ag. 78.

436. Gates.   **Seventh Generation.**   **Tower.**

186. MARY ANN[6], JONAS[5], JOSEPH[4], AMBROSE[3], BENJAMIN[2], JOHN[1].

Mary Ann[6], dau. of Jonas[5] and Fanny (Parmenter) Tower, b. Aug. 11, 1812; mar. Charles Gates in Petersham, Mass., March 5, 1836, by Rev. Mr. Tracy. C. Gates b. 1808.

Childr. born in Petersham.

I. MARCIA J.[7]   born Feb. 3, 1837; mar. E. F. Clark, of Framingham, Mass.
II. MARY JOSEPHINE[7] " Feb. 22, 1839.
III. ELLA FRANCES[7] " April 20, 1841; unmar.; died Feb. 20, 1871, ag. 29 y. 10 m.

IV. John Tower [7]   born Sept. 20, 1843.
V. Lizzie L. [7]   " April 20, 1818; unmar.; died Dec. 31, 1873,
                                         ag. 25 y. 8 m. 11 d.
VI. Charles Willie [7]   " Oct. 20, 1855.

Charles Gates died in Petersham, April 5, 1872, ag. 64.

437.   Seventh Generation.   Tower.

186. Samuel S.[6], Jonas [5], Joseph [4], Ambrose [3], Benjamin [2], John [1].
Samuel S.[6], son of Jonas [5] and Nancy (Stone) Tower, b.
July 17, 1817; mar. Relief Rice, of New Salem, Mass.,
April 29, 1845, by Rev. S. Clark. She was b.
           1819, and was dau. of William and Joanna (   )
     Rice.
                              Child.

957.   I. Albert R.[7] born Sept. 14, 1849.

Relief (Rice) Tower died Sept. 23, 1849, ag. 30?
Samuel S. Tower [6] mar., 2d, Mary M. Chamberlain,
April 14, 1859, by Rev. A. L. Thompson. She was b.
Jan. 24, 1832, and was dau. of Ebenezer and Lucy (Hard-
wick) Chamberlain.
                              Childr.

II. Mary C.[7]   born Nov. 4, 1861; died July 31, 1872, ag. 10 y.
                                         8 m. 27 d.
III. Lucy S.[7]   "   June 9, 1863; died Dec. 10, 1875, ag, 12 y.
                                         6 m. 1 d.
IV. Samuel A.[7]   "   June 26, 1865; died May 12, 1869, ag. 3 y.
                                         10 m. 16 d.
V. Eben Lincoln [7] " May 10, 1868; died Aug. 15, 1868.

438. McCullock. Seventh Generation.   Tower.

186. Nancy [6], Jonas [5], Joseph [4], Ambrose [3], Benjamin [2], John [1].
Nancy [6], dau. of Jonas [5] and Nancy (Stone) Tower, b.
Dec. 23, 1818; mar. Solomon McCullock, of Barre, Mass.,
April 10, 1844, by Rev. L. Gage. S. McCullock, b.
Aug. 14, 1814, was son of William and Dency (Dennis)
McCullock.
                              Childr.

I. Mary H.[7]   born Nov. 1, 1845, in Petersham, Mass.
II. Jeraline D.[7] " Sept. 1, 1848, in Barre; died Dec. 19, 1879, ag. 31 y.
                                         3 m. 18 d.
III. Julia T.[7]   " March 19, 1851,   "   died Oct. 29, 1866, ag. 15 y.
                                         7 m. 10 d.
IV. Harriet M.[7] " June 19, 1853,   "
V. Dency E.[7]   " Oct. 30, 1856, in Oakham, Mass.

VI. SAMUEL H.[7] born Sept. 9, 1858, in Holden, Mass.; died June 26, 1859.
VII. OREN H.[7]   "   July 3, 1860, in Barre,   "   "   Jan. 7, 1871,
                                       ag. 10 y. 6 m. 4 d.
VIII. IDA L.[7]   "   Aug. 2, 1863   "

Solomon McCullock died in Barre, June 25, 1883, ag. 68 y.
10 m. 11 d.

439.   **Seventh Generation.**   **Tower.**

187. RUSSELL[6], JOHN[5], JOSEPH[4], AMBROSE[3], BENJAMIN[2], JOHN[1].
Russell[6], son of John[5] and Catherine (Haynes) Tower, b.
Feb. 8, 1796; mar. Carissa E. Cole.

Child.
958.   I.   AMELIA[7] born

Carissa E. (Cole) Tower died   .
Russell Tower[6] mar., 2d, Sarah Ackley.

Child.
II.   ACKLEY[7] born

Russell Tower[6] died Dec. 16, 1866, ag. 70 y. 10 m. 8 d.

440.   **Seventh Generation.**   **Tower.**

187. WILLIAM[6], JOHN[5], JOSEPH[4], AMBROSE[3], BENJAMIN[2], JOHN[1].
William[6], son of John[5] and Catherine (Haynes) Tower, b.
Feb. 5, 1802; mar. Elizabeth Beebe, of Marshall, N. Y.

Childr.
I.   MILTON[7] born   ; died at sea.
II.   ELLEN[7]   "   ; mar. Amos Rowley. She died in Pennsylvania.

William Tower[6] died in Brothertown, Calumet Co., Wis.,
April 29, 1837, ag. 35 y. 2 m. 24 d.

441.   **Seventh Generation.**   **Tower.**

187. JOHN H.[6], JOHN[5], JOSEPH[4], AMBROSE[3], BENJAMIN[2], JOHN[1].
John H.[6], son of John[5] and Catherine (Haynes) Tower, b.
Feb. 22, 1807; mar. Elizabeth Stebbins, of Clinton, N. Y.
Elizabeth (Stebbins) Tower d.
John H. Tower mar., 2d, Jane W. Willis.

Child.
I.   ELIZABETH[7] born Aug. 10, 1833; mar. David G. Saxton, of Charles City,
      Ia.; ch. Fred[8].

Jane W. (Willis) Tower died
John H. Tower mar., 3d, Harriet Marvin.

Child.

II. JAY H.[7] born Sept. 29, 1843 ; died Sept. 29, 1865, ag. 22.

Harriet (Marvin) Tower died
John H. Tower mar., 4th, Martha Lent.

Child.

III. FREDDIE L.[7] born Sept. 16, 1853.

Martha (Lent) Tower died
John H. Tower mar., 5th, Emma Johnson in Rome, N.Y.,
Aug. 19, 1863. She was born in England,
, 1838.
John H. Tower[6] died in Clinton, N. Y., Jan. 2, 1885, ag.
77 y. 10 m. 9 d.

442. Look. **Seventh Generation.** **Tower.**

187. CHARLOTTE H.[6], JOHN[5], JOSEPH[4], AMBROSE[3], BENJAMIN[2],
JOHN[1].
Charlotte H.[6], dau. of John[5] and Catherine (Haynes)
Tower, b.
Oct. 4, 1813 ; mar. Noah Look, of Waterville, N. Y.,
Oct. 7, 1832. He was b. in Sangerfield, N. Y.,
April 30, 1807, and was son of William and Sally Look.

Childr.

I. JUDSON W.[7] born Sept. 4, 1833.
II. FRANCES C.[7] " April 5, 1840.
III. CHARLES T.[7] " May 14, 1843.
IV. JULIAN H.[7] " June 28, 1850; died July 8, 1853, ag. 3 y. 10 d.

Noah Look died in Plank Road, Onondaga Co., N. Y., July
16, 1883.

443. Cleaveland. Seventh Generation. **Tower.**

188. MARY ANN[6], JOTHAM[5], JOSEPH[4], AMBROSE[3], BENJAMIN[2],
JOHN[1].
Mary Ann[6], dau. of Jotham[5] and Polly (Barrett) Tower, b.
Nov. 2, 1808; mar. William P. Cleaveland,
Feb. 17, 1830. He was b. in Westmoreland, N. Y.,
Aug. 10, 1800, and was son of Anson and Mehitable (Ham-
mond) Cleaveland.

Childr. born in Waterville, N. Y.

I. ELLEN CORNELIA[7] born Aug. 2, 1831.
II. MARY B.[7] " May 5, 1833; died July 27, 1833.
III. WILLIAM ALBERT[7] " May 6, 1834.

IV.	MARY JANE[7]	born Jan. 21, 1836.
V.	EMERY BISSELL[7]	" March 29, 1839; died June 24, 1845, ag. 6 y. 2 m. 26 d.
VI.	EMMA CELINA[7]	" Dec. 31, 1842.
VII.	HERBERT COBURN[7]	" Jan. 21, 1847 ; died July 17, 1851, ag. 4 y. 5 m. 26 d.
VIII.	ANNA CAROLINE[7]	" Nov. 1, 1849.
IX.	HARRIET REED[7]	" Nov. 21, 1851.
X.	CATHERINE[7]	" Dec. 9, 1853; died Dec. 19, 1853.

444. Montgomery. Seventh Generation. Tower.

188. URSULA CALISTA[6], JOTHAM[5], JOSEPH[4], AMBROSE[3], BENJA-MIN[2], JOHN[1].

Ursula C.[6], dau. of Jotham[5] and Polly (Barrett) Tower, b. Jan. 4, 1811; mar. Bradford C. Montgomery in Sangerfield, N. Y.,

May   , 1831, by Rev. E. S. Barrows. B. C. Montgomery, b. in Sangerfield,

May 4, 1803, was son of Elias and Lydia (Campbell) Montgomery.

Childr. born in Marshall, N. Y.

I.	CHARLES MILTON[7]	born Aug. 12, 1832 ; unmar.
II.	EDWARD TOWER[7]	" April 25, 1835; died Sept. 17, 1880, ag. 45 y. 4 m. 23 d.
III.	JULIUS HENRY[7]	" Nov. 6, 1839.

Bradford C. Montgomery died in Marshall, Oct. 13, 1868, ag. 64 y. 5 m. 9 d.

Ursula C. (Tower) Montgomery died in Utica, N. Y., April 3, 1881, ag. 70 y. 2 m. 30 d.

445. Seventh Generation. Tower.

188. JULIUS CANDEE[6], JOTHAM[5], JOSEPH[4], AMBROSE[3], BENJAMIN[2], JOHN[1].

Julius C.[6], son of Jotham[5] and Polly (Barrett) Tower, b. Nov. 23, 1821 ; mar. Harriet Willis, of Sangerfield, N. Y., July 6, 1841.

Child.

I. JULIUS WILLIS[7] born Nov. 12, 1849; mar. Anna Babcock, of Mohawk, N. Y. ; *s. p.*

Julius Candee Tower[6] died in Herkimer, N.Y., June 8, 1882, ag. 60 y. 6 m. 16 d.

446.   Seventh Generation.   Tower.

188. ALONZO BACON [6], JOTHAM [5], JOSEPH [4], AMBROSE [3], BENJAMIN [2],
     JOHN [1].
     Alonzo B.[6], son of Jotham [5] and Polly (Barrett) Tower, b.
     May 6, 1824 ; mar. Eliza Winchell in Waterville, N. Y.,
     March 14, 1852, by Rev. E. Williams.   She was b.
     Sept. 12, 1832.

                          Child.

     I. GEORGE WINCHELL [7] born March 19, 1853 ; unmar.

     Alonzo B. Tower [6] died in Waterville, Nov. 24, 1874, ag. 50 y.
     6 m. 18 d.

447. Reed.   Seventh Generation.   Tower.

188. HARRIET ELIZABETH [6], JOTHAM [5], JOSEPH [4], AMBROSE [3], BEN-
     JAMIN [2], JOHN [1].
     Harriet E.[6], dau. of Jotham [5] and Polly (Barrett) Tower, b.
     Dec. 14, 1826 ; mar. Ira L. Reed in Utica, N. Y.,
     July 14, 1844, by Rev. Dr. Barrows.   I. L. Reed, b.
     July 7, 1820, was son of Ira and Betsey (Kenyon) Reed.

                Child born in Waterville, N. Y.

     I. MARY ANTOINETTE [7] born Oct. 12, 1845.

448. Hunt, Black. Seventh Generation.   Tower.

190. POLLY [6], SILAS [5], AMBROSE [4], AMBROSE [3], BENJAMIN [2], JOHN [1].
     Polly [6], dau. of Silas [5] and Ruth (Smith) Tower, b.
     July 29, 1781 ; mar. Stewart Black in Sudbury, Mass.,
     July 7, 1802, by Rev. J. Bigelow.

                          Childr.

     I. SUSAN [7].   II. WILLIAM [7].   III. GEORGE [7].

     Stewart Black died, and Polly (Tower) Black mar., 2d,
     Newell Hunt, of Cambridge, Vt.

449. Wellington. Seventh Generation.   Tower.

190. SUKEY [6], SILAS [5], AMBROSE [4], AMBROSE [3], BENJAMIN [2], JOHN [1].
     Sukey [6], dau. of Silas [5] and Ruth (Smith) Tower, b.
     March 18, 1783 ; mar. Ephraim Wellington, of Watertown,
     Mass.,
     April 7, 1805, by Rev. J. Bigelow.

Childr.

I. VARNUM[7].	III. LUCY[7]
II. GEORGE[7].	IV. RUTH[7].

450. Brown.   **Seventh Generation.**   **Tower.**

190. JERUSHA[6], SILAS[5], AMBROSE[4], AMBROSE[3], BENJAMIN[2], JOHN[1].
Jerusha[6], dau. of Silas[5] and Ruth (Smith) Tower, b.
March 27, 1785 ; mar. Israel Brown, of Sudbury, Mass.,
May 11, 1806, by Rev. J. Bigelow.

Childr.

I.	ELIZA[7]	born	; mar.	Knight; ch. Charles T.[8]
II.	OTIS[7]	"		
III.	ISRAEL[7]	"	; unmar.	
IV.	HARRIET[7]	"	May 27, 1816.	
V.	CHARLES[7]	"	June 12, 1819.	

Israel Brown died in Framingham, Mass., Feb. , 1852.
Jerusha (Tower) Brown died in Framingham, Feb. 22, 1864,
ag. 78 y. 10 m 26 d.

451.   **Seventh Generation.**   **Tower.**

190. THADDEUS[6], SILAS[5], AMBROSE[4], AMBROSE[3], BENJAMIN[2],
JOHN[1].
Thaddeus[6], son of Silas[5] and Ruth (Smith) Tower, b.
July 27, 1787 ; mar. Ruth Maynard in Sudbury, Mass.,
, 1812, by Rev. J. Bigelow. She was b. in Sudbury
Feb. 16, 1791, and was dau. of Isaac and Rebecca (Haynes)
Maynard.

Childr. born in Sudbury.

	I.	MARY[7]	born Oct. 27, 1814; unmar.
959.	II.	WILLIAM PARKER[7]	" Feb. 6, 1821.
	III.	GEORGE HENRY[7]	" Nov. 5, 1823 ; unmar.

Thaddeus Tower[6] died in Lexington, Mass., April 5, 1872,
ag. 84 y. 8 m. 9 d.

452. Howe.   **Seventh Generation.**   **Tower.**

190. RUTH[6], SILAS[5], AMBROSE[4], AMBROSE[3], BENJAMIN[2], JOHN[1].
Ruth[6], dau. of Silas[5] and Ruth (Smith) Tower, b.
Sept. 17, 1789 ; mar. Reuben Howe, of Rutland, Mass.,
April 30, 1809, by Rev. J. Bigelow. R. Howe, b.
May 18, 1780, was son of Matthias and Azubah ( ) Howe.

Childr. born in Rutland.

I.   HENRY[7]   born Feb. 2, 1810; died Feb. 24, 1826, ag. 16 y. 22 d.
II. RUTH H.[7]   "   April 1, 1812.
III. WILLIAM[7]   "   Jan. 11, 1816; died   1836, ag. 20 ?
IV. DEXTER[7]   "   April 11, 1818.

Reuben Howe died Sept.   , 1835, ag. 46.
Ruth (Tower) Howe died July   , 1818, ag. 28 y. 10 m. 0 d. ?

453. **Seventh Generation.** **Tower.**

190. JONAS[6], SILAS[5], AMBROSE[4], AMBROSE[3], BENJAMIN[2], JOHN[1].
Jonas[6], son of Silas[5] and Ruth (Smith) Tower, b.
Nov. 28, 1793; mar. Almira Perry, of Sudbury, Mass.,
June 3, 1828, by Rev. Rufus Hurlburt. She was b.
March 1, 1803, and was dau. of Joshua and Azubah (Knight)
Perry.

Childr. born in Sudbury.

I.   EMILY[7]   born Dec. 15, 1828; died Sept. 16, 1831, ag. 2 y.
                                      9 m. 1 d.
II. ALMIRA[7]   "   Feb. 11, 1831; died May 19, 1831, ag. 3 m. 8 d.
III. EMILY[7]   "   March 18, 1832; "   Feb. 16, 1833, ag. 10 m. 28 d.
IV. LAURA[7]   "   Jan. 7, 1834; "   June 9, 1834, ag. 5 m. 2 d.
960. V.   LOUISA[7]   "   July 3, 1835.
VI. LUCY[7]   "   March 9, 1838; "   March 13, 1838.
VII. SUSAN[7]   "   Feb. 2, 1839; "   Nov. 9, 1839.
961. VIII. CATHERINE[7] "   Nov. 9, 1845.

Jonas Tower[6] died in Sudbury, April 5, 1870, ag. 76 y. 4 m. 8 d.

454. Howe. **Seventh Generation.** **Tower.**

190. SALLY[6], SILAS[5], AMBROSE[4], AMBROSE[3], BENJAMIN[2], JOHN[1].
Sally[6], dau. of Silas[5] and Ruth (Smith) Tower, b.
Feb. 28, 1796; mar. Buckley Howe, of Sudbury, Mass.,
May 6, 1816. He was b. in Sudbury
Dec. 23, 1794, and was son of Joseph and Hepsibeth (Belk-
nap) Howe.

Childr. born in Sudbury.

I.   JOSEPH CALVIN[7]   born Dec. 6, 1817.
II. BUCKLEY HUBBARD[7] "   April 11, 1819.
III. GEORGE MARSHAL[7]   "   July 2, 1824.
IV. GILBERT WARREN[7]   "   June 21, 1828.
V.   SARAH EMELINE[7]   "   March 16, 1834.

Buckley Howe died in Sudbury, April 19, 1876, ag. 81 y. 3 m.
27 d.
Sally (Tower) Howe died in Sudbury, July 5, 1877, ag. 81 y.
4 m. 7 d.

455. Holman. Seventh Generation. **Tower.**

190. ELIZABETH [6], SILAS [5], AMBROSE [4], AMBROSE [3], BENJAMIN [2], JOHN [1].

Elizabeth [6], dau. of Silas [5] and Ruth (Smith) Tower, b.
April 10, 1800; mar. Oren Holman, of Lancaster, Mass.,
Sept. 26, 1821. He was b.
Dec. 5, 1797, and was son of Jonathan and Eunice (Rush)
Holman.

Childr.

I. JAMES H.[7]   born April 20, 1825.
II. ELIZABETH J.[7] "   Oct. 23, 1829; unmar.
III. AMANDA M.[7]   "   Dec. 10, 1833.
IV. HELEN M.[7]   "   Oct. 9, 1836.
V. CHARLES A.[7]   "   May 28, 1839; died Oct. 6, 1857, ag. 18 y. 4 m.
                         9 d.

Oren Holman died in Lancaster, Mass., April 20, 1868, ag.
70 y. 4 m. 15 d.
Elizabeth (Tower) Holman died in Lancaster, Feb. 25, 1883,
ag. 82 y. 10 m. 15 d.

456. Colburn. Seventh Generation. **Tower.**

190. RELIEF [6], SILAS [5], AMBROSE [4], AMBROSE [3], BENJAMIN [2], JOHN [1].
Relief [6], dau. of Silas [5] and Ruth (Smith) Tower, b.
July 11, 1802; mar. Charles Colburn, of Leominster, Mass.,
June , 1823. He was b.
Dec. 13, 1796, and was son of Elijah and Sally (Hosley)
Colburn.

Childr.

I. SARAH A.[7]   born July , 1825; died Aug. 8, 1828, ag. 3 y. 1 m.
II. GEORGE E.[7] "   Jan. 3, 1829.
III. SARAH A.[7] "   Jan. 29, 1831.
IV. JAMES A.[7]   "   Oct. 21, 1835.

Charles Colburn died in Clinton, Mass., April 14, 1872, ag.
75 y. 4 m. 1 d.

457. Seventh Generation. **Tower.**

191. ABEL [6], ABEL [5], AMBROSE [4], AMBROSE [3], BENJAMIN [2], JOHN [1].
Abel [6], son of Abel [5] and Eleanor (Parmenter) Tower, b.
Dec. 7, 1780; mar. Mary Moore, of Wilmington, Vt.,
        1805. She was b.
Sept. 10, 1779, and was dau. of Judah and Polly (McMasters) Moore.

Childr.

962.   I.   GEORGE[7]   born Aug. 30, 1805.
       II. JOHN[7]   "   May 9, 1807; died Jan. 2, 1861, ag. 53 y. 7 m. 24 d.
963.   III. CHARLES[7]   "   Jan. 19, 1811.
964.   IV. MARY[7]   "   Feb. 21, 1815.
965.   V.   DAVID[7]   "   Feb. 13, 1818.

Abel Tower[6] died in Illinois, Aug. 29, 1846, ag. 65 y. 8 m.
22 d.

Mary (Moore) Tower died in Illinois, Sept. 11, 1839, ag.
60 y. 1 d.

458.   Babbitt.   Seventh Generation.   Tower.

191.   POLLY[6], ABEL[5], AMBROSE[4], AMBROSE[3], BENJAMIN[2], JOHN[1].
Polly[6], dau. of Abel[5] and Eleanor (Parmenter) Tower, b.
Sept. 10, 1782; mar. Benajah Babbitt, of Boston,
May 13, 1805.   He was b. in Barre, Mass.,
Nov. 6, 1782.

Child.

   I.   WILLIAM W.[7] born Dec. 14, 1805, in Wayland, Mass.

Benajah Babbitt died Dec. 2, 1858, ag. 76 y. 26 d.
Polly (Tower) Babbitt died Oct. 14, 1849, ag. 67 y. 1 m. 4 d.

459.   Seventh Generation.   Tower.

191.   DAVID[6], ABEL[5], AMBROSE[4], AMBROSE[3], BENJAMIN[2], JOHN[1].
David[6], son of Abel[5] and Eleanor (Parmenter) Tower, b.
May 5, 1787; mar. Sarah Howe in Sudbury, Mass.,
Sept. 30, 1810, by Rev. J. Bigelow.

Child.

I.   SARAH E.[7] bapt. Aug.   , 1813; mar. Hiram Kimball, of Boston, Sept. 28,
        1835, by Rev. Chandler Robbins.

David Tower[6] died in Dedham, Mass., Aug.   , 1812, ag.
25 y. 3 m. 0 d.?

460.   Wheeler.   Seventh Generation.   Tower.

191.   ELEANOR[6], ABEL[5], AMBROSE[4], AMBROSE[3], BENJAMIN[2], JOHN[1].
Eleanor[6], dau. of Abel[5] and Eleanor (Parmenter) Tower, b.
July 16, 1791; mar. Elisha Wheeler, of Sudbury, Mass.,
Jan. 3, 1816, by Rev. J. Bigelow.   E. Wheeler was b.
Nov. 18, 1783.

Childr.

   I.   ELEANOR[7]   born Feb. 10, 1817.
   II. MARY W.[7]   "   Feb. 2, 1819.
   III. JOEL[7]   "   Feb. 13, 1821.

IV. HANNAH [7]   born Nov. 2, 1822.
V. NANCY [7]   " March 6, 1827.
VI. GEORGE [7]   " July 19, 1829; died July 26, 1829.
VII. LUCY W. [7]   " Sept. 2, 1830.
VIII. HENRY [7]   " Sept. 21, 1831; died Oct. 3, 1844, ag. 13 y. 12 d.
IX. ELBRIDGE [7]   " Oct. 31, 1833.

Elisha Wheeler died in Concord, Mass., Feb. 10, 1856, ag. 72 y. 2 m. 23 d.

Eleanor (Tower) Wheeler died in Concord, Mass., Aug. 30, 1861, ag. 70 y. 1 m. 14 d.

461.   Wheeler.   Seventh Generation.   Tower.

191. NANCY [6], ABEL [5], AMBROSE [4], AMBROSE [3], BENJAMIN [2], JOHN [1].
Nancy [6], dau. of Abel [5] and Eleanor (Parmenter) Tower, b. Nov. 12, 1793; mar. Joel Wheeler, of Boston, Mass., Nov. 26, 1815, by Rev. Horace Holley.

Childr.

I. Infant	died	IV. Infant	died
II. Infant	"	V. GEORGE AMBROSE [7] " April 5,	
III. FREDERICK SEAVER [7] "		1854.	

Nancy (Tower) Wheeler died   1826.

462.   Seventh Generation.   Tower.

191. CALEB [6], ABEL [5], AMBROSE [4], AMBROSE [3], BENJAMIN [2], JOHN [1].
Caleb [6], son of Abel [5] and Eleanor (Parmenter) Tower, b. Aug. 17, 1796; mar. Julia Edwards, of Acton, Mass., April 10, 1828. She was b. in Acton
June 29, 1802, and was dau. of John and Susanna (Harrington) Edwards.

Childr.

	I. ANNA EDWARDS [7]	born Nov. 12, 1829, in Stow, Mass.; died March 11, 1851, ag. 21 y. 3 m. 27 d.
966.	II. SUSAN ADDIE [7]	" Jan. 5, 1835, in Edwardsville, Ill.
967.	III. JULIA ELLA [7]	" Dec. 16, 1836, " "
968.	IV. CALEB EDWARDS [7]	" Nov. 14, 1841, " "

Caleb Tower [6] died in Edwardsville, June 17, 1841, ag. 44 y. 10 m.

Julia (Edwards) Tower mar., 2d, Nathaniel Wilder in Rockford, Ill.

She died Dec. 9, 1880, ag. 78 y. 5 m. 10 d.

463.   Seventh Generation.   Tower.

192. ASAHEL [6], ASAHEL [5], AMBROSE [4], AMBROSE [3], BENJAMIN [2], JOHN [1].
Asahel [6], son of Asahel [5] and Milicent (Wyman) Tower, b.
Aug. 11, 1787 ; mar. Mary Palmer, of Sterling, Mass.,
Sept.   , 1817. She was b.
Sept. 16, 1792, and was dau. of William and Mary (Willard)
Palmer.

Childr.

969.	I.	MARY ELIZA [7]	born Aug. 25, 1818.
970.	II.	HENRY AMBROSE [7]	" Feb. 5, 1821.
971.	III.	JULIA ANN [7]	" Feb. 21, 1823.
972.	IV.	GEORGE FRANKLIN [7]	" June 3, 1825.
973.	V.	SARAH MARIA [7]	" June 21, 1827.
974.	VI.	RUFUS ELLIS [1]	" Feb. 26, 1830.
	VII.	HANNAH S. [7]	" Nov. 3, 1832; unmar.
	VIII.	FRANCES ELLEN [7]	" May 2, 1835; "

Asahel Tower [6] died in Winchester, N. H., Oct. 18, 1859, ag.
72 y. 2 m. 7 d.
Mary (Palmer) Tower died in Winchester, N. H., Dec. 24,
1880, ag. 88 y. 3 m. 8 d.

464.   Seventh Generation.   Tower.

192. JAMES [6], ASAHEL [5], AMBROSE [4], AMBROSE [3], BENJAMIN [2], JOHN [1].
James [6], son of Asahel [5] and Milicent (Wyman) Tower, b.
May 16, 1796 ; mar. Sarah E. Baker, of Littleton, Mass.,
April 30, 1827, by Rev. Paul Dean. She was b.
May 23, 1799, and was dau. of Edward and Elizabeth (   )
Baker.

Childr.

	I.	JAMES BAKER [7]	born Dec. 26, 1829; unmar.; died in California, Aug. 15, 1853, ag. 23 y. 7 m. 20 d.
975.	II.	SARAH ELIZABETH [7]	" Feb. 22, 1831.
976.	III.	FRANCES M. [7]	" Dec. 25, 1836.
	IV.	THOMAS THAYER [7]	" Feb. 26, 1839; unmar.; died in Lowell, June 2, 1871, ag. 32 y. 3 m. 6 d.

Sarah E. (Baker) Tower died in Lowell, May 13, 1859, ag.
59 y. 11 m. 20 d.
James Tower [6] mar., 2d, widow Hannah (Hastings) Frost
Oct. 16, 1860, by Rev. A. P. Cleverly. She was b.
        1824, and was dau. of Benjamin and Abigail (   )
Hastings.

465. Seventh Generation. **Tower.**

192. HENRY [6], ASAHEL [5], AMBROSE [4], AMBROSE [3], BENJAMIN [2], JOHN [1].
Henry [6], son of Asahel [5] and Milicent (Wyman) Tower, b.
March 13, 1803 ; mar. Hannah Harrington
June 18, 1828. She was b. in Worcester, Mass.,
1812, and was dau. of Noah Harrington.

Childr. born in Millbury, Mass.

	I.	HANNAH MARIA [7]	born April 23, 1830; died Nov. 3, 1832, ag. 2 y. 6 m. 10 d.
	II.	ANNA MARIA [7]	" Aug. 5, 1833; died April , 1836, ag. 2 y. 8 m.
977.	III.	EDWARD HENRY [7]	" Oct. 19, 1835.
	IV.	CHARLES NOYES [7]	" Nov. 27, 1840; died March 13, 1849, ag. 8 y. 3 m. 14 d.
	V.	GEORGE HARRINGTON [7]	" Nov. 27, 1845; died Sept. 28, 1849, ag. 3 y. 10 m. 1 d.

Henry Tower [6] died in Worcester, Nov. 13, 1876, ag. 73 y. 6 m.
Hannah (Harrington) Tower died in Columbia, S. C., March
23, 1853, ag. 41 ?

466. Seventh Generation. **Tower.**

194. SAMUEL GORE [6], DANIEL [5], AMBROSE [4], AMBROSE [3], BENJAMIN [2],
JOHN [1].
Samuel Gore [6], son of Daniel [5] and Mary (Leeds) Tower, b.
March 27, 1806 ; mar. Ann Clark, of Epsom, N. H.,
Aug. 25, 1830. She was b.
June 3, 1808, and was dau. of James and Hannah (Robinson) Clark.

Childr.

	I.	DANIEL CLARK [7]	born May 4, 1831; died Jan. 2, 1836, ag. 4 y. 7 m. 29 d.
	II.	ANN [7]	" Nov. 3, 1833; died Nov. 6, 1833.
	III.	GEORGE CLARK [7]	" April 7, 1836; " May 23, 1850, ag. 14 y. 1 m. 16 d.
	IV.	ANN MARIA [7]	" March 15, 1840; died June 4, 1840.
978.	V.	MARY LEEDS [7]	" Sept. 10, 1843.
979.	VI.	LUCY ANN [7]	" Jan 13, 1849.
	VII.	ELIZABETH ABBOTT [7]	" July 7, 1850.

Samuel Gore Tower [6] died in Cambridge, Mass., Dec. 29,
1883, ag. 77 y. 9 m. 3 d.
Ann (Clark) Tower died in Cambridge, Mass., Aug. 30,
1881, ag. 73 y. 2 m. 27 d.

467. Jones.   Seventh Generation.   Tower.

194. MARY LEEDS[6], DANIEL[5], AMBROSE[4], AMBROSE[3], BENJAMIN[2],
JOHN[1].
Mary Leeds[6], dau. of Daniel[5] and Mary (Leeds) Tower, b.
March 10, 1809; mar. Thomas C. Jones, of Norridgewock,
Me.,
Nov. 7, 1842.

Childr.

I. LUCY ELLEN[7]   mar. Edward Pierson.   Child, Alice[8].
II. JOHN CODMAN.[7]   IV. SARAH[7] died   .
III. GEORGE T.[7] died   .

Thomas C. Jones died in Norridgewock, Jan. 8, 1876.
Mary L. (Tower) Jones died in Norridgewock, July 17, 1876,
ag. 67 y. 4 m. 7 d.

468. Moore.   Seventh Generation.   Tower.

194. LUCY A.[6], DANIEL[5], AMBROSE[4], AMBROSE[3], BENJAMIN[2],
JOHN[1].
Lucy A.[6], dau. of Daniel[5] and Lucy (Cushing) Tower, b.
March 7, 1818; mar. Horatio Moore, of Bolton, Mass.,
March 22, 1836, by Rev. Samuel Ripley. H. Moore, b. in
Bolton,
June 10, 1810, was son of Henry and Mary (Cook) Moore.

Childr. born in Waltham, Mass.

I. Infant   born   ; died
II. Infant   "   ; "
III. Infant   "   ; "
IV. JOHN F.[7]   "   Feb. 10, 1843; mar.   Feb. 20, 1866.
V. HATTIE R.[7]   "   Jan. 18, 1845.
VI. ANNIE[7]   "   Sept. 20, 1847.
VII. MARY L.[7]   "   April 11, 1850; mar. Samuel Epes Turner, Jr., of
                              Baltimore, Sept. 14, 1878.
VIII. CAROLINE A.[7] " Nov. 1, 1852.
IX. GEORGE[7]   "   Aug. 10, 1855.

469.   Seventh Generation.   Tower.

197. JONATHAN[6], JONATHAN[5], JONATHAN[4], AMBROSE[3], BENJAMIN[2],
JOHN[1].
Jonathan[6], son of Jonathan[5] and Anna (Park) Tower, b.
1794; mar. Mary E.

Childr.

I. CHARLES [7]   ; living in San Francisco, 1883.
980. II. JOHN S.[7] born   1827.
III. MARY [7]   "   ; mar. William Keen, of East Boston.

Mary E. (   ) Tower died in Cambridge, Mass., March   ,
    1831, ag. 30.
Jonathan Tower [6] mar., 2d, Martha
Jonathan Tower [6] died in Boston, Feb. 3, 1854, ag. 60 ?

470.   **Seventh Generation.**   **Tower.**

197. DANIEL [6], JONATHAN [5], JONATHAN [4], AMBROSE [3], BENJAMIN [2],
    JOHN [1].
    Daniel [6], son of Jonathan [5] and Anna (Park) Tower, b.
        1796; mar. Mary Ann Clark in Attleborough, Mass.,
    Aug. 4, 1822, by Rev. R. L. Killam. She was b. in Amherst,
    N. H.,
        1801.

Childr.

981. I. MARY ANN [7]   born Feb. 3, 1823.
982. II. GEORGE FRANCIS [7]   "   June 3, 1825.
983. III. DANIEL ABNER [7]   "   May 11, 1827.
984. IV. JOHN H.[7]   "   Nov. 12, 1829.
985. V. LEVI QUINCY ADAMS [7]   "   April 17, 1832.
      VI. NINA JANE [7]   "   1833; died   1833.
986. VII. SUSANNA HANNAH LOUISA [7] " Jan. 15, 1835.
      VIII. ELIZABETH ANN VICTORIA [7] "

Mary Ann (Clark) Tower died Sept. 24, 1838, ag. 37.

471.   **Seventh Generation.**   **Tower.**

197. CALVIN [6], JONATHAN [5], JONATHAN [4], AMBROSE [3], BENJAMIN [2],
    JOHN [1].
    Calvin [6], son of Jonathan [5] and Anna (Park) Tower, b.
    July 4, 1798; mar. Ann R. Bailey, of Concord, Mass.,
    March 1, 1821. She was b. in Waltham, Mass.,
    June 20, 1804, and was dau. of David and Amelia (   )
        Bailey.

Childr.

987. I. ELIZA ANN [7] born Dec. 25, 1821.
      II. JOHN [7]   "   April 21, 1823.
988. III. HENRY C.[7]   "   July 2, 1826.
      IV. ROSELLA C.[7]   "   Sept. 7, 1828; mar.   Rawson.
      V. EMMA D.[7]   "   Aug. 31, 1830; unmar.; died in Idaho,   1865 ?
989. VI. CALVIN D.[7]   "   July 16, 1832.
990. VII. ISAAC [7]   "   Sept. 24, 1834.
      VIII. BETSEY M.[7]   "   Oct. 26, 1836; died Sept. 16, 1838, ag. 1 y.
                10 m. 20 d.

991.   IX.   George E.[7] born Oct. 23, 1838.
       X.   Amelia E.[7]   "   Dec. 20, 1840; unmar.
       XI.   William M.[7] "   May 4, 1843; died May 16, 1846, ag. 3 y. 12 d.
       XII. Charles A.[7] "   May 5, 1847; died Jan. 28, 1851, ag. 3 y. 8 m.
                            23 d.

472. Cate.   Seventh Generation.   Tower.

197. Anna P.[6], Jonathan [5], Jonathan [4], Ambrose [3], Benjamin [2], John [1].
      Anna P.[6], dau. of Jonathan [5] and Anna (Park) Tower, b.
      Sept. 12, 1800 ; mar. James Cate, of Sanbornton, N. H.,
      Feb. 20, 1825, by Rev. Hosea Ballou.

Childr.

I.	Ammon T.[7]	born Dec. 8, 1825, in Newburyport, Mass.		
II.	Mary D.[7]	" Feb. 8, 1827,	" Sanbornton, N. H.	
III.	Elizabeth [7]	" March 5, 1828,	" " "	
IV.	James D.[7]	" Nov. 22, 1829,	" " "	
V.	Daniel T.[7]	" Aug. 15, 1831,	" Franklin, "	
VI.	George E.[7]	" May 9, 1833,	" " "	
VII.	Richard J.[7]	" Nov. 16, 1834,	" " "	
VIII.	Emily D.[7]	" Feb. 19, 1838,	" " "	
IX.	Susan A.[7]	" July 19, 1841,	" " " ; unmar.	
X.	Helen A.[7]	" July 21, 1847,	" " " ; died March	

                    30, 1849, ag. 1 y. 8 m. 9 d.

James Cate died   1872.

473. Stone.   Seventh Generation.   Tower.

197. Mary Ann [6], 'Jonathan [5], Jonathan [4], Ambrose [3], Benja-
      min [2], John [1].
      Mary Ann [6], dau. of Jonathan [5] and Abigail(Dudley)Tower,b.
      Dec. 7, 1802; mar. Levi Stone, of Amesbury, Mass.,
                    He was b. in Chester, Vt.,
      July 25, 1803, and was son of Joel and Sally (   ) Stone.

Childr. born in Amesbury.

I.	William [7] born	1826; mar.; died Oct. 25, 1851, ag. 25?			
II.	Mary A.[7]	" March 6, 1839;	" 1857, ag. 18?		
III.	Charles [7]	" June 4, 1841; mar.; died May 29, 1865, ag. 23 y.			

                    11 m. 25 d.

Levi Stone died in Amesbury, Oct. 25, 1873, ag. 70 y. 3 m.
Mary Ann (Tower) Stone died in Amesbury, Feb. 19, 1866,
      ag. 63 y. 2 m. 12 d.

474. Wight.   Seventh Generation.   Tower.

197. Cynthia [6], Jonathan [5], Jonathan [4], Ambrose [3], Benjamin [2], John [1].

Cynthia [6], dau. of Jonathan [5] and Abigail (Dudley) Tower, b. Sept. 29, 1805 ; mar. William Wight, of New York State.

Child.

I. Charles [7].

475. Buttrick. Seventh Generation. Tower.

198. Lydia[6], Daniel[5], Jonathan[4], Ambrose[3], Benjamin[2], John[1].
Lydia[6], dau. of Daniel[5] and Mary (Childs) Tower, b.
; mar. John Buttrick, of Lunenburg, Mass.

Childr. born in Lunenburg.

I. Eliza Ann [7] born March 10, 1820.	V. Aaron[7] ; died in infancy.
II. John [7].	VI. Alexander[7]; " " "
III. Walter [7].	VII. Charles [7].
IV. Abiel [7].	VIII. George Tower [7] born April 2, 1836.

John Buttrick died in Lunenburg.
Lydia (Tower) Buttrick died in Groton, Mass.

476. Wright. Seventh Generation. Tower.

198. Varazina [6], Daniel [5], Jonathan [4], Ambrose [3], Benjamin [2], John [1].
Varazina [6], dau. of Daniel [5] and Mary (Childs) Tower, bapt.
Feb. 4, 1798 ; mar. Abel Wright, of Pepperell, Mass.

Childr.

I. Emeline [7] born   ; mar. Luther Smith; both died.
II. Prescott [7] "

477. Tyler. Styles. Seventh Generation. Tower.

198. Mary [6], Daniel [5], Jonathan [4], Ambrose [3], Benjamin [2], John [1].
Mary [6], dau. of Daniel [5] and Rebecca (Farrar) Tower, b.
May 28, 1803 ; mar. Asahel Foster Styles in Lunenburg, Mass.,
Jan.   , 1826, by Rev. Mr. Damon.

Childr.

I. Daniel [7]   born Jan. 5, 1827; died   1830.
II. Mary Ann [7]   " Sept. 3, 1828.
III. George Henry [7] " May 12, 1831.
IV. Asahel F.[7]   " July 12, 1833.

Asahel F. Styles died, and Mary (Tower) Styles mar., 2d, Zebadiah Tyler.

Childr.

V. JOHNNY T.[7] born April 17, 1838; died July 8, 1845, ag. 7 y. 2 m. 21 d.
VI. CLARISSA[7]   " Jan. 10, 1844.

Zebadiah Tyler died May 20, 1854, ag. 67.

478.   **Seventh Generation.**   **Tower.**

198. ELI[6], DANIEL[5], JONATHAN[4], AMBROSE[3], BENJAMIN[2], JOHN[1].
Eli[6], son of Daniel[5] and Rebecca (Farrar) Tower, b.
Jan. 15, 1807 ; mar. Mary Fletcher,
Dec. 3, 1833. She was b.
Jan. 1, 1813, and was dau. of Thomas and Orpah (Fletcher)
    Fletcher.
Childr. born in Westford, Mass.

992.   I. AMANDA[7]   born April 4, 1834.
993.   II. ABBIE[7]   "   Jan. 5, 1836.
994.   III. ADALINE[7]   "   March 15, 1838.
       IV. WALDO[7]   "   June 21, 1840; died Dec. 5, 1841, ag. 1 y. 5 m.
                             14 d.
995.   V. AMY[7]   "   June 22, 1842.
996.   VI. HELEN[7]   "   July 30, 1844.
      VII. ALBRO W.[7]   "   Oct. 1, 1846; died Aug. 29, 1848, ag. 1 y. 10 m.
                             18 m.
997. VIII. FRANCES A.[7]   "   Dec. 6, 1848.
998.   IX. EMMA F.[7]   "   March 22, 1851.
        X. LILIAN EVA[7]   "   Aug. 11, 1853; unmar.
999.   XI. MARY LUELLA[7] "   Nov. 28, 1856.

Mary (Fletcher) Tower died April 22, 1878, ag. 63 y. 3 m.
    21 d.

479.   **Seventh Generation.**   **Tower.**

198. MELZAR T.[6], DANIEL[5], JONATHAN[4], AMBROSE[3], BENJAMIN[2],
    JOHN[1].
Melzar T.[6], son of Daniel[5] and Rebecca (Farrar) Tower, b.
June 15, 1821 ; mar. Ann Prescott.

Child.

1000.   I. WALDO TURNER[7] born Jan. 8, 1844.

Melzar T. Tower died in Fitzwilliam, N. H.
Ann (Prescott) Tower died in Fitzwilliam, N. H.

480.   **Seventh Generation.**   **Tower.**

199. LEWIS[6], NATHAN[5], JONATHAN[4], AMBROSE[3], BENJAMIN[2],
    JOHN[1].
Lewis[6], son of Nathan[5] and Sevia (Warren) Tower, b.
May 6, 1806 ; mar. Martha Thomas in Cumberland, R. I.,

Sept. 23, 1832, by Rev. Mr. Cutler. She was b.
Jan 20, 1799, and was dau. of George Christian and Lydia
(Mason) Thomas.

Childr. born in Cumberland, R. I.

I. Lewis Warren [7] born July 14, 1833; unmar.
II. William Cullen [7] " Jan. 18, 1835 ; died April 13, 1848, ag.
13 y. 2 m. 26 d.
III. Nathan Allen [7] " May 23, 1837; died March 11, 1840, ag.
2 y. 9 m. 17 d.
1001. IV. Sarah Thomas [7] " July 15, 1841.

Lewis Tower [6] died in Cumberland, Aug. 17, 1872, ag. 66 y.
3 m. 11 d.
Martha (Thomas) Tower died in Cumberland, May 22,
1888, ag. 89 y. 4 m. 2 d.

481. Lambert. Seventh Generation. Tower.

200. Sally [6], Peter [5], Benjamin [4], Ambrose [3], Benjamin [2], John [1].
Sally [6], dau. of Peter [5] and Sarah (Putnam) Tower, b.
Aug. 16, 1790 ; mar. Ebenezer Lambert, of South Dover, Me.,
Oct.   , 1818, by Augustus Tower, J. P. E. Lambert, b. in
Winthrop, Me.,
April 4, 1793, was son of Paul and Mercy (Dexter) Lambert.

Childr. b. in Dover, Me.

I. Silas [7] born July 17, 1819; died July   , 1822, ag. 3 ?
II. Horace [7] " March 20, 1821; unmar.; died March 1, 1873, ag. 51 y.
11 m. 9 d.
III. Emily [7] " Dec. 28, 1824;   "
IV. Sarah [7] " March 28, 1826;   "   " May 28, 1853, ag. 27 y. 2 m.
V. Edwin [7] " Oct. 21, 1828.

Ebenezer Lambert died in Dover, July 8, 1876, ag. 83 y.
3 m. 4 d.
Sally (Tower) Lambert died in Dover, Jan. 15, 1869, ag.
77 y. 4 m. 30 d.

482. Seventh Generation. Tower.

200. Ruel [6], Peter [5], Benjamin [4], Ambrose [3], Benjamin [2], John [1].
Ruel [6], son of Peter [5] and Sarah (Putnam) Tower, b.
May 30, 1792 ; mar. Nancy Nevers.

Childr. born in Sweden, Me.

I. Nancy [7] born May 31, 1817; mar. David Moulton.
1002. II. Eli [7] " Feb. 4, 1819.
III. Sally [7] " Sept. 6, 1820; died Dec. 27, 1839, ag. 19 y.
3 m. 21 d.

      IV. BETSEY M.[7] born Oct. 11, 1822; mar. Augustus Cushman. He died April 21, 1867.

1003.	V.	LUTHER[7]	"	March 19, 1825.
1004.	VI.	WILLIAM W.[7]	"	July 20, 1827.
1005.	VII.	LYDIA M.[7]	"	Jan. 1, 1831.
1006.	VIII.	SYLVESTER[7]	"	April 14, 1833.
1007.	IX.	MARTHA E.[7] }	"	April 4, 1835. Mary E. mar. Henry Cur-
	X.	MARY E.[7] }		rier, of Lowell, Mass., 1860; died 1861, ag. 26 ?

Ruel Tower [6] died June 13, 1878, ag. 86 y. 14 d.

Nancy (Nevers) Tower died July 17, 1849, ag. 54.

483. Beckford.   Seventh Generation.   Tower.

200. NANCY [6], PETER [5], BENJAMIN [4], AMBROSE [3], BENJAMIN [2], JOHN [1].

Nancy [6], dau. of Peter [5] and Sarah (Putnam) Tower, b.
Aug. 17, 1797 ; mar. Daniel Beckford, of Dover, Me.,
Feb. 23, 1823. He was b. in Salem, Mass.,
Dec. 22, 1793, and was son of Daniel and Hannah (Picker-
ing) Beckford.

Childr.

	I.	AUGUSTUS F.[7]	born Nov. 28, 1823, in Charleston, Me.
	II.	CLARA H.[7]	" April 21, 1825, " "
	III.	HANNAH[7]	" Nov. 24, 1827, " "
	IV.	EMILY F.[7]	" Feb. 1, 1831, " " ; unmar.
	V.	CHARLES H.[7]	" July 3, 1840, in Bangor, Me.

Daniel Beckford died in Dover, Me., March 23, 1870, ag.
76 y. 3 m. 1 d.

Nancy (Tower) Beckford died in Dover, Me., Dec. 6, 1848,
ag. 51 y. 3 m. 19 d.

484.   Seventh Generation.   Tower.

202. CHARLES [6], AUGUSTUS [5], BENJAMIN [4], AMBROSE [3], BENJAMIN [2], JOHN [1].

Charles [6], son of Augustus [5] and Polly (Leathe) Tower, b.
May 19, 1794; mar. Lucretia Maynard, of Stow, Mass.,
April 9, 1820. She was b. in Marlborough, Mass.,
Dec. 23, 1799, and was dau. of Uriah and Mary (   )
Maynard.

Childr.

	I.	CHARLES AUGUSTUS[7]	born Sept. 8, 1821; died Aug. 20, 1824, ag. 2 y. 11 m. 12 d.
1008.	II.	ELIZA MAYNARD[7]	" Nov. 14, 1823.
	III.	CHARLES AUGUSTUS[7]	" March 24, 1826.
1009.	IV.	HENRY[7]	" June 24, 1829.

1010.	V.	ALBERT[7]	born Oct. 16, 1833.
1011.	VI.	ALONZO[7]	" Jan. 10, 1837.
	VII.	MARY LOUISA[7]	" Jan. 11, 1840, died July 12, 1859, ag. 19 y. 6 m. 1 d.

Lucretia (Maynard) Tower died in Stow, Nov. 12, 1856, ag. 56 y. 10 m. 11 d.

Charles Tower[6] mar., 2d, Joanna Haynes, of Sudbury, Mass., April 10, 1858, by Rev. Reuben Bates. She was b. March 1, 1809, and was dau. of Josiah and Lydia ( ) Haynes ; *s. p.*

Charles Tower[6] died in Stow, Mass., April 14, 1874, ag. 79 y. 10 m. 25 d.

485. Fletcher, Whitney. Seventh Generation. Tower.

202. HARRIET[6], AUGUSTUS[5], BENJAMIN[4], AMBROSE[3], BENJAMIN[2], JOHN[1].

Harriet[6], dau. of Augustus[5] and Polly (Leathe) Tower, b. Sept. 28, 1799 ; mar. John Whitney, of Stow, Mass., June 13, 1819. He was b. May 28, 1789, and was son of Daniel and Sarah ( ) Whitney ; *s. p.*

John Whitney died in Stow, Feb. 2, 1854, ag. 64 y. 8 m. 5 d.

Harriet (Tower) Whitney mar., 2d, Peter Fletcher in Stow, June 18, 1857. He was b. in Stow Feb. 22, 1799, and was son of Peter and Lucy (Wood) Fletcher ; *s. p.*

Harriet (Tower) Fletcher died in Stow, March 16, 1873, ag. 73 y. 5 m. 16 d.

486. Seventh Generation. Tower.

202. AUGUSTUS[6], AUGUSTUS[5], BENJAMIN[4], AMBROSE[3], BENJAMIN[2], JOHN[1].

Augustus[6], son of Augustus[5] and Polly (Leathe) Tower, b. Aug. 16, 1801 ; mar. Nancy Bright, of Acton, Mass. Int. pub. March 7, 1826.

Childr. born in Concord, Mass.

	I.	MARTHA A.[7]	born March 25, 1833 ; unmar.
1012.	II.	NANCIE B.[7]	" Dec. 31, 1834.
1013.	III.	HATTIE W.[7]	" May 2, 1836.

Nancy (Bright) Tower died

Augustus Tower[6] mar., 2d, Martha D. Brown.

Child born in Lowell, Mass.

IV. MARTHA ANN[7] born

487. Robinson.   Seventh Generation.   Tower.

202. LUCY[6], AUGUSTUS[5], BENJAMIN[4], AMBROSE[3], BENJAMIN[2], JOHN[1].

Lucy[6], dau. of Augustus[5] and Polly (Leathe) Tower, b. June 14, 1803 ; mar. Nathan S. Robinson, of Stow, Mass., April 18, 1838. He was b. July 10, 1807, and was son of Keene and Axie (Leathe) Robinson.

Child.

I. AUGUSTUS TOWER[7] born April 14, 1840, in Stow; mar. Sarah J. Atkinson, Sept. 20, 1870.

Lucy (Tower) Robinson died in Lynn, Mass., March 11, 1876, ag. 72 y. 8 m. 26 d.

488.   Seventh Generation.   Tower.

202. JEDEDIAH L.[6], AUGUSTUS[5], BENJAMIN[4], AMBROSE[3], BENJAMIN[2], JOHN[1].

Jedediah L.[6], son of Augustus[5] and Polly (Leathe) Tower, b. April 25, 1805 ; mar. Mary Jane Noyes, of Wayland, Mass. Int. pub. March 2, 1839. She was dau. of Samuel S. and Mary (Plympton) Noyes.

Childr. born in Stow, Mass.

	I.	CHARLES HENRY[7]	born	Jan. 10, 1840; died Oct. 29, 1841, ag. 1 y. 9 m. 19 d.
1014.	II.	HELEN PLYMPTON[7]	"	Jan. 5, 1842.
1015.	III.	HERMAN C.[7]	"	March 8, 1843.
1016.	IV.	JOHN NOYES[7]	"	May 30, 1846.

Jedediah L. Tower[6] died in Stow, Jan. 3, 1858, ag. 52 y. 8 m. 8 d.

489. Soper.   Seventh Generation.   Tower.

202. ELIZA[6], AUGUSTUS[5], BENJAMIN[4], AMBROSE[3], BENJAMIN[2], JOHN[1].

Eliza[6], dau. of Augustus[5] and Polly (Leathe) Tower, b. Dec. 30, 1807 ; mar. Jacob Soper. Int. pub. Oct. 27, 1838. He was b. Nov. 7, 1799, and was son of Jacob and Sally (Blood) Soper.

Childr.

I. FANNY [7] born Feb. 28, 1841; unmar.
II. GEORGIA [7] " Oct. 2, 1843; died Sept. 28, 1846, ag. 2 y. 11 m. 26 d.
III. JOSEPH [7] " Sept. 19, 1845.

Jacob Soper died Sept. 3, 1872, ag. 72 y. 9 m. 27 d.
Eliza (Tower) Soper died June , 1876, ag. 68 y. 6 m. 0 d. ?

490. Seventh Generation. **Tower.**

205. MATTHEW [6], MATTHEW [5], MATTHEW [4], SAMUEL [3], SAMUEL [2], JOHN [1].
Matthew [6], son of Matthew [5] and Lydia (Beal) Tower, b.
1769; mar. Nabby Bates in Cummington, Mass.,
Oct. 27, 1791, by Rev. James Briggs. She was b. in Weymouth, Mass.,
, and was dau. of Abraham and Sarah (Tower) Bates.

BATES. TOWER.
Nabby [6], Sarah [5], Peter [4], Jeremiah [3], Jeremiah [2], John [1].

Childr.

1017.	I.	LYDIA [7]	born July 8, 1792, in Cummington, Mass.
1018.	II.	MATTHEW [7]	" Nov. 13, 1793, "
1019.	III.	COTTON [7]	" March 24, 1795, "
1020.	IV.	ABRAHAM BATES [7]	" April 27, 1798, "
1021.	V.	SARAH J. [7]	" Feb. 8, 1800, "
1022.	VI.	HULL [7]	" Feb. 28, 1802, "
1023.	VII.	NABBY [7]	" May 23, 1806, "
1024.	VIII.	JONATHAN W. [7]	" Dec. 8, 1809, in New York State.
1025.	IX.	NEHEMIAH [7]	" Dec. 17, 1814, " " "
1026.	X.	HARRIET [7]	" Sept. 21, 1821, in Kentucky.

Matthew Tower [6] died Sept. 21, 1845, ag. 76 ?
Nabby (Bates) Tower died May 26, 1833.

491. Seventh Generation. **Tower.**

207. LUTHER [6], ABNER [5], JOSEPH [4], JOSEPH [3], SAMUEL [2], JOHN [1].
Luther [6], son of Abner [5] and Lucina (Spencer) Tower, b.
May 15, 1793; mar. Sally Reed
July 11, 1816. She was b.
June 6, 1799, and was dau. of Samuel and Betsey (Smith) Reed.

Childr.

1027.	I.	LOREN LUTHER [7]	born Nov. 25, 1816.
1028.	II.	SALLY IRENE [7]	" Nov. 25, 1819.
	III.	Infant [7]	; died Jan. 17, 1822.

1029.	IV.	LUCINA S.[7]	born Oct. 21, 1825.
1030.	V.	BETSEY SMITH[7]	" June 20, 1827.
1031.	VI.	JANE E.[7]	" May 19, 1829.
1032.	VII.	MARTHA ALMIRA[7]	" June 16, 1833.
1033.	VIII.	MARY ADELAIDE[7]	" June 22, 1836.
	IX.	ELLEN CORDELIA[7]	" Nov. 20, 1842; died July 6, 1843.

Luther Tower[6] died in Northampton, Mass., April 14, 1882,
ag. 88 y. 10 m. 30 d.

Sally (Reed) Tower died in Northampton, Mass., July 11,
1882, ag. 83 y. 1 m. 5 d.

492.   Thayer.   Seventh Generation.   Tower.

207. SALLY AMELIA[6], ABNER[5], JOSEPH[4], JOSEPH[3], SAMUEL[2],
JOHN[1].

Sally A.[6], dau. of Abner[5] and Lucina (Spencer) Tower, b.
Nov. 13, 1795; mar. John Thayer
July 22, 1819. He was b. in Northampton, Mass.,
April 27, 1794.

Childr.

I.	LUCINA CORDELIA[7]	born Sept. 18, 1820; died Nov. 15, 1820.
II.	ABNER MARSHAL[7]	" 1824.
III.	CEPHAS[7]	" Aug. 24, 1826; died in East Saginaw, Mich., 1865, ag. 49.
IV.	SPENCER TOWER[7]	" Feb. 3, 1828.
V.	WILLIAM LUTHER[7]	" April 25, 1830.
VI.	LUCINA ADRIANA[7]	" July 18, 1832.
VII.	OPHELIA R.[7]	" Nov. 28, 1834; died in Troy, N. Y., Sept. 9, 1848, ag. 13 y. 9 m. 12 d.
VIII.	AMELIA FLINT[7]	" Sept. 18, 1836; died in Northampton, Mass. Feb. 15, 1839, ag. 2 y. 4 m. 28 d.
IX.	HENRY F.[7]	" March 9, 1839.

John Thayer died in Troy, N. Y., July 29, 1856, ag. 62 y.
3 m. 2 d.

Sally A. (Tower) Thayer died in Troy, N. Y., April 14,
1854, ag. 58 y. 5 m. 1 d.

493.   Bruce.   Seventh Generation.   Tower.

207. MARY[6], ABNER[5], JOSEPH[4], JOSEPH[3], SAMUEL[2], JOHN[1].

Mary[6], dau. of Abner[5] and Lucina (Spencer) Tower, b.
July 10, 1798; mar. Seth Bruce, of New York State,
March 18, 1826. He was b. in Blandford, Mass.,
April 26, 1804, and was son of Jesse and Anna (Sinnott)
Bruce.

Childr.

I. DEBORAH TOWER [7] born Feb. 18, 1827.
II. JESSE [7]   "   Jan. 26, 1829; unmar.
III. ANN ELIZA [7]   "   Feb. 10, 1831.
IV. MARY ROMAINE [7]   "   April 14, 1833.
V. ALEXANDER [7]   "   Jan. 29, 1836.
VI. JOSEPH WARNER [7]   "   April 25, 1840;   "

494.   **Seventh Generation.**   **Tower.**

207. ABNER [6], ABNER [5], JOSEPH [4], JOSEPH [3], SAMUEL [2], JOHN [1].
Abner [6], son of Abner [5] and Lucina (Spencer) Tower, b.
Feb. 5, 1804; mar. Lydia Sampson, of Chester, Mass.,
Oct. 9, 1842, by Rev. William Taylor. She was b.
Dec. 5, 1813.

Child.

MARY, an adopted daughter, died Nov. 6, 1844, ag. 15.

Abner Tower [6] died in Chesterfield, Feb. 16, 1851, ag. 47 y.
11 d.
Lydia (Sampson) Tower mar., 2d, Nehemiah Luce, of Ches-
terfield, Mass.,
July 12, 1852. He was son of Jonathan and Mehitable
(Bates) Luce.

LUCE, BATES.   TOWER.
Nehemiah [7], Mehitable [6], Nehemiah [5], Solomon [4], Rachel [3], Ibrook [2],
John [1].

495. Streeter, Lawson.   **Seventh Generation.**   **Tower.**

207. ELVIRA J. [6], ABNER [5], JOSEPH [4], JOSEPH [3], SAMUEL [2], JOHN [1].
Elvira J. [6], dau. of Abner [5] and Lucina (Spencer) Tower, b.
Aug. 15, 1806; mar. John M. Lawson
May 16, 1835. He was b.
June 10, 1810, and was son of William and Mary (Mont-
gomery) Lawson.

Childr. born in Worthington, Mass.

I. MARY ELIZABETH [7] born Oct. 26, 1836.
II. AMELIA LOUISA [7]   "   Nov. 28, 1838.
III. SARAH G. [7]   "   Oct. 21, 1840.
IV. OPHELIA J. [7]   "   Feb. 9, 1846.

John M. Lawson died in Worthington, Mass., April 20,
1862, ag. 61 y. 10 m. 10 d.
Elvira J. (Tower) Lawson mar., 2d, Oren Streeter in Halifax, Vt.,

Jan. 6, 1881, by J. Stark, J. P.   O. Streeter, born in Rowe, Mass.,

July 11, 1813, was son of James and Prudence (Baker) Streeter; *s. p.*

496.   Seventh Generation.   Tower.

207. Spencer [6], Abner [5], Joseph [4], Joseph [3], Samuel [2], John [1].
Spencer [6], son of Abner [5] and Lucina (Spencer) Tower, b.
Aug. 17, 1813; mar. Elizabeth Tirrell
Nov. 17, 1852. She was b.
July 28, 1834, and was dau. of Arza and Electa (Snow) Tirrell.

> Childr. born in Chesterfield, Mass.
>
> I. Abner Luther [7]   born June 4, 1854.
> II. Spencer Mitchel [7] " Dec. 27, 1857.

497. Hitchcock.   Seventh Generation.   Tower.

209. Lydia [6], Pyam [5], Joseph [4], Joseph [3], Samuel [2], John [1].
Lydia [6], dau. of Pyam [5] and Rachel (Cowing) Tower, b.
Oct. 1, 1801; mar. Eri Hitchcock, of Perrysburg, N. Y.

> Child.
>
> I. Alfred A. [7] born July 3, 1829.

Lydia (Tower) Hitchcock died June   , 1837, ag. 35 y. 8 m. 0 d. ?

498.   Seventh Generation.   Tower.

209. Salmon Pyam [6], Pyam [5], Joseph [4], Joseph [3], Samuel [2], John [1].
Salmon Pyam [6], son of Pyam [5] and Rachel (Cowing) Tower, b.
  ; mar. Louisa   .

> Childr.
>
> I. Miron [7] bórn   .   II. Daughter [7] born   .
>   III. Daughter [7] born   .

Salmon P. Tower [6] died in Meadville, Pa.

499. Hitchcock.   Seventh Generation.   Tower.

209. Susan [6], Pyam [5], Joseph [4], Joseph [3], Samuel [2], John [1].
Susan [6], dau. of Pyam [5] and Rachel (Cowing) Tower, b.
Aug. 23, 1816; mar. Eri Hitchcock, of Perrysburg, N. Y.

Childr. born in Perrysburg.

I. Louisa A.[7] born May 14, 1841.
II. Eri [7]   " Nov. 17, 1844; unmar.

Eri Hitchcock died in Perrysburg, June , 1872, ag. 71 y.
8 m. 0 d. ?

500.   **Seventh Generation.**   **Tower.**

210. Joseph P.[6], Ezekiel [5], Joseph [4], Joseph [3], Samuel [2], John [1].
Joseph P.[6], son of Ezekiel [5] and Betsey E. (Josselyn) Tower, b.
1805; mar. Julia A. Denton, of Monmouth Co., N. J.

Childr. born in Brooklyn, N. Y.

1034.	I.	William F.[7] born Jan. 25, 1839.			
	II.	Nelson H.[7]	"	1841; died young.	
1035.	III.	Emily J.[7]	"	1843.	
1036.	IV.	Nelson H.[7]	"	1845.	
	V.	Edgar D.[7]	"	1847; died young.	
1037.	VI.	Charles B.[7]	" Nov. 5, 1850.		
	VII.	Granville [7]	"	1852; died young.	
	VIII.	Edgar D.[7]	"	1854; " 1860.	

Joseph P. Tower [6] died in the war, 1864.
Julia A. (Denton) Tower died in Brooklyn, N. Y., March
31, 1881, ag. 61 ?

501.   **Seventh Generation.**   **Tower.**

210. Lyman Josselyn [6], Ezekiel [5], Joseph [4], Joseph [3], Samuel [2],
John [1].
Lyman J.[6], son of Ezekiel [5] and Betsey (Josselyn) Tower, b.
May 29, 1809; mar. Lucy C. Converse, of Worthington,
Mass.,
March 21, 1832, by Rev. J. L. Pomeroy. She was b.
Nov. 12, 1806.

Childr. born in Worthington, Mass.

1038.	I.	Hersey E.[7]	born Dec. 3, 1833.
1039.	II.	Elisha C.[7]	" Dec. 10, 1834.
1040.	III.	Oscar F [7]	" Dec. 27, 1838.
1041.	IV.	Welthea A.[7]	" Jan. 17, 1841.
	V.	Lorenza J.[7]	" April 17, 1843.
1042.	VI.	Esther Josephine [7]	" Sept. 19, 1846.
1043.	VII.	Lucy E [7]	" Dec. 26, 1850.

Lucy C. (Converse) Tower died in Worthington, May 21,
1877, ag. 70 y. 6 m. 9 d.

502.   Seventh Generation.   Tower.

210. WILLIAM E.[6], EZEKIEL,[5] JOSEPH [4], JOSEPH [3], SAMUEL [2], JOHN [1].
    William E.[6], son of Ezekiel [5] and Betsey (Josselyn) Tower, b.
        1812; mar. Lucy M. Gilbert, of Cummington, Mass.,
    April, 1836, by Rev. H. Adam. She was b. in Peru, Mass.,
        1814.

            Childr. born in Worthington, Mass.

1044.	I.	JOSEPH H.[7]	born July 14, 1836.
	II.	JULIA M.[7]	" 1839; died Aug. 4, 1854, ag. 15.
	III.	MARY E.[7]	" June , 1842; " Sept. 15, 1843, ag. 1 y. 3 m. 0 d. ?
	IV.	MUNROE A.[7]	" April 30, 1844; died Sept. 30, 1845, ag. 1 y. 5 m.
1045.	V.	SARAH J.[7]	" Oct. 20, 1848.
1046.	VI.	WILLIAM MUNROE [7]	" Jan. 18, 1851.
	VII.	MARY R.[7]	" Dec. 5, 1852.
1047.	VIII.	HELEN L.[7]	" Aug. 1, 1855.

William E. Tower [6] died in Worthington, Aug. 3, 1866, ag. 54 ?
Lucy M. (Gilbert) Tower mar., 2d, William Frissell, of Peru,
    Mass., May 18, 1869.

503. Weston.   Seventh Generation.   Tower.

210. ELIZABETH [6], EZEKIEL [5], JOSEPH [4], JOSEPH [3], SAMUEL [2], JOHN [1].
    Elizabeth [6], dau. of Ezekiel [5] and Betsey (Josselyn) Tower, b.
        1818; mar. G. D. Weston, of Dalton, Mass.

                    Child.
        I. Daughter [7] born   ; died   .

Elizabeth (Tower) Weston died in Dalton, May 7, 1857,
    ag. 39 ?

            EIGHTH GENERATION.

504. Newton, Ballou.   Eighth Generation.   Tower.

211. LUCY [7], WANTON [6], ENOCH [5], GIDEON [4], BENJAMIN [3], JOHN [2],
    JOHN [1].
    Lucy [7], dau. of Wanton [6] and Finis (Cook) Tower, b.
                ; mar. Augustus Ballou, son of Richard Ballou,
        Aug. 8, 1814.
                    Childr.

| I. | LYDIA [8] | ; mar. Learned Shepardson, of Wrentham, Mass. They removed to Killingly, Windham Co., Conn |
| II. | ADILLA [8] | ; mar., 1st,   Ballou, 2d,   Henry; live in Blackstone, Mass. |

Lucy (Tower) Ballou and her husband were divorced, and both again married. She mar.   Newton.

505. Morse.   Eighth Generation.   Tower.

211. MARY[7], WANTON[6], ENOCH[5], GIDEON[4], BENJAMIN[3], JOHN[2], JOHN[1].

Mary[7], dau. of Wanton[6] and Finis (Cook) Tower, b.
May 6, 1801; mar. Nahum Morse
July 4, 1826. He was b. in Whitestone, N. Y.,
March 30, 1797, and was son of Nahum and Olive (Comstock) Morse.

Childr.

I.   ADELINE[8] born Sept. 5, 1828.
II.   LYDIA A.[8] "   Dec. 11, 1830.
III. NELSON[8] "   April 21, 1833; died Oct. 11, 1833.
IV.   LOUISA[8] "   Aug. 4, 1835;   " Feb. 9, 1840, ag. 4 y. 6 m. 5 d.
V.   HENRY S.[8] "   Feb. 15, 1837.
VI.   CHARLES[8] "   May 30, 1839; died July 3, 1840; ag. 1 y. 1 m. 4 d.

Nahum Morse died in Uxbridge, Mass., April 14, 1874, ag. 77 y. 15 d.

Mary (Tower) Morse was living with her daughter Lydia in Whitinsville, Worcester Co., Mass., 1884.

506. Thayer.   Eighth Generation.   Tower.

215. JANE G.[7], DAVID[6], ICHABOD[5], GIDEON[4], BENJAMIN[3], JOHN[2], JOHN[1].

Jane G.[7], dau. of David[6] and Pamelia (Darrow) Tower, b.
1809; mar. Nelson L. Thayer.

Childr.

I. CYNTHIA O.[8]   II. ELLEN[8]

507. Bixler.   Eighth Generation.   Tower.

215. MARY R.[7], DAVID[6], ICHABOD[5], GIDEON[4], BENJAMIN[3], JOHN[2], JOHN[1].

Mary R.[7], dau. of David[6] and Pamelia (Darrow) Tower, b.
1813; mar. William Bixler,
1842.

Childr.

I.   ORRIN[8].   IV. ALBERT[8].
II.   FLORENCE[8].   V.   ALICE CAREY[8].
III. THOMAS[8].

William Bixler died in Oberlin, Ohio, Feb. 27, 1886.

508. Hoskinson. Eighth Generation. Tower.

215. LORA A.[7], DAVID[6], ICHABOD[5], GIDEON[4], BENJAMIN[3], JOHN[2], JOHN[1].

Lora A.[7], dau. of David[6] and Pamelia (Darrow) Tower, b. 1813; mar. Josiah Hoskinson.

Childr.

I. MARTHA[8].   III. ELON[8].
II. GEORGE[8].   IV. JOSEPHINE[8].

509. Hedges. Eighth Generation. Tower.

215. CYNTHIA[7], DAVID[6], ICHABOD[5], GIDEON[4], BENJAMIN[3], JOHN[2], JOHN[1].

Cynthia[7], dau. of David[6] and Pamelia (Darrow) Tower, b. 1815; mar. Elias Hedges.

Child.

I. ELIZABETH[8] died

510. Eighth Generation. Tower.

215. DAVID[7], DAVID[6], ICHABOD[5], GIDEON[4], BENJAMIN[3], JOHN[2], JOHN[1].

David[7], son of David[6] and Pamelia (Darrow) Tower, b. 1817; mar. Louisa Gunn.

Child.

I. CHARLES[8].

511. Sheldon, Hall. Eighth Generation. Tower.

215. PAMELIA E.[7], DAVID[6], ICHABOD[5], GIDEON[4], BENJAMIN[3], JOHN[2], JOHN[1].

Pamelia E.[7], dau. of David[6] and Pamelia (Darrow) Tower, b. 1820; mar. Samuel R. Hall.

Childr.

I. JULIUS TOWER[8].   III. EDWARD[8].
II. JAMES GUIN[8].

Samuel R. Hall died   .
Pamelia E. (Tower) Hall mar., 2d, Rev. H. O. Sheldon; *s. p.*
H. O. Sheldon died in Oberlin, Lorain Co., Ohio.
Pamelia E. (Tower) Sheldon was living in Oberlin   1884.

512.   Eighth Generation.   Tower.

215. GEORGE W.[7], DAVID[6], ICHABOD[5], GIDEON[4], BENJAMIN[3], JOHN[2], JOHN[1].

George W.[7], son of David[6] and Pamelia (Darrow) Tower, b. June 7, 1822; mar. Jane Elizabeth Morse in Bradford, Iowa, April 15, 1855. She was b. in Rock Island, Ill., April 12, 1840, and was dau. of Leonard and Elizabeth (Stearns) Morse.

Childr.

I. ARTHUR SEWARD[8]   born Oct. 12, 1857; died Aug. 29, 1864, ag. 6 y. 10 m. 17 d.

II. FREDERICK WILLIAM[8]   "   April 3, 1861; died March 28, 1868, ag. 6 y. 11 m. 25 d.

III. MARY ELLEN[8]   "   April 21, 1863.

IV. CHARLES JOHN[8]   "   June 21, 1865; died June 3, 1873, ag. 7 y. 11 m. 13 d.

V. CARRIE BELLE[8]   "   April 21, 1868.

VI. GEORGIA WINONA[8]   "   April 7, 1870, died June 14, 1873, ag. 3 y. 2 m. 7 d.

VII. JENNIE GALE[8]   "   April 8, 1872; "   Aug. 21, 1872, ag. 4 m. 13 d.

George W. Tower[7] was living in Faribault, Rice Co., Minn., 1884.

513.   Eighth Generation.   Tower.

215. JAMES M.[7], DAVID[6], ICHABOD[5], GIDEON[4], BENJAMIN[3], JOHN[2], JOHN[1].

James M.[7], son of David[6] and Pamelia (Darrow) Tower, b. June 6, 1824; mar. Phebe Jane Scott in Oberlin, Ohio, 1856. She was born in Clarksfield, Ohio, July 14, 1836, and was dau. of Hiler and Mary (Bedell) Scott.

Childr.

I. ELLA MARY[8]   born March 18, 1858; died in Faribault, Minn, 1862.

II. AMY LORA[8]   "   Oct. 16, 1861;   "   "   "   1861.

III. E. MONROE[8]   "   March 30, 1863.

IV. ADDIE JANE[8]   "   July 31, 1866.

V. FRANKLIN JAMES[8]   "   Jan. 1, 1869; died   1877.

514. Marble.   Eighth Generation.   Tower.

217. ANN E.[7], ISAAC[6], ICHABOD[5], GIDEON[4], BENJAMIN[3], JOHN[2], JOHN[1].

Ann E.[7], dau. of Isaac[6] and Rebecca (Dexter) Tower, b. Nov. 28, 1802; mar. Freegrace Marble, of Charlton, Mass., July 1, 1827.

Childr.

I. LOUISA JANE [8] born July 12, 1828 ; mar. William S. Goodell, of Charlton ; *s. p.* She died Jan. 20, 1879, ag. 50 y. 6 m. 8 d.

II. CORDELIA [8]   "   ; mar. Charles Converse, of Charlton.
III. ABIGAIL D. [8]   "   Aug. 18, 1831, in New Salem, Mass.
IV. MARCUS M. [8]   "   Aug. 26, 1833,   "   "
V. MARSHAL M. [8]   "   ; mar. Emma Burr, of Providence.
VI. FRANK H. [8]   "   April 9, 1837, in New Salem.
VII. JAMES M. [8]   "   May 11, 1840,   "
VIII. ANN ELIZA [8]   "   ; mar. Whitman S. Steer, of Springfield, Mass.

515.   **Eighth Generation.**   **Tower.**

217. WILLIAM [7], ISAAC [6], ICHABOD [5], GIDEON [4], BENJAMIN [3], JOHN [2], JOHN [1].

William [7], son of Isaac [6] and Rebecca (Dexter) Tower, b. Feb. 6, 1806 ; mar. Sallie Wood, of Charlton, Mass., Nov. 23, 1828. She was b. Jan. 22, 1805, and was dau. of William and Margaret (Howe) Wood.

Childr. born in Charlton.

1048. I. ALBERT [8]   born Sept. 21, 1829.
1049. II. MARY LUCY [8]   "   July 1, 1831.
III. WILLIAM HENRY [8] "   March 15, 1833 ; unmar.
IV. GEORGE MARION [8] "   May 31, 1835 ; mar. Maggie Moore ; ch. ; three girls.

William Tower [8] died in Galesville, Wis., Dec. 17, 1883, ag. 77 y. 10 m. 8 d.
Sallie (Wood) Tower died in Charlton, Mass., Dec. 7, 1837, ag. 32 y. 10 m. 16 d.

516. Pike.   **Eighth Generation.**   **Tower.**

217. ELSEY [7], ISAAC [6], ICHABOD [5], GIDEON [4], BENJAMIN [3], JOHN [2], JOHN [1].

Elsey [7], dau. of Isaac [6] and Rebecca (Dexter) Tower, b. Sept. 27, 1807 ; mar. Stillman Pike, of Charlton, Mass., April 15, 1835. He was b. in Charlton June 24, 1801, and was son of Jacob and Sally (Early) Pike.

Childr.

I. HORACE SMITH [8] born Jan. 19, 1839.
II. LOUISA [8]   "   Nov. 11, 1842.
III. EDDY AURIN [8]   "   Oct. 30, 1849 ; died Sept. 18, 1850.

517.   Eighth Generation.   Tower.

217. ISAAC[7], ISAAC[6], ICHABOD[5], GIDEON[4], BENJAMIN[3], JOHN[2], JOHN[1].

Isaac[7], son of Isaac [6] and Rebecca (Dexter) Tower, b.
March 27, 1810; mar. Paulina Buckman, of Woodstock, Conn.,
March 4, 1832. She was b.
Aug. 26, 1805, and was dau. of Abel and Cynthia (Edwards) Buckman.

Childr.

I.	MARY ANN [8]	born Sept. 10, 1834; unmar.
II.	SARAH FRANCES [8]	" June 28, 1842; died March 21, 1846, ag. 3 y. 8 m. 23 d.
1050. III.	FRANCES PAULINA [8]	" Oct. 22, 1847.

Paulina (Buckman) Tower died in Charlton, Oct. 29, 1847, ag. 42 y. 2 m. 3 d.
Isaac Tower[7] mar., 2d, Catherine Sprague, of Northbridge, Mass.,
April 1, 1857. She was born in Danby, Vt.,
Sept. 30, 1806, and was dau. of Zebulon and Silama (Aldrich) Sprague.
Isaac Tower[7] died in Charlton, Mass., April 7, 1881, ag. 70 y. 10 m. 11 d.

518.   Eighth Generation.   Tower.

217. ALANSON P.[7], ISAAC [6], ICHABOD[5], GIDEON[4], BENJAMIN[3], JOHN[2], JOHN[1].

Alanson P.[7], son of Isaac [6] and Rebecca (Dexter) Tower, b.
May 30, 1814; mar. Mary N. Fales, of Holden, Mass.,
Feb. 6, 1839. She was b. in Holden
June 29, 1820, and was dau. of Ambrose and Amy (Newell) Fales.

Childr.

1051. I.	REBECCA JANE [8]	born Nov. 12, 1839.
1052. II.	ELLEN MARIA [8]	" June 28, 1841.
III.	EMMA FRANCES [8]	" Dec. 29, 1849; died Jan. 30, 1850.
IV.	IDA ADELA[8]	" Feb. 13, 1858; " in Chatfield, Minn., May 19, 1883, ag. 25 y. 3 m. 3 d.
1053. V.	AMY EUDORA [8]	" May 10, 1859.
VI.	MARY ISABELLA [8]	" Dec. 7, 1861; died June 22, 1862.

Alanson P. Tower[7] died in Chatfield, Minn., Sept. 17, 1888, ag. 74 y. 3 m. 18 d.

519.   Eighth Generation.   **Tower.**

217. JOHN[7], ISAAC[6], ICHABOD[5], GIDEON[4], BENJAMIN[3], JOHN[2], JOHN[1].

John[7], son of Isaac[6] and Rebecca (Dexter) Tower, b.
July 27, 1820 ; mar. Mary Lucy Bellows in Charlton, Mass.,
April 14, 1844. She was b. in Leverett, Mass.,
Feb. 29, 1820, and was dau. of Jonathan and Abigail (Simpson) Bellows.

Childr.

1054.	I.	CHARLEMAGNE[8]	born May 16, 1847, in Charlton.
1055.	II.	ISAAC DEXTER[8]	" Nov. 16, 1849, " "
	III.	THEODORE EUGENE[8]	" Dec. 7, 1854; unmar.; died in Worcester, Mass., April 26, 1878, ag. 23 y. 4 m. 20 d.
	IV.	WILLIAM J.[8]	" Jan. 12, 1864.

John Tower[7] died at Tower Hill, in Harney, Meeker Co.,
Minn., March 17, 1873, ag. 52 y. 7 m. 21 d.

520. Moore.   Eighth Generation.   **Tower.**

218. PAMELIA[7], JOSEPH P.[6], ICHABOD[5], GIDEON[4], BENJAMIN[3], JOHN[2], JOHN[1].

Pamelia[7], dau. of Joseph P.[6] and Cynthia (Pullen) Tower, b.
Jan. 23, 1806 ; mar. Silas Moore ; *s. p.*
Silas Moore died in Quincy, Branch Co., Mich., subsequent
to 1849.
Pamelia (Tower) Moore died in Quincy about 1849.

521. Bigelow.   Eighth Generation.   **Tower.**

218. SALLY[7], JOSEPH P.[6], ICHABOD[5], GIDEON[4], BENJAMIN[3], JOHN[2], JOHN[1].

Sally[7], dau. of Joseph P.[6] and Cynthia (Pullen) Tower, b.
May 15, 1809 ; mar. William Bigelow, of Geneva, N. Y.,
            1829. He was b. in Phelps, Ontario Co., N. Y.,
Feb. 9, 1809, and was son of Abner and Lovice (Guilford)
    Bigelow.

Childr.

I.	HENRY L.[8]	born Sept. 16, 1830, in Phelps.
II.	FRANCIS M.[8]	" Aug. 28, 1833, " " ; died June 3, 1868, ag. 32 y. 9 m. 6 d.
III.	CYNTHIA L.[8]	" Aug. 1, 1835; died in Plymouth, Wayne Co., Mich., Nov. 7, 1836, ag. 1 y. 3 m. 6 d.
IV.	MARY L.[8]	" ; died March 23, 1856. She was drowned in Grand River, Mich.
V.	MARY LUCY[8]	" , in Plymouth, Mich.

Sally (Tower) Bigelow died in Plymouth, July 5, 1845, ag. 36 y. 1 m. 21 d.

522. Bigelow.   Eighth Generation.   Tower.

218. Lucinda[7], Joseph P.[6], Ichabod[5], Gideon[4], Benjamin[3], John[2], John[1].

Lucinda[7], dau. of Joseph P.[6] and Cynthia (Pullen) Tower, b. Sept. 11, 1810; mar. William Bigelow
Sept. , 1845. He was b.
Feb. 9, 1809, and was son of Abner and Lovice (Guilford) Bigelow.

Child.

526. I. Guilford[8] born May , 1846.

Lucinda (Tower) Bigelow died in Grand Ledge, Eaton Co., Mich., Nov. , 1880, ag. 70 y. 2 m.

523.   Eighth Generation.   Tower.

218. Joseph H.[7], Joseph P.[6], Ichabod[5], Gideon[4], Benjamin[3], John[2], John[1].

Joseph H.[7], son of Joseph P.[6] and Cynthia (Pullen) Tower, b. Feb. 1, 1812; mar. Phebe Ann Thomas
Oct. 5, 1854. She was b. in Eagle, Clinton Co., Mich.,
, and was dau. of Heman and Lucy (Benson) Thomas.

Childr. born in Grand Ledge, Eaton Co., Mich.

	I.	Julius[8]	born July 13, 1855; died Jan. 15, 1856.
	II.	Elizabeth A[8]	" Nov. 7, 1856.
	III.	Lucy A[8]	" April 21, 1858; mar. William Sharp, Dec. 25, 1879.
1056.	IV.	Vernon J.[8]	" Jan. 19, 1860.
	V.	Seward[8]	" Oct. 25, 1861.
1057.	VI.	Alice L.[8]	" Sept. 28, 1864.
1058.	VII.	Cynthia B.[8]	" July 10, 1869.

Joseph H. Tower lives at Grand Ledge (1884).

524.   Eighth Generation.   Tower.

218. Isaac W.[7], Joseph P.[6], } Ichabod[5], Gideon[4], Benjamin[3],
217. Mary D.[7], Isaac[6], } John[2], John[1].

Isaac W.[7], son of Joseph P.[6] and Cynthia (Pullen) Tower, b. Aug. 1, 1813; mar. Mary Dexter Tower[7]
May 28, 1843. She was b. in Charlton, Mass., Sept. 20, 1817, and was dau. of Isaac[6] and Rebecca (Dexter) Tower.

Child.

I. CLARA CYNTHIA [8] born July 4, 1845, in Charlton; died in Providence, R. I.,
　　　　　unmar., Dec. 23, 1868, ag. 24 y. 5 m. 19 d.

Isaac Wilson Tower was living in Providence, R. I., 1877.

525.　　　　**Eighth Generation.**　　　　**Tower.**

218. WILLIAM P.[7], JOSEPH P.[6], ICHABOD [5], GIDEON [4], BENJAMIN [3],
　　JOHN [2], JOHN [1].

William P.[7], son of Joseph P.[6] and Cynthia (Pullen)Tower, b.
Sept. 12, 1815; mar. Rosette Clarissa Barnes in Rollin,
Lenawee Co., Mich.,
Jan. 10, 1840.

Childr.

1059.	I.	ICHABOD HARRISON [8] born Dec. 7, 1840, in Wheatland, Mich.	
	II.	CYNTHIA ELIZABETH [8] "	Jan. 8, 1843, " Plymouth, "
	III.	GEORGE LEWIS [6] "	Nov. 17, 1846, " Woodstock, "
	IV.	JOHN BARNES [8] "	June 29, 1848, " " "
			died Dec. 19, 1851, ag. 3 y. 5 m. 20 d.
	V.	ANDREW EUGENE [8] "	Oct. 9, 1852, in Woodstock, Mich.
	VI.	WILLIAM PORTER [8] "	Nov. 23, 1854, " " "
	VII.	CHARLES FREEMAN [8] "	Feb. 4, 1857, " Minnesota; died in Grand Ledge, Mich.

Rosette C. (Barnes) Tower died in Rice Co., Minn., Jan. 6,
1863.
William P. Tower [7] was living in Motley, Morrison Co., Minn.,
1883.

526.　　　　**Eighth Generation.**　　　　**Tower.**

218. JAMES P.[7], JOSEPH P.[6], ICHABOD [5], GIDEON [4], BENJAMIN [3],
　　JOHN [2], JOHN [1].

James P.[7], son of Joseph P.[6] and Cynthia (Pullen) Tower, b.
May 31, 1817; mar. Lucena Jenkins
July 26, 1849. She was b. in Allegany Co., N. Y.,
April 22, 1833, and was dau. of Richard L. and Ann Maria
(Lake) Jenkins.

Childr.

	I.	ISAAC RINALDO [8] born July 29, 1851, in Burr Oak, St. Joseph's Co., Mich.	
1060.	II.	CARL KOSSUTH [8] "	Nov. 3, 1852, in Burr Oak.
1061.	III.	VIOLA F.[8] "	June 26, 1855, " "
1062.	IV.	JAY B.[8] "	Jan. 26, 1859, " "

James P. Tower [7] died in Grand Ledge, Mich., Feb. 5, 1873,
ag. 55 y. 8 m. 5 d.

Lucena (Jenkins) Tower mar., 2d, Guilford Bigelow [8]
Sept.   , 1874. He was born
May   , 1846, and was son of William and Lucinda [7] (Tower)
Bigelow.

527.   **Eighth Generation.**   **Tower.**

218. SAMUEL R.[7], JOSEPH P.[6], ICHABOD [5], GIDEON [4], BENJAMIN [3],
JOHN [2], JOHN [1].
Samuel R.[7], son of Joseph P.[6] and Cynthia (Pullen)Tower, b.
Dec.   , 1823 ; mar. Sophronia Wilson, of Potsdam, St. Lau-
rence Co., N. Y.,
July   , 1848. She was b.
Aug. 13, 1827, and was dau. of Harry W. and Levisa L.
(Ames) Wilson.

Childr.

	I.	ARGAMENTO C.[8]	born	Dec. 19,1850, in Faun River, St. Joseph's Co., Mich.
1063.	II.	JOSEPHINE A.[8]	"	Aug. 13, 1852, in Somerset, Lenawee Co., Mich.
1064.	III.	CYNTHIA LEVISA [8]	"	March 24, 1854, in Somerset.
	IV.	ELLA ESTELLA [8]	"	July 21, 1855, in Litchfield, Hillsdale Co., Mich. ; died 1857.
1065.	V.	DELIA DELL [8]	"	Dec. 19, 1858, in Burr Oak, St. Joseph's Co., Mich.
	VI.	CLARISSA ANN [8]	"	Jan. 21, 1860, in Addison, Lenawee Co., Mich.
	VII.	WILLIAM C.[8]	"	March 5, 1862, in Addison ; died 1862.
1066.	VIII.	NETTIE ELIZABETH [8]	"	June 26, 1863, " "

Samuel R. Tower [7] died at Deep Bottom, Va., Aug. 18, 1863,
ag. 39 y. 8 m.

528. **Whitney.** **Eighth Generation.**   **Tower.**

218. HARRIET D.[7], JOSEPH P.[6], ICHABOD [5], GIDEON [4], BENJAMIN [3],
JOHN [2], JOHN [1].
Harriet D.[7], dau. of Joseph P.[6] and Cynthia (Pullen) Tower, b.
May 15, 1825 ; mar. Samuel G. Whitney, of Grand Ledge,
Mich.,
June 25, 1856. He was b. in Jefferson Co., N. Y.,
Oct. 26, 1827.

Childr. born in Grand Ledge.

I. GEORGE A.[8]   born May 15, 1857. III. EVA [8]   born Aug. 15, 1861.
II. PATTIE MARIA [8] " April 7, 1859. IV. ALBERT S.[8] " Feb. 1, 1866.

529. Lewis.   **Eighth Generation.**   **Tower.**

218. ELIZABETH B.[7], JOSEPH P.[6], ICHABOD[5], GIDEON[4], BENJAMIN[3], JOHN[2], JOHN[1].

Elizabeth B.[7], dau. of Joseph P.[6] and Cynthia (Pullen) Tower, b.

Feb. 22, 1828; mar. George M. Lewis in Addison, Lenawee Co., Mich.,

Nov. 26, 1846. He was b.

Aug. 28, 1825, and was son of John and Rizpah (Smith) Lewis.

Childr. born in Addison.

I.	IMOGENE [8]	born Oct. 21, 1847.
II.	CASSPARATA [8]	" May 6, 1850.
III.	BARTHA L.[8]	" Nov. 26, 1851.
IV.	JOHN [8]	" Feb. 20, 1854; died Aug. 27, 1854.
V.	BYRON [8]	" Feb. 3, 1856; " Feb. 17, 1856.
VI.	FRANKIE R.[8]	" July 4, 1857.
VII.	ALICE [8]	" Jan. 1, 1860; died Aug. 15, 1860.
VIII.	CHARLES [8] } Twins	" Oct. 15, 1861; died Oct. 30, 1861.
IX.	GEORGE [8] }	
X.	JOHN FREDDIE [8]	" Aug. 1, 1864.

George Lewis died in Addison, Feb. 6, 1887, ag. 61 y. 5 m. 9 d.

530. Bowen.   **Eighth Generation.**   **Tower.**

218. CORNELIA N.[7], JOSEPH P.[6], ICHABOD[5], GIDEON[4], BENJAMIN[3], JOHN[2], JOHN[1].

Cornelia N.[7], dau. of Joseph P.[6] and Cynthia (Pullen) (Tower) b.

Sept. 16, 1829; mar. Thomas Bowen

June 16, 1851. He was b. in Norwich, Chenango Co., N. Y.,

June 1, 1821, and was son of James and Annie (Williams) Bowen.

Childr.

I.	EVA L.[8]	born April 14, 1853, in Burr Oak, Mich.
II.	MATTIE [8]	" May 1, 1855, in Grand Ledge.
III.	ELLA [8]	" July 4, 1857, in Addison.
IV.	ORA B.[8]	" Nov. 18, 1859, "
V.	IMOGENE [8]	" Feb. 17, 1862, in Plainville, Allegan Co., Mich.
VI.	GEORGE [8]	" Sept. 1, 1864, in Addison.
VII.	Infant [8] } Twins	" ; died in infancy.
VIII.	Infant [8] }	

Thomas Bowen's residence, 1883, was in Addison, Mich.

531. Carmichael. Eighth Generation. Tower.

218. EMMA[7], JOSEPH P.[6], ICHABOD[5], GIDEON[4], BENJAMIN[3], JOHN[2], JOHN[1].

Emma[7], dau. of Joseph P.[6] and Cynthia (Pullen) Tower, b.
March 18, 1831; mar. Charles Carmichael
March 5, 1854. He was b.
June 29, 1831, and was son of Charles and Ann (Langdon)
Carmichael.

Childr.

I.	EDITH M.[8]	born June 17, 1855, in Somerset, Hillsdale Co., Mich.
II.	LANNES E.[8]	" Jan. 22, 1857, in Woodstock, Lenawee Co., "
III.	ALICE E.[8]	" June 24, 1860, in Wheatland, Hillsdale Co., "
IV.	BYRON[8]	" Oct. 10, 1861; died Nov. 9, 1861.
V.	GEORGE L.[8]	" Nov. 18, 1862, in Rollin, Lenawee Co., Mich.
VI.	RACHEL M.[8]	" Jan. 24, 1866, " " "
VII.	BURTZ[8]	" June 19, 1869; died in Wheatland Oct. 9, 1869.

Charles Carmichael was living in Wheatland in 1883.

532. Eighth Generation. Tower.

222. JOHN C.[7], LEVI[6], LEVI[5], GIDEON[4], BENJAMIN[3], JOHN[2], JOHN[1].
John C.[7], son of Levi[6] and Elizabeth W. (Cook) Tower, b.
Feb. 7, 1809; mar. Sarah G. Le Favour, of Marblehead,
Mass.,
She was b.
March 23, 1801.

Childr.

I.	ELIZABETH DAY[8] born Sept. 11, ; mar. William J. Doyle.
II.	LEVI[8] " Aug. 18, 1835; died at Bull Run, Va., July 21, 1861, ag. 25 y. 11 m. 3 d.
III.	CAROLINE MINERVA[8] " ; mar. George H. Potter.
1067. IV.	SARAH MARGARET[8] "

John C. Tower[7] died   .

533. De Jongh. Eighth Generation. Tower.

222. AMELIA C.[7], LEVI[6], LEVI[5], GIDEON[4], BENJAMIN[3], JOHN[2], JOHN[1].

Amelia C.[7], dau. of Levi[6] and Elizabeth W. (Cook) Tower, b.
  ; mar. William De Jongh.

Child.

I. BERTHA[8].

534.   **Eighth Generation.**   **Tower.**

224. WILLIAM E.[7], JASON [6], LEVI [5], GIDEON [4], BENJAMIN [3], JOHN [2],
JOHN [1].
William E.[7], son of Jason [6] and Philena (Howard) Tower, b.
May 13, 1811; mar. Betsey Ann Parlow, of New Bedford,
Mass.,
April 20, 1833.

Child.

1068. I. WILLIAM F.[8] born   1839.

William E. Tower [7] died at Gabena, Africa, Oct. , 1857, ag.
46 y. 5 m.
Betsey A. (Parlow) Tower died in Milford, Mass.

535. Coombs.   **Eighth Generation.**   **Tower.**

224. MARY [7], JASON [6], LEVI [5], GIDEON [4], BENJAMIN [3], JOHN [2], JOHN [1].
Mary [7], dau. of Jason [6] and Philena (Howard) Tower, b.
Jan. 10, 1813; mar. Amos Coombs, of Bellingham, Mass.,
March 27, 1833. He was b. in Bellingham
Oct. 20, 1808, and was son of Jesse and Sarah (Adams)
Coombs.

Childr.

I. SARAH ADAMS [8]   born Feb. 28, 1835, in Medway, Mass.
II. CAROLINE THOMPSON [8] " Aug. 30, 1836; died Dec. 13, 1839, ag. 3 y.
3 m. 14 d.

Amos Coombs died in Bellingham, March 7, 1840, ag. 31 y.
4 m. 18 d.

BREWER.   TOWER.
Mary (Tower) Coombs mar., 2d, Cyrus Albert Brewer, of
Brewer, Me.,
Oct. 29, 1843.

Child.

III. ALBERT GLEASON [8] born April   , 1845.

Mary (Tower) Brewer died in Brewer, Me., May 25, 1845,
ag. 32 y. 4 m. 15 d.

536.   **Eighth Generation.**   **Tower.**

224. JOHN H.[7], JASON [6], LEVI [5], GIDEON [4], BENJAMIN [3], JOHN [2],
JOHN [1].
John H.[7], son of Jason [6] and Philena (Howard) Tower, b.
Dec. 6, 1814; mar. Sarah Smith

Dec. 7, 1844. She was b. in Orrington, Me.,
Feb. 14, 1815, and was dau. of Zenas and Abigail (Harden)
Smith.

Childr. born in Brewer, Me.

1069.	I.	JASON HOWARD [8]	born Sept. 28, 1845.	
1070.	II.	MARY ELCENA [8]	" Dec. 18, 1846.	
1071.	III.	ANDERSON COOK [8]	" July 16, 1849.	
	IV.	ADRIAN LEVI [8]	" Jan. 12, 1851; unmar., 1885.	
1072.	V.	ETTA SOPHIA [8]	" March 1, 1852.	
	VI.	IDA EZOLE [8]	" Sept. 10, 1854.	

Sarah (Smith) Tower died in Brewer, Me., Aug. 10, 1882,
ag. 67 y. 5 m. 24 d.

537. Cook. Eighth Generation. Tower.

224. LYDIA [7], JASON [6], LEVI [5], GIDEON [4], BENJAMIN [3], JOHN [2], JOHN [1].
Lydia [7], dau. of Jason [6] and Philena (Howard) Tower, b.
July 13, 1816 ; mar. Winslow Cook, of Franklin, Mass.,
June 2, 1861. He was b.
1801, and was son of Whipple and Lucy Cook ; *s. p.*

538. Metcalf. Eighth Generation. Tower.

224. NANCY R .[7], JASON [6], LEVI [5], GIDEON [4], BENJAMIN [3], JOHN [2],
JOHN [1].
Nancy R.[7], dau. of Jason [6] and Philena (Howard) Tower, b.
Aug. 19, 1818 ; mar. Welcome Metcalf, of Cumberland, R. I.,
Feb. 1, 1841.

Child.

I. MARY CAROLINE [8] born May 1, 1841.

Welcome Metcalf died in Cumberland about 1853.

539. Eighth Generation. Tower.

224. LEVI [7], JASON [6], LEVI [5], GIDEON [4], BENJAMIN [3], JOHN [2], JOHN [1].
Levi [7], son of Jason [6] and Philena (Howard) Tower, b.
Sept. 10, 1820 ; mar. Mary Jane Shepalton, of Illinois; *s. p.*
Levi Tower [7] died in San Francisco, Cal., 1870, ag. 50.

540. Camden. Eighth Generation. Tower.

224. PHILENA [7], JASON [6], LEVI [5], GIDEON [4], BENJAMIN [3], JOHN [2],
JOHN [1].
Philena [7], dau. of Jason [6] and Philena (Howard) Tower, b.
Sept. 27, 1822 ; mar. Charles Camden

Nov. 11, 1853. He was born in Aston Magnor, Worcestershire, England,

1817, and was son of Joseph and Mary (Smith) Camden.

Childr.

I. ADA HOWARD [8] born Aug. 11, 1854.
II. GRACE [8]   "   Jan.   6, 1856.
III. MARY ELECTA [8]   "   March 8, 1861.

---

541.   Eighth Generation.   **Tower.**

224. JASON [7], JASON [6], LEVI [5], GIDEON [4], BENJAMIN [3], JOHN [2], JOHN [1]. Jason [7], son of Jason [6] and Philena (Howard) Tower, b. Nov. 16, 1824; mar. Electa Ross Fisher, of Cumberland, R. I., Aug. , 1856. She was b. in Cumberland

1833, and was dau. of Charles and Julia Ann (Whipple) Fisher.

Child.

I. CHARLES WELCOME [8] born April 9, 1857; died Aug. , 1857.

Electa R. (Fisher) Tower died June 13, 1857, ag. 22.
Jason Tower [7] mar., 2d, Mary E. Jardin, of Newcastle, N. B., Sept. 24, 1870. She was b. in Newcastle

1849, and was dau. of Richard and Helen (Kingston) Jardin.

Childr.

II. LEVI HOWARD [8]   born July 18, 1871.
III. LUCY ELLEN [8]   "   Sept. 20, 1872.
IV. WILLIAM EMERSON [8] "   Sept. 1, 1874.
V. PHILENA CAMDEN [8]   "   May 25, 1876.

---

542. Follett.   Eighth Generation.   **Tower.**

225. POLLY T. [7], EMERSON [6], LEVI [5], GIDEON [4], BENJAMIN [3], JOHN [2], JOHN [1].
Polly T. [7], dau. of Emerson [6] and Sally (Thurston) Tower, b. March 31, 1811; mar. Nelson Follett, of Cumberland, R. I., Oct. 2, 1828. He was son of Luther Follett.

Childr.

I. MARY ANN [8] born Aug. 21, 1829, in Cumberland; mar. Jerome Coombs. She died
II. SANFORD N. [8]   "   Feb. 14, 1832, in Wrentham, Mass; died Oct. 18, 1832.

Polly T. (Tower) Follett died Aug. 15, 1832.

543. Follett. Eighth Generation. Tower.

225. DELIA[7], EMERSON[6], LEVI[5], GIDEON[4], BENJAMIN[3], JOHN[2], JOHN[1].

Delia[7], dau. of Emerson[6] and Sally (Thurston) Tower, b. Dec. 2, 1812; mar. John G. Follett April 4, 1830. He was b. in Wrentham, Mass., April 22, 1801, and was son of Benjamin and Katura (Hayden) Follett.

Childr.

I.	ADIN E.[8]	born May 17, 1831.	
II.	JOHN S.[8]	" April 29, 1833.	
III.	ANNA FRANCES[8]	" Oct. 22, 1835.	
IV.	DELIA[8]	"	; died in infancy.
V.	NAPOLEON B.[8]	" April 14, 1839.	
VI.	EMERSON TOWER[8]	" Oct. 4, 1841.	
VII.	EUGENE B.[8]	" Nov. , 1843.	
VIII.	MARY E.[8]	" Nov. , 1845.	
IX.	HENRY G.[8]	" Dec. , 1847.	

John G. Follett died in Smithfield, R. I.
Delia (Tower) Follett died in Attleborough, Mass., 1874.

544. Follett. Eighth Generation. Tower.

225. CALISTA[7], EMERSON[6], LEVI[5], GIDEON[4], BENJAMIN[3], JOHN[2], JOHN[1].

Calista[7], dau. of Emerson[6] and Sally (Thurston) Tower, b. Sept. 25, 1814; mar. Benjamin Follett in Cumberland, R. I., Oct. 2, 1844. He was b. in Wrentham, Mass., March 2, 1811, and was son of Benjamin and Ketura (Hayden) Follett.

Childr.

I.	FRANK F.[8]	born March 6, 1846, in Wrentham, Mass.	
II.	EMMA K.[8]	" May 22, 1848,	" "
III.	SARAH CALISTA[8]	" June 9, 1850,	" "
IV.	ANGIE P.[8]	" Nov. 8, 1852, in Stratton, Vt.	
V.	LIZZIE TOWER[8]	" April 21, 1855, in Wrentham.	

Benjamin Follett died in Wrentham, May 11, 1878, ag. 67 y. 2 m. 9 d.

545. Darling. Eighth Generation. Tower.

225. LYDIA[7], EMERSON[6], LEVI[5], GIDEON[4], BENJAMIN[3], JOHN[2], JOHN[1].

Lydia[7], dau. of Emerson[6] and Sally (Thurston) Tower, b.

Sept. 19, 1816; mar. John W. Darling in Wrentham, Mass., Aug. 31, 1836. He was b. in Cumberland, R. I., April 15, 1813, and was son of John and Mary (Weeden) Darling.

Childr.

I. JOHN EMERSON [8] born March 23, 1838.
II. ERASTUS C.[8] " Sept. 28, 1842, in Franklin, Mass.; died June 25, 1849, ag. 6 y. 8 m. 27 d.
III. JULIUS A.[8] " Aug. 14, 1845, in Wrentham; died Feb. 6, 1849, ag. 3 y. 5 m. 23 d.
IV. JOANNA A.[8] " Aug. 14, 1845, in Wrentham; died March 11, 1849, ag. 3 y. 6 m. 28 d.
V. LYDIA TOWER [8] " Aug. 14, 1848, in Wrentham; died March 4, 1849.

Lydia (Tower) Darling died in Wrentham, June 21, 1849, ag. 32 y. 9 m. 2 d.

546. **Eighth Generation.** **Tower.**

225. EMERSON [7], EMERSON [6], LEVI [5], GIDEON [4], BENJAMIN [3], JOHN [2], JOHN [1].

Emerson [7], son of Emerson [6] and Sally (Thurston) Tower, b. June 29, 1818; mar. Elizabeth Adeline Hidden Aug. 9, 1838. She was b. May 23, 1815, and was dau. of James and Mary W. (Clifford) Hidden.

Child.

1073. I. JAMES H.[8] born May 21, 1847, in Providence, R. I.

Emerson Tower [7] died in Providence, April 23, 1870, ag. 51 y. 9 m. 24 d.

547. Prue. **Eighth Generation.** **Tower.**

225. DELILA [7], EMERSON [6], LEVI [5], GIDEON [4], BENJAMIN [3], JOHN [2], JOHN [1].

Delila [7], dau. of Emerson [6] and Sally (Whipple) Tower, b. Nov. 14, 1828; mar. Francis Prue Dec. 18, 1849. He was b. in Canada Dec. 17, 1828, and was son of Paul and Agnes (Allee) Prue.

Childr.

I. ELMIRA WHIPPLE [8] born March 11, 1850, in Smithfield, R. I.
II. CORNELIUS W.[8] " July 4, 1851, in Woonsocket, "
III. ELLA G.[8] " March 25, 1854, " "
IV. RUTH ANN [8] " Sept. 5, 1856, in Cumberland, "

548. Knight. **Eighth Generation.** **Tower.**

225. CHLOE [7], EMERSON [6], LEVI [5], GIDEON [4], BENJAMIN [3], JOHN [2], JOHN [1].

Chloe[7], dau. of Emerson[6] and Sally (Whipple) Tower, b. Nov. 19, 1830; mar. William Knight, of Johnson, R. I., May 6, 1850. He was son of Daniel Knight.

Child.

I. WINFIELD SCOTT[8] born Aug. 19, 1850.

CAPRON. TOWER.

Chloe (Tower) Knight mar., 2d, E. M. Capron, of Taunton, Oct. 19, 1859; *s. p.*

549. Baylies. Eighth Generation. Tower.

225. ZILLA[7], EMERSON[6], LEVI[5], GIDEON[4], BENJAMIN[3], JOHN[2], JOHN[1].

Zilla[7], dau. of Emerson[6] and Sally (Whipple) Tower, b. Sept. 27, 1834; mar. Hiram W. Baylies, of Taunton, Mass., Nov. , 1859. He was son of Horatio and Rhoda Baylies.

Childr.

I.	EMERSON HORATIO[8]	born	
II.	ANNIE[8]	"	
III.	NICHOLAS[8]	"	Aug. 12, 1864.
IV.	HARRIET ELIZA[8]	"	May 13, 1869.
V.	ADELINE FRANCES[8]	"	Jan. 3, 1871; died Aug. , 1874.
VI.	HELEN PATIENCE[8]	"	Nov. 3, 1875.
VII.	MARY ELIZABETH[8]	"	Jan. 15, 1878.

550. Wilder. Eighth Generation. Tower.

226. OMYRA[7], JOSEPH[6], SAMUEL[5], GIDEON[4], BENJAMIN[3], JOHN[2], JOHN[1].

Omyra[7], dau. of Joseph[6] and Polly (Stewart) Tower, b. 1809; mar. Artemas Wilder, of Rutland Co., Vt., 1834.

Childr.

Two daughters.

Artemas Wilder died in Royalton, Niagara Co., N. Y., 1838.

551. Eighth Generation. Tower.

226. SAMUEL[7], JOSEPH[6], SAMUEL[5], GIDEON[4], BENJAMIN[3], JOHN[2], JOHN[1].

Samuel[7], son of Joseph[6] and Polly (Stewart) Tower, b. Aug. 11, 1811; mar. Chloe Hurlburt, of Brandon, Rutland Co., Vt., 1857; *s. p.*

Samuel Tower[7] died in Brandon, July 22, 1872, ag. 60 y. 11 m. 11 d.

Chloe (Hurlburt) Tower died in Brandon Sept. 22, 1872.

552. **Eighth Generation.** **Tower.**

226. HARVEY[7], JOSEPH[6], SAMUEL[5], GIDEON[4], BENJAMIN[3], JOHN[2], JOHN[1].

Harvey[7], son of Joseph[6] and Polly (Stewart) Tower, b. March 3, 1817; mar. Laura Mallet, of Barry Co., Mich., Dec. 16, 1846. She was b. Feb. 16, 1829, and was dau. of Miner and Marietta (Parker) Mallet.

Childr.

	I.	RU[8]	born	1848, in Barry Co.; died 1865, ag. 17.
1074.	II.	EMMA[8]	"	Dec. 27, 1850, in Oceana Co., Mich.
1075.	III.	ADA[8]	"	Sept. 7, 1853, " " "
1076.	IV.	LEE L.[8]	"	Sept. 17, 1856, " " "
	V.	DON[8]	"	1858, " " "
	VI.	URI[8]	"	1860, " " "
	VII.	WARD[8]	"	1862, " " "
	VIII.	INA[8]	"	1865, " " " ; died 1867.
	IX.	EFFIE[8]	"	1867, " " "
	X.	EMMOR[8]	"	1870, " " "
	XI.	JOSEPH[8]	"	1872, " " "

553. Stearns. **Eighth Generation.** **Tower.**

226. HARRIET[7], JOSEPH[6], SAMUEL[5], GIDEON[4], BENJAMIN[3], JOHN[2], JOHN[1].

Harriet[7], dau. of Joseph[6] and Polly (Stewart) Tower, b. ; mar. John Stearns, of Middlebury, Vt., 1844.

Childr.

I. ELIZA[8]. III. CORA[8].
II. WALTER[8]. IV. CLARENCE[8]

Harriet (Tower) Stearns died .

554. **Eighth Generation.** **Tower.**

233. ROBERT[7], JONATHAN[6], GIDEON[5], JOHN[4], BENJAMIN[3], JOHN[2], JOHN[1].

Robert[7], son of Jonathan Tower[6]; mar. Rebecca Stone in Dearborn Co., Ind., Nov. 7, 1833.

Child.

I. BENJAMIN S.[8] He lives in Holton, Ind. (1885).

555. **Eighth Generation.** **Tower.**

233. JOHN[7], JONATHAN[6], GIDEON[5], JOHN[4], BENJAMIN[3], JOHN[2], JOHN[1].

John[7], son of Jonathan Tower[6]; mar. Lucinda Lacey.

Childr.

I. OLIVER [8].   He lives in Wyandotte, Kansas.
II. Daughter [8],   ; mar. She   "   "   "

Lucinda (Lacey) Tower died   .
John Tower [7] mar., 2d, Ester Lemon, of Dearborn Co., Ind.

556. Ellis.   **Eighth Generation.**   **Tower.**

233. AMANDA [7], JONATHAN [6], GIDEON [5], JOHN [4], BENJAMIN [3], JOHN [2], JOHN [1].

Amanda [7], dau. of Jonathan Tower [6],
        ; mar. Hezekiah Ellis, of Dearborn Co., Ind.,
Oct. 2, 1832.

Childr.

I. HIRAM [8].   He lives in Rockport, Ind.
II. MARVIN [8].   "   "   "

Amanda (Tower) Ellis died   .

557.   **Eighth Generation.**   **Tower.**

233. ALFRED [7], JONATHAN [6], GIDEON [5], JOHN [4], BENJAMIN [3], JOHN [2], JOHN [1].

Alfred [7], son of Jonathan Tower [6], mar. Almira   .

Childr.

I. LEVI [8].   He lives in Rockport, Ind.
II. OLIVER [8].   "   "   "

Alfred Tower [7] died   .

558.   **Eighth Generation.**   **Tower.**

233. LEWIS [7], JONATHAN [6], GIDEON [5], JOHN [4], BENJAMIN [3], JOHN [2], JOHN [1].

Lewis [7], son of Jonathan Tower [6], b.
    1824 ; mar. Susan   .

Child.

I. LEWIS SCRANTON [8].

Lewis Tower [7] died in Switzerland Co., Ind., June,   1884,
    ag. 60.

559. Orem.   **Eighth Generation.**   **Tower.**

235. ALMA [7], GIDEON [6], GIDEON [5], JOHN [4], BENJAMIN [3], JOHN [2], JOHN [1].
Alma [7], dau. of Gideon [6] and Roxana (Scranton) Tower, b.
Dec. 3, 1822 ; mar. James Orem, of Switzerland Co., Ind.,
    1843.   He was b. in Switzerland Co.
Sept. 15, 1822.

Childr. born in Switzerland Co.

I. JAMES G.[8] born Feb. 9, 1844.
II. WILLIAM Z.[8] " Nov. 12, 1846; mar. Clara B. Woody, of Switzerland Co.
III. ROXANA[8] " Dec. 20, 1848; mar. Francis M. McMaken, of Switzerland Co.
IV. MARY E.[8] ⎫ ⎧ died Sept. 9, 1852, ag. 1 y. 18 d.
V. SARAH J.[8] ⎬ Twins " Aug. 22, 1851 ⎨ " Sept. 23, 1852, ag. 1 y. 1 m. 2 d.
 ⎭ ⎩
VI. LYDIA A.[8] ⎫ " " Oct. 30, 1854; John S. died Nov. 23, 1856,
VII. JOHN S.[8] ⎭ ag. 2 y. 24 d.
VIII. GEORGE H.[8] " Feb. 1, 1856; died Feb. 4, 1859, ag. 3 y. 3 d.
IX. JOSIAH W.[8] " May 22, 1858; mar. Elizabeth E. Cotton, of Switzerland Co.
X. NANCY T.[8] " Nov. 28, 1860; mar. James P. Orem, of Switzerland Co.

James Orem lives in Moorfield, Switzerland Co., Ind. (1885).

560.   **Eighth Generation.**   **Tower.**

235. WILLIAM S.[7], GIDEON[6], GIDEON[5], JOHN[4], BENJAMIN[3], JOHN[2], JOHN[1].

William S.[7], son of Gideon[6] and Roxana (Scranton) Tower, b. June 10, 1826; mar. Tabitha Jane Ricketts, of Switzerland Co., Ind.,

Nov. 28, 1844. She was born in Dearborn Co., Ind., Oct. 25, 1825.

Childr. born in Switzerland Co.

1077. I. MARY ANN[8] born Oct. 11, 1846.
1078. II. ALMA ELIZABETH[8] " May 29, 1848.
1079. III. LOUISA MARIA[8] " April 2, 1850.
 IV. CINDERILLA JANE[8] " July 11, 1852.
1080. V. IRA[8] " May 1, 1854.
 VI. LOVINIA[8] " May 13, 1856.
1081. VII. DANIEL RICKETTS[8] " June 10, 1858.
1082. VIII. JAMES WILLIAM[8] " Oct. 15, 1860.
 IX. ALLEN[8] " March 11, 1863; died Nov., 1863, ag. 8 m.
 X. RACHEL[8] " March 12, 1865; " March 30, 1885, ag. 20 y. 18 d.

William S. Tower[7] lives in Vevay, Switzerland Co., Ind.

561.   **Eighth Generation.**   **Tower.**

235. GIDEON[7], GIDEON[6], GIDEON[5], JOHN[4], BENJAMIN[3], JOHN[2], JOHN[1].

Gideon [7], son of Gideon [6] and Roxana (Scranton) Tower, b. June 2, 1830 ; mar. Susanna Woltz
Oct. 29, 1848. She was daughter of Henry and Hannah Woltz.

Childr.

I. WILLIAM HENRY [8] born Feb. 1, 1851, in Switzerland Co., Ind.; mar. Sallie A. Matthews June 11, 1874.
II. JOSEPH [8] " June 15, 1853, in Switzerland Co.; died July 18, 1854, ag. 1 y. 1 m. 3 d.
III. ARMENIA [8] " Feb. 20, 1856, in Decatur Co., Ind.
IV. MELISSA [8] " Feb. 1, 1858, in Switzerland Co.; mar. Jacob Christman, Sept. 14, 1881.
1083. V. ROXANA [8] " Aug. 9, 1860, in Switzerland Co.
VI. OLIVE ANNA [8] " Oct. 21, 1862, " "
VII. JAMES HARVEY [8] " Feb. 2, 1864, in Jefferson Co., Ind.
VIII. ALMA [8] " April 30, 1867, in Switzerland Co.
IX. MARY ELLEN [8] " May 5, 1869, " " ; died June 10, 1869.

Gideon Tower [7] lives in Madison, Jefferson Co., Ind. (1885).

562. Munger. Eighth Generation. Tower.

237. ROXSENA [7], ALPHEUS P.[6], GIDEON [5], JOHN [4], BENJAMIN [3], JOHN [2]. JOHN [1].

Roxsena [7], dau. of Alpheus P.[6] and Orpah (Hunter) Tower, b. May 20, 1820; mar. Freeman Munger, of Worcester, Mass., Jan. 1, 1842. He was b. in Wales, Mass., Jan. 1, 1809.

Childr.

I. FREEMAN WASHINGTON [8] born Sept. 10, 1842, in Ohio Co., Ind.; died Feb. 3, 1862, in Louisville, Ky., ag. 19 y. 4 m. 23 d.
II. SAMANTHA SOPHIA [8] " March 24, 1844, in Ripley Co., Ind.; died Oct. 16, 1865, ag. 21 y. 6 m. 23 d.
III. AMASA [8] " Dec. 7, 1846, in Ripley Co.

Roxsena (Tower) Munger died Jan. 12, 1860, ag. 39 y. 7 m. 23 d.

563. Eighth Generation. Tower.

237. JOSEPH H.[7], ALPHEUS P.[6], GIDEON [5], JOHN [4], BENJAMIN [3], JOHN [2], JOHN [1].

Joseph H.[7], son of Alpheus P.[6] and Orpah (Hunter) Tower, b. Feb. 24, 1825; mar. Philena Melvina Burton
May 31, 1849. She was b. in Warren Co., Ohio,
Dec. 13, 1828, and was dau. of Hiram and Sibyl (Dudley) Burton.

Childr.

1084.	I.	SIBYL S.[8]	born March 18, 1850, in Ripley Co., Ind.
	II.	MARY ELLA[8]	" Feb. 24, 1852, " " " ;
			mar. J. V. Clark.
1085.	III.	JULIA JOSEPHINE[8]	" May 20, 1854, in Ripley Co.
	IV.	FRANKLIN BURTON[8]	" Oct 2, 1857, in Wapello Co., Iowa.
1086.	V.	WILLIAM EVERETT[8]	" Jan. 4, 1860, " " "
	VI.	EMMA ORPAH[8]	" Aug. 3, 1864, " " "

Philena M. (Burton) Tower died in Van Buren Co., Iowa,
Dec. 14, 1867, ag. 39 y. 1 d.

Joseph H. Tower[7] lives in Dowds Station, Van Buren Co.,
Iowa (1885).

564. Stickel.   Eighth Generation.   Tower.

237. CINDERELLA L.[7], ALPHEUS P.[6], GIDEON[5], JOHN[4], BENJAMIN[3],
JOHN[2], JOHN[1].

Cinderella L.[7], dau. of Alpheus P.[6] and Orpah (Hunter)
Tower, b.

Nov. 14, 1827; mar. George W. Stickel

Feb. 8, 1846. He was b. in Fayette Co., Penn.,

April 7, 1822, and was son of Peter and Rebecca (Boyd)
Stickel.

Childr.

I.	FLORENCE J.[8]		born Dec. 9, 1846, in Indiana; died
			March 7, 1862, ag. 15 y. 2 m. 29 d.
II.	HUNTER L.[8]		" Oct. 10, 1848, in Indiana.
III.	ETTIE M.[8]		" Nov. 27, 1850, " ; mar.
			John Q. McKinney.
IV.	RALPH D.[8]		" Jan. 13, 1853, in Indiana.
V.	ERNEST C.[8]		" Dec. 9, 1854, "
VI.	VALENTINE G.[8]	} Twins	" Jan. 20, 1856, "
VII.	DAYTON CONSTANTINE[8]	}	
VIII.	JOSEPH E.[8]		" June 13, 1858, "
IX.	FRANK ROSCOE[8]		" Feb. 1, 1862, in Iowa; died March
			20, 1863, ag. 1 y. 1 m. 19 d.
X.	WALTER H.[8]		" June 18, 1866, in Iowa.
XI.	ORPAH R.[8]		" Jan. 18, 1870, "

George W. Stickel died in Council Bluffs, Omaha, Sept. 1,
1870, ag. 48 y. 4 m. 24 d.

565. Parker.   Eighth Generation.   Tower.

238. LUCY[7], JOSEPH[6], JOSEPH[5], JOSEPH[4], BENJAMIN[3], JOHN[2],
JOHN[1].

Lucy[7], dau. of Joseph[6] and Priscilla (Edmonds) Tower, b.
Sept. 21, 1797; mar. Calvin Parker, of Ira, Vt.

Childr.

I. JAMES E.[8]   born June 14, 1819, in Ira.
II. THORNTON [8]   "   ; died ag. about 2 years.
III. FRANKLIN[8]   "   ; " in Middleton, Vt., ag. about 20 years.
IV. LYDIA[8]   "   , in Clarendon, Vt.; mar. James Richardson, of Middleton, Vt.
V. JOSEPH WASHINGTON[8] " Sept. 25, 1828.
VI. ELIZA[8]   " died ag. about 2 years.
VII. LEONARD V.[8]   "
VIII. EZRA M.[8]   "

566.   **Eighth Generation.**   **Tower.**

238. AMOS [7], JOSEPH [6], JOSEPH [5], JOSEPH [4], BENJAMIN [3], JOHN [2], JOHN [1].

Amos [7], son of Joseph [6] and Priscilla (Edmonds) Tower, b.
246. Feb. 21, 1799; mar. Emeline Tower [7], of Ira, Vt., March 10, 1836. She was b. in Ira Feb. 13, 1816, and was dau. of Thomas [6] and Polly (McCoy) Tower.

Childr. born in Ira, Vt.

1087. I. ELSE EMELINE [8] born Sept. 10, 1837.
1088. II. THOMAS AMOS [8] " Aug. 17, 1841.

Amos Tower [7] died in Ira, Vt., July 11, 1871, ag. 72 y. 4 m. 18 d.
Emeline (Tower) Tower died in Ira, June 17, 1863, ag. 47 y. 4 m. 4 d.

567.   **Eighth Generation.**   **Tower.**

238. HENRY [7], JOSEPH [6], JOSEPH [5], JOSEPH [4], BENJAMIN [3], JOHN [2], JOHN [1].

Henry [7], son of Joseph [6] and Priscilla (Edmonds) Tower, b.
Nov. 26, 1805; mar. Marcia Worcester, of Clarendon, Vt., April , 1834. She was born in Salem, Mass., , and was dau. of John and Abigail (Benjamin) Worcester.

Child.

1089. I. HENRY F.[8] born July 2, 1835.

Henry Tower [7] died near Momence, Ill., June , 1840, ag. 34 y. 7 m.
Marcia (Worcester) Tower died near Momence June , 1840.

568. Perry.   **Eighth Generation.**   **Tower.**

238. ABIGAIL [7], JOSEPH [6], JOSEPH [5], JOSEPH [4], BENJAMIN [3], JOHN [2], JOHN [1].

Abigail[7], dau. of Joseph[6] and Priscilla (Edmonds) Tower, b.
April 1, 1808; mar. John H. Perry, of Ira, Vt.,
Feb. 13, 1832. He was b. in Chelsea, Vt.,
Dec. 17, 1808, and was son of Nathaniel G. and Roxana
(Hutchinson) Perry.

Childr.

I.	ELLEN M.[8]	born May 5, 1833, in Ira.
II.	ALDEN J.[8]	" July 18, 1835; died in Mound City, Ill., Oct. 26, 1864, ag. 29 y. 3 m. 8 d.
III.	MARY E.[8]	" Oct. 25, 1836, in Ira; died, unmar., in Aroma, Ill., Oct. 28, 1873, ag. 37 y. 3 d.
IV.	EDETHA F.[8]	" April 18, 1838, in Ira.
V.	LUCY E.[8]	" May 16, 1840, in Rutland, Vt.
VI.	PHIANIA[8]	" Oct. 19, 1841, " "
VII.	WEALTHY P.[8]	" Aug. 17, 1843, in Saline, Mich.

John H. Perry died in Saline, Mich., Aug. 9, 1844, ag. 35 y.
7 m. 23 d.
Abigail (Tower) Perry lives in Waldron, Kankakee Co.,
Ill. (1885).

569. **Eighth Generation.** **Tower.**

238. JOSEPH[7], JOSEPH[6], JOSEPH[5], JOSEPH[4], BENJAMIN[3], JOHN[2],
JOHN[1].

Joseph[7], son of Joseph[6] and Priscilla (Edmonds) Tower, b.
Dec. 20, 1811; mar. Sarah A. Bates, of Ira, Vt.,
Feb. 6, 1840. She was b.
March 28, 1821, and was dau. of Elias and Nancy (Whipple)
Bates.

Childr. born in Ira, Vt.

1090.	I.	GEORGE WASHINGTON[8]	born June 14, 1840.
1091.	II.	HENRY CLAY[8]	" June 25, 1841.
1092.	III.	EMMET MASON[8]	" Dec. 20, 1842.
1093.	IV.	JOSEPH W.[8]	" March 9, 1846.

Sarah A. (Bates) Tower died in Rutland, Vt., May 1, 1872,
ag. 51 y. 1 m. 4 d.
Joseph Tower[7] mar., 2d, widow E. A. (Whitcomb) Marston,
of Fairfield, Vt.,
May 10, 1875. She was b. in Hartford, Vt.,
1821, and was dau. of Rufus and Martha (Oliver)
Whitcomb.

570. Stoddard. **Eighth Generation.** **Tower.**

238. ALPHA L.[7], JOSEPH[6], JOSEPH[5], JOSEPH[4], BENJAMIN[3], JOHN[2],
JOHN[1].

Alpha L.[7], dau. of Joseph[6] and Priscilla (Edmonds) Tower, b.

Oct. 21, 1816 ; mar. Ichabod Stoddard, of Ira, Vt.,
Nov. 8, 1853. He was born in Bastard, Canada,
April 14, 1808, and was son of Sheldon and Olive (Chipman)
Stoddard.

Childr.

I. WILLIAM [8] born Oct. 17, 1854, in Momence, Ill.
II. GEORGE H.[8] " Aug. 12, 1856, " " "

Ichabod Stoddard lives in Momence (1885).

---

571.   **Eighth Generation.**   **Tower.**

243. GALUSHA A [7], MASON [6], JOSEPH [5], JOSEPH [4], BENJAMIN [3], JOHN [2], JOHN [1].

Galusha A.[7], son of Mason [6] and Mabel ( ) Tower, b.
1819 ; mar.   Mabbitt, of Fredonia, N. Y.

Childr.

I. BRYANT M.[8] born Dec. 10, 1858. II. CHARLES W.[8] born July 9, 1863.

Galusha A. Tower [7] is living (1887).

---

572.   **Eighth Generation.**   **Tower.**

245. ALANSON [7], OTIS [6], NATHANIEL [5], JOSEPH [4], BENJAMIN [3], JOHN [2], JOHN [1].

Alanson [7], son of Otis [6] and Sarah (Edmonds) Tower, b.
April 22, 1805 ; mar. Diana Perham,
June 2, 1833. She was b. in Upton, Mass.,
April 14, 1815, and was dau. of Aaron and Betsey (Hill)
Perham.

Childr. born in Hanover, Chautauqua Co., N. Y.

1094.	I.	HANIBAL L.[8]	born May 29, 1836.
1095.	II.	MARINDA P.[8]	" Sept. 25, 1838.
1096.	III.	MALINDA D.[8]	" July 15, 1844.
1097.	IV.	BETSEY S.[8]	" Sept. 29, 1846.
1098.	V.	PERHAM O.[8]	" Feb. 27, 1849.
	VI.	Infant	" Aug. 19, 1854; died in infancy.

Diana (Perham) Tower died in Hanover, Dec. 20, 1881, ag.
66 y. 8 m. 5 d.
Alanson Tower [7] died in Hanover, April 15, 1888, ag. 82 y.
11 m. 23 d.

---

573.   **Eighth Generation.**   **Tower.**

245. LYMAN [7], OTIS [6], NATHANIEL [5], JOSEPH [4], BENJAMIN [3], JOHN [2], JOHN [1].

Lyman [7], son of Otis [6] and Sarah (Edmonds) Tower, b.

July 10, 1810 ; mar. Julia Ann Buxton
Sept. , 1833. She was b.
Nov.   , 1813, and was dau. of Timothy and Mary Buxton.

Childr.

1099.	I.	MARY M.[8]	born Aug. 1, 1835.
	II.	TIMOTHY [8]	" May 3, 1837; died Sept. 8, 1843, ag. 6 y. 4 m. 5 d.
1100.	III.	EMELINE V.[8] } Twins " April 22, 1839.	
1101.	IV.	EMILY J.[8] }	

Lyman Tower [7] lives in Hanover, N. Y. (1883).

---

574. Hunt.   **Eighth Generation.**   **Tower.**

245. ALMIRA [7], OTIS [6], NATHANIEL [5], JOSEPH [4], BENJAMIN [3], JOHN [2], JOHN [1].
Almira [7], dau. of Otis [6] and Sarah (Edmonds) Tower, b.
June 7, 1812 ; mar. Ephraim Hunt, son of Lewis Hunt.

Childr.

I. ZERUAH [8] born April 10, 1836.   II. WALLACE W.[8] born Jan. 21, 1841.

Ephraim Hunt died in Hanover, N. Y.,   1842.

BLACKMAN.   TOWER.

Almira (Tower) Hunt mar., 2d, William Blackman
Jan. 1, 1849.

Childr.

III. THEODORE [8] born Dec. 20, 1849.
IV.   MARY JANE [8] " May 15, 1856 ; mar.   Watkins, of Almena, Mich.

William Blackman died in Alamo, Mich., Feb. 28, 1862.
Almira (Tower) Blackman lives in Alamo (1883).

---

575.   **Eighth Generation.**   **Tower.**

245. LOAMI [7], OTIS [6], NATHANIEL [5], JOSEPH [4], BENJAMIN [3], JOHN [2], JOHN [1].
Loami [7], son of Otis [6] and Sarah (Edmonds) Tower, b.
Aug. 4, 1814 ; mar Betsey Townsend.

Childr.

I.	POLLY [8].	
II.	NATHANIEL [8]	; lives in Kansas (1883).
III.	LUCY SARAH [8]	; mar.
IV.	CYNTHIA [8].	
V.	TIMOTHY [8]	; died in Christian Co., Ill., 1864.
VI.	AMANDA M.[8]	; mar. Frank Freeman.
VII.	Son [8].	
VIII.	MARY [8].	

Loami Tower [7] died in Christian Co., Ill.,　1864.
Betsey (Townsend) Tower died

576.　　　　**Eighth Generation.**　　　　**Tower.**

245. RIAL [7], OTIS [6], NATHANIEL [5], JOSEPH [4], BENJAMIN [3], JOHN [2], JOHN [1].
Rial [7], son of Otis [6] and Sarah (Edmonds) Tower, b. and mar.
Childr. Three.
Rial Tower [7] died in Lockport, Westmoreland Co., Penn.

577. Haven.　　　**Eighth Generation.**　　　**Tower.**

246. CHARLOTTE [7], THOMAS [6], NATHANIEL [5], JOSEPH [4], BENJAMIN [3], JOHN [2], JOHN [1].
Charlotte [7], dau. of Thomas [6] and Polly (McCoy) Tower, b.
Feb. 15, 1803 ; mar. Solomon Haven,
Jan. 1, 1823. He was born in Ludlow, Windsor Co., Vt.,
Sept. 25, 1799, and was son of Jedediah and Jemima (Snell) Haven.

Childr.

I. CHARLOTTE [8] born Oct. 16, 1823, in Ludlow; died May 17, 1849, ag. 25 y. 7 m. 1 d.
II. ADELINE [8]　"　Jan. 26, 1825, in Ludlow.
III. SILAS W. [8]　"　March 3, 1826, "　"
IV. HORACE [8]　"　Sept. 26, 1827, "　"　; died Sept. 2, 1829, ag. 1 y. 11 m. 6 d.
V. HORACE T. [8]　"　April 6, 1830, in Ludlow.
VI. WILLARD [8]　"　Aug. 8, 1831, "　"　; died May 3, 1832, ag. 8 m. 26 d.
VII. LYMAN T. [8]　"　Feb. 15, 1833, in Ludlow; died Jan. 30, 1835, ag. 1 y. 11 m. 12 d.
VIII. EMILY L [8]　"　April 26, 1835, in Clarendon, Vt.
IX. GEORGE R. [8]　"　March 4, 1837, "　"　"
X. LAURA L. [8]　"　Dec. 4, 1838, "　"　"
XI. JAMES H. [8]　"　Jan. 15, 1841, "　"　"
XII. IDA A. [8]　"　April 16, 1843, "　"　"
XIII. INEZ A. [8]　"　Feb. 17, 1845, "　"　"
XIV. MELINDA L [8]　"　Feb. 3, 1847, " Harlem, Ill.; died July 26, 1848, ag. 1 y. 5 m. 23 d.
XV. MARK A. [8]　"　Aug. 20, 1849, in Harlem, Ill.

Solomon Haven died Oct. 21, 1873, ag. 74 y. 26 d.
Charlotte (Tower) Haven lives in Dyersville, Iowa (1884).

578.　　　　**Eighth Generation.**　　　　**Tower.**

246. DAVID [7], THOMAS [6], NATHANIEL [5], JOSEPH [4], BENJAMIN [3], JOHN [2], JOHN [1].
David [7], son of Thomas [6] and Polly (McCoy) Tower, b.

July 31, 1804 ; mar. Fanny Spring

Nov. 23, 1826. She was b. in Clarendon, Vt.,

Nov. 11, 1806, and was dau. of Amos and Azula (Gates) Spring.

Childr.

1102.   I.   HANNIBAL[8] born Aug. 27, 1827.

1103.   II.   WALLACE[8]   "   1830.

III.   HORACE[8]   "   Jan.   8, 1833 ; unmar.

1104. IV.   HELEN[8]   "   July 16, 1835.

David Tower[7] died in Clarendon, Feb. 4, 1879, ag. 74 y. 6 m. 4 d.

Fanny (Spring) Tower died in Clarendon, May 7, 1881, ag. 74 y. 5 m. 26 d.

---

579. Wilkinson.   Eighth Generation.   Tower.

246. CYNTHIA[7], THOMAS[6], NATHANIEL[5], JOSEPH[4], BENJAMIN[3], JOHN[2], JOHN[1].

Cynthia[7], dau. of Thomas[6] and Polly (McCoy) Tower, b.

March 26, 1806 ; mar. George Wilkinson[7], of Ira, Vt.,

He was b.

Sept. 4, 1802, and was son of George and Lydia[6] (Whipple) Wilkinson.

Childr. born in Ira.

I.   SIMEON[8] born April 5, 1832.

II.   LYDIA A.[8]   "   Jan. 19, 1835.

III.   JAY[8]   "   Aug. 27, 1842.

WILKINSON, WHIPPLE.   TOWER.

George[7], Lydia[6], Christopher[5], John[4], William[3], Hannah[2], John[1].

---

580. Bates.   Eighth Generation.   Tower.

246. ELECTA[7], THOMAS[6], NATHANIEL[5], JOSEPH[4], BENJAMIN[3], JOHN[2], JOHN[1].

Electa[7], dau. of Thomas[6] and Polly (McCoy) Tower, b.

Dec. 8, 1807 ; mar. Milton M. Bates, of Ira, Vt.,

Dec. 2, 1830.   He was b. in Ira,

Dec. 29, 1804, and was son of Elias and Nancy (Whipple) Bates.

Childr. born in Ira.

I.   ALBERT ELLIOT[8] born April 19, 1833.

II.   MARY JANE[8]   "   Oct. 18, 1834.

III.   CHARLES EDWIN[8]   "   Sept. 15, 1836.

Milton M. Bates died March 13, 1879, ag. 74 y. 2 m. 15 d.

Electa (Tower) Bates lives in Londonderry, Vt. (1884).

581. **Eighth Generation.** **Tower.**

246. LYMAN[7], THOMAS[6], NATHANIEL[5], JOSEPH[4], BENJAMIN[3], JOHN[2], JOHN[1].

Lyman[7], son of Thomas[6] and Polly (McCoy) Tower, b.
Jan. 4, 1812; mar. Alvira Mason,
Oct. 21, 1839. She was b.
Oct. 18, 1819.

Child.

I. ALANSON[8] born Aug. 12, 1840; died Aug. 27, 1842, ag. 2 y. 15 d.

Lyman Tower died in Ira, Vt., July 27, 1886, ag. 74 y. 6 m. 23 d.

Alvira (Mason) Tower died in Ira, Vt., Feb. 22, 1882, ag. 62 y. 4 m. 7 d.

582. Gilmore. **Eighth Generation.** **Tower.**

246. LAURA[7], THOMAS[6], NATHANIEL[5], JOSEPH[4], BENJAMIN[3], JOHN[2], JOHN[1].

Laura[7], dau. of Thomas[6] and Polly (McCoy) Tower, b.
June 13, 1818; mar. Gilman Gilmore, of Ira, Vt. He was b. , 1813.

Childr. born in Ira.

I. MARTHA L.[8] born 1842. III. AMELIA[8] born March , 1850.
II. MARY[8] " 1844.

583. **Eighth Generation.** **Tower.**

246. BRADLEY C.[7], THOMAS[6], NATHANIEL[5], JOSEPH[4], BENJAMIN[3], JOHN[2], JOHN[1].

Bradley C.[7], son of Thomas[6] and Polly (McCoy) Tower, b.
Oct. 2, 1820; mar. Laura Olivia Bruce, of Wallingford, Vt.,
Sept. 17, 1853. She was b. in Wallingford,
Dec. 21, 1827, and was dau. of Ransom and Philena (Jewell) Bruce.

Childr. born in East Wallingford, Vt.

1105. I. FRANK BRADLEY[8] born Aug. 25, 1854.
II. LYMAN ALANSON[8] " Feb. 18, 1857.
III. MARY INEZ[8] " Feb. 6, 1859; died Nov. 5, 1859.

Bradley C. Tower lives in East Wallingford (1887).

584. **Eighth Generation.** **Tower.**

249. FRANKLIN R.[7], WELCOME[6], NATHANIEL[5], JOSEPH[4], BENJAMIN[3], JOHN[2], JOHN[1].

Franklin R.[7], son of Welcome[6] and Betsey (Rowe) Tower, b.

July 26, 1815 ; mar. Elizabeth Ettredge, of Springville, La.,
Feb. 6, 1853. She was born in Natchitoches, La.,
Nov. 21, 1828, and was dau. of William and Nancy (Brown)
    Ettredge.

Childr.

	I.	WILLIE E.[8]	born June 10, 1854, in Springville.
1106.	II.	FRANK C.[8]	" Jan. 2, 1856, " "
1107.	III.	CHARLES A.[8]	" Jan. 16, 1858, " Natchitoches.
1108.	IV.	GEORGE M.[8]	" June 22, 1860, " Campti, La.
	V.	EDWARD ROWE [8]	" Sept. 5, 1863.
1109.	VI.	MARY MATTIE MELISSA [8]	" Oct. 8, 1866.
	VII.	MINERVA [8]	" Jan. 27, 1868, in Red River ; died Feb. 17, 1868.

Franklin R. Tower [7] died in East Point, La., March 6, 1870,
    ag. 54 y. 7 m. 11 d.
Elizabeth (Ettredge) Tower died in East Point, La., June
    25, 1884, ag. 55 y. 7 m. 4 d.

585. Peck.   Eighth Generation.   Tower.

249. MELISSA [7], WELCOME [6], NATHANIEL [5], JOSEPH [4], BENJAMIN [3],
    JOHN [2], JOHN [1].
Melissa [7], dau. of Welcome [6] and Betsey (Rowe) Tower, b.
May 7, 1819 ; mar. Daniel H. Peck, of Ira, Vt.,
Sept. 9, 1838. He was born in Clarendon, Vt.,
Jan. 29, 1815, and was son of Noah and Mehitable (Yeaw)
    Peck.

Childr.

I.	BETSEY M.[8]	born July 28, 1839.
II.	SARAH ADDIE [8]	" June 19, 1842.
III.	BYRON EUGENE [8]	" March 3, 1845 ; died April 24, 1845.
IV.	MARY ANNA TOWER [8]	" Dec. 10, 1846.
V.	FRANK WELCOME [8]	" July 26, 1851.
VI.	LEWIS WILLIAM [8]	" Oct. 8, 1854.
VII.	ISABELLA LAVINA [8]	" April 22, 1859.
VIII.	BLANCHE H.[8]	" Sept. 21, 1862.
IX.	WILHELMINA M.[8]	" April 15, 1865.

Daniel H. Peck died in Harford, Pa., Oct. 8, 1872, ag. 57 y.
    8 m. 10 d.
Melissa (Tower) Peck lives in Harford, Pa. (1883).

586.   Eighth Generation.   Tower.

249. WILLIAM O.[7], WELCOME [6], NATHANIEL [5], JOSEPH [4], BENJAMIN [3],
    JOHN [2], JOHN [1].
William O.[7], son of Welcome [6] and Betsey (Rowe) Tower, b.
June 30, 1823 ; mar. Mary Ann Gambell

Jan. 26, 1846. She was b. in Hillsdale, N. H.,
June 23, 1824, and was dau. of Samuel and Sally (Risley)
Gambell.

Child.

1110. I. MINNIE H.[8] born April 17, 1855.

William O. Tower [7] lives in Albany, N. Y. (1883).

---

587. **Eighth Generation.** **Tower.**

249. ROLLIN C.[7], WELCOME [6], NATHANIEL [5], JOSEPH [4], BENJAMIN [3], JOHN [2], JOHN [1].
Rollin C.[7], son of Welcome [6] and Betsey (Rowe) Tower, b.
June 7, 1828; mar. Deborah M. Russell
May 11, 1854. She was dau. of Laban Russell.

Child.

I. JAMES RUSSELL [8] born　　　; died　　.

Rollin C. Tower [7] died in Winona, Minn., Jan. 12, 1856, ag.
27 y. 7 m. 5 d.
Deborah M. (Russell) Tower mar., 2d, M. Lamarr, of Philadelphia, Penn.

---

588. Stockton. **Eighth Generation.** **Tower.**

250. MARYETTE D.[7], CEPHAS [6], NATHANIEL [5], JOSEPH [4], BENJAMIN [3], JOHN [2], JOHN [1].
Maryette D.[7], dau. of Cephas [6] and Sophia (Comstock) Tower, b.
Dec. 3, 1818; mar. James B. Stockton, of Milan, Ind.,
Sept. 4, 1838. He was b. in Dearborn Co., Ind.,
June 2, 1818, and was son of Israel F. and Sallie Hall (Lord) Stockton.

Childr.

I. TERESA [8]　　　born Oct. 24, 1840, in Milan.
II. SOPHIA [8]　　　 " 　Nov. 18, 1843, in Rozetta, Ill.
III. EUGENE [8]　　　 " 　Feb. 23, 1846,　　 " 　; died Sept. 16, 1846.
IV. ORILLA EUGENIA [8]　" 　June 8, 1848　　 "
V. WILBUR F [8]　　 " 　Aug. 5, 1859.

Maryette D. (Tower) Stockton died May 5, 1886, ag. 67 y.
5 m. 2 d.
James B. Stockton lives in Springfield, Mo. (1886).

---

589. **Eighth Generation.** **Tower.**

250. NATHANIEL F.[7], CEPHAS [6], NATHANIEL [5], JOSEPH [4], BENJAMIN [3], JOHN [2], JOHN [1].

Nathaniel F.[7], son of Cephas[6] and Sophia (Comstock) Tower, b.

Feb. 10, 1821 ; mar. Rachel Stephens

April 7, 1850. She was b.

May 11, 1829, and was dau. of Henry and Hannah (Bennett) Stephens.

Childr.

	I.	CARVOSSO B.[8]	born Feb. 12, 1852; died Oct. 4, 1854, ag. 2 y. 7 m. 21 d.
1111.	II.	ALICE S.[8]	" May 15, 1854.
	III.	FAYETTE S.[8]	" Sept. 9, 1855, died Jan. 24, 1857, ag. 1 y. 4 m. 14 d.
	IV.	EMMA J.[8]	" Sept. 28, 1857; " Dec. 10, 1881.
	V.	WILLIAM WHEELER [8]	" July 4, 1859.
	VI.	SCEOLA B.[8]	" June 4, 1862.
	VII.	ERASTUS P.[8]	" July 28, 1864.

Nathaniel F. Tower [7] lives in Laurel, Franklin Co., Ind. (1883).

590. Millard.   Eighth Generation.   Tower.

251. SALLY E.[7], RIAL [6], NATHANIEL [5], JOSEPH [4], BENJAMIN [3], JOHN [2], JOHN [1].

Sally E.[7], dau. of Rial [6] and Betsey P. (Car) Tower, b.

Oct. 28, 1823 ; mar. Stephen S. Millard

Oct. 4, 1839. He was b.

Dec. 7, 1818, and was son of John and Sally (Buck) Millard.

Childr.

I.	MARY ABIGAIL [8]	born Feb. 9, 1841.
II.	HUMPHREY JUDSON [8]	" Dec. 24, 1843.
III.	FREEMAN TINGLEY [8]	" March 4, 1846; died 1867, ag. 21.
IV.	ROSANNA PIERCE [8]	" Sept. 11, 1848.

Stephen S. Millard died in Rush, Penn.

Sally E. (Tower) Millard died in East Lenox, Penn., Feb. 28, 1850, ag. 26 y. 4 m. 3 d.

591. Callender.   Eighth Generation.   Tower.

251. POLLY M.[7], RIAL [6], NATHANIEL [5], JOSEPH [4], BENJAMIN [3], JOHN [2], JOHN [1].

Polly M.[7], dau. of Rial [6] and Betsy P. (Car) Tower, b.

Nov. 16, 1825 ; mar. Nathan Callender

Sept. 9, 1847.

Polly M. (Tower) Callender died Nov. 22, 1847, ag. 22 y. 6 d.

Nathan Callender is a Baptist minister.

592. Moore. Eighth Generation. Tower.

251. EMILY F.[7], RIAL[6], NATHANIEL[5], JOSEPH[4], BENJAMIN[3], JOHN[2], JOHN[1].

Emily F.[7], dau. of Rial[6] and Betsey P. (Car) Tower, b. Sept. 9, 1827 ; mar. Elias N. Moore, of Carbondale, Penn., Feb. 20, 1851. He was b. in Clifford, Penn., Oct. 3, 1827, and was son of William and Elizabeth (Ferris), Moore.

Childr.

I. CLEMENT WARNER[8] born Feb. 1, 1852; unmar ; died June 13, 1879 ag. 27 y. 4 m. 12 d.
II. RIAL TOWER[8]   "   Sept. 24, 1853; died Jan. 9, 1854.
III. FRANCES EMILY[8]   "   Oct. 22, 1854.
IV. ARTHUR MERVIN[8]   "   Dec. 5, 1856.
V. RIAL[8]   "   ; died in infancy.
VI. JAMES EDWARD[8]   "   July 16, 1859; mar. Sally Gallaher in Pierre, Dakota.
VII. MARIA JOSEPHINE[8] " June 16, 1861; died Aug. 16, 1864, ag. 3 y. 2 m.
VIII. MIRIAM[8]   "   Dec. 22, 1863.
IX. MARY DIANTHE[8]   "   Oct. 11, 1865.

Elias N. Moore died in West Lenox, Penn., May 15, 1868, ag. 40 y. 7 m. 12 d.
Emily F. (Tower) Moore mar., 2d, William H. Pope, of Burlington, N. Y.,
June 14, 1877. He was b. in Burlington,
Jan. 18, 1814, and was son of William S. and Abba (Stanton) Pope.
William H. Pope lives in Gibson, Penn. (1883).

593. Eighth Generation. Tower.

251. WARNER C.[7], RIAL[6], NATHANIEL[5], JOSEPH[4], BENJAMIN[3], JOHN[2], JOHN[1].

Warner C.[7], son of Rial[6] and Betsey P. (Car) Tower, b. Sept. 17, 1829; mar. Teressa M. Tiffany, of Lenox, Penn., April 24, 1852. She was b.
April 16, 1832, and was dau. of Alson and Fanny (Ely) Tiffany.

Childr.

1112.   I. WILLIS RIAL[8]   born March 7, 1855.
     II. HERBERT LLEWLYN[8] " April 17, 1859; mar. Emily Beecher June 24, 1885.
1113.   III. ELMER ELLSWORTH[8] " Feb. 22, 1861.
     IV. MARY JENETTE[8]   "   Dec. 24, 1863; died Oct. 1, 1866, ag. 2 y. 9 m. 8 d.

Warner C. Tower[7] died in West Lenox, Sept. 11, 1867, ag. 37 y. 11 m. 24 d.

Teressa M. (Tiffany) Tower mar., 2d, Hubbard M. Smith, of Lenox, Penn.,
Oct. 1, 1868.

594. White. Eighth Generation. Tower.

251. DIANTHA E.[7], RIAL[6], NATHANIEL[5], JOSEPH[4], BENJAMIN[3], JOHN[2], JOHN[1].

Diantha E.[7], dau. of Rial[6] and Betsey P. (Car) Tower, b.
Dec. 20, 1831; mar. John W. White
Aug. 28, 1851. He was b.
July 2, 1829.

Childr.

I.	ANGUS CAMERON[8] }	Twins born June 5, 1852, in Carbondale, Penn.;
II.	ARGUS CARLTON[8] }	Angus C. died Sept. 20, 1859, ag. 7 y. 3 m. 15 d.
III.	ALBAN M.[8]	" March 8, 1854, in Carbondale.
IV.	CLARENCE LINCOLN[8]	" Sept. 23, 1860, in Lenox, Penn.
V.	EMMA DIANTHA[8]	" July 25, 1862, " " ; mar. J. H. Emley in Wisner, Neb., 1884.
VI.	WILLIAM RIAL[8]	" Dec. 20, 1866, in Harford, Penn.
VII.	LEAH BETSEY[8]	" Dec. 9, 1876, in Factoryville, "

595. Eighth Generation. Tower.

251. PURRINGTON R.[7], RIAL[6], NATHANIEL[5], JOSEPH[4], BENJAMIN[3], JOHN[2], JOHN[1].

Purrington R.[7], son of Rial[6] and Betsey P. (Car) Tower, b.
March 22, 1834; mar. Mary D. Lyon, of Herrick, Penn.,
Oct. 8, 1857. She was b.
Nov. 24, 1831, and was dau. of Henry and Harlian (Kent) Lyon.

Childr. none.

596. Eighth Generation. Tower.

251. WILLIAM N.[7], RIAL[6], NATHANIEL[5], JOSEPH[4], BENJAMIN[3], JOHN[2], JOHN[1].

William N.[7], son of Rial[6] and Betsey P. (Car) Tower, b.
Oct. 24, 1836; mar. Jennie A. Mackey, of New Milford, Penn.,
Oct. 22, 1861. She was b. in Clifford, Penn.,
April 25, 1839, and was dau. of David and Miranda (Smith) Mackey.

Childr. none.

WILLIE (THAYER) TOWER, born Aug. 4, 1876, in Clark's Summit, Penn., is an adopted son, and son of William H. and Ada M. (Mackey) Thayer.

William N. Tower [7] died in North Hector, N. Y., Aug. 26, 1882, ag. 45 y. 10 m. 2 d.

597. Oakley. **Eighth Generation.** **Tower.**

251. LUCY Z.[7], RIAL [6], NATHANIEL [5], JOSEPH [4], BENJAMIN [3], JOHN [2], JOHN [1].

Lucy Z [7], dau. of Rial [6] and Betsey P. (Car) Tower, b. April 8, 1839 ; mar. Daniel C. Oakley, of West Lenox, Penn., Nov. 25, 1860. He was b. Feb. 17, 1835, and was son of Milbourn and Nancy (Carpenter) Oakley.

Childr.

  I. LIZZIE [8] born Jan. 3, 1867.
  II. WILLISTON [8] " Feb. 19, 1879.

Daniel C. Oakley lives in West Lenox (1883).

598. **Eighth Generation.** **Tower.**

251. CHARLES M.[7], RIAL [6], NATHANIEL [5], JOSEPH [4], BENJAMIN [3], JOHN [2], JOHN [1].

Charles M.[7], son of Rial [6] and Betsey P. (Car) Tower, b. June 19, 1844; mar. Mary Ellen Sainter, of Philadelphia, Penn., March 12, 1865. She was b. May 23, 1845, and was dau. of William J. and Pamelia (Morse) Sainter.

Childr.

 I. FRANK SAINTER [8] born Feb. 1, 1866.
 II. WILLIAM JAMES [8] " June 25, 1867.
 III. BERTHA JANE [8] " April 12, 1869.
 IV. WALTER BOWMAN [8] " March 2, 1871.
 V. CHARLES CARLTON [8] " June 28, 1873.
 VI. MARY EMILY [8] " May 3, 1875.
 VII. HARRY FREAR [8] " July 7, 1876; died Sept. 17, 1883, ag. 7 y. 2 m. 10 d.
 VIII. LAURA [8] " March 3, 1878; " April 17, 1878.

Charles M. Tower [7] lives in Dundee, N. Y. (1888).

599. **Eighth Generation.** **Tower.**

254. CHARLES [7], JOHN [6], JAMES [5], JOHN [4], JOSEPH [3], JOHN [2], JOHN [1].

Charles [7], son of John [6] and Betsey (Parker) Tower, b. ; mar. Elizabeth

Childr.

I. HARRIET [8]   born   ; 1841; mar. Christopher Morey, of New-
                              buryport, Mass., Aug. 16, 1864. He
                              was born in 1834, and was son of
                              Christopher and Sarah Morey.

II. DAVID WOODMARY [8] "   Feb. 27, 1845.

600. Swan.   **Eighth Generation.**   **Tower.**

257. ANNIE E.[7], EBENEZER [6], JAMES [5], JOHN [4], JOSEPH [3], JOHN [2],
     JOHN [1].
     Annie E.[7], dau. of Ebenezer [6] and Roxanna (Blackman)
     Tower, b.
     Oct. 20, 1836; mar. John Edwin Swan, of Dorchester, Mass.,
     Nov. 3, 1857. He was b.
          , 1834, and was son of John and Julia Swan.

Child.

I. WILLIAM UPHAM [8] born May 26, 1864, in Dorchester.

600 a.   **Eighth Generation.**   **Tower.**

258. JAMES [7], MEHITABLE [6], JOHN [5], JOHN [4], JOSEPH [3], JOHN [2],
     JOHN [1].
     James [7], son of Mehitable Tower [6], b.
          1798; mar. Susannah Thayer, of Braintree, Mass.,
     July 1, 1823. She was b.
     Dec. 3, 1806, and was dau. of Betheel and Anna Thayer.

Childr. born in Braintree.

| 1114. I. SUSAN [8]   born   1824. | 1116. III. JOHN [8]   born   1828. |
| 1115. II. WILLIAM E.[8] "   1826. | IV. NEWTON J.[8] "   1831. |

James Tower [7] died
Susannah (Thayer) Tower mar., 2d, Benjamin Pratt, of
     Holbrook, Mass.,
Dec. 10, 1843. She died
April , 1873, ag. 66 y. 4 m.

PRATT.   TOWER.
Benjamin [6], Robert [5], Benjamin [4], Christian [3], Benjamin [2], John [1].

601.   **Eighth Generation.**   **Tower.**

261. ISAAC P.[7], ALEXANDER [6], JOHN [5], JOHN [4], JOSEPH [3], JOHN [2],
     JOHN [1].
     Isaac P.[7], son of Alexander [6] and Celia (Pratt) Tower, b.

Jan. 25, 1809; mar. Ruth H. Pool. Int. pub.
April 3, 1826. She was b.
June 10, 1810.

Childr.

1116 a.	I.	RUTH J.[8]	born Dec.	9, 1826.
1117.	II.	CHARLOTTE A.[8]	" Oct.	30, 1827.
1118.	III.	ISAAC AVERY[8]	" Sept.	, 1829.
1119.	IV.	CHARLES L.[8]	" April	6, 1831.
	V.	GEORGE[8]	"	, 1832; died in infancy.
1120.	VI.	SUSANNAH M.[8]	" Aug.	31, 1834.
	VII.	SARAH[8]	"	, 1836; died in infancy.
	VIII.	ELIZABETH[8]	" Aug.	, 1837, " " "
	IX.	ALEXANDER[8]	" Dec.	, 1838, " Feb. 10, 1847, ag. 8 y. 2 m.

Ruth H. (Pool) Tower died Dec. , 1838, ag. 28 y. 6 m.
Isaac P. Tower [7] mar., 2d, Susan Snow
Aug. 2, 1840. She was b. in Lyman, N. H.,
    , 1823, and was dau. of Ira and Pamela Snow.

Childr.

	X.	ALONZO[8]	born	1841; died in infancy.
	XI.	ALONZO[8]	"	1843.
1121.	XII.	CHRISTOPHER P.[8]	"	1845.
1122.	XIII.	MINOTT A.[8]	"	1846.
1123	XIV.	NANCY A.[8]	" July	2, 1848.
	XV.	ORA SANFORD[8]	" July	19, 1853.

Isaac P. Tower [7] died June 25, 1854, ag. 45 y. 5 m. 1 d.
Susan (Snow) Tower mar., 2d, Elbridge L. Leach, of Randolph, Mass., Jan. 27, 1868.

602. Belcher.   **Eighth Generation.**   **Tower.**

261. MARY [7], ALEXANDER [6], JOHN [5], JOHN [4], JOSEPH [3], JOHN [2], JOHN [1].
Mary [7], dau. of Alexander [6] and Celia (Pratt) Tower, b.
June 17, 1811; mar. Samuel Belcher, of Randolph, Mass.,
Dec. 19, 1833. He was b.
Feb. 13, 1810, and was son of Samuel and Dorcas (Thayer)
Belcher.

Childr.

I.	ELLEN M.[9]	born Dec.	22, 1834; died Aug. 19, 1835.
II.	MARY A.[8]	" April	3, 1837; " Feb. 22, 1838.
III.	FRANKLIN M.[8]	" Oct.	19, 1838.
IV.	ORIN H.[8]	" Aug	30, 1841.
V.	ALEXANDER TOWER[8]	" April	9, 1844.
VI.	MARY E.[8]	" July	10, 1846.
VII.	SAMUEL W.[8]	" May	5, 1849.

VIII. Lucy A.[8]   born May   6, 1851; died Oct. 10, 1851.
IX.   Myron L.[8]   "   Aug. 19, 1852; " Sept. 17, 1853.
X.   Laura[8]   "   Sept. 19, 1853.

603. Holbrook.   Eighth Generation.   Tower.

261. EMELINE K.[7], ALEXANDER[6], JOHN[5], JOHN[4], JOSEPH[3], JOHN[2], JOHN[1].

Emeline K.[7], dau. of Alexander[6] and Celia (Pratt) Tower, b. Feb. 13, 1813; mar. Charles Holbrook, of Braintree, Mass., April 2, 1831. He was b. in Braintree, and was son of Abiezer and Patty (Taunt) Holbrook.

Childr.

I.   EMELINE[8]   born Feb. 28, 1832.
II.   LEWIS[8]   "   July 2, 1834; died Oct. 7, 1835, ag. 1 y. 3 m. 5 d.
III. CHARLES LEWIS[8]   "   Sept. 28, 1835.
IV.   RELIEF[8]   "   Dec. 24, 1838; died May 20, 1841, ag. 2 y. 4 m. 27 d.
V.   CHARLOTTE MARIA[8] "   Nov. 13, 1840.

Charles Holbrook died   1846.
Emeline K. (Tower) Holbrook mar., 2d, Elijah Wild Beals, Aug. 24, 1848. He was born
Oct. 24, 1827, and was son of Abijah and Deborah (Wild) Beal.

Childr.

VI.   ELIJAH WINSLOW[8] born Dec. 17, 1848.
VII. BETSEY ANN[8]   "   Aug. 15, 1851.
VIII. LUCY ALLEN[8]   "   Oct. 19, 1856; mar. William E. Hawes, June 10, 1874.

Emeline K.[7] (Tower) Beals died

604. Blackman.   Eighth Generation.   Tower.

261. LUCY A.[7], ALEXANDER[6], JOHN[5], JOHN[4], JOSEPH[3], JOHN[2], JOHN[1].

Lucy A.[7], dau. of Alexander[6] and Celia (Pratt) Tower, b. March 27, 1816; mar. Eben H. Blackman.

Childr.

I.   ANN E.[8]   born July 31, 1833; died March 22, 1836, ag. 2 y. 7 m. 22 d.
II.   RUTHY H.[8]   "   Feb. 17, 1835.
III. LEMUEL[8]   "   June 28, 1836; " May 19, 1837, ag. 10 m. 21 d.
IV.   LEMUEL S.[3]   "   Oct. 31, 1837; " May 29, 1838, ag. 6 m. 29 d.
V.   EBEN H.[8]   "   April 2, 1839; " April 20, 1842, ag. 3 y. 18 d.
VI.   JAMES H.[8]   "   May 3, 1840; " April 19, 1842, ag. 1 y. 11 m. 16 d.
VII. ALEXANDER T.[8]   "   June 7, 1841; died April 29, 1842, ag. 10 m. 22 d.

Eben H. Blackman died in Dorchester, Mass.

605. Belcher. Eighth Generation. Tower.

261. SELAH[7], ALEXANDER[6], JOHN[5], JOHN[4], JOSEPH[3], JOHN[2], JOHN[1].
Selah[7], dau. of Alexander[6] and Celia (Pratt) Tower, b.
March 23, 1819; mar. Munroe Belcher, of Braintree, Mass.,
Jan. 29, 1837. He was b. in Braintree
      and was son of Asa and Charlotte (Thayer)
  Belcher.

Childr.

I.	ANN MARIA[8] born	1838.	IV.	ADDIE[8] born
II.	ELLEN D. Q.[8] "	1840.	V.	LUCY JANE[8] " May 29,
III.	ROYAL[8] "			1844; unmar.

606. French. Eighth Generation. Tower.

263. JULIA[7], JOHN[6], GIDEON[5], GIDEON[4], JOSEPH[3], JOHN[2], JOHN[1].
Julia[7], dau. of John[6] and Polly (Holbrook) Tower, b.
July 18, 1802; mar. Zenas French, of Holbrook, Mass.,
Nov. 25, 1825.

Childr.

I.	JULIA ANN[8].		V.	RUTH WHITE[8].
II.	ELIZABETH PORTER[8].		VI.	SARAH RELIEF[8].
III.	MARY HOLBROOK[8].		VII.	CAROLINE FRANCES[8].
IV.	CHARLES F.[8], born 1835; died		VIII.	ZENAS AARON[8], born 1844.
	March 26, 1853, ag. 18.			

Zenas French died in Holbrook
Julia (Tower) French died in Holbrook, Feb. 24, 1877, ag.
 74 y. 7 m. 9 d.

607. Eighth Generation. Tower.

263. JOHN[7], JOHN[6], GIDEON[5], GIDEON[4], JOSEPH[3], JOHN[2], JOHN[1].
John[7], son of John[6] and Polly (Holbrook) Tower, b.
Sept. 28, 1800; mar. Sarah Stearns Hewett
Dec. 20, 1835. She was b.
Aug. 28, 1810, and was dau. of Job and Rachel (Billings)
 Hewett.

Childr.

1124.	I.	MARY HORTON[8]	born Sept. 18, 1836.
	II.	JOHN[8]	" Nov. 17, 1838; died Dec. 10, 1865, ag.
			27 y. 23 d.
	III.	EBEN BAILEY[8]	" Nov. 23, 1840.
1125.	IV.	ELISHA HORTON[8]	" Aug. 1, 1844.
	V.	FANNY MOREY[8]	" Dec. 9, 1850; died Oct. 27, 1869, ag.
			18 y. 10 m. 18 d.

Sarah S. (Hewett) Tower died Feb. 27, 1871, ag. 60 y. 6 m.
 2 d.

608.   **Eighth Generation.**   **Tower.**

270. GEORGE[7], JOSEPH[6], GIDEON[5], GIDEON[4], JOSEPH[3], JOHN[2], JOHN[1].

George[7], son of Joseph[6] and Polly (Hayden) Tower, b.
      ; mar. Fanny M. White.

Childr. born in Randolph, Mass.

1126.	I.	MATILDA ANN[8]	born	Nov. 11, 1845.	
	II.	ELLEN[8]	"		; died
1127.	III.	ELLEN A.[8]	"	1850.	
1128.	IV.	MARY A.[8]	"	1852.	
1129.	V.	EMILY J.[8]	"	Feb. 13, 1857.	
	VI.	GEORGE W.[8]	"	Jan. 20, 1858.	
	VII.	Daughter[8]	"	Oct. 30, 1863.	

609. Holmes.   **Eighth Generation.**   **Tower.**

272. ELIZA ANN[7], WASHINGTON[6], GIDEON[5], GIDEON[4], JOSEPH[3], JOHN[2], JOHN[1].

Eliza Ann[7], dau. of Washington[6] and Rebecca T. (French)
      Tower, b.

Oct. 16, 1822; mar. Wadsworth Holmes, of Stoughton,
      Mass.

Childr.

I.	ANN ELIZA[8]	born	Feb. 3, 1841, in Stoughton; died June 18, 1842, ag. 1 y. 4 m. 15 d.
II.	BERTHIER WADSWORTH[8]	"	Sept. 9, 1842, in Stoughton.
III.	JAMES ALBERT[8]	"	March 9, 1844. " ; died Sept. 12, 1844.
IV.	HERBERT OSCAR[8]	"	April 16, 1845.
V.	ORLANDO HOLMES[8]	"	May 7, 1846; died Aug. 15, 1846.
VI.	LUELLA ANN[8]	"	Aug. 23, 1847.
VII.	ELIZA MARIA[8]	"	Feb. 8, 1849, in Lynn, Mass.
VIII.	CHARLES ERNEST[8]	"	Aug. 25, 1850, in Stoughton.
IX.	LAURA JANE[8]	"	Oct. 21, 1851, " ; died Nov. 13, 1851.
X.	EDRICK TOWER[8]	"	Jan. 10, 1853, in " ; " July 10, 1853.
XI.	HENRY JOSEPH GARDNER[8]	"	March 9, 1856.
XII.	NATHAN ALBERT[8]	"	June 21, 1858.
XIII.	ELDON FOREST[8]	"	May 31, 1860.
XIV.	LIZZIE E.[8]	"	April 16, 1864.
XV.	GERTIE FRANCES[8]	"	July 11, 1867.

610.   **Eighth Generation.**   **Tower.**

272. WASHINGTON[7], WASHINGTON[6], GIDEON[5], GIDEON[4], JOSEPH[3], JOHN[2], JOHN[1].

Washington[7], son of Washington[6] and Rebecca T. (French) Tower, b.

Dec. 13, 1824; mar. Maria E. Holmes, of Sharon, Mass., March 5, 1844. She was b. in Sharon June 24, 1824, and was dau. of Enoch and Susan (Marsh) Holmes.

Childr. none.

Maria E. (Holmes) Tower died June 9, 1860, ag. 35 y. 11 m. 15 d.

Washington Tower[7] mar., 2d, Hannah Howard Hartwell, of West Bridgewater, Mass., May 1, 1861. She was b. in West Bridgewater Jan. 6, 1831, and was dau. of Jonas and Sally (Howard) Hartwell.

Childr. born in Stoughton, Mass.

    I. HARRIET MARIA[8] born Aug. 23, 1862.
    II. CORDELIA F.[8]   " April 25, 1865.

Washington Tower[7] died   1887.

611.   **Eighth Generation.**   **Tower.**

272. IRA F.[7], WASHINGTON[6], GIDEON[5], GIDEON[4], JOSEPH[3], JOHN[2], JOHN[1].

Ira F.[7], son of Washington[6] and Rebecca T. (French) Tower, b.

Oct. 2, 1826; mar. Elizabeth B. Southworth, of Stoughton, Mass., July 18, 1848. She was b. Feb. 27, 1826, and was dau. of Luther and Chloe (Henry) Southworth.

Childr. born in Stoughton.

    1130. I. HORACE BAKER[8] born March 13, 1849.
    1131. II. WILLIAM SARGENT[8] " Feb. 16, 1852.

Ira F. Tower[7] died in Stoughton, Jan. 1, 1870, ag. 43 y. 2 m. 30 d.

612.   **Eighth Generation.**   **Tower.**

272. FRANCIS W. D.[7], WASHINGTON[6], GIDEON[5], GIDEON[4], JOSEPH[3], JOHN[2], JOHN[1].

Francis W. D.[7], son of Washington[6] and Rebecca T. (French) Tower, b.

Jan. 19, 1828; mar. Maretta Turner Gill, of Stoughton, Mass.,

Dec. 31, 1848. She was b. in Stoughton

March 1, 1832, and was dau. of Jason and Mary Ann (Talbot) Gill.

Childr. born in Stoughton.

I. CELIA MARIA [8]   born March 28, 1853.
II. FREDERIC LINCOLN [8] " Aug. 23, 1860; mar. Julia M. Crocker, Dec. 6, 1882, in Dorchester, Mass.

---

613.   **Eighth Generation.**   **Tower.**

272. GEORGE EDWIN [7], WASHINGTON [6], GIDEON [5], GIDEON [4], JOSEPH [3], JOHN [2], JOHN [1].

George Edwin [7], son of Washington [6] and Rebecca T. (French) Tower, b.

March 16, 1832; mar. Mary F. Crane

March 2, 1851. She was b.

1831, and was dau. of Eben and Mary F. Crane.

---

614. Reynolds.   **Eighth Generation.**   **Tower.**

272. REBECCA F. [7], WASHINGTON [6], GIDEON [5], GIDEON [4], JOSEPH [3], JOHN [2], JOHN [1].

Rebecca F. [7], dau. of Washington [6] and Rebecca T. (French) Tower, b.

July 6, 1836; mar. Lewis Whitcomb Reynolds, of North Bridgewater, Mass.,

Dec. 22, 1855. He was b. in North Bridgewater

July 14, 1834, and was son of Thomas and Nancy (Pike) Reynolds.

Childr.

I.   EDWARD FRANCIS [8] born Aug. 5, 1857; died Nov. 15, 1859, ag. 2 y. 3 m. 10 d.
II.   CLINTON LEWIS [8]   " March 18, 1859.
III. ANNA MARIA [8]   " Oct.   11, 1860.
IV.   EDWARD FRANCIS [8]   " Sept. 16, 1863.
V.   INEZ REBEKAH [8]   " Sept.   1, 1866.
VI.   CARA EVELYN [8]   " Feb. 3, 1868; died Feb. 27, 1870, ag. 2 y. 24 d.
VII. NELLIE EVELYN [8]   " Aug.   6, 1869.

Lewis W. Reynolds lives in Stoughton, Mass. (1880).

---

615. Caffrey.   **Eighth Generation.**   **Tower.**

272. MARY E. [7], WASHINGTON [6], GIDEON [5], GIDEON [4], JOSEPH [3], JOHN [2], JOHN [1].

Mary E. [7], dau. of Washington [6] and Rebecca T. (French) Tower, b.

Aug. 3, 1840 ; mar. Charles Caffrey, of Stoughton, Mass., Jan. 17, 1856.

Mary E. (Tower) Caffrey died in Stoughton, Jan. 24, 1873, ag. 32 y. 5 m. 21 d.

616. Crooks.   Eighth Generation.   Tower.

285. ELIZA ANN[7], ORRAMELL[6], ISAAC[5], JOSEPH[4], JOSEPH[3], JOHN[2], JOHN[1].
Eliza Ann[7], dau. of Orramell[6] and Phebe (Thayer) Tower, b. Aug. 9, 1821 ; mar. Thomas C. Crooks, of Farmington, Iowa, March 4, 1841.

Childr.

I. ORRAMELL CLAY[8] born Dec. 31, 1841; died in infancy.
II. CAROLINE[8]   "   July 4, 1844;   "   "   "
III. SUSAN VIRGINIA[8] " Sept. 3, 1846; mar. John O. Barton. She died.
IV. WILLIAM C.[8]   "   ; lives in Angel's Camp, Cal.
V. ELLEN MAYNARD[8] "   ; died. She was drowned, by breaking through the ice, with two other children.

Thomas C. Crooks died in Farmington, June 12, 1853
Eliza Ann (Tower) Crooks died in Farmington, Feb. 26, 1868, ag. 46 y. 6 m. 19 d.

617. Williams.   Eighth Generation.   Tower.

285. GEORGIANA[7], ORRAMELL[6], ISAAC[5], JOSEPH[4], JOSEPH[3], JOHN[2], JOHN[1].
Georgiana[7], dau. of Orramell[6] and Sarah A. (Doran) Tower, b. Jan. 15, 1837 ; mar. Egbert Williams July 28, 1856.

Childr.

I. STELLA E.[8] born July 1, 1860.
II. Infant   "   ; died.
III. Infant   "   ; "

Egbert Williams lives in Cedar Springs, Mich. (1880).

618.   Eighth Generation.   Tower.

285. DANIEL W.[7], ORRAMELL[6], ISAAC[5], JOSEPH[4], JOSEPH[3], JOHN[2], JOHN[1].
Daniel W.[7], son of Orramell[6] and Sarah A.(Doran)Tower, b. Jan. 26, 1841 ; mar. Laura Rowleys, of Mt. Pleasant, Iowa, Sept. 11, 1867. She was dau. of Rev. L. T. Rowleys.

Childr.

I. CHARLIE [8] born Oct. 3, 1868.
II. MABEL [8] " Oct. 30, 1873.
III. LILLIAN [8] " Nov. 29, 1874, in Ottumwa, Iowa; died Dec. 9, 1875,
　　　　　ag. 1 y. 10 d.

Daniel W. Tower lives in Ottumwa (1883).

619. **Eighth Generation.** **Tower.**

286. ISAAC H. [7], ISAAC [6], ISAAC [5], JOSEPH [4], JOSEPH [3], JOHN [2],
　　JOHN [1],
　　　　Isaac H. [7], son of Isaac [6] and Minora A. (Bracket) Tower, b.
　　　　　　1829 ; mar. Abby Belcher, of Randolph, Mass.,
　　　　Sept. 5, 1854. She was b. in Randolph, Mass.,
　　　　　　1830, and was dau. of Jonathan and Hannah Belcher.

620. Mann. **Eighth Generation.** **Tower.**

286. MINORA A. [7], ISAAC [6], ISAAC [5], JOSEPH [4], JOSEPH [3], JOHN [2],
　　JOHN [1].
　　　　Minora A. [7], dau. of Isaac [6] and Minora A. (Bracket) Tower, b.
　　　　　　1830 ; mar. Seth Mann, of Boston,
　　　　Oct. 18, 1849. He was born in Vermont,
　　　　　　1820, and was son of Elisha and Ruth Mann.

621. **Eighth Generation.** **Tower.**

286. JAMES A. [7], ISAAC [6], ISAAC [5], JOSEPH [4], JOSEPH [3], JOHN [2],
　　JOHN [1].
　　　　James A. [7], son of Isaac [6] and Minora A. (Bracket) Tower, b.
　　　　　　1833 ; mar. Emma D. Whittier
　　　　May 27, 1868. She was b.
　　　　　　1846.
　　　　　　　　Child. born in Randolph, Mass.
　　　　　　　　I. JAMES A. [8] born May 14, 1875.

622. **Eighth Generation.** **Tower.**

286. MORTON [7], ISAAC [6], ISAAC [5], JOSEPH [4], JOSEPH [3], JOHN [2], JOHN [1].
　　　　Morton [7], son of Isaac [6] and Minora A. (Bracket) Tower, b.
　　　　　　1840 ; mar. Annie M. London, of Dorchester, Mass.,
　　　　Feb. 23, 1869. She was b. in Liverpool, England,
　　　　　　1844, and was dau. of Thomas and Margaret London.

623. London. **Eighth Generation.** **Tower.**

286. MARY E. [7], ISAAC [6], ISAAC [5], JOSEPH [4], JOSEPH [3], JOHN [2],
　　JOHN [1].

Mary E.⁷, dau. of Isaac ⁶ and Minora A. (Bracket) Tower, b.
1847 ; mar. John L. London, of Dorchester, Mass.,
Oct. 2, 1867. He was b. in Liverpool, England,
1842, and was son of Thomas and Margaret London.

Child.

1. THOMAS H.⁸ born May 28, 1869, in Brooklyn, N. Y.; died June 29, 1869.

624. Gray.   Eighth Generation.   Tower.

288. ANN⁷, BENJAMIN F.⁶, ISAAC⁵, JOSEPH⁴, JOSEPH³, JOHN²,
JOHN¹.
Ann⁷, dau. of Benjamin F.⁶ and Esther (Hollis) Tower, b.
Jan. 16, 1831 ; mar. Robert B. Gray,
Jan. 25, 1849. He was b.
March 22, 1824.

Childr.

I. FRANKLIN T.⁸   born Oct. 26, 1850; died Sept. 20, 1852, ag. 1 y.
10 m. 25 d.
II. ADA JOSEPHINE ⁸ "   April 11, 1854; died May 30, 1858, ag. 4 y. 1 m.
18 d.
III. CLYDE ⁶   "   June 4, 1857; died June 5, 1858, ag. 1 y. 1 d.
IV. AUSTIN G.⁸   "   Aug. 30, 1859.
V. FLORA H.⁸   "   Aug. 20, 1863.
VI. MYRA T.⁸   "   July 7, 1866.
VII. WILLIE H.⁸   "   Nov. 29, 1869.
VIII. JERRY ⁸   "   Aug. 26, 1875.

Robert B. Gray lives in Farmington, Iowa (1880).

625.   Eighth Generation.   Tower.

291. SILAS F.⁷, LUTHER⁶, ISAAC⁵, JOSEPH⁴, JOSEPH³, JOHN²,
JOHN¹.
Silas F.⁷, son of Luther ⁶ and Adah (Warren) Tower, b.
Sept. 3, 1837 ; mar. Malinda S. Ellis, of Brockton, Mass.,
Nov. 27, 1862. She was b. in West Waterville, Me.,
May 16, 1841.

Childr.

1132. I. ADA F.⁸   born Jan. 15, 1866, in Brockton, Mass.
II. LENA MAY ⁸ " June 28, 1869, "   "   "   ; died in West
Bridgewater, Mass., June 22, 1872, ag. 2 y.
11 m. 24 d.

Malinda S. (Ellis) Tower died in Brockton, Sept. 6, 1874,
ag. 33 y. 3 m. 21 d.
Silas F. Tower mar., 2d, Mary Emma Tobey, of Fairfield, Me.,
Jan. 14, 1878. She was born in Fairfield,
April , 1847, and was dau. of Charles and Relief (Lowe)
Tobey.

Child.

III. RALPH E.[8] born July 5, 1880, in Easton, Md.; died Aug. 1, 1880.

626. Lakin.   Eighth Generation.   Tower.

291. L. ADDIE[7], LUTHER[6], ISAAC[5], JOSEPH[4], JOSEPH[3], JOHN[2], JOHN[1].

 L. Addie[7], dau. of Luther[6] and Adah (Warren) Tower, b.
Dec. 30, 1845; mar. J. Alfred Lakin, of Westfield, Mass.,
July 3, 1870. He was b. in Boston,
   1841, and was son of Jones R. and Sarah E. Lakin.

627.   Eighth Generation.   Tower.

291. GEORGE M.[7], LUTHER[6], ISAAC[5], JOSEPH[4], JOSEPH[3], JOHN[2], JOHN[1].

 George M.[7], son of Luther[6] and Adah (Warren) Tower, b.
June 6, 1848; mar. Othalia C. Soule, of East Bridgewater,
 Mass.,
Dec. 31, 1868. She was b. in New Orleans,
   1847, and was dau. of Nathan and Catherine Soule.

Child.

I. HERMAN WARREN[8] born Sept. 24, 1871, in East Bridgewater.

628.   Eighth Generation.   Tower.

292. L. AUGUSTUS[7], LORENZO[6], ISAAC[5], JOSEPH[4], JOSEPH[3], JOHN[2], JOHN[1].

 L. Augustus[7], son of Lorenzo[6] and Hannah L. (Perry)
Tower, b.
July 11, 1846; mar. Mary S. Thompson,
July 10, 1869. She was b.
Dec. 10, 1848, and was dau. of John T. Z. and Sage B.
Thompson.

Childr.

  I. WILLIAM LAWRENCE[8] born Dec. 22, 1872.
  II. ALICE BAILEY[8]   " March 3, 1875.
  III. EDITH ALLERTON[8]   " June 1, 1879.

629. Churchill.   Eighth Generation.   Tower.

292. HELEN A.[7], LORENZO[6], ISAAC[5], JOSEPH[4], JOSEPH[3], JOHN[2], JOHN[1].

 Helen A.[7], dau. of Lorenzo[6] and Hannah (Perry) Tower, b.

Nov. 15, 1852; mar. Nathan Delano Churchill, of Middle-
borough, Mass.,
June 11, 1871. He was born in Plympton, Mass.,
1852, and was son of Ansel, Jr., and Sarah Churchill.

Childr.

I. CARRIE DELANO [8] born April 6, 1875.
II. FRANK WILSON [8] " April 25, 1879.

630. **Eighth Generation.** **Tower.**

293. ABRAHAM W. [7], JOSEPH [6], JOSEPH [5], JOSEPH [4], JOSEPH [3],
JOHN [2], JOHN [1].
Abraham W. [7], son of Joseph [6] and Eliza A. (Thayer) Tower, b.
Sept. 10, 1829; mar. Lydia Ann Clark, of Randolph, Mass.,
Sept. 12, 1852. She was b.
June 4, 1833, and was dau. of Benjamin Clark.

Childr.

I. ABRAHAM WALTER [8] born June 30, 1853.
II. CARRIE DAISEY [8] " Feb. 28, 1872.

631. Springer. **Eighth Generation.** **Tower.**

293. ELIZA ANN [7], JOSEPH [6], JOSEPH [5], JOSEPH [4], JOSEPH [3], JOHN [2],
JOHN [1].
Eliza Ann [7], dau. of Joseph [6] and Eliza A. (Thayer) Tower, b.
March 14, 1835; mar. Benjamin F. Springer, of Natick,
Mass.,
Oct. 12, 1856. He was b.
1830, and was son of Stephen Springer.

632. **Eighth Generation.** **Tower.**

296. ELISHA [7], ISAIAH [6], ELISHA [5], ELISHA [4], RICHARD [3], IBROOK [2],
JOHN [1].
Elisha [7], son of Isaiah [6] and Silvia (Tobey) Tower, b.
May 10, 1788; mar. Filenah Morgan, of Berne, N. Y.,
June 1, 1815. She was dau. of Simeon and Rhobe (Allen)
Morgan.

Childr.

	I.	EMILY [8]	born	; died July 21, 1817.
1133.	II.	ELISHA [8]	" Jan. 13, 1818.	
1134.	III.	RHOBE ALLEN [8]	" May 4, 1820.	
1135.	IV.	SIMEON MORGAN [8]	" Sept. 11, 1822.	
	V.	CLARISSA DEBORAH [8]	" June , 1826; unmar.	
1136.	VI.	EMILY MINERVA [8]	" Jan. , 1829.	
1137.	VII.	CORYDON LAZELL [8]	" 1834.	

Elisha Tower [7] died in Ellery, N. Y., Jan. 9, 1866, ag. 77 y. 7 m. 30 d.

Filenah (Morgan) Tower died in Ellery, N. Y., Dec.   , 1860.

633. Bolles.   Eighth Generation.   Tower.

296. RHUAMY [7], ISAIAH [6], ELISHA [5], ELISHA [4], RICHARD [3], IBROOK [2], JOHN [1].

Rhuamy [7], dau. of Isaiah [6] and Silvia (Tobey) Tower, b. Sept. 9, 1790 ; mar. Julius Bolles, of Schenectady, N. Y., May 6, 1807.

Childr.

I.	JOANNA [8].	
II.	ELISHA TOWER [8]	born June 2, 1809.
III.	GEORGE NELSON [8].	
IV.	BENJAMIN TOWER [8].	
V.	EMILY [8]	Twins born Nov. 23, 1815.
VI.	AMANDA [8]	
VII.	HARRIET [8].	; mar. Stephen Henry Griffith.
VIII.	SILVIA [8].	
IX.	DEBORAH [8]	; died, ag. about 16 years.
X.	WILLIAM S. [8]	born 1822.
XI.	ABIGAIL JONES [8]	; died, ag. about 18 years.
XII.	JULIUS [8]	; " " " 4 days.
XIII.	REBECCA [8].	
XIV.	MARY JONES [8].	

Julius Bolles died in Marengo, Calhoun Co., Mich.

Rhuamy (Tower) Bolles died in Marengo, 1867, ag. 77.

634.   Eighth Generation.   Tower.

296. ISAIAH [7], ISAIAH [6], ELISHA [5], ELISHA [4], RICHARD [3], IBROOK [2], JOHN [1].

Isaiah [7], son of Isaiah [6] and Silvia (Tobey) Tower, b. March 7, 1795 ; mar. Mary Sherburne, of Rensselaer Co., N. Y.,

Feb. 23, 1825. She was b. in Duanesburg, N. Y., April 24, 1805, and was dau. of John and Nancy (Simmons) Sherburne.

Childr.

	I.	JOHN SHERBURNE [8]	born Oct. 14, 1826; unmar.
1138.	II.	WILLIAM JAMES [8]	" Jan. 24, 1828.
1139.	III.	ALONZO D. [8]	" Dec. 2, 1831.
1140.	IV.	CAROLINE ROSINA [8]	" July 16, 1835.
	V.	JANE SOPHIA [8]	" March 12, 1840; died Jan. 4, 1844, ag. 3 y. 9 m. 23 d.
1141.	VI.	ANSON KNIBLOE [8]	" Jan. 1, 1842.

Isaiah Tower [7] died in Rochester, N. Y., Sept. 27, 1850, ag. 55 y. 6 m. 21 d.

635. Eighth Generation. Tower.

296. JOHN A.[7], ISAIAH [6], ELISHA [5], ELISHA [4], RICHARD [3], IBROOK [2], JOHN [1].

John A.[7], son of Isaiah [6] and Silvia (Tobey) Tower, b.

Aug. 17, 1799 ; mar. Eunice C. Schauber, of Clifton Park, N. Y.,

Dec. 28, 1830. She was b.

June 1, 1803, and was dau. of David and Maplet (Budlow) Schauber.

Child.

1142. I. BENJAMIN S.[8] born March 11, 1832.

Eunice C. (Schauber) Tower died May 13, 1832, ag. 28 y. 11 m. 12 d.

John A. Tower [7] mar., 2d, Jane Turnbull, of Schenectady, N. Y.,

May 11, 1842. She was b. in Edinburgh, Scotland, Sept. 22, 1811.

Childr.

II. FANNY MEEKER [8] born March 8, 1843; died Dec. 27, 1849, ag. 6 y. 9 m. 19 d.

III. EUNICE S.[8] " Aug. 29, 1844; died Dec. 27, 1866, ag. 22 y. 3 m. 29 d.

IV. CHARLES ALBERT [8] " March 20, 1847; mar.

V. EDWARD A.[8] " May 1, 1851; died Nov. 22, 1852, ag. 1 y. 6 m. 21 d.

John A. Tower [7] died near Cedar Springs, Mich., Nov. 14, 1869, ag. 70 y. 2 m. 28 d.

636. Eighth Generation. Tower.

296. JEREMIAH B.[7], ISAIAH [6], ELISHA [5], ELISHA [4], RICHARD [3], IBROOK [2], JOHN [1].

Jeremiah B.[7], son of Isaiah [6] and Silvia (Tobey) Tower, b.

Dec. 8, 1801 ; mar. Mary Barkhoff, of Duanesburg, N. Y.,

Sept. 19, 1833. She was b.

Oct. 7, 1812, and was dau. of William and Rhoda (Cummings) Barkhoff.

Childr.

I. EUNICE S.[8] born June 23, 1834 ; died Aug. 27, 1834.

II. WILLIAM B.[8] " Oct. 6, 1836; died Jan. 19, 1863, ag. 26 y. 3 m. 13 d.

1143. III. HULDAH [8] " Sept. 7, 1838.

IV. JOHN NELSON [8] " Feb. 18, 1840; mar. Lucelia Barnes, of Newton, Mich.

V.   Julius T.[8]   born Sept. 21, 1843; died at Gettysburg, July, 1863,
            ag. 19 y. 10 m.
VI.   Lewis P.[8]   "   June 17, 1846.
VII.   Charles E.[8]   "   June 9, 1849.
VIII.   James M.[8]   "   Feb. 28, 1852.

Jeremiah B. Tower[7] died in Michigan, June 10, 1856, ag.
54 y. 6 m. 2 d.

Mary (Barkhoff) Tower mar., 2d, Elihu G. Kyes, of Fredonia,
Mich. He died Oct. 2, 1870, ag. 77 y. 10 m. 24 d.

637.   **Eighth Generation.**   **Tower.**

296. Joseph [7], Isaiah [6], Elisha [5], Elisha [4], Richard [3], Ibrook [2],
       John [1].
Joseph [7], son of Isaiah [6] and Silvia (Tobey) Tower, b.
Nov. 16, 1803 ; mar. Elizabeth Richards in Galloway, N. Y.,
Aug. 29, 1832.
Joseph Tower[7] died in Ballston, N. Y.,   1858, ag. 55.
Elizabeth (Richards) Tower died   .

638. Beal.   **Eighth Generation.**   **Tower.**

296. Silvia [7], Isaiah [6], Elisha [5], Elisha [4], Richard [3], Ibrook [2],
       John [1].
Silvia [7], dau. of Isaiah [6] and Silvia (Tobey) Tower, b.
March 7, 1806 ; mar. Thomas Brownell Beal.

Childr.

I. Thomas [8].	III. George [8].
II. Edward [8].	IV. Henrietta [8].

Silvia (Tower) Beal died near Rome, N. Y., about 1873.

639.   **Eighth Generation.**   **Tower.**

296. Stephen G.[7], Isaiah [6], Elisha [5], Elisha [4], Richard [3],
       Ibrook [2], John [1].
Stephen G.[7], son of Isaiah [6] and Silvia (Tobey) Tower, b.
March 8, 1808 ; mar. Martha W. Ruddock,
Jan. 3, 1844. She was b.
Dec. 22, 1812.

Child.

I. S. Whitman [8] born Nov. 18, 1847; died in New Orleans, Aug. 2, 1864,
            ag. 16 y. 8 m. 14 d.

Martha W. (Ruddock) Tower died   .
Stephen G. Tower[7] mar., 2d, Mary Abigail Pinckney,
Dec. 1, 1852. She was b. in Albany Co., N. Y.,
Sept. 2, 1828.

Childr.

II. P. WILLARD [8]   born Nov. 28, 1853; died Dec. 9, 1854, ag. 1 y. 11 d.
III. ELLIS LEIGHTON [8] " Sept. 1, 1855.
IV. Infant [8]   " Jan. 12, 1860; died Feb. 17, 1860.
V. MARY ALICE [8]   " Sept. 23, 1862.

Stephen G. Tower [7] died Dec. 28, 1868, ag. 60 y. 9 m. 20 d.

640. Hoyt.   Eighth Generation.   Tower.

297. ELIZABETH [7], SYLVANUS [6], ELISHA [5], ELISHA [4], RICHARD [3], IBROOK [2], JOHN [1].
Elizabeth [7], dau. of Sylvanus [6]   b.
Feb. , 1792 ; mar Samuel Hoyt.

Childr.

I. JOHN [8].   II. JOEL [8].   III. VELINA [8].   IV. ELIZA [8].

641.   Eighth Generation.   Tower.

297. DANIEL [7], SYLVANUS [6], ELISHA [5], ELISHA [4], RICHARD [3], IBROOK [2], JOHN [1].
Daniel [7], son of Sylvanus [6]   b.
Oct. 22, 1794 ; mar. Mary Pratt.

Childr.

I. SYLVANUS [8].   II. ELIZABETH [8].   III. MERCY [8].
IV. SARAH [8].   V. VELINA [8].

Mary (Pratt) Tower died
Daniel Tower [7] mar., 2d,

Childr.

VI. ALVAH W. [8]   VII. ALFRED [8].

Daniel Tower died in Delaware, Ind., March 28, 1885, ag.
90 y. 5 m. 6 d.

642.   Eighth Generation.   Tower.

298. ELISHA [7], ELISHA [6], ELISHA [5], ELISHA [4], RICHARD [3], IBROOK [2], JOHN [1].
Elisha [7], son of Elisha [6] and Hannah (Baxter) Tower, b.
Jan. 25, 1802 ; mar. Elizabeth Stevens, of Andover, Mass.
She was dau. of John Stevens.

Childr.

1144.   I. ELISHA [8]   born Oct. 11, 1824.
1145.   II. CHARLES B. [8] " March 13, 1826.
1146. III. MARY [8]   " May 17, 1830.
1147. IV. EMELINE A. [8] " June 9, 1834.

Elizabeth (Stevens) Tower died
Elisha Tower[7] mar., 2d, Lucy A. Fay
May 18, 1848.   She was born in Northborough, Mass.,
   1819, and was dau. of John F. and Charlotte Fay.

Childr.

V. Lucy Louisa[8] born May 12, 1859; died Aug. , 1859.
VI. Frederick[8] "

Elisha Tower[7] died in Lexington, Mass., Sept. 20, 1880, ag.
  78 y. 7 m. 26 d.

643.   **Eighth Generation.**   **Tower.**

300. Daniel W. P.[7], Cornelius[6], Isaac[5], Cornelius[4], John[3],
   Ibrook[2], John[1].
  Daniel W. P.[7], son of Cornelius[6] and Abby (Potter) Tower, b.
  June 7, 1803; mar. Emily Hill, of East Hampton, Conn.,
  Sept. 24, 1824.   She was b. in East Hampton,
  April 23, 1803, and was dau. of David and Polly (Welch)
   Hill.

Childr.

  I. Daniel[8] born Dec. 25, 1826, in New Hartford, N. Y.; died
         1827.
1148. II. David H.[8] " March 2, 1828, "   "   "
1149. III. James[8] " Aug. 7, 1829, "   "   "
1150. IV. Henry E.[8] " June 7, 1831, "   "   "

Daniel W. P. Tower[7] died in Algonquin, Ill., April 14, 1847,
  ag. 43 y. 10 m. 7 d.
He was killed at his mill by logs rolling over him.
Emily (Hill) Tower was living in Woodstock, Ill., 1883.

644.   **Eighth Generation.**   **Tower.**

301. Joseph F.[7], Elkanah[6], Isaac[5], Cornelius[4], John[3], Ibrook[2],
   John[1].
  Joseph F.[7], son of Elkanah[6] and Elizabeth (Frissell) Tower, b.
  Aug. 14, 1805; mar. Clarissa Peck,
  April 7, 1827.   She was b. in Amherst, Mass.,
  Sept. 22, 1794, and was dau. of Winchester and Lydia
   (Perkins) Peck.

Child, an adopted daughter.

Elizabeth Maria born July 11, 1848; mar Andrew Hutchinson, of
        Worcester, Mass.

Joseph F. Tower lives in Huntington, Mass. (1880).
His wife was living at the same date.
He is a mason by trade.

645. Strong. Eighth Generation. Tower.

301. MARIA [7], ELKANAH [6], ISAAC [5], CORNELIUS [4], JOHN [3], IBROOK [2],
JOHN [1].

Maria [7], dau. of Elkanah [6] and Elizabeth (Frissell) Tower, b.
March 3, 1807; mar. Lewis Strong, of Hatfield, Mass.,
Nov. 7, 1825. He was b.
1796, and was son of Elijah and Elizabeth (Morton)
Strong.

Childr.

I. ELIZABETH M. [8] born Sept. 22, 1826.
II. LEWIS C. [8]   " June 24, 1831; died June 29, 1839, ag. 8 y. 5 d.

Lewis Strong died Aug. 2, 1831, ag. 35.
Maria (Tower) Strong mar., 2d, R. W. Walker, of Belcher-
town, Mass.,
April 29, 1835. He was b.
Oct. 26, 1800, and was son of Nathaniel and Thankful
(Morse) Walker.

Child.

III. LEWIS C. [8] born April 7, 1836; died May 6, 1836.

646. Eighth Generation. Tower.

301. EDWARD [7], ELKANAH [6], ISAAC [5], CORNELIUS [4], JOHN [3], IBROOK [2],
JOHN [1].
Edward [7], son of Elkanah [6] and Elizabeth (Stone) Tower, b.
Oct. 5, 1815; mar. Mary Hubbard, of Brimfield, Mass.,
May 27, 1841.

Childr.

I. ANN ELIZABETH [8] born Aug. 4, 1843, in Brimfield; died Aug.
6, 1857, ag. 13 y. 8 m. 2 d.
1151. II. GEORGE EDWARD [8] " Jan. 10, 1846, in Brimfield.
III. WARREN HUBBARD [8] " Nov. 20, 1849, in Sturbridge; died Feb.
22, 1854, ag. 4 y. 3 m. 4 d.
IV. FRANK WARREN [8] " Feb. 26, 1854, in Sturbridge.
V. CHARLES HUBBARD [8] " Aug. 6, 1861, " Chicopee.

Edward Tower [7] died in West Springfield, Dec. 15, 1870, ag.
55 y. 2 m. 10 d.

647. Wood. Eighth Generation. Tower.

301. ELIZABETH F. [7], ELKANAH [6], ISAAC [5], CORNELIUS [4], JOHN [3],
IBROOK [2], JOHN [1].
Elizabeth F. [7], dau. of Elkanah [6] and Elizabeth (Stone)
Tower, b.
Aug. 5, 1817; mar. Luton Wood, of Rochester, N. Y.

Childr.

I. Elizabeth M.[8].   III. Frances[8].
II. Sarah[8].   IV. William[8].

648.   **Eighth Generation.**   **Tower.**

301. George A.[7], Elkanah[6], Isaac[5], Cornelius[4], John[3], Ibrook[2], John[1].

George A.[7], son of Elkanah[6] and Elizabeth (Stone) Tower, b. Oct. 29, 1821; mar. widow Ellen M. Hall in Dyersburg, Tenn., July 6, 1870.

Childr. none.

George A. Tower[7] died in Dyersburg, May 20, 1876, ag. 54 y. 6 m. 22 d.

649.   **Eighth Generation.**   **Tower.**

301. Eli[7], Elkanah[6], Isaac[5], Cornelius[4], John[3], Ibrook[2], John[1].

Eli[7], son of Elkanah[6] and Elizabeth (Stone) Tower, b. March 10, 1823; mar. Alice G. Watson, Dec. 10, 1867. She was b. in Chapel Hill, N. C., Oct.   , 1841, and was dau. of William F. and Mary (Pelletier) Watson.

Child.

I. Lizzie Beall[8] born June 4, 1872, in Tuscaloosa, Ala.

Eli Tower[7] lives in Tuscaloosa (1882).

650. Howes.   **Eighth Generation.**   **Tower.**

301. Frances A.[7], Elkanah[6], Isaac[5], Cornelius[4], John[3], Ibrook[2], John[1].

Frances A.[7], dau. of Elkanah[6] and Elizabeth (Stone) Tower, b. Jan. 6, 1828; mar. Roswell F. Howes, of Brooklyn, N. Y., Sept. 10, 1851.

Childr.

I. Clara[8].   II. Minnie[8].

Roswell F. Howes lives in Brooklyn, N. Y. (1882).

651. Lavake.   **Eighth Generation.**   **Tower.**

302. Lucinda[7], Isaac W.[6], Isaac[5], Cornelius[4], John[3], Ibrook[2], John[1].

Lucinda[7], dau. of Isaac W.[6] and Zeruah (Hitchcock) Tower, b. Sept. 25, 1800; mar. Thomas Lavake, of Northampton, Mass., 1816.

Childr.

I. CHARLES W.[8] born April 9, 1817.
II. MARY ANN [8] " Aug. 18, 1818; mar.

Thomas Lavake died in Northampton, July 24, 1872, ag. 78.
Lucinda (Tower) Lavake died in Northampton, Dec. 5, 1877,
ag. 77 y. 2 m. 10 d.

652. French.   Eighth Generation.   Tower.

302. SOPHIA [7], ISAAC W. [6], ISAAC [5], CORNELIUS [4], JOHN [3], IBROOK [2],
JOHN [1].
Sophia [7], dau. of Isaac W.[6] and Zeruah (Hitchcock) Tower, b.
1808; mar. Ambrose French.

Childr.

I. HENRY M. [8].   II. CHARLES [8].   III. EDWARD [8].
IV. SALLY ANN [8].   V. MARY ESTHER [8].

Ambrose French died   1858.
Sophia (Tower) French died Feb. 22, 1875, ag. 67.

653. Hutchinson.   Eighth Generation.   Tower.

302. ELIZABETH F.[7], ISAAC W.[6], ISAAC [5], CORNELIUS [4], JOHN [3],
IBROOK [2], JOHN [1].
Elizabeth F.[7], dau. of Isaac W.[6] and Zeruah (Hitchcock)
Tower, b.
1810; mar. John Hutchinson.

Childr.

I. CHARLES S.[8]   II. ALEXANDER [8].

Elizabeth (Tower) Hutchinson died in Alleghany, Penn.

654. Perigo.   Eighth Generation.   Tower.

302. SALLY [7], ISAAC W.[6], ISAAC [5], CORNELIUS [4], JOHN [3], IBROOK [2],
JOHN [1].
Sally [7], dau. of Isaac W.[6] and Zeruah (Hitchcock) Tower, b.
1814; mar. John Perigo, of Northampton, Mass.

Childr.

I. GEORGE W.[8] born   1840; died in Baton Rouge, La., April 27,
1863, ag. 23.
II. FREDERICK [8].
III. MARY [8].

655. Lepard. **Eighth Generation.** **Tower.**

302. NANCY[7], ISAAC W.[6], ISAAC[5], CORNELIUS[4], JOHN[3], IBROOK[2], JOHN[1].

Nancy[7], dau. of Isaac W.[6] and Zeruah (Hitchcock) Tower, b. 1820 ; mar. Frederick Lepard.

Child.

I. FREDERICK[8]

Frederick Lepard lives in Hartford, Conn.

656. **Eighth Generation.** **Tower.**

303. LEWIS C.[7], MICAH[6], ISAAC[5], CORNELIUS[4], JOHN[3], IBROOK[2], JOHN[1].

Lewis C.[7], son of Micah[6] and Pamela (Clark) Tower, b. May 17, 1803 ; mar Margaret S. White, April 30, 1828. She was b. in Hadley, Mass., March 20, 1811, and was dau. of Elijah and Lucy (Pierce) White.

Childr.

1152.	I.	LUCY F.[8]	born May 20, 1829.
1153.	II.	PAMELA CLARK[8]	" Aug. 17, 1831.
	III.	CHARLES S.[8]	" Jan. 4, 1835.	He went to Colorado.
1154.	IV.	LEWIS C.[8]	" Aug. 24, 1839.
	V.	JULIA[8]	" Dec. 3, 1842 ; died Sept. 3, 1843.

Lewis C. Tower[7] died April 30, 1868, ag. 64 y. 11 m. 14 d. Margaret S. (White) Tower is living in Rochester, N. Y. (1883).

657. Frary. **Eighth Generation.** **Tower.**

303. DELIA[7], MICAH[6], ISAAC[5], CORNELIUS[4], JOHN[3], IBROOK[2], JOHN[1].

Delia[7], dau. of Micah[6] and Pamela (Clark) Tower, b. Aug. 29, 1805 ; mar. John Frary, of Southampton, Mass., Aug. 24, 1828.

Childr.

I. CORDELIA[8].	III. JULIA[8].	V. MARIA[8].
II. CORNELIA[8].	IV. CHARLES[8].	VI. MARTHA[8].

658. **Eighth Generation.** **Tower.**

304. SOLOMON[7], JOSEPH[6], ISAAC[5], CORNELIUS[4], JOHN[3], IBROOK[2], JOHN[1].

Solomon [7], son of Joseph [6] and Naomi (Strong) Tower, b.
; mar. Polly Baldwin. She was b. in the State of
New York,
June 28, 1817, and was dau. of Benedict and Permelia
(Potter) Baldwin.

Childr.

	I.	RUFUS [8]	born March 22, 1844.		
	II.	CYNTHIA [8]	"	; mar.	Wellman, of Belding, Mich.
1155.	III.	LOUSIA S. [8]	"	1848.	
1156.	IV.	BURTON J. [8]	"	1850.	
	V.	NAOMI [8]	"	; mar. John Myers, of Belding.	
	VI.	HENRY [8]	"	1856. He lives in Groton, Dakota, (1883).	

Solomon Tower [7] died in Grattan, Mich.
Polly (Baldwin) Tower died in Grattan, May 14, 1880,
ag. 62 y. 10 m. 16 d.

---

659.   **Eighth Generation.**   **Tower.**

304. SAMUEL S. [7], JOSEPH [6], ISAAC [5], CORNELIUS [4], JOHN [3], IBROOK [2],
JOHN [1].
Samuel S. [7], son of Joseph [6] and Naomi (Strong) Tower, b.
; mar. Mary F.

Childr.

I.	SOLOMON [8]	born	1834.	IV.	THO. L. [8] born	1845.
II.	WILLIAM C. [8]	"		V.	DAVID J. [8] "	
III.	SAMUEL S.	"				

---

660.   **Eighth Generation.**   **Tower.**

304. DAVID J. [7], JOSEPH [6], ISAAC [5], CORNELIUS [4], JOHN [3], IBROOK [2],
JOHN [1].
David J. [7], son of Joseph [6] and Naomi (Strong) Tower, b.
July 6, 1807 ; mar.

Childr.

I.	RACHEL C. [8] born	; mar. John L. Tyler, of Shaftsburg, Mich.	
II.	MARY S. [8]	"	; " James Eddy, of Isabella Co., "

---

661.   **Eighth Generation.**   **Tower.**

304. JOSEPH [7], JOSEPH [6], ISAAC [5], CORNELIUS [4], JOHN [3], IBROOK [2],
JOHN [1].
Joseph [7], son of Joseph [6] and Naomi (Strong) Tower, b.
Aug. 20, 1812 ; mar. Palura

Childr.

BENEDICT [8].	He lives in Otisco, Mich (1883).
BENJAMIN [8].	" " " "
FRANCIS [8].	" " " "
CORDELIA [8].	She " " "
JOSEPH [8].	He " " "
LEMUEL [8].	" " " "
PERMELIA [8].	She " Watertown, Mich.
SARAH ELLEN [8].	" " Lansing, "
EMMET [8].	He " Ensley, "
ELIZABETH [8].	She " " "
ALVAH [8].	He " " "
DAVID [8] born Sept. 8, 1850,	" Grattan, "

Joseph Tower [7] died in Grattan, Oct. 11, 1874, ag. 62 y. 1 m. 22 d.

Palura (   ) Tower is living in Otisco (1883).

662.   Eighth Generation.   Tower.

306. CHARLES H.[7], ELIJAH [6], ISAAC [5], CORNELIUS [4], JOHN [3], IBROOK [2], JOHN [1].

Charles H.[7], son of Elijah [6] and Elvira (Russell) Tower, b. Aug. 23, 1829; married Sarah Young Dec. 24, 1868. She was b. in Huntingdon, Mass., May 11, 1844, and was dau. of James and Agnes (Allen) Young.

Child.

I. JAMES WALLACE [8] born Oct. 4, 1871, in Holyoke, Mass.

663.   Eighth Generation.   Tower.

306. HARVEY R.[7], ELIJAH [6], ISAAC [5], CORNELIUS [4], JOHN [3], IBROOK [2], JOHN [1].

Harvey R.[7], son of Elijah [6] and Elvira (Russell) Tower, b. Oct. 19, 1831; mar. Angeline A. Wilson, of Holyoke, Mass., March 21, 1861. She was born Sept. 24, 1837.

Childr.

I. ALICE WILSON [8]   born May 17, 1862, in Agawam, Mass.; died Aug. 5, 1864, ag. 2 y. 2 m. 19 d.
II. CHARLES HENRY [8]   "   Oct. 1, 1865, in Hartford, Conn.
III. FRANK ELIJAH [8]   "   May 15, 1874, in Holyoke, Mass.

664. Loomis.   Eighth Generation.   Tower.

306. LUCY ELVIRA [7], ELIJAH [6], ISAAC [5], CORNELIUS [4], JOHN [3], IBROOK [2], JOHN [1].

Lucy Elvira [7], dau. of Elijah [6] and Elvira (Russell) Tower, b.

Dec. 21, 1833; mar. Samuel J. Loomis, of Southampton, Mass.,
Jan. 13, 1861. He was b.
Sept. 11, 1809, and was son of Alexander and Miriam (   ) Loomis.

665.   **Eighth Generation.**   **Tower.**

307. BENJAMIN [7], OSWIN [6], ISAAC [5], CORNELIUS [4], JOHN [3], IBROOK [2], JOHN [1].

Benjamin [7], son of Oswin [6] and Clarissa (Ludden) Tower, b.
June 6, 1814; mar. Lavina Twiss, of Northampton, Mass.,
Sept. 25, 1839. She was b. in Northampton
March 19, 1815, and was dau. of Elias and Lavina (Bird) Twiss.

Childr.

1157.	I.	MARY E. [8]	born July 23, 1840.
1158.	II.	SARAH P. [8]	" Dec. 12, 1841.
1159.	III.	HENRY B. [8]	" Dec. 27, 1843.
1160.	IV.	HARRIET P. [8]	" April 4, 1847.
	V.	FRANK S. [8]	" May 6, 1852; died in Chesterfield, Mass., Jan. 10, 1854, ag. 1 y. 8 m. 4 d.
1161.	VI.	FRED L. [8]	" June 12, 1855.

Benjamin Tower [7] died in Richmond, Mass., March 15, 1870, ag. 55 y. 9 m. 9 d.

666.   **Eighth Generation.**   **Tower.**

307. LEVI [7], OSWIN [6], ISAAC [5], CORNELIUS [4], JOHN [3], IBROOK [2], JOHN [1].
Levi [7], son of Oswin [6] and Clarissa (Ludden) Tower, b.
Sept. 19, 1816; mar. Julia A. Wheeler
Feb. 14, 1841. She was b. in Westfield, Mass.,
Aug. 1, 1818, and was dau. of Joseph and Elizabeth (Bush) Wheeler.

Childr.

	I.	JAMES [8]	born July 4, 1842; died May 10, 1843.
1162.	II.	HENRY L. [8]	" Aug. 28, 1843.
1163.	III.	FRANKLIN D. [8]	" July 28, 1848.

667. Warriner, Montague. Eighth Generation. Tower.

307. FRANCES J. [7], OSWIN [6], ISAAC [5], CORNELIUS [4], JOHN [3], IBROOK [2], JOHN [1].

Frances J. [7], dau. of Oswin [6] and Clarissa (Ludden) Tower, b.
March 9, 1818; mar. Sylvester Montague
Nov. 26, 1839. He died in Belchertown, Mass.
She mar., 2d, Alfred Warriner, of Southampton, Mass.
He died Sept. 18, 1856.

668. Peck.   Eighth Generation.   Tower.

307. ANISE[7], OSWIN[6], ISAAC[5], CORNELIUS[4], JOHN[3], IBROOK[2],
      JOHN[1].

Anise[7], dau. of Oswin[6] and Clarissa (Ludden) Tower, b.
June 21, 1820; mar. Arnold M. Peck, of Hatfield, Mass.,
Dec. 31, 1840. He was son of James Peck.

Child.

I. HATTIE LILLYBELL[8].

Anise (Tower) Peck died   1863.

669.   Eighth Generation.   Tower.

307. QUARTUS[7], OSWIN[6], ISAAC[5], CORNELIUS[4], JOHN[3], IBROOK[2],
      JOHN[1].

Quartus[7], son of Oswin[6] and Clarissa (Ludden) Tower, b.
Aug. 27, 1822; mar. Mary Cowls, of Goshen, Mass.,
Nov. 28, 1844. She was b.
        1823, and was dau. of Simon Cowls.

Child.

1164. I. ELLEN[8] born   1847.

Quartus Tower[7] died in Granby, Mass., Dec. 7, 1875, ag.
53 y. 3 m. 11 d.

670.   Eighth Generation.   Tower.

307. ASA D.[7], OSWIN[6], ISAAC[5], CORNELIUS[4], JOHN[3], IBROOK[2],
      JOHN[1].

Asa D.[7], son of Oswin[6] and Clarissa (Ludden) Tower, b.
Oct. 4, 1825; mar. Elizabeth Carter
Nov. 1, 1853. She was b.
        1831, and was dau. of Timothy and Sophronia Carter.

Childr. none.

Elizabeth (Carter) Tower died Aug. 2, 1854, ag. 23.
Asa D. Tower[7] mar., 2d, Mary Ann Drury, of Warren, Mass.,
April 24, 1861. She was b.
June 6, 1829, and was dau. of Franklin and Sophia Drury.

Childr. born in Warren.

I.   FRANK FORREST[8] born March 10, 1862; died April 29, 1862.
II.   ABBY FLORENCE[8] " July 21, 1863.
III. WALTER STARR[8] " Nov. 19, 1865.

671.   **Eighth Generation.**   **Tower.**

307. GEORGE [7], OSWIN [6], ISAAC [5], CORNELIUS [4], JOHN [3], IBROOK [2], JOHN [7].

George [7], son of Oswin [6] and Clarissa (Ludden) Tower, b. March 24, 1830 ; mar. Dolly Ann Cole March 6, 1854. She was born 1829, and was dau. of Harvey Cole.

Childr.

I.   JULIET JOSEPHINE [8] born April 4, 1855.
II.   EMMA JANE [8]   "   Dec. 23, 1856.

672.   **Eighth Generation.**   **Tower.**

311. ASA C.[7], JESSE [6], ROBERT [5], DAVID [4], HEZEKIAH [3], IBROOK [2], JOHN [1].

Asa C.,[7] son of Jesse [6] and Rebecca (Cushing) Tower, bapt. March 25, 1787 ; mar. Charlotte Mann.

Childr. born in Cohasset, Mass.

1165.	I.	THOMAS [8]	born July	3, 1807.
1166.	II.	CHARLOTTE [8]	" Sept.	18, 1809.
1167.	III.	ASA C.[8]	" May	4, 1811.
	IV.	MARY [8]	" May	13, 1813.
	V.	Infant [8]	" Jan.	, 1816; died Feb. 16, 1816.
	VI.	Daughter [8]	" Sept.	, 1817; " Sept. 26, 1819, ag. 2.
1168.	VII.	HANNAH K.[8]	" Sept.	9, 1819.

Charlotte (Mann) Tower died March 23, 1826, ag. 48.
Asa C. Tower [7] mar., 2d, Ruth Willcutt, of Cohasset, Sept. 23, 1827. She was b.
Sept.   , 1789, and was widow of David Willcutt.

Child.

1169.   VIII.   ALVAN [8] born Sept. 13, 1832.

Asa C. Tower [7] died in Cohasset, April 5, 1840, ag. 53.
Ruth Tower mar., 3d, Mordecai Lincoln, of Cohasset.
She died in Cohasset, March 14, 1852, ag. 62 y. 6 m.

673. Hersey.   **Eighth Generation.**   **Tower.**

311. ELIZABETH BURBANK [7], JESSE [6], ROBERT [5], DAVID [4], HEZEKIAH [3], IBROOK [2], JOHN [1].

Elizabeth B.[7], dau. of Jesse [6] and Rebecca (Cushing) Tower, b.

June 28, 1790; mar. William Hersey, of Hingham, Mass.,
Oct. 24, 1819. He was b.
Oct. 16, 1798, and was son of William and Polly (Dill)
Hersey.

Childr. born in Hingham.

I.	WILLIAM [8]	born	Jan. 30, 1820.
II.	SARAH ELIZABETH [8]	"	Oct. 13, 1821, died Sept. 6, 1822.
III.	HENRY W.[8]	"	Aug. 16, 1823.
IV.	ISAAC LINCOLN [8]	"	July 21, 1825.
V.	SARAH MARIA [8]	"	Dec. 21, 1827; died Jan. 5, 1829, ag. 1 y. 15 d.
VI.	JOHN QUINCY [8]	"	Sept. 23, 1829.
VII.	MARY [8]	"	Aug. 15, 1831; mar. Ebenezer H. Elmes, and died in Boston, Sept. 20, 1857, ag. 26 y. 1 m. 6 d.

William Hersey died in Hingham, July 27, 1874, ag. 75 y.
10 m.

Elizabeth B. (Tower) Hersey died in Hingham, June 30, 1858,
ag. 68 y. 2 d.

674.   **Eighth Generation.**   **Tower.**

311. JESSE [7], JESSE [6], ROBERT [5], DAVID [4], HEZEKIAH [3], IBROOK [2],
JOHN [1].

Jesse [7], son of Jesse [6] and Rebecca (Cushing) Tower, b.
June   , 1792; mar. Grace Souther, of Hingham, Mass.,
Sept. 26, 1813. She was b. in Hingham
Nov. 20, 1784, and was dau. of Daniel [5] and Grace (Sprague)
Souther.

SOUTHER.   TOWER.

Grace [6], Daniel [5], Joseph [4], Content [3], Ibrook [2], John [1].

Childr. born in Cohasset.

1170.	I.	REBECCA C.[8]	born June	1, 1814.
1171.	II.	JESSE [8]	"	March 28, 1817.
1172.	III.	JOHN [8]	"	Jan. 18, 1821.
1173.	IV.	MARTHA B.[8]	"	Dec. 17, 1822.
	V.	JOSEPH [8]	"	March 1, 1825; died Sept. 25, 1825.
1174.	VI.	ABIGAIL K.[8]	"	Sept. 29, 1826.
	VII.	JAMES [8]	"	Aug. 27, 1830; " July 4, 1831.

Grace (Souther) Tower died in Cohasset, Aug. 8, 1851, ag.
66 y. 8 m. 18 d.

Jesse Tower [7] mar., 2d, widow Mary [8] (Beal) Robinson, of
Hingham,
Feb. 16, 1861. She was b. in Cohasset
          1797, and was dau. of Joshua Beal [7] and widow of
Joseph Robinson.

Jesse Tower [7] died in Cohasset, Nov. 1, 1871, ag. 79 y. 5 m.
Mary [8] (Beal) Tower died in Cohasset, May 22, 1878, ag. 81.

675. Souther. Eighth Generation. Tower.

311. $\left\{ \begin{array}{l} \text{REBECCA [7], JESSE [6], ROBERT [5], DAVID [4],} \\ \quad \text{HEZEKIAH [3]} \\ \text{DANIEL [6], DANIEL [5], JOSEPH [4], CONTENT [3]} \end{array} \right\}$ IBROOK [2], JOHN [1].

Rebecca [7], dau. of Jesse [6] and Rebecca (Cushing) Tower, b.
June 12, 1794 ; mar. Daniel Souther [6], in Hingham,
Feb.   1815, by Rev. Joseph Richardson. D. Souther, b.
Jan. 14, 1786, was son of Daniel [5] and Grace (Sprague)
Souther.

Childr.

I.	DANIEL [8]	born March	8, 1816; died at sea.
II.	GRACE SPRAGUE [8]	" Dec.	29, 1817.
III.	ELIZABETH [8]	" May	25, 1820.
IV.	MARTIN [8]	" March	20, 1822.
V.	SAMUEL CUSHING [8]	" July	8, 1824.
VI.	REBECCA TOWER [8]	" Feb.	22, 1827.
VII.	HARRIET ATWOOD [8]	" Aug.	29, 1829.
VIII.	SARAH LOUISA [8]	" July	19, 1834.
IX.	NATHAN BARNES [8]	" Sept.	17, 1836; died 1837, ag. 9 m.

Daniel Souther died in Hingham, Aug. 1, 1845, ag. 59 y.
6 m. 18 d.
Rebecca (Tower) Souther died in Hingham, Nov. 2, 1864, ag.
70 y. 4 m. 21 d.

676. Lincoln. Eighth Generation. Tower.

311. $\left\{ \begin{array}{l} \text{RUTH L. [7], JESSE [6], ROBERT [5], DAVID [4],} \\ \quad \text{HEZEKIAH [3]} \\ \text{JOHN M. [7], LYDIA [6], HANNAH [5], RACHEL [4]} \\ \quad \text{RACHEL [3]} \end{array} \right\}$ IBROOK [2], JOHN [1].

Ruth L. [7], dau. of Jesse [6] and Rebecca (Cushing) Tower, bapt.
Oct. 28, 1798 ; mar. John M. Lincoln [7]
May 24, 1841. He was b.
July 25, 1784, and was son of Lydia [6] (Barnes) and Urbane
Lincoln.
John M. Lincoln [7] died in Hingham, Dec. 31, 1848, ag. 64 y.
5 m. 6 d.
Ruth L. (Tower) Lincoln died in Hingham, Aug. 12, 1859,
ag. 61.

677. Eighth Generation. Tower.

312. ABRAHAM H. [7], ABRAHAM H. [6], ABRAHAM [5], DANIEL [4], DANIEL [3],
IBROOK [2], JOHN [1].

Abraham H.[7], son of Abraham H.[6] and Charlotte (Bates[8])
Tower, b.
April 1, 1829; mar. Mary L. Brown, of Cohasset, Mass.,
Dec. 24, 1851. She was b.
Aug. 16, 1829, and was dau. of Thomas J. and Sarah (Pratt)
Brown.

Childr. born in Cohasset.

   1175. I. MARY HOBART[8]   born Oct. 30, 1852.
   1176. II. ABRAHAM HOBART[8] " Sept. 8, 1858.

Mary L. (Brown) Tower died in Cohasset, Oct. 16, 1871, ag.
42 y. 2 m.
Abraham H. Tower[7] mar., 2d, Fannie Hincks, of Cohasset,
Nov. 20, 1873. She was b. in York, England,
    1831, and was dau. of William and Maria Ann
    (Sandel) Hincks.

678.   **Eighth Generation.**   **Tower.**

312. HENRY C.[7], ABRAHAM H.[6], ABRAHAM[5], DANIEL[4], DANIEL[3],
IBROOK[2], JOHN[1].
Henry C.[7], son of Abraham H.[6] and Charlotte[8] (Bates)
Tower, b.
April 16, 1831; mar. Martha D. Joy, of Cohasset, Mass.,
Oct. 31, 1861. She was b. in Cohasset,·
Nov. 28, 1836, and was dau. of Bela and Paulina (Snow)
Joy.

Child. born in Cohasset.

   1177. I. LAURA SNOW[8] born Jan. 4, 1864.

679.   **Eighth Generation.**   **Tower.**

312. CHARLES C.[7], ABRAHAM H.[6], ABRAHAM[5], DANIEL[4], DANIEL[3],
IBROOK[2], JOHN[1].
Charles C.[7], son of Abraham H.[6] and Charlotte (Bates)
Tower, b.
Sept. 26, 1833; mar. Clarissa L. Pratt, of Cohasset, Mass.,
Nov. 29, 1860. She was b. in Boston,
Jan. 3, 1834, and was dau. of Charles and Ruth Nichols
    (Pratt) Pratt.

Childr.

  I. Daughter[8]   born Sept. 15, 1861; died Sept. 17, 1861.
  II. CARRIE APPLETON[8] " July 18, 1862.
  III. CHARLOTTE BATES[8] " Nov. 22, 1863; mar. Arthur Clifton Heald,
                            Dec. 31, 1883.
  IV. HELEN MERRIEL[8] " Aug. 5, 1868.
  V. RUTH NICHOLS[8] " Nov. 15, 1873.

680.   **Eighth Generation.**   **Tower.**

312. NEWCOMB B.[7], ABRAHAM H.[6], ABRAHAM [5], DANIEL [4], DANIEL [3],
  IBROOK [2], JOHN [1].
  Newcomb B.[7], son of Abraham H.[6] and Charlotte (Bates)
  Tower, b.
  Feb. 20, 1840; mar. Sophronia L. Parker, of Cohasset, Mass.,
  Feb. 19, 1862. She was b.
  Feb. 18, 1842, and was dau. of John and Mary (Laurence)
  Parker.

Childr. born in Cohasset.

	I.	MARTHA BATES [8]	born Feb. 12, 1863; died Oct. 22, 1868, ag. 5 y. 8 m. 7 d.
1178.	II.	GEORGE PARKER [8]	"	Feb. 1, 1865.
	III.	ELLA GERTRUDE [8]	"	May 2, 1867; mar. Edward Nichols, of Cohasset, Oct. 17, 1888.
	IV.	MARY PARKER [8]	"	July 31, 1870.
	V.	CHARLOTTE SOPHRONIA [8]	"	May 25, 1876.

681.   **Eighth Generation.**   **Tower.**

312. DANIEL N.[7], ABRAHAM H.[6], ABRAHAM [5], DANIEL [4], DANIEL [3],
  IBROOK [2], JOHN [1].
  Daniel N.[7], son of Abraham H.[6] and Charlotte [8] (Bates)
  Tower, b.
  Feb. 28, 1846 ; mar. Josephine Smith, of Cohasset, Mass.,
  Oct. 21, 1871. She was b. in Cohasset,
  Feb. 4, 1846, and was dau. of Joseph H. and Almatia
  (Pool) Smith.

Childr. born in Cohasset.

I.	BESSIE LORD [8]	born	July 31, 1875.
II.	GILBERT SANDERS [8]	"	Feb. 15, 1885.

682.   **Eighth Generation.**   **Tower.**

316. LUTHER F.[7], ABRAHAM [6], ISAAC [5], DANIEL [4], DANIEL [3], IBROOK [2],
  JOHN [1].
  Luther F.[7], son of Abraham [6] and Bethia (Field) Tower, b.
  Nov. 5, 1808 ; mar. Catherine E. Yuille,
  July 4, 1853. She was b. in Hamilton, Scotland.

Childr. none.

Luther F. Tower resided in New Orleans about forty years.
He removed to Daphne. Baldwin Co., Ala., in 1877.

683.   Eighth Generation.   Tower.

316. IBROOK[7], ABRAHAM[6], ISAAC[5], DANIEL[4], DANIEL[3], IBROOK[2], JOHN[1].

Ibrook[7], son of Abraham[6] and Bethia (Field) Tower, b. Sept. 10, 1810; mar. Mary Wheeler, of Brighton, N. Y., Sept. 23, 1839. She was b. in Lebanon, N. Y., Sept. 12, 1818, and was dau. of Elmore and Aurelia Wheeler.

Childr.

	I.	EDMUND W.[8] born Feb. 12, 1842, in Hartland, Mich.; died Feb. 18, 1851, ag. 9 y. 6 d.
1179.	II.	FRED E.[8]	" Feb. 22, 1845, in Ann Arbor, Mich.
1180.	III.	DECKER F.[8]	" Dec. 27, 1848, " " "
1181.	IV.	IDA MAY[8]	" Aug. 13, 1853, " Milford, "

684.   Eighth Generation.   Tower.

316. ABRAHAM[7], ABRAHAM[6], ISAAC[5], DANIEL[4], DANIEL[3], IBROOK[2], JOHN[1].

Abraham[7], son of Abraham[6] and Bethia (Field) Tower, b. Jan. 12, 1815; mar. Nancy L. Thornton, of Springfield, Vt.. March 20, 1839. She was b. in Springfield, and was dau. of Solomon and Rosetta (Earl) Thornton.

Childr.

I.	PLINY[8]	born Dec. 24, 1839.	
II.	FRANK[8]	" May 20, 1841; mar.	
III.	CHARLES[8]	" Aug. 21, 1843, unmar.	
IV.	NETTIE[8]	" 1845; died about 1851.	
V.	NELLIE[8]	" 1847; " " "	
VI.	ANN ELIZA[8]	" April 17, 1849.	
VII.	ABBY[8]	" May 6, 1851; unmar.	

Nancy L. (Thornton) Tower died in Springfield, May 27, 1853.

Abraham Tower[7] mar., 2d, widow Clorinda Haskell, of Weathersfield, Vt., May 26, 1857. She was dau. of Jacob Kimball.

685.   Eighth Generation.   Tower.

316. JOHN[7], ABRAHAM[6], ISAAC[5], DANIEL[4], DANIEL[3], IBROOK[2], JOHN[1].

John[7], son of Abraham[6] and Bethia (Field) Tower, b. Nov. 14, 1819; mar. Tila O. Eaton, Jan. 1, 1845.

Childr. none.

John Tower[7] died in Springfield, Vt., May 6, 1850, ag. 30 y.
5 m. 22 d.

686. **Eighth Generation.** **Tower.**

316. ISAAC[7], ABRAHAM[6], ISAAC[5], DANIEL[4], DANIEL[3], IBROOK[2],
JOHN[1].
Isaac[7], son of Abraham[6] and Bethia (Field) Tower, b.
June 13, 1822 ; mar. Mary Corbin.

Childr.

I. WILLIS H.[8] born Nov. 15, 1855.   II. NEWTON E.[8] born Nov. 27, 1857.

687. Hazeltine, Latham. **Eighth Generation.** **Tower.**

316. JANE M.[7], ABRAHAM[6], ISAAC[5], DANIEL[4], DANIEL[3], IBROOK[2],
JOHN[1].
Jane M.[7], dau. of Abraham[6] and Bethia (Field) Tower, b.
May 10, 1832 ; mar. James Henry Latham,
March 27, 1859.   He was b.
1826, and was son of Harvey and Jemima (Ellis)
Latham.

Childr. none.

James H. Latham died Aug. 20, 1860, ag. 34.

Jane M. (Tower) Latham mar., 2d, William Hazeltine,
May 1, 1871.   He was b.
1829, and was son of Chauncey and Mary (Sanderson)
Hazeltine.

Child.

I. KATIE E.[8] born May 20, 1872.

688. Johnson. **Eighth Generation.** **Tower.**

317. ELIZABETH S.[7], ISAAC[6], ISAAC[5], DANIEL[4], DANIEL[3], IBROOK[2],
JOHN[1].
Elizabeth S.[7], dau. of Isaac[6] and Susanna (Field) Tower, b.
Nov. 10, 1805 ; mar. Nelson Johnson.

Childr.

I. SAMUEL[8]   ; unmar.; died. III. ELIZABETH[8]   ; unmar.; died.
II. ISAAC N.[8]   ;   "   "

Nelson Johnson died in Springfield, Vt.

Elizabeth S. (Tower) Johnson died in Springfield, June 11,
1844, ag. 38 y. 7 m. 1 d.

689.   **Eighth Generation.**   **Tower.**

317. DANIEL F.[7], ISAAC[6], ISAAC[5], DANIEL[4], DANIEL[3], IBROOK[2], JOHN[1].

Daniel F.[7], son of Isaac[6] and Susanna (Field) Tower, b.
Aug. 29, 1807 ; mar. Caroline White
Dec. 19, 1832; *s. p.*
He mar., 2d, widow Prudence (Dexter) Dallas
June 24, 1847. She was b.
April 22, 1822, and was dau. of Samuel and Anna (Fargo) Dexter.

Childr.

I.	HELEN E.[8]	born Aug. 1, 1848.
II.	ISABELLA M.[8]	" May 11, 1850.
III.	ELLEN AMELIA[8]	" Jan. 13, 1853; died April 14, 1854, ag. 1 y. 3 m. 1 d.
IV.	DANIEL WEBSTER[8]	" Aug. 13, 1855.
V.	CARL SCHURZ[8]	" Nov. 9, 1859 ; died Jan. 6, 1864, ag. 4 y. 1 m. 27 d.

Daniel F. Tower[7] died in Grand Rapids, Mich., Dec. 9, 1878, ag. 71 y. 3 m. 11 d.

690.   **Eighth Generation.**   **Tower.**

317. LEVI[7], ISAAC[6], ISAAC[5], DANIEL[4], DANIEL[3], IBROOK[2], JOHN[1].
Levi[7], son of Isaac[6] and Susanna (Field) Tower, b.
Oct. 18, 1810; mar. in Virginia.

Childr.

I. Son[8].	II. ELIZABETH[8].

Levi Tower[7] died in Springfield, Vt.

691.   **Eighth Generation.**   **Tower.**

317. STEPHEN S.[7], ISAAC[6], ISAAC[5], DANIEL[4], DANIEL[3], IBROOK[2], JOHN[1].

Stephen S.[7], son of Isaac[6] and Susanna (Field) Tower, b.
Aug. 16, 1812 ; mar. Mary Eddy.

Childr.

I. FRANCES[8].   II. SCHUYLER[8].   III. HENRY[8].   IV. SARAH[8].
V. ISAAC[8] born Oct.   , 1850 ; died in Oakfield, Mich., Oct. 29, 1880, ag. 30.

Mary (Eddy) Tower died
Stephen S. Tower[7] mar., 2d, Mary Ann Mumey.

Childr.

VI.	IDA MAY[8] born	1856.	IX. JOB A.[8] born Aug. 14, 1868.	
VII.	CLYD O.[8] "	1858.	X. ERNEST A.[8] " Dec. 28, 1872.	
VIII.	GERTRUDE E.[8] "	1864.		

692.   **Eighth Generation.**   **Tower.**

317. LEWIS[7], ISAAC[6], ISAAC[5], DANIEL[4], DANIEL[3], IBROOK[2], JOHN[1].

Lewis[7], son of Isaac[6] and Susanna (Field) Tower, b. Jan. 10, 1814; mar. Mary

Childr.

I. MAY[8].   II. LEWIS[8].   III. BELLE[8].

693.   **Eighth Generation.**   **Tower.**

317. ISAAC N.[7], ISAAC[6], ISAAC[5], DANIEL[4], DANIEL[3], IBROOK[2], JOHN[1].

Isaac N.[7], son of Isaac[6] and Susanna (Field) Tower, b. May 11, 1816; mar. Mary Jane Welsh.

Childr.

I. ALBERT LEWIS[8].	V. DE WITT CLINTON[8].
II. THOMAS JENKINS[8].	VI. ISAAC NICHOLS[8].
III. LEVI DURANT[8].	VII. THEODA[8], ; mar. George
IV. LUTHER AUBREY[8].	Washington Bennet, of Louisiana.

Isaac N. Tower[7] died in Big Bend, La., 1881.

694.   **Eighth Generation.**   **Tower.**

317. WINSLOW[7], ISAAC[6], ISAAC[5], DANIEL[4], DANIEL[3], IBROOK[2], JOHN[1].

Winslow[7], son of Isaac[6] and Susanna (Field) Tower, b. Sept. 1, 1817; mar. Elizabeth Johnson.

Childr.

I. EUSTACE[8].   II. ADELBERT[8].   III. EMMA[8].   IV. ALMY[8].

Winslow Tower[7] died in Rockford, Mich., 1854.

695.   **Eighth Generation.**   **Tower.**

317. SAMUEL[7], ISAAC[6], ISAAC[5], DANIEL[4], DANIEL[3], IBROOK[2], JOHN[1].

Samuel[7], son of Isaac[6] and Susanna (Field) Tower, b.

July 20, 1819; mar. Sarah Burns, of Albany, N. Y.,

Aug. 1, 1841. She was b.

1817, and was dau. of George and Sarah M. (Dougal) Burns.

Childr.

I. ISAAC LEWIS [8] born May 16, 1842.

II. GEORGE [8]   "   1844; died in Murfresboro', Tenn.,   1862.

Sarah (Burns) Tower died Aug.   , 1847, ag. 30.

Samuel Tower [7] mar., 2d, Editha Newton,

1847. She was dau. of Dudley Newton.

Childr.

    III. SARAH [8]   born   ; died in infancy.

    IV. RAY [8]   "   Feb. 1, 1859.

    V. AUGUSTA [8]   "

    VI. Infant [8]   ; died.

Editha (Newton) Tower died Aug. 15, 1863, ag. 39.

Samuel Tower [7] mar., 3d, Hepzibah E. B. Nichols, of Cohasset, Mass.,

April, 7, 1864. She was b. in Cohasset

Nov. 24, 1827, and was dau. of Levi [7] and Mary [6] (Hall) Nichols.

{ NICHOLS, BATES.   TOWER.

{ HALL, LINCOLN.   TOWER.

Hepzibah, E. B. [8] { Levi [7], Zibiah [6], Joshua [5], Joshua [4] / Rachel [3] / Mary [6], Persis [5], Daniel [4], Daniel [3] } Ibrook [2], John [1].

Samuel Tower [7] mar., 4th, Fannie Bosworth,

Feb. 22, 1872. She was dau. of (   ) and Mary (Henderson) Bosworth.

696. Thornton.   Eighth Generation.   Tower.

317. SUSAN [7], ISAAC [6], ISAAC [5], DANIEL [4], DANIEL [3], IBROOK [2], JOHN [1].

Susan [7], dau. of Isaac [6] and Susanna (Field) Tower, b.

May 18, 1821; mar. William Thornton,

May 14, 1839. He was b.

Dec. 29, 1814, and was son of Salmon and Rosetta (Earl) Thornton.

Childr.

    I. ABBY ELIZABETH [8] born Jan.   3, 1841.

    II. MARTHA HATTON [8]   "   March 28, 1842.

    III. CHARLES EDWARD [8]   "   April 25, 1847.

    IV. MARY VIOLA [8]   "   Feb. 5, 1851.

    V. EDITH LODISA [8]   "   Sept. 5, 1855; unmar.

697. Winsor. Eighth Generation. Tower.

317. HANNAH[7], ISAAC[6], ISAAC[5], DANIEL[4], DANIEL[3], IBROOK[2], JOHN[1].

Hannah[7], dau. of Isaac[6] and Susanna (Field) Tower, b.
May 27, 1824; mar. Zenas G. Winsor in Courtland, Mich.,
Aug. 1, 1840. He was b. in Skeneateles, N. Y.,
Dec. 28, 1814, and was son of Darius and Sally (Yates)
Winsor.

Childr.

I. EMILY L.[8]	born Oct. 18, 1842, in Plainfield, Mich.
II. HENRY H.[8]	" April 20, 1845, " Grand Rapids, Mich.
III. ALICE ADELL[8]	" July 10, 1847, " " "
IV. ADELAIDE ELIZABETH[8]	" March 3, 1850, " " "
V. FRANCES ESTELLA[8]	" July 21, 1854, " " "

Hannah (Tower) Winsor died in Grand Rapids, Sept. 28,
1869, ag. 45 y. 4 m. 2 d.

698. Eighth Generation. Tower.

317 DAVID[7], ISAAC[6], ISAAC[5], DANIEL[4], DANIEL[3], IBROOK[2], JOHN[1].

David[7], son of Isaac[6] and Susanna (Field) Tower, b.
Dec. 23, 1825; mar. Sarah D. Chapin in Oakfield, Mich.,
Oct. 18, 1857. She was dau. of Zelotes and Mary (Marvin)
Chapin.

Childr.

1182.	I. ALICE[8]	born Sept. 7, 1859.
	II. NELLIE M.[8]	" Dec. 13, 1861.
	III. THEODA[8]	" Feb. 20, 1864.
	IV. MERIBA[8]	" July 12, 1866.
	V. BYRON[8]	" April 3, 1869.
	VI. FOSTER D.[8]	" April 18, 1873.

699. Severns. Eighth Generation. Tower.

317. THEODA[7], ISAAC[6], ISAAC[5], DANIEL[4], DANIEL[3], IBROOK[2], JOHN[1].

Theoda[7], dau. of Isaac[6] and Susanna (Field) Tower, b.
Sept. 21, 1827; mar. Henry Severns, of California.

Childr. none.

Theoda (Tower) Severns died in California, Aug. 18, 1869,
ag. 41 y. 10 m. 27 d.

700.   **Eighth Generation.**   **Tower.**

321. ISAAC S.[7], STODDARD[6], ISAAC[5], DANIEL[4], DANIEL[3], IBROOK[2],
       JOHN[1].
       Isaac S.[7], son of Stoddard[6] and Sally (Bates) Tower, b.
       Feb. 5, 1830 ; mar. Mary Evelyn Smith[8] of Richmond,Va.,
              She was b. in Richmond,
       Feb. 22, 1846, and was dau. of Hiram M.[7] and Elizabeth L.
       (Ames) Smith.

                   Childr. born in Richmond.

     I.   GEORGE AMES[8]   born Jan. 29, 1872.
    II.   FREDERICK CHARLES[8] "   Aug. 19, 1873.
   III.   FRANK WALLIS[8]   "   Jan. 4, 1875.
    IV.   JESSIE[8]   "   Nov. 18, 1878; died young.
     V.   BESSIE LOUISE[8]   "   June 2, 1880.
    VI.   EVELYN STODDARD[8]   "   July 11, 1882.
   VII.   GRACE[8]   "   Jan. 2, 1886; died young.

701. Adams.   **Eighth Generation.**   **Tower.**

325. ABIGAIL[7], LEVI[6], SAMUEL[5], DANIEL[4], DANIEL[3], IBROOK[2],
       JOHN[1].
       Abigail[7], dau. of Levi[6] and Anstis (Stratton) Tower, b.
       Aug. 11, 1807 ; mar. Jonathan S. Adams, of Plainfield, Conn.,
       Feb. 6, 1833. He was b.
       Sept. 22, 1802, and was son of Joshua and Abigail (Sabin)
       Adams.

                 Childr. born in Fitzwilliam, N. H.

     I.   MARY A.[8]   born Nov. 22, 1833.
    II.   LYSANDER TOWER[8]   "   April 16, 1836; died May 25, 1836.
   III.   HANNAH AURILLA[8]   "   June 2, 1837.
    IV.   CATHERINE AMBRA[8]   "   June 25, 1840.
     V.   JOHN SABIN[8]   "   April 29, 1842; died Aug. 16, 1863, ag.
                                     21 y. 3 m. 17 d.
    VI.   REBECCA ANSTIS[8]   "   Sept. 30, 1844; died April 27, 1850, ag. 5 y.
                                     6 m. 27 d.
   VII.   MARTHA AMELIA[8]   "   March 17, 1847; died Jan. 7, 1856, ag. 8 y.
                                     9 m. 21 d.

702. Spaulding. **Eighth Generation.**   **Tower.**

325. AMBRA[7], LEVI[6], SAMUEL[5], DANIEL[4], DANIEL[3], IBROOK[2],
       JOHN[1].
       Ambra[7], dau. of Levi[6] and Anstis (Stratton) Tower, b.
       May 26, 1813 ; mar. Alvah Spaulding, of Jaffrey, N. H.,
       Nov. 17, 1835.

Childr.

I. LYSANDER TOWER [8] born   1837.
II. ELLEN [8]   ; mar. Edwin Johnson, of Cornish, N. H.
III. FIDELIA [8]   ; unmar.; died in Windsor, Vt.
IV. ABBY S.[8]   "   1847.
V. LUCIA [8]   ; unmar.
VI. AMBRA [8]   ; died, ag. 2 years.

703. Pond.   Eighth Generation.   Tower.

326. MARIA [7], DANIEL [6], SAMUEL [5], DANIEL [4], DANIEL [3], IBROOK [2], JOHN [1].

Maria [7], dau. of Daniel [6] and Mary (Buswell) Tower, b. July 30, 1820 ; mar. Nathaniel Pond, of Dedham, Mass., July 9, 1850.

Childr. born in Dedham.

I. MARY ELIZABETH [8] born May 8, 1853; died in Dedham.
II. ABBIE MARIA [8]   " Oct. 7, 1855.

Nathaniel Pond died in Dedham, April 29, 1861.
Maria (Tower) Pond died in Dedham, Oct. 27, 1860, ag. 40 y. 3 m. 26 d.

704. Treat.   Eighth Generation.   Tower.

326. REBECCA B.[7], DANIEL [6], SAMUEL [5], DANIEL [4], DANIEL [3], IBROOK [2], JOHN [1].

Rebecca B.[7], dau. of Daniel [6] and Mary (Buswell) Tower, b. May 14, 1825; mar. Edward H. Treat, of Enfield, Me., Oct. 26, 1847. He was b. in Orono, Me., Nov. 15, 1820.

Childr.

I. ANNA MARY [8]   born Sept. 13, 1851, in Foxcroft, Me.
II. FLORA ELIZABETH [8] " Feb. 5, 1853, " Enfield, "
III. EVA MARIA [8]   " Sept. 9, 1862, " " " ; mar. C. S. Sullivan, of Maine, in Riverside, Dec. 15, 1886.

705. Huntting.   Eighth Generation.   Tower.

326. MARY [7], DANIEL [6], SAMUEL [5], DANIEL [4], DANIEL [3], IBROOK [2], JOHN [1].

Mary [7], dau. of Daniel [6] and Mary (Buswell) Tower, b. Aug. 10, 1827; mar. Leonard Huntting, of Lee, Me., Aug. 10, 1852. He was b. in Mt. Desert, Me., June 1, 1824, and was son of Enoch and Joanna Huntting.

Childr.

I.	HENRY HALE [8]	born March 6, 1854, in Lincoln, Me.
II.	CHARLES WOODBURY [8]	" Aug. 11, 1857, " Saybrook, Ohio.
III.	LEON WALTER [8]	" Oct. 17, 1860, " Fremont, Kansas.
IV.	EDWIN TOWER [8]	" Feb. 28, 1862, " Nashville, "
V.	WILLIS CARLTON [8]	" July 6, 1865, " Osawatomie, "

706. Woodbury.   Eighth Generation.   Tower.

326. LUCINDA B.[7], DANIEL [6], SAMUEL [5], DANIEL [4], DANIEL [3], IBROOK [2], JOHN [1].

Lucinda B.[7], dau. of Daniel [6] and Mary (Buswell) Tower, b. June 28, 1829 ; mar. Charles H. B. Woodbury, of Dover, Me., Sept. 20, 1854.

Child. born in Dover, Me.

I. WILLIAM CHALMERS [8] born Dec. 15, 1857.

707.   Eighth Generation.   Tower.

326. LEVI N. C.[7], DANIEL [6], SAMUEL [5], DANIEL [4], DANIEL [3], IBROOK [2], JOHN [1].

Levi N. C.[7] son of Daniel [6] and Mary (Buswell) Tower, b. March 6, 1834 ; mar. Ellen Maria Dudley in Presideo, Cal., March 30, 1865. She was b. in Lowell, Mass., March 14, 1847, and was dau. of Charles F. and Lydia (Davis) Dudley.

Childr. born in California.

I.	CHARLES DUDLEY [8]	born Feb. 19, 1866; died May , 1866.
II.	MARY LYDIA [8]	" March 11, 1867.
III.	AGNES FULLER [8]	" July 4, 1872.
IV.	EDWARD HENDERSON [8]	" Oct. 11, 1874.

708. Dakin.   Eighth Generation.   Tower.

326. ABBY FRANCES [7], DANIEL [6], SAMUEL [5], DANIEL [4], DANIEL [3], IBROOK [2], JOHN [1].

Abby Frances [7], dau. of Daniel [6] and Mary (Buswell) Tower, b. Jan. 1, 1837 ; mar. William Justus Dakin, of San Francisco, May 24, 1860. He was b. in Wilton, Me., May 26, 1832, and was son of Levi and Edee (Richardson) Dakin.

Childr.

I.	CHARLES W.[8]	born March 3, 1861, in Mokelumne, Cal.
II.	EDWIN TOWER [8]	" Sept. 18, 1864, " " " ; died Oct. 16, 1867, ag. 3 y. 28 d.
III.	MARY EDEE [8]	" Nov. 13, 1868, in San Andreas, "

709. Bates.   Eighth Generation.   Tower.

329. ANNA H.[7], LEVI[6], LEVI[5], DANIEL[4], DANIEL[3], IBROOK[2], JOHN[1].

Anna H.[7], dau. of Levi[6] and Abigail (Nichols) Tower, b.
Dec. 15, 1803; mar. Zealous Bates[7],
Jan. 1, 1822. He was born in Cohasset,
May 19, 1799, and was son of Daniel and Sally[6] (Tower) Bates.

BATES.   TOWER.
Zealous[7], Sally[6], Levi[5], Daniel[4], Daniel[3], Ibrook[2], John[1].

Childr. born in Cohasset.

I.	OTIS BRIGHAM[8]	born April 7, 1823.
II.	JAMES B.[8]	" March 26, 1825.
III.	CAROLINE LOTHROP[8]	" Feb. 5, 1827.
IV.	BETHIAH T. L.[8]	" July , 1829; died.
V.	ABIGAIL N.[8]	" Jan. 29, 1833.
VI.	SARAH B. D.[8]	" June 29, 1835.
VII.	DANIEL T.[8]	" Jan. 5, 1838.
VIII.	LEWIS NICHOLS[8]	" Oct. 1, 1841; died May 28, 1842.
IX.	LEWIS NICHOLS[8]	" Dec. 29, 1843.
X.	ELIZABETH JOSEPHINE[8]	" June 29, 1846.

Zealous Bates[7] died in Hempstead, N. Y., Jan. 18, 1867, ag. 67 y. 7 m. 30 d.

710.   Eighth Generation.   Tower.

329. NICHOLS[7], LEVI[6], LEVI[5], DANIEL[4], DANIEL[3], IBROOK[2], JOHN[1].

Nichols[7], son of Levi[6] and Abigail (Nichols) Tower, b.
Feb. 10, 1805; mar. Caroline Lothrop[6], of Cohasset, Mass.,
March 29, 1831. She was b. in Cohasset,
March 29, 1806, and was dau. of John J. and Bethia[5] (Tower) Lothrop.

LOTHROP.   TOWER.
Caroline[6], Bethiah[5], Daniel[4], Daniel[3], Ibrook[2], John[1].

Childr. born in Cohasset.

I.	NICHOLS[8]	born Aug. 14,1832; unmar.; died Feb. 28,1859, ag. 26 y. 6 m. 17 d.
II.	THOMAS LOTHROP[8]	" Feb. 3, 1835; unmar.; died Sept. 13, 1863, ag. 28 y. 7 m. 10 d.
III.	CAROLINE LOUISA[8]	" Aug. 11, 1837; died Feb. 9, 1853, ag. 15 y. 6 m. 1 d.
IV.	GEORGE WASHINGTON[8]	" June 24, 1840; died.
V.	DANIEL LOTHROP[8]	" Oct. 10, 1842; mar.

Nichols Tower [7] died in Boston, Aug. 19, 1842, ag. 37 y. 6 m. 9 d.

Caroline (Lothrop) Tower died May 10, 1861, ag. 55 y. 1 m. 12 d.

711.   **Eighth Generation.**   **Tower.**

329. EDWARD [7], LEVI [6], LEVI [5], DANIEL [4], DANIEL [3], IBROOK [2], JOHN [1].

Edward [7], son of Levi [6] and Abigail (Nichols) Tower, b. Dec. 3, 1807 ; mar. Elizabeth B. Delano, of Cohasset, Mass., April 20, 1837. She was b.

Aug. 18, 1815, and was dau. of Samuel and Hannah (Bates) Delano.

Childr. born in Cohasset.

1183. I. SAMUEL DELANO [8]   born March 31, 1838.
1184. II. HANNAH ELIZABETH DELANO [8] " March 4, 1849.

Edward Tower [7] died in Cohasset, March 6, 1873, ag. 65 y. 3 m. 3 d.

Elizabeth B. (Delano) Tower died in Cohasset, Jan. 10, 1874, ag. 58 y. 4 m. 23 d.

712.   **Eighth Generation.**   **Tower.**

329. LEVI [7], LEVI [6], LEVI [5], DANIEL [4], DANIEL [3], IBROOK [2], JOHN [1].

Levi [7], son of Levi [6] and Abigail (Nichols) Tower, b. Jan. 1, 1810 ; mar. Rebecca Bates, of Cohasset, Mass., Sept. 1, 1833. She was b. in Cohasset,

1815, and was dau. of Bela and Rebecca Bates.

Childr. born in Cohasset.

1185. I. EDWARD EVERETT [8] born Feb. 1, 1834.
1186. II. LEVI [8]   " June 8, 1836.
       III. HORATIO BATES [8]   " Sept. 20, 1840 ; died March 5, 1843, ag. 2 y. 5 m. 15 d.

713.   **Eighth Generation.**   **Tower.**

329. WILLIAM B. [7], LEVI [6], LEVI [5], DANIEL [4], DANIEL [3], IBROOK [2], JOHN [1].

William B. [7], son of Levi [6] and Abigail (Nichols) Tower, b. Aug. 11, 1817 ; mar. Sarah E. Souther [7], of Cohasset, Mass., June 8, 1853. She was b. in Cohasset

May 1, 1825, and was dau. of Laban [6] and Elizabeth [6] (Tower) Souther.

SOUTHER.   TOWER.
  Laban [6], Asa [5], Joseph [4], Content [3]   } Ibrook [2], John [1].
  Elizabeth [6], Abraham [5], Daniel [4], Daniel [3] }

Childr.

I. ABRAHAM SOUTHER [8] born June 23, 1855, in Dedham, Mass.
II. LIZZIE ELLA [8]   "   April 21, 1859, "   "   "
III. CAROLINE E. [8]   "   Jan.   4, 1864, " Cambridge, "

Sarah E. (Souther) Tower died in Boston, July 19, 1887, ag. 62 y. 2 m. 18 d.

714.   **Eighth Generation.**   **Tower.**

329. LEWIS [7], LEVI [6], LEVI [5], DANIEL [4], DANIEL [3], IBROOK [2], JOHN [1].
Lewis [7], son of Levi [6] and Abigail (Nichols) Tower, b. April 17, 1822; mar. Abby N. Bates.

Childr.

I. Son [8]   born Oct. 21, 1855, in Boston, Mass.
II. LEWIS NICHOLS [8] "   Feb. 20, 1862, " Weymouth, Mass.

715. Lincoln.   **Eighth Generation.**   **Tower.**

329. PRISCILLA N. [7], LEVI [6], LEVI [5], DANIEL [4], DANIEL [3], IBROOK [2], JOHN [1].
Priscilla N. [7], dau. of Levi [6] and Abigail (Nichols) Tower, b. Dec. 19, 1824; mar. Joel W. Lincoln, of Cohasset, Mass., May 1, 1853. He was b. in Cohasset, Jan. 19, 1829, and was son of Joseph and Mary H. (Nichols) Lincoln.

Childr. none.

Joel W. Lincoln died in Cohasset, June 5, 1873, ag. 44 y. 4 m. 17 d.

716.   **Eighth Generation.**   **Tower.**

331. DAVID B. [7], NICHOLS [6], LEVI [5], DANIEL [4], DANIEL [3], IBROOK [2], JOHN [1].
David B. [7], son of Nichols [6] and Anne [7] (Bates) Tower, b. May 7, 1808; mar. Elizabeth Bates.

Childr.

1187.   I. GEORGE B. N. [8] born   1834.   III. ANNA B. [8]
       II. CHARLES B. [8]

David B. Tower [7] died July 28, 1858, ag. 50 y. 2 m. 21 d.

717.   **Eighth Generation.**   **Tower.**

331. GEORGE [7], NICHOLS [6], LEVI [5], DANIEL [4], DANIEL [3], IBROOK [2], JOHN [1].
George [7], son of Nichols [6] and Anne (Bates) Tower, b. April 9, 1811; mar. Adeline Lane.

Childr.

1188.   I. Benjamin L. M.[8]   born   1848.
    II. George Homer [8]   " Jan. 31, 1850; unmar.; died April 14, 1878, ag. 28 y. 2 m. 14 d.
    III. Levi [8]   " May 17, 1854; died   1857.
    IV. John Foster Williams [8] " Feb. 3, 1860; died   .
    V. Frederic Russell [8]   " Oct. 15, 1861.

George Tower [7] died in Boston, May 11, 1876, ag. 62 y. 1 m. 2 d.

718.   **Eighth Generation.**   **Tower.**

331. Thomas N.[7], Nichols [6], Levi [5], Daniel [4], Daniel [3], Ibrook [2], John [1].

Thomas N.[7], son of Nichols [6] and Anne [7] (Bates) Tower, b. June 18, 1813; mar. Jane B. Bates [7 & 8], of Cohasset, Mass., Dec. 29, 1837. She was b. in Cohasset Jan. 3, 1813, and was dau. of Paul [7] and Priscilla [6] (Tower) Bates.

BATES.   TOWER.

Jane B.[7 & 8] { Paul [7], Zealous [6], Joshua [5], Joshua [4], Rachel [3], Priscilla [6], Levi [5], Daniel [4], Daniel [3] } Ibrook [2], John [1].

Childr. born in Cohasset.

    I. Bethiah Nichols [8]   born June 27, 1839; died March 29, 1842, ag. 2 y. 9 m. 2 d.
1189. II. Elizabeth Hall [8]   " July 17, 1841.
1190. III. Nichols [8]   " July 20, 1844.
    IV. Martha Jane Bates [8] " Nov. 19, 1846.

Thomas N. Tower [7] died in Cohasset, April 11, 1887, ag. 73 y. 9 m. 23 d.

719.   **Eighth Generation.**   **Tower.**

331. Daniel [7], Nichols [6], Levi [5], Daniel [4], Daniel [3], Ibrook [2], John [1].

Daniel [7], son of Nichols [6] and Anne [7] (Bates) Tower, b. Jan. 25, 1815; mar. Susan S. Bates Feb. 16, 1840. She was b. , and was dau. of J. Beal Bates.

Childr.

1186.   I. Mary Rebecca [8]   born Aug. 18, 1840.
    II. Margaret Louisa [8] " Jan. 16, 1843; died Oct. 12, 1843.
    III. Walter Scott [8]   " Feb. 5, 1844.
1191. IV. Clement Bates [8]   " March 13, 1848.
    V. Jonathan B. B.[8]   " May 20, 1851; died Dec. 31, 1851.

720.   **Eighth Generation.**   Tower.

331. FREDERIC[7], NICHOLS[6], LEVI[5], DANIEL[4], DANIEL[3], IBROOK[2], JOHN[1].

Frederic[7], son of Nichols[6] and Anne[7] (Bates) Tower, b.
330. Oct. 21, 1820; mar. Elizabeth Bates[7] [8], of Cohasset, Mass., Feb. 8, 1844. She was b. in Cohasset April 12, 1823, and was dau. of Paul[7] and Priscilla[6] (Tower) Bates.

Childr. born in Cohasset.

I.	ANNA BATES[8]	born May 6, 1845.	
II.	SARAH NICHOLS[8]	"	Sept. 5, 1849; died April 27, 1868, ag. 18 y. 7 m. 22 d
III.	DAVID BATES[8]	"	Oct. 24, 1855.
IV.	ELIZABETH BATES[8]	"	Dec. 17, 1857; " Jan. 14, 1865, ag. 7 y. 28 d.
V.	Child[8]	"	Jan. 16, 1860; " same day.
VI.	"	"	Jan. 15, 1861; " " "
VII.	"	"	June 24, 1864; " " "

721. Keene.   **Eighth Generation.**   Tower.

331. ABIGAIL[7], NICHOLS[6], LEVI[5], DANIEL[4], DANIEL[3], IBROOK[2], JOHN[1].

Abigail[7], dau. of Nichols[6] and Anne[7] (Bates) Tower, b.
Sept. 7, 1826; mar. Cyrus Keene, of Cohasset, Mass., June 6, 1854. He was b. in Buckfield, Me.,
1829, and was son of Simeon Keene.

Childr. born in Cohasset.

I.	SARAH ELWELL[8]	born March 26, 1855.	
II.	ARTHUR RICHMOND[8]	"	Oct. 30, 1857.
III.	ANNA BATES[8]	Twins "	March 15, 1860; died June 3, 1860.
IV.	ABBY TOWER[8]		
V.	GRACE[8]	"	Feb. 4, 1862.
VI.	ANNA NICHOLS[8]	"	Jan. 25, 1866.

722. Foster.   **Eighth Generation.**   Tower.

331. ADELINE[7], NICHOLS[6], LEVI[5], DANIEL[4], DANIEL[3], IBROOK[2], JOHN[1].

Adeline[7], dau. of Nichols[6] and Anne[7] (Bates) Tower, b.
Feb. 9, 1828; mar. Fordyce Foster in Cohasset, Mass., March 24, 1847. He was b. in Southbridge, Mass.,
Dec. 10, 1815, and was son of Fordyce and Elizabeth B. (Wolcott) Foster.

Childr. born in Cohasset.

I.	ELLEN FRANCES[8]	born June 23, 1848.
II.	JULIA SIMMONS[8]	" Jan. 27, 1852.

III. NICHOLS TOWER [8]   born Sept. 9, 1856.
IV.   ADDIE JANE [8]   "   Oct. 7, 1860; died Feb. 8, 1863, ag. 2 y.
                                   4 m. 1 d.
V.   HARRIET RICHARDS [8]   "   Nov. 17, 1863.

723. Pratt.   Eighth Generation.   Tower.

331. SARAH P. N.[7], NICHOLS [6], LEVI [5], DANIEL [4], DANIEL [3], IBROOK [2],
      JOHN [1].
      Sarah P. N.[7], dau. of Nichols [6] and Anne [7] (Bates) Tower, b.
      March 20, 1830; mar. Thomas Pratt, of Cohasset, Mass.,
      Oct. 22, 1850. He was b. in Cohasset
      April 7, 1822, and was son of Job and Lucretia (Oakes)
          Pratt.
                            Childr.

      I.   FLORA LESLIE [8] born May 31, 1852, in Cohasset.
      II.   MARIANNIE [8]   "   July 7, 1855,   "
      III. ISABEL [8]   "   Sept. 17, 1861, in Cambridge, Mass.

724. Beal.   Eighth Generation.   Tower.

333. MARCIA DUNLAP [7], ABRAHAM [6], LEVI [5], DANIEL [4], DANIEL [3],
      IBROOK [2], JOHN [1].
      Marcia D.[7], dau. of Abraham [6] and Marcia D. (Lothrop)
          Tower, b.
      Feb. 19, 1843; mar. Zacheus L. Beal [9]
      Feb. 21, 1864. He was b.
      Sept. 8, 1839, and was son of Zacheus L.[8] and Harriet S.
          (Barnes) Beal.

      BEAL.   TOWER.

      Zacheus L.[9], Zacheus L.[8], Caleb [7], Daniel [6], Joshua [5], Rachel [4], Rachel [3],
      Ibrook [2], John [1].
                            Childr.

      I.   Son [8]   born Dec. 31, 1864.
      II.   SARAH CUMMINGS [8]   "   Aug. 6, 1870.
      III. JULIA MARCIA [8]   "   Dec. 31, 1876.

725.   Eighth Generation.   Tower.

333. ABRAHAM [7], ABRAHAM [6], LEVI [5], DANIEL [4], DANIEL [3], IBROOK [2],
      JOHN [1].
      Abraham [7], son of Abraham [6] and Marcia D. (Lothrop)
          Tower, b.
      March 6, 1851; mar. Julia Annie Hall, of Brookline, Mass.,
      Nov. 23, 1876. She was b. in Brookline
          1853, and was dau. of William and Elizabeth L.
      (Lothrop) Hall.

726.   Eighth Generation.   Tower.

334. JOB [7], JOB [6], LEVI [5], DANIEL [4], DANIEL [3], IBROOK [2], JOHN [1].
Job [7], son of Job [6] and Louisa L. (Lothrop) Tower, b.
Aug. 15, 1826 ; mar. Susan Brown Hodgkins
Dec.   , 1850.   She was b.
    1832.

Child.

I. SUSAN E. [8] born April 22, 1852; mar. Benjamin Robinson Horton, of
                        Ipswich, Mass., Sept. 16, 1877.

Job Tower [7] died Sept. 28, 1851, ag. 25 y. 1 m. 14 d.
Susan B. (Hodgkins) Tower mar., 2d, Wentworth R. Sargent
July 29, 1857. She died Jan. 10, 1882.

727.   Eighth Generation.   Tower.

334. WARREN L. [7], JOB [6], LEVI [5], DANIEL [4], DANIEL [3], IBROOK [2],
JOHN [1].
Warren L. [7], son of Job [6] and Louisa L. (Lothrop) Tower, b.
Jan. 14, 1831 ; mar. Lucinda Pratt Stoddard, of Cohasset,
Mass.,
April 10, 1856. She was b. in Cohasset
May 11, 1831, and was dau. of Zenas and Ann (   )
Stoddard.

Childr.

I. LUCINDA WARREN [8] born Sept. 28, 1858; died Nov. 15, 1862, ag. 4 y.
                       1 m. 17 d.
II. ANNA LOUISA [8]   "   March 22, 1860; "   Sept. 12, 1865, ag. 5 y.
                       5 m. 21 d.
III. JENNIE BRACKET [8]   "   April 9, 1862 ; died Oct. 17, 1862, ag. 6 m. 8d.
IV. WARREN AUGUSTUS [8] "   Oct. 2, 1866; "   March 29, 1871, ag. 4 y.
                       5 m. 27 d.

728.   Eighth Generation.   Tower.

334. JOHN J. [7], JOB [6], LEVI [5], DANIEL [4], DANIEL [3], IBROOK [2], JOHN [1].
John J. [7], son of Job [6] and Louisa L. (Lothrop) Tower, b.
April 6, 1837 ; mar. Aletta Emily Virginia Merwin
April 25, 1865.

Childr. born in Brooklyn, N. Y.

I. ALETTA LOUISA [8]   born Oct. 6, 1867.
II. WILLIAM HOGARTH [8] "   Feb. 1, 1871.
III. WARREN MERWIN [8]   "   Nov. 24, 1873.
IV. GRACE VIRGINIA [8]   "   Nov 9, 1876.

729.   Bates.   **Eighth Generation.**   **Tower.**

835. MARY JANE[7], DAVID[6], LEVI[5], DANIEL[4], DANIEL[3], IBROOK[2],
      JOHN[1].

Mary Jane[7], dau. of David[6] and Jane (Laurence) Tower, b.
Dec. 31, 1825 ; mar. Lorenzo Bates[7]
Dec. 31, 1848. He was b.
Feb. 11, 1824, and was son of Daniel and Sally[6] (Tower)
Bates.

     BATES.   TOWER.

Lorenzo[7], Sally[6], Levi[5], Daniel[4], Daniel[3], Ibrook[2], John[1].

Childr. born in Cohasset.

I.	DAVID TOWER[8]	born Sept. 25, 1849.	
II.	HENRIETTA LINCOLN[8]	" April 19, 1851; died Sept. 16, 1871, ag.	
		20 y. 4 m. 27 d.	
III.	MARY LOVELL[8]	" Nov. 27, 1852.	
IV.	LORENZO WARREN[8]	" March 27, 1854.	
V.	Son[8]	" Nov. 28, 1857.	
VI.	HARRIET JANE[8]	" Oct. 2, 1862.	

Lorenzo Bates[7] died in Quincy, Ill., Aug. 22, 1867, ag. 43 y.
6 m. 9 d.

730.   **Eighth Generation.**   **Tower.**

835. JAMES J.[7], DAVID[6], LEVI[5], DANIEL[4], DANIEL[3], IBROOK[2],
      JOHN[1].

James J.[7], son of David[6] and Jane (Laurence) Tower, b.
May 25, 1832; mar. Chloe Lincoln Kent[8], of Cohasset,
Mass.,
July 4, 1855. She was b. in Cohasset
Sept. 20, 1828, and was dau. of Isaac[7] and Sarah (Worrick)
Kent.

    KENT, LINCOLN, WHITCOMB.   TOWER.

Chloe L.[8], Isaac[7], Chloe[6], Elizabeth[5], Sarah[4], Daniel[3], Ibrook[2],
John[1].

James J. Tower[7] died in Newton, Mass., May 6, 1888, ag.
55 y. 11 m. 12 d.

731.   **Eighth Generation.**   **Tower.**

835. JOHN W.[7], DAVID[6], LEVI[5], DANIEL[4], DANIEL[3], IBROOK[2],
      JOHN[1].

John W.[7], son of David[6] and Jane (Laurence) Tower, b.
Nov. 13, 1842; mar. Emily A. Litchfield, of Cohasset, Mass.,
Oct. 4, 1864. She was b.
1845, and was dau. of Charles and Deborah (   )
Litchfield.

Childr.

I. DEBORAH FRANCIS [8] born April 23, 1866.
II. GEORGE A. [8]   "   Oct. 18, 1867.
III. CHARLES AUGUSTUS [8]   "   April 23, 1870; died.
IV. CHARLES AUGUSTUS [8]   "   July 31, 1872.
V. HENRIETTA B. [8]   "   Dec. 13, 1873.
VI. Daughter [8]   "   Dec. 22, 1875.

732.   **Eighth Generation.**   **Tower.**

335. FRANCIS C. [7], DAVID [6], LEVI [5], DANIEL [4], DANIEL [3], IBROOK [2], JOHN [1].

Francis C. [7], son of David [6] and Jane (Laurence) Tower, b.
Feb. 17, 1845 ; mar. Margaret E. Sloan, of Scituate, Mass.,
June 2, 1867. She was b. in Scituate
       1848, and was dau. of John and Christiana (Hill)
Sloan.

Childr.

I. CHRISTIANA [8] born Oct. 9, 1867; died Feb. 15, 1869, ag. 1 y. 4 m. 6 d.
II. REUBEN [8].

733.   Robinson.   **Eighth Generation.**   **Tower.**

337. ANNA [7], STEPHEN [6], PETER [5], PETER [4], JEREMIAH [3], JEREMIAH [2], JOHN [1].

Anna [7], dau. of Stephen [6] and Anna (Bowker) Tower, b.
Sept. 15, 1776 ; mar. Samuel Robinson, of Cummington,
     Mass.,
Sept. 13, 1801. He was b.
     1773.

Childr. born in Cummington.

I. GALEN [8]   born July 30, 1802.
II. ANNA ALVIRA [8]   "   Sept. 29, 1804.
III. ROBERT CLARK [8]   "   Aug. 17, 1806.
IV. STEPHEN [8]   "   Sept. 28, 1808.
V. MELISSA JANE [8]   "   ; mar.; *s. p.*
VI. SAMUEL [8]   "   Aug. 17, 1811.
VII. NAHUM [8]   "   ; died,   ag. 2 years.
VIII. FIDELIA [8]   "   Dec. 24, 1817.

Samuel Robinson died in Batavia, N. Y.,   1856, ag. 83.
Anna (Tower) Robinson died in Harmony, N. Y., Nov. 17,
     1871, ag. 95 y. 2 m. 2 d.

734.   **Eighth Generation.**   **Tower.**

337. STEPHEN [7], STEPHEN [6], PETER [5], PETER [4], JEREMIAH [3], JERE-MIAH [2], JOHN [1].

Stephen [7], son of Stephen [6] and Anna (Bowker) Tower, b.

March 8, 1778; mar. Melatiah Bartlett, of Cummington, Mass.,

Dec. 15, 1803. She was b. in Stoughton, Mass.,

Dec. 14, 1783, and was dau. of Edward and Zilpha (Sylvester) Bartlett.

Childr. born in Cummington.

1192.	I.	WEALTHY T.[8]	born	Jan. 18, 1805.
	II.	PERMELIA [8]	"	Oct. 20, 1806; died May 24, 1812, ag. 5 y. 7 m. 4 d.
1193.	III.	CALVIN BOWKER [8]	"	Nov. 4, 1808.
1194.	IV.	PERMELIA [8]	"	Nov. 24, 1811.
	V.	ZILPHA [8]	"	May 5, 1814; died May 5, 1814.
	VI.	ANNA ALMINA [8]	"	Oct. 11, 1816; " Jan. 5, 1820, ag. 3 y. 2 m. 25 d.
1195.	VII.	LUTHER BARTLETT [8]	"	Dec. 13, 1819.

Stephen Tower[7] died in Cummington, June 7, 1856, ag. 78 y. 2 m. 30 d.

Melatiah (Bartlett) Tower died in Cummington, Aug. 18, 1864, ag. 80 y. 8 m. 4 d.

735. **Eighth Generation.** **Tower.**

337. JOHN[7], STEPHEN[6], PETER[5], PETER[4], JEREMIAH[3], JEREMIAH[2], JOHN[1].

John[7], son of Stephen[6] and Anna (Bowker) Tower, b.

July 8, 1781; mar. Ruth Reed, of Charlemont, Mass.,

March 1, 1809. She was b. in Charlemont

March 29, 1785, and was dau. of Rev. Jesse and Ruth (Whitman) Reed.

Childr.

1196.	I.	JOHN MADISON [8]	born	April 5, 1810.
	II.	SALOME [8]	"	March 14, 1812; died June 3, 1816, ag. 4 y. 2 m. 20 d.
1197.	III.	CELEMNA [8]	"	May 5, 1815.
1198.	IV.	DEXTER [8]	"	March 12, 1817.
1199.	V.	LAURA [8]	"	May 13, 1819.
1200.	VI.	ROSWELL [8]	"	Sept. 4, 1821.
1201.	VII.	RUSSELL [8]	"	May 31, 1826.

John Tower[7] died in Youngstown, N. Y., Sept. 30, 1827, ag. 46 y. 2 m. 23 d.

Ruth (Reed) Tower died in Cummington, Mass., Nov. 17, 1833, ag. 48 y. 7 m. 19 d.

736. **Eighth Generation.** **Tower.**

337. DAVID[7], STEPHEN[6], PETER[5], PETER[4], JEREMIAH[3], JEREMIAH[2], JOHN[1].

David[7], son of Stephen[6] and Anna (Bowker) Tower, b.

Dec. 11, 1782 ; mar. Elsie Mason Dean, of Adams, Mass. Int. pub.

Dec. 12, 1812. She was b.

March 26, 1792, and was dau. of Dr. Dean, of Adams.

Childr.

1202.	I.	DAVID DEAN [8]	born Nov. 14, 1814.
	II.	PETER G.[8]	" Nov. 26, 1816.
1203	III.	CHRISTOPHER MASON [8]	" Sept. 20, 1818.
1204.	IV.	LUKE BOWKER [8]	" May 21, 1820.
	V.	ANNA [8]	" May 26, 1822 ; died Sept. 24, 1838, ag. 16 y. 3 m. 29 d.
1205.	VI.	STEPHEN ASA [8]	" Sept. 27, 1824.
1206.	VII.	LEVI LINCOLN [8]	" Oct. 15, 1826.
1207.	VIII.	JOHN W.[8]	" Oct. 20, 1828.
1208.	IX.	DANIEL TIMOTHY [8]	" Aug. 13, 1831.

Elsie M. (Dean) Tower died April 6, 1833, ag. 41 y. 11 d.

David Tower [7] mar., 2d, Mary Bassett, of Adams. Int. pub. April 26, 1834.

He died in Wilson, N. Y., March 13, 1870, ag. 87 y. 3 m. 2 d.

---

737. Miner.   Eighth Generation.   Tower.

337. JOANNA [7], STEPHEN [6], PETER [5], PETER [4], JEREMIAH [3], JEREMIAH [2], JOHN [1].

Joanna [7], dau. of Stephen [6] and Anna (Bowker) Tower, b. Sept. 27, 1784 ; mar. Lemon Miner, of Windsor, Mass., Jan. 21, 1807. He was b.

June 28, 1785, and was son of Ephraim and Elizabeth ( ) Miner.

Childr.

I.	EMMERETTA [8]	born July 30, 1809.
II.	AUSTIN T.[8]	" Feb. 9, 1811.
III.	EPHRAIM HARRISON [8]	" Dec. 5, 1813.
IV.	JOHN TOWER [8]	" Jan. 3, 1815.
V.	STEPHEN TOWER [8]	" Dec. 30, 1816.
VI.	NORMAN F.[8]	" Jan. 12, 1819 ; died June 28, 1845, ag. 26 y. 5 m. 17 d.
VII.	ELIZABETH ANN [8]	" March 22, 1822 ; mar. Jerome Thompson ; *s. p.*
VIII.	LA FAYETTE [8]	" Aug. 12, 1825.
IX.	JULIA A.[8]	" June 1, 1828.

Lemon Miner died in Batavia, N. Y., May 12, 1836, ag. 48 y. 10 m. 14 d.

Joanna (Tower) Miner died in Batavia, N. Y., March 6, 1885, ag. 100 y. 5 m. 9 d.

738.   Ford.   Eighth Generation.   Tower.

337. DEBORAH [7], STEPHEN [6], PETER [5], PETER [4], JEREMIAH [3], JERE-
         MIAH [2], JOHN [1].
         Deborah [7], dau. of Stephen [6] and Anna (Bowker) Tower, b.
         July 16, 1786 ; mar. Anselm Ford, of Cummington, Mass.,
         June 7, 1807. He was b.
         June 27, 1788, and was son of Hezekiah and Huldah (   )
            Ford.

Childr. born in Cummington.

I.	DEBORAH [8]	born	Aug. 15, 1807; died Aug. 15, 1807.
II.	CHARLES [8]	"	Jan. 22, 1809.
III.	HOSEA [8]	"	April 4, 1810.
IV.	OTIS [8]	"	Jan. 5, 1812.
V.	AMOS [8]	"	Dec. 6, 1813.
VI.	LUCIUS [8]	"	Nov. 9, 1815.
VII.	DEBORAH ELMINA [8]	"	March 11, 1818.
VIII.	ANNA [8].		

X. DELIA [8].
XI FRANK [8].

IX. CYRUS [8].

739. Timothy.   Eighth Generation.   Tower.

337. CLARISSA [7], STEPHEN [6], PETER [5], PETER [4], JEREMIAH [3], JERE-
         MIAH [2], JOHN [1].
         Clarissa [7], dau. of Stephen [6] and Anna (Bowker) Tower, b.
         May 3, 1788 ; mar. Elkanah Timothy, of Pownal, Vt.,
         Aug. 16, 1807. He was b.
         April 8, 1789, and was son of Daniel and Anna (Boyd)
            Timothy.

Childr.

I.	HIRAM [8]	born	Feb. 16, 1809; died March 3, 1809.
II.	MARY ANN [8]	"	April 9, 1810.
III.	HELAN B. [8]	"	Nov. 25, 1811.
IV.	OTIS [8]	"	Aug. 30, 1813.
V.	FRANCES [8]	"	Aug. 1, 1815.
VI.	CLARISSA ANN [8]	"	July 16, 1817.
VII.	CHARLES DEWEY [8]	"	Sept. 14, 1819.
VIII.	JOHN HENRY [8]	"	Nov. 17, 1821.

Elkanah Timothy died in Porter, N. Y., Nov. 30, 1850, ag.
   61 y. 7 m. 22 d.
Clarissa (Tower) Timothy died in Porter, N. Y., May 29,
   1876, ag. 88 y. 26 d.

740.   Eighth Generation.   Tower.

337. PETER [7], STEPHEN [6], PETER [5], PETER [4], JEREMIAH [3], JEREMIAH [2],
         JOHN [1].
         Peter [7], son of Stephen [6] and Anna (Bowker) Tower, b.

July 10, 1790 ; mar. Hannah Bailey [7], of Cummington, Mass.,

April 5, 1819. She was b.

1798, and was dau. of John and Lucy [6] (Tower) Bailey.

BAILEY.   TOWER.

Hannah [7], Lucy [6], Peter [5], Peter [4], Jeremiah [3], Jeremiah [2], John [1].

Childr. born in Porter, N. Y.

1209.	I.	LYANDA [8]	born Oct. 19, 1819.
1210.	II.	JOHN EDWIN [8]	"	Jan. 3, 1821.
1211.	III.	WILLIAM [8]	"	Oct. 1, 1822.
1212.	IV.	JAMES MUNROE [8]	"	Oct. 1, 1824.
	V.	OCTAVIA [8]	"	Jan. 18, 1827; died Oct. 18, 1830, ag. 3 y. 9 m.
	VI.	ELIZABETH ANN [8]	"	July 16, 1829; " Aug. 31, 1854, ag. 25 y. 1 m. 15 d.

Hannah [7] (Bailey) Tower died in Porter, Dec. 27, 1831, ag. 33. Peter Tower [7] mar., 2d, widow Olive (Baldwin) Smith June 13, 1833. She was b.

May 22, 1803, and was dau. of Guy and Tryphena (Harmon) Baldwin.

Childr.

1213.	VII.	LUKE [8]	born May 24, 1834.
1214.	VIII.	GEORGE PEARCE [8]	"	May 19, 1836.
1215.	IX.	HARMON BALDWIN [8]	"	Aug. 28, 1838.
1216.	X.	EMUGENE [8] } Twins	"	Oct. 9, 1840. Eugene died Nov. 22, 1849, ag. 9 y. 1 m. 13 d.
	XI.	EUGENE [8]		
1217.	XII.	PETER SMITH [8]	"	March 22, 1843.
1218.	XIII.	OLIVE ALMENA [8]	"	June 15, 1846.

Peter Tower [7] died in Porter, N. Y., April 1, 1882, ag. 91 y. 8 m. 22 d.

Olive (Baldwin) Tower died in Porter, N. Y., March 17, 1886, ag. 82 y. 9 m. 26 d.

741.   **Eighth Generation.**   **Tower.**

337. OTIS [7], STEPHEN [6], PETER [5], PETER [4], JEREMIAH [3], JEREMIAH [2], JOHN [1].

Otis [7], son of Stephen [6] and Anna (Bowker) Tower, b. Oct. 28, 1791 ; mar. Susanna Bowker in Granville, N. Y., Feb. 10, 1817. She was b. in Rutland Co., Vt., Oct. 26, 1792, and was dau. of Liberty Bowker.

Childr. born in Porter and Wilson, N. Y.

1219.	I.	LUCETTA [8]	born Jan. 18, 1818.
	II.	NAOMI [8]	"	Aug. 20, 1820; died Sept. 24, 1820.

1220.	III.	MARY [8]	born Dec. 19, 1821.
1221.	IV.	ANNA [8]	" Oct. 15, 1823.
	V.	OTIS FRANKLIN [8]	" Aug. 10, 1825; died Sept. 12, 1847, ag. 22 y. 1 m. 2 d.
1222.	VI.	JOHN [8]	" Sept. 23, 1827.
1223.	VII.	CAROLINE [8]	" April 6, 1830.
1224.	VIII.	ADELINE SOPHIA [8]	" July 16, 1832.

Otis Tower [7] died in Bethel, Mich., Oct. 11, 1870, ag. 78 y. 11 m. 14 d.

Susanna (Bowker) Tower died in Bethel, Mich., Jan. 22, 1869, ag. 76 y. 2 m. 27 d.

742.   **Eighth Generation.**   **Tower.**

338. RUFUS [7], RUFUS [6], PETER [5], PETER [4], JEREMIAH [3], JEREMIAH [2], JOHN [1].

Rufus [7], son of Rufus [6] and Sally Tower, b. 1783; mar. Caroline Cutter, of Cohasset, Mass., Nov. 2, 1805; and mar., 2d, Elizabeth Frances in Boston Nov. 2, 1809.

He died in Boston, Feb. 9, 1815, ag. 32.

743.   **Eighth Generation.**   **Tower.**

340. ASA [7], ASA [6], PETER [5], PETER [4], JEREMIAH [3], JEREMIAH [2], JOHN [1].

Asa [7], son of Asa [6] and Deborah (Dyer) Tower, b. Oct. 15, 1784; mar. Clarissa Bates, of Plainfield, Mass., Nov. 23, 1815. She was b.

Aug. 8, 1792, and was dau. of Calvin and Mary (Bemis) Bates.

Childr. born in Cummington, Mass.

1225.	I.	BETSEY [8]	born Sept. 12, 1816.
1226.	II.	WILLIAM [8]	" May 20, 1818.
	III.	LUCRETIA [8]	" Feb. 18, 1820; unmar.; died June 11, 1843, ag. 23 y. 3 m. 22 d.
1227.	IV.	CLARISSA [8]	" Jan. 19, 1822.
	V.	ORLANDO BEMIS [8]	" Dec. 17, 1825; died June 27, 1827, ag. 1 y. 6 m. 11 d.
1228.	VI.	ALMOND J. [8]	" May 18, 1828.
	VII.	ASA BEMIS [8]	" Sept. 21, 1830; died Nov. 12, 1843, ag. 13 y. 1 m. 21 d.
1229.	VIII.	MARY SOPHIA [8]	" April 24, 1834.

Asa Tower [7] died in Cummington, Dec. 15, 1855, ag. 71 y. 2 m.

Clarissa (Bates) Tower died in Cummington, June 21, 1865, ag. 72 y. 10 m. 13 d.

744. Grover.   Eighth Generation.   Tower.

340. POLLY⁷, ASA⁶, PETER⁵, PETER⁴, JEREMIAH³, JEREMIAH², JOHN¹.

Polly⁷, dau. of Asa⁶ and Deborah (Dyer) Tower, b.
Jan. 19, 1787; mar. Charles N. Grover, of Cummington, Mass.,
Dec. 4, 1821. He was b. in Pownal, Vt.

Child.

I. MARY ANN⁸ born   1824; mar.   Boyington.

Charles N. Grover died in Cummington.
Polly (Tower) Grover died in Cummington.

745. Jacobs.   Eighth Generation.   Tower.

340. HANNAH W.⁷, ASA⁶, PETER⁵, PETER⁴, JEREMIAH³, JEREMIAH², JOHN¹.

Hannah W.⁷, dau. of Asa⁶ and Deborah (Dyer) Tower, b.
Sept. 23, 1789; mar. Richard Jacobs, of Cummington, Mass.,
Feb.   , 1811. He was b. in Sheffield, Mass.,
March 5, 1792, and was son of Sherman and Sylvina (Carver) Jacobs.

Childr.

I. SYLVINA C.⁸   born Sept. 28, 1813, in Lyons, N. Y.
II. RICHARD FRANCIS⁸ " July 24, 1825,   "   "

Richard Jacobs died in Windsor, Mass., Jan. 16, 1875, ag.
82 y. 10 m. 11 d.
Hannah (Tower) Jacobs died in Windsor, Mass., March 31,
1863, ag. 73 y. 6 m. 7 d.

746. Lent, Robinson.   Eighth Generation.   Tower.

340. JANE⁷, ASA⁶, PETER⁵, PETER⁴, JEREMIAH³, JEREMIAH², JOHN¹.

Jane⁷, dau. of Asa⁶ and Deborah (Dyer) Tower, b.
May 5, 1792; mar.   Robinson.

Child.

I. SAMUEL⁸.

Jane (Tower) Robinson mar., 2d, Andrew Lent, of Wilson, N. Y.,

Childr.

II. DEBORAH⁸.   III. ESTHER⁸   ; unmar.; died.

Jane (Tower) Lent died in Wilson.

747. Bowker.   Eighth Generation.   Tower.

340. LEAH[7], ASA[6], PETER[5], PETER[4], JEREMIAH[3], JEREMIAH[2], JOHN[1].

Leah[7], dau. of Asa[6] and Deborah (Dyer) Tower, b.
Sept. 24, 1801; mar. Franklin Bowker
Nov. 23, 1825. He was b.
Oct. 19, 1797.

Childr.

I.   ELIZABETH M.[8] born July 22, 1829.
1396. II.   CALVIN[8]   "   Oct. 7, 1831.

Franklin Bowker died in Wilson, N. Y., Nov. 1, 1876, ag. 79 y. 13 d.
Leah (Tower) Bowker died in Wilson, N. Y., July 18, 1861, ag. 59 y. 9 m. 24 d.

748.   Eighth Generation.   Tower.

340. DYER[7], ASA[6], PETER[5], PETER[4], JEREMIAH[3], JEREMIAH[2], JOHN[1].

Dyer[7], son of Asa[6] and Deborah (Dyer) Tower, b.
Aug. 24, 1804; mar. Lydia Wilkes, of Windsor, Mass.,
Jan. 19, 1832. She was b. in Abington, Mass.,
Feb. 14, 1808, and was dau. of Thomas and Nancy (Porter) Wilkes.

Childr.

I.   RICHARD P.[8] born March 18, 1833; died Sept. 24, 1836, ag.
          3 y. 6 m. 7 d.
II.   DIANTHA S.[8]   "   April 25, 1835;   "   July 18, 1836, ag.
          1 y. 2 m. 23 d.
III. Infant[8]   "   ; died Mar. 16, 1837.
1230. IV.   LYDIA[8]   "   March 16, 1838.
1231. V.   CYRUS R.[8]   "   May 23, 1843.
VI.   CLARENCE[8]   "   July 10, 1850; mar. Mary Streeter, of Plain-
          field, Mass., Oct. 29, 1879.

Dyer Tower[7] died in Cummington, Mass., Dec. 9, 1851, ag. 47 y. 3 m. 16 d.
Lydia (Wilkes) Tower died in Cummington, Mass., Aug. 16, 1850, ag. 42 y. 6 m. 2 d.

749.   Eighth Generation.   Tower.

340. STEPHEN D.[7], ASA[6], PETER[5], PETER[4], JEREMIAH[3], JEREMIAH[2], JOHN[1].

Stephen D.[7], son of Asa[6] and Deborah (Dyer) Tower, b.
Dec. 9, 1807; mar. Esther E. Beale, of Windsor, Mass.,

June 2, 1831. She was b.

May 20, 1811, and was dau. of David and Lucy (Bridges) Beale.

Childr. born in Cummington and Windsor.

1232.	I.	DAVID HORATIO [6]	born March 7, 1832.
	II.	DWIGHT GIDEON [8]	" July 20, 1833; unmar.
1233.	III.	JARVIS EDSON [8]	" Sept. 18, 1834.
1234.	IV.	HENRY ALPHONZO [8]	" May 27, 1836.
1235.	V.	EMMA ELIZA [8]	" Aug. 22, 1838.
1236.	VI.	ELMA LOUISA [8]	" May 8, 1840.
	VII.	LUCY BEALE [8]	" March 15, 1842; unmar.
1237.	VIII.	LUCIA DEBORAH DYER [8]	" Sept. 29, 1844.
1238.	IX.	ASHLEY BEMIS [8]	" June 26, 1847.
1239.	X.	MAHALA JANE [8]	" March 21, 1850.

Stephen D. Tower [7] died in Dalton, Mass., Oct. 13, 1881, ag. 73 y. 10 m. 4 d.

750.	Eighth Generation.	Tower.

343. MOSES [7], MALACHI [6], MALACHI [5], PETER [4], JEREMIAH [3], JEREMIAH [2], JOHN [1].

Moses [7], son of Malachi [6] and Bathshebee (Weatherbee) Tower, b.

April 5, 1785; mar. Mary Binney, of Hull, Mass.,

May 7, 1809. She was b. in Hull

June 14, 1790, and was dau. of Spencer and Mary (Jones) Binney.

Childr. born in Hingham.

1240.	I.	MARY JONES [8]	born Feb. 24, 1810.
1241.	II.	MOSES BINNEY [8]	" April 26, 1814.
1242.	III.	THOMAS JONES [8]	" Sept. 29, 1818.
1243.	IV.	JOHN WESLEY [8]	" Aug. 11, 1821.
	V.	SPENCER BINNEY [8]	" Nov. 18, 1823; died May 26, 1841, ag. 17 y. 6 m. 7 d.

Mary (Binney) Tower died in Hingham, June 12, 1825, ag. 34 y. 11 m. 28 d.

Moses Tower [7] mar., 2d, Abigail Andrews Gould, of Hingham, Dec. 25, 1825. She was. b. in Hull

April 11, 1786, and was dau. of Robert and Mary (Lincoln) Gould.

Child.

VI. ABNER JONES [8] born Jan. 19, 1827; died May 22, 1828, ag. 1 y. 4 m. 3 d.

Moses Tower [7] died in Hingham, Aug. 31, 1862, ag. 77 y. 4 m. 25 d.

Abigail A. (Gould) Tower died in Hingham, Aug. 26, 1870, ag. 84 y. 4 m. 14 d.

751.   Eighth Generation.   **Tower.**

343. PETER[7], MALACHI[6], MALACHI[5], PETER[4], JEREMIAH[3], JERE-
      MIAH[2], JOHN[1].

Peter[7], son of Malachi[6] and Bathshebee (Weatherbee)
    Tower, b.
April 14, 1787 ; mar. Susan Churchill, of Plymouth, Mass.,
    Jan. 25, 1806. She was b. in Plymouth
April 14, 1785, and was dau. of Joseph and Eunice Churchill.

Childr.

1244.	I.	MARTIN WINDSOR [8]	born	Nov. 10, 1806, in Plympton, Mass.
1245.	II.	MALACHI [8]	"	June 30, 1808.
1246.	III.	EUNICE CHURCHILL [8]	"	May 12, 1810.
	IV.	SARAH ANN [8]	"	Nov. 10, 1812; died in Belmont, Me., May 29, 1842, ag. 29 y. 6 m. 19 d.
1247.	V.	WARNER COTTRELL [8]	"	Jan. 2, 1814.
1248.	VI.	PETER [8]	"	April 24, 1816.
1249.	VII.	ELBRIDGE GERRY [8]	"	March 29, 1818.
1250.	VIII.	SUSAN GIBBS [8]	"	Dec. 16, 1819.
1251.	IX.	NEHEMIAH HAYWARD [8]	"	July 31, 1822.
	X.	JEROME ADAMS [8]	"	Nov. 7, 1823; unmar.; died in Belmont, Aug. 10, 1872, ag. 48 y. 9 m. 3 d.
1252.	XI.	JOHN CROSBY [8]	"	April 24, 1825.

Peter Tower[7] died in Belmont, Sept. 30, 1865, ag. 78 y. 5 m.
    16 d.
Susan (Churchill) Tower died in Belmont, Feb.   , 1868, ag.
    82 y. 2 m.

752.   Eighth Generation.   **Tower.**

343. COMFORT[7], MALACHI[6], MALACHI[5], PETER[4], JEREMIAH[3], JERE-
      MIAH[2], JOHN[1].

Comfort[7], son of Malachi[6] and Bathshebee (Weatherbee)
    Tower, b.
Aug. 26, 1790 ; mar. Priscilla Hobart, of Hingham, Mass.,
    April 19, 1829. She was b. in Hingham,
March 14, 1797, and was dau. of Hawkes and Elizabeth
    (Stoddard) Hobart.

Childr. born in Hingham.

1253.	I.	SARAH ELIZABETH [8]	born	May 15, 1834.
1254.	II.	JOHN MARTIN [8]	"	July 21, 1836.

Comfort Tower[7] died in Hingham, June 27, 1852, ag. 61 y. 10 m. 2 d.

Priscilla (Hobart) Tower died in Hingham, April 11, 1873, ag. 76 y. 28 d.

753. **Eighth Generation.** **Tower.**

343. JOHN H.[7], MALACHI[6], MALACHI[5], PETER[4], JEREMIAH[3], JEREMIAH[2], JOHN[1].

John H.[7], son of Malachi[6] and Bathshebee (Weatherbee) Tower, b.

Oct. 6, 1794; mar. Phebe Poland, of North Brookfield, Mass.,

Aug. 31, 1817. She was b.

1791.

Childr. born in Underhill, Vt.

	I.	Daughter[8]	born May 23, 1818; died in infancy.
1255.	II.	JOHN H.[8]	" March 1, 1819.
1256.	III.	JOSEPH P.[8]	" Aug. 18, 1821.
	IV.	THOMAS W.[8]	" April 21, 1824.
	V.	SARAH A.[8]	" June 11, 1826; died Jan. 30, 1827.
	VI.	WILLIAM LORING[8]	" July 18, 1829; " March 23, 1845, ag. 15 y. 8 m. 5 d.
	VII.	SARAH A.[8]	" May 2, 1833; " Feb. 17, 1841, ag. 7 y. 9 m. 15 d.

John H. Tower[7] died in Wisconsin, April 7, 1856, ag. 61 y. 6 m. 1 d.

Phebe (Poland) Tower died in Wisconsin, Oct. 23, 1860, ag. 69.

754. Thomasson. **Eighth Generation.** **Tower.**

345. REBECCA P.[7], GAD H.[6], LYNDE[5], JAMES[4], BENJAMIN[3], BENJAMIN[2], JOHN[1].

Rebecca P.[7], dau. of Gad H.[6] and Martha (Cook) Tower, b. Dec. 27, 1806; mar. Andrew Thomasson.

Childr.

I.	GAD TOWER[8] born	IV.	THEODORE TOWER[8] born
II.	ANDREW[8] "	V.–IX.	Five other sons.
III.	EDWIN[8] "		

755. Baker. **Eighth Generation.** **Tower.**

345. ANGELINE W.[7], GAD H.[6], LYNDE[5], JAMES[4], BENJAMIN[3], BENJAMIN[2], JOHN[1].

Angeline W.[7], dau. of Gad H.[6] and Martha (Cook) Tower, b. June 27, 1808; mar. Lewis Baker

May 10, 1860.   He was b.
1794.
Lewis Baker died May 10, 1875, ag. 81.

756.   **Eighth Generation.**   **Tower.**

345. EDWIN W.[7], GAD H.[6], LYNDE[5], JAMES[4], BENJAMIN[3], BEN-
JAMIN[2], JOHN[1].
Edwin W.[7] son of Gad H.[6] and Martha (Cook) Tower, b.
Feb. 3, 1810; mar. Mary A. Deering,
Dec. 25, 1839. She was b. in Morganstown, West Virginia,
May 14, 1814, and was dau. of George S. and Ann L.
(McNeely) Deering.

Childr. born in Morganstown.

1257.	I.	ROSALIE[8]	born Oct. 28, 1840.
1258.	II.	MARY M.[8]	" May 8, 1842.
1259.	III.	CAROLINE J.[8]	" March 30, 1844.
	IV.	EMMA E.[8]	" ; mar. Frank R. Layng, Sept. 16, 1869.
	V.	VIRGIL D.[8]	" , died Aug. 1, 1851.
1260.	VI.	ANNA L.[8]	" Dec. 11, 1850.
	VII.	EDWIN W.[8]	" ; died Feb. 19, 1869.
1261.	VIII.	HARRY G.[8]	" July 5, 1856.
	IX.	JESSE ELLICUTT[8]	" ; unmar.

Edwin W. Tower [7] died   1869, ag. 59.

757.   **Eighth Generation.**   **Tower.**

345. EDWARD C.[7], GAD H.[6], LYNDE[5], JAMES[4], BENJAMIN[3], BEN-
JAMIN[2], JOHN[1].
Edward C.[7], son of Gad H.[6] and Martha (Cook) Tower, b.
June 1, 1814; mar. Mary H. Haffelfinger, of Covington, Ky.,
Aug. 19, 1855. She was b. in Kingsess, Penn.,
Jan. 1, 1815, and was dau. of John J. and Barbara A.
(Kantze) Haffelfinger.

Child born in Covington, Ky.

I. VIRGIL GORHAM [8] born Oct. 30, 1857; unmar.

Edward C. Tower died in Cincinnati, Ohio, Jan. 27, 1881,
ag. 66 y. 7 m. 26 d.

758. Morgan.   Eighth Generation.   **Tower.**

345. MARTHA [7], GAD H.[6], LYNDE[5], JAMES[4], BENJAMIN[3], BENJA-
MIN[2], JOHN[1].
Martha[7], dau. of Gad H.[6] and Martha (Cook) Tower, b.
`   ; mar.   Morgan.

Childr.

I. VIRGIL TOWER [8] born   IV. AGGIE [8].
II. EDWARD [8].   V.-VII. Three others.
III. FRANK [8].

Martha (Tower) Morgan died   1877 ?

759.   Eighth Generation.   Tower.

345. GAD H.[7], GAD H.[6], LYNDE[5], JAMES[4], BENJAMIN [3], BENJAMIN[2],
JOHN [1].
Gad H.[7], son of Gad H.[6] and Martha (Cook) Tower, b.
April 14, 1820 ; mar. Rebecca H. Smith,
April 19, 1849. She was b. in Union, Penn.,
Oct. 26, 1824, and was dau. of James and Martha (Wallace)
Smith.

Childr. born in Elizabeth, Penn., except the last.

1262. I. ADA MAY [8]   born
     II. CHARLES THEODORE [8] " April 10, 1853; died April 1, 1863, ag.
                                   9 y. 11 m. 21 d.
     III. JAMES SUMNER [8]   " Feb. 27, 1857 ; died Feb. 19, 1859, ag.
                                   1 y. 11 m. 20 d.
     IV. WILLIAM EDWARD [8]   " Sept. 9, 1860; unmar.
     V. HARRIE WEDDLE [8]   " March 30, 1863; "
     VI. BIRDIE [8]   " May 25, 1866, in Pittsburg, Penn.; died
                                   June 22, 1868, ag. 2 y. 28 d.

760. Harrison.   Eighth Generation.   Tower.

345. ORELLA [7], GAD H.[6], LYNDE [5], JAMES [4], BENJAMIN [3], BENJAMIN [2],
JOHN [1].
Orella [7], dau. of Gad H.[6] and Martha (Cook) Tower, b.
     ; mar. Joseph Harrison,
          1867. He was b. in Berkley Co., Md.,
               , and was son of James and   (Kredgel)
Harrison.

Childr. born in Washington Co., Penn.

I. JOSEPH TOWER [8] born   1869.   II. MARY ORELLA [8] born   1873.

761.   Eighth Generation.   Tower.

345. THEODORE S.[7], GAD H.[6], LYNDE [5], JAMES [4], BENJAMIN [3], BEN-
JAMIN [2], JOHN [1].
Theodore S.[7], son of Gad H.[6] and Martha (Cook) Tower, b.
     1824 ; mar.

Childr.

I.	ALICE MAY [8]	born July 3, 1856.
II.	ZELOS BAKER [8]	" Feb. , 1860.
III.	MARY LEE [8]	" 1862.
IV.	HARRY McKNIGHT [8] "	1864.
V.	FRANK [8]	" 1866.

Theodore S. Tower died

762.   **Eighth Generation.**   **Tower.**

346. LYNDE [7], JAMES [6], LYNDE [5], JAMES [4], BENJAMIN [3], BENJAMIN [2], JOHN [1].

Lynde [7], son of James [6] and Persis (Averill) Tower, b. April 22, 1824 ; mar. Almeda Fairbrother Jan. 13, 1849. She was b. May 14, 1826, and was dau. of Amos and Maria (Sergeant) Fairbrother.

Childr.

1263. I. JENNIE A. [8] born April 13, 1850, in Westminster, Vt.
       II. FRANK E. [8] " Nov. 22, 1854, "   "   "

763. Smith.   Eighth Generation.   Tower.

346. BETSEY A. [7], JAMES [6], LYNDE [5], JAMES [4], BENJAMIN [3], BENJA-MIN [2], JOHN [1].

Betsey A. [7], dau. of James [6] and Persis (Averill) Tower, b. Feb. 18, 1827 ; mar. Joseph Smith Dec. 24, 1849. He was b. 1823.

Child.

    I. JAMES OTIS [8] born Oct. 15, 1850.

Betsey A. (Tower) Smith died in Westminster, Vt., March 28, 1875, ag. 48 y. 1 m. 7 d.

764. Wiley.   Eighth Generation.   Tower.

346. ANGELINE P. [7], JAMES [6], LYNDE [5], JAMES [4], BENJAMIN [3], BEN-JAMIN [2], JOHN [1].

Angeline P. [7], dau. of James [6] and Persis (Averill) Tower, b. Nov. 25, 1828 ; mar. Frederick Wiley, of Rockingham, Vt., Nov. 1, 1847. He was b. 1822, and was son of John and Mary (Barry) Wiley.

Child.

    I. MARY ELLEN [8] born Nov. 10, 1848, in Rockingham.

Angeline P. (Tower) Wiley died in Rockingham, Oct. 17, 1861, ag. 32 y. 10 m. 22 d.

765. Wiley. **Eighth Generation.** **Tower.**

346. CYNTHIA H.[7], JAMES[6], LYNDE[5], JAMES[4], BENJAMIN[3], BEN-
JAMIN[2], JOHN[1].

Cynthia H.[7], dau. of James[6] and Persis (Averill) Tower, b.
Nov. 21, 1832; mar. George Wiley, of Rockingham, Vt.,
Feb. 19, 1854. He was b.
April 3, 1828, and was son of John and Mary (Barry) Wiley.

Childr. born in Rockingham.

I. OSCAR G.[8] born Nov. 24, 1856.
II. WALTER P.[8] " Sept. 26, 1858.
III. JAMES O.[8] " Oct. 20, 1862.
IV. ANGELINE P.[8] " Dec. 21, 1864.

766. **Eighth Generation.** **Tower.**

349. BENJAMIN[7], BENJAMIN T.[6], BENJAMIN[5], JAMES[4], BENJAMIN[3],
BENJAMIN[2], JOHN[1].

Benjamin[7], son of Benjamin T.[6] and Chloe (Bates) Tower, b.
156. July 17, 1799; mar. Lucy Tower[6], of Westminster, Vt.,
March 24, 1822. She was b. in Westminster
1803, and was dau. of Lynde[5] and Lucy (Gary)
Tower.

Childr.

I. BETSEY FILETTA[8] born Jan. 28, 1829; mar. F. Ballou, of Springfield, Mass.
II. MARY ELLEN[8] " ;
1264. III. JAMES SARDELL[8] " Jan. 8, 1833.

Benjamin Tower[7] died in Westmoreland, N. H., 1869?
Lucy[6] (Tower) Tower died in Westminster, Vt. Aug. 25,
1872, ag. 69.

767. **Eighth Generation.** **Tower.**

349. WASHINGTON[7], BENJAMIN T.[6], BENJAMIN[5], JAMES[4], BENJA-
MIN[3], BENJAMIN[2], JOHN[1].

Washington[7], son of Benjamin T.[6] and Chloe (Bates)
Tower, b.
Aug. 11, 1801; mar. Marcia Chaffee
Oct. 27, 1824. She was b.
Jan. 11, 1804, and was dau. of John and Sally (Evans)
Chaffee.

Childr.

1265. I. JOHN T.[8] born Nov. 24, 1825.
II. AUGUSTA[8] " Feb. 24, 1827, died in infancy.
1266. III. BENJAMIN F.[8] " April 5, 1828.

1267.	IV.	JANE [8]	born June 6, 1830.
1268.	V.	LYMAN C.[8]	" May 19, 1832.
	VI.	GEORGE [8]	" April 3, 1837; died Oct. 3, 1839, ag. 2 y.6 m.
1269.	VII.	ELLEN [8]	" April 24, 1839.
	VIII.	GEORGE [8]	" April 27, 1841; unmar.

Washington Tower [7] died in Rochester, Vt., March 20, 1869, ag. 67 y. 7 m. 9 d.

768.   'Eighth Generation.   **Tower.**

349. AMASA [7], BENJAMIN T.[6], BENJAMIN [5], JAMES [4], BENJAMIN [3], BENJAMIN [2], JOHN [1].

Amasa [7], son of Benjamin T.[6] and Chloe (Bates) Tower, b. 1804; mar. Lucy Warrington, of Westminster, Vt.

Childr.

1270.	I. MARY [8] born 1848.	1271. III. RHODA [8] born 1857.
	II. WILLARD [8] " 1853.	

Amasa Tower [7] died April 18, 1870, ag. 66.

769.   **Eighth Generation.**   **Tower.**

349. GARDNER [7], BENJAMIN T.[6], BENJAMIN [5], JAMES [4], BENJAMIN [3], BENJAMIN [2], JOHN [1].

Gardner [7], son of Benjamin T.[6] and Chloe (Bates) Tower, b. Jan. 26, 1811; mar. Mary A. Darling, of Westminster, Vt., Sept. 14, 1835. She was b.
Aug. 28, 1815, and was dau. of Joel and Lucy (Reed) Darling.

Childr.

1272.	I.	JOEL M.[8]	born June 8, 1836.
	II.	JULIA ANN [8]	" Sept. 18, 1837; died Dec. 12, 1840, ag. 3 y. 2 m. 24 d.
1273.	III.	JULIUS[8]	" June 16, 1839.
	IV.	LUCY C.[8]	" Dec. 24, 1841; died March 14, 1848, ag. 6 y. 2 m. 21 d.
1274.	V.	GEORGE RILEY [8]	" Jan. 8, 1844.
1275.	VI.	MARY ELLEN[8]	" Nov. 8, 1846.
	VII.	LOUISA A.[8]	" July 6, 1850; died Sept. 23, 1851, ag. 1 y. 2 m. 17 d.
	VIII.	EDWARD GARDNER [8]	" Jan. 17, 1853; unmar.
	IX.	CHARLES HENRY [8]	" March 6, 1857; "

770. Emerson.   Eighth Generation.   Tower.

353. LUCY [7], EPHRAIM D.[6], BENJAMIN [5], JAMES [4], BENJAMIN [3], BENJAMIN [2], JOHN [1].

Lucy [7], dau. of Ephraim D.[6] and Betsey (Emery) Tower, b. March   , 1812; mar. Reuben Emerson in Bangor, N. Y., July   , 1832.

Childr. born in Rochester, N. Y.

I. DORCAS [8]   born July 4, 1833.
II. FRANCIS [8]   "
III. MORTIMER [8]   "   ; died at the age of two years.
IV. CATHERINE E. [8]   "   Dec. 20, 1837.
V. CHARLES [8]   "   1849; unmar.

Reuben Emerson died in Werner, Wis., June 5, 1877.
Lucy (Tower) Emerson died in Werner, Feb. 22, 1875, ag.
62 y. 11 m.

771.   **Eighth Generation.**   **Tower.**

353. LYNDE [7], EPHRAIM D. [6], BENJAMIN [5], JAMES [4], BENJAMIN [3],
BENJAMIN [2], JOHN [1].

Lynde [7], son of Ephraim D. [6] and Betsey (Emery) Tower, b.
May 14, 1820; mar. Cynthia M. Blood
March 3, 1844. She was b. in Northfield, Vt.,
Feb. 27, 1819, and was dau. of Joel and Polly (Cummings)
Blood.

Childr.

1276.   I. LIZZIE [8] born April 6, 1847.
1277.   II. LUCY [8]   "   Feb. 27, 1849.
    III. HEBER [8]   "   March 6, 1851; died Oct. 19, 1852, ag. 1 y. 7 m. 13 d.
    IV. ALICE [8]   "   Dec. 29, 1852;   "   April 10, 1863, ag. 10 y. 3 m.
                                      12 d.

Lynde Tower [7] died Aug. 1, 1877, ag. 57 y. 2 m. 18 d.
Cynthia (Blood) Tower died June 12, 1858, ag. 39 y. 3 m.
13 d.

772.   **Eighth Generation.**   **Tower.**

354. AMBROSE [7], JACOB [6], BENJAMIN [5], JAMES [4], BENJAMIN [3], BENJA-
MIN [2], JOHN [1].

Ambrose [7], son of Jacob [6] and Lucia (Prentiss) Tower, b.
Dec. 17, 1825; mar. Caroline C. Lyon, of Chicopee, Mass.,
Sept. 26, 1850. She was b.
               1824, and was dau. of Stephen and Patience Lyon.

Child born in Westville, N. Y.

I. LUCIA B. [8] born March 31, 1855; died March 27, 1870, ag. 14 y. 11 m. 27 d.

Caroline C. (Lyon) Tower died Jan. 3, 1859, ag. 35.
Ambrose Tower [7] mar., 2d, Elizabeth Conner, of Hopkinton,
N. Y.,
July 27, 1862. She was b.
May 5, 1832, and was dau. of John and Margaret (Stone)
Conner.

Childr. born in Dickinson, N. Y.

II. CARRIE C.[8] born June 10, 1863.
III. SARAH E.[8] "   April 18, 1865.
IV. HORACE J.[8] "   Sept. 23, 1869.

773.   **Eighth Generation.**   **Tower.**

354. WARREN J.[7], JACOB[6], BENJAMIN[5], JAMES[4], BENJAMIN[3], BEN-
JAMIN[2], JOHN[1].

Warren J.[7], son of Jacob[6] and Sevona (Kingsbury) Tower, b.
Feb. 4, 1829; mar. Elizabeth H. Freeman, of Westville,
N. Y.,
Dec. 28, 1854. She was b. in Westville
July 30, 1834, and was dau. of David and Lovina (Water-
man) Freeman.

Childr.

1278. I.   IDA E.[8]   born Oct. 20, 1855.
II.   VINA M.[8]   "   July 17, 1859.
III. EMMA S.[8]   "   March 23, 1862.
IV.   BERTHA M.[8] "   Oct. 4, 1868.

774. Young.   **Eighth Generation.**   **Tower.**

354. ROXANA[7], JACOB[6], BENJAMIN[5], JAMES[4], BENJAMIN[3], BENJA-
MIN[2], JOHN[1].

Roxana[7], dau. of Jacob[6] and Sevona (Kingsbury) Tower, b.
Sept. 15, 1831; mar. Lyndon Young, of Dickinson, N. Y.,
Sept. 9, 1855. He was b. in Westville, N. Y.,
Aug. 12, 1834, and was son of Hiram and Emily (King)
Young.

Childr.

I.   WARREN P.[8]   born May   4, 1857.
II.   EUGENE C.[8]   "   May 26, 1859.
III. EDSON TOWER[8]   "   Dec. 28, 1861.
IV.   LYNDON[8] } Twins "   Oct. 27, 1864.
V.   LILLIAN[8] }
VI.   HIRAM J.[8]   "   Aug. 12, 1866.
VII. NEWTON H.[8]   "   Dec. 18, 1867.
VIII. MARTIN R.[8]   "   Sept. 10, 1872.

775.   **Eighth Generation.**   **Tower.**

354. RANSOM J.[7], JACOB[6], BENJAMIN[5], JAMES[4], BENJAMIN[3], BEN-
JAMIN[2], JOHN[1].

Ransom J.[7], son of Jacob[6] and Sevona (Kingsbury) Tower, b.
March 31, 1833; mar. Amelia Young

Nov. 4, 1862. She was b. in Constable, N. Y., Oct. 19, 1843, and was dau. of Hiram and Emily (King) Young.

Childr.

I. WALLACE [8] born Aug. 12, 1863; died May 19, 1864.
II. WALLACE G. [8] " April 30, 1865.
III. EMILY [8] " Oct. 4, 1866.

Ransom J. Tower [7] died in West Constable, Dec. 6, 1872, ag. 39 y. 8 m. 6 d.

776. **Eighth Generation.** **Tower.**

354. ALBERT [7], JACOB [6], BENJAMIN [5], JAMES [4], BENJAMIN [3], BENJA-MIN [2], JOHN [1].

Albert [7], son of Jacob [6] and Sevona (Kingsbury) Tower, b. Aug. 29, 1835; mar. Lucy Freeman, of Westville, N. Y., Oct. 23, 1858. She was b. in Westville Aug. 1, 1833, and was dau. of David and Lovina (Waterman) Freeman.

Childr. born in Westville.

I. CHARLIE [8] born July 20, 1859; died March 29, 1870, ag. 10 y. 8 m. 9 d.
II. EDITH [8] born Oct. 12, 1863.
III. ELLA [8] " April 20, 1865.
IV. MARY [8] born April 9, 1869.
V. LAURA [8] " March 13, 1872.
VI. HERBERT [8] " Feb. 26, 1874.
VII. ALBERT [8] " Feb. 5, 1876.

Lucy (Freeman) Tower died in Westville, March 25, 1880, ag. 46 y. 7 m. 24 d.
Albert Tower [7] mar., 2d, widow Ellen Lovett, of Fort Covington, N. Y., Aug. 20, 1882. She was b. in Fort Covington April 3, 1833, and was dau. of John and Nancy (McCabe) Foster.

777. **Eighth Generation.** **Tower.**

354. ALMON N. [7], JACOB [6], BENJAMIN [5], JAMES [4], BENJAMIN [3], BENJA-MIN [2], JOHN [1].

Almon N. [7], son of Jacob [6] and Sevona (Kingsbury) Tower, b. Aug. 14, 1842; mar. Emma Haskell, of Dickinson, N. Y., Jan. 2, 1867. She was b. 1846, and was dau. of James and Esther (Moffit) Haskell.

Childr.

I. MAMIE E. [8] born Oct. 9, 1871; died Sept. 18, 1872.
II. ARCHIE R. [8] " Aug. 19, 1874.
III. MAMIE E. [8] " July 28, 1877.
IV. HERMON J. [8] " March 20, 1882

778. Gleason.   Eighth Generation.   Tower.

354. ADELINE P.[7], JACOB[6], BENJAMIN[5], JAMES[4], BENJAMIN[3], BEN-
JAMIN[2], JOHN[1].

Adeline P.[7], dau. of Jacob[6] and Sevona (Kingsbury) Tower, b.
April 11, 1845 ; mar. Samuel W. Gleason, of Westville, N. Y.,
Nov. 10, 1872. He was b. in Norwich, Vt.,
Jan. 4, 1826, and was son of Sewall and Hannah (Bissell)
Gleason.

Childr.

I.   EDWIN W.[8]   born Aug. 2, 1874; died May 9, 1880.
II.   ADA AUGUSTA[8]   "   May 29, 1876.
III. NINA CATHERINE[8]   "   May 25, 1880.

779.   Eighth Generation.   Tower.

354. EDWIN R.[7], JACOB[6], BENJAMIN[5], JAMES[4], BENJAMIN[3], BENJA-
MIN[2], JOHN[1].

Edwin R.[7], son of Jacob[6] and Sevona (Kingsbury) Tower, b.
April 5, 1848; mar. Nettie Willis, of West Parishville, N. Y.,
Nov. 5, 1873. She was b. in Parishville
Oct. 11, 1851, and was dau. of Samuel and Mary (Gould)
Willis.

Childr.

I.   RANSOM WRIGHT[8] born Feb. 14, 1876.
II.   WEST WARREN[8]   "   Dec. 24, 1877.

780. Hood, Martin   Eighth Generation.   Tower.

357. ABBY J.[7], HORACE S.[6], SOLOMON[5], JAMES[4], BENJAMIN[3], BEN-
JAMIN[2], JOHN[1].

Abby J.[7], dau. of Horace S.[6] and Malinda (Hammond)
Tower, b.
      1839 ; mar. James Hood
June 3, 1855. He was b.
      1829, and was son of Charles and Mary Hood.

Childr. born in New Bedford, Mass.

I.   WARREN H.[8]   born
II.   ABBY FRANCES[8]   "   ; died

James Hood died
Abby J. (Tower) Hood mar., 2d, Thomas Martin
Dec. 30, 1874. He was born in England
      1834, and was son of William and Frances Martin.

Child.

III. GWENDOLINE MARTINA[8] born Nov. 29, 1877.

781.   Eighth Generation.   Tower.

357. LEWIS F.[7], HORACE S.[6], SOLOMON[5], JAMES[4], BENJAMIN[3], BEN-
JAMIN[2], JOHN[1].

Lewis F.[7], son of Horace S.[6] and Malinda (Hammond)
Tower, b.

Nov. 2, 1842 ; mar. Ella Kelsey.

Childr.

I. LILLA[8].   II. JESSIE[8].

Lewis F. Tower[7] died in Sterling, Ill., Aug. 14, 1877, ag.
34 y. 9 m. 12 d.

782. Waterman.   Eighth Generation.   Tower.

357. MALINDA F.[7], HORACE S.[6], SOLOMON[5], JAMES[4], BENJAMIN[3],
BENJAMIN[2], JOHN[1].

Malinda F.[7], dau. of Horace S.[6] and Malinda (Hammond)
Tower, b.

May 10, 1849 ; mar. Dexter Franklin Waterman,
April 30, 1873. He was b. in Bucksport, Me.,
1849, and was son of Luther and Eliza Waterman.

Child born in New Bedford, Mass.

I. LUCY E.[8] born Feb. 6, 1874.

783.   Eighth Generation.   Tower.

359. JAMES A.[7], JOHN S.[6], SOLOMON[5], JAMES[4], BENJAMIN[3],
BENJAMIN[2], JOHN[1].

James A.[7], son of John S.[6] and Jane[6] (Tower) Tower, b.
1838 ; mar. Eliza E. Arnold, of Abington, Mass.,
Oct. 22, 1857. She was b.
1841, and was dau. of Jonathan and Mary W.
Arnold.

Childr.

I.	MARY JANE[8]	born Sept. 16, 1858.
II.	FRANK ELLIOT[8]	" April 19, 1862.
III.	LILLIE M.[8]	" Feb. , 1866.
IV.	JAMES L.[8]	" Feb. 25, 1870; died April 3, 1871, ag. 1 y. 1 m. 6 d.
V.	HATTIE PRESCOTT[8]	" March 7, 1873; died Aug. 23, 1873.
VI.	CHESTER ADELBERT[8]	" Oct. 2, 1874.

28

784.   Eighth Generation.   Tower.

363. HORACE S.[7], JOHN [6], DAVID [5], JAMES [4], BENJAMIN [3], BENJA-
      MIN [2], JOHN [1].

      Horace S.[7], son of John [6] and Nancy (Sylvester) Tower, b.
      May 11, 1847 ; mar. Helen A. Barker, of Hanover, Mass.,
      Feb. 10, 1870. She was b. in Hanover
                  1852, and was dau. of Lot P. and Deborah (Damon)
      Barker.
                    Childr. born in Hanover.

      I.   CHESTER MORTON [8] born
      II. EDGAR [8]   "   June 19, 1874; died Oct. 8, 1874.

785.   Eighth Generation.   Tower.

366. LUTHER W.[7], EZRA [6], JONATHAN [5], JONATHAN [4], BENJAMIN [3],
      BENJAMIN [2], JOHN [1].

      Luther W.[7], son of Ezra [6] and Sally (Fuller) Tower, b.
      Dec. 23, 1813 ; mar. Elizabeth C. Bruce, of Wallingford,Vt.,
      Dec. 16, 1841. She was b. in Wallingford
      March 16, 1822, and was dau. of Ransom and Filena (Jewell)
      Bruce.
                    Child born in Wallingford.

      I. EUGENE IMLEY [8] born Sept. 29, 1842; died April 2, 1862, ag. 19 y. 6 m. 3 d.

      Luther W. Tower [7] died in Wallingford, Aug. 26, 1878, ag.
      64 y. 8 m. 3 d.

786. Johnson.   Eighth Generation.   Tower.

366. BELINDA B. B.[7], EZRA [6], JONATHAN [5], JONATHAN [4], BENJAMIN [3],
      BENJAMIN [2], JOHN [1].

      Belinda B. B.[7], dau. of Ezra [6] and Sally (Fuller) Tower, b.
      May 16, 1816 ; mar. Nehemiah Johnson, of Wallingford, Vt.

                    Childr. none.

      She died in Wallingford, Jan. 13, 1864, ag. 47 y. 7 m. 28 d.

787. Warner.   Eighth Generation.   Tower.

366. JERUSHA E. E.[7], EZRA [6], JONATHAN [5], JONATHAN [4], BENJAMIN [3],
      BENJAMIN [2], JOHN [1].

      Jerusha E. E.[7], dau. of Ezra [6] and Sally (Fuller) Tower, b.
      July 8, 1821 ; mar. Anson Warner, of Brandon, Vt.,
      Jan. 1, 1843. He was b. in Wallingford, Vt.,
      Nov. 3, 1821, and was son of Oliver and Hannah (Maxham)
      Warner.

Childr. born in Wallingford, Vt.

I.	FITCH MERTON [8]	born Sept 19, 1843.
II.	CATHERINE TOWER [8]	" July 16, 1845.
III	PITT MELEOSE [8]	" Jan. 10, 1850.
IV.	MOTT DEVOS [8]	" May 17, 1853.

788 Packard. Eighth Generation. Tower.

366. EMILY H. [7], EZRA [6], JONATHAN [5], JONATHAN [4], BENJAMIN [3], BENJAMIN [2], JOHN [1].

Emily H. [7], dau. of Ezra [6] and Sally (Fuller) Tower, b. Dec. 11, 1825; mar. David Packard, of Wallingford, Vt., Jan. 22, 1849. He was b. in Londonderry, Vt., April 25, 1825.

Childr. none.

789. Johnson. Eighth Generation. Tower.

368. ALMIRA [7], JOSHUA [6], JONATHAN [5], JONATHAN [4], BENJAMIN [3], BENJAMIN [2], JOHN [1].

Almira [7], dau. of Joshua [6] and Eliza (Crouch) Tower, b. Nov. 13, 1805; mar. Samuel Jones Johnson.

Childr.

I.	HENRY [8]	born	
II.	SUSAN [8]	"	; mar. Frank Metcalf.
III.	FREDDIE [8]	"	
IV.	MIRA [8]	"	
V.	NATHAN [8]	"	; died
VI.	SAMUEL JONES [8]	"	

Almira (Tower) Johnson died in Cambridge, Mass., 1848, ag. 43.

790. Eighth Generation. Tower.

368. JOSHUA H. [7], JOSHUA [6], JONATHAN [5], JONATHAN [4], BENJAMIN [3], BENJAMIN [2], JOHN [1].

Joshua H. [7], son of Joshua [6] and Elizabeth (Woodcock) Tower, b. Jan. 31, 1828; mar. Philena Maria Knowlton, of Hopkinton, Mass., June 17, 1850. She was b. Nov. 25, 1831, and was dau. of Marshal and Mary Ann (Holmes) Knowlton.

Childr. none.

Joshua H. Tower [7] died in Savannah, Ga., Oct. 10, 1864, ag. 36 y. 8 m. 10 d.

Philena M. (Knowlton) Tower mar., 2d, Roswell Nichols, of
Holliston, Mass.,
March 13, 1870. He was born in Franklin, Mass.,
          1842, and was son of Job and Betsey (Temple)
Nichols.

791.   **Eighth Generation.**   **Tower.**

368. SAMUEL W.[7], JOSHUA [6], JONATHAN [5], JONATHAN [4], BENJAMIN [3],
BENJAMIN [2], JOHN [1].
Samuel W.[7], son of Joshua [6] and Elizabeth (Woodcock)
Tower, b.
Oct. 29, 1829; mar. Anna Louisa Claflin, of Medway, Mass.,
April 3, 1872. She was b. in Medway
Dec. 29, 1837, and was dau. of William and Susan (Fairbanks) Claflin.

Childr.

   I. EUNICE ALMA [8]   born March 16, 1873.
  II. EDITH B. CLAFLIN [8]   "   March 27, 1875.
 III. HOLLIS ALTON [8]   "   June 20, 1879.

Samuel W. Tower [7] died in Charlton, Mass., Aug. 25, 1885,
ag. 55 y. 9 m. 27 d.

792. Stevens.   **Eighth Generation.**   **Tower.**

368. SARAH P.[7], JOSHUA [6], JONATHAN [5], JONATHAN [4], BENJAMIN [3],
BENJAMIN [2], JOHN [1].
Sarah P.[7], dau. of Joshua [6] and Elizabeth(Woodcock)Tower, b.
May 17, 1832; mar. Albert Stevens, of Milford, Mass.,
Sept. 13, 1854. He was b. in Claremont, N. H.,
March 3, 1824, and was son of Charles and Friendly(Thomas)
Stevens.

Childr. born in Holliston, Mass.

   I. ELLEN MARTHA [8] born Jan. 4, 1856.
  II. PARAN ALBERT [8]   "   Feb. 15, 1858.
 III. WARREN HARVEY [8] "   Dec. 6, 1859.

793. Barney.   **Eighth Generation.**   **Tower.**

368. CAROLINE E.[7], JOSHUA [6], JONATHAN [5], JONATHAN [4], BENJAMIN [3],
BENJAMIN [2], JOHN [1].
Caroline E.[7], dau. of Joshua [6] and Elizabeth (Woodcock)
Tower, b.
March 16, 1835; mar. Homer John Barney, of Milford, Mass.,
May 11, 1853. He was b. in Williston, Vt.,
        1831, and was son of Benjamin F. Barney.

Childr.

I. THOMAS CHITTENDEN [8] born May 16, 1854, in Medway, Mass.
II. WILLIAM PITT [8] " Dec. 9, 1855, " Upton, "

Caroline E. (Tower) Barney died in Holliston, Mass., March
5, 1864, ag. 28 y. 11 m. 20 d.

794.   Eighth Generation.   Tower.

368. WILBER I.[7], JOSHUA [6], JONATHAN [5], JONATHAN [4], BENJAMIN [3],
BENJAMIN [2], JOHN [1].
Wilber I.[7], son of Joshua [6] and Elizabeth(Woodcock)Tower, b.
Feb. 24, 1839; mar. Mariana Abigail Emerson, of Uxbridge,
Mass.,
March 9, 1863. She was b. in Grafton, Mass.,
June 26, 1833, and was dau. of Willard C. and E. H. (Childs)
Emerson.

Child born in Holliston, Mass.

I. GEORGE WALTER [8] born Nov. 26, 1863.

795.   Eighth Generation.   Tower.

370. SANFORD M.[7], JONATHAN H.[6], JONATHAN [5], JONATHAN [4], BEN-
JAMIN [3], BENJAMIN [2], JOHN [1].
Sanford M.[7], son of Jonathan H.[6] and Hannah(Ross)Tower, b.
Sept. 1, 1809; mar. Jane Robinson Crane
Sept. 1, 1832. She was b.
March 13, 1814, and was dau. of Moses and Sarah Crane.

Childr.

1279.	I.	EMMA VIRGINIA [8]	born Oct. 24, 1833, in Bloomfield, N. Y.
1280.	II.	OSCAR MERTON [8]	" Nov. 1, 1835, " " "
	III.	ROBERT HOLLIS [8]	" June 25, 1839, " Newark, N. J.; unmar.
	IV.	GEORGE WASHINGTON [8] "	Sept. 29, 1841, " in New York; died in Bloomfield, Jan. 31, 1844, ag. 2 y. 4 m. 2 d.
1281.	V.	SARAH ADELINE [8]	" Oct. 4, 1843, in New York.
	VI.	GEORGE WINFIELD [8]	" Nov. 6, 1845, " " ; died in Harlem, N. Y., Aug. 26, 1864, ag. 18 y. 9 m. 19 d.
1282.	VII.	PHEBE ARAMINTHA [8]	" April 8, 1848, in New York.
	VIII.	CHARLES FREDERICK [8] "	July 4, 1850, " "
	IX.	ESTELLA C.[8]	" March 20, 1855, " " ; died in Harlem, Oct. 17, 1873, ag. 18 y. 6 m. 28 d.

796. Redgate.   Eighth Generation.   Tower.

370. HARRIET H.[7], JONATHAN H.[6], JONATHAN[5], JONATHAN[4], BENJAMIN[3], BENJAMIN[2], JOHN[1].
Harriet H.[7], dau. of Jonathan H.[6] and Hannah(Ross)Tower, b. Oct. 19, 1811 ; mar. William Redgate May 16, 1828.

Childr.

I.   FRANCES[8] born   ; mar. Bennet   ; three children.
   Five other children.

Harriet H. (Tower) Redgate died in Canarsie, N. Y., July , 1881, ag. 70.

797.   Eighth Generation.   Tower.

370. JAMES L.[7], JONATHAN H.[6] JONATHAN[5], JONATHAN[4], BENJAMIN[3], BENJAMIN[2], JOHN[1].
James L.[7], son of Jonathan H.[6] and Hannah (Ross) Tower, b. June 4, 1817 ; mar. Joanna Crane June , 1853.

Childr.

I.   ALFRED[8] born   II.   Daughter[8] born   ; mar. William B. Oakley.

798. Dugan.   Eighth Generation.   Tower.

370. LUCY A.[7], JONATHAN H.[6], JONATHAN[5], JONATHAN[4], BENJAMIN[3], BENJAMIN[2], JOHN[1].
Lucy A.[7], dau. of Jonathan H.[6] and Hannah (Ross) Tower, b. April 8, 1819 ; mar. Francis Dugan May 20, 1840.

Childr. three.

Francis Dugan died Aug. , 1849.
Lucy Ann (Tower) Dugan died Jan. 8, 1853, ag. 33 y. 9 m.

799.   Eighth Generation.   Tower.

370. WILLIAM W.[7], JONATHAN H.[6], JONATHAN[5], JONATHAN[4], BENJAMIN[3], BENJAMIN[2], JOHN[1].
William W.[7], son of Jonathan H.[6] and Hannah (Ross) Tower, b.
Sept. 10, 1821 ; mar. Matilda F. Minkler Dec. 3, 1845.

Child.

I.   EDWARD B. HALE[8] b.   .

William W. Tower[7] died April 25, 1855, ag. 33 y. 7 m. 15 d.

800. Burnett, Parse. Eighth Generation. Tower.

370. MARY J.[7], JONATHAN H.[6], JONATHAN [5], JONATHAN [4], BENJA-MIN [3], BENJAMIN [2], JOHN [1].

Mary J.[7], dau. of Jonathan H.[6] and Hannah (Ross) Tower, b. March 28, 1824 ; mar. John Parse
Jan. 8, 1843. He was b.
Oct. 9, 1817.

Childr. three.

John Parse died Dec. 28, 1847, ag. 30 y. 2 m. 19 d.
Mary J. (Tower) Parse mar., 2d, James Milton Burnett.

Child one.

801. Lyon. Eighth Generation. Tower.

370. MARIAH L.[7], JONATHAN H.[6], JONATHAN [5], JONATHAN [4], BENJA-MIN [3], BENJAMIN [2], JOHN [1].

Mariah L.[7], dau. of Jonathan H.[6] and Hannah (Ross) Tower, b.
Dec. 4, 1827 ; mar. James Hammond Lyon
May 8, 1848.

Childr.

I. GEORGE [8].   II. MILLARD [8].   III. One other.

802. Gibson. Eighth Generation. Tower.

370. PAMELA L.[7], JONATHAN H.[6], JONATHAN [5], JONATHAN [4], BENJA-MIN [3], BENJAMIN [2], JOHN [1].

Pamela L.[7], dau. of Jonathan H.[6] and Hannah (Ross) Tower, b.
April 19, 1830; mar. William Augustus Gibson
May 3, 1852. He was son of Hugh and Mary (Johnson) Gibson.

Childr.

EDWARD [8].   EUGENE [8].   HENRY M.[8]   Four others.

803. Kopp. Eighth Generation. Tower.

371. HANNAH [7], GRENVILLE [6], JONATHAN [5], JONATHAN [4], BENJAMIN [3], BENJAMIN [2], JOHN [1].

Hannah [7], dau. of Grenville [6] and Mary (Sage) Tower, b.
June 29, 1817 ; mar. John Kopp in Elizabeth, N. J.

Childr. none.

Hannah (Tower) Kopp died April 3, 1842, ag. 24 y. 9 m. 4 d.

804.   **Eighth Generation.**   **Tower.**

371. EZRA [7], GRENVILLE [6], JONATHAN [5], JONATHAN [4], BENJAMIN [3],
    BENJAMIN [2], JOHN [1].
    Ezra [7], son of Grenville [6] and Mary (Sage) Tower, b.
    Jan. 24, 1819 ; mar.   .

Childr.

I.   Daughter [8] born   ; died at the age of 16 years.
II. Son [8]   "   ; mar. One child. Both died.

805.   **Eighth Generation.**   **Tower.**

371. JOB S. [7], GRENVILLE [6], JONATHAN [5], JONATHAN [4], BENJAMIN [3],
    BENJAMIN [2], JOHN [1].
    Job S. [7], son of Grenville [6] and Mary (Sage) Tower, b.
    Jan. 9, 1821 ; mar. Mary Crane, of Newark, N. J.,
    Oct. 1, 1845. She was b. in Newark.

Childr. born in Elizabeth, N. J.

1283.   I.   MARY ALICE [8]   born June 14, 1846.
        II. EMMA R. [8]   "   April 18, 1851; died July 21, 1852, ag.
                                        1 y. 3 m. 2 d.
        III. SPENCER P. [8]   "   Dec. 16, 1853.
        IV. EDWARD SAYRE [8]   "   Nov. , 1860.
        V.   WILLIAM ARTHUR [8]   "   Feb. 14, 1862.

Mary (Crane) Tower died Dec. 20, 1863.
Job S. Tower [7] mar., 2d, widow Elizabeth (Farrar) Elliott,
    of Elizabeth,
Jan. 31, 1867. She was b. in Newark
April 17, 1830, and was dau. of John and Eliza (Fillow)
    Farrar.

Childr. none.

806. Shed.   **Eighth Generation.**   **Tower**

372. MARY P. [7], LUTHER [6], JONATHAN [5], JONATHAN [4], BENJAMIN [3],
    BENJAMIN [2], JOHN [1].
    Mary P. [7], dau. of Luther [6] and Mary (Ware) Tower, b.
    Feb. 17, 1818 ; mar. Edward D. Shed, of Needham, Mass.,
    Nov. 29, 1838.
                        Childr.

I.   HENRY DUNSTER [8] born July 12, 1839; died Sept. 12, 1839.
II.   MARIA TOWER [8]   "   Sept. 21, 1841; " Sept. 23, 1842, ag. 1 y. 2 d.
III. EDWARD FRANCIS [8] "   Aug. 27, 1843.

Mary P. (Tower) Shed died Jan. 14, 1845, ag. 26 y. 10 m. 25 d.

807. Eighth Generation. Tower.

372. LUTHER W.[7], LUTHER [6], JONATHAN [5], JONATHAN [4], BENJAMIN [3], BENJAMIN [2], JOHN [1].

Luther W.[7], son of Luther [6] and Mary (Ware) Tower, b. Sept. 24, 1823; mar. Fanny E. Cobb, of Dedham, Mass., May 4, 1847. She was b. Aug. 13, 1825, and was dau. of Daniel and Mary Cobb.

Childr.

I. HOLLIS [8]   born Feb. 16, 1851, died Oct. 9, 1852, ag. 1 y. 7 m. 21 d.
II. CALVIN L.[8] "   Nov. 18, 1852.

808. Winchester. Eighth Generation. Tower

372. ADELINE R.[7], LUTHER [6], JONATHAN [5], JONATHAN [4], BENJAMIN [3], BENJAMIN [2], JOHN [1].

Adeline R.[7], dau. of Luther [6] and Mary (Ware) Tower, b. Aug. 2, 1831; mar. J. H. Winchester, of Southborough, Mass., May 11, 1873. He was b. in Salem, Mass., 1830, and was son of William D. and Cynthia Winchester.

809. Eighth Generation. Tower.

372. CHARLES E.[7], LUTHER [6], JONATHAN [5], JONATHAN [4], BENJAMIN [3], BENJAMIN [2], JOHN [1].

Charles E.[7], son of Luther [6] and Mary (Ware) Tower, b. March 14, 1839; mar. Margaret Dougherty, of French Village, N. S., Aug. 16, 1865. She was b. in French Village Jan. 1, 1842, and was dau. of John and Mary Dougherty.

Childr. born in Dedham, Mass.

I. CHARLES H. W.[8] born March 1, 1867.
II. WILLIAM F.[8] "   Jan. 18, 1869.
III. MARY ELLEN [8] "   Feb. 8, 1870.
IV. ADELINE R.[8] "   May 4, 1872.
V. FRANCIS [8] "   Aug. 29, 1874.
VI. GEORGE E.[8] "   Nov. 21, 1877.

810. Childs. Eighth Generation. Tower.

373. ELIZABETH [7], RUFUS [6], JONATHAN [5], JONATHAN [4], BENJAMIN [3], BENJAMIN [2], JOHN [1].

Elizabeth [7], dau. of Rufus [6] and Elizabeth (Willis) Tower, b. , 1828; mar. James A. Childs, of Framingham, Mass., Sept. 9, 1856. He was b. 1827, and was son of Windsor and Roxana Childs.

373.　FRANK [7], RUFUS [6], JONATHAN [5], JONATHAN [4], BENJAMIN [3], BENJAMIN [2], JOHN [1].

Frank [7], son of Rufus [6] and Elizabeth (Willis) Tower, b. Jan. 25, 1834; mar. Ann Shaw, of Framingham, Mass. Int. pub.

Sept. 28, 1855.

Childr.

I.　FRANK RANDALL [8]　　born Aug. 5, 1857, in Framingham.
II.　HARRIET ELIZABETH [8]　　" 　July 9, 1859, in 　" 　; mar. George Osborn, of Waltham.
III.　CHARLES H. [8]　　" 　Nov. 9, 1860, in Waltham.

Frank Tower [7] died in Waltham, Jan. 1, 1877, ag. 42 y. 11 m. 7 d.

373.　JOHN H. [7], RUFUS [6], JONATHAN [5], JONATHAN [4], BENJAMIN [3], BENJAMIN [2], JOHN [1].

John H. [7], son of Rufus [6] and Elizabeth (Willis) Tower, b. ; mar. Mary E. Lewis, of Windham, Me. Int. pub.

June 20, 1847.

Child.

I.　FRANK WEBSTER [8] born May 31, 1852, in Stoneham, Mass.

373.　FREEMAN G. [7], RUFUS [6], JONATHAN [5], JONATHAN [4], BENJAMIN [3], BENJAMIN [2], JOHN [1].

Freeman G. [7], son of Rufus [6] and Elizabeth (Willis) Tower, b. 1840; mar. Elizabeth Faulkner, of Framingham, Mass.,

Nov. 13, 1865.　She was b. in Scotland 1838.

Child.

GEORGE H. [8] born Nov. 24, 1870.

375.　AMANDA [7], NATHANIEL [6], NATHANIEL [5], NATHANIEL [4], THOMAS [3], BENJAMIN [2], JOHN [1].

Amanda [7], dau. of Nathaniel [6] and Hannah (Reed) Tower, b. July 25, 1800; mar. Arunah Bartlett, of Cummington, Mass., Feb. , 1825.　He was b. in Cummington March 30, 1797, and was son of Edward and Polly Bartlett.

Childr. none.

815. Hutchins.   Eighth Generation.   Tower.

375. AMELIA [7], NATHANIEL [6], NATHANIEL [5], NATHANIEL [4], THOMAS [3], BENJAMIN [2], JOHN [1].

Amelia [7], dau. of Nathaniel [6] and Hannah (Reed) Tower, b. July 28, 1804; mar. Allen Hutchins.

Childr. none.

Amelia [7] (Tower) Hutchins died May 23, 1838, ag. 33 y. 9 m. 26 d.

816.   Eighth Generation.   Tower.

375. ALDEN [7], NATHANIEL [6], NATHANIEL [5], NATHANIEL [4], THOMAS [3], BENJAMIN [2], JOHN [1].

Alden [7], son of Nathaniel [6] and Hannah (Reed) Tower, b. March 2, 1808; mar. Laura Everett, of Cummington, Mass., Dec. 15, 1832. She was b.

1810, and was dau. of James Everett.

Childr. born in Cummington.

1284. I.   SARAH AMELIA [8] born June 15, 1835.
       II. EUGENE ALDEN [8] "   June 25, 1838; died April 4, 1839.
1285. III. AMANDA [8]   "   Sept. 6, 1840.

Laura (Everett) Tower died in Cummington, Sept. 16, 1849, ag. 39.

Alden Tower [7] mar., 2d, widow Mary (Trow) Pierce, of Cummington,

Jan. 2, 1856. She was b. in Cummington

Jan. 4, 1828, and was dau. of James and Sarah (Mason) Trow.

Childr.

       IV. EVA LILLIAN [8]   born Jan. 10, 1857.
1286. V.   NELLY ALMA [8]   "   Jan. 10, 1858.
       VI. ALDEN EUGENE [8]   "   Feb. 28, 1859; died Aug. 29, 1859.
       VII. MARY ISADORE [8]   "   April 4, 1864.

Alden Tower [7] died in Cummington, March 27, 1880, ag. 72 y. 25 d.

817.   Eighth Generation.   Tower.

375. OSMOND [7], NATHANIEL [6], NATHANIEL [5], NATHANIEL [4], THOMAS [3], BENJAMIN [2], JOHN [1].

Osmond [7], son of Nathaniel [6] and Hannah (Reed) Tower, b. Feb. 16, 1811; mar. Martha Gallagher, of Watervliet, N. Y., Sept. 1, 1834.

Childr.

    I. GEORGE WARREN [8] born July 26, 1836; mar. Eliza Edwards.
1287. II. OSMOND SELWIN [8] " May 27, 1840.
1288. III. ANGELO EMERY [8] " Aug. 16, 1842.
1289. IV. JAMES FREDERICK [8] " May 26, 1849.

818.   **Eighth Generation.**   **Tower.**

375. AMBROSE [7], NATHANIEL [6], NATHANIEL [5], NATHANIEL [4], THOMAS [3], BENJAMIN [2], JOHN [1].
Ambrose [7], son of Nathaniel [6] and Hannah (Reed) Tower, b. March 9, 1813; mar. Phebe Ferguson, of New York.

Child.
HOWARD [8].

819. Dexter.   **Eighth Generation.**   **Tower.**

375. LOUISA H. [7], NATHANIEL [6], NATHANIEL [5], NATHANIEL [4], THOMAS [3], BENJAMIN [2], JOHN [1].
Louisa H. [7], dau. of Nathaniel [6] and Hannah (Williams) Tower, b.
Oct. 22, 1820; mar. John C. Dexter, of Ionia, Mich.

Childr. none.
John C. Dexter died in Evarts, Mich., July   , 1880.

820. Ball.   **Eighth Generation.**   **Tower.**

375. ALMIRA C. [7], NATHANIEL [6], NATHANIEL [5], NATHANIEL [4], THOMAS [3], BENJAMIN [2], JOHN [1].
Almira C. [7], dau. of Nathaniel [6] and Hannah (Williams) Tower, b.
March 24, 1823; mar. Warren J. Ball, of Goshen, Mass.,
Oct. 3, 1845. He was born in Chesterfield, Mass.,
Oct. 22, 1822, and was son of Brewer and Rhoda (Willcutt) Ball.

Childr. born in Goshen.

   I. DELIA A. [8] born Aug. 7, 1846.
  II. CHARLES W. [8] " July 3, 1849; mar. Lucy M. Lancashire, Nov. 5, 1878.
III. JOHN TOWER [8] " April 8, 1855; " Rose Ruby, May 30, 1880.

821. Tillson.   **Eighth Generation.**   **Tower.**

377. LEAH [7], AMBROSE [6], NATHANIEL [5], NATHANIEL [4], THOMAS [3], BENJAMIN [2], JOHN [1].
Leah [7], dau. of Ambrose [6] and Rachel (Bartlett) Tower, b.

Dec. 5, 1802 ; mar. Welcome Tillson, of Halifax, Mass.,
Sept. 4, 1820. He was b. in Halifax
Sept. 1, 1800, and was son of Ephraim and Fear (Waterman)
Tillson.

Childr.

I.	AMBROSE.[8]	born	June 16, 1821.
II.	RACHEL BARTLETT[8]	"	June 7, 1825.
III.	CHARLES WATERMAN[8]	"	Feb. 16, 1827.
IV.	LUTHER B.[8]	"	Aug. 3, 1829.
V.	CYRUS MORTON[8]	"	Nov. 6, 1831.

Welcome Tillson died Aug. 10, 1877, ag. 76 y. 11 m. 9 d.
Leah[7] (Tower) Tillson died in Cummington, March 27,
1876, ag. 73 y. 9 m. 22 d.

822. Eighth Generation. **Tower.**

377. HOLLISTON[7], AMBROSE[6], NATHANIEL[5], NATHANIEL[4], THOMAS[3],
BENJAMIN[2], JOHN[1].

Holliston[7], son of Ambrose[6] and Rachel (Bartlett) Tower, b.
Oct. 20, 1810 ; mar. Lydia   . She was b.
1816.

Holliston Tower[7] died in Halifax, Mass., May 9, 1834, ag.
23 y. 6 m. 20 d.

Lydia (   ) Tower died in Hanover, Mass., Oct. 26, 1843,
ag. 27.

823. Bartlett. Eighth Generation. **Tower.**

379. SALOME[7], WARREN[6], NATHANIEL[5], NATHANIEL[4], THOMAS[3],
BENJAMIN[2], JOHN[1].

Salome[7], dau. of Warren[6] and Rhoda (Tower) Tower, b.
Oct. 9, 1817 ; mar. Ephraim T. Bartlett.   Int. pub.
May 27, 1837. He was b.
Aug. 13, 1813, and was son of Ephraim and Eliza (Tillson)
Bartlett.

Childr.

I.	RHODA ELIZA[8]	born	April 11, 1838; died Nov. 10, 1842, ag. 4 y. 6 m. 29 d.
II.	AROLINE PRATT[8]	"	Sept. 19, 1839; died Nov. 11, 1842, ag. 3 y. 1 m. 22 d.
III.	LUCIUS W.[8]	"	April 3, 1841.
IV.	ERMINA DRURY[8]	"	Sept. 1, 1844 ; unmar.
V.	ALICE PRATT[8]	"	July 1, 1847.
VI.	VERTA EMERETTA[8]	"	April 16, 1849 ; mar.
VII.	ANN ELIZA[8]	"	May 25, 1855; died Aug. 29, 1867, ag. 12 y. 3 m. 4 d.
VIII.	FLORA LOUISA[8]	"	Dec. 6, 1856.

Ephraim T. Bartlett died   Sept. 16, 1857, ag. 44 y.
1 m. 3 y.

823 a.   Bartlett.   Eighth Generation.   Tower.

379. ELMINA [7], WARREN [6], NATHANIEL [5], NATHANIEL [4], THOMAS [3], BENJAMIN [2], JOHN [1].
Elmina [7], dau. of Warren [6] and Rhoda [7] (Tower) Tower, b.
Oct. 6, 1822; mar. Otis B. Bartlett [9]
May 1, 1851. He was b.
May 15, 1828, and was son of Peter and Wealthy [8] (Tower) Bartlett.

BARTLETT.   TOWER.
Otis B.[9], Wealthy T.[8], Stephen [7], Stephen [6], Peter [5], Peter [4], Jeremiah [3], Jeremiah [2], John [1].

Childr. born in Cummington.

   I.   GRANVILLE OTIS [8]   born April 18, 1852.
  II.   ELMER ELLSWORTH [8]   "   Feb. 27, 1862.

824.   Eighth Generation.   Tower.

379. WARREN E.[7], WARREN [6], NATHANIEL [5], NATHANIEL [4], THOMAS [3], BENJAMIN [2], JOHN [1].
Warren E.[7], son of Warren [6] and Rhoda (Tower) Tower, b.
April 5, 1824; mar. Agnes Lyman, of Cummington, Mass.,
Nov. 27, 1851. She was b. in Cummington
May 30, 1834, and was dau. of Benjamin B. and Roxana (Packard) Lyman.

Child born in Cummington.

  1290.   EDITH MARION [8] born April 22, 1857.

825.   Eighth Generation.   Tower.

379. LORENZO H.[7], WARREN [6], NATHANIEL [5], NATHANIEL [4], THOMAS[3], BENJAMIN [2], JOHN [1].
Lorenzo H.[7], son of Warren [6] and Rhoda (Tower) Tower, b.
Aug. 14, 1830; mar. Vesta A. Bartlett, of Cummington,
Nov. 27, 1856. She was b. in Cummington
Oct. 16, 1830, and was dau. of Ephraim and Betsey (Marshal) Bartlett.

Childr. born in Cummington.

    I.   ARTHUR L.[8]   born March 1, 1858; died Oct. 8, 1859, ag. 1 y. 7 m. 7 d.
   II.   THEODORE P.[8]   "   July 18, 1860.
  III.   BESSIE M.[8]   "   April 9, 1867;   "   Sept. 22, 1867.

826. Hersey.   Eighth Generation.   Tower.

381. MARY ANN [7], MARTIN [6], MARTIN [5], SHADRACH [4], THOMAS [3], BENJAMIN [2], JOHN [1].

Mary Ann [7], dau. of Martin [6] and Nancy (Christy) Tower, b. June 11, 1803; mar. Gridley F. Hersey, of Hingham, Mass., Nov. 3, 1831. He was b. in Hingham

Aug. 11, 1809, and was son of Gridley and Lucy (Cudworth) Hersey.

Childr. born in Hingham.

I. HENRY FOSTER [8] born July 20, 1833.
II. THOMAS [8]   "   Aug. 6, 1834.
III. EDWIN [8]   "   March 14, 1843.
IV. MARY ANN [8]   "   Nov. 12, 1845; died Nov. 25, 1847, ag. 2 y. 13 d.

Gridley F. Hersey died in Hingham, May 19, 1882, ag. 72 y. 9 m. 8 d.

Mary Ann (Tower) Hersey died in Hingham, March 15, 1866, ag. 62 y. 9 m. 4 d.

827. Hibbard.   Eighth Generation.   Tower.

382 SALLY [7], THOMAS [6], THOMAS G. [5], SHADRACH [4], THOMAS [3], BENJAMIN [2], JOHN [1].

Sally [7], dau. of Thomas [6] and Sarah (Mann) Tower, b. Oct. 19, 1807; mar. Alanson Hibbard, of Rowe, Mass., 1827. He was b. 1805.

Childr.

I. SARAH [8] born   ; mar. Robert Messinger, of Jefferson, Iowa.
II. OLIVE [8]   "   ;   "   Samuel A. Sessions, of Travers City, Mich.
III. ALFRED [8].   IV. OLVARD. [8]   V. EDWARD. [8]

Alanson Hibbard died in Rowe, June   , 1859, ag. 54.
Sally (Tower) Hibbard mar., 2d, Sumner Hemingway, of Schoolcraft, Mich.,
Oct.   , 1869.

828.   Eighth Generation.   Tower.

382. HORACE [7], THOMAS [6], THOMAS G. [5], SHADRACH [4], THOMAS [3], BENJAMIN [2], JOHN [1].

Horace [7], son of Thomas [6] and Sarah (Mann) Tower, b. Jan. 18, 1809; mar. Lucinda Witt, of Florida, Mass., Jan. 1, 1833. She was b. in Belchertown, Mass., April 30, 1810, and was dau. of Pliny and Lucinda Witt.

Childr. born in Florida.

I.	Son [8]		born Dec. 30, 1833; died Dec. 30, 1833.
II.	ANGELINA [8]		"	April 20, 1835; " Oct. 5, 1842, ag. 7 y. 5 m. 15 d.

1291. III. CHARLES FREDERICK [8] " Aug. 10, 1837.
1292. IV. HENRY A. [8] " Oct. 14, 1839.
1293. V. EDWARD A. [8] " March 5, 1842.
VI. Daughter [8] } Twins " Jan. 12, 1844; died March 5, 1846,
VII. Daughter [8] } ag. 2 y. 1 m. 24 d.
1294. VIII. HORACE A. [8] " Feb. 3, 1845.

Horace Tower [7] died in Florida, May 17, 1846, ag. 37 y. 3 m. 30 d.

829. **Eighth Generation.** **Tower.**

382. EPHRAIM [7], THOMAS [6], THOMAS G. [5], SHADRACH [4], THOMAS [3], BENJAMIN [2], JOHN [1].
Ephraim [7], son of Thomas [6] and Sarah (Mann) Tower, b. March 28, 1811 ; mar. Minerva Brown, of Florida, Mass., April 26, 1840. She was b. in Florida June 2, 1819, and was dau. of Harvey and Rizpah (Thatcher) Brown.

Childr. born in Florida.

I. JENETTE [8] born Feb. 23, 1844; died March 20, 1852, ag. 8 y. 26 d.
1295. II. AUSTIN [8] " Sept. 24, 1845.
1296. III. RUSSELL B. [8] " Aug. 27, 1846.

Minerva (Brown) Tower died in Florida, Sept. 14, 1846, ag. 27 y. 3 m. 12 d.
Ephraim Tower [7] mar., 2d, widow Sally Maria (Bushnell) Brown, of Florida, April 26, 1848. She was b. in Cheshire, Mass., 1824, and was dau. of Rev. N. Y. and Sally Bushnell, and widow of Harvey Russell Brown.

Child.

1297. IV. JANE [8] born Sept. 18, 1853.

Sally M. (Bushnell) Tower died in Florida, Oct. 3, 1857, ag. 33.
Ephraim Tower [7] mar., 3d, Mary Brown, of Rowe, Mass., May 10, 1860. She was b. 1820, and was dau. of James and Lucretia Brown ;
s. p.
She died in Florida, July 28, 1868, ag. 48.

830. Whitcomb. Eighth Generation. Tower.

382. CLARISSA T.[7], THOMAS [6], THOMAS G.[5], SHADRACH [4], THOMAS [3], BENJAMIN [2], JOHN [1].

Clarissa T.[7], dau. of Thomas [6] and Sarah (Mann) Tower, b. Dec. 9, 1813; mar. Israel Whitcomb, of Florida, Mass., Nov. 28, 1832. He was b. in Florida Aug. 4, 1806, and was son of Nathaniel and Emma (Piper) Whitcomb.

Childr. born in Florida.

I.	LORENZO [8]	born Dec. 4, 1833.	
II.	ADRIANA [8]	" May 26, 1838; died July 25, 1842, ag. 4 y. 1 m. 30 d.
III.	LYMAN T.[8]	" Jan. 1, 1843; " Oct. 11, 1868, ag. 25 y. 9 m. 10 d.
IV.	EMORY S.[8]	" Jan. 24, 1846.	
V.	CLARISSA A.[8]	" Nov. 19, 1851.	

Israel Whitcomb died in Florida, March 27, 1877, ag. 70 y. 7 m. 23 d.

831. Eighth Generation. Tower.

383. ALVIN [7], MARTIN [6], THOMAS G.[5], SHADRACH [4], THOMAS [3], BENJAMIN [2], JOHN [1].

Alvin [7], son of Martin [6] and Fanny (Clark) Tower, b. Dec. 9, 1817; mar. Mary B. Roberts, of Monroe, Mass., Jan. 10, 1844. She was b. in Monroe May 4, 1820, and was dau. of Jeduthun and Olive (Ballou) Roberts.

Childr. born in Monroe.

1298.	I.	MARYETTE [8]	born Feb. 23, 1845.
1299.	II.	NANCY ELLEN [8]	" July 27, 1847.
	III.	NATHAN ALVIN [8]	" March 4, 1850; unmar.
	IV.	LYMAN JEDUTHUN [8]	" Aug. 27, 1852; died Dec. 12, 1854, ag. 2 y. 3 m. 16 d.
	V.	OLIVE SYLVANIA [8]	" April 17, 1854; died .
	VI.	MARTIN JEDUTHUN [8]	" May 5, 1856; " Aug. 23, 1857, ag. 1 y. 3 m. 18 d.
	VII.	Daughter [8]	" April 9, 1858; died April 13, 1858.
	VIII.	WILLIAM MINOR [8]	" June 27, 1859; " Aug. , 1878, ag. 19 y. 2 m.
	IX.	Son [8]	" Feb. 9, 1861; " Feb. 9, 1861.

Mary B. (Roberts) Tower died in Monroe, Jan. 13, 1862, ag. 41 y. 8 m. 9 d.

Alvin Tower [7] mar., 2d, Lemira Goodell, of Readsboro', Vt., Feb. 14, 1864. She was born in Readsboro' Nov. 24, 1834, and was dau. of Daniel and Diana (Stearns) Goodell.

Childr.

X.	EMMA CALISTA [8]	born Nov. 29, 1864.
XI.	MURRY HENRY [8]	" Sept. 25, 1866; died Feb. 11, 1867.
XII.	RUTH ESTHER [8]	" April 28, 1870.
XIII.	HUEL STANLEY [8] } Twins	" Dec. 2, 1872.
XIV.	RUEL STEARNS [8] }	

832. Eighth Generation. Tower.

383. CALVIN [7], MARTIN [6], THOMAS G. [5], SHADRACH [4], THOMAS [3], BENJAMIN [2], JOHN [1].
Calvin [7], son of Martin [6] and Fanny (Clark) Tower, b.
Jan. 8, 1819 ; mar. Louisa Blanchard, of Savoy, Mass.,
April 17, 1846. She was b.
1824.

Childr.

I.	FREEMAN C. [8]	born May 26, 1847.
II.	PHILO A. [8]	" 1850.

Louisa (Blanchard) Tower died   .
Calvin Tower [7] mar., 2d, Mary Ann Bridges
Aug. 20, 1874.

833. Eighth Generation. Tower.

383. ORRIN [7], MARTIN [6], THOMAS G. [5], SHADRACH [4], THOMAS [3], BENJAMIN [2], JOHN [1].
Orrin [7], son of Martin [6] and Fanny (Clark) Tower, b.
April 1, 1820 ; mar. Florinda Granger, of Rowe, Mass.,
May 21, 1841. She was b. in Rowe
March 23, 1820, and was dau. of George and Florinda
(Dickenson) Granger.

Childr. born in Savoy, Mass.

I.	WAREHAM [8]	born April 23, 1843; died July 6, 1854, ag. 11 y. 2 m. 13 d.
II.	ELANSFORD [8]	" Jan. 30, 1845; died July 6, 1854, ag. 9 y. 5 m. 7 d.
III.	MINERVA A. [8]	" Feb. 10, 1848; died Aug. 10, 1852, ag. 4 y. 6 m.
IV.	MELINDA FRANCES [8]	" May 10, 1849; died July 28, 1852, ag. 3 y. 2 m. 18 d.
1300. V.	LUCY E. [8]	" Oct. 23, 1850.
1301. VI.	GILBERT JUDSON [8]	" April 1, 1854.
VII.	CLARISSA M. [8]	" Aug. 25, 1856; mar. Alfred W. Burnett, of Savoy.
VIII.	HARRIET L. [8]	" April 5, 1859; died Dec. 15, 1866, ag. 7 y. 8 m. 10 d.
IX.	GEORGE ORRIN [8]	" Aug. 3, 1861.

834. Phelps. **Eighth Generation.** **Tower.**

383. FANNY[7], MARTIN[6], THOMAS G.[5], SHADRACH[4], THOMAS[3], BEN-JAMIN[2], JOHN[1].

Fanny[7], dau. of Martin[6] and Fanny (Clark) Tower, b. Dec. 14, 1822; mar. Cyrus Phelps, of Monroe, Mass., June 29, 1841. He was b. Jan. 19, 1819, and was son of Dana and Prudas (Bullock) Phelps.

Childr. born in Monroe.

I. CYRUS MARTIN[8] born Nov. 29, 1841.
II. FANNY MARIA[8] " May 11, 1843.
III. MANLY[8] " July 21, 1844.
IV. ORRIN M.[8] " May 10, 1850; unmar.; died Dec. 7, 1874, ag. 24 y. 6 m. 28 d.
V. LUCY M.[8] " July 6, 1852.
VI. PHILA C.[8] " Feb. 27, 1856.

Cyrus Phelps died .
Fanny (Tower) Phelps mar., 2d, Samuel J. Allen, of Adams, Mass., Feb. 25, 1869. He was b. 1843, and was son of Samuel L. and Lodicea (Walker) Allen.

835. Hicks. **Eighth Generation.** **Tower.**

383. PHILA D.[7], MARTIN[6], THOMAS G.[5], SHADRACH[4], THOMAS[3], BENJAMIN[2], JOHN[1].

Phila D.[7], dau. of Martin[6] and Fanny (Clark) Tower, b. Dec. 14, 1822; mar. Miles B. Hicks, of Florida, Mass.

Child.

I. POLLY PHINNET[8] born .

Phila D. (Tower) Hicks died in Florida, Nov. 23, 1853, ag. 30 y. 11 m. 8 d.

836. **Eighth Generation.** **Tower.**

383. WARREN F.[7], MARTIN[6], THOMAS G.[5], SHADRACH[4], THOMAS[3], BENJAMIN[2], JOHN[1].

Warren F.[7], son of Martin[6] and Fanny (Clark) Tower, b. April 23, 1828; mar. Nancy S. Roberts, of Monroe, Mass., Jan. 17, 1854. She was dau. of Jeduthun K. and Olive (Ballou) Roberts.

Childr. none.

She died, and Warren F. Tower[7] mar., 2d, Elgada Polly, of Savoy, Mass.,

May 7, 1857. She was born in Savoy

July 13, 1832, and was dau. of Asa and Mary (Blanchard) Polly.

Childr. born in Monroe.

I.	NANCY S.[8]	born April 11, 1858; died Jan. 18, 1862, ag. 3 y. 9 m. 7 d.	
II.	SARAH R.[8]	" June 2, 1860.	
III.	EMMA JANE[8]	" June 2, 1862.	
IV.	MARIETTE[8]	" July 14, 1864.	
V.	MINNIE HANNAH[8]	" Aug. 7, 1867.	
VI.	WILLIS HARVEY[8]	" May 8, 1871.	
VII.	EDIE L.[8]	" Jan. 18, 1874; died June 23, 1875, ag. 1 y. 5 m. 6 d.	
VIII.	NELLIE ARABEL[8]	" Oct. 23, 1876.	

837. Phelps.   **Eighth Generation.**   **Tower.**

383. CALISTA[7], MARTIN[6], THOMAS G.[5], SHADRACH[4], THOMAS[3], BENJAMIN[2], JOHN[1].

Calista[7], dau. of Martin[6] and Fanny (Clark) Tower, b. May 16, 1831; mar. Walter Phelps, of Florida, Mass.

Child.

SARAH[8] born   ; mar   .

Calista (Tower) Phelps died July 27, 1860, ag. 29 y. 2 m. 11 d.

838.   **Eighth Generation.**   **Tower.**

383. HOUGHTON[7], MARTIN[6], THOMAS G.[5], SHADRACH[4], THOMAS[3], BENJAMIN[2], JOHN[1].

Houghton[7], son of Martin[6] and Fanny (Clark) Tower, b. Aug. 2, 1835; mar. Louisa J. Bassett, of Florida, Mass., Dec. 28, 1853. She was b.

1835, and was dau. of Harvey and Emily Bassett.

Childr. born in Florida.

I.	FRANCIS HOUGHTON[8]	born March 31, 1855; died June 8, 1856, ag. 1 y. 2 m. 8 d.	
II.	ARTHUR F.[8]	" Sept. 27, 1857; mar.	
III.	MERRITT H.[8]	" Nov. 10, 1859.	
IV.	MELVIN M.[8]	" March 4, 1862; died Nov. 5, 1874, ag. 14 y. 8 m. 1 d.	

Houghton Tower [7] died Nov. 19, 1864, ag. 29 y. 3 m. 17 d.
Louisa J. (Bassett) Tower mar., 2d, Minor Tower [7], brother
to Houghton [7]. See 842.

839.   Eighth Generation.   Tower.

383. ELI [7], MARTIN [6], THOMAS G.[5], SHADRACH [4], THOMAS [3], BENJA-
MIN [2], JOHN [1].
Eli [7], son of Martin [6] and Fanny (Clark) Tower, b.
Nov. 15, 1836 ; mar. Sarah M. Phelps
March 3, 1858. She was b. in Monroe, Mass.,
; and was dau. of Dana Phelps.

Child.

IDA ELIZA [8] born May 21, 1861, in Lanesborough, Mass.

840.   Eighth Generation.   Tower.

383. SIDNEY [7], MARTIN [6], THOMAS G.[5], SHADRACH [4], THOMAS [3], BEN-
JAMIN [2], JOHN [1].
Sidney [7], son of Martin [6] and Fanny (Clark) Tower, b.
June 15, 1839 ; mar. Lucinda M. Phelps, of Monroe, Mass.,
July 22, 1863. She was b.
March 22, 1843, and was dau. of Alfred and Sally (Hough-
ton) Phelps.

Childr.

I.	ROSEA MELVINA [8]	born	July 19, 1864.
II.	WILLIAM ALFRED [8]	"	Jan. 24, 1867.
III.	HUBERT ALLEN [8]	"	June 8, 1872 ; died Feb. 4, 1873.
IV.	CHARLES RILEY [8]	"	Dec. 23, 1874; " March 11, 1876; ag. 1 y. 2 m. 19 d.
V.	EDGAR STERGIE [8]	"	Feb. 22, 1877.
VI.	SIDNEY BURTON [8]	"	Aug. 11, 1880.

841.   Eighth Generation.   Tower.

383. MILES [7], MARTIN [6], THOMAS G.[5], SHADRACH [4], THOMAS [3], BEN-
JAMIN [2], JOHN [1].
Miles [7], son of Martin [6] and Fanny (Clark) Tower, b.
Aug. 29, 1844 ; mar. Orrilla E. Brown, of Florida, Mass.,
May 22, 1866. She was b. in Florida
Sept. 5, 1847, and was dau. of Nahum P. and Sarah (Pettin-
gill) Brown.

Child born in Florida.

I. OZRO MILES [8] born Oct. 31, 1866 ; died Nov. 21, 1874, ag. 8 y. 21 d.

383. MINOR[7], MARTIN[6], THOMAS G.[5], SHADRACH[4], THOMAS[3], BEN-
      JAMIN[2], JOHN[1].
      Minor[7], son of Martin[6] and Fanny (Clark) Tower, b.
      Aug. 29, 1844; mar. widow Louisa J. (Basset) Tower, of
      Florida, Mass.,
      Dec. 26, 1864. She was b.
            1835, and was dau. of Harvey and Emily Bassett,
      and widow of Houghton Tower[7].

                 Childr. born in Florida.

 I. CARRIE LEONA[8]   born Nov. 29, 1865; died Oct. 29, 1866.
II. LUTHERA LOUISA[8]   "   Sept. 27, 1868;   "   Nov 8, 1874, ag. 6 y.
                               1 m. 11 d.

      Louisa J. (Bassett) Tower died in Florida, Jan. 29, 1871,
      ag. 36.
      Minor Tower[7] mar., 2d, Loretta C. Ross, of Readsboro', Vt.,
      May 8, 1871. She was b. in Readsboro'
      May 8, 1852, and was dau. of David and Eliza Ross.

                      Childr.

III. ELLIS MINOR[8]   born April 24, 1872, died Sept. 11, 1874, ag. 2 y.
                               4 m. 17 d.
IV.   WALTER CYRUS[8] "   Oct 24, 1874;   "   Nov. 8, 1874.
 V.   FRANCIS LEON[8] "   March 10, 1876.
VI.   DILLA ELIZA[8]   "   June 6, 1878.
VII. ROYAL ELI[8]   "   Sept. 20, 1879.

384. DENNIS[7], WILLIAM[6], THOMAS G.[5], SHADRACH[4], THOMAS[3],
      BENJAMIN[2], JOHN[1].
      Dennis[7], son of William[6] and Anna (Thatcher) Tower, b.
      July 28, 1817; mar. Abigail Alden, of Ashfield, Mass.,
      Oct. 18, 1837. She was b. in Ashfield
      Dec. 8, 1817, and was dau. of Henry and Hannah (Smith)
      Alden.
                 Childr. born in Florida.

1302.   I. ALONZO D.[8]   born Oct. 4, 1839.
1303.   II. SARAH A.[8]   "   Jan. 23, 1842.
1304. III. SYLVANUS C.[8]   "   Feb. 17, 1844.
1305.   IV. SELINA L.[8]   "   July 23, 1846.
         V. GEORGE HENRY[8]   "   March 19, 1849; died Jan. 25, 1875, ag.
                                       25 y. 10 m. 13 d.
        VI. JOHN W.[8]   "   Feb. 9, 1851; died Dec. 20, 1871, ag.
                                       20 y. 10 m. 11 d.

1306.   VII.   Rizpah Anna [8] born May 4, 1853.
        VIII.   Addie L. [8]   "   July 11, 1859; died Feb. 19, 1875, ag.
                     15 y. 7 m. 11 d.

844.   Kemp.   Eighth Generation.   Tower.

384.   Rispah [7], William [6], Thomas G. [5], Shadrach [4], Thomas [3], Benjamin [2], John [1].

Rispah [7], dau. of William [6] and Anna (Thatcher) Tower, b. Aug. 4, 1820; mar. Gideon Kemp, of Florida, Mass., Jan. 10, 1843. He was b. Sept. 9, 1813, and was son of Nathan and Molly (Hartwell) Kemp.

Childr. born in Florida.

I.   Morris G. [8] born Sept. 29, 1848.   III.   Anna R. [8] born Sept. 23, 1858.
II.   Nathan W. [8] "   May 22, 1853.

845.   Bryant.   Eighth Generation.   Tower.

384.   Sarah [7], William [6], Thomas G. [5], Shadrach [4], Thomas [3], Benjamin [2], John [1].

Sarah [7], dau. of William [6] and Anna (Thatcher) Tower, b. Jan. 27, 1822; mar. Arad Bryant, of Stamford, Vt., March 26, 1840.

Childr.

I.   William Elisha [8] born April 20, 1841.
II.   Edna [8]   "
III.   Elbert [8]   "   ; mar. Lilian Keyes, of North
                                     Adams; s. p.
IV.   Dolly [8]   "   1864.

846.   Wheeler.   Eighth Generation.   Tower.

384.   Nancy [7], William [6], Thomas G. [5], Shadrach [4], Thomas [3], Benjamin [2], John [1].

Nancy [7], dau. of William [6] and Anna (Thatcher) Tower, b. Jan. 29, 1827; mar. Freebun Wheeler, of Charlemont, Mass., March 14, 1850. He was b. 1829, and was son of James and Candace Wheeler.

Childr. born in Florida, Mass.

I.   James W. [8]   born March 2, 1851; died June 14, 1867, ag. 16 y. 3 m.
                                         12 d.
II.   Lauretta N. [8] "   1859.   IV.   James F. [8] born   1868.
III.   Algene [8]   "   1861.

Nancy (Tower) Wheeler died in Florida, Nov. 20, 1880, ag. 53 y. 9 m. 22 d.

847.   **Eighth Generation.**   **Tower.**

384. SEDATE T.[7], WILLIAM [6], THOMAS G.[5], SHADRACH [4], THOMAS [3], BENJAMIN [2], JOHN [1].

Sedate T.[7], son of William [6] and Anna (Thatcher) Tower, b. Sept. 10, 1838; mar. Lyanda M. Thatcher, of Florida, Mass., July 3, 1860. She was b. in Florida July 3, 1836, and was dau. of Leonard and Abigail (Manning) Thatcher.

Childr.

I. LEONARD S.[8] born June 15, 1863.   III. ELLEA [8] born Nov. 15, 1868.
II. WILLIAM E.[8]   "   Sept. 11, 1867.   IV. EFFIE E.[8] "   March 5, 1879.

848.   **Eighth Generation.**   **Tower.**

384. MARSHAL W.[7], WILLIAM [6], THOMAS G.[5], SHADRACH [4], THOMAS [3], BENJAMIN [2], JOHN [1].

Marshal W.[7], son of William [6] and Anna (Thatcher) Tower, b. Aug. 26, 1840; mar. Sylvia G. Negus Nov. 21, 1861. She was b. 1843, and was dau. of Lorin and Emily (Clark) Negus.

Childr. none.

Marshal W. Tower [7] died in Florida, Aug. 11, 1867, ag. 26 y. 11 m. 16 d.

Sylvia G. (Negus) Tower mar., 2d, Thomas Mallory, of Adams, Mass.

849.   **Eighth Generation.**   **Tower.**

387. CHESTER L.[7], CHESTER [6], THOMAS G.[5], SHADRACH [4], THOMAS [3], BENJAMIN [2], JOHN [1].

Chester L.[7], son of Chester [6] and Grateful (Thatcher) Tower, b. Oct. 16, 1826; mar. Mary Ann Nelson, of Florida, Mass., Nov. 28, 1850. She was b. in Florida Nov. 30, 1832, and was dau. of David and Mary E. (Kemp) Nelson.

Childr.

1307.   I.   HOBART CHESTER [8] born Sept. 16, 1852.
1308.   II.   LIDA E.[8]   "   Sept. 23, 1858.

850.   **Eighth Generation.**   **Tower.**

387. FRANCIS O.[7], CHESTER [6], THOMAS G.[5], SHADRACH [4], THOMAS [3], BENJAMIN [2], JOHN [1].

Francis O.[7], son of Chester[6] and Grateful (Thatcher) Tower, b.
Jan. 1, 1834; mar. Almira Blanchard, of Florida, Mass.,
Jan. 16, 1859. She was b. in Florida
    1841, and was dau. of Robert and Nancy (Cutler) Blanchard.

Childr.

I. CLIFTON O.[8] born July 30, 1865.   II. LILLIE M.[8] born March 4, 1870.

---

851. Sherman, Burnett.   Eighth Generation.   Tower.

387. MATILDA R.[7], CHESTER[6], THOMAS G.[5], SHADRACH[4], THOMAS[3], BENJAMIN[2], JOHN[1].
Matilda R.[7], dau. of Chester[6] and Grateful (Thatcher) Tower, b.
April 28, 1835; mar. William F. Burnett, of Florida, Mass.,
Nov. 5, 1854. He was b. in Florida
    1832, and was son of Isaac and Rhoda (Smith) Burnett.

Childr. none.

William F. Burnett died in Florida, Sept. 1, 1863, ag. 31.
Matilda R. (Tower) Burnett mar., 2d, Henry Sherman, of Florida,
Sept. 30, 1866. He was b.
June 16, 1820, and was son of Abiel and Sarah (Harkness) Sherman.

---

852.   Eighth Generation.   Tower.

387. HARVEY B.[7], CHESTER[6], THOMAS G.[5], SHADRACH[4], THOMAS[3], BENJAMIN[2], JOHN[1].
Harvey B.[7], son of Chester[6] and Grateful (Thatcher)Tower, b.
Nov. 22, 1838; mar. Mary Hunt, of Florida, Mass.,
Nov. 21, 1861. She was b. in Florida
    1845, and was dau. of Charles and Mary (Blanchard) Hunt.

Child.

I. CHARLIE[8] born April 1, 1874.

---

853. Warfield.   Eighth Generation.   Tower.

389. BETSEY S.[7], LYMAN[6], SAMUEL[5], SAMUEL[4], PETER[3], BENJAMIN[2], JOHN[1].
Betsey S.[7], dau. of Lyman[6] and Julia (Welton) Tower, b.

May 15, 1823 ; mar. Chester Warfield, of Franklin, N. Y.,
Dec. 28, 1842. He was b. in Franklin
July 2, 1823, and was son of Curtice and Polly (Chapman)
Warfield.

Child born in Franklin.

    I. CHARLES [8] born May 25, 1850.

Betsey S. (Tower) Warfield died in Franklin, April 25, 1870,
ag. 46 y. 11 m. 11 d.

---

854. Brown.   **Eighth Generation.**   **Tower.**

393. MARY AMELIA [7], WILLIAM [6], SHUBAEL [5], SAMUEL [4], PETER [3],
    BENJAMIN [2], JOHN [1].
Mary A.[7], dau. of William [6] and Diana (Sacket) Tower, b.
May 21, 1835 ; mar. Robert W. Brown, of Utica, Wis.,
Sept. 21, 1867.

Childr.

    I. NELLIE MAY [8]   born March 7, 1870.
    II. MATTIE D.[8]   " Nov. 16, 1871.
    III. ROBERT WILLIAM [8] " June 20, 1873.

---

855.   **Eighth Generation.**   **Tower.**

394. MIRON [7], ALMON [6], SHUBAEL [5], SAMUEL [4], PETER [3], BENJAMIN [2],
    JOHN [1].
Miron [7], son of Almon [6] and Mary (Sexton) Tower, b.
March 20, 1834 ; mar. Chloe L. Maynard, of Whitehall, N. Y.,
Oct. 14, 1860. She was b.
Jan. 8, 1838, and was dau. of Rufus and Patience Maynard.

Childr.

    I. ALMON [8] born June 7, 1863, in Saratoga, Minn.
    II. MARY [8]   " March 13, 1866, "   "

Chloe (Maynard) Tower died Dec. 5, 1868, ag. 30 y. 10 m.
28 d.
Miron Tower [7] mar., 2d, Mary Evans, of Lansing, Minn.,
Jan. 13, 1870. She was born in Caermarthenshire, North
Wales,
Nov. 12, 1834.

Childr.

    III. DAISY [8] born May 25, 1873, in Lincoln, Neb.
    IV. PEARLE [8] " June 7, 1875, " Geneva, " ; died Sept. 5, 1875.
    V. ROSETTA [8] " May 29, 1876, " " " ; " Sept. 1, 1876.

856. Eighth Generation. Tower.

394. ADDISON[7], ALMON[6], SHUBAEL[5], SAMUEL[4], PETER[3], BENJA-
MIN[2], JOHN[1],

Addison[7], son of Almon[6] and Mary (Sexton) Tower, b.
Nov. 15, 1836; mar. Adeline Lough in California.
She was b. in Elkart Co., Ind.,
Dec. 16, 1846, and was dau. of Thomas and Mary Ann
(Nichols) Lough.

Childr.

I.	IRENA FRANCES[8]	born May 29, 1863, in Markeville, Cal.
II.	MARY A.[8]	" Dec. 22, 1864, " " "
III.	EMMA JANE[8]	" Dec. 29, 1866, " Lockeford, Cal.; died in Plymouth, N. Y., Dec. 4, 1867.
IV.	WILLIAM H.[8]	" Aug. 25, 1868, in Troy, Minn.
V.	AMASA[8]	" Oct. 26, 1870, " Lancaster Co., Neb.
VI.	ADA MARY[8]	" Nov. 17, 1872, " Ashland, "
VII.	FLORA EDNA[8]	" Dec. 18, 1874, " " "
VIII.	ALBERT[8]	" Feb. 18, 1877, " " "

857. Eighth Generation. Tower.

394. AMASA[7], ALMON[6], SHUBAEL[5], SAMUEL[4], PETER[3], BENJAMIN[2],
JOHN[1].

Amasa[7], son of Almon[6] and Mary (Sexton) Tower, b.
March 24, 1839; mar. Juliet West, of Partlett, Vt., in St.
Charles, Minn.,
March 27, 1866. She was b. in Partlett,
and was dau. of Leander and Alta (Davis) West.

858. Phelps. Eighth Generation. Tower.

394. NANCY A.[7], ALMON[6], SHUBAEL[5], SAMUEL[4], PETER[3], BENJA-
MIN[2], JOHN[1].

Nancy A.[7], dau. of Almon[6] and Mary (Sexton) Tower, b.
April 14, 1841; mar. Isaac E. Phelps, of Wahoo, Neb.,
Dec. 28, 1876. He was b. in Warsaw, N. Y.,
May 14, 1841, and was son of Isaac N. and Mary (Perkins)
Phelps.

859. Eighth Generation. Tower.

394. WARREN[7], ALMON[6], SHUBAEL[5], SAMUEL[4], PETER[3], BENJAMIN[2],
JOHN[1]

Warren[7], son of Almon[6] and Mary (Sexton) Tower, b.
Aug. 17, 1843; mar. Lucy Helen Glover in Sarpy Co., Neb.,
March 3, 1875. She was b. in Indiana
Oct. 28, 1840, and was dau. of John B. and Eliza W. (Child)
Glover.

Child.

I. BERTHA[8] born Jan. 21, 1876, in Lancaster Co., Neb.

860. West.   Eighth Generation.   Tower.

394. MARY A.[7], ALMON[6], SHUBAEL[5], SAMUEL[4], PETER[3], BENJAMIN[2], JOHN[1].
Mary A.[7], dau. of Almon[6] and Mary (Sexton) Tower, b.
Nov. 23, 1846 ; mar. Charles West in Plymouth, N. Y.,
Nov. 12, 1872. He was b. in Morrisville, N. Y.,
March 3, 1850, and was son of Charles and Orinda (Birdwin)
West.

Child.

I. FERN E.[8] born April 6, 1877, in Lancaster Co., Neb.

861. Stewart.   Eighth Generation.   Tower.

394. FLORA ELIZA[7], ALMON[6], SHUBAEL[5], SAMUEL[4], PETER[3], BENJAMIN[2], JOHN[1].
Flora E.[7], dau. of Almon[6] and Mary (Sexton) Tower, b.
Sept. 12, 1854 ; mar. William B. Stewart
Feb. 22, 1878.

Child.

LEON TOWER[8] born Jan. 27, 1879.

862. Swain.   Eighth Generation.   Tower.

395. MARIA H.[7], OBADIAH[6], SHUBAEL[5], SAMUEL[4], PETER[3], BENJAMIN[2], JOHN[1].
Maria H.[7], dau. of Obadiah[6] and Fidelia (Munroe) Tower, b.
April 21, 1833 ; mar. John M. Swain, of Plymouth, N. Y.,
Sept. 12, 1852. He was b.
Sept. 3, 1831, and was son of Oliver and Sarah W. (Merrihen) Swain.

Childr.

I.	ELLA M.[8]	born Sept. 22, 1853.
II.	CLARA E.[8]	" March 19, 1859.
III.	WILLIAM A.[8]	" April 20, 1862.
IV.	EDWARD M.[8]	" March 5, 1865.
V.	SYLVIA B.[8]	" Sept. 3, 1867.
VI.	ALLEN D.[8]	" Oct. 17, 1870.

863.   Eighth Generation.   Tower.

395. EDWIN M.[7], OBADIAH[6], SHUBAEL[5], SAMUEL[4], PETER[3], BENJAMIN[2], JOHN[1].

Edwin M.[7], son of Obadiah [6] and Fidelia (Munroe) Tower, b.
March 24, 1835; mar. Emily J. Morley, of Smyrna, N. Y.,
Oct. 3, 1859. She was b. in Smyrna
Aug. 14, 1831, and was dau. of Luther and Mary (Bunker)
Morley.

Childr.

I. ALICE FIDELIA [8] born Nov. 18, 1861, in Smyrna.
II. BERTHA AMELIA [8] " Feb 2, 1863; died Aug. 19, 1874, ag. 11 y.
6 m. 17 d.
III. MYRA L.[8] " April 25, 1865, in Oxford, N. Y.

864. **Eighth Generation.** **Tower.**

395. CYRUS O.[7], OBADIAH [6], SHUBAEL [5], SAMUEL [4], PETER [3] BEN-
JAMIN [2], JOHN [1].
Cyrus O.[7], son of Obadiah [6] and Fidelia (Munroe) Tower, b.
July 19, 1845; mar. Emma Johnson.

Child.

I. EMMA [8] born Sept. 7, 1878.

Emma (Johnson) Tower died Sept. 17, 1878.
Cyrus O. Tower [7] mar., 2d, Eva Kohlsact, of Chicago,
Oct. 12, 1882.

865. Fuller. **Eighth Generation.** **Tower.**

396. LAURA D.[7], RODNEY [6], SHUBAEL [5], SAMUEL [4], PETER [3], BENJA-
MIN [2], JOHN [1].
Laura D.[7], dau. of Rodney [6] and Fidelia (Robinson) Tower, b.
Feb. 28, 1834; mar. Anthony Putnam Fuller, of Jackson,
Wis.,
May 31, 1855. He was b. in Pike, N. Y.,
July 6, 1827.

Child born in Jackson.

I. LILIAN M.[8] born Aug. 31, 1856; died Sept. 8, 1863, ag. 7 y. 8 d.
II. VIVIAN M.[8] " Oct. 5, 1860.
III. EDGAR P.[8] " Sept. 1, 1863.
IV. EARL RODNEY [8] " Sept. 24, 1867.

866. Gilfallan. **Eighth Generation.** **Tower.**

396. HELEN S.[7], RODNEY [6], SHUBAEL [5], SAMUEL [4], PETER [3], BENJA-
MIN [2], JOHN [1].
Helen S.[7], dau. of Rodney [6] and Fidelia (Robinson) Tower, b.
Feb. 7, 1840; mar. William Gilfallan, of Burns, Wis.,
Dec. 22, 1857. He was b. in Barnet, Vt.,
March 6, 1835.

Childr.

I.   ELBERT O.[8] born April 20, 1859, in Burns.
II. SHERMAN L.[8] "   June 26, 1860, " Hamilton, Wis.
III. MARGARET A.[8] " Dec. 26, 1861, " Burns.
IV. MILFORD I.[8] "   Oct. 27, 1875, " Farmington, Wis.; died Jan. 3,
                        1877, ag. 1 y. 2 m. 7 d.
V.   SUSIE F.[8]   "   Feb.   , 1882.

867. Adams.   Eighth Generation.   Tower.

396. ADELINE F.[7], RODNEY [6], SHUBAEL [5], SAMUEL [4], PETER [3], BEN-
        JAMIN [2], JOHN [1].
     Adeline F.[7], dau. of Rodney [6] and Fidelia (Robinson) Tower, b.
     April 8, 1846; mar. Charles E. Adams, of Burns, Wis.,
     Oct. 5, 1867.

Childr.

I.   FRANK D.[8] born June 28, 1869, in Hamilton, Wis.
II. ELLA F.[8]   "   March 29, 1873, "   "   " ; died April 9, 1874,
                        ag. 1 y. 11 d.

Charles E. Adams died

ROBINSON.   TOWER.

Adeline F.[7] (Tower) Adams mar., 2d, George Robinson.

Child.

III. GEORGE [8] born   1883.

868.   Eighth Generation.   Tower.

396. ORVILLE R.[7], RODNEY [6], SHUBAEL [5], SAMUEL [4], PETER [3], BEN-
        JAMIN [2], JOHN [1].
     Orville R.[7], son of Rodney [6] and Fidelia (Robinson) Tower, b.
     March 3, 1849; mar. Clara W. Cook, of Farmington, Wis.,
     Jan. 20, 1871. She was b. in Cambridge, Mass.,
     Sept. 6, 1849.

Childr. born in Farmington.

I.   EFFIE MAUD [8] born June 5, 1873.
II. LIZZIE MAY [8]   "   April 11, 1875.
III. LAURA VIRNE [8] "   1883.

869.   Eighth Generation.   Tower.

396. EDGAR A.[7], RODNEY [6], SHUBAEL [5], SAMUEL [4], PETER [3], BENJA-
        MIN [2], JOHN [1].
     Edgar A.[7], son of Rodney [6] and Fidelia (Robinson) Tower, b.
     Nov. 13, 1851; mar. Margaret Florin Hodge, of Mindora,
     Wis.,

Sept. 10, 1882. She was b. in Mindora April 6, 1857, and was dau. of Thomas and Jessie (Haliburton) Hodge.

Child.

I. ETHEL FLORIN [8] born Aug. 4, 1884, in North Bend, Wis.

870. **Eighth Generation.** **Tower.**

397. JAMES B.[7], JAMES B.[6], SHUBAEL [5], SAMUEL [4], PETER [3], BENJAMIN [2], JOHN [1].

James B.[7], son of James B.[6] and Amanda F. (Powell) Tower, b.

Aug. 24, 1840; mar. widow Matilda (Doolan) Rock, of Chicago,

Feb. 10, 1865. She was born in Tipperary, Ireland,

Jan. 28, 1837, and was dau. of John and Amelia (Palmer) Doolan.

Child.

MARY LULU [8] born July 21, 1870.

871. **Eighth Generation.** **Tower.**

397. FRANKLIN H.[7], JAMES B.[6], SHUBAEL [5], SAMUEL [4], PETER [3], BENJAMIN [2], JOHN [1].

Franklin H.[7], son of James B.[6] and Amanda F. (Powell) Tower, b.

Jan. 6, 1847; mar. Mary Doolan, of Chicago,

Aug. 1, 1867. She was b. in Tipperary, Ireland,

Aug. 2, 1846, and was dau. of John and Amelia (Palmer) Doolan.

Childr.

I. JAMES FRANKLIN [8] born March 7, 1868.
II. HARRY DOOLAN [8] " Aug. 21, 1873.
III. MARY CELESTINE [8] " Jan. 4, 1877.
IV. MARTHA ZELLA [8] " June 2, 1881.

872. Hay. **Eighth Generation.** **Tower.**

398. HANNAH A.[7], SAMUEL N.[6], SHUBAEL [5], SAMUEL [4], PETER [3], BENJAMIN [2], JOHN [1].

Hannah A.[7], dau. of Samuel N.[6] and Hannah (Lewis) Tower, b. March 2, 1843; mar. Francis Marion Hay, of Annawan, Ill., Nov. , 1868.

Childr.

I. MARK [8] born Sept. 25, 1869. III. ROY C.[8] born Aug. , 1874.
II. LOUIS M.[8] " Jan. 16, 1872.

873. Eighth Generation. Tower.

398. LEWIS N.[7], SAMUEL N.[6], SHUBAEL[5], SAMUEL[4], PETER[3], BEN-
JAMIN[2], JOHN[1].

Lewis N.[7], son of Samuel N.[6] and Hannah (Lewis) Tower, b.
Aug. 19, 1848; mar. Elizabeth Boremore
Oct. 16, 1867.

Childr.

I. MAY[8] born May 1, 1872. II. JOSEPHINE[8] born Dec. 24, 1874.

874. Crozier, Loveland. Eighth Generation. Tower.

400. LUCINA A.[7], LABAN[6], PETER[5], SAMUEL[4], PETER[3], BENJAMIN[2],
JOHN[1].

Lucina A.[7], dau. of Laban[6] and Patty (Johnson) Tower, b.
April 14, 1826; mar. William Loveland, of Hinsdale, Mass.,
Feb. 10, 1847. He was b.
Feb. 28, 1817; and was son of Erastus and Olive (Ford)
Loveland.

Childr. born in Hinsdale.

I. MARY E.[8]   born March 25, 1848.
II. GEORGE WILLIAM[8] " Sept. 11, 1849.
III. CHARLES ELMER[8] " May 16, 1853.
IV. DEXTER B.[8]   " May 31, 1855; died Aug. 28, 1855.
V. ETTA MARIA[8]   " Dec. 3, 1857.
VI. DEXTER B.[8]   " May 18, 1861, died Dec. 10, 1861.

William Loveland died Nov. 11, 1872, ag. 55 y. 8 m. 12 d.

CROZIER.   TOWER.

Lucina (Tower) Loveland mar., 2d, Lewis Crozier, of
Dalton, Mass.,
Sept. 16, 1876. He was born in Peru, Mass.,
Aug. 6, 1827, and was son of Joseph and Sarah (Babbitt)
Crozier.

875. Cleveland. Eighth Generation. Tower.

400. AURELIA M.[7], LABAN[6], PETER[5], SAMUEL[4], PETER[3], BENJA-
MIN[2], JOHN[1].

Aurelia M.[7], dau. of Laban[6] and Patty (Johnson) Tower, b.
July 22, 1829; mar. George L. Cleveland, of Dalton, Mass.,
Sept. 21, 1851. He was b.
1828, and was son of Cyrus and Betsey Cleveland.

Childr. born in Dalton.

I. EMMA G.[8]   born Aug 11, 1852.
II. ELIZABETH[8]   "   1855.

III.	MARY [8]	born	1858.
IV.	HARMONY [8]	"	Sept. 2, 1859.
V.	HATTIE B. [8]	"	1860.
VI.	GEORGE WESLEY [8]	"	Feb. 16, 1864; died April 14, 1865, ag. 1 y. 1 m. 26 d.
VII.	EGBERT C. [8]	"	Aug. 17, 1865.
VIII.	Child [8]	"	Dec. 20, 1871; died Dec. 20, 1871.

876.   **Eighth Generation.**   **Tower.**

400. JOHN W. [7], LABAN [6], PETER [5], SAMUEL [4], PETER [3], BENJAMIN [2], JOHN [1].

John W. [7], son of Laban [6] and Patty (Johnson) Tower, b.
May 16, 1839, mar. Elizabeth Dillingham, of Watertown,
N. Y.,
Sept. 7, 1864. She was b. in Toronto, Canada,
    1840, and was dau. of Isaac and Caroline Dillingham.

Child born in Hinsdale, Mass.

Daughter [8] born May 24, 1865; died May 27, 1865.

Elizabeth (Dillingham) Tower died May 27, 1865, ag. 25.
John W. Tower [7] mar., 2d, Maria Downes, of Bennington, Vt.,
    1871. She was b. in Bennington
    1838, and was dau. of Jesse and Adelia Downes.

877.   **Eighth Generation.**   **Tower.**

400. SAMUEL D. [7], LABAN [6], PETER [5], SAMUEL [4], PETER [3], BENJAMIN [2], JOHN [1].

Samuel D. [7], son of Laban [6] and Patty (Johnson) Tower, b.
Jan. 5, 1842; mar. Sylvina S. Lewis, of Dalton, Mass.,
Nov. 14, 1867. She was b. in Maryland, N. Y.,
April 10, 1849, and was adopted daughter of John and Sarah
    Lewis.

Childr. born in Dalton.

I. EDITH [8] born Nov. 20, 1871.   II. CHARLES [8] born March , 1881.

878.   **Eighth Generation.**   **Tower.**

405. EDWIN O. [7], SALLY [6], PETER [5], SAMUEL [4], PETER [3], BENJAMIN [2], JOHN [1].

Edwin O. [7], son of Sally [6] and   , b.
Dec. , 1832; mar. Lucy A. Montgomery, of Pownal, Vt.,
Sept. 30, 1853. She was b. in Pownal
Sept. 29, 1837, and was dau. of Henry and Betsey (Barber)
    Montgomery.

Child born in Adams, Mass.

I. EDITH[8] born June 29, 1854; mar. Everett D. Streeter, of Adams, Mass.,
                    July 7, 1875.

Edwin O. Tower[7] died in Adams, June 15, 1864, ag. 31 y. 7 m.

879. Roberts.   Eighth Generation.   Tower.

406. HANNAH J.[7], ISAIAH [6], ISAIAH [5], ISAIAH [4], PETER [3], BENJAMIN [2],
        JOHN [1].
        Hannah J.[7], dau. of Isaiah [6] and Polly (Wilder) Tower, b.
        Sept. 4, 1811; mar. Ebenezer Roberts, of Hingham, Mass.,
        May 11, 1834. He was b. in Portland, Me.,
        Aug. 8, 1808, and was son of Ebenezer and Jane (Richards)
        Roberts.
                    Child born in Hingham.
                I. EBENEZER W.[8] born Aug. 23, 1837.

Hannah J. (Tower) Roberts died in Hingham, Dec. 2, 1842,
        ag. 31 y. 2 m. 28 d.
Ebenezer Roberts mar., 2d, widow Nancy A. (Patterson)
        Libby.

880.   Eighth Generation.   Tower.

406. ISAIAH G.[7], ISAIAH [6], ISAIAH [5], ISAIAH [4], PETER [3], BENJAMIN [2],
        JOHN [1].
        Isaiah G.[7], son of Isaiah [6] and Polly (Wilder) Tower, b.
        Aug. 26, 1813; mar. Mary A. Fearing, of Hingham, Mass.,
        Feb. 21, 1836. She was b. in Hingham
        June 25, 1817, and was dau. of Ezekiel and Anna (Cushing)
        Fearing.
                    Child born in Hingham.
        1309.   I. ISAIAH F.[8] born Nov. 24, 1838.

Mary A. (Fearing) Tower died in Hingham, Dec. 4, 1838,
        ag. 21 y. 5 m. 9 d.
Isaiah G. Tower[7] mar., 2d, Sally Higgins, of Hingham,
        Oct. 10, 1840. She was b.
        Sept. 25, 1818, and was dau. of Sylvanus and Sally (Linel)
        Higgins.
                        Child.
        1310.   II. MARY ADAMS[8] born Aug. , 1841.

Isaiah G. Tower[7] died in Hingham, Dec. 25, 1841, ag. 28 y.
        4 m. 29 d.
Sally (Higgins) Tower died in Hingham, Sept. 10, 1843, ag.
        25 y. 2 m. 15 d.

881.   Eighth Generation.   Tower.

406. GEORGE A.[7], ISAIAH [6], ISAIAH [5], ISAIAH [4], PETER [3], BENJAMIN [2], JOHN [1].

George A.[7], son of Isaiah [6] and Chloe (Gardner) Tower, b. July 6, 1818; mar. Lucy Ann Marble, of Hingham, Mass., June 9, 1844. She was. b. in Hingham Sept. 8, 1823, and was dau. of Othniel S. and Lucy (Hoba Marble.

Childr.

I. GEORGE F [8] born Nov. 2, 1845.   III. Son [8]   born Oct. 27, 1850.
II. CHARLES I [8] "   May 16, 1849.   IV. LEAVITT J.[8] "   Dec. 4, 1851.

Lucy A. (Marble) Tower died in Fall River, Mass. George A. Tower [7] mar., 2d,   .

882.   Eighth Generation.   Tower.

406. CHARLES F.[7], ISAIAH [6], ISAIAH [5], ISAIAH [4], PETER [3], BENJAMIN [2], JOHN [1].

Charles F.[7], son of Isaiah [6] and Chloe (Gardner) Tower, b. April 19, 1823; mar. Harriet Newell Bisbee Dec. 19, 1852. She was b.
     1830. She died, and he mar., 2d, Ann Judson Bisbee. She was b. Dec. 15, 1833.

Child.

I. CARL VERNON [8] born Dec. 14, 1869.

883.   Eighth Generation.   Tower.

407. JOSHUA [7], JOSHUA [6], ISAIAH [5], ISAIAH [4], PETER [3], BENJAMIN [2], JOHN [1].

Joshua [7], son of Joshua [6] and Hannah (Hersey) Tower, b. Aug. 27, 1812; mar. Louisa Wilder, of Hingham, Mass., Dec. 19, 1839. She was b. in Hingham
     1812, and was dau. of Crocker and Deborah (Jacob) Wilder.

Childr. none.

Joshua Tower [7] died in Hingham, March 22, 1884, ag. 71 y. 5 m. 26 d.

884. Cushing.   Eighth Generation.   Tower.

407. ANGELINA H.[7], JOSHUA [6], ISAIAH [5], ISAIAH [4], PETER [3], BENJA-MIN [2], JOHN [1].

Angelina H.[7], dau. of Joshua [6] and Anna (Hersey) Tower, b.

Feb. 9, 1818 ; mar. Henry Cushing, of Hingham, Mass.,
May 2, 1839. He was b. in Hingham
Jan. 29, 1798, and was son of Henry and Sarah (Whiton)
    Cushing.
                    Childr. born in Hingham.

I. ANGELINA [8] born   1843.   II. HENRY W.[8] born May 27, 1848.

Henry Cushing died in Hingham, Jan. 25, 1864, ag. 65 y.
    11 m. 14 d.

885.   **Eighth Generation.**   **Tower.**

407. EDWIN [7], JOSHUA [6], ISAIAH [5], ISAIAH [4], PETER [3], BENJAMIN [2],
    JOHN [1].
Edwin [7], son of Joshua [6] and Anna (Hersey) Tower, b.
Dec. 11, 1821 ; mar. Maria Churchill, of Hingham, Mass.,
Jan. 1, 1851. She was. b. in Hingham
        1829, and was dau. of Rufus and Eunice (Lewis)
    Churchill.
                    Childr. none.

Maria (Churchill) Tower died in Hingham, Jan. 12, 1853,
    ag. 23.
Edwin Tower [7] mar., 2d, Martha Collamore Kilby, of Den-
    nysville, Me.,
Aug. 30, 1859. She was b. in Dennysville
        1827, and was dau. of Theophilus and Deborah
    (Wilder) Kilby.
                    Childr. none.

886. Whitcomb. Eighth Generation.   **Tower.**

407. MARY J.[7], JOSHUA [6], ISAIAH [5], ISAIAH [4], PETER [3], BENJAMIN [2],
    JOHN [1].
Mary J.[7], dau. of Joshua [6] and Anna (Hersey) Tower, b.
July 16, 1824 ; mar. Edwin Barker Whitcomb, of Hingham,
Jan. 16, 1848. He was b. in Hingham
        1827, and was son of Ezekiel and Lucy (Whitcomb)
    Whitcomb.
                    Childr. born in Hingham.

        I. JANE B.[8]   born June 2, 1849.
       II. ANNA L.[8]   "   May 28, 1851.
      III. ARTHUR RAYNOR [8] " Nov. 11, 1856.

887. Spooner.   Eighth Generation.   **Tower.**

408. MARY R.[7], LEAVITT [6], ISAIAH [5], ISAIAH [4], PETER [3], BENJAMIN [2],
    JOHN [1].
Mary R.[7], dau. of Leavitt [6] and Mary J. (Jacob) Tower, b.

Nov. 26, 1824; mar. Richard H. Spooner, of Boston,
July 12, 1846. He was b.
1818, and was son of William and Lydia Spooner.

Childr. none.

Richard H. Spooner died in Hingham, Nov. 16, 1853, ag. 35.
Mary R. (Tower) Spooner died in Hingham, Oct. 7, 1849,
ag. 24 y. 10 m. 11 d.

888. Eighth Generation. Tower.

409. REUBEN [7], REUBEN [6], ISAIAH [5], ISAIAH [4], PETER [3], BENJAMIN [2],
JOHN [1].
Reuben [7], son of Reuben [6] and Rebecca (Hathaway) Tower, b.
Dec. 30, 1820; mar. Hannah D. Snow, of Maine,
Dec. 20, 1843.

Childr.

I. HANNAH LOUISE [8] born Nov. 5, 1844, died March 11, 1847, ag.
2 y. 4 m. 6 d.
1311. II. REUBEN EDWARDS [8] " April 12, 1847.
1312. III. HANNAH LOUISE [8] " Oct. 5, 1848.

889. Wilder. Eighth Generation. Tower.

409. REBECCA [7], REUBEN [6], ISAIAH [5], ISAIAH [4], PETER [3], BENJAMIN [2],
JOHN [1].
Rebecca [7], dau. of Reuben [6] and Rebecca (Hathaway) Tower, b.
Feb. 18, 1822; mar. Ezra Wilder, of Hingham, Mass.,
Feb. 28, 1841. He was b. in Hingham
June 13, 1819, and was son of Joshua and Judith (Sherman)
Wilder.

Childr. born in Hingham.

I. LUCY SHERMAN [8] born Jan. 30, 1842; died Oct. 10, 1842
II. EZRA [8] " Nov. 26, 1843.
III. ELLEN REBECCA [8] " July 1, 1845; died Feb. 13, 1846.
IV. FREDERICK [8] " Aug. 23, 1846.
V. JOSHUA SHERMAN [8] " Nov. 16, 1847.

Ezra Wilder died in Weymouth, Mass., Oct. 21, 1886, ag.
67 y. 4 m. 7 d.

889 a. Stoddard. Eighth Generation. Tower.

409. BETSEY A. [7], REUBEN [6], ISAIAH [5], ISAIAH [4], PETER [3], BENJAMIN [2],
JOHN [1].
Betsey A. [7], dau. of Reuben [6] and Rebecca (Hathaway)
Tower, b.

Sept. 3, 1823 ; mar. Peter Stoddard [8]

Nov. 3, 1844. He was b.

1820, and was son of Peter [7] and Jane M. (Wilder) Stoddard.

Childr. born in Hingham.

I.   ROSALIE ANN [8] born Nov. 28, 1845.

II.   Son [8]   " Dec. 16, 1850.

STODDARD.   TOWER.

Peter [8], Peter [7], Mary [6], Rachel [5], David [4], Hezekiah [3], Ibrook [2], John [1].

---

890. Bowditch.   Eighth Generation.   Tower.

409. CAROLINE [7], REUBEN [6], ISAIAH [5], ISAIAH [4], PETER [3], BENJAMIN [2], JOHN [1].

Caroline [7], dau. of Reuben [6] and Rebecca (Hathaway)Tower, b.

March 17, 1825 ; mar. William W. Bowditch in Hingham, Mass.,

Nov. 26, 1854.   He was b. in Braintree, Mass.,

1829.

891.   Eighth Generation.   Tower.

409. WILLIAM S.[7], REUBEN [6], ISAIAH [5], ISAIAH [4], PETER [3], BENJAMIN [2], JOHN [1].

William S.[7], son of Reuben [6] and Rebecca (Hathaway) Tower, b.

July 7, 1826 ; mar. Mary A. Wilder [7], of Hingham, Mass.,

Nov. 24, 1850. She was b. in Hingham

Nov. 22, 1822, and was dau. of Joseph and Lydia [6] (Loring) Wilder.

Childr. born in Hingham.

I.   MARY A.[8]   born Dec. 11, 1854; died Dec. 14, 1854.

II.   MARY ADDIE [8] " Sept. 12, 1857.

1313.   III.   NELLIE JACOB [8] "   Feb. 7, 1863.

892.   Eighth Generation.   Tower.

409. JOHN B.[7], REUBEN [6], ISAIAH [5], ISAIAH [4], PETER [3], BENJAMIN [2], JOHN [1].

John B.[7], son of Reuben [6] and Rebecca (Hathaway) Tower, b.

Jan. 3, 1828 ; mar. Lucy A. Whitmarsh, of Weymouth, Mass.,

Jan. 7, 1848. She was b. in Weymouth

July 15, 1829, and was dau. of Freeman and Lucy Whitmarsh.

Childr. born in Weymouth.

I.   JOHN E.[8]   born May 16, 1849; died Feb. 8, 1850.

II.   ANNA BROOKS [8] "   July 25, 1850; mar. James H. Stetson, of Littleton, Mass., Dec. 31, 1871.

III.   Daughter[8]   born Oct. 13, 1855.
IV.   OSCAR AUGUSTUS[8] "   May 27, 1859.

John B. Tower[7] died in Weymouth, April 15,1880, ag. 52 y.
    3 m. 12 d.

893.   **Eighth Generation.**   **Tower.**

409. ANDREW[7], REUBEN[6], ISAIAH[5], ISAIAH[4], PETER[3], BENJAMIN[2],
        JOHN[1].
    Andrew[7], son of Reuben[6] and Rebecca (Hathaway)Tower, b.
    May 26, 1829; mar. Anna A. Mead, of Lawrence, Mass.,
    Nov. 7, 1853. She was b. in Lowell, Mass.,
    May 22, 1833, and was dau. of William and Nancy (Berry)
        Mead.

Childr.

I.   LOUISA A.[8]   born Nov. 5, 1856.
II.   EMMA REBECCA[8] "   Jan. 27, 1864.

894.   **Eighth Generation.**   **Tower**

409. JAMES G.[7], REUBEN[6], ISAIAH[5], ISAIAH[4], PETER[3], BENJAMIN[2],
        JOHN[1].
    James G.[7], son of Reuben[6] and Rebecca (Hathaway) Tower, b.
    March 26, 1831; mar. Maria H. Lincoln, of Charlestown,
    Dec. 2, 1862. She was b.
        1842, and was dau. of Joshua M. and Mercy Lincoln.
    James G. Tower[7] died in Boston, July 6, 1884, ag. 53 y. 3 m.
        11 d.

895.   **Eighth Generation.**   **Tower.**

409. HENRY T.[7], REUBEN[6], ISAIAH[5], ISAIAH[4], PETER[3], BENJAMIN[2],
        JOHN[1].
    Henry T.[7], son of Reuben[6] and Rebecca (Hathaway)Tower, b.
    April 9, 1833; mar. Drucilla Swift, of Plymouth, Mass.,
    Oct. · 7, 1853. She was b. in Plymouth
    May 16, 1832, and was dau. of Thomas and Lois (Briggs)
        Swift.

Childr. born in Plymouth.

1314.   I.   ALICE MELVILLE[8] born Aug. 15, 1857.
        II.   HERBERT E.[8]   "   May 24, 1862.

Drucilla (Swift) Tower died March 6, 1865, ag. 32 y. 9 m.
    21 d.
Henry T. Tower[7] mar., 2d, widow Mary E. Edwards
Jan. 21, 1866. She was born in Lynn, Mass.,
        1840, and was dau. of Michael and Mary Mulligan.

Child.

III. FLORIMOND EDWARD [8] born April 2, 1868.

896.   **Eighth Generation.**   **Tower.**

409. CHARLES S.[7], REUBEN [6], ISAIAH [5], ISAIAH [4], PETER [3], BENJA-
MIN [2], JOHN [1].

Charles S.[7], son of Reuben [6] and Rebecca (Hathaway)
Tower, b.
Dec. 27, 1838 ; mar. Lucy Torrey, of South Scituate, Mass.,
Dec. 26, 1858. She was b. in South Scituate (Norwell),
Jan. 2, 1840, and was dau. of George and Eliza (Day)
Torrey.

Childr. none.

897. Gardner.   Eighth Generation.   Tower.

410. LUCY A.[7], WILLIAM [6], LUCY [5], LABAN [4], PETER [3], BENJAMIN [2],
JOHN [1].

Lucy A.[7], dau. of William [6] and Lucy A. (Young) Tower, b.
Oct. 17, 1853 ; mar. Henry C. Gardner [9], of Hingham,
Jan. 12, 1869. He was b. in Hanover, Mass.,
March 13, 1841, and was son of Thomas H.[8] and Sally
(Chubbuck) Gardner.

Childr. born in Hingham.

I.   ROBERT H.[8]   } Twins born May 27, 1870; { died May 28, 1870.
II. WILLIAM H.[8] }   { "   Sept. 9, 1870.
III. EDGAR FRANCIS [8]   "   June 11, 1872.
IV. ELIZABETH MARIA [8]   "   Nov. 27, 1873 ; died Oct. 23, 1874.
V.   KATY GERTRUDE [8]   "   Dec. 30, 1874.

Lucy A. (Tower) Gardner died in Hingham, Feb. 8, 1876,
ag. 22 y. 3 m. 22 d.

898.   **Eighth Generation.**   **Tower.**

410. WILLIAM A.[7], WILLIAM [6], LUCY [5], LABAN [4], PETER [3], BENJA-
MIN [2], JOHN [1].

William A.[7], son of William [6] and Lucy A. (Young) Tower, b.
July 26, 1855 ; mar. Laura Frances Tilden, of Hingham,
Dec. 15, 1882. She was b. in Hingham, Mass.,
Dec. 20, 1859, and was dau. of George W. and Jane (Mor-
rison) Tilden.

Child born in Hingham.

I. GEORGE ARTHUR [8] born Dec. 15, 1883.

899. Eighth Generation. Tower.

410. CHARLES S. [7], WILLIAM [6], LUCY [5], LABAN [4], PETER [3], BEN-JAMIN [2] JOHN [1].

Charles S.[7], son of William [6] and Lucy A. (Young) Tower, b. June 18, 1856; mar. Alice Mayhew, of Turner, Me., 1877.

Child.

I. ELLA [8] born Aug. , 1879.

900. Clark. Eighth Generation. Tower.

410. ELIZABETH M.[7], WILLIAM [6], LUCY [5], LABAN [4], PETER [3], BEN-JAMIN [2], JOHN [1].

Elizabeth M.[7], dau. of William [6] and Lucy A. (Young) Tower, b.
Dec. 31, 1861; mar. Charles Munroe Clark, of Boston, Oct. 7, 1879.

Childr. born in Hingham.

I. JEANNETTE TOWER [8] born Aug. 5, 1881.
II. RALPH ALEXANDER [8] " Aug. 25, 1886.

901. Eighth Generation. Tower.

412. PHILO [7], ISAAC [6], ISAAC [5], JOSEPH [4], AMBROSE [3], BENJAMIN [2], JOHN [1].

Philo [7], son of Isaac [6] and Polly (Haskell) Tower, b.
Jan. 1, 1812; mar. Cynthia Beecher, of Avon, N. Y., Sept. 17, 1837. She was b. in Sharon, Conn., 1816, and was dau. of Ransom and Adelia (Deming) Beecher.

Childr.

1315. I. MARY ADELIA BEECHER [8] born Oct. 12, 1841.
II. JOHN DEMPSTER [8] " July 11, 1847; died Jan. , 1850, ag. 2 y. 6 m.

Cynthia (Beecher) Tower died in Adrian, Mich., June 30, 1860, ag. 44.
Philo Tower [7] mar., 2d, Abby Ann Bills in Lowell, N Y., Aug. 2, 1863. She was b. in Bennington, Vt., and was dau. of Thomas and Eliza (Hollenbeck) Bills.

Childr. born in Lowell.

III. JOHN WESLEY [8] born Jan. 17, 1865.
IV. DOCTOR DEMPSTER [8] " May 16, 1866.
V. WILBUR FISK [8] " Aug 17, 1868.

902. Travis.   Eighth Generation.   Tower.

412. Louisa[7], Isaac[6], Isaac[5], Joseph[4], Ambrose[3], Benjamin[2], John[1].

Louisa[7], dau. of Isaac[6] and Polly (Haskell) Tower, b. June 23, 1813; mar. John Travis, of Canandaigua, N. Y.

Child.
I. Child; died at the age of 10 years.

John Travis died in Canandaigua.
Louisa (Tower) Travis died in Canandaigua, 1873, ag. 60.

903.   Eighth Generation.   Tower.

412. Andrew J.[7], Isaac[6], Isaac[5], Joseph[4], Ambrose[3], Benjamin[2], John[1].

Andrew J.[7], son of Isaac[6] and Polly (Haskell) Tower, b. July 4, 1815; mar. Susan Chase.

Child.
I. Ellen[8] born   ; mar. Thomas Stillson, of Detroit, Mich.

Andrew J. Tower[7] died March   , 1837, ag. 21 y. 8 m.
Susan (Chase) Tower died in Flint, Mich.

904. Moore.   Eighth Generation.   Tower.

412. Hannah[7], Isaac[6], Isaac[5], Joseph[4], Ambrose[3], Benjamin[2], John[1].

Hannah[7], dau. of Isaac[6] and Polly (Haskell) Tower, b. April 25, 1819; mar. Joel Moore   1840. He was b. Sept. 30, 1809, and was son of Joel and Sarah (Gillet) Moore.

Childr.
I. Edwin R.[8]   born March 16, 1843.
II. Diantha R[8]   " Aug. 28, 1846.
III. William W.[8] } Twins " March 2, 1852.
IV. Wilson W.[8] }

Joel Moore died Jan. 9, 1877, ag. 67 y. 3 m. 9 d.
Hannah (Tower) Moore died March 19, 1852, ag. 32 y. 10 m. 24 d.

905.   Eighth Generation.   Tower.

412. Charles H.[7], Isaac[6], Isaac[5], Joseph[4], Ambrose[3], Benjamin[2], John[1].

Charles H.[7], son of Isaac[6] and Polly (Haskell) Tower, b.

Jan. 28, 1825 ; mar. Rowena Moreland

Jan. 20, 1859. She was b.

Aug. 28, 1839, and was dau. of William and Olive (Powers) Moreland.

Childr.

I.	LIBBIE [8]	born Aug. 6, 1859; died Sept. 25, 1876, ag. 17 y. 1 m. 20 d.
II.	LEWIS ELMER [8]	" May 3, 1861.
III.	WILLIAM LAWRENCE [8]	" June 9, 1863.
IV.	CHARLES EDWIN [8]	" Dec. 6, 1865; died Oct. 19, 1867, ag. 1 y. 10 m. 13 d.
V.	CHARLES LEE [8]	" May 28, 1869; " April 10, 1883, ag. 13 y. 10 m. 13 d.

906.   **Eighth Generation.**   **Tower.**

414. ISAAC [7], JOB [6], ISAAC [5], JOSEPH [4], AMBROSE [3], BENJAMIN [2], JOHN [1].

Isaac [7], son of Job [6] and Nancy (Sanger) Tower, b.

Nov. 24, 1823 ; mar. Mary Eleanor Ackerman, of Portsmouth, N. H.,
        1850.

Childr.

	I.	CARRIE FRENCH [8] born July 6, 1851.	
1316.	II	SUSAN LURANA [8] " June 2, 1857.	

Mary E. (Ackerman) Tower died in   , 1860.

Isaac Tower [7] mar., 2d, widow Harriet A. Hill, of Boston.

907. Sweetzer.   Eighth Generation.   **Tower.**

414. ALICE M. [7], JOB [6], ISAAC [5], JOSEPH [4], AMBROSE [3], BENJAMIN [2], JOHN [1].

Alice M. [7], dau. of Job [6] and Nancy (Sanger) Tower, b.

Aug. 14, 1825 ; mar. George H. Sweetzer, of Boston,

Feb. 16, 1852. He was b. in Boston

April 7, 1831, and was son of George H. and Sarah (Wiley) Sweetzer.

Childr. born in New York city.

I.	MARY AUGUSTA [8]	born Nov. 5, 1853.
II.	CLARA JANE [8]	" Oct. 7, 1855; died Aug. 31, 1856.
III.	GEORGETTA [8]	" June 25, 1858.
IV.	WILLIE WALLACE [8]	" May 5, 1860; died Aug. 16, 1862, ag. 2 y. 3 m. 11 d.
V.	CHARLES EDWARD [8]	" Jan. 11, 1862; died July 30, 1862.
VI.	ALICE MARIA [8] } Twins	" Jan. 6, 1867; { died June 20, 1867.
VII.	VESTA VEAZIE [8] }	{ " June 4, 1867.

908. Flood.   **Eighth Generation.**   **Tower.**

414. MARY[7], JOB[6], ISAAC[5], JOSEPH[4], AMBROSE[3], BENJAMIN[2],
JOHN[1].

Mary[7], dau. of Job[6] and Nancy (Sanger) Tower, b.
Feb. 24, 1828; mar. Christopher Flood
Aug. 20, 1856. He was born in Dublin, Ireland,
April 25, 1829, and was son of Christopher and Marianna
(Mollen) Flood.

Childr. born in Morrisania, N. Y.

I.   MARY ALICE[8]   born Oct. 31, 1858.
II. CHRISTABEL[8]   "   Dec. 8, 1861.
III. WILLIAM TOWER[8]   died May 20, 1870,
                                                                      ag. 2 y. 8 m.
IV. LILIAN TOWER[8]   Twins   "   Sept. 19, 1867;   died Nov. 17, 1867,
                                                                      ag. 1 m. 28 d.

909.   **Eighth Generation.**   **Tower.**

414. CHARLES[7], JOB[6], ISAAC[5], JOSEPH[4], AMBROSE[3], BENJAMIN[2],
JOHN[1].

Charles[7], son of Job[6] and Nancy (Sanger) Tower, b.
July 24, 1836; mar. Frances Ann Badger, of Brooklyn, N. Y.,
March 21, 1868. She was b. in Brooklyn
Sept. 23, 1846, and was dau. of Augustus Henry and Fran-
ces (Higby) Badger.

Childr. born in Brooklyn.

I.   NELLY FRANCES[8] born Jan. 21, 1869.
II. CHARLES HENRY[8]   "   June 29, 1871.
III. ALICE LURANA[8]   "   Aug. 3, 1873.
IV. SUSAN ADELAIDE[8] "   Feb. 14, 1877.

910.   **Eighth Generation.**   **Tower.**

417. JOSHUA C.[7], SAMUEL[6], ISAAC[5], JOSEPH[4], AMBROSE[3], BENJA-
MIN[2], JOHN[1].

Joshua C.[7], son of Samuel[6] and Asenath (Dickenson)
Tower, b.
July 19, 1823; mar. Charlotte Nash, of Amherst, Mass.,
April 11, 1849. She was b.
Feb. 28, 1825, and was dau. of Luther and Salva Nash.

Childr. born in Amherst.

1317.   I. SAMUEL DWIGHT[8] born June 10, 1852.
        II. MYRON LUTHER[8]   "   Sept.   , 1860.

911.   **Eighth Generation.**   **Tower.**

417. SAMUEL M.[7], SAMUEL [6], ISAAC [5], JOSEPH [4], AMBROSE [3], BENJA-
MIN [2], JOHN [1].

Samuel M.[7], son of Samuel [6] and Mary (Clark) Tower, b.
Aug. 14, 1832; mar. Lucia Davis, of Cazenovia, N. Y.,
April , 1858. She was dau. of Joseph Davis. ˙
Samuel M. Tower [7] died in Hadley, Mass., Dec. 19, 1860, ag.
28 y. 4 m. 5 d.

912.   **Eighth Generation.**   **Tower.**

417. J. EDWIN [7], SAMUEL [6], ISAAC [5], JOSEPH [4], AMBROSE [3], BENJA-
MIN [2], JOHN [1].

J. Edwin [7], son of Samuel [6] and Mary (Clark) Tower, b.
June 9, 1834 ; mar. Harriet I. Eaton, of Groton, Mass.,
March 13, 1862. She was b. in Stoddard, N. H.,
Jan. 5, 1835, and was dau. of Joel W. and Indiana (Green)
Eaton.

Child born in North Brookfield, Mass.

I. JAMES E.[8] born March 17, 1863.

J. Edwin Tower [7] died in Groton, Aug. 18, 1862, ag. 28 y,
2 m. 9 d.
Harriet I. (Eaton) Tower mar., 2d, Timothy Mason Duncan,
of North Brookfield,
Sept. 27, 1871. He was b.
1822.

913. Fish.   **Eighth Generation.**   **Tower.**

417. MARY ANN [7], SAMUEL [6], ISAAC [5], JOSEPH [4], AMBROSE [3], BENJA-
MIN [2], JOHN [1].

Mary Ann [7], dau. of Samuel [6] and Mary (Clark) Tower, b.
May 23, 1837 ; mar. Lauriston C. Fish, of Hadley, Mass.,
June 6, 1860. He was son of Lewis and Polly Fish.

Childr. none.

Mary Ann (Tower) Fish died March 6, 1863, ag. 25 y. 9 m.
14 d.

914.   **Eighth Generation.**   **Tower.**

418. CHARLEMAGNE [7], REUBEN [6], JEDUTHUN [5], JOSEPH [4], AMBROSE [3],
BENJAMIN [2], JOHN [1].

Charlemagne [7], son of Reuben [6] and Deborah T. (Pierce)
Tower, b.

April 18, 1809 ; mar. Amelia Malvina Bartle in Orwigsburg,
Penn.,

June 14, 1847. She was b.

Dec. 12, 1819, and was dau. of Lambert B. and Sarah (Herring) Bartle.

Childr.

1318.	I.	CHARLEMAGNE [8]	born April 17, 1848, in Philadelphia, Penn.
	II.	SARAH LOUISA [8]	" Aug. 6, 1849, in Orwigsburg; died in Pottsville, Penn., June 16, 1868, ag. 18 y. 10 m. 10 d.
1319.	III.	DEBORAH TAYLOR [8]	" Feb. 4, 1851, in Orwigsburg.
1320.	IV.	EMMA [8]	" June 15, 1852, in Pottsville.
	V.	ELIZABETH [8]	" March 2, 1854, " ; died Sept. 20, 1855, ag. 1 y. 6 m. 18 d.
	VI.	HENRIETTA [8]	" Oct. 26, 1856, in Pottsville.
1321.	VII.	GRACE WILLIAMS [8]	" May 15, 1859.

915.   **Eighth Generation.**   **Tower.**

418. JULIUS [7], REUBEN [6], JEDUTHUN [5], JOSEPH [4], AMBROSE [3], BENJA-
MIN [2], JOHN [1].

Julius [7], son of Reuben [6] and Deborah T. (Pierce) Tower, b.

April 17, 1811 ; mar. Delia Hearsey, of Waterville, N. Y.,

Sept. 12, 1832. She was b. in Waterville

Oct. 13, 1811, and was dau. of Henry and Nancy (Bartholomew) Hearsey.

Childr.

1322.	I.	WALTER SCOTT [8]	born May 10, 1834.
	II	ROBERT [8]	" Sept. 5, 1837; unmar.

Delia (Hearsey) Tower died in Philadelphia, Dec. 23, 1881,
ag. 70 y. 2 m. 10 d.

916. Page.   **Eighth Generation.**   **Tower.**

418. HENRIETTA [7], REUBEN [6], JEDUTHUN [5], JOSEPH [4], AMBROSE [3],
BENJAMIN [2], JOHN [1].

Henrietta [7], dau. of Reuben [6] and Deborah T. (Pierce)
Tower, b.

Aug. 30, 1814 ; mar. Putnam Page, of Waterville, N. Y.,

Oct. 10, 1833. He was b. in Sangerfield, N. Y.,

Dec. 9, 1809, and was son of William and Margaret (Terry)
Page.

Childr.

I.	REUBEN TOWER [8]	born July 3, 1834; died April 24, 1838, ag. 3 y. 9 m. 21 d.
II.	DEBORAH TOWER [8]	" June 29, 1837.
III.	HENRIETTA TOWER [8]	" June 3, 1840.
IV.	ARABELLA PUTNAM [8]	" April 29, 1860; died May 22, 1860.

Putnam Page died in New York city, April 25, 1881, ag. 71 y. 4 m. 17 d.

917. **Eighth Generation.** **Tower.**

418. FAYETTE B.[7], REUBEN[6], JEDUTHUN[5], JOSEPH[4], AMBROSE[3], BENJAMIN[2], JOHN[1].

Fayette Bartholomew[7], son of Reuben[6] and Deborah Taylor (Pierce) Tower, b.

Jan. 29, 1817; mar. Elizabeth Huntington Phelps July 11, 1839. She was b. in Guilford, Vt.,

Dec. 7, 1818, and was dau. of John and Lucy (Lovell) Phelps.

Childr. none.

Elizabeth H. (Phelps) Tower died in New York city, Jan. 31, 1841, ag. 22 y. 1 m. 25 d.

Fayette B. Tower[7] mar., 2d, Ann Regina Phelps Sept. 5, 1843. She was b. in Guilford, Vt.,

Jan. 17, 1822, and was dau. of John and Lucy (Lovell) Phelps.

Childr.

1322 a.	I. LAWRENCE[8] born Oct. 16, 1845, at Oriskany Falls, N. Y.	
	II. CLARENCE[8] " March 14, 1847, " " " ;	
	died Sept. 19, 1849, at Waterville, N. Y., ag. 2 y. 6 m. 6 d.	

Ann R. (Phelps) Tower died at Oriskany Falls, March 30, 1847, ag. 25 y. 2 m. 13 d.

Fayette B. Tower[7] mar., 3d, Anna L. Frary at Cumberland, Md.,

Aug. 1, 1850. She was b. in New Lisbon, N. Y., Nov. 19, 1831.

Childr.

	III. FLOYD[8] born Nov. 7, 1851, in Cumberland, Md.	
1322 b.	IV. EMILY[8] " Nov. 12, 1854, " "	

Fayette B. Tower[7] died at Waterville, N. Y., Feb. 16, 1857, ag. 40 y. 18 d.

Anna L. (Frary) Tower died at Fort Wayne, Ind., Jan. 5, 1883.

918. **Eighth Generation.** **Tower.**

418. DE WITT C.[7], REUBEN[6], JEDUTHUN[5], JOSEPH[4], AMBROSE[3], BENJAMIN[2], JOHN[1].

De Witt C.[7] son of Reuben[6] and Deborah T. (Pierce) Tower, b.

Jan. 20, 1821; mar. Anne Williams, of Waterloo, N. Y.,
   She was b.
Feb. 24, 1824, and was dau. of Samuel and Philanda (Brooks)
  Williams.

Childr.

1323.	I.	BLANCHE [8]	born June 22, 1845, in Waterville, N. Y.	
	II.	FRANCIS EARL [8]	" Aug. 30, 1847, " ; unmar.	
1324.	III.	DE WITT CLINTON [8]	" Sept. 27, 1856, in Brooklyn, N. Y.	
	IV.	ARTHUR [8]	" Aug. 16, 1859, " "	

De Witt Clinton Tower [7] died in Brooklyn, Oct. 18, 1873,
 ag. 52 y. 8 m. 29 d.

919.   **Eighth Generation.**   **Tower.**

418. JAMES M. [7], REUBEN [6], JEDUTHUN [5], JOSEPH [4], AMBROSE [3], BEN-
  JAMIN [2], JOHN [1].
 James M. [7], son of Reuben [6] and Deborah T. (Pierce) Tower, b.
 March 21, 1823; mar. Mary Catherine Osborn in Waterville,
  N. Y.,
 Aug. 4, 1847. She was b.
 May 6, 1823, and was dau. of Amos Osborn.

Childr. none.

Mary Catherine (Osborn) Tower died Jan. 2, 1875, ag. 51 y.
 7 m. 27 d.

920.   **Eighth Generation.**   **Tower.**

418. FRANCIS M. [7], REUBEN [6], JEDUTHUN [5], JOSEPH [4], AMBROSE [3],
  BENJAMIN [2], JOHN [1].
 Francis M. [7], son of Reuben [6] and Deborah T. (Pierce) Tower, b.
 July 31, 1825; mar. Sarah A. Ransom in Brooklyn, N. Y.,
 Sept. 2, 1852.

Childr.

I.	CORA [8]	born 1855, in Pottsville, Penn.	
II.	ANNA [8]	" Feb. 29, 1860, " Boston.	
III.	SARAH [8]	" " Bridgeport, Conn.	
IV.	FLORENCE [8]	" " " "	

921. Seabury. **Eighth Generation.** **Tower.**

419. HARRIET A. [7], DANIEL [6], JEDUTHUN [5], JOSEPH [4], AMBROSE [3],
  BENJAMIN [2], JOHN [1].
 Harriet A. [7], dau. of Daniel [6] and Thirza (Whitmarsh)
  Tower, b.
 Oct. 30, 1815; mar. Micah Seabury, of Waterville, N. Y.,
 May 6, 1833.

Childr.

I. JULIA[8] born March 4, 1834, in Waterville, N. Y.
II. HARRIET[8] " May 17, 1837, "   "   "

Harriet A. (Tower) Seabury died May 22, 1837, ag. 21 y.
6 m. 21.

922. Sprague, Dyer.   Eighth Generation.   Tower.

419. MARY J.[7], DANIEL[6], JEDUTHUN[5], JOSEPH[4], AMBROSE[3], BEN-
JAMIN[2], JOHN[1].

Mary J.[7], dau. of Daniel[6] and Thirza (Whitmarsh) Tower, b.
Sept. 3, 1817 ; mar. Andrew N. Dyer
June 12, 1837. He was b. in Oneida Co., N. Y.,
            and was son of Sylvanus and Amor (Norton) Dyer.

Childr. none.

Andrew N. Dyer died in Fulton, Ill., Dec. 23, 1854.
Mary J.[7] (Tower) Dyer mar., 2d, Barney Sprague in Che-
nango, N. Y.
April 29, 1856. He was born in Chenango
April 19, 1819, and was son of Charles and Lurana (Bennet)
Sprague.

Childr.

I. FRANK H.[8] born March 16, 1857, in Chenango.
II. CARRIE L.[8] " Oct. 13, 1860, in Waterville ; died Sept. 19, 1875, ag.
            14 y. 11 m. 7 d.

923.   Eighth Generation.   Tower.

419. CHARLES[7], DANIEL[6], JEDUTHUN[5], JOSEPH[4], AMBROSE[3], BEN-
JAMIN[2], JOHN[1].

Charles[7], son of Daniel[6] and Thirza (Whitmarsh) Tower, b.
Jan. 18, 1819; mar. Elvira Whitney, of Truxton, N. Y.,
March 13, 1843. She was b. in Augusta, N. Y.,
            , and was dau. of James H. and Lydia (Gates)
      Whitney.

Childr. born in Homer, N. Y.

1325. I. FRANK C.[8]   born Sept. 21, 1846.
       II. FREDERICK E.[8] " June 22, 1852.

Elvira (Whitney) Tower died June 22, 1852.
Charles Tower[7] mar., 2d, Lucina Stone, of Chenango, N. Y.,
Jan. 23, 1854. She was born in Chenango
March 17, 1823, and was dau. of Stephen and Eliza (Allen)
Stone.

Childr. none.

Lucina (Stone) Tower died Feb. 14, 1870, ag. 46 y. 11 m.

Charles Tower[7] mar., 3d, widow Sally M. Gates, of Homer,
Nov. 10, 1870. She was born in Salem, N. Y.,
Feb. 8, 1818, and was dau. of Charles and Orra (Merrill)
Withey.

Charles Tower[7] died in Homer, N. Y., Sept. 17, 1887, ag.
68 y. 8 m.

---

924.   **Eighth Generation.**   **Tower.**

419. LENTHEL[7], DANIEL[6], JEDUTHUN[5], JOSEPH[4], AMBROSE[3], BEN-
JAMIN[2], JOHN[1].

Lenthel[7], son of Daniel[6] and Thirza (Whitmarsh) Tower, b.
Dec. 23, 1820 ; mar. Cornelia M. Hull, of Volney, N. Y.,
She was b.
Nov. 18, 1823.

Childr. born in Gaines, N. Y.

> 1326.   I.   JAMES A.[8]   born July 29, 1843.
> 1327.   II.   LYMAN H.[8]   "   July 11, 1845.

Lenthel Tower[7] died in Ottawa, Ill., Sept. 21, 1867, ag. 46 y.
8 m. 29 d.

Cornelia M. (Hull) Tower died in Volney, N. Y., Aug. 14,
1865, ag. 41 y. 8 m. 26 d.

---

925.   **Eighth Generation.**   **Tower.**

422. ALBERT[7], JONAS[6], JEDUTHUN[5], JOSEPH[4], AMBROSE[3], BENJA-
MIN[2], JOHN[1].

Albert[7], son of Jonas[6] and Almira (Stone) Tower, b.
Nov. 8, 1817 ; mar. Mary Ann Bidwell, of Madison, Ohio,
Feb. 4, 1841. She was b.
July 15, 1815, and was dau. of William and Mary Bidwell.

Childr. none.

Mary Ann (Bidwell) Tower died April 15, 1848, ag. 39 y.
9 m.

Albert Tower[7] mar., 2d, Anna M. Underhill, of Pough-
keepsie, N. Y.,
Sept. 11, 1860. She was born in Hudson, N. Y.,
Aug. 28, 1828, and was dau. of Josiah I. and Hannah
Underhill.

Childr. born in Poughkeepsie.

I.   ALBERT EDWARD [8]   born Jan. 4, 1863.
II.   JOSEPH TUCKERMAN [8]   " Aug. 22, 1864.
III. MARY FRANCES [8]   " March 10, 1866; died March 13, 1866.
IV.   FREDERICK [8]   " Aug. 6, 1867; died Sept. 17, 1867.

926. Blackman.   Eighth Generation.   Tower.

422. SARAH J.[7], JONAS [6], JEDUTHUN [5], JOSEPH [4], AMBROSE [3], BEN-
JAMIN [2], JOHN [1].

Sarah J.[7], dau. of Jonas [6] and Almira (Stone) Tower, b.
Feb. 13, 1824; mar. Benjamin Franklin Blackman, of Madi-
son, Ohio,
Jan. 10, 1847.

Childr. none.

Sarah J. (Tower) Blackman died in Ironton, Wis., Aug. 6,
1872, ag. 48 y. 5 m. 22 d.

927. Williams.   Eighth Generation.   Tower.

425. LOUISA [7], LUKE [6], JONATHAN [5], JOSEPH [4], AMBROSE [3], BENJA-
MIN [2], JOHN [1].

Louisa [7], dau. of Luke [6] and Mary (May) Tower, b.
April 21, 1817; mar. Jerry H. Williams, of Bakersfield, Vt.,
April 3, 1839. He was b.
July 21, 1816, and was son of Ebenezer and Keziah (Per-
ham) Williams.

Childr.

I.   SARAH AMANDA [8] born Jan. 28, 1840.
II.   MARY ALVINA [8]   " Aug. 22, 1842.
III. ELLA AURILLA [8]   " Oct. 8, 1853; died Nov. 28, 1858, ag. 5 y. 1 m.
21 d.

Jerry H. Williams died Feb. 2, 1868, ag. 51 y. 6 m. 12 d.
Louisa (Tower) Williams died in Oakham, Mass., Feb. 5,
1885, ag. 67 y. 9 m. 14 d.

928. Wood.   Eighth Generation.   Tower.

425. LURANA [7], LUKE [6], JONATHAN [5], JOSEPH [4], AMBROSE [3], BENJA-
MIN [2], JOHN [1].

Lurana [7], dau. of Luke [6] and Mary (May) Tower, b.
Nov. 24, 1818; mar. Isaac Sumner Wood, of Monson, Mass.,
He was b. in Monson
March 24, 1821, and was son of Levi and Esther (Roberts)
Wood.

Childr. none.

Lurana (Tower) Wood died in Spencer, Mass., Sept. 2, 1859, ag. 40 y. 9 m. 8 d.

929.   **Eighth Generation.**   **Tower.**

425. AMBROSE M.[7], LUKE[6], JONATHAN[5], JOSEPH[4], AMBROSE[3], BENJAMIN[2], JOHN[1].
Ambrose M.[7], son of Luke[6] and Mary (May) Tower, b. March 27, 1821; mar. Rosamond Draper Adams in Spencer Oct. 13, 1846. She was b. in Brookfield, Mass., Sept. 20, 1828.

Childr. born in Spencer, Mass.

1328. I. HENRY MENDELL[8] born July 23, 1847.
       II. IDA MARIA[8]   "   Nov. 29, 1856; died Dec. 10, 1856.

Ambrose M. Tower[7] died in Spencer, May 3, 1874, ag. 53 y. 1 m. 7 d.

930.   **Eighth Generation.**   **Tower.**

425. LORENZO[7], LUKE[6], JONATHAN[5], JOSEPH[4], AMBROSE[3], BENJAMIN[2], JOHN[1].
Lorenzo[7], son of Luke[6] and Mary (May) Tower, b. Nov. 24, 1824; mar. Melissa C. Harrington, of Adams, Mass., July 18, 1850. She was b.
May 19, 1825, and was dau. of Thaddeus and Susanna (Mason) Harrington.

Childr. none.

931.   **Eighth Generation.**   **Tower.**

425. MARVIN G.[7], LUKE[6], JONATHAN[5], JOSEPH[4], AMBROSE[3], BENJAMIN[2], JOHN[1].
Marvin G.[7], son of Luke[6] and Mary (May) Tower, b. Oct. 5, 1831; mar. Althea Elizabeth Jones, of Spencer, Mass., July 16, 1858. She was b. in Spencer March 15, 1842, and was dau. of Jacob W. and Martha (Buch) (Stratton) Jones.

Childr. none.

Althea E. (Jones) Tower died April 24, 1859, ag. 17 y. 1 m. 10 d.

Marvin G. Tower[7] mar., 2d, Harriet Olivia Merriam, of Burlington, Vt.,
She was dau. of Stedman G. and Harriet N. (Morton) Merriam.

Childr.

I. WINFRED MARVIN [8] born Aug. 21, 1863, in West Randolph, Vt.
II. HAROLD STEDMAN [8] " July 10, 1868, in Charles City, Iowa.

932. Hubbard. Eighth Generation. Tower.

427. JULIA S.[7], HORACE D.[6], JUSTUS [5], JOSEPH [4], AMBROSE [3], BENJA-
MIN [2], JOHN [1].

Julia S.[7], dau. of Horace D.[6] and Susan (Wolcott) Tower, b.
July 16, 1821; mar. John W. Hubbard
Jan. 22, 1851. He was b. in Pittsfield, Mass.,
Jan. 9, 1819, and was son of Henry and Sophia (Whitney)
Hubbard.

Childr. born in Waterville, N. Y.

I. FRED H.[8] born June 21, 1852.   III. IDA J.[8] born Aug. 31, 1859.
II. HATTIE T.[8] " Jan. 11, 1855.

933.   Eighth Generation. Tower.

427. HORACE W.[7], HORACE D.[6], JUSTUS [5], JOSEPH [4], AMBROSE [3],
BENJAMIN [2], JOHN [1].

Horace W.[7], son of Horace D.[6] and Susan (Wolcott) Tower, b.
July 19, 1824; mar. Cornelia S. Stafford, of Sangerfield, N.Y.,
Oct. 21, 1847. She was b.
July 4, 1825, and was dau. of Truman and Sarepta (Haw-
ley) Stafford.

Childr.

I. HORACE S.[8] born Dec. 11, 1848, in Sangerfield; died Aug. 9,
1849.
1329. II. WILLIAM S.[8] " July 13, 1850,   "
1330. III. CLARA S.[8] " Oct. 8, 1854, in Waterville, N. Y.

934.   Eighth Generation. Tower.

427. HENRY N.[7], HORACE D.[6], JUSTUS [5], JOSEPH [4], AMBROSE [3],
BENJAMIN [2], JOHN [1].

Henry N.[7], son of Horace D.[6] and Susan (Wolcott) Tower, b.
Sept. 17, 1830; mar. Sarah M. Simmons, of Paris, N. Y.,
Aug. 29, 1865. She was dau. of Philip Simmons.

Child.

I. FRANK S.[8] born Aug. 26, 1873.

Sarah M. (Simmons) Tower died April 26, 1874.
Henry N. Tower [7] mar., 2d, Phebe Hitchcock, of Madison,
N. Y.,
June 20, 1875.

935. Stafford.　Eighth Generation.　　Tower.

428. LAURA H.[7], HENRY[6], JUSTUS[5], JOSEPH[4], AMBROSE[3], BENJA-
MIN[2], JOHN[1].
Laura H.[7], dau. of Henry[6] and Eliza (Haynes) Tower, b.
Aug. 15, 1820 ; mar. John W. Stafford, of Sangerfield, N. Y.,
June 22, 1840. He was b. in Madison, N. Y.,
Sept. 7, 1814, and was son of Freeman and Sarepta (Haw-
ley) Stafford.

Child.

I. TRUMAN HENRY[8] born Aug. 3, 1845, in Waterville, N. Y.

936. Grant.　Eighth Generation.　　Tower.

428. MARY W.[7], HENRY[6], JUSTUS[5], JOSEPH[4], AMBROSE[3], BENJA-
MIN[2], JOHN[1].
Mary W.[7], dau. of Henry[6] and Eliza (Haynes) Tower, b.
April 30, 1822 ; mar. Rev. Stillman B. Grant, of Sangerfield,
N. Y.,
Aug. 25, 1847.

Child.

I. LILLIE[8] born May 8, 1851.

Stillman B. Grant died in Fitchburg, Mass., Dec. 17, 1874.
Mary W. (Tower) Grant died in Fitchburg, Sept. 23, 1885,
ag. 60 y. 4 m. 23 d.

937. Hayhurst.　Eighth Generation.　　Tower.

428. ELIZABETH H.[7], HENRY[6], JUSTUS[5], JOSEPH[4], AMBROSE[3],
BENJAMIN[2], JOHN[1].
Elizabeth H.[7], dau. of Henry[6] and Eliza (Haynes) Tower, b.
July 30, 1825 ; mar. Rev. Lamar W. Hayhurst, of Sanger-
field, N. Y.
Oct. 1, 1850. He was b.
April 3, 1823, and was son of Benajah and Martha (Kinsey)
Hayhurst.

Child.

I. HENRY TOWER[8] born Dec. 12, 1852, in Mohawk, N. Y.

Elizabeth H. (Tower) Hayhurst died in Waterville, N. Y.,
March 17, 1865, ag. 39 y. 7 m. 18 d.

938. Tolman.　Eighth Generation.　　Tower.

430. JANE A.[7], JUSTUS[6], JUSTUS[5], JOSEPH[4], AMBROSE[3], BENJAMIN[2],
JOHN[1].

Jane A.[7], dau. of Justus[6] and Emeline A. (Talcott) Tower, b. March 11, 1830; mar. Albert Tolman, of Pittsfield, Mass., Sept. 23, 1853. He was b. in Dorchester, Mass., Feb. 13, 1824, and was son of Stephen and Mary (Pierce) Tolman.

Childr.

I. CARLTON TOWER [8] born Aug. 23, 1854.
II. ALBERT HARRIS [8]   "   June 17, 1856.
III. WILLIAM [8]   "   June   2, 1858.
IV. GEORGE [8]   "   April 15, 1860.
V. EDWARD [8]   "   May 20, 1862.

Jane A. (Tower) Tolman died Sept. 30, 1871, ag. 41 y. 6 m. 20 d.

939.   **Eighth Generation.**   **Tower.**

430. EDWARD J.[7], JUSTUS [6], JUSTUS [5], JOSEPH [4], AMBROSE [3], BENJA-MIN [2], JOHN [1].

Edward J.[7], son of Justus [6] and Emeline A. (Talcott) Tower, b.

Oct. 4, 1832; mar. Sarah A. Wood, of Lanesborough, Mass., Oct. 1, 1857. She was b.

     1826, and was dau. of Titus and Elizabeth Wood.

Childr. none.

940.   **Childs.**   **Eighth Generation.**   **Tower.**

430. HARRIET N.[7], JUSTUS [6], JUSTUS [5], JOSEPH [4], AMBROSE [3], BEN-JAMIN [2], JOHN [1].

Harriet N.[7], dau. of Justus [6] and Emeline A. (Talcott) Tower, b.

Sept. 2, 1834; mar. Edwin L. Childs, of Pittsfield, Mass., Sept. 15, 1856. He was b. in Whately, Mass.,

     1829, and was son of Horace B. and Mary C. (Jennings) Childs.

Child.

I. CLARA [8] born   1859, in Pittsfield; died in Lanesborough, 1859.

941.   **Francis.**   **Eighth Generation.**   **Tower.**

430. MARTHA L.[7], JUSTUS [6], JUSTUS [5], JOSEPH [4], AMBROSE [3], BEN-JAMIN [2], JOHN [1].

Martha L.[7], dau. of Justus [6] and Emeline A. (Talcott) Tower, b.

May 8, 1838; mar. James Dwight Francis, of Lanesborough, Mass.,

June 15, 1859. He was b. in Pittsfield, Mass.,
Dec. 23, 1837, and was son of A. D. and Lucy (Churchill)
Francis.

Childr.

I.   HENRY A.[8] born Oct. 12, 1861.   IV. CLIFFORD [8] born March 3, 1872.
II. GEORGE D.[8] " Jan. 22, 1866.   V.   ROBERT T.[8] " Dec. 7, 1873.
III. FRED T.[8]   " Nov. 21, 1869.

Martha L. (Tower) Francis died in Pittsfield, Aug. 29, 1882,
ag. 44 y. 3 m. 21 d.

942. Hemming. Eighth Generation.   Tower.

430. MARY [7], JUSTUS [6], JUSTUS [5], JOSEPH [4], AMBROSE [3], BENJAMIN [2],
JOHN [1].
Mary [7], dau. of Justus [6] and Emeline A. (Talcott) Tower, b.
April 6, 1853; mar. John F. Hemming, of Lanesborough,
Oct. 22, 1874. He was b. in Cherry Valley, N. Y.,
Dec. 25, 1849, and was son of Robert H. and Minerva
(Walter) Hemming.

Childr.

I.   CLARA WALTON [8] born Nov. 9, 1875.
II. LAWRENCE [8]   "   April 4, 1880.

943. Fox.   Eighth Generation.   Tower.

431. MARIA E.[7], CHARLES [6], JONAS [5], JOSEPH [4], AMBROSE [3], BENJA-
MIN [2], JOHN [1].
Maria E.[7], dau. of Charles [6] and Sarah (Pratt) Tower, b.
July 17, 1823 ; mar. Walter W. Fox, of Westville, Conn.,
Aug. 22, 1842. He was b. in Manchester, Conn.,
May 20, 1818, and was son of Wait and Jerusha (Hunt) Fox.

Childr.

I.   WALTER T.[8]   born May 19, 1843.
II. FRANKLIN W.[8] " Aug. 6, 1844.

Maria E. (Tower) Fox died May 2, 1851, ag. 27 y. 9 m. 16 d.

944. Wolcott.   Eighth Generation.   Tower.

431. SARAH A.[7], CHARLES [6], JONAS [5], JOSEPH [4], AMBROSE [3], BEN-
JAMIN [2], JOHN [1].
Sarah A.[7], dau. of Charles [6] and Sarah (Pratt) Tower, b.
Nov. 17, 1826 ; mar. Daniel F. Wolcott, of Southbridge,
Jan. 12, 1846. He was b. in Southbridge, Mass.,
                    and was son of Peres B. and Isabella (Foster)
Wolcott.

Childr. none.

945. Williams. Eighth Generation. Tower.

431. FRANCES E.[7], CHARLES [6], JONAS [5], JOSEPH [4], AMBROSE [3], BEN-
JAMIN [2], JOHN [1].

Frances E.[7], dau. of Charles [6] and Sarah (Pratt) Tower, b.
Feb. 14, 1831; mar. Lyman U. Williams, of Indianapolis,
Sept. 17, 1851. He was b. in Thompson, Conn.,
July 9, 1829, and was son of David and Hannah (Stone)
Williams.

Childr.

I. DAVID TOWER [8]   born May 2, 1853, in Thompson.
II. CHARLES HENRY [8]   "   June 6, 1856, " Dudley, Mass.
III. LYMAN F.[8]   "   Feb. 28, 1864, " Dedham, "

Frances E. (Tower) Williams died in Indianapolis, Ind.,
May 31, 1881, ag. 50 y. 3 m. 14 d.

946. Eighth Generation. Tower.

431. LENDALL P.[7], CHARLES [6], JONAS [5], JOSEPH [4], AMBROSE [3], BEN-
JAMIN [2], JOHN [1].

Lendall P.[7], son of Charles [6] and Sarah (Pratt) Tower, b.
Jan. 13, 1833; mar. Debby Ann Bottom, of Southbridge,
March 27, 1856. She was b. in Southbridge, Mass.,
1827, and was dau. of Jedd and Emeline (Morse)
Bottom.

Child.

I. MARYETT PAMELIA [8] born April 14, 1857.

Debby Ann (Bottom) Tower died Dec. 6, 1867, ag. 40.
Lendall P. Tower [7] mar., 2d, Hettie E. Braman.
March 13, 1870. She was born in Blanford, Mass.,
April 14, 1847, and was dau. of William and Harriet (Bart-
lett) Braman.

Childr.

II. FLORA H.[8] born Jan. 22, 1875. III. FREEMAN A.[8] born March 5, 1877.

947. Eighth Generation. Tower.

431. CHARLES H.[7], CHARLES [6], JONAS [5], JOSEPH [4], AMBROSE [3], BEN-
JAMIN [2], JOHN [1].

Charles H.[7], son of Charles [6] and Sarah (Pratt) Tower, b.
May 12, 1835; mar. Lizzie M. Mellamy
May 12, 1860. She was b. in Dublin, Ireland.

Childr.

I. IDA L.[8]   born Feb. 28, 1861; died Nov. 11, 1880, ag. 19 y. 8 m. 11 d.
II. C. LENDALL [8] " Oct. 7, 1863.

Lizzie (Mellamy) Tower died June 9, 1869.

Charles H. Tower[7] mar., 2d, Mary Braman
April 23, 1871. She was b. in Coleraine, Mass.,
Sept. 20, 1848, and was dau. of William and Harriet (Bart-
lett) Braman.

Childr.

III.   WILLIE B.[8]   born Sept. 4, 1872.
IV.   EMMA MAY[8]   " April , 1878.

---

948.   **Eighth Generation.**   **Tower.**

431. FREEMAN P.[7], CHARLES[6], JONAS[5], JOSEPH[4], AMBROSE[3], BEN-
JAMIN[2], JOHN[1].

Freeman P.[7], son of Charles[6] and Sarah (Pratt) Tower, b.
Feb. 13, 1838; mar. Julia A. Cleveland, of Barre, Mass.,
Aug. 20, 1863. She was b. in Barre
Jan. 20, 1840, and was dau. of Newcomb and Sophronia
(Gilbert) Cleveland.

Childr.

I.   Son[8]   born June 20, 1864; died June 20, 1864.
II.   FLORENCE HAMILTON[8]   "   Aug. 22, 1870; " Sept. 5, 1870.
III. OLIVE FREEMAN[8]   "   March 19, 1872.

---

949. Blodget.   Eighth Generation.   Tower.

431. SUSAN N.[7], CHARLES[6], JONAS[5], JOSEPH[4], AMBROSE[3], BENJA-
MIN[2], JOHN[1].

Susan N.[7], dau. of Charles[6] and Sarah (Pratt) Tower, b.
Jan. 23, 1842; mar. John B. Blodget
April 3, 1862. He was b. in Holland, Mass.,
        and was son of Winthrop and Elizabeth (Bracket)
Blodget.

Childr. none.

John B. Blodget died Sept. 26, 1864.

Susan N. (Tower) Blodget died Oct. 15, 1869, ag. 27 y. 8 m.
23 d.

---

950. Goodell.   Eighth Generation.   Tower.

431. ELLEN R.[7], CHARLES[6], JONAS[5], JOSEPH[4], AMBROSE[3], BEN-
JAMIN[2], JOHN[1].

Ellen R.[7], dau. of Charles[6] and Sarah (Pratt) Tower, b.
March 17, 1843; mar. W. Waldo Goodell, of Brookfield,
Mass.,
June 6, 1868. He was b. in Dudley, Mass.,
        , 1838, and was son of Warren and Clarinda (Healey)
Goodell.

951.   **Eighth Generation.**   **Tower.**

432. WILLIAM A.[7], OREN[6], JONAS[5], JOSEPH[4], AMBROSE[3], BENJA-
MIN[2], JOHN[1].

William A.[7], son of Oren[6] and Harriet (Gleason) Tower, b.
Feb. 26, 1824 ; mar. Julia Davis, of Lancaster, Mass.,
April 29, 1847. She was b. in Princeton, Mass.,
July 21, 1824, and was dau. of Austin and Sally (Welling-
ton) Davis.

Childr.

I.   ELLEN MAY[8]   born Feb. 28, 1848, in Lancaster.
II.   CHARLOTTE GRAY[8]   "   Feb. 12, 1851, " Cambridge.
III. AUGUSTUS CLIFFORD[8]   "   July 3, 1853, "   "   ; mar. Louisa
                            G. Dreer, of Philadelphia, June 7, 1883.
IV. RICHARD GLEASON[8]   "   Oct. 11, 1858, in Lexington, Mass.

952. Hale.   **Eighth Generation.**   **Tower.**

432. SUSAN W.[7], OREN[6], JONAS[5], JOSEPH[4], AMBROSE[3], BENJAMIN[2],
JOHN[1].

Susan W.[7], dau. of Oren[6] and Harriet (Gleason) Tower, b.
July 22, 1828 ; mar. Abraham G. R. Hale
Jan. 12, 1865. He was b. in Stow, Mass.,
Aug. 16, 1834, and was son of Calvin and Hannah Hale.

Childr.

I.   WILLIE A.[8] born Feb. 28, 1866; died March 4, 1866.
II. WILLIE A.[8]   "   May 8, 1867;   "   Oct. 11, 1867.

Susan W. (Tower) Hale died May 9, 1867, ag. 38 y. 9 m.
18 d.

953.   **Eighth Generation.**   **Tower.**

432. FRANCIS EMERY[7], OREN[6], JONAS[5], JOSEPH[4], AMBROSE[3], BEN-
JAMIN[2], JOHN[1].

Francis E.[7], son of Oren[6] and Lucy L. (Foster) Tower, b.
Nov. 30, 1836 ; mar. Ella S. Shepardson, of Petersham, Mass.,
Nov. 30, 1868. She was b. in New Salem, Mass.,
June 29, 1847, and was dau. of John and Maria N. (Cham-
berlain) Shepardson.

Childr.

I.   RALPH WINFRED[8] born May 24, 1870.
II. MAUD HELEN[8]   "   Sept. 13, 1873.
III. ETHEL ELLA[8]   "   July 25, 1876.

954.   Eighth Generation.   Tower.

432. GEORGE H.[7], OREN [6], JONAS [5], JOSEPH [4], AMBROSE [3], BENJAMIN [2],
    JOHN [1].
    George H.[7], son of Oren [6] and Lucy L. (Foster) Tower, b.
    Sept. 1, 1839 ; mar. Frances E. Farrar.
    Jan. 22, 1873. She was dau. of Charles and Elizabeth (Fitch)
    Farrar.

955.   Eighth Generation.   Tower.

435. GEORGE N.[7], HORATIO N.[6], JONAS [5], JOSEPH [4], AMBROSE [3], BEN-
    JAMIN [2], JOHN [1].
    George N.[7], son of Horatio N.[6] and Emeline (Goodnow)
    Tower, b.
    March 6, 1850 ; mar. Louise Chichester Butts, of Jersey
    City, N. J.,
    Oct. 25, 1882. She was b.
    Jan. 17, 1861, and was dau. of John H. and Elizabeth P.
    (Chichester) Butts.

Child.

I. NELSON BUTTS [8] born Oct. 14, 1883.

956.   Eighth Generation.   Tower.

435. FRANK G.[7], HORATIO N.[6], JONAS [5], JOSEPH [4], AMBROSE [3], BEN-
    JAMIN [2], JOHN [1].
    Frank G.[7], son of Horatio N.[6] and Mary (Goodnow) Tower, b.
    Oct. 28, 1853 ; mar. Margaret S. Haynie, of Austin, Texas,
    June 3, 1881. She was b.
    Dec. 15, 1861, and was dau. of Samuel G. and Hannah M.
    (Trask) Haynie.

Child.

I. GEORGE HAYNIE [8] born Oct. 19, 1882, in Bloomfield, N. J.

957.   Eighth Generation.   Tower.

437. ALBERT R.[7], SAMUEL S.[6], JONAS [5], JOSEPH [4], AMBROSE [3], BEN-
    JAMIN [2], JOHN [1].
    Albert R.[7], son of Samuel S.[6] and Relief (Rice) Tower, b.
    Sept. 14, 1849 ; mar. Narcissa N. White, of New Salem, Mass.,
    Oct. 15, 1873. She was b. in the Sandwich Islands
    Sept. 25, 1850, and was dau. of Rev. Lorenzo and Elizabeth
    (Babcock) White.

Childr. born in Athol, Mass.

I. JENNY WHITE [8] born April 4, 1875.
II. MARY ELIZABETH [8] " Feb. 25, 1876.
III. LUCY NARCISSA [8] " Feb. 13, 1878; died Aug. 25, 1878.
IV. ALBERT R. [8] " July 25, 1879.

958. Carpenter. Eighth Generation. Tower.

439. AMELIA [7], RUSSELL [6], JOHN [5], JOSEPH [4], AMBROSE [3], BENJAMIN [2], JOHN [1].
Amelia [7], dau. of Russell [6] and Carissa E. (Cole) Tower, b.
; mar. Milton Carpenter.

Childr.

I. ALICE [8]. II. FRED [8]. III. CHARLES [8].

Milton Carpenter died in Syracuse, N. Y.

959. Eighth Generation. Tower.

451. WILLIAM P. [7], THADDEUS [6], SILAS [5], AMBROSE [4], AMBROSE [3], BENJAMIN [2], JOHN [1].
William P.[7], son of Thaddeus [6] and Ruth (Maynard) Tower, b.
Feb. 6, 1821 ; mar. Nancy Morgan Atkins, of Roxbury, Mass.,
Feb. 26, 1859. She was b. in Boston,
1824, and was dau. of John and Jane (Dunn) Atkins.

Childr.

I. CAROLINE REGALLY [8] born Sept. 26, 1860, in Boston.
II. HENRY ATKINS [8] " Oct. 20, 1865, " Malden ; died July 3, 1872, ag. 6 y. 8 m. 14 d.

960. Robinson. Eighth Generation. Tower.

453. LOUISA [7], JONAS [6], SILAS [5], AMBROSE [4], AMBROSE [3], BENJAMIN [2], JOHN [1].
Louisa [7], dau. of Jonas [6] and Almira (Perry) Tower, b.
July 3, 1835 ; mar. Fitz A. Robinson, of Weston, Mass.,
May 5, 1858. He was b. in Sudbury, Mass.,
Jan. 21, 1835, and was son of Dexter and Anna (Hapgood)
Robinson.

Childr. born in Weston.

I. FREDERICK EUGENE [8] born Aug. 3, 1859; died Aug. 21, 1863, ag. 4 y. 18 d.
II. ALICE LOUISE [8] " Dec. 17, 1861.
III. GERTRUDE [8] " April 28, 1864.
IV. EDNA LUTHERA [8] " March 15, 1866.

V.   IDA ALMA [8]   born July   2, 1868.
VI.   HERBERT ALVAN [8]   "   March 21, 1871.
VII. GEORGE ALBERT [8]   "   Aug. 26, 1873.
VIII. ELLA ALMIRA [8]   "   April 2, 1876.

961. Hurlburt.   Eighth Generation.   Tower.

453. CATHERINE [7], JONAS [6], SILAS [5], AMBROSE [4], AMBROSE [3], BEN-
     JAMIN [2], JOHN [1].
     Catherine [7], dau. of Jonas [6] and Almira (Perry) Tower, b.
     March 2, 1845 ; mar. Rufus Hurlburt, of Sudbury, Mass.,
     Nov. 18, 1867. He was b. in Sudbury
     July 16, 1842, and was son of Thomas P. and Mary (Moore)
     Hurlburt.

                        Childr.

     I.   ARTHUR SCOLLAY [8] born Sept. 12, 1868.
     II.   MARIAN BELLE [8]   "   Aug. 14, 1870.
     III. GRACE PERRY [8]   "   Oct. 4, 1876.
     IV.   ANZA PRENTISS [8]   "   Feb. 20, 1878.

962.   Eighth Generation.   Tower.

457. GEORGE [7], ABEL [6], ABEL [5], AMBROSE [4], AMBROSE [3], BENJAMIN [2],
     JOHN [1].
     George [7], son of Abel [6] and Mary (Moore) Tower, b.
     Aug. 30, 1805 ; mar. Mary A. Castle
     March 23, 1829. She was b.
     July 22, 1809, and was dau. of Philo and Jerusha (Dix)
     Castle.
                        Childr.

1331. I.   JUSTUS DAVID [8]   born Jan. 18, 1830.
1332. II.   AUGUSTUS CHARLES [8]   "   July 4, 1833.
1333. III. MARY JERUSHA [8]   "   May 4, 1840.
1334. IV.   CAROLINE ELIZABETH [8] "   July 2, 1843.
       V.   DANIEL GEORGE [8]   "   April 30, 1846; died July 21, 1865,
                                          ag. 19 y. 2 m. 21 d.

     George Tower [7] died in Troy Grove, Ill., Oct. 1, 1864, ag.
     59 y. 1 m.

963.   Eighth Generation.   Tower.

457. CHARLES [7], ABEL [6], ABEL [5], AMBROSE [4], AMBROSE [3], BENJAMIN [2],
     JOHN [1].
     Charles [7], son of Abel [6] and Mary (Moore) Tower, b.
     Jan. 19, 1811 ; mar Amanda Salisbury, of Freetown, N. Y.

Child.

I. MARY EMMA [8] born   .

Charles Tower[7] died Aug. , 1839, ag. 28 y. 7 m.
Amanda (Salisbury) Tower mar., 2d,   Jennings.

964. Knights.   Eighth Generation.   Tower.

457. MARY[7], ABEL[6], ABEL[5], AMBROSE[4], AMBROSE[3], BENJAMIN[2], JOHN[1].
Mary[7], dau. of Abel[6] and Mary (Moore) Tower, b.
Feb. 21, 1815 ; mar. Samuel Knights, of Columbus, Ill.,
March 20, 1839. He was b. in Maryland
June 28, 1816, and was son of Peter and Anna (Dell)
Knights.

Childr.

I.	HARRIET MATILDA [8]	born June 5, 1840.
II.	MARY ELIZABETH [8]	" May 24, 1842.
III.	AMANDA JANE [8]	" Jan. 5, 1845.
IV.	GEORGE WASHINGTON[8]	" April 14, 1847 ; died Aug. 13, 1850, ag. 3 y. 3 m. 29 d.
V.	JOHN HARLOW [8]	" April 16, 1849; " May 19, 1850, ag. 1 y. 1 m. 2 d.
VI.	LAURA EMMA [8]	" May 23, 1851.
VII.	LYDIA AUGUSTA [8]	" March 14, 1853.
VIII.	SARAH ANN [8]	" March 16, 1855.
IX.	CHARLES M.[8]	" June 27, 1857.
X.	ALICE ADA [8]	" Dec. 5, 1859; died Nov. 26, 1863, ag. 3 y. 11 m. 22 d.

965.   Eighth Generation.   Tower.

457. DAVID[7], ABEL[6], ABEL[5], AMBROSE[4], AMBROSE[3], BENJAMIN[2], JOHN[1].
David[7], son of Abel[6] and Mary (Moore) Tower, b.
Feb. 13, 1818 ; mar. Mary A. Daily
June 6, 1847. She was b.
June 6, 1831.

Childr.

1335.	I.	GEORGE W.[8] born Sept. 22, 1853.
	II.	HARRIET [8]	" April 2, 1856; mar. Joseph Lanan, July 5, 1881.
	III.	DAVID [8]	" Dec. 30, 1868.

966. Clarke.   Eighth Generation.   Tower.

462. SUSAN A.[7], CALEB[6], ABEL[5], AMBROSE[4], AMBROSE[3], BENJAMIN[2], JOHN[1].
Susan A.[7], dau. of Caleb[6] and Julia (Edwards) Tower, b.

Jan. 5, 1835; mar. Orlando Clarke
July 5, 1855. He was b. in Brookfield, N. Y.,
Dec. 12, 1822, and was son of Ethan and Amy (Crandall)
Clarke.

Childr.

I.	JULIA [8]	born April 26, 1857; died in Portland, Ore., Oct. 31, 1882, ag. 25 y. 6 m. 4 d.
II.	CHARLIE [8]	" Feb. 11, 1859; died March 11, 1859.
III.	NELLIE [8]	" Dec. 2, 1860.
IV.	HARRY TOWER [8]	" Dec. 4, 1864.
V.	MARY ESTELLE [8]	" April 1, 1868.

967. Miller.   Eighth Generation.   Tower.

462. JULIA ELLA [7], CALEB [6], ABEL [5], AMBROSE [4], AMBROSE [3], BEN-JAMIN [2], JOHN [1].
Julia E.[7], dau. of Caleb [6] and Julia (Edwards) Tower, b.
Dec. 16, 1836; mar. Cyrus T. Miller
Nov. 14, 1858. He was b.
Feb. 13, 1815, and was son of Luther and Phebe (Wright)
Miller.

Childr.

I. BELLE EDWARDS [8] born Dec. 29, 1862.
II. LUTHER LINCOLN [8] " Sept. 18, 1868.

Julia E. (Tower) Miller died June 1, 1876, ag. 39 y. 5 m. 16 d.

968.   Eighth Generation.   Tower.

462. CALEB E.[7], CALEB [6], ABEL [5], AMBROSE [4], AMBROSE [3], BENJAMIN [2], JOHN [1].
Caleb E.[7], son of Caleb [6] and Julia (Edwards) Tower, b.
Nov. 14, 1841; mar. widow Nellie (Dunn) Hollister, of
Battle Creek, Mich.,
Oct. 4, 1866.

Childr. none.

969. Buffum.   Eighth Generation.   Tower.

463. MARY E.[7], ASAHEL [6], ASAHEL [5], AMBROSE [4], AMBROSE [3], BEN-JAMIN [2], JOHN [1].
Mary E.[7], dau. of Asahel [6] and Mary (Palmer) Tower, b.
Aug. 25, 1818; mar. Sampson Wilder Buffum
Feb. 9, 1842.

Childr.

I.	CHARLES S. W.[8]	born April 12, 1844; died Aug. 19, 1846, ag. 2 y. 4 m. 7 d.
II.	GEORGE TOWER [8]	" March 16, 1846.

III. FRANKLIN D.[8] born May 31, 1849; died Sept. 18, 1858, ag. 9 y.
3 m. 18 d.
IV. MARY EMMA [8] " May 21, 1852.
V. JENNIE GERTRUDE [8] " May 28, 1854.
VI. TRYLENA WILDER [8] " May 2, 1860.
VII. WILDER STODDARD [8] " Feb. 8, 1862.

970. **Eighth Generation.** **Tower.**

463. HENRY A.[7], ASAHEL [6], ASAHEL [5], AMBROSE [4], AMBROSE [3], BENJAMIN [2], JOHN [1].
Henry A.[7], son of Asahel [6] and Mary (Palmer) Tower, b.
Feb. 5, 1821 ; mar. Caroline Valeria Burton, of Boston,
March 26, 1846. She was b. in Warren, N. H.,
March 27, 1823, and was dau. of Amos and Sarah (Merrill)
Burton.

Childr. born in Winchester, N. H.

I. CHARLES H. B.[8] born May 3, 1847; died Jan. 31, 1853, ag. 5 y. 8 m. 28 d.
II. WILLIAM A.[8] " July 1, 1848; " Aug. 9, 1850, ag. 2 y. 1 m. 8 d.
III. BURTON L.[8] " Aug. 8, 1858; mar. Mary E. Beals.
IV. EVA VALERIA [8] " Jan. 24, 1861.

971. Gould. **Eighth Generation.** **Tower.**

463. JULIA A.[7], ASAHEL [6], ASAHEL [5], AMBROSE [4], AMBROSE [3], BEN-JAMIN [2], JOHN [1].
Julia A.[7], dau. of Asahel [6] and Mary (Palmer) Tower, b.
Feb. 21, 1823 ; mar. Henry Gould
March 13, 1852. He was b.
March 7, 1829, and was son of Thomas and Abigail (Briggs)
Gould.

Childr. born in Winchester, N. H.

I. MARY C.[8] born Aug. 5, 1853.
II. FREDERICK B.[8] " May 2, 1859.
III. WALTER P.[8] " July 23, 1860; died April 18, 1861.

972. **Eighth Generation.** **Tower.**

463. GEORGE F.[7], ASAHEL [6], ASAHEL [5], AMBROSE [4], AMBROSE [3], BENJAMIN [2], JOHN [1].
George F.[7], son of Asahel [6] and Mary (Palmer) Tower, b.
June 3, 1825 ; mar. Julia A. Torrey
Aug. 23, 1854. She was b. in Michigan
March 20, 1835, and was dau. of Erastus and Julia Torrey.

Childr. born in St Louis, Mo.

I. FLORENCE [8] born March , 1856, died Aug. , 1856.
II. HELEN P.[8] " Dec. 27, 1858.

Julia A. (Torrey) Tower died in St. Louis, March 30, 1859,
  ag. 24 y. 10 d.

George F. Tower [7] mar., 2d, Martha A. Smith
Jan. 30, 1860. She was b.
Dec. 26, 1825, and was dau. of Rominor and Sarah Smith.

Childr.

III.	GEORGE F.[8]	born Dec. 23, 1861.	
IV.	SARAH LOUISA [8]	" Nov. 8, 1863.	
V.	MARTHA I.[8]	" Jan. 17, 1866.	
VI.	JOHN J.[8]	" Sept. 15, 1868; died Sept. , 1868.	

973. Bliss.   Eighth Generation.   Tower.

463. SARAH M.[7], ASAHEL [6], ASAHEL [5], AMBROSE [4], AMBROSE [3],
      BENJAMIN [2], JOHN [1].

Sarah M.[7], dau. of Asahel [6] and Mary (Palmer) Tower, b.
June 21, 1827; mar. Harvey W. Bliss, of Royalston, Mass.,
April 23, 1857. He was b. in Royalston
Sept. 19, 1827, and was son of Daniel and Harriet (Peek)
Bliss.

Childr.

I.	KATE M.[8]	born March 14, 1858; died Feb.26, 1865, ag. 16 y. 11 m. 15 d.
II.	JAMES H.[8]	" Sept. 2, 1860.
III.	JULIA T.[8]	" May 24, 1863.

Sarah M. (Tower) Bliss died March 31, 1865, ag. 37 y. 9 m.
  9 d.

974.   Eighth Generation.   Tower.

463. RUFUS E.[7], ASAHEL [6], ASAHEL [5], AMBROSE [4], AMBROSE [3], BEN-
      JAMIN [2], JOHN [1].

Rufus E.[7], son of Asahel [6] and Mary (Palmer) Tower, b.
Feb. 26, 1830; mar. Sarah I. Chapin, of Grafton, Mass.,
        1855. She was b. in Milford, Mass.

Childr.

I.	KATE C.[8]	born June , 1856; died in St. Louis, Mo., March,1857.
II.	CAROLINE [8]	" "
III.	RUFUS CHAPIN [8]	" July , 1862; " " July, 1864, ag. 2.

975. Chellis.   Eighth Generation.   Tower.

464. SARAH E.[7], JAMES [6], ASAHEL [5], AMBROSE [4], AMBROSE [3], BEN-
      JAMIN [2], JOHN [1].

Sarah E.[7], dau. of James [6] and Sarah E. (Baker) Tower, b.

Feb. 22, 1831; mar. Seth G. Chellis, of Rockford, Ill.,
Oct. 5, 1854. He was b.
　　1831, and was son of Seth and Myra Chellis.

Child.

I. ARTHUR SETH [8] born May 10, 1858.

976. Knowles.　Eighth Generation.　Tower.

464. FRANCES M.[7], JAMES [6], ASAHEL [5], AMBROSE [4], AMBROSE [3], BEN-
JAMIN [2], JOHN [1].
　　Frances M.[7], dau. of James [6] and Sarah E. (Baker) Tower, b.
Dec. 25, 1836; mar. Jefferson A. Knowles
Nov. 8, 1864.　He was b.
　　1833, and was son of Jonathan and Mary P. Knowles.

Childr.

I. BLANCHE [8]　　　born March 12, 1866; died Aug. 16, 1866.
II. HERBERT T.[8]　　　"　Aug. 3, 1871; died Oct. 13, 1874, ag. 3 y. 2 m. 10 d.
III. ANNIE FRANCES [8] "　Oct. 9, 1873.

977.　　　Eighth Generation.　Tower.

465. EDWARD H.[7], HENRY [6], ASAHEL [5], AMBROSE [4], AMBROSE [3],
BENJAMIN [2], JOHN [1].
　　Edward H.[7], son of Henry [6] and Hannah (Harrington)
Tower, b.
Oct. 19, 1835; mar. Martha Redding, of Linens, Mo.,
Feb.　, 1867.

Childr.

I. WILLIAM HENRY [8] born Aug. 7, 1868.
II. MARY [8]　　　"　Aug.　, 1871.
III. GEORGIE [8]　　　"　June 29, 1875.

978. Martin.　Eighth Generation.　Tower.

466. MARY L.[7], SAMUEL G.[6], DANIEL [5], AMBROSE [4], AMBROSE [3],
BENJAMIN [2], JOHN [1].
　　Mary L[7], dau. of Samuel G.[6] and Ann (Clark) Tower, b.
Sept. 10, 1843; mar. Lemuel B. Martin, of Cambridge, Mass.,
Dec. 20, 1870.　He was b. in Bristol, R. I.,
　　1843, and was son of George H. and Elizabeth H.
Martin.

Childr. none.

979. Jacobs.　Eighth Generation.　Tower.

466. LUCY A.[7], SAMUEL G.[6], DANIEL [5], AMBROSE [4], AMBROSE [3], BEN-
JAMIN [2], JOHN [1].

Lucy A.[7], dau. of Samuel G.[6] and Ann (Clark) Tower, b.
Jan. 13, 1849 ; mar. Dr. Judson L. Jacobs, of Boston,
Jan. 10, 1880.

980.   **Eighth Generation.**   **Tower.**

469. JOHN S.[7], JONATHAN [6], JONATHAN [5], JONATHAN [4], AMBROSE [3],
      BENJAMIN [2], JOHN [1].
      John S.[7], son of Jonathan [6] and Mary E. (   ) Tower, b.
            1827 ; mar. Mary E. Fraser, of Boston,
      July 12, 1863. She was b.
            1837.

981. Barrett.   **Eighth Generation.**   **Tower.**

470. MARY A.[7], DANIEL [6], JONATHAN [5], JONATHAN [4], AMBROSE[3],
      BENJAMIN [2], JOHN [1].
      Mary A.[7], dau. of Daniel [6] and Mary Ann (Clark) Tower, b.
      Feb. 3, 1823 ; mar. Charles Barrett, of Lowell, Mass.,
      Jan. 16, 1845. He was b.
      Jan. 20, 1823, and was son of Charles T. and Susan (Seaver)
      Barrett.

Childr.

I. MARY ANN [8]   born July 15, 1845; died Feb. 7, 1863, ag. 17 y. 6 m.
                    23 d.
II. ELLEN AUGUSTA [8] " July 6, 1847 ; mar. Henry H. Hoyt, of White-
                    field, Vt.
III. CHARLES HENRY [8] " June 15, 1853.

Mary Ann (Tower) Barrett died Sept. 15, 1858, ag. 35 y.
      7 m. 12 d.

982.   **Eighth Generation.**   **Tower.**

470. GEORGE F.[7], DANIEL [6], JONATHAN [5], JONATHAN [4], AMBROSE[3],
      BENJAMIN [2], JOHN [1].
      George F.[7], son of Daniel [6] and Mary Ann (Clark) Tower, b.
      June 3, 1825 ; mar. Sarah Jane Warren, of Waltham, Mass.,
      Nov. 26, 1851. She was b. in Waltham
      July 29, 1829, and was dau. of Jonathan and Mary (Hast-
      ings) Warren.

Childr.

I. ADDIE E.[8]   born Feb. 9, 1854; died Aug. 25, 1855, ag. 1 y. 6 m.
                    13 d.
1336. II. IDA F.[8]   " Jan. 15, 1856.
1337. III. EVA A.[8]   " April 9, 1858.
      IV. CARA EVELINE [8] " April 10, 1864.

983.   **Eighth Generation.**   **Tower.**

470. DANIEL A.[7], DANIEL [6], JONATHAN [5], JONATHAN [4], AMBROSE [3], BENJAMIN [2], JOHN [1].

Daniel A.[7], son of Daniel [6] and Mary Ann (Clark) Tower, b. May 11, 1827 ; mar. Frances M. Chase, of Lowell, Mass., April 16, 1849. She was b.
1832.

Childr.

1338.   I.   GEORGE A.[8]   born Aug. 11, 1853, in Biddeford, Me.
      II.   WILLIAM MUNROE [8] "   " Waterville, "
      III.   NELLIE F.[8]   "   "   "   ·   "

984.   **Eighth Generation.**   **Tower.**

470. JOHN H. [7], DANIEL [6], JONATHAN [5], JONATHAN [4], AMBROSE [3], BENJAMIN [2], JOHN [1].

John H.[7], son of Daniel [6] and Mary Ann (Clark) Tower, b. Nov. 12, 1829 ; mar. Adeline Emerson, of Haverhill, Mass., May 4, 1854. She was b. in Pelham, Mass., Feb. 22, 1833, and was dau. of Samuel and Mary (Wilson) Emerson.

Childr. born in Haverhill.

    I.   LOIS ADDIE [8]   born Sept.   , 1857.
   II.   WALTER HENRY [8]   "   June 16, 1862; died Aug. 5, 1864, ag. 2 y. 1 m. 19 d.
  III.   MARY WILSON [8]   "   July 21, 1866; " June 10, 1867.
  IV.   ALICE EMERSON [8]   "   Dec. 7, 1868.
   V.   HERBERT MURRAY [8] "   Nov. 20, 1870; " May 22, 1873, ag. 2 y. 6 m. 1 d.

985.   **Eighth Generation.**   **Tower.**

470. LEVI Q. A.[7], DANIEL [6], JONATHAN [5], JONATHAN [4], AMBROSE [3], BENJAMIN [2], JOHN [1].

Levi Q. A.[7], son of Daniel [6] and Mary Ann (Clark) Tower, b. April 17, 1832 ; mar. Frances A. Wheelock, of Leominster, Mass., Sept. 22, 1856. She was b. in Leominster 1831.

Childr. none.

986. Battles.   **Eighth Generation.**   **Tower.**

470. SUSANNA H. L.[7], DANIEL [6], JONATHAN [5], JONATHAN [4], AMBROSE [3], BENJAMIN [2], JOHN [1].

Susanna H. L.[7], dau. of Daniel [6] and Mary Ann (Clark) Tower, b.

Jan. 15, 1835 ; mar. George F. Battles, of New London, N. H.,
May 11, 1863. He was b.
    1836, and was son of Henry and Clarissa Battles.

Childr.

I. DANIEL FRANCIS [8] born March 11, 1864, in Haverhill, Mass.
II. GEORGE HENRY [8]   " Oct.   30, 1866, " Londonderry, N. H.
III. WILLIE GORDON [8]   " Jan.   15, 1869, "   "   "
IV. CORA ELLA [8]   " Dec.   8, 1870; died April 18, 1872, ag. 1 y.
                                        4 m. 10 d.
V. ALFRED WILSON [8]   " Dec. 8, 1873, in Haverhill.

987.   Eaton.   Eighth Generation.   Tower.

471. ELIZA A.[7], CALVIN [6], JONATHAN [5], JONATHAN [4], AMBROSE [3],
    BENJAMIN [2], JOHN [1].
    Eliza A.[7], dau. of Calvin [6] and Ann R. (Bailey) Tower, b.
    Dec. 25, 1821 ; mar. John Eaton, of Providence, R. I.,
    May   , 1837.

Childr.

I. SARAH M. AMELIA [8] born   ; died Sept. 15, 1840.
II. MARY ELIZA [8]   "   1840.

John Eaton died
Eliza Ann (Tower) Eaton mar., 2d, Ira L. Myrick, of Fox-
borough, Mass.,
April 1, 1846. He was b. in Vermont
    1821, and was son of Nathan and Harriet Myrick.

Childr. none.

Eliza Ann (Tower) Myrick died in Amesbury, Mass., April
    25, 1850, ag. 38 y. 4 m. 1 d.
Ira L. Myrick died

988.   Eighth Generation.   Tower.

471. HENRY C.[7], CALVIN [6], JONATHAN [5], JONATHAN [4], AMBROSE [3],
    BENJAMIN [2], JOHN [1].
    Henry C.[7], son of Calvin [6] and Ann R. (Bailey) Tower, b.
    July 2, 1826 ; mar. Eliza A. Paine, of Salisbury, Mass.,
    Oct. 14, 1849. She was b. in Salisbury
        1831, and was dau. of Edward and Mary (Blake)
    Paine.

Childr.

1339.   I. MARY ELLA [8] born March 4, 1851.
1340. II. CHARLES [8]   " Sept. 19, 1852.
       III. WILLIAM [8]   " Dec. 13, 1853 ; mar. Sept. 18, 1872 ; ch.
                            Fred [9], born June 9, 1874.

IV.   HARRY [8]   born Jan. 19, 1862.
V.   JOHN [8]   "   June 8, 1866.
VI.   LEROY [8]   "   Dec. 25, 1873.

989.   Eighth Generation.   Tower.

471. CALVIN D.[7], CALVIN [6], JONATHAN [5], JONATHAN [4], AMBROSE [3], BENJAMIN [2], JOHN [1].

Calvin D.[7], son of Calvin [6] and Ann R. (Bailey) Tower, b. July 16, 1832; mar. Sarah Jane Richardson, of Nashua, N. H.,

Dec. 30, 1857. She was b.

Dec. 30, 1836, and was dau. of Henry R. and Hannah (Badger) Richardson.

Child.

1341. I. GRACE ELIZA [8] born Sept. 30, 1858.

990.   Eighth Generation.   Tower.

471. ISAAC [7], CALVIN [6], JONATHAN [5], JONATHAN [4], AMBROSE [3], BENJAMIN [2], JOHN [1].

Isaac [7], son of Calvin [6] and Ann R. (Bailey) Tower, b.

Sept. 24, 1834; mar. Sarah Jane Hale, of Aurora, Ill.,

1855. She was b.

1836, and was dau. of John and Mary (Goodale) Hale.

She died   1870; *s. p.*

991.   Eighth Generation.   Tower.

471. GEORGE E.[7], CALVIN [6], JONATHAN [5], JONATHAN [4], AMBROSE [3], BENJAMIN [2], JOHN [1].

George E.[7], son of Calvin [6] and Ann R. (Bailey) Tower, b.

Oct. 23, 1838; mar. widow Sarah (West) Robinson

1861.

Childr. none.

She died in Springfield, Ill.

992. Fisher.   Eighth Generation.   Tower.

478. AMANDA [7], ELI [6], DANIEL [5], JONATHAN [4], AMBROSE [3], BENJAMIN [2], JOHN [1].

Amanda [7], dau. of Eli [6] and Mary (Fletcher) Tower, b.

April 4, 1834 ; mar. Alvan Fisher, of Westford, Mass.,

Dec. 19, 1854. He was b. in Canton, Mass.,

Dec. 2, 1821, and was son of Alexander and Clarissa Fisher.

Childr. born in Westford.

I.	FREDERICK J.[8]	born Oct.	9, 1855.	
II.	MARY[8]	"	July 12, 1857;	died March 3, 1858.
III.	HARRY[8]	"	April 9, 1858;	" March 17, 1859.
IV.	ADALINE MARIA[8]	"	Dec. 25, 1860.	
V.	CLARA AMANDA[8]	"	July 6, 1863.	
VI.	ALICK[8]	"	Aug. 22, 1865.	
VII.	JOHN[8]	"	May 1, 1868.	
VIII.	ELIZA CAPEN[8]	"	Oct. 17, 1870.	
IX.	THOMAS FLETCHER[8]	"	Aug. 25, 1872.	
X.	EDWARD[8]	"	Aug. 22, 1874.	
XI.	RUTH[8]	"	Nov. 15, 1876.	

993. Hamlin.   Eighth Generation.   Tower.

478. ABBIE[7], ELI[6], DANIEL[5], JONATHAN[4], AMBROSE[3], BENJAMIN[2], JOHN[1].

Abbie[7], dau. of Eli[6] and Mary (Fletcher) Tower, b.
Jan. 5, 1836; mar. Samuel A. Hamlin, of Westford, Mass.,
May 21, 1855. He was b.
1832, and was son of Nathan S. and Harriet Hamlin.

Childr. born in Westford.

I.	EDWARD AUGUSTUS[8]	born May 22, 1857.	
II.	GEORGE S.[8]	" April 7 1860.	
III.	GERTRUDE REBECCA FLETCHER[8]	" Jan. 3, 1871.	

994. Burbeck.   Eighth Generation.   Tower.

478. ADALINE[7], ELI[6], DANIEL[5], JONATHAN[4], AMBROSE[3], BENJAMIN[2], JOHN[1].

Adaline[7], dau. of Eli[6] and Mary (Fletcher) Tower, b.
March 15, 1838; mar. John Burbeck, of Westford, Mass.,
March 26, 1862. He was b. in Dorchester, Mass.,
Feb. 21, 1833, and was son of Samuel N. and Eliza P
(Irving) Burbeck.

Childr. born in Westford.

I.	HARRY IRVING[8]	born Jan. 24, 1863; died Aug. 13, 1865, ag. 2 y. 6 m. 20 d.
II.	WILLIE J.[8]	" Nov. 8, 1864.
III.	FREDERICK ALVAN[8]	" Dec. 12, 1868.
IV.	ELI TOWER[8]	" Nov. 17, 1871.
V.	MARY ELIZA[8]	" April 3, 1874.
VI.	GRACE AMANDA[8]	" May 27, 1876.

995. Clark.   Eighth Generation.   Tower.

478. AMY[7], ELI[6], DANIEL[5], JONATHAN[4], AMBROSE[3], BENJAMIN[2], JOHN[1].

Amy [7], dau. of Eli [6] and Mary (Fletcher) Tower, b.
June 22, 1842; mar. Paul Francis Stillman Clark, of West-
ford, Mass.,
Aug. 2, 1864. He was b. in Jaffrey, N. H.,
July 12, 1844, and was son of Rev. Stillman S. and Susan
(Litchfield) Clark.

Childr.

I.	ANNA [8]	born Feb. 17, 1865, in Webster, N. H.
II.	WILLIAM [8]	" April 5, 1867, " " " ; died Aug. 13, 1867.
III.	DELOS [8]	" June 13, 1868.
IV.	WILLIAM ELLERY [8]	" Dec. 5, 1872.
V.	BENGIE STILLMAN [8]	" Nov. 15, 1875, in Westford.
VI.	HELEN AMANDA [8]	" Feb. 16, 1881, " " ; died March 3, 1881.

996. Fletcher.   Eighth Generation.   Tower.

478. HELEN [7], ELI [6], DANIEL [5], JONATHAN [4], AMBROSE [3], BENJAMIN,[2] JOHN [1].

Helen [7], dau. of Eli [6] and Mary (Fletcher) Tower, b.
July 30, 1844; mar. Francis Leighton Fletcher, of Westford,
Jan. 1, 1865. He was b. in Westford, Mass.,
Sept. 22, 1832, and was son of John B. and Joanna (Hildreth)
Fletcher.

Child.

I. LENIE HELEN [8] born Feb. 28, 1869.

997. Prescott.   Eighth Generation.   Tower.

478. FRANCES A.[7], ELI [6], DANIEL [5], JONATHAN [4], AMBROSE [3], BEN-JAMIN [2], JOHN [1].

Frances A.[7], dau. of Eli [6] and Mary (Fletcher) Tower, b.
Dec. 6, 1848; mar. Noah Prescott, of Westford, Mass.,
Dec. 31, 1868. He was b. in Vershire, Vt.,
1845, and was son of Nathan P. and Bethiah Prescott.

Childr. born in Westford.

I.	FANNY BETHIAH [8]	born July 8, 1872.
II.	HARRY BROOKS [8]	" Oct. 12, 1874.
III.	WALDO FLETCHER [8]	" July 10, 1877.
IV.	PHILIP REGINALD [8]	" Sept. 19, 1880.

998. Pickering.   Eighth Generation.   Tower.

478. EMMA F.[7], ELI [6], DANIEL [5], JONATHAN [4], AMBROSE [3], BENJA-MIN [2], JOHN [1].

Emma F.[7], dau. of Eli [6] and Mary (Fletcher) Tower, b.

March 22, 1851; mar. Charles Henry Pickering, of Braintree, Mass.,
Dec. 31, 1872. He was b. in Northfield, Mass.,
          1848, and was son of Rufus and Julia Pickering.

Child.

    I. Leon Dexter[8] born Jan. 3, 1886, in Braintree.

999. Smith.   Eighth Generation.   Tower.

478. Mary L.[7], Eli[6], Daniel[5], Jonathan[4], Ambrose[3], Benja-
min[2], John[1].
Mary L.[7], dau. of Eli[6] and Mary (Fletcher) Tower, b.
Nov. 28, 1856; mar. James Frederic Smith, of Westford,
Mass.,
Dec. 25, 1887. He was b. in Brooklyn, N. Y.,
          1837, and was son of John C. and Louisa (Foulkes)
Smith.

1000.   Eighth Generation.   Tower.

479. Waldo T.[7], Melzar T.[6], Daniel[5], Jonathan[4], Ambrose[3],
Benjamin[2], John[1].
Waldo T.[7], son of Melzar T.[6] and Ann (Prescott) Tower, b.
Jan. 8, 1844 ; mar. Mary A. Wyman, of Westminster, Mass.,
March 7, 1868. She was b.
May 17, 1848, and was dau. of Abijah W. and Phebe A.
Wyman.

Childr.

    I. Eleanor May[8]   born Aug. 15, 1869.
    II. Charlotte Anna[8] " Aug. 28, 1871.
    III. Waldo Ernest[9]   " Dec. 9, 1873; died April 19, 1874.

Mary A. (Wyman) Tower died Oct. 26, 1874, ag. 26 y. 5 m.
9 d.

1001. Bellows. Eighth Generation.   Tower.

480. Sarah T.[7], Lewis[6], Nathan[5], Jonathan[4], Ambrose[3], Ben-
jamin[2], John[1].
Sarah T.[7], dau. of Lewis[6] and Martha (Thomas) Tower, b.
July 15, 1841; mar. John O. Bellows, of Cumberland, R. I.,
May 30, 1867. He was son of Willard and Lydia (Martin)
Bellows.

Childr. born in Cumberland.

    I. Annie Tower[8]   born Dec. 2, 1868.
    II. Carrie Maria[8]   " May 15, 1871.
    III. Walter Everett[8] " May 2, 1873.

1002. **Eighth Generation.** **Tower.**

482. ELI[7], RUEL[6], PETER[5], BENJAMIN[4], AMBROSE[3] BENJAMIN[2], JOHN[1].

Eli[7], son of Ruel[6] and Nancy (Nevers) Tower, b.
Feb. 4, 1819; mar. Susan Farrington, of Sweden, Me.,
Dec. 21, 1850. She was b. in Fryburg, Me.,
1824, and was dau. of Jacob and Mehitable (Fry) Farrington.

Childr. born in Sweden.

1342. I. DEXTER[8] born Oct. 22, 1851.
1343. II. EDGAR C.[8] " Aug. , 1853.
III. ORRISON[8] " Nov. 27, 1854; died 1858, ag. 4.

1003. **Eighth Generation.** **Tower.**

482. LUTHER[7], RUEL[6], PETER[5], BENJAMIN[4], AMBROSE[3], BENJAMIN[2], JOHN[1].

Luther[7], son of Ruel[6] and Nancy (Nevers) Tower, b.
March 19, 1825; mar. Rebecca Whitney, of Bridgton, Me.

Child.

I. OZRO MELVIN[8] born Aug. 1, 1858, in Burlington, Mass.

1004. **Eighth Generation.** **Tower.**

482. WILLIAM W.[7], RUEL[6], PETER[5], BENJAMIN[4], AMBROSE[3], BENJAMIN[2], JOHN[1].

William W.[7], son of Ruel[6] and Nancy (Nevers) Tower, b.
July 20, 1827; mar. Miriam E. Deane, of Canton, Mass.,
May 26, 1859. She was b. in Canton
Aug. 26, 1837, and was dau. of Francis W. and Mary (Adams) Deane.

Child.

I. EMMA E.[8] born Feb. 19, 1863, in Canton, Mass.; mar. Arthur L. Hewett, of Canton, Nov. 14, 1883.

1005. **Bolster.** **Eighth Generation.** **Tower.**

482. LYDIA M.[7], RUEL[6], PETER[5], BENJAMIN[4], AMBROSE[3], BENJAMIN[2], JOHN[1].

Lydia M.[7], dau. of Ruel[6] and Nancy (Nevers) Tower, b.
Jan. 1, 1831; mar. Oliver Franklin Pierce Bolster, of Charlestown, Mass.,
Feb. 3, 1858. He was b. in Harrison, Me.,
Sept. 6, 1828, and was son of Isaac and Mary (Cushman) Bolster.

Childr.

I. ADER E.[8] born Jan. 19, 1859, in Auburn, Me.
II. JAMES L.[8] " Aug. 13, 1860, in Burlington, Mass.
III. NELLY M.[8] " Feb. 3, 1863, in Lawrence, "

1006. Eighth Generation. Tower.

482. SYLVESTER [7], RUEL [6], PETER [5], BENJAMIN [4], AMBROSE [3], BEN-JAMIN [2], JOHN [1].

Sylvester [7], son of Ruel [6] and Nancy (Nevers) Tower, b. April 14, 1833; mar. Elizabeth Bang, of Cambridge, Mass., Feb. 14, 1861. She was b.
1838, and was dau. of Jacob N. and Eliza Bang.

Childr.

I. Child [8] } Twins born Dec. 5, 1861, in Burlington, Mass.
II. Child [8] }
III. Son [8]   " Oct. 1, 1865,   "   "
IV. EDWARD [8]   " Sept. 11, 1870, in Cambridge, "

1007. Nevers. Eighth Generation. Tower.

482. MARTHA E.[7], RUEL [6], PETER [5], BENJAMIN [4], AMBROSE [3], BEN-JAMIN [2], JOHN [1].

Martha E.[7], dau. of Ruel [6] and Nancy (Nevers) Tower, b. April 4, 1835 ; mar. Wyman Nevers, of Sweden, Me., Jan. 19, 1859. He was son of William and Abby P. (Knee-land) Nevers.

Child.

I. EUGENE E.[8] born Dec. 5, 1861, in Sweden.

1008. Robinson. Eighth Generation. Tower.

484. ELIZA M.[7], CHARLES [6], AUGUSTUS [5], BENJAMIN [4], AMBROSE [3], BENJAMIN [2], JOHN [1].

Eliza M.[7], dau. of Charles [6] and Lucretia (Maynard) Tower, b. Nov. 14, 1823 ; mar. Charles H. Robinson, of Sudbury, Mass., Oct. 26, 1848. He was b. in Sidney, Me., Feb. 14, 1821, and was son of John and Susannah (Mason) Robinson.

Childr. none.

Eliza M. (Tower) Robinson died in Stow, Mass., April 30, 1853, ag. 29 y. 5 m. 16 d.

1009. Eighth Generation. Tower.

484. HENRY [7], CHARLES [6], AUGUSTUS [5], BENJAMIN [4], AMBROSE [3], BENJAMIN [2], JOHN [1].

Henry [7], son of Charles [6] and Lucretia (Maynard) Tower, b.
June 24, 1829; mar. Betsey C. Wilmot, of Stow, Mass.,
Feb. 12, 1854. She was b. in Haverhill, N. H.,
Sept. 25, 1830, and was dau. of Timothy and Mary Wilmot.

Childr. b. in Stow.

I. CHARLES A.[8] born Aug. 6, 1855; died Sept. 11, 1855.
II. ALICE E.[8] " Aug. 26, 1856.

1010. **Eighth Generation.** **Tower.**

484. ALBERT [7], CHARLES [6], AUGUSTUS [5], BENJAMIN [4], AMBROSE [3],
BENJAMIN [2], JOHN [1].
Albert [7], son of Charles [6] and Lucretia (Maynard) Tower, b.
Oct. 16, 1833 ; mar. Angelia S. Gragg, of Boston,
May 5, 1858. She was b.
Oct. 10, 1836, and was dau. of William and Rebecca (Willard) Gragg.

Childr.

I. ALBERT PHINEAS [8] born Dec. 10, 1859, in Charlestown, Mass.
II. CHARLES AUGUSTUS [8] " Jan. 14, 1870.

1011. **Eighth Generation.** **Tower.**

484. ALONZO [7], CHARLES [6], AUGUSTUS [5], BENJAMIN [4], AMBROSE [3],
BENJAMIN [2], JOHN [1].
Alonzo [7], son of Charles [6] and Lucretia (Maynard) Tower, b.
Jan. 10, 1837 ; mar. Tryphena Clark, of Concord, Mass.,
March 22, 1859. She was b. in Lancaster, Mass.,
May 1, 1834, and was dau. of Joseph and Lucinda (Davis)
Clark.

Child.

I. FREDERICK ALONZO [8] born Feb. 10, 1871.

1012. Fletcher. **Eighth Generation.** **Tower.**

486. NANCIE B.[7], AUGUSTUS [6], AUGUSTUS [5], BENJAMIN [4], AMBROSE [3],
BENJAMIN [2], JOHN [1].
Nancie B.[7], dau. of Augustus [6] and Nancy (Bright) Tower, b.
Dec. 31, 1834 ; mar. John S. Fletcher, of Stow, Mass.,
July 5, 1859. He was son of Peter and Betsey (Patch)
Fletcher.

Childr. none.

1013. Wilder. **Eighth Generation.** **Tower.**

486. HATTIE W.[7], AUGUSTUS [6], AUGUSTUS [5], BENJAMIN [4], AMBROSE [3],
BENJAMIN [2], JOHN [1].

510 THE TOWER GENEALOGY.

Hattie W.[7], dau. of Augustus [6] and Nancy (Bright) Tower, b.
May 2, 1836 ; mar. Henry Windsor Wilder, of Stow, Mass.,
May 26, 1857. He was b. in Stow
May 31, 1834, and was son of Henry and Ann S. Wilder.

Childr. born in Stow.

I. NELLIE SOPHIA [8] born June 25, 1858; died Jan. 10, 1874, ag. 15 y. 6 m.
15 d.
II. IDA FRANCES [8]   " Feb. 1, 1861.

1014. Whitcomb. Eighth Generation.   Tower.

488. HELEN P.[7], JEDEDIAH L.[6], AUGUSTUS [5], BENJAMIN [4], AMBROSE [3],
BENJAMIN [2], JOHN [1].
Helen P.[7], dau. of Jedediah L.[6] and Mary Jane (Noyes)
Tower, b.
Jan. 5, 1842 ; mar. John Whitcomb, of Harvard, Mass.,
June 13, 1868. He was b.
Sept. 8, 1837, and was son of John and Susan (Brown)
Whitcomb.

Childr.

I. FRED JOSIAH [8]   born Jan. 27, 1869.
II. GEORGE LEVI [8]   " March 24, 1870.
III. HERMAN PLYMPTON [8] " April 8, 1871.
IV. MARY JANE [8]   " Aug. 16, 1874.

1015.   Eighth Generation.   Tower.

488. HERMAN C.[7], JEDEDIAH L.[6], AUGUSTUS [5], BENJAMIN [4], AMBROSE [3],
BENJAMIN [2], JOHN [1].
Herman C.[7], son of Jedediah L.[6] and Mary Jane (Noyes)
Tower, b.
March 8, 1843 ; mar. Mary A. Walker, of Providence, R. I.,
March 16, 1871. She was b.
Aug. 31, 1845, and was dau. of Samuel and Martha (Belling) Walker.

Childr.

I. FRED HERMAN [8] born June 22, 1872.
II. GRACE WALKER [8] " Feb. 24, 1877.

1016.   Eighth Generation.   Tower.

488. JOHN N.[7], JEDEDIAH L.[6], AUGUSTUS [5], BENJAMIN [4], AMBROSE [3],
BENJAMIN [2], JOHN [1].
John N.[7], son of Jedediah L.[6] and Mary Jane (Noyes)
Tower, b.
May 30, 1846 ; mar. Elsie Hunt, of Marlborough, Mass.,

March 14, 1874. She was b. in Marlborough Aug. 24, 1853, and was dau. of Edward and Clementine (Tarbell) Hunt.

Child.

I. MARY WARREN [8] born Aug. 8, 1874.

1017. Gardner. Eighth Generation. Tower.

490. LYDIA [7], MATTHEW [6], MATTHEW [5], MATTHEW [4], SAMUEL [3], SAMUEL [2], JOHN [1].

Lydia [7], dau. of Matthew [6] and Nabby [6] (Bates) Tower, b. July 8, 1792; mar. Samuel P. Gardner, of New York State, Dec. 6, 1810. He was b. June 28, 1786.

Childr.

I.	SAMUEL ABBOTT [8]	born	March 24, 1812; died April 30, 1830, ag. 18 y. 1 m. 7 d.
II.	EDMUND [8]	"	April 28, 1815; died June 27, 1830, ag. 15 y. 1 m. 29 d.
III.	JERUSHA L. [8]	"	Feb. 9, 1817.
IV.	BETSEY C. [8]	"	Sept. 21, 1819.
V.	WILLIAM WESLEY [8]	"	July 18, 1821.
VI.	MATTHEW TOWER [8]	"	July 8, 1824.

Samuel P. Gardner died in Crawford Co., Ind., Oct. 13, 1867, ag. 81 y. 3 m. 15 d.

Lydia (Tower) Gardner died in Crawford Co., Ind., Oct. 26, 1867, ag. 75 y. 3 m. 18 d.

1018. Eighth Generation. Tower.

490. MATTHEW [7], MATTHEW [6], MATTHEW [5], MATTHEW [4], SAMUEL [3], SAMUEL [2], JOHN [1].

Matthew [7], son of Matthew [6] and Nabby [6] (Bates) Tower, b. Nov. 13 1793; mar. Lydia Brookhart, of Jeffersontown, Ky., 1822. She was b. in Virginia, and was dau. of Jacob and (Killer) Brookhart.

Childr.

1344.	I.	DAVID BROOKHART [8]	born	July 27, 1823, in Kentucky.
	II.	JAMES W. [8]	"	1827; unmar.
	III.	ABIGAIL [8]	"	; mar. J. Newton Mallet, 1854. She died 1856.
1345.	IV.	SAVINA [8]	"	
	V.	MIRIAM [8]	"	; mar. Cronic.

Matthew Tower [7] died near York, Ill., Oct. , 1872, ag. 78 y. 11 m.

Lydia (Brookhart) Tower died near York, Ill., Oct. 18, 1869.

1019.   Eighth Generation.   Tower.

490. COTTON [7], MATTHEW [6], MATTHEW [5], MATTHEW [4], SAMUEL [3],
      SAMUEL [2], JOHN [1].
      Cotton [7], son of Matthew [6] and Nabby [6] (Bates) Tower, b.
      March 24, 1795; mar. Hannah Edson in Kentucky
                    She was b. in New York State,
                        and was dau. of Isaac and Sarah (Ford) Edson.

Childr.

1346.	I.	JULIA ANN [8]	born July 19, 1817.	
	II.	CHARLES WESLEY [8]	"	; mar. Elizabeth Rogers.
	III.	AMBROSE [8]	"	; " Mary J. Totten.
1347.	IV.	ELIZABETH [8]	" Dec. 31, 1827.	
	V.	WILLIAM WALLACE [8]	"	; mar. Catherine Bailey.
	VI.	SAMUEL ALBERT [8]	"	; " Sarah Jenkins.
	VII.	ROBERT BRUCE [8]	"	; " Martha Totten.
	VIII.	MARY [8]	"	; " John Collins.
	IX.	JAMES BURTON [8]	"	; " Lizzie Carter.

Cotton Tower [7] died in Crawford Co., Ind., Jan. 11, 1881, ag.
    85 y. 9 m. 18 d.
Hannah (Edson) Tower died in Crawford Co., Ind., Aug.
    , 1873.

1020.   Eighth Generation.   Tower.

490. ABRAHAM B. [7], MATTHEW [6], MATTHEW [5], MATTHEW [4], SAMUEL [3],
      SAMUEL [2], JOHN [1].
      Abraham B. [7], son of Matthew [6] and Nabby [6] (Bates) Tower, b.
      April 27, 1798; mar. Delilah Lynch.

Childr.

1348.	I.	MARY ANN [8]	born		
1349.	II.	NANCY JANE [8]	"		
	III.	GEORGE BURTON [8]	"	; mar.	Humphrey.
1350.	IV.	HARRIET SOPHIA [8]	"		

Abraham B. Tower [7] died in Crawford Co., Ind.,   1855,
    ag. 56.

1021. Reynolds.   Eighth Generation.   Tower.

490. SARAH J. [7], MATTHEW [6], MATTHEW [5], MATTHEW [4], SAMUEL [3],
      SAMUEL [2], JOHN [1].
      Sarah J. [7], dau. of Matthew [6] and Nabby [6] (Bates) Tower, b.
      Feb. 8, 1800; mar. William Rhodes Reynolds, of Hardin
          Co., Ky.,
      Nov.   , 1819. He was b.
      Dec. 25, 1798, and was son of Richard and Esther Reynolds.

Childr.

I. WILLIAM VALENTINE [8] born Sept. 15, 1820, in Hardin Co., Ky.
II. ALONZO DAVIS [8]   " May 26, 1822, " Grayson Co., "
III. THOMAS HUMPHREY [8]   " Aug. 23, 1825, " Leavenworth, Ind. ;
       died 1845, ag. 20.
IV. JAMES MORTIMER [8]   " May 27, 1827, in Leavenworth.
V. MARY ELIZA [8]   " July 26, 1831, " "
VI. SARAH ROSALTHA [8]   "   "   " ; died
       in infancy.
VII. MARTHA LYDIA [8]   "   "   "
VIII. HARRIET URSULA [8]   " .   "   " ; mar.
       Thomas Murphy.

William R. Reynolds died in Rome, Ind.
Sarah J. (Tower) Reynolds died in Rome.

1022.   **Eighth Generation.**   **Tower.**

490. HULL [7], MATTHEW [6], MATTHEW [5], MATTHEW [4], SAMUEL [3], SAM-
UEL [2], JOHN [1].
Hull [7], son of Matthew [6] and Nabby [6] (Bates) Tower, b.
Feb. 27, 1802 ; mar. Sarah Edson
Nov. 21, 1821. She was b. in New York State
Nov. 5, 1804, and was dau. of Isaac and Sarah (Ford) Edson.

Childr. born in Kentucky, Indiana, and Illinois.
1351. I. SARAH JANE [8]   born Sept. 28, 1822.
     II. PHILANDER [8]   " Nov. 16, 1824; died Aug. 18,
       1851, ag. 26 y. 9 m. 1 d. ; s. p.
1352. III. ABIGAIL BATES [8]   " Nov. 6, 1826.
     IV. PRESTON [8]   " Feb. 2, 1829 ; died Nov. 15,
       1830, ag 1 y. 9 m. 13 d.
1353. V. WASHINGTON LAFAYETTE [8] " Feb. 27, 1831.
     VI. LYDIA [8]   " March 24, 1833.
     VII. DANIEL EDSON [8]   " July 25, 1835; mar. Flora A.
       Kenoyer. Nine children.
1354. VIII. HARRIET NEWELL [8]   " Oct. 12, 1837.
     IX. JOHN WESLEY [8]   " Jan. 30, 1840.
1355. X. HANNAH [8]   " March 16, 1841.
1356. XI. MARTHA ELLEN [8]   " May 25, 1844.
     XII. MARY RACHEL [8]   " Dec. 8, 1846; died in Oregon,
       Aug. 11, 1857, ag. 10 y. 8 m. 3 d.

Hull Tower [7] died in Oakland, Oregon, Nov. 19, 1880, ag.
78 y. 8 m. 21 d.

1023. West.   **Eighth Generation.**   **Tower.**

490. NABBY [7], MATTHEW [6], MATTHEW [5], MATTHEW [4], SAMUEL [3],
SAMUEL [2], JOHN [1].
Nabby [7], dau. of Matthew [6] and Nabby [6] (Bates) Tower, b.

May 23, 1806 ; mar. William West, of Crawford Co., Ind.,
Sept. 22, 1825. He was b. in Kentucky,
May 6, 1803, and was son of Jesse and Nancy Ann (French)
West.

Childr. born near Leavenworth, Ind.

I.   HESTER ANN [8] born Aug. 1, 1826; unmar.
II.   CHARLOTTE [8]   "   Oct. 20, 1827; died June 3, 1833, ag. 5 y. 7 m.
         14 d.
III.   FRANCES [8]   "   March 18, 1829; mar.   Parker, of Quincy,
         Adams Co , Iowa.
IV.   JAMES [8]   "   Jan. 30, 1831.
V.   NANCY E. [8]   "   March 26, 1833.
VI.   WILLIAM F. [8]   "   May 11, 1835.
VII.   CHARLES [8]   "   March 30, 1837; died in Cairo, Ill., Sept. 15,
         1865, ag. 28 y. 5 m. 16 d.
VIII.   JOSEPH B. [8]   "   May 28, 1839.
IX.   LILA J. [8]   "   Dec. 6, 1841.
X.   LUCY B. [8]   "   Jan. 11, 1844; mar.   Mazzola, of New Al-
         bany, Ind.
XI.   ENOCH W. [8]   "   Feb. 16, 1846; unmar.
XII.   SARAH [8]   "   Jan. 20, 1848; died Aug. 21, 1849.

William West died Dec. 24, 1866, ag. 63 y. 7 m. 18 d.
Nabby (Tower) West died Aug. 6, 1874, ag. 68 y. 2 m. 14 d.

1024.   **Eighth Generation.**   **Tower.**

490.   JONATHAN W. [7], MATTHEW [6], MATTHEW [5], MATTHEW [4], SAMUEL [3],
   SAMUEL [2], JOHN [1].
   Jonathan W. [7], son of Matthew [6] and Nabby [6] (Bates) Tower, b.
   Dec. 8, 1809; mar. Sarah Vest Munroe, of Crawford Co.,
   Ind.
   Feb. 28, 1831. She was b.
   July 10, 1811, and was dau. of James and Nancy (Lemastris)
   Munroe.

Childr.

1357.   I.   MATTHEW [8]   born March 25, 1832.
1358.   II.   LOUISA CAROLINE [8]   "   June 22, 1834.
   III.   ISABEL [8]   "   Oct. 18, 1836; died Oct. 18, 1836.
1359.   IV.   ABRAHAM BATES [8]   "   Oct. 16, 1837.
1360.   V.   ROSANNAH CASSIDY [8]   "   May 10, 1840.
   VI.   HARRIET NEAL [8]   "   Nov. 16, 1842; died July 27, 1843.
   VII.   JAMES MORTIMER [8]   "   June 23, 1844; died July 7, 1844.
1361. VIII.   CHARLOTTE TEMPLE [8]   "   Sept. 3, 1845.
1362.   IX.   JONATHAN WARREN [8]   "   Aug. 21, 1848.
1363.   X.   SARAH JANE [8]   "   Sept. 17, 1853.
1364.   XI.   LEVI GIFFORD [8]   "   Sept. 27, 1856.

Sarah V. (Munroe) Tower died in Alton, Ind., Sept. 4, 1884,
  ag. 73 y. 1 m. 25 d.

1025.   **Eighth Generation.**   **Tower.**

490. NEHEMIAH[7], MATTHEW[6], MATTHEW[5], MATTHEW[4], SAMUEL[3], SAMUEL[2], JOHN[1].

Nehemiah[7], son of Matthew[6] and Nabby[6] (Bates) Tower, b. Dec. 17, 1814; mar. Betsey Pope.

Childr.

I.	ALVAN[8]	; mar.	Rachel Blind.
II.	SARAH JANE[8]	; "	James Summers.
III.	ELIJAH[8]	; "	
IV.	JOHN W.[8]	; "	

Betsey (Pope) Tower died
Nehemiah Tower[7] mar., 2d, Lucinda Donner.

Childr.

V. JOSEPH[8]   mar.   VI. JAMES L.[8]   ; mar.

Lucinda (Donner) Tower died.
Nehemiah Tower[7] mar., 3d,
He died about   1877.

1026. Bullington.   **Eighth Generation.**   **Tower.**

490. HARRIET[7], MATTHEW[6], MATTHEW[5], MATTHEW[4], SAMUEL[3], SAMUEL[2], JOHN[1].

Harriet[7], dau. of Matthew[6] and Nabby[6] (Bates) Tower, b. Sept. 21, 1821; mar. Daniel Bullington
Oct.   , 1839. He was b. in Crawford Co., Ind., May   4, 1818, and was son of Robert and Mary (Mathers) Bullington.

Child.

I. HENRY NEWELL[8] born   1840.

Harriet (Tower) Bullington died April , 1841, ag. 19 y. 7 m.

1027.   **Eighth Generation.**   **Tower.**

491. LOREN L.[7], LUTHER[6], ABNER[5], JOSEPH[4], JOSEPH[3], SAMUEL[2], JOHN[1].

Loren L.[7], son of Luther[6] and Sally (Reed) Tower, b. Nov. 25, 1816; mar. Sophronia Bates
April 22, 1841. She was b. in Westford, Vt., July 15, 1815, and was dau. of Moses and Rebecca (Macomber) Bates.

Childr. born in Chesterfield, Mass.

1365.	I. ELLEN O.[8]	born Sept. 4, 1843.
1366.	II. ALICE L.[8]	" Oct. 15, 1845.

1367.	III.	WALTER M.[8]	born Sept. 19, 1847.
1368.	IV.	VIETTA E.[8]	" Dec. 20, 1849.
1369.	V.	ANN ELIZA[8]	" June 13, 1852.
	VI.	ALMIRA J.[8]	" July 14, 1855.
	VII.	LUCY J.[8]	" July 27, 1860.

1028. Capen.   Eighth Generation.   Tower.

491. SALLY I.[7], LUTHER[6], ABNER[5], JOSEPH[4], JOSEPH[3], SAMUEL[2],
JOHN[1].
Sally I.[7], dau. of Luther[6] and Sally (Reed) Tower, b.
Nov. 25, 1819; mar. Daniel Capen, of Worthington, Mass.,
April 28, 1840. He was b. in Windsor, Mass.,
Dec. 2, 1816, and was son of Asa H. and Amey (Price)
Capen.

Childr. born in Worthington.

I.	SARAH R.[8]	born June 14, 1841; died Nov. 17, 1855, ag. 14 y. 5 m. 3 d.
II.	WARD D.[8]	" March 15, 1844; died May 17, 1845, ag. 1 y. 2 m. 2 d.
III.	GRANVILLE D.[8]	" March 1, 1857.

Daniel Capen died in Worthington, Jan. 5, 1874, ag. 57 y.
1 m. 3 d.

1029. Tyler.   Eighth Generation.   Tower.

491. LUCINA S.[7], LUTHER[6], ABNER[5], JOSEPH[4], JOSEPH[3], SAMUEL[2],
JOHN[1].
Lucina S.[7], dau. of Luther[6] and Sally (Reed) Tower, b.
Oct. 21, 1825; mar. Elijah Tyler, of Conway, Mass.,
April 22, 1847. He was b. in Chesterfield, Mass.,
Feb. 24, 1816, and was son of Elijah and Lavisa (Hewitt)
Tyler.

Childr.

I.	ELLA ADELAIDE[8]	born Feb. 9, 1849.
II.	LUTHER ELY[8]	" Dec. 31, 1851.
III.	ISABELL LUCINA[8]	" Dec. 25, 1853.

1030. Smith.   Eighth Generation.   Tower.

491. BETSEY S.[7], LUTHER[6], ABNER[5], JOSEPH[4], JOSEPH[3], SAMUEL[2],
JOHN[1].
Betsey S.[7], dau. of Luther[6] and Sally (Reed) Tower, b.
June 20, 1827; mar. Martin Smith, of Ashfield, Mass.,
June 18, 1851. He was b. in Ashfield
April 20, 1828, and was son of Justus and Sibyl (Maynard)
Smith.

Childr.

I.   LUTHER MAYNARD [8] born Nov. 9, 1855, in Windsor; died May 28, 1863, ag. 7 y. 6 m. 18 d.
II. EDNA JOSEPHINE [8]   "   April 9, 1857, in Windsor.
III. ELVA ETTA SIBYL [8]   "   Dec. 11, 1859, in Conway.
IV. WILLIE HERBERT [8]   "   Sept. 28, 1861,   "   ; died March 4, 1865, ag. 3 y. 5 m. 6 d.
V.   SARAH IRENE [8]   "   April 9, 1863,   "
VI. MARTIN EUGENE [8]   "   May 28, 1865,   "

1031. Bigelow.   Eighth Generation.   Tower.

491. JANE E.[7], LUTHER [6], ABNER [5], JOSEPH [4], JOSEPH [3], SAMUEL [2], JOHN [1].

Jane E.[7], dau. of Luther [6] and Sally (Reed) Tower, b.
May 19, 1829; mar. Silas Bigelow, of Windsor, Mass.,
Oct. 18, 1848. He was b. in Conway, Mass.,
April 25, 1820, and was son of Samuel and Electa (Wilder)
Bigelow.

Childr.

I.   EMMA JANE [8] born Jan. 12, 1850, in Conway.
II. SARAH ELECTA [8] "   Jan. 17, 1852,   "
III. EDWIN SILAS [8]   "   June 6, 1863, in Buckland; died June 13, 1863.

1032. Prince.   Eighth Generation.   Tower.

491. MARTHA A.[7], LUTHER [6], ABNER [5], JOSEPH [4], JOSEPH [3], SAMUEL [2], JOHN [1].

Martha A.[7], dau. of Luther [6] and Sally (Reed) Tower, b.
June 16, 1833 ; mar. Arial Avery Prince, of Windsor, Mass.,
Sept. 25, 1855. He was b. in Windsor
Feb. 10, 1832, and was son of Arial and Emma (Avery)
Prince.

Child born in Pittsfield, Mass.

I.   ELMER ARIAL [8] born Aug. 4, 1862; died in Springfield, Aug. 2, 1876, ag. 13 y. 11 m. 29 d.

1033. Pierce.   Eighth Generation.   Tower.

491. MARY A.[7], LUTHER [6], ABNER [5], JOSEPH [4], JOSEPH [3], SAMUEL [2], JOHN [1].

Mary A.[7], dau. of Luther [6] and Sally (Reed) Tower, b.
June 22, 1836 ; mar. Julius F. Pierce [8], of Windsor, Mass.,
Oct. 6, 1858. He was b. in Windsor
Nov. 7, 1836, and was son of Isaac and Joanna (Bailey)
Pierce.

PIERCE, BAILEY.   TOWER.

Julius F.[8], Joanna[7], Lucy[6], Peter[5], Peter[4], Jeremiah[3], Jeremiah[2],
John[1].

Childr.

I.   ELWIN LEWELLYN[8], born Nov. 26, 1860, in Windsor; died Feb. 4, 1861.
II. MARTHA ALICE[8]   "   Aug. 6, 1864, in Conway, Mass.
III. MARY ADELAIDE[8]   "   June 10, 1868, in Buckland, Mass.
IV. BERTIE JULIA[8]   "   May 24, 1876, in Conway; died in North-
                              ampton, Mass., Aug. 2, 1877, ag. 1 y.
                              2 m. 9 d.

1034.   **Eighth Generation.**   **Tower.**

500. WILLIAM F.[7], JOSEPH P.[6], EZEKIEL[5], JOSEPH[4], JOSEPH[3],
     SAMUEL[2], JOHN[1].
     William F.[7], son of Joseph P.[6] and Julia A. (Denton) Tower, b.
     Jan. 25, 1839; mar. Mary Rheel, of Pittsfield, Mass.,
     Dec. 13, 1877. She was b. in Poughkeepsie, N. Y.,
               1849, and was dau. of George and Mary E. (Boss)
          Rheel.

Child.

I.   HENRY FAYETTE[8] born Dec. 3, 1878, in Hinsdale, Mass.

1035. McDonough. Eighth Generation.   **Tower.**

500. EMILY J.[7], JOSEPH P.[6], EZEKIEL[5], JOSEPH[4], JOSEPH[3],
     SAMUEL[2], JOHN[1].
     Emily J.[7], dau. of Joseph P.[6] and Julia A. (Denton) Tower, b.
          1843; mar. Franklin McDonough, of Brooklyn, N. Y.

Childr.

I.   FRANK[8].   II. JOSEPH[8]   ; died ag. 4 y.

Franklin McDonough died   .
Emily J. (Tower) McDonough mar., 2d, Oliver H. Taylor.

Child.

III. ARTHUR A.[8] born Aug. 27, 1880.

1036.   **Eighth Generation.**   **Tower.**

500. NELSON H.[7], JOSEPH P.[6], EZEKIEL[5], JOSEPH[4], JOSEPH[3],
     SAMUEL[2], JOHN[1].
     Nelson H.[7], son of Joseph P.[6] and Julia A. (Denton) Tower, b.
          1845; mar. Clara Middleton, of San Francisco, Cal.

Childr.

I.   CLARA[8].   II. Son[8].

1037.   Eighth Generation.   Tower.

500. CHARLES B.[7], JOSEPH P.[6], EZEKIEL[5], JOSEPH[4], JOSEPH[3], SAMUEL[2], JOHN[1].

Charles B.[7], son of Joseph P.[6] and Julia A. (Denton) Tower, b. Nov. 5, 1850; mar. Mary Louisa Dunn, of Green Point, N.Y., June 16, 1875. She was b. in New York city Feb. 6. 1851, and was dau. of Robert and Mary (Dansbury) Dunn.

Childr.

I.   ESTELLA LOUISA   born April 13, 1876.
II.   LILLIANS EMMA[8]   "   May   4, 1878.
III. MABEL D.[8]   "   Aug. 28, 1880.

1038.   Eighth Generation.   Tower.

501. HERSEY E.[7], LYMAN J.[6], EZEKIEL[5], JOSEPH[4], JOSEPH[3], SAMUEL[2], JOHN[1].

Hersey E.[7], son of Lyman J.[6] and Lucy C. (Converse) Tower, b. Dec. 3, 1833; mar. Rosa A. Doran, of Pittsfield, Mass., Sept. 5, 1866. She was b. in Worcester, Mass., Dec. 14, 1842.

Childr. born in Worthington, Mass.

I.   ELIZABETH[8] } Twins born Dec. 15, 1867 { died Dec. 16, 1867.
II.   ELLEN[8]   }   { "   Dec. 18, 1867.
III. MATTHEW D. E.[8]   "   May 4, 1869.
IV.   ELISHA M. L.[8]   "   Feb. 7, 1871; died Jan. 20, 1872.
V.   JOHN MILTON[8]   "   Oct. 9, 1872.

1039.   Eighth Generation.   Tower.

501. ELISHA C.[7], LYMAN J.[6], EZEKIEL[5], JOSEPH[4], JOSEPH[3], SAMUEL[2], JOHN[1].

Elisha C.[7], son of Lyman J.[6] and Lucy C. (Converse) Tower, b. Dec. 10, 1834; mar. Ebzina Stebbins, of Hinsdale, Mass., July 4, 1856. She was b. in Hinsdale April 23, 1836, and was dau. of Randall S. Stebbins.

Childr.

I.   ELISHA CLIFTON[8] born Aug. 30, 1857, in Worthington, Mass.
II.   MEDA ISABEL F.[8]   "   May 6, 1859,   "   "
III. ADDIE IMOGENE[8]   "   Aug. 16, 1862,   "   "   ; died
                              Aug. 22, 1863, ag. 1 y. 6 d.
IV.   WILLARD R.[8]   "   Sept. 16, 1864, in Worthington; died Sept. 16,
                              1865, ag. 1. y.
V.   ROSA GEORGIANA[8]   "   July 20, 1866,   "

VI.   Eva Ebzina [8]   born May 6, 1868, in Hinsdale; died Sept. 19, 1869,
                              ag. 1 y. 4 m. 13 d.
VII. Maud Josephine [8] "   Sept. 7, 1873, in Hinsdale; "   Sept. 17, 1874,
                              ag. 1 y. 10 d.

1040.   Eighth Generation.   Tower.

501. Oscar F. [7], Lyman J. [6], Ezekiel [5], Joseph [4], Joseph [3], Samuel [2],
          John [1].
          Oscar F. [7], son of Lyman J. [6] and Lucy C. (Converse) Tower, b.
          Dec. 27, 1838; mar. Ellen Ryan, of Hudson, N. Y.,
          Dec. 15, 1869. She was b. in Hudson
                  1851, and was dau. of Henry and Mary Ryan.

Childr. born in Hinsdale, Mass.

  I.   Zenas Seymour [8]   born Nov. 12, 1870.
 II.   Bainbridge York [8]   "   May 8, 1872; died Feb. 24, 1873.
III.   Mabel Frothingham [8]   "   March 29, 1874; died Aug. 19, 1874.
 IV.   Oscar Fayette [8]   "   July 30, 1877.

          Oscar F. Tower [7] died in Hinsdale, July 25, 1877, ag. 37 y.
          6 m. 29 d.

1041. Mailey.   Eighth Generation.   Tower.

501. Welthea A. [7], Lyman J. [6], Ezekiel [5], Joseph [4], Joseph [3],
          Samuel [2], John [1].
          Welthea A. [7], dau. of Lyman J. [6] and Lucy C. (Converse)
          Tower, b.
          Jan. 17, 1841 ; mar. Charles Mailey, of Brooklyn, N. Y.,
          Feb. 10, 1864. He was b.
                  1838, and was son of Charles and Elizabeth Mailey.

1042. Kelly.   Eighth Generation.   Tower.

501. Esther J. [7], Lyman J. [6], Ezekiel [5], Joseph [4], Joseph [3], Sam-
          uel [2], John [1].
          Esther J. [7], dau. of Lyman J. [6] and Lucy C. (Converse)
          Tower, b.
          Sept. 19, 1846 ; mar. John Kelly, of Worthington, Mass.,
          Jan. 13, 1867. He was b. in Worthington
                  1843, and was son of James and Martha B. Kelly.

Childr. born in Worthington.

I.   James L. [8] born Jan. 4, 1868.   III. Charles M. [8] born Nov. 1, 1872.
II. Bertha J. [8] "   Feb. 14, 1870.

1043. Dewey. Eighth Generation. Tower.

501. LUCY E.[7], LYMAN J.[6], EZEKIEL [5], JOSEPH [4], JOSEPH [3], SAMUEL [2], JOHN [1].
Lucy E.[7], dau. of Lyman J.[6] and Lucy C. (Converse) Tower, b.
Dec. 26, 1850; mar. Edward A. Dewey, of Worcester, Mass.,

Child.

I. JENNIE [8].

1044. Eighth Generation. Tower.

502. JOSEPH H.[7], WILLIAM E.[6], EZEKIEL [5], JOSEPH [4], JOSEPH [3], SAMUEL [2], JOHN [1].
Joseph H.[7], son of William E.[6] and Lucy M. (Gilbert) Tower, b.
July 14, 1836; mar. Ellen E. Mason, of Cummington, Mass., July 12, 1862. She was b.
March 20, 1844, and was dau. of Justus and Lydia P. Mason.

Childr. born in Worthington, Mass.

I. JULIA L.[8]   born Nov. 2, 1863.
II. GEORGE W.[8]   "   April 26, 1865.
III. CLARENCE P.[8] "   Nov. 18, 1866.
IV. WILLIS W.[8]   "   March 18, 1871.
V. IDA V.[8]   "   June 23, 1875.

1045. Mason. Eighth Generation. Tower.

502. SARAH J.[7], WILLIAM E.[6], EZEKIEL [5], JOSEPH [4], JOSEPH [3], SAMUEL [2], JOHN [1].
Sarah J.[7], dau. of William E.[6] and Lucy M. (Gilbert) Tower, b.
Oct. 20, 1848; mar. Newell A. Mason
July 4, 1869. He was b.
1850, and was son of Justus and Lydia (Tirrell) Mason.

Childr.

I. MARY [8] born May 1, 1870.   II. EMMA [8] born June 17, 1872.

1046. Eighth Generation. Tower.

502. WILLIAM M.[7], WILLIAM E.[6], EZEKIEL [5], JOSEPH [4], JOSEPH [3], SAMUEL [2], JOHN [1].
William M.[7], son of William E.[6] and Lucy M. (Gilbert) Tower, b.
Jan. 18, 1851; mar. Ida Elizabeth Mason, of Cummington,

May 2, 1871. She was b. in Cummington, Mass.,
Oct. 19, 1852, and was dau. of Justus and Lydia (Tirrell)
Mason.

Childr. born in Dalton, Mass.

I.   CLARIBEL [8]   born Nov. 14, 1871; died Dec. 3, 1871.
II. MABEL ROMAINE [8]   "   Feb. 1, 1876.
III. FRANCIS WILLIAM [8] "   Feb. 2, 1878.
IV. LEO JUSTUS [8]   "   Aug. 16, 1879.

1047. Parker.   Eighth Generation.   Tower.

502. HELEN L.[7], WILLIAM E.[6], EZEKIEL [5], JOSEPH [4], JOSEPH [3],
SAMUEL [2], JOHN [1].

Helen L.[7], dau. of William E.[6] and Lucy M. (Gilbert) Tower, b.
Aug. 1, 1855 ; mar. Cushing M. Parker, of Dalton, Mass.,
June 1, 1877. He was b. in Dalton
and was son of H. M. and Lucinda Parker.

NINTH GENERATION.

1048.   Ninth Generation.   Tower.

515. ALBERT [8], WILLIAM [7], ISAAC [6], ICHABOD [5], GIDEON [4], BENJA-
MIN [3], JOHN [2], JOHN [1].

Albert [8], son of William [7] and Sallie (Wood) Tower, b.
Sept. 21, 1829 ; mar. Adaline S. Grover in Fitchburg, Mass.,
April 7, 1859. She was b. in Millbury, Mass.,
Sept. 26, 1832, and was dau. of Zina and Lydia (Sprague)
Grover.

Childr.

I.   WILLIAM ALBERT [9] born May 17, 1860, in Bristol, Ill.
II. MARY ADDIE [9]   "   Aug. 25, 1861, " Aurora, "
III. HATTIE D.[9]   "   Nov. 4, 1867, " Galesville, Wis.
IV. MILDRED SPRAGUE [9] "   Oct. 28, 1874, "   "   "

1049. Bacon.   Ninth Generation.   Tower.

515. MARY L. [8], WILLIAM [7], ISAAC [6], ICHABOD [5], GIDEON [4], BEN-
JAMIN [3], JOHN [2], JOHN [1].

Mary L.[8], dau. of William [7] and Sallie (Wood) Tower, b.
July 1, 1831 ; mar. Theodore F. Bacon, of Charlton, Mass.,
Oct. 21, 1855. He was son of Asa and Elizabeth (Comins)
Bacon.

Childr. none.

Mary L.[8] (Tower) Bacon died Sept. 20, 1861, ag. 30 y. 2 m.
19 d.

1050. Horn.   Ninth Generation.   Tower.

517. FRANCES P.[8], ISAAC [7], ISAAC [6], ICHABOD [5], GIDEON [4], BENJA-
      MIN [3], JOHN [2], JOHN [1].
      Frances P.[8], dau. of Isaac [7] and Paulina (Buckman) Tower, b.
      Oct. 22, 1847 ; mar. Adelbert Horn, of Charlton, Mass.,
           1869.

Child.
I. NELLIE ELIZA.[9]

1051. Lamb.   Ninth Generation.   Tower.

518. REBECCA J.[8], ALANSON P.[7], ISAAC [6], ICHABOD [5], GIDEON [4], BEN-
      JAMIN [3], JOHN [2], JOHN [1].
      Rebecca J. [8], dau. of Alanson P. [7] and Mary N. (Newell)
           Tower, b.
      Nov. 12, 1839 ; mar. Edward Lamb, of Charlton, Mass.,
           Feb. 20, 1857.

Childr. none.

Rebecca J.[8] (Tower) Lamb died May 23, 1857, ag. 17 y. 6 m.
      10 d.

1052. Edwards.   Ninth Generation.   Tower.

518. ELLEN M.[8], ALANSON P.[7], ISAAC [6], ICHABOD [5], GIDEON [4], BEN-
      JAMIN [3], JOHN [2], JOHN [1].
      Ellen M.[8], dau. of Alanson P.[7] and Mary N. (Newell) Tower, b.
      June 28, 1841 ; mar. William Edwards, of Chatfield, Minn.,
           May 24, 1860.

Childr. none.

Ellen M. (Tower) Edwards died April 11, 1862, ag. 20 y.
      9 m. 13 d.

1053. Hassett.   Ninth Generation.   Tower.

518. AMY EUDORA [8], ALANSON P.[7], ISAAC [6], ICHABOD [5], GIDEON [4],
      BENJAMIN [3], JOHN [2], JOHN [1].
      Amy E.[8], dau. of Alanson P.[7] and Mary N. (Newell) Tower, b.
      May 10, 1859 ; mar. Henry Melbern Hassett, of Chatfield,
           Minn.,
      Oct. 1, 1878. He was b. in Pennsylvania
      Dec. 6, 1851, and was son of John E. and Bessey Ann (Good-
           rich) Hassett.

Child.

      I. EARL PORTER [9] born March 1, 1881, in Chatfield.

1054.   **Ninth Generation.**   **Tower.**

519. CHARLEMAGNE [8], JOHN [7], ISAAC [6], ICHABOD [5], GIDEON [4], BENJA-
MIN [3], JOHN [2], JOHN [1].

Charlemagne [8], son of John [7] and Lucy (Bellows) Tower, b.
May 16, 1847 ; mar. Ella A. Andrews in Burbank, Minn.,
Jan. 8, 1874. She was b. in Yellowhead, Ill.,
Jan. 27, 1853, and was dau. of Elijah and Asenath (Jacobs)
Andrews.

Childr.

I. EARL BERDET [9]   born Sept. 20, 1875, in Manannah, Minn.
II. WILLIS ANDREWS [9]   " Dec.   4, 1880, " Burbank ; died Aug. 31,
                             1883, ag. 2 y. 8 m. 27 d.
III. ROY CHARLIE [9]   " Jan. 17, 1883, in Burbank.

1055.   **Ninth Generation.**   **Tower.**

519. ISAAC D. [8], JOHN [7], ISAAC [6], ICHABOD [5], GIDEON [4], BENJAMIN [3],
JOHN [2], JOHN [1].

Isaac D. [8], son of John [7] and Lucy (Bellows) Tower, b.
Nov. 16, 1849 ; mar. Carrie A. Launsbury in Tower Hill,
Minn.,
Nov. 16, 1873. She was b. in Java, N. Y.,
March 19, 1849, and was dau. of Benjamin W. and Sarah A.
(Jackson) Launsbury.

Childr. none.

1056.   **Ninth Generation.**   **Tower.**

523. VERNON J. [8], JOSEPH H. [7], JOSEPH P. [6], ICHABOD [5], GIDEON [4],
BENJAMIN [3], JOHN [2], JOHN [1].

Vernon J. [8], son of Joseph H. [7] and Phebe Ann (Thomas)
Tower, b.
Jan. 19, 1860 ; mar. Amy Beach [9] in Houghton Lake, Mich.,
1881. She was b.
May   , 1867, and was dau. of Mary L. [8] (Bigelow) and Cyrus
Beach.

BEACH, BIGELOW.   TOWER.
Amy [9], Mary L. [8], Sally [7], Joseph P. [6], Ichabod [5], Gideon [4], Benjamin [3],
John [2], John [1].

1057. Space.   **Ninth Generation.**   **Tower.**

523. ALICE L. [8], JOSEPH H. [7], JOSEPH P. [6], ICHABOD [5], GIDEON [4], BEN-
JAMIN [3], JOHN [2], JOHN [1].

Alice L.[8], dau. of Joseph H.[7] and Phebe Ann (Thomas) Tower, b.

Sept. 28, 1864; mar. Philip Space in Grand Ledge, Mich., Nov. 18, 1882.

Childr.

I. MILLIE R.[9] born June 19, 1884.   II. ELLSWORTH[9] born Oct. 13, 1885.

1058. Eastman.   Ninth Generation.   Tower.

523. CYNTHIA B.[8], JOSEPH H.[7], JOSEPH P.[6], ICHABOD[5], GIDEON[4], BENJAMIN[3], JOHN[2], JOHN[1].

Cynthia B.[8], dau. of Joseph H.[7] and Phebe Ann (Thomas) Tower, b.

July 10, 1869; mar. William Eastman in Grand Ledge, Mich., March 31, 1886.   He was b. in Lansing, Mich., March 31, 1864.

1059.   Ninth Generation.   Tower.

525. ICHABOD H.[8], WILLIAM P.[7], JOSEPH P.[6], ICHABOD[5], GIDEON[4], BENJAMIN[3], JOHN[2], JOHN[1].

Ichabod H.[8], son of William P.[7] and Rosette C. (Barnes) Tower, b.

Dec. 7, 1840; mar. Hannah Ellen Dix in Middleville, Minn., Sept. 17, 1868.   She was b. in Clark Co., Ill., April 9, 1846.

Childr.

I.	GRANT[9]	born July 20, 1869, in Middleville.
II.	JESSIE FREMONT[9]	" Feb. 2, 1871, " "
III.	JIMMIE ARTHELLOW[9]	" June 24, 1872, " " ; died Sept. 24, 1882, ag. 10 y. 3 m.
IV.	SHERMAN[9]	" Sept. 2, 1873, in Middleville.
V.	ELLSWORTH[9]	" Dec. 17, 1874, " Greenwood, Minn.; died Sept. 27, 1882, ag. 7 y. 9 m. 11 d.
VI.	ANNIE[9]	" July 29, 1876, in Middleville.
VII.	GEORGE WESLEY[9]	" Dec. 17, 1879, " Willard, Minn. ; died Sept. 23, 1882, ag. 2 y. 9 m. 7 d.
VIII.	EDITH MAY[9]	" June 13, 1881.

1060.   Ninth Generation.   Tower.

526. CARL K.[8], JAMES P.[7], JOSEPH P.[6], ICHABOD[5], GIDEON[4], BENJAMIN[3], JOHN[2], JOHN[1].

Carl K.[8], son of James P.[7] and Lucena (Jenkins) Tower, b.

Nov. 3, 1852; mar. Minnie R. Harris in Midland, Mich., Jan. 1, 1878.   She was b. in Midland, Dec. 3, 1862, and was dau. of Watson and Nancy (Cady) Harris.

Child.

I. WATSON EARL[9] born July 6, 1882, in Midland.

1061. Dickinson.   Ninth Generation.   Tower.

526. VIOLA F.[8], JAMES P.[7], JOSEPH P.[6], ICHABOD[5], GIDEON[4], BEN-
JAMIN[3], JOHN[2], JOHN[1].
Viola F.[8], dau. of James P.[7] and Lucena (Jenkins) Tower, b.
June 26, 1855; mar. Orlando P. Dickinson
June 2, 1875. He was b. in the State of New York,
Sept. 8, 1849, and was son of John F. and Helen (Ferguson)
Dickinson.

Childr.

I.   EFFIE[9] born April 27, 1878, in Houghton Lake, Mich.
II. Son[9]   "   March 14, 1880; died June 27, 1882, ag. 2 y. 3 m. 14 d.

1062.   Ninth Generation.   Tower.

526. JAY B.[8], JAMES P.[7], JOSEPH P.[6], ICHABOD[5], GIDEON[4], BEN-
JAMIN[3], JOHN[2], JOHN[1].
Jay B.[8], son of James P.[7] and Lucena (Jenkins) Tower, b.
Jan. 26, 1859; mar. Zoe Woolworth in Denton, Mich.,
Aug. 23, 1881. She was b. in Jackson, Mich.,
1865, and was dau. of Henry and Hannah (Knick-
erbocker) Woolworth.

Childr. none.

1063. Miller.   Ninth Generation.   Tower.

527. JOSEPHINE A.[8], SAMUEL R.[7], JOSEPH P.[6], ICHABOD[5], GIDEON[4],
BENJAMIN[3], JOHN[2], JOHN[1].
Josephine A.[8], dau. of Samuel R.[7] and Sophronia (Wilson)
Tower, b.
Aug. 13, 1852; mar. Samuel D. Miller
June 28, 1868. He was b. in Manchester, Penn.,
July 3, 1835, and was son of Michael and Phebe (Kelley)
Miller.

Childr.

I.   VERNON S.[9]   born June 30, 1869.
II.   ELMER JAY[9]   "   May 30, 1872.
III. ELDA BELL[9]   "   Aug. 18, 1878.

1064. Hagar.   Ninth Generation.   Tower.

527. CYNTHIA L.[8], SAMUEL R.[7], JOSEPH P.[6], ICHABOD[5], GIDEON[4],
BENJAMIN[3], JOHN[2], JOHN[1].

Cynthia L.[8], dau. of Samuel R.[7] and Sophronia (Wilson) Tower, b.

March 24, 1854 ; mar. Calvin J. Hagar

March 10, 1872. He was b. in Schoharie Co., N. Y.,

March 16, 1837, and was son of Jonas V. and Clarissa (Brown) Hagar.

Childr. born in Branch Co., Mich.

I. JENNIE DERETA [9] born Sept. 24, 1874.
II. LEONA [9]   "   April 20, 1878.

1065. Yates.   Ninth Generation.   Tower.

527. DELIA D.[8], SAMUEL R.[7], JOSEPH P.[6], ICHABOD[5], GIDEON[4], BENJAMIN[3], JOHN[2], JOHN[1].

Delia D.[8], dau. of Samuel R. and Sophronia (Wilson) Tower, b.

Dec. 19, 1858 ; mar. John Franklin Yates, of the State of New York,

March 5, 1876. He was b. in Cayuga Co., N. Y.,

Oct. 14, 1853, and was son of John V. and Martha J. (Wilson) Yates.

Child.

I. JOHN REMINGTON [9] born Feb. 6, 1877, in Butler, Mich.

1066. Flowers.   Ninth Generation.   Tower.

527. NETTIE E.[8], SAMUEL R.[7], JOSEPH P.[6], ICHABOD[5], GIDEON[4], BENJAMIN[3], JOHN[2], JOHN[1].

Nettie E.[8], dau. of Samuel R.[7] and Sophronia (Wilson) Tower, b.

June 26, 1863 ; mar. George W. Flowers in Quincy, Mich.,

March 20, 1879. He was b. in Saint Paris, Ohio,

Jan. 5, 1856, and was son of William F. and Sarah E. (Martindale) Flowers.

1067. Goodwin.   Ninth Generation.   Tower.

532. SARAH M.[8], JOHN C.[7], LEVI[6], LEVI[5], GIDEON[4], BENJAMIN[3], JOHN[2], JOHN[1].

Sarah M.[8], dau. of John C.[7] and Sarah G. (Le Favour) Tower, b.

; mar. Almon K. Goodwin, of Providence, R. I.

Child.

I. MARGARET KENT [9].

1068. Ninth Generation. Tower.

534. WILLIAM F.[8], WILLIAM E.[7], JASON [6], LEVI [5], GIDEON [4], BENJA-
MIN [3], JOHN [2], JOHN [1].
William F.[8], son of William E.[7] and Betsey Ann (Parlow)
Tower, b.
1839 ; mar. Sarah S. Johnson, of Dartmouth, Mass.,
Nov. 6, 1861. She was b. in Dartmouth
1839, and was dau. of Samuel and Sarah Johnson.

1069. Ninth Generation. Tower.

536. JASON H.[8], JOHN H.[7], JASON [6], LEVI [5], GIDEON [4], BENJAMIN [3],
JOHN [2], JOHN [1].
Jason H.[8], son of John H.[7] and Sarah (Smith) Tower, b.
Sept. 28, 1845 ; mar. Mary Covell
Dec. 25, 1866. She was b.
April 16, 1847.
Childr.
I. MARY [9] born Aug. 22, 1870.
II. ELLERY D.[9] " April 24, 1872; died Sept. 4, 1872.

1070. Adams. Ninth Generation. Tower.

536. MARY E.[8], JOHN H.[7], JASON [6], LEVI [5], GIDEON [4], BENJAMIN [3],
JOHN [2], JOHN [1].
Mary E.[8], dau. of John H.[7] and Sarah (Smith) Tower, b.
Dec. 18, 1846 ; mar. Edwin S. Adams
Dec. 7, 1864. He was b. in Bellingham, Mass.,
Aug. 27, 1841, and was son of Ruel and Julia M. (Smith)
Adams.

1071. Ninth Generation. Tower.

536. ANDERSON C.[8], JOHN H.[7], JASON [6], LEVI [5], GIDEON [4], BENJA-
MIN [3], JOHN [2], JOHN [1].
Anderson C.[8], son of John H.[7] and Sarah (Smith) Tower, b.
July 16, 1849 ; mar. Katy Gessure
She was b. in Fond Du Lac, Wis.,
Dec. 20, 1859, and was dau. of Fred and Carrie Gessure.

Childr. born in Fergus Falls, Minn.
I. GRADY PHILLIPS [9] born Sept. , 1882.
II. IDA ESOLA [9] " Sept. 4, 1883; died Sept. 26, 1883.

1072. Doane. Ninth Generation. Tower.

536. ETTA S.[8], JOHN H.[7], JASON [6], LEVI [5], GIDEON [4], BENJAMIN [3],
JOHN [2], JOHN [1].

Etta S.[8], dau. of John H.[7] and Sarah (Smith) Tower, b.
March 1, 1852; mar. Ephraim L. Doane
May 27, 1874. He was b. in Brewer, Me.,
Jan. 5, 1850, and was son of Charles M. and Ellen (Hodgdon) Doane.

Childr.

I. CHARLES EDWIN [9] born June 15, 1878, in Brewer.
II. SARAH E.[9]   " Nov. 3, 1880, in Orrington, Me.
III. MARY LEE[9]   " Jan. 10, 1883.

1073.   **Ninth Generation.**   **Tower.**

546. JAMES H.[8], EMERSON [7], EMERSON [6], LEVI [5], GIDEON [4], BENJAMIN [3], JOHN [2], JOHN [1].

James H.[8], son of Emerson [7] and Elizabeth A. (Hidden) Tower, b.
May 21, 1847; mar. Julia Wilkinson Sayles
Dec. 19, 1866. She was dau. of Welcome B. and Deborah C. (Watson) Sayles.

Childr. born in Providence, R. I.

I. CLIFFORD SAYLES [9] born Nov. 13, 1867.
II. LEWIS PHILIP [9]   " March 6, 1869.
III. MONA ELIZABETH [9]   " March 9, 1871.

1074. Huston.   **Ninth Generation.**   **Tower.**

552. EMMA [8], HARVEY [7], JOSEPH [6], SAMUEL [5], GIDEON [4], BENJAMIN [3], JOHN [2], JOHN [1].

Emma [8], dau. of Harvey [7] and Laura (Mallet) Tower, b.
Dec. 27, 1850; mar. Orin Huston
June 5, 1870. He was b. in Cumberland Co., Me.,
Dec. 5, 1847, and was son of Adam and Eliza (Lord) Huston.

Childr. born in Clay Banks, Oceana Co., Mich.

I. WILLIE HENRY [9] born Nov. 23, 1872.
II. MABEL CLAIR [9]   " Feb. 8, 1874.
III. LESLY J.[9]   " March 15, 1877.
IV. ETHEL M.[9]   " June 30, 1879; died April 25, 1880.
V. ORIN [9]   " Dec. 5, 1882.
VI. PEARL [9]   " March 27, 1884.

1075. Hanson.   **Ninth Generation.**   **Tower.**

552. ADA [8], HARVEY [7], JOSEPH [6], SAMUEL [5], GIDEON [4], BENJAMIN [3], JOHN [2], JOHN [1].

Ada [8], dau. of Harvey [7] and Laura (Mallet) Tower, b.
Sept. 7, 1853; mar. John D. S. Hanson in White Hall, Mich.,

Oct. 22, 1876. He was b.

Jan. 1, 1852, and was son of John D. and Betsey (Austin) Hanson.

Childr. born in Clay Bank, Oceana Co., Mich.

I. LAURA BELL[9]   born Dec.   7, 1877.
II. EDITH BESSIE[9]   "   April 21, 1879.
III. VERNI IDEL[9]   "   July 16, 1880.
IV. MINNIE ESTELLA[9] "   Oct. 14, 1882; died Aug. 10, 1884, ag. 1 y.
                9 m. 27 d.

1076.   **Ninth Generation.**   **Tower.**

552. LEE L.[8], HARVEY[7], JOSEPH[6], SAMUEL[5], GIDEON[4], BENJAMIN[3], JOHN[2], JOHN[1].

Lee L.[8], son of Harvey[7] and Laura (Mallet) Tower, b.

Sept. 17, 1856 ; mar. Sarah Bezzo, of Clay Bank, Oceana Co., Mich.,

July 27, 1879. She was b.

June 17, 1858, and was dau. of John and Esther (Tapley) Bezzo.

Sarah (Bezzo) Tower died in Newago Co., Mich., Aug. 11, 1879, ag. 21 y. 1 m. 24 d.

Lee L. Tower[8] mar., 2d, Lizzie Boynton, of Litchfield, Minn., June 19, 1884. She was b. in Bradley, Me.,

Sept. 25, 1865, and was dau. of Henry and Ruth (Eaton) Boynton.

1077. Kerth.   **Ninth Generation.**   **Tower.**

560. MARY A.[8], WILLIAM S.[7], GIDEON[6], GIDEON[5], JOHN[4], BENJAMIN[3], JOHN[2], JOHN[1].

Mary A.[8], dau. of William S.[7] and Tabitha J. (Ricketts) Tower, b.

Oct. 11, 1846 ; mar. George Kerth

May 23, 1867. He was b. in New York city

Feb. 14, 1846, and was son of Jacob and Christina (Troutman) Kerth.

Childr.

I. WILLMER[9] }
II. GILLMER[9] } Twins born April 21, 1873, in Vevay, Ind.
III. ELMER[9]   "   Feb. 19, 1878; died Jan. 12, 1880; ag. 1 y.
                10 m. 21 d.
IV. HARRY[9]   "   June 29, 1883.

1078. Bevis.   **Ninth Generation.**   **Tower.**

560. ALMA E.[8], WILLIAM S.[7], GIDEON[6], GIDEON[5], JOHN[4], BENJAMIN[3], JOHN[2], JOHN[1].

Alma E.[8], dau. of William S.[7] and Tabitha J. (Ricketts) Tower, b.

May 29, 1848 ; mar. William Levi Bevis

Sept. 24, 1867. He was b. in Louisville, Ky.,

1845, and was son of Ely and Elizabeth (Stevens) Bevis.

Childr.

I. WILLIAM M.[9] born Sept. 10, 1868, in Centre Square, Ind.
II. TABITHA E.[9] " April 27, 1870, " " "
III. LYDIA L.[9] " July 12, 1873, in Kohomo, Ind.
IV. JAMES OTIS[9] " Oct. 5, 1875, " "
V. CHARLES D.[9] " June 8, 1878, in Great Bend, Kan.
VI. OLIVER P. M.[9] " Sept. 1, 1880, " " " ; died March 29, 1884, ag. 3 y. 6 m. 28 d.
VII. LEVI P.[9] " Feb. 5, 1883.

1079. Orem. Ninth Generation. Tower.

560. LOUISA M.[8], WILLIAM S.[7], GIDEON [6], GIDEON [5], JOHN [4], BENJAMIN [3], JOHN [2], JOHN [1].

Louisa M.[8], dau. of William S.[7] and Tabitha J. (Ricketts) Tower, b.

Apr. 2, 1850 ; mar. John William Orem in Moorefield, Ind., May 23, 1867. He was b. in Bennington, Ind.,

Jan. 27, 1846, and was son of Lorenzo and Mary E. (Johnson) Orem.

Childr.

I. CLARENCE IRVINE [9] born April 30, 1868.
II. MARY ELEANOR [9] " Oct. 31, 1869; died near Buena Vista, Kan., April 1, 1884, ag. 14 y. 5 m. 1 d.
III. ALICE BELLE [9] " Nov. 11, 1871.
IV. NOEL SCRANTON [9] " April 10, 1873.
V. DORA.[9] " Dec. 19, 1875.

1080. Ninth Generation. Tower.

560. IRA [8], WILLIAM S.[7], GIDEON [6], GIDEON [5], JOHN [4], BENJAMIN [3], JOHN [2], JOHN [1].

Ira [8], son of William S.[7] and Tabitha J. (Ricketts) Tower, b.

May 1, 1854 ; mar. Mary O. Orem

Jan. 1, 1873. She was b. in Jefferson Co., Ind.,

April 5, 1855, and was dau. of Lorenzo and Mary E. (Johnson) Orem.

Childr.

I. ANDREW T.[9] born Oct. 20, 1873, in Switzerland Co., Ind.
II. JOHN C.[9] " March 2, 1876, " "
III. ALFRED [9] " Feb. 6, 1878, " "
IV. FLORENCE MABEL [9] " Feb. 9, 1880, in Barton Co., Kan.
V. CHARLEY B.[9] " May 9, 1882, in Switzerland Co., Ind.

1081. Ninth Generation. Tower.

560. DANIEL R.[8], WILLIAM S.[7], GIDEON [6], GIDEON [5], JOHN [4], BENJA-MIN [3], JOHN [2], JOHN [1].

Daniel R.[8], son of William S.[7] and Tabitha J. (Ricketts) Tower, b.
June 10, 1858; mar. Emma McKenzie
Nov. 14, 1878. She was b. in Switzerland Co., Ind.,
Nov. 2, 1858, and was dau. of Alexander and Elizabeth (Locke) McKenzie.

Childr.

I. BESSIE [9] born Jan. 15, 1880.
II. OLLIE BELL [9] " Nov. 20, 1881.
III. EDNA PEARL [9] " Aug. 29, 1883, died in Cherryville, Ind., Sept. 24, 1884, ag. 1 y. 26 d.

1082. Ninth Generation. Tower.

560. JAMES W.[8], WILLIAM S.[7], GIDEON [6], GIDEON [5], JOHN [4], BEN-JAMIN [3], JOHN [2], JOHN [1].

James W.[8], son of William S.[7] and Tabitha (Ricketts) Tower, b.
Oct. 15, 1860; mar. Malinda Banta in Queen's Grove, Ind.,
Nov. 16, 1882. She was b. in Vevay, Ind.,
July 7, 1861, and was dau. of Henry H. and Malinda (Violes) Banta.

Child.

I. LINA MABEL [9] born Aug. 19, 1883, in Vevay, Ind.

1083. Barnhardt. Ninth Generation. Tower.

561. ROXANA [8], GIDEON [7], GIDEON [6], GIDEON [5], JOHN [4], BENJAMIN [3], JOHN [2], JOHN [1].

Roxana [8], dau. of Gideon [7] and Roxana (Scranton) Tower, b.
Aug. 9, 1860; mar. Charles Barnhardt in Madison, Ind.,
July 3, 1878. He was b.
Nov. 13, 1854, and was son of Adam and Margaret (Scholler) Barnhardt.

Childr.

I. CHARLEY [9] born July 18, 1879, in Madison, Ind.
II. HATTIE [9] " April 8, 1881; died April 8, 1881.

1084. Green. Ninth Generation. Tower.

563. SIBYL [8], JOSEPH H.[7], ALPHEUS [6], GIDEON [5], JOHN [4], BENJAMIN [3], JOHN [2], JOHN [1].

Sibyl [8], dau. of Joseph H. [7] and Philena M. (Burton) Tower, b.
March 18, 1850; mar. Francis Marion Green
April 23, 1871. He was b.
May 10, 1844, and was son of Richard and Mary (Smith)
Green.

Childr. born in Van Buren Co., Iowa.

I.	PHILENA BELLE [9]		born April 2, 1872.
II.	GRACE ALMA [9]	} Twins "	June 1, 1874; Gertrude A. died Aug.
III.	GERTRUDE ALTA [9]		4, 1875, ag. 1 y. 2 m. 3 d.
IV.	FRANK LEROY [9]	"	Feb. 27, 1876.
V.	ARCHIE EVERETT [9]	"	Sept. 5, 1880.
VI.	ETHEL ORPHA [9]	} Twins "	June 5, 1882, Effie J. died Feb. 6, 1883.
VII.	EFFIE JULIA [9]		
VIII.	BLANCHE [9]	"	Aug. 18, 1884.

1085. Carr.   **Ninth Generation.**   **Tower.**

563. JULIA J. [8], JOSEPH H. [7], ALPHEUS P. [6], GIDEON [5], JOHN [4], BEN-
JAMIN [3], JOHN [2], JOHN [1].
Julia J. [8], dau. of Joseph H. [7] and Philena M. (Burton) Tower, b.
May 20, 1854; mar. Thomas J. Carr
Oct. 18, 1882. He was b.
Sept. 15, 1852, and was son of Claybourn M. and Martha F.
(Plasket) Carr.

Child.

I. Infant, born March 1, 1884, died March 1, 1884.

1086.   **Ninth Generation.**   **Tower.**

563. WILLIAM E. [8], JOSEPH H. [7], ALPHEUS P. [6], GIDEON [5], JOHN [4],
BENJAMIN [3], JOHN [2], JOHN [1].
William E. [8], son of Joseph H. [7] and Philena M. (Burton)
Tower, b.
Jan. 4, 1860; mar. Isabella Ferguson
July 26, 1832. She was b. in Van Buren Co., Iowa,
Oct. 12, 1862, and was dau. of Daniel W. and Sarah A.
(Alcorn) Ferguson.

1087. Giddings.   **Ninth Generation.**   **Tower.**

566. ELSE E. [8], AMOS [7], JOSEPH [6], JOSEPH [5], JOSEPH [4], BENJAMIN [3],
JOHN [2], JOHN [1].
Else E. [8], dau. of Amos [7] and Emeline (Tower) Tower, b.
Sept. 10, 1837; mar. Jeremiah P. Giddings in Ira, Vt.,

Feb. 25, 1855.   He was b. in Rutland, Vt.,
                    and was son of Elijah S. and Lydia (Powers)
Giddings.

Childr.

I.	AMOS ELIJAH[9]	born June	7, 1856, in Ira.
II.	JAMES COOK[9]	" May	17, 1858, " Rutland.
III.	ELMER ELLSWORTH[9] "	Feb.	18, 1860, " "
IV.	LYDIA EMELINE[9]	" Nov.	29, 1861, " Ira; died April 17, 1862.
V.	THOMAS SMITH[9]	" March	15, 1863, " "
VI.	MARY ELLEN[9]	" Oct.	6, 1865, " "
VII.	DAN JEREMIAH[9]	" Aug.	27, 1869, " Pittsford.
VIII.	FRANK LEROY[9]	" April	4, 1874, " Castleton.

1088.   **Ninth Generation.**   **Tower.**

566. THOMAS A.[8], AMOS[7], JOSEPH[6], JOSEPH[5], JOSEPH[4], BENJA-
        MIN[3], JOHN[2], JOHN[1].
      Thomas A.[8], son of Amos[7] and Emeline (Tower) Tower, b.
      Aug. 17, 1841; mar. Jane M. Clark, of Canada East,
      Aug. 21, 1864.   She was b. in East Sutton, Canada East,
      Dec. 25, 1841, and was dau. of Samuel O. and Betsey (Bul-
      lock) Clark.

Childr.

I.	BETSEY E.[9]	born Oct. 16, 1865, in Ira, Vt.
II.	HELEN ELIZABETH[9] "	Sept. 24, 1867, " " "

Jane M. (Clark) Tower died in Clarendon, Vt., Oct. 16, 1870,
    ag. 28 y. 9 m. 22 d.
Thomas A. Tower[8] mar., 2d, Martha J. Brewster, of Castle-
    ton, Vt.,
June 20, 1872.   She was b. in Castleton
May 15, 1841, and was dau. of Eathen A. and Martha J.
    (Hinchen) Brewster.

Childr.

III	EDMONDS A.[9]	born Oct. 20, 1878.
IV.	HERBERT I.[9]	" March 30, 1881.

1089.   **Ninth Generation.**   **Tower.**

567. HENRY F.[8], HENRY[7], JOSEPH[6], JOSEPH[5], JOSEPH[4], BENJAMIN[3],
        JOHN[2], JOHN[1].
      Henry F.[8], son of Henry[7] and Marcia (Worcester) Tower, b.
      July 2, 1835; mar. Clara Bell Smith in Denver, Col.,
      July 18, 1873.   She was b. in Attica, Ind.,
      Nov. 1, 1853, and was dau. of John N. and Martha A.
        (Davis) Smith.

Childr.

I. EFFIE MARTHA [9]   born April 10, 1874, in Del Norte, Cal.
II. PEARL ELLEN [9]   " March 6, 1876, "   "   "
III. WALTER WORCESTER [9] " Oct. 17, 1878, " Bushnell, Ill.

1090.   **Ninth Generation.**   **Tower.**

569. GEORGE W.[8], JOSEPH [7], JOSEPH [6], JOSEPH [5], JOSEPH [4], BENJAMIN [3], JOHN [2], JOHN [1].

George W.[8], son of Joseph [7] and Sarah A. (Bates) Tower, b. June 14, 1840 ; mar. Emeline Malvina Streeter.

Childr.

I. GEORGE E.[9] born Feb. 1, 1865, in Ira, Vt.
II. SARAH E.[9]   "   1866.

1091.   **Ninth Generation.**   **Tower.**

569. HENRY C.[8], JOSEPH [7], JOSEPH [6], JOSEPH [5], JOSEPH [4], BENJAMIN [3], JOHN [2], JOHN [1].

Henry C.[8], son of Joseph [7] and Sarah A. (Bates) Tower, b. June 25, 1841 ; mar. Almira Wilkinson [8], of Ira, Vt., Jan. 22, 1863. She was b.

May 1, 1845, and was dau. of Ira and Emeline (Greggs) Wilkinson.

WILKINSON, WHIPPLE.   TOWER.

Almira [8], Ira [7], Lydia [6], Christopher [5], John [4], William [3], Hannah [2], John [1].

Childr.

I. CLAYTON H.[9] born Jan. 1, 1865; died May 25, 1877, ag. 12 y. 4 m. 24 d.
II. HERBERT [9]   " Jan. 5, 1867, " May 25, 1877, ag. 10 y. 4 m. 20 d.
III. SARAH E.[9]   " July 11, 1870.
IV. Son [9]   " Jan. 4, 1873; died Jan. 4, 1873.

Almira [8] (Wilkinson) Tower died in Clarendon, Vt., Jan. 8, 1873, ag. 27 y. 8 m. 7 d.

Henry C. Tower [8] mar., 2d, widow Kate M. (Brewer) Cheney, of Rutland, Vt.,

Oct. 6, 1874. She was born in Rutland, Vt.,

April 13, 1841, and was dau. of Samuel and Philena (Eastman) Brewer.

Childr. born in Clarendon.

V. W. ROY [9]   born June 11, 1876; died Oct. 17, 1881, ag. 5 y. 4 m. 6 d.
VI. Daughter [9]   " Jan. 6, 1878; " Jan. 6, 1878.

1092.   **Ninth Generation.**   **Tower.**

569. EMMET M.[8], JOSEPH [7], JOSEPH [6], JOSEPH [5], JOSEPH [4], BENJA-
MIN [3], JOHN [2], JOHN [1].
Emmet M.[8], son of Joseph[7] and Sarah A. (Bates) Tower, b.
Dec. 20, 1842 ; mar. Lucinda H. Rider.
                She was b.
      1843.
                        Childr.
      I. JAMES EMMET [9] born Oct. 10, 1864.
      II. HARRIS G.[9]   " Jan. 24, 1869.

1093.   **Ninth Generation.**   **Tower.**

569. JOSEPH W.[8], JOSEPH [7], JOSEPH [6], JOSEPH [5], JOSEPH [4], BENJA-
MIN [3], JOHN [2], JOHN [1].
Joseph W.[8], son of Joseph[7] and Sarah A. (Bates) Tower, b.
March 9, 1846 ; mar. Helen M. Clark
Oct. 5, 1869. She was b. in Ganeer, Ill.,
Dec. 27, 1851, and was dau. of Bela T. and Charlotte T.
(Thayer) Clark.

          Childr. born in Ganeer.
      I. JOSEPH BELA [9] born Aug. 25, 1872.
      II. ELWYN HENRY [9] " Aug. 19, 1875.

1094.   **Ninth Generation.**   **Tower.**

572. HANIBAL L.[8], ALANSON [7], OTIS [6], NATHANIEL [5], JOSEPH [4], BEN-
JAMIN [3], JOHN [2], JOHN [1].
Hanibal L.[8], son of Alanson[7] and Diana (Perham) Tower, b.
May 29, 1836 ; mar. Helen A. Matthews, of Hopkinton,
Mass.,
Sept. 20, 1865. She was b.
June 2, 1844, and was dau. of P. R. H. and Calista (Ellery)
Matthews.

        Childr. born in Hanover, N. Y.
      I. CLARENCE [9]   born Sept. 19, 1868; died Oct. 22, 1868.
      II. CLARA HELENA [9] " June 2, 1871.

1095. Green.   **Ninth Generation.**   **Tower.**

572. MARINDA P.[8], ALANSON [7], OTIS [6], NATHANIEL [5], JOSEPH [4], BEN-
JAMIN [3], JOHN [2], JOHN [1].
Marinda P.[8], dau. of Alanson[7] and Diana (Perham) Tower, b.
Sept. 25, 1838 ; mar. Julius Green, of Hanover, N. Y.,

Sept. 25, 1870. He was b.

Oct.   4, 1842, and was son of Levi and Mary A. (White) Green.

Child.

    I. ADA M.[9] born July 23, 1872.

Julius Green died in Dunkirk, N. Y., Sept. 23, 1873, ag. 30 y. 11 m. 19 d.

1096. Everhart.   Ninth Generation.   Tower.

572. MALINDA D.[8], ALANSON[7], OTIS[6], NATHANIEL[5], JOSEPH[4], BEN-JAMIN[3], JOHN[2], JOHN[1].

Malinda D.[8], dau. of Alanson[7] and Diana (Perham) Tower, b. July 15, 1844; mar. Adam Everhart, of Hanover, N. Y., Dec. 21, 1874. He was b.

Jan. 3, 1849, and was son of Jacob and Mary (Hostater) Everhart.

Childr.

    I.   ARTHUR J.[9] born Aug. 8, 1875.
   II. HERBERT E.[9] "   July 3, 1877.
  III. PERHAM O.[9]   "   Dec. 26, 1879.

1097. Hancock.   Ninth Generation.   Tower.

572. BETSEY S.[8], ALANSON[7], OTIS[6], NATHANIEL[5], JOSEPH[4], BEN-JAMIN[3], JOHN[2], JOHN[1].

Betsey S.[8], dau. of Alanson[7] and Diana (Perham) Tower, b. Sept. 29, 1846; mar. Royal T. Hancock, of Hanover, N. Y., April 21, 1875. He was b.

Nov. 6, 1839, and was son of Zina and Lucy (McIntyre) Hancock.

Child.

    I. ALICE E.[9] born Sept. 10, 1880.

1098.   Ninth Generation.   Tower.

572. PERHAM O.[8], ALANSON[7], OTIS[6], NATHANIEL[5], JOSEPH[4], BEN-JAMIN[3], JOHN[2], JOHN[1].

Perham O.[8], son of Alanson[7] and Diana (Perham) Tower, b. Feb. 27, 1849; mar. Melissa Mitchel

Sept. 15, 1876. She was b. in Triangle, N. Y.,

and was dau. of George and Sarah (Perham) Mitchel.

Child.

    I. FLORENCE E.[9] born April 20, 1879, in Hanover, N. Y.

1099. Hitchcock.   Ninth Generation.   Tower.

573. MARY M.[8], LYMAN[7], OTIS[6], NATHANIEL[5], JOSEPH[4], BENJA-
      MIN[3], JOHN[2], JOHN[1].

Mary M.[8], dau. of Lyman[7] and Julia A. (Buxton) Tower, b.
Aug. 1, 1835; mar. Alfred A. Hitchcock[7]
April 2, 1876. He was b.
July 3, 1829, and was son of Eri and Lydia[6] (Tower)
   Hitchcock.

HITCHCOCK.   TOWER.

Alfred A.[7], Lydia[6], Pyam[5], Joseph[4], Joseph[3], Samuel[2], John[1].

1100. Chapman.   Ninth Generation.   Tower.

573. EMELINE V.[8], LYMAN[7], OTIS[6], NATHANIEL[5], JOSEPH[4], BENJA-
      MIN[3], JOHN[2], JOHN[1].

Emeline V.[8], dau. of Lyman[7] and Julia Ann (Buxton)
   Tower, b.
April 22, 1839; mar. Uriah Chapman
Oct.   9, 1860. He was b. in Hanover, N. Y.,
Feb. 13, 1825, and was son of Thomas and Anna (Welton)
   Chapman.

Childr.

I.	SARAH[9]	born Oct. , 1861; died Feb , 1862.
II.	CHARLES L.[9] "	1866.
III.	CLARA[9] "	1868.
IV.	ALBERT[9] "	1870.

Uriah Chapman died in Forestville, N. Y., Aug. 7, 1884, ag.
   59 y. 5 m. 23 d.

1101. Story, Underwood.   Ninth Generation.   Tower.

573. EMILY J.[8], LYMAN[7], OTIS[6], NATHANIEL[5], JOSEPH[4], BENJA-
      MIN[3], JOHN[2], JOHN[1].

Emily J.[8], dau. of Lyman[7] and Julia Ann (Buxton) Tower, b.
April 22, 1839; mar. John Underwood, of Hanover, N. Y.,
Sept. 29, 1869.

Child.

I. ALICE V.[9] born July 26, 1874.

John Underwood died in Virginia, March 26, 1874.

STORY.   TOWER.

Emily J. (Tower) Underwood mar., 2d, Andrew Story, of
   Hanover, Feb. 27, 1881.

1102.   Ninth Generation.   Tower.

578. HANNIBAL [8], DAVID [7], THOMAS [6], NATHANIEL [5], JOSEPH [4], BENJAMIN [3], JOHN [2], JOHN [1].

Hannibal [8], son of David [7] and Fanny (Spring) Tower, b.
Aug. 27, 1827; mar. Polly Elizabeth Potter in Clarendon
Jan. 1, 1850. She was b. in Clarendon, Vt.,
April 19, 1831, and was dau. of J. W. and Lucy R. (Fisk)
Potter.

Childr.

1370.   I.   IDA A. [9] born July 31, 1852, in Clarendon.
      II.   Infant [9]   "   March 18, 1859, in Palmyra, Wis.; died March 29, 1859.
    III.   NOEL D. [9] "   Dec. 1, 1862,   "   "

1103.   Ninth Generation.   Tower.

578. WALLACE [8], DAVID [7], THOMAS [6], NATHANIEL [5], JOSEPH [4], BENJAMIN [3], JOHN [2], JOHN [1].

Wallace [8], son of David [7] and Fanny (Spring) Tower, b.
1830; mar. Julia A.   .

Childr.

    I.   HELEN H. [9] born July 3, 1858, died April 24, 1860, ag. 1 y. 9 m. 21 d.
   II.   EMILY T. [9]   "   Dec 18, 1859, in Rutland, Vt.; died May 18, 1860.
  III.   GEORGE [9]   "   1861.
  IV.   MINNIE J. [9]   "   1863.
   V.   HORACE H. [9] "   1867.

1104. Hall.   Ninth Generation.   Tower.

578. HELEN [8], DAVID [7], THOMAS [6], NATHANIEL [5], JOSEPH [4], BENJAMIN [3], JOHN [2], JOHN [1].

Helen [8], dau. of David [7] and Fanny (Spring) Tower, b.
July 16, 1835; mar. Isaac S. Hall in Sudbury, Vt.,
July 3, 1852. He was b. in Clarendon, Vt.,
Nov. 6, 1829, and was son of David and Electa (Wheaton)
Hall.

Childr.

   I.   MAHLON SCOTT [9] born April 11, 1855, in Rutland, Vt.; died in Pittsford, Vt., Aug. 30, 1873, ag. 18 y. 4 m. 18 d.
  II.   DAVID PERRY [9]   "   April 16, 1860, in Clarendon, Vt.; died in Rutland, Aug. 11, 1861, ag. 1 y 3 m 25 d.

1105.   Ninth Generation.   Tower.

583. FRANK B. [8], BRADLEY C. [7], THOMAS [6], NATHANIEL [5], JOSEPH [4], BENJAMIN [3], JOHN [2], JOHN [1].

Frank B.[8], son of Bradley C.[7] and Laura O. (Bruce) Tower, b.
Aug. 25, 1854; mar. Mary Adeline Cummings in Walling-
ford, Vt.,
Aug. 26, 1884. She was b. in Wallingford
Jan. 18, 1868, and was dau. of W. H. H. and Malvira E.
(Preston) Cummings.

Child.

I.   Infant [9] born March 20, 1887.

1106.   **Ninth Generation.**   **Tower.**

584. FRANK C.[8], FRANKLIN R.[7], WELCOME [6], NATHANIEL [5], JOSEPH [4],
BENJAMIN [3], JOHN [2], JOHN [1].
Frank C.[8], son of Franklin R.[7] and Elizabeth (Ettredge)
Tower, b.
Jan. 2, 1856; mar. Louella Mayfield
Nov. 3, 1887. She was b. in Chester Co., S. C.,
Dec. 4, 1866, and was dau. of William and Mary E. (Smith)
Mayfield.

1107.   **Ninth Generation.**   **Tower.**

584. CHARLES A.[8], FRANKLIN R.[7], WELCOME [6], NATHANIEL [5], JO-
SEPH [4], BENJAMIN [3], JOHN [2], JOHN [1].
Charles A.[8], son of Franklin R.[7] and Elizabeth (Ettredge)
Tower, b.
Jan. 16, 1858; mar. Helen V. Saunders at Cooper, Tex.,
Jan. 16, 1878. She was b.
Aug. 10, 1860, and was dau. of James K. and Nellie W.
(Motley) Saunders.

Childr.

I.   Son [9]   born April 10, 1879; died aged a few days.
II.   PEARL E. T.[9]   "   July 18, 1880, in Red River Parish, La.
III. LIZZIE W.[9]   "   Jan. 28, 1882,   "   "   "
IV.   EDDIE F.[9]   "   July 7, 1883, in Cooper; died Aug. 19, 1885, ag.
                            2 y. 1 m. 12 d.

1108.   **Ninth Generation.**   **Tower.**

584. GEORGE M.[8], FRANKLIN R.[7], WELCOME [6], NATHANIEL [5], JO-
SEPH [4], BENJAMIN [3], JOHN [2], JOHN [1].
George M.[8], son of Franklin R.[7] and Elizabeth (Ettredge)
Tower, b.
June 22, 1860; mar. Helen Saunders.

Childr.

I.   PEARL [9].   II   LIZZIE [9].

1109. Williams. Ninth Generation. Tower.

584. MARY M. M.[8], FRANKLIN R.[7], WELCOME[6], NATHANIEL[5], JOSEPH[4], BENJAMIN[3], JOHN[2], JOHN[1].

Mary M. M.[8], dau. of Franklin R.[7] and Elizabeth (Ettredge) Tower, b.

Oct. 8, 1866 ; mar. Charles C. Williams

Jan. 1, 1885. He was b. in Monticello, Fla.,

Oct. 17, 1863, and was son of Hampden S. and Flora (Tryon) Williams.

Child.

I. CLAUD[9] born Aug 17, 1886.

1110. Mayer. Ninth Generation. Tower.

586. MINNIE H.[8], WILLIAM O.[7], WELCOME[6], NATHANIEL[5], JOSEPH[4], BENJAMIN[3], JOHN[2], JOHN[1].

Minnie H.[8], dau. of William O.[7] and Mary A. (Gambell) Tower, b.

April 17, 1855 ; mar. Henry A. Mayer

Oct. 30, 1872. He was b in Scranton, Penn.,

March 3, 1853, and was son of John and Mary T. (Hultzshoe) Mayer.

Childr.,

I. MINNIE MAUD[9]   born Nov. 18, 1873, in Scranton.
II. MARIAN THERESA[9] "   Feb. 28, 1875,   "   ; died July 15, 1875.
III. WILLIAM ALBERT[9] "   Nov. 13, 1876, in South Gibson, Penn.

1111. Roberts. Ninth Generation. Tower.

589. ALICE S.[8], NATHANIEL F.[7], CEPHAS[6], NATHANIEL[5], JOSEPH[4], BENJAMIN[3], JOHN[2], JOHN[1].

Alice S.[8], dau. of Nathaniel F.[7] and Rachel (Stephens) Tower, b.

May 15, 1854 ; mar. Jaspar W. Roberts

Feb. 2, 1879. He was b.

May 7, 1857, and was son of William Roberts.

Childr.

I. LEOTIS ALVA[9] born Aug. 28, 1880, in Blooming Grove, Ind.
II. LURA BELL[9]   "   Dec. 3, 1882, in Fairfield, Ind.

1112. Ninth Generation. Tower.

593. WILLIS R.[8], WARNER C.[7], RIAL[6], NATHANIEL[5], JOSEPH[4], BENJAMIN[3], JOHN[2], JOHN[1].

Willis R.[8], son of Warner C.[7] and Teresa M. (Tiffany) Tower, b.
March 7, 1855 ; mar. Inez E. Smith, of Lenox, Penn.,
March 2, 1880. She was b.
Aug. 6, 1853, and was dau. of James F. and Roxana (Joselyn) Smith.

Childr.

I. WARNER CARL[9] born Dec. 25, 1880.
II. PEARL ELOISE[9]   "   Sept. 30, 1882; died April 10, 1883.
III. GRACE ELLA[9]   "   Nov. 23, 1884.

1113.   **Ninth Generation.**   **Tower.**

593. ELMER E.[8], WARNER C.[7], RIAL[6], NATHANIEL[5], JOSEPH[4], BEN-
JAMIN[3], JOHN[2], JOHN[1].
Elmer E.[8], son of Warner C.[7] and Teresa M. (Tiffany) Tower, b.
Feb. 22, 1861 ; mar. Laura Loomis, of Lenox, Penn.,
Nov. 22, 1883. She was b.
Feb. 8, 1866, and was dau. of Griswold and Mary (West) Loomis.

Child.

I. JEAN LOOMIS[9] born Aug. 31, 1884.

1114. Holbrook. Ninth Generation.   **Tower.**

600 a. SUSAN[8], JAMES[7], MEHITABLE[6], JOHN[5], JOHN[4], JOSEPH[3],
JOHN[2], JOHN[1].
Susan[8], dau. of James[7] and Susannah (Thayer) Tower, b.
1824 ; mar. Elias Holbrook, of Braintree, Mass.,
He was b. in Braintree
1822.

Childr.

I. GEORGE W.[9] born   1843, in Randolph; died   .
II. GEORGE W.[9]   "   1845,   "   "
III. CHARLES F.[9]   "   1847,   "
IV. MARILLE I.[9]   " March 6, 1848,   "   " Dec. 6, 1862, ag.
                    14 y. 9 m.
V. MARY E.[9]   "   1851,   "
VI. GEORGE W.[9]   " April 5, 1852, in Braintree.
VII. HARRIET A.[9]   " Dec.   , 1854,   "   " June 2, 1857, ag.
                    2 y. 6 m.
VIII. HATTIE A.[9]   " May   , 1857,   "
IX. EUGENE W.[9]   " Feb. 28, 1859, in Weymouth.
X. EMMA A.[9]   "   1861.

1115.   Ninth Generation.   **Tower.**

600 *a*. WILLIAM E.[8], JAMES[7], MEHITABLE[6], JOHN[5], JOHN[4], JOSEPH[3], JOHN[2], JOHN[1].

William E.[8], son of James[7] and Susannah (Thayer) Tower, b. 1826; mar. Urania M. Wakefield in Woonsocket, R. I., June 11, 1848. She was b. in Smithfield, R. I., May 31, 1830, and was dau. of Leonard and Mary (Carroll) Wakefield.

Childr.

1371.	I.	GEORGE OSCAR[9]	born Feb. 28, 1849, in Cumberland, R. I.
	II.	MARY FRANCIS[9]	" March 14, 1851, in Holbrook. Mass.; died Sept. 14, 1851.
1372.	III.	MARY MINERVA[9]	" July 18, 1852, in Holbrook.
	IV.	CHARLES LEONARD[9]	" June 29, 1854, in Milford, Mass.
	V.	ANNA WAKEFIELD[9]	" Nov. 12, 1856, " " ; died April 21, 1863, ag. 6 y. 5 m. 9 d.
1373.	VI.	EVA VIOLA[9]	" May 3, 1860.
	VII.	WILLIAM ALBERT[9]	" Aug. 8, 1862.
	VIII.	JAMES EUSTACE[9]	" July 4, 1868.

1116.   Ninth Generation.   **Tower.**

600 *a*. JOHN[8], JAMES[7], MEHITABLE[6], JOHN[5], JOHN[4], JOSEPH[3], JOHN[2], JOHN[1].

John[8], son of James[7] and Susannah (Thayer) Tower, b. 1828; mar. Susan Langley. Int. pub. Sept. 14, 1844. She was b. in Weymouth, Mass., 1822, and was dau. of John and Abigail (Jeffers) Langley.

Childr.

I.	ANN MARIA[9]	born Dec. 8, 1847.
II.	FANNY WALES[9]	" July 14, 1851, in Braintree, Mass.
III.	MARY ABIGAIL[9]	" Dec. 12, 1852; died July 26, 1853.
IV.	MARY I.[9]	" April 30, 1854; " Nov. 30, 1854.

Susan (Langley) Tower died in Braintree, Nov. 20, 1861, ag. 39.

John Tower[8] mar., 2d, widow Alice (Simpson) ———.
Sept. 2, 1867. She was b. in Dartmouth, Mass., 1828, and was dau. of Stephen and Lucinda Simpson.

1116 a.   Porter, Lovell.   Ninth Generation.   **Tower.**

601. RUTH J.[8], ISAAC P.[7], ALEXANDER[6], JOHN[5], JOHN[4], JOSEPH[3], JOHN[2], JOHN[1].

Ruth J.[8], dau. of Isaac P.[7] and Ruth H. (Pool) Tower, b.

Dec. 9, 1826; mar. William R. Lovell[8]. Int. pub.

Feb. 26, 1843. He was b.

Oct. 24, 1824, and was son of Jacob[7] and Zereviah (Bates) Lovell.

LOVELL.	TOWER.

William R.[8], Jacob[7], Jacob[6], Mary[5], Peter[4], Jeremiah[3], Jeremiah[2], John[1].

Childr. born in Weymouth.

I.	JANE ELIZABETH[9]	born Jan. 25, 1844.
II.	ALBINA[9]	" June 30, 1846; died Sept. 14, 1846.
III.	ALICE ANN[9]	" Aug. 14, 1848; " Jan. 22, 1853, ag. 4 y. 5 m. 8 d.
IV.	WILLIAM HORACE[9]	" May 13, 1850.
V.	ALICE ALVIRA[9]	" Sept. 23, 1853; died Aug. 15, 1854.
VI.	CHARLES WARREN[9]	" Oct. 4, 1855.
VII.	GEORGE A.[9]	" Dec. 3, 1857; died Oct. 1, 1858.
VIII.	ETTA MAY[9]	" Sept. 8, 1861; " Oct. 12, 1862, ag. 1 y. 1 m. 4 d.

William R. Lovell[8] died in Weymouth, Dec. 16, 1864, ag. 40 y. 1 m. 23 d.

Ruth J.[8] (Tower) Lovell mar., 2d, Hiram Porter, of Weymouth,

May 24, 1873. He was b. in Weymouth

July 17, 1826, and was son of Laban and Deborah (Thompson) Porter.

Childr. none.

1117. Hayden. Ninth Generation. Tower.

601. CHARLOTTE A.[8], ISAAC P.[7], ALEXANDER[6], JOHN[5], JOHN[4], JOSEPH[3], JOHN[2], JOHN[1].

Charlotte A.[8], dau. of Isaac P.[7] and Ruth H. (Pool) Tower, b. Oct. 30, 1827; mar. Hosea Ballou Hayden, of Braintree, Oct. 7, 1844. He was b. in Braintree, Mass., March 29, 1825.

Childr. born in Braintree.

I.	EMILY JANE[9]	born Sept. 14, 1845.
II.	Son[9]	" April 28, 1847; died Jan. 21, 1848.
III.	AMATIA[9]	" Aug 4, 1848; died June 6, 1850, ag. 1 y. 10 m. 2 d.
IV.	EDGAR[9]	" June 24, 1850.
V.	INDIANA[9]	" July 7, 1851; " Aug. 29, 1851.
VI.	SUSAN MARIA[9]	" June 20, 1852.
VII.	INDIANA[9]	" July 14, 1853; " Sept. 28, 1853.
VIII.	ISAAC WILLIE[9]	" Oct. 17, 1855.

1118.   Ninth Generation.   **Tower.**

601. Isaac A.[8], Isaac P.[7], Alexander[6], John[5], John[4], Joseph[3], John[2], John[1].

Isaac A.[8], son of Isaac P.[7] and Ruth H. (Pool) Tower, b. Sept. , 1829; mar. Eunice Roberts, of Weymouth, Mass., Nov. 13, 1850. She was b. in Nova Scotia 1823, and was dau. of Henry Roberts.

Childr.

1373 a.	I.	Eunice Ann[9]	born	Oct. 27, 1851.
1374.	II.	Elizabeth S.[9]	"	May , 1853.
	III.	Jacob H.[9]	"	Nov. 5, 1857.
	IV.	Nathaniel Herbert[9]	"	June 2, 1860.
	V.	Jacob Nelson[9]	"	Nov. 10, 1862.
	VI.	Rosena[9]	"	Oct. 5, 1866.

1119.   Ninth Generation.   **Tower.**

601. Charles L.[8], Isaac P.[7], Alexander[6], John[5], John[4], Joseph[3], John[2], John[1].

Charles L.[8], son of Isaac P.[7] and Ruth H. (Pool) Tower, b. April 6, 1831; mar. Rebecca M. Stetson, of Hanover, Sept. 28, 1851. She was b. in Hanover, Mass., Jan. 19, 1822, and was dau. of Samuel and Abigail (Munroe) Stetson.

Childr. born in Hanover.

1375.	I.	Rebecca E.[9] born Jan. 16, 1854.
	II.	Ruth Ella[9] " Aug. 3, 1862; died Aug. 30, 1864, ag. 2 y. 27 d.

1120. Curtis.   Ninth Generation.   **Tower.**

601. Susannah M.[8], Isaac P.[7], Alexander[6], John[5], John[4], Joseph[3], John[2], John[1].

Susannah M.[8], dau. of Isaac P.[7] and Ruth H. (Pool) Tower, b. Aug. 31, 1834; mar. William H. Curtis, of Hanover, Mass., Nov. 7, 1852. He was b. in Hanover 1825, and was son of Luther and Bashua (Curtis) Curtis.

1121.   Ninth Generation.   **Tower.**

601. Christopher P.[8], Isaac P.[7], Alexander[6], John[5], John[4], Joseph[3], John[2], John[1].

Christopher P.[8], son of Isaac P.[7] and Susan (Snow) Tower, b. 1845; mar. Ella J. Abbott, of Randolph, Aug. 28, 1869. She was b. 1850, and was dau. of John S. and   (Goldthwaite) Abbott.

Childr. born in Weymouth.

I. JOHN LESTER [9] born March 27, 1871; died Aug. 21, 1874, ag. 3 y. 4 m. 25 d.
II. LEON ELMER [9] " Nov. 16, 1873.
III. GRACE EVELYN [9] " June 21, 1875.

1122. **Ninth Generation.** **Tower.**

601. MINOTT A.[8], ISAAC P.[7], ALEXANDER [6], JOHN [5], JOHN [4], JOSEPH [3], JOHN [2], JOHN [1].
Minott A.[8], son of Isaac P.[7] and Susan (Snow) Tower, b.
    1846; mar. Nancy S. Mackintosh
Sept. 4, 1869. She was b. in West Roxbury
    1844, and was dau. of William and Adeline Mackintosh.

1123. Wood. **Ninth Generation.** **Tower.**

601. NANCY A.[8], ISAAC P.[7], ALEXANDER [6], JOHN [5], JOHN [4], JOSEPH [3], JOHN [2], JOHN [1].
Nancy A.[8], dau. of Isaac P.[7] and Susan (Snow) Tower, b.
July 2, 1848; mar. William H. Wood
Aug. 31, 1865. He was b. in Braintree, Mass.,
    1836, and was son of Joel and Eliza (Howard) Wood.

Child.

I. MARIAN ETHEL [9] born Feb. 14, 1878; died Feb. 25, 1879, ag. 1 y. 11 d.

1124. Marston. **Ninth Generation.** **Tower.**

607. MARY H.[8], JOHN [7], JOHN [6], GIDEON [5], GIDEON [4], JOSEPH [3], JOHN [2], JOHN [1].
Mary H.[8], dau. of John [7] and Sarah S. (Hewett) Tower, b.
Sept. 18, 1836; mar. William H. Marston, of Gloucester,
Jan. 28, 1866. He was b. in Gloucester, Mass.,
    1836, and was son of Benjamin S. and Betsey
Marston.
Child born in Braintree.

I. HENRY HEWETT [9] born March 10, 1867.

1125. **Ninth Generation.** **Tower.**

607. ELISHA H.[8], JOHN [7], JOHN [6], GIDEON [5], GIDEON [4], JOSEPH [3], JOHN [2], JOHN [1].
Elisha H.[8], son of John [7] and Sarah S. (Hewett) Tower, b.
Aug. 1, 1844; mar. Ann Eliza Mulliken
April 29, 1874. She was dau. of Emery A. and Avis (Wellington) Mulliken.

1126. Jones. Ninth Generation. Tower.

608. MATILDA A.[8], GEORGE [7], JOSEPH [6], GIDEON [5], GIDEON [4],
JOSEPH [3], JOHN [2], JOHN [1].
Matilda A.[8], dau. of George [7] and Fanny M. (White) Tower, b.
Nov. 11, 1845; mar. Adam W. Jones, of Randolph, Mass.,
May 11, 1867. He was b. in Randolph,
1847, and was son of Adam F. and Jane (Mann)
Jones.

1127. Bryant. Ninth Generation. Tower.

608. ELLEN A.[8], GEORGE [7], JOSEPH [6], GIDEON [5], GIDEON [4], JOSEPH [3],
JOHN [2], JOHN [1].
Ellen A.[8], dau. of George [7] and Fanny M. (White) Tower, b.
1850; mar. Conrad E. Bryant, of Stoughton, Mass.,
July 24, 1875. He was b. in Stoughton,
1854, and was son of Luther S. and Hannah F.
(Allen) Bryant.

1128. Badger. Ninth Generation. Tower.

608. MARY A.[8], GEORGE [7], JOSEPH [6], GIDEON [5], GIDEON [4], JOSEPH [3],
JOHN [2], JOHN [1].
Mary A.[8], dau. of George [7] and Fanny M. (White) Tower, b.
1852; mar. Hiram M. Badger, of Stoughton, Mass.,
Nov. 16, 1872. He was b. in Bridgewater, Mass.,
1851, and was son of George H. and Clarissa
Badger.

1129. Keith. Ninth Generation. Tower.

608. EMILY J.[8], GEORGE [7], JOSEPH [6], GIDEON [5], GIDEON [4], JOSEPH [3],
JOHN [2], JOHN [1].
Emily J.[8], dau. of George [7] and Fanny M. (White) Tower, b.
Feb. 13, 1857; mar. Lucien B. Keith, of North Bridgewater,
Mass.,
June 14, 1873. He was b. in Stoughton, Mass.,
1853, and was son of Nathaniel and Sally E. Keith.

1130. Ninth Generation. Tower.

611. HORACE B.[8], IRA F.[7], WASHINGTON [6], GIDEON [5], GIDEON [4],
JOSEPH [3], JOHN [2], JOHN [1].
Horace B.[8], son of Ira F.[7] and Elizabeth B. (Southworth)
Tower, b.

March 13. 1849; mar. Sarah Curley in Stoughton, Mass.,
Jan. 31, 1869. She was b. in Boston
Feb. 28, 1849, and was dau. of Brian and Sarah (Dunleny)
Curley.

1131. **Ninth Generation.** **Tower.**

611. WILLIAM S.[8], IRA F.[7], WASHINGTON[6], GIDEON[5], GIDEON[4],
JOSEPH[3], JOHN[2], JOHN[1].
William S.[8], son of Ira F.[7] and Elizabeth B. (Southworth)
Tower, b.
Feb. 16, 1852; mar. Mary D. Kennedy in Racine, Wis.,
Nov. 27. 1873. She was b. in Hickory, Ill.,
March 17, 1849, and was dau. of James and Margaret
(Gleason) Kennedy.

Child born in Racine.

I. IRA F.[9] born May 7, 1875; died Jan. 18, 1877, at Millburn.

Mary D. (Kennedy) Tower died in Racine, Oct. 23, 1883,
ag. 34 y. 7 m. 6 d.

1132. Coney. **Ninth Generation.** **Tower.**

625. ADA F.[8], SILAS F.[7], LUTHER[6], ISAAC[5], JOSEPH[4], JOSEPH[3],
JOHN[2], JOHN[1].
Ada F.[8], dau. of Silas F.[7] and Malinda S. (Ellis) Tower, b.
Jan. 15, 1866; mar. William M. Coney, of Easton, Md.,
June 27, 1883.

1133. **Ninth Generation.** **Tower.**

632. ELISHA[8], ELISHA[7], ISAIAH[6], ELISHA[5], ELISHA[4], RICHARD[3],
IBROOK[2], JOHN[1].
Elisha[8], son of Elisha[7] and Filenah (Morgan) Tower, b.
Jan. 13, 1818; mar. Electa Moon, of Gerry, N. Y.

Childr.

I. EMMA CERELLE[9] born   ; mar. Daniel Farrington.
II. HARLAN[9]   "   1868.

Electa (Moon) Tower died in Portland, N. Y.

1134. Moon. **Ninth Generation.** **Tower.**

632. RHOBE A.[8], ELISHA[7], ISAIAH[6], ELISHA[5], ELISHA[4], RICHARD[3],
IBROOK[2], JOHN[1].
Rhobe A.[8], dau. of Elisha[7] and Filenah (Morgan) Tower, b.

May 4, 1820 ; mar. Ebenezer Moon
Aug. 9, 1840. He was b.
June 22, 1811, and was son of Charles H. and Lucy (Briggs)
Moon.

Childr.

I. ADELBERT A.[9]   born Dec. 4, 1841, in Ellery, N. Y.
II. DELEVAN ADOLPHUS[9] " April 23, 1844, " Gerry, "
III. DE WITT C.[9]   " July 24, 1856, " Stockton, "

1135.   **Ninth Generation.**   **Tower.**

632. SIMEON M.[8], ELISHA[7], ISAIAH[6], ELISHA[5], ELISHA[4], RICHARD[3],
IBROOK[2], JOHN[1].
Simeon M.[8], son of Elisha[7] and Filenah (Morgan) Tower, b.
Sept. 11, 1822 ; mar. Sarah Dennison, of Ellery, N. Y.,
She was b.
1831.

Childr.

I. LEONA[9] born Aug. , 1856.   II. ALTON[9] born   1858.

1136. Benison.   **Ninth Generation.**   **Tower.**

632. EMILY M.[8], ELISHA[7], ISAIAH[6], ELISHA[5], ELISHA[4], RICHARD[3],
IBROOK[2], JOHN[1].
Emily M.[8], dau. of Elisha[7] and Filenah (Morgan) Tower, b.
Jan. , 1829 ; mar. Benjamin Franklin Benison, of Charlotte,
N. Y.

Childr.

I. CHARLES[9].   II. BENJAMIN FRANKLIN[9].

1137.   **Ninth Generation.**   **Tower.**

632. CORYDON L.[8], ELISHA[7], ISAIAH[6], ELISHA[5], ELISHA[4], RICHARD[3],
IBROOK[2], JOHN[1].
Corydon L.[8], son of Elisha[7] and Filenah (Morgan) Tower, b.
1834 ; mar. Harriet Felt, of Ellington, N. Y.

Childr.

I. LAZELL H.[9] born   1863. IV. FANNY[9] born   1875.
II. FILA R.[9]   "   1871.   V. BENN[9] "   1877 ; died.
III. SHERAL[9]   "   1873.

1138.   **Ninth Generation.**   **Tower.**

634. WILLIAM J.[8], ISAIAH[7], ISAIAH[6], ELISHA[5], ELISHA[4], RICHARD[3],
IBROOK[2], JOHN[1].
William J.[8], son of Isaiah[7] and Mary (Sherburne) Tower, b.

Jan. 24, 1828; mar. Adelaide C. Smith, of Watertown, N.Y.,
June 1, 1871. She was b. in Rutland, N. Y.,
May 5, 1837, and was dau. of Charles D. and Ann (Brooks)
Smith.

Childr. none.

1139. Ninth Generation. Tower.

634. ALONZO D.[8], ISAIAH [7], ISAIAH [6], ELISHA [5], ELISHA[4], RICHARD [3],
IBROOK [2], JOHN [1].

Alonzo D.[8], son of Isaiah [7] and Mary (Sherburne) Tower, b.
Dec. 2, 1831; mar. Helen V. Smith in San Francisco, Cal.,
Oct. 25, 1864. She was b. in New York City
Sept. 24, 1841.

Childr. born in Nevada City, Cal.

I. MAY VIRGINIA [9] born Aug. 16, 1865; died July 21, 1866.
II. CHARLES KNIBLOE [9] " March 9, 1867.
III. CORINE EMILY [9] " Sept. 14, 1873.

1140. Read. Ninth Generation. Tower.

634. CAROLINE R.[8], ISAIAH [7], ISAIAH [6], ELISHA [5], ELISHA [4], RICHARD[3]
IBROOK [2], JOHN [1].

Caroline R.[8], dau. of Isaiah [7] and Mary(Sherburne)Tower, b.
July 16, 1835; mar. Isaac F. Read, of Rochester, N. Y.,
May 8, 1862. He was b. in Carlton, Bedfordshire, England,
Jan. 21, 1827.

Child.

I. JOHN SHERBURNE [9] born April 19, 1864.

Isaac F. Read died in Rochester, Oct. 24, 1867, ag. 40 y.
9 m. 3 d.

Caroline R. (Tower) Read died in Rochester, July 2, 1879,
ag. 43 y. 11 m. 17 d.

1141. Ninth Generation. Tower.

634. ANSON K.[8], ISAIAH [7], ISAIAH [6], ELISHA [5], ELISHA [4], RICHARD [3],
IBROOK [2], JOHN [1].

Anson K.[8], son of Isaiah [7] and Mary (Sherburne) Tower, b.
Jan. 1, 1842; mar. Julia E. M. Richmond, of Churchville, N.Y.,
Oct. 1, 1878. She was b. in Sacramento, Cal.,
Aug. 3, 1857, and was dau. of John W. and Julia (Moore)
Richmond.

Childr. born in Rochester, N. Y.

I. ARTHUR RICHMOND [9] born Aug. 28, 1879.
II. CARRIE MARY [9] " Sept. 28, 1883.

1142. **Ninth Generation.** **Tower.**

635. BENJAMIN S.[8], JOHN A.[7], ISAIAH [6], ELISHA [5], ELISHA [4], RICH-
ARD [3], IBROOK [2], JOHN [1].

Benjamin S.[8], son of John A.[7] and Eunice (Schauber)
Tower, b.

March 11, 1832; mar. Elizabeth Ann Stevenson, of Brooklyn, N. Y.,

Dec. 22, 1859. She was b. in New Brunswick, N. J.,

Sept. 10, 1836, and was dau. of Henry Stevenson.

Childr. none.

1143. **Wilson.** **Ninth Generation.** **Tower.**

636. HULDAH [8], JEREMIAH B.[7], ISAIAH [6], ELISHA [5], ELISHA [4], RICH-
ARD [3], IBROOK [2], JOHN [1].

Huldah [8], dau. of Jeremiah B.[7] and Mary (Barkhoff) Tower, b.

Sept. 7, 1838; mar. William Wilson

May 24, 1858. He was b.

May 22, 1838.

Childr.

I. MARY [9]   born Aug. 9, 1860; died July 9, 1869, ag. 8 y. 11 m.
II. JOHN C. FREMONT [9] " Feb. 16, 1862; " Sept. 9, 1862.

William Wilson died at South Mountain, 1862, ag. 24.

DAYTON.   TOWER.

Huldah (Tower) Wilson mar., 2d, Smith Dayton, of Illinois,
Sept. , 1863. He was b.
1814.

Child.

III. CHAUNCEY F.[9] born Dec. 28, 1874.

Smith Dayton died March , 1874, ag. 60.

CLARK.   TOWER.

Huldah (Tower) Dayton mar., 3d, William M. Clark, of
Fredonia, Mich.,
April , 1875.

Childr.

IV. MENOMIA MIRIAM [9] born June 20, 1876.
V. PHEBE ANN [9]   " April 26, 1878.

1144. **Ninth Generation.** **Tower.**

642. ELISHA [8], ELISHA [7], ELISHA [6], ELISHA [5], ELISHA [4], RICHARD [3],
IBROOK [2], JOHN [1].

Elisha [8], son of Elisha [7] and Elizabeth (Stevens) Tower, b.
Oct. 11, 1824; mar. Mary Ann Heath
Nov. 6, 1850.   She was b.
1828, and was dau. of Dana Heath.

Childr.

I.   MARIA ADELIA [9]   born Aug. 23, 1851.
II. CHARLES DANA [9]   "   March 27, 1853.
III. REUBEN HUNTRESS [9] "   Sept. 4, 1854; died Dec. 3, 1882, ag. 28 y.
                                 2 m. 29 d.
IV. EDWIN CLARENCE [9]   "   Nov. 18, 1859.

1145.   **Ninth Generation.**   **Tower.**

642. CHARLES B. [8], ELISHA [7], ELISHA [6], ELISHA [5], ELISHA [4], RICH-
      ARD [3], IBROOK [2], JOHN [1].
      Charles B. [8], son of Elisha [7] and Elizabeth (Stevens) Tower, b.
      March 13, 1826; mar. Harriet L. Putnam
      March 30, 1853.   She was b. in Topsham, Vt.,
              1827, and was dau. of Jesse and Eliza (Grow)
      Putnam.

Childr.

1376. I.   CHARLES PUTNAM [9] born Feb. 6, 1854, in Charlestown, Mass.
       II. HARRIET ELIZA [9]   "   April 25, 1856, in Attleborough, Mass.
       III. HARRY ELDREDGE [9]   "   July 7, 1858, in Somerville, Mass.
       IV. SAMUEL F. [9]   "   Feb. 24, 1861, in Roxbury,   "
       V.   JESSIE BAXTER [9]   "   Dec. 13, 1867,   "   "; died
                                       Dec. 16, 1867.
       VI. WALTER STEVENS [9]   "   Dec. 23, 1870, in Hyde Park.

1146. Huntress.   **Ninth Generation.**   **Tower.**

642. MARY [8], ELISHA [7], ELISHA [6], ELISHA [5], ELISHA [4], RICHARD [3],
      IBROOK [2], JOHN [1].
      Mary [8], dau. of Elisha [7] and Elizabeth (Stevens) Tower, b.
      May 17, 1830; mar. Reuben Huntress, of Chelsea, Mass.,
      Dec. 24, 1851.   He was b. in Shapleigh, Me.,
      June 13, 1821, and was son of Reuben and Martha (Went-
      worth) Huntress.

Childr.

I. REUBEN WENTWORTH [9] born Nov. 16, 1852, in Attleborough, Mass.
II. ELIZABETH STEVENS [9]   "   Aug. 30, 1860, in Charlestown,   "; died
                                July 2, 1880, in Chelsea, ag. 19 y. 10 m. 3 d.

Mary (Tower) Huntress died in Charlestown, Nov. 28, 1861,
    ag. 31 y. 6 m. 12 d.
Reuben Huntress died in Chelsea, March 17, 1878, ag. 56 y.
    9 m. 4 d.

1147. Tucker. Ninth Generation. Tower.

642. EMELINE A.[8], ELISHA[7], ELISHA[6], ELISHA[5], ELISHA[4], RICH-
ARD[3], IBROOK[2], JOHN[1].
Emeline A.[8], dau. of Elisha[7] and Elizabeth (Stevens) Tower, b.
June 9, 1834; mar. William Tucker, of Boston,
Oct. 29, 1869. He was b. in Milford, N. H.,
Aug. 2, 1817, and was son of Joseph and Lydia (Crehore)
Tucker.

Childr. none.

1148. Ninth Generation. Tower.

643. DAVID H.[8], DANIEL W. P.[7], CORNELIUS[6], ISAAC[5], CORNELIUS[4],
JOHN[3], IBROOK[2], JOHN[1].
David H.[8], son of Daniel W. P.[7], and Emily (Hill) Tower, b.
March 2, 1828; mar. Jennie Booth in California.

Child.
I. EMILY JANE[9] born Nov. 9, 1875.

David H. Tower[8] died in Los Angeles, Cal., Aug. 13, 1877,
ag. 49 y. 5 m. 11 d.

1149. Ninth Generation. Tower.

643. JAMES[8], DANIEL W. P.[7], CORNELIUS[6], ISAAC[5], CORNELIUS[4],
JOHN[3], IBROOK[2], JOHN[1].
James[8], son of Daniel W. P.[7] and Emily (Hill) Tower, b.
Aug. 7, 1829; mar. Emma J. Gates
April 26, 1859. She was dau. of Silas Gates.

Child.
I. GEORGE J.[9] born March 17, 1860.

James Tower[8] mar., 2d, Anna M. Anderson
Sept. 11, 1866.

Childr. none.

1150. Ninth Generation. Tower.

643. HENRY E.[8], DANIEL W. P.[7], CORNELIUS[6], ISAAC[5], CORNELIUS[4],
JOHN[3], IBROOK[2], JOHN[1].
Henry E.[8], son of Daniel W. P.[7] and Emily (Hill) Tower, b.
June 7, 1831; mar. Rachel A. Miller
Nov. 13, 1855. She was b.
Dec. 8, 1836, and was dau. of Howard and Damask (Kil-
bourn) Miller.

Childr.

I. FRANK G.[9] born Oct. 30, 1856; died Oct. 16, 1858, ag. 1 y. 11 m. 17 d.
II. HATTIE[9] " Dec. 12, 1859.
III. EMILY L.[9] " Nov. 1, 1861; " March 13, 1875, ag. 13 y. 4 m. 12 d.
IV. HITTIE[9] " Nov. 12, 1864.
V. JAMES H.[9] " March 24, 1868; died March 26, 1868.
VI. MERTIE B.[9] " April 25, 1871; died Dec. 20, 1873, ag. 2 y. 7 m. 25 d.
VII. HENRY H.[9] " Sept. 1, 1875.
VIII. IRMA J.[9] " Jan. 19, 1881.

1151. **Ninth Generation.** **Tower.**

646. GEORGE E.[8], EDWARD[7], ELKANAH[6], ISAAC[5], CORNELIUS[4], JOHN[3], IBROOK[2], JOHN[1].

George E.[8], son of Edward[7] and Mary (Hubbard) Tower, b. Jan. 10, 1846; mar. widow Delia Babcock Aug. 27, 1866. She was b.
1845, and was dau. of Francis and Celinda Bartlett.

1152. Newman. **Ninth Generation.** **Tower.**

656. LUCY F.[8], LEWIS C.[7], MICAH[6], ISAAC[5], CORNELIUS[4], JOHN[3], IBROOK[2], JOHN[1].

Lucy F.[8], dau. of Lewis C.[7] and Margaret S. (White) Tower, b. May 20, 1829; mar. Le Roy Newman, of Rochester, N. Y., 1847.

Lucy F. (Tower) Newman died in Rochester, Feb. 9, 1852, ag. 22 y. 8 m. 20 d.

1153. Case. **Ninth Generation.** **Tower.**

656. PAMELA C.[8], LEWIS C.[7], MICAH[6], ISAAC[5], CORNELIUS[4], JOHN[3], IBROOK[2], JOHN[1].

Pamela C.[8], dau. of Lewis C.[7] and Margaret S. (White) Tower, b.

Aug. 17, 1831; mar. Isaac L. Case, of Binghampton, N. Y.

Child.

I. CHARLES C.[9] born 1859, in Rochester, N. Y.

Isaac L. Case died 1871.

HALE. TOWER.

Pamela C. (Tower) Case mar., 2d, C. H. Hale, of Olympia, Wash.,
1874

1154. **Ninth Generation.** **Tower.**

656. LEWIS C.[8], LEWIS C.[7], MICAH [6], ISAAC [5], CORNELIUS [4], JOHN [3], IBROOK [2], JOHN [1].

Lewis C.[8], son of Lewis C.[7] and Margaret S. (White) Tower, b. Aug. 24, 1839; mar. Maria H. Dennis Aug. 24, 1865. She was b. March 9, 1842, and was dau. of James and Harriet (Chamberlain) Dennis.

Childr. born in Rochester, N. Y.

I. CLIFFORD HAMILTON [9] born April 13, 1867.
II. LUCY DENNIS [9]   " June 8, 1868.
III. FRED EVERETT [9] } Twins " March 7, 1870.
IV. FRANK CLARK [9] }

1155. Eddy. **Ninth Generation.** **Tower.**

658. LOUISA S.[8], SOLOMON [7], JOSEPH [6], ISAAC [5], CORNELIUS [4], JOHN [3], IBROOK [2], JOHN [1].

Louisa S.[8], dau. of Solomon [7] and Polly (Baldwin) Tower, b. 1848; mar. William G. Eddy, of Grattan, Mich., Jan. 21, 1871. He was b. in Chili, N. Y., 1835.

Childr. born in Grattan.

I. S. J.[9]   born   1872.   III. RUFUS H.[9] born   1876.
II. MARY P.[9]   "   1874.   IV. CHARLES [9]   "   1879.

1156. **Ninth Generation.** **Tower.**

658. BURTON J.[8], SOLOMON [7], JOSEPH [6], ISAAC [5], CORNELIUS [4], JOHN [3], IBROOK [2], JOHN [1].

Burton J.[8], son of Solomon [7] and Polly (Baldwin) Tower, b. 1850; mar. Mary Stevens in Oakfield, Mich., June 8, 1873. She was b. in Oakfield 1855.

Child born in Oakfield.

I. FREDERICK N.[9] born Sept. 5, 1877.

1157. Thompson. **Ninth Generation.** **Tower.**

665. MARY E.[8], BENJAMIN [7], OSWIN [6], ISAAC [5], CORNELIUS [4], JOHN [3], IBROOK [2], JOHN [1].

Mary E.[8], dau. of Benjamin [7] and Lavina (Twiss) Tower, b. July 23, 1840; mar. Charles W. Thompson, of Pittsfield, Mass.,

Jan. 3, 1860. He was b. in Hudson, Mass.,
Sept. 6, 1837, and was son of Ezra and Angelina (Barber)
Thompson.

Childr.

I.	CHARLES F.[9]	born Oct. 19, 1860 ; died Aug. 1, 1862, ag. 1 y. 9 m. 13 d.
II.	FRED H.[9]	" Nov. 7, 1863, in Pittsfield.
III.	INEZ R.[9]	" Nov. 18, 1868, " " ; died Oct. 11, 1870, ag. 1 y. 10 m. 23 d.
IV.	JESSIE I.[9]	" Oct. 23, 1870, in Pittsfield; " July 22, 1872, ag. 1 y. 8 m. 30 d.
V.	HENRY E.[9] } Twins	" June 6, 1874, in Pittsfield.
VI.	HELEN M.[9] }	

1158. Thompson.   Ninth Generation.   Tower.

665.   SARAH P.[8], BENJAMIN [7], OSWIN [6], ISAAC [5], CORNELIUS [4], JOHN [3],
IBROOK [2], JOHN [1].
Sarah P.[8], dau. of Benjamin [7] and Lavina (Twiss)Tower, b.
Dec. 12, 1841 ; mar. Henry E. Thompson, of Pittsfield, Mass.,
June 14, 1864. He was b.
1842, and was son of Ezra and Angelina (Barber)
Thompson.

Childr. none.

1159.   Ninth Generation.   Tower.

665.   HENRY B.[8], BENJAMIN [7], OSWIN [6], ISAAC [5], CORNELIUS [4], JOHN [3],
IBROOK [2], JOHN [1].
Henry B.[8], son of Benjamin [7] and Lavina (Twiss) Tower, b.
Dec. 27, 1843 ; mar. Carrie E. Phillips
Nov. 20, 1867. She was b.
Aug. 12, 1848, and was dau. of Henry and Caroline Phillips.

Childr. born in Richmond, Mass.

I.	BERTHA P.[9]	born April 20, 1869.
II.	CORA L.[9]	" April 7, 1871.
III.	CARRIE B.[9]	" Aug. 3, 1872.
IV.	JESSIE M.	" Jan. 13, 1875.
V.	ALICE I.[9]	" March 20, 1876.
VI.	MILDRED CLAPP [9]	" March 25, 1880.
VII.	RUBY ELIZABETH [9]	" March 5, 1882.
VIII.	HENRY BENJAMIN [9]	" March 8, 1885.

1160. Ransehausen.   Ninth Generation.   Tower.

665.   HARRIET P. [8], BENJAMIN [7], OSWIN [6], ISAAC [5], CORNELIUS [4],
JOHN [3], IBROOK [2], JOHN [1].

Harriet P.[8], dau. of Benjamin [7] and Lavina(Twiss)Tower, b.
April 4, 1847; mar. William Ransehausen, of Pittsfield,
Mass.,

Sept. 6, 1865. He was b.

1840, and was son of William and Louisa Ransehausen.

Childr.

I.	LILIAN L.[9]	born July 24, 1866, in Pittsfield.
II.	JAMES W.[9]	" Sept. 5, 1868, " "
III.	BENJAMIN TOWER [9]	" July 6, 1870, " "
IV.	HATTIE L.[9]	" Dec. 27, 1872, " "
V.	BESSIE B.[9]	" Sept. 13, 1874, " "
VI.	FRANCES M.[9]	" Feb. 24, 1877, " Providence, R. I.
VII.	GEORGE Y.[9]	" Jan. 5, 1879, " " " ; died Dec. 17, 1880, ag. 1 y. 11 m. 12 d.

VIII. MARTHA [9] } Twins " July 31, 1881, " Richmond, Mass.
IX. MIRIAM [9] }

X. ANNIE GERTRUDE [9] " Sept. 16, 1882, " Pittsfield.
XI. RICHARD WARREN [9] " Dec. 10, 1884, " "

1161. **Ninth Generation.** **Tower.**

665. FRED L.[8], BENJAMIN [7], OSWIN [6], ISAAC [5], CORNELIUS [4], JOHN [3],
IBROOK [2], JOHN [1].

Fred L.[8], son of Benjamin [7] and Lavina (Twiss) Tower, b.
June 12, 1855; mar. Edith L. Twiss in Northampton, Mass.,
Sept. 27, 1882. She was b. in Northampton
June 13, 1853, and was dau. of Horace and Lima (Metcalf)
Twiss.

Childr. none.

Edith L. (Twiss) Tower died in Northampton, March 9,
1884, ag. 30 y. 8 m. 26 d.

Fred L. Tower [8] mar., 2d, Martha Maud Granger, of
Northampton
Sept. 22, 1885. She was. b. in Chester, Mass.,
Dec. 14, 1864, and was dau. of Paul and Laura (Ballou)
Granger.

1162. **Ninth Generation.** **Tower.**

666. HENRY L.[8], LEVI [7], OSWIN [6], ISAAC [5], CORNELIUS [4], JOHN [3],
IBROOK [2], JOHN [1].

Henry L.[8], son of Levi [7] and Julia A. (Wheeler) Tower, b.
Aug. 28, 1843; mar. Fanny Jane Overbaugh, of Catskill,
N. Y.,

Oct. 29, 1869. She was b.

Jan. 8, 1844, and was dau. of William and Fanny (Smith) Overbaugh.

Child.

I. WILLIAM HENRY [9] born May 27, 1877.

1163. **Ninth Generation.** **Tower.**

666. FRANKLIN D.[8], LEVI [7], OSWIN [6], ISAAC [5], CORNELIUS [4], JOHN [3], IBROOK [2], JOHN [1].

Franklin D.[8], son of Levi [7] and Julia A. (Wheeler) Tower, b. July 23, 1848 ; mar. Catherine Blessing, of Albany, N. Y., Oct. 29, 1868.

Childr. born in Albany.

I. LIZZIE B.[9] born Dec. 20, 1869.
II. MINNIE [9]   "   ; died, ag. 2 weeks.
III. FLORENCE C.[9] " Nov. 15, 1874.
IV. MABEL F.[9]   " Aug. 14, 1877.

1164. **Lyman.** **Ninth Generation.** **Tower.**

669. ELLEN [8], QUARTUS [7], OSWIN [6], ISAAC [5], CORNELIUS [4], JOHN [3], IBROOK [2], JOHN [1].

Ellen [8], dau. of Quartus [7] and Mary (Cowls) Tower, b.
    1847 ; mar. Auret M. Lyman
May 14, 1865. He was b.
    1843, and was son of Israel F. and Catherine A.
Lyman.

Childr. three.

1165. **Ninth Generation.** **Tower.**

672. THOMAS [8], ASA C.[7], JESSE [6], ROBERT [5], DAVID [4], HEZEKIAH [3], IBROOK [2], JOHN [1].

Thomas [8] son of Asa C.[7] and Charlotte (Mann) Tower, b.
July 3, 1807 ; mar. Rebecca Lambert [8], of Cohasset, Mass.,
April 27, 1831. She was b. in Cohasset
Dec. 17, 1812, and was dau. of Isaac and Mary (Barrell)
    Lambert

LAMBERT, BEAL, BATES.   TOWER.

Rebecca [8], Isaac [7], Hannah [6], Joshua [5], Rachel [4], Rachel [8], Ibrook [2], John [1].

Childr. born in Cohasset.

1377.	I.	THOMAS [9]	born Feb. 19, 1832.
1378.	II.	SARAH JANE [9]	" Feb. 25, 1834.
1379.	III.	LEVI C.[9]	" Oct. 17, 1835.

1380.	IV.	Ruth C.[9]	born	1839.
1381.	V.	Polly N.[9]	"	Feb. 10, 1841.
1382.	VI.	Rebecca [9]	"	June 30, 1843.
1383.	VII.	Isaac Henry [9]	"	May 26, 1846.
1384.	VIII.	Harriet [9]	"	Oct. 26, 1848.
	IX.	Daughter [9]	"	Oct. 25, 1850; died Oct. 25, 1850.
1385.	X.	Caroline Lambert [9]	"	Feb. 26, 1852.

Thomas Tower [8] died in Cohasset, Aug. 13, 1854, ag. 47 y. 1 m. 10 d.

Rebecca [8] (Lambert) Tower mar., 2d, John Tyrer in Cohasset June 20, 1857. He was born in England 1813, and was son of Thomas and Elizabeth Tyrer.

1166. Williston. Ninth Generation. Tower.

672. Charlotte [8], Asa C. [7], Jesse [6], Robert [5], David [4], Hezekiah [3], Ibrook [2], John [1].

Charlotte [8], dau. of Asa C. [7] and Charlotte (Mann) Tower, b. Sept. 18, 1809; mar. Henry Williston, of Cohasset, Mass., Dec. 10, 1831. He was b. in Boston Nov. , 1804, and was son of Friend and Elizabeth (Brewer) Williston.

Childr. born in Cohasset.

I.	Maria [9]	born Oct.	1, 1832.
II.	Elizabeth B. [9]	" Dec.	31, 1834.
III.	Mary L [9]	" March	17, 1837.
IV.	Hannah T. [9]	" May	8, 1840.
V.	Thomas [9]	" Oct.	6, 1843.

Henry Williston died in Cohasset, April 27, 1873, ag. 68 y. 5 m.

Charlotte (Tower) Williston died in Braintree, July 26, 1887, ag. 77 y. 10 m. 7 d.

1167. Ninth Generation. Tower.

672. Asa C. [8], Asa C. [7], Jesse [6], Robert [5], David [4], Hezekiah [3], Ibrook [2], John [1].

Asa C. [8], son of Asa C. [7] and Charlotte (Mann) Tower, b. May 4, 1811; mar. Eliza Stoddard, of Scituate, Mass., June 30, 1834.

Eliza (Stoddard) Tower died in Hingham, 1836.

Asa C. Tower [8] mar., 2d, Sarah W. Lambert [8] of Cohasset, April 16, 1837. She was b. in Cohasset, Mass., Feb. 6, 1822, and was dau. of Isaac [7] and Mary (Barrell) Lambert.

LAMBERT, BEAL, BATES.   TOWER.

Sarah W.[8], Isaac[7], Hannah[6], Joshua[5], Rachel[4], Rachel[3], Ibrook[2], John[1].

Childr. born in Hingham.

1386. I. SARAH CUSHING[9] born June 6, 1840.
      II. CHARLES[9]   " May 10, 1844; mar. Sarah J. Davis, of Boston, Oct. 4, 1881.
387. III. OLIVER[9]   " Dec. 25, 1848.
      IV. ALICE MARIA[9]   " Aug. 23, 1864; died Sept. 5, 1865, ag. 1 y. 13 d.

Asa C. Tower[8] died in Hingham, Dec. 31, 1883, ag. 72 y. 7 m. 27 d.

1168. Corthell.   Ninth Generation.   Tower.

672. HANNAH K.[8], ASA C.[7], JESSE[6], ROBERT[5], DAVID[4], HEZEKIAH[3], IBROOK[2], JOHN[1].

Hannah K.[8], dau. of Asa C.[7] and Charlotte (Mann)Tower, b. Sept.   9, 1819; mar. Nelson Corthell[7], 'of Hingham, May   28, 1843.   He was b.

March 28, 1815, and was son of Robert[6] and Charlotte (Hersey) Corthell.

CORTHELL.   TOWER.

Nelson[7], Robert[6], Robert[5], Robert[4], Deborah[3], Benjamin[2], John[1].

Childr.

   I. GUSTAVUS P.[9] born Feb. 23, 1845.
  II. SARAH ANN[9]   " Aug. 29, 1852.

1169.   Ninth Generation.   Tower.

672. ALVAN[8], ASA C,[7] JESSE[6], ROBERT[5], DAVID[4], HEZEKIAH[3], IBROOK[2], JOHN[1].

Alvan[8], son of Asa C.[7] and Ruth (   ) Tower, b. Sept. 13, 1832; mar. Rebecca T. Souther[7], of Hingham, June 4, 1854.   She was b. in Hingham, Mass., Feb. 22, 1827, and was dau. of Daniel[6] and Rebecca[7] (Tower) Souther.

SOUTHER.   TOWER.

Rebecca T.[7] { Daniel[6], Daniel[5], Joseph[4], Content[3]   } Ibrook[2], John[1].
              { Rebecca T.[7], Jesse[6], Robert[5], David[4], Hezekiah[3] }

Childr. born in Hingham.

   I. EMMA CLARK[9] born Feb. 27, 1855; died Aug. 9, 1855.
  II. LOUISA ATWOOD[9] " April 19, 1856 ; died Jan. 24, 1861, ag. 4 y. 9 m. 4 d.
 III. FRANKLIN A.[9]   " June 3, 1860; died Sept. 6, 1860.

Alvan Tower[8] died in Virginia, June 8, 1862, ag. 29 y. 8 m. 25 d.

Rebecca T.[7] (Souther) Tower mar., 2d, Benjamin C. Morse, of Hingham,

Aug. 6, 1867. He was born in Horton, N. S.,
1806, and was son of John and Cynthia (Cleveland) Morse.

1170. Vinal. Ninth Generation. Tower.

674. REBECCA C.[8], JESSE[7], JESSE[6], ROBERT[5], DAVID[4], HEZEKIAH[3], IBROOK[2], JOHN[1].

Rebecca C.[8], dau. of Jesse[7] and Grace[6] (Souther) Tower, b. June 1, 1814; mar. David Vinal[7]

Feb. 19, 1830. He was b.

May 1, 1801, and was son of Clitus and Nabby[6] (Souther) Vinal.

VINAL. TOWER.

David[7], Nabby[6], Joseph[5], Joseph[4], Content[3], Ibrook[2], John[1].

Childr.

I. ABIGAIL[9] born Aug. 6, 1830.
II. MARY ANN[9] " Oct. 7, 1831; mar. George Fish.

Rebecca C.[8] (Tower) Vinal died in Cohasset, April 11, 1877, ag. 62 y. 10 m. 10 d.

1171. Ninth Generation. Tower.

674. JESSE[8], JESSE[7], JESSE[6], ROBERT[5], DAVID[4], HEZEKIAH[3], IBROOK[2], JOHN[1].

Jesse[8], son of Jesse[7] and Grace[6] (Souther) Tower, b.

March 28, 1817; mar. Grace S. Souther[7], of Hingham,

Aug. 10, 1837. She was b. in Hingham, Mass.,

Dec. 29, 1817, and was dau. of Daniel[6] and Rebecca[7] (Tower) Souther.

SOUTHER. TOWER.

Grace S.[7] { Daniel[6], Daniel[5], Joseph[4], Content[3] } Rebecca[7], Jesse[6], Robert[5], David[4], } Ibrook[2], John[1]. Hezekiah[3]

Childr. born in Cohasset.

1388. I. HARRIET ELIZABETH[9] born March 15, 1838.
1389. II. GRACE ELLEN[9] " March 25, 1844.
III. STEPHEN PUFFER[9] " March 16, 1849; died Feb. 14, 1863, ag. 13 y. 10 m. 29 d.

Jesse Tower[8] died in Cohasset, Feb. 26, 1876, ag. 58 y. 10 m. 29 d.

Grace S. (Souther) Tower died in Cohasset, June 30, 1849, ag. 31 y. 6 m. 2 d.

1172.   **Ninth Generation.**   **Tower.**

674. JOHN [8], JESSE [7], JESSE [6], ROBERT [5], DAVID [4], HEZEKIAH [3],
      IBROOK [2], JOHN [1].
      John [8], son of Jesse [7] and Grace [6] (Souther) Tower, b.
      Jan. 18, 1821; mar. Susan Dady [9]
      July 24, 1845. She was b. in Cohasset, Mass.,
      Oct. 22, 1827, and was dau. of John and Hannah [8] (Lam-
      bert) Dady.

      DADY, LAMBERT, BEAL, BATES.   TOWER.
      Susan [9], Hannah [8], Isaac [7], Hannah [6], Joshua [5], Rachel [4], Rachel [3],
      Ibrook [2], John [1].

Childr. born in Cohasset.

1390. I.   HELEN LOUISA [9] born
       II. SERENO HOWE [9]   "   July 7, 1848.
       III. JAMES D. [9]   "   Aug. 3, 1850; died
       IV. JAMES D. [9]   "   April 2, 1853 ; " May 2, 1853.
       V.   SUSAN M. [9]   "   May 30, 1854; " Aug. 31, 1856, ag. 2 y.
                                    3 m. 1 d.

1173. Barnes.   **Ninth Generation.**   **Tower.**

674. MARTHA B. [8], JESSE [7], JESSE [6], ROBERT [5], DAVID [4], HEZEKIAH [3],
      IBROOK [2], JOHN [1].
      Martha B. [8], dau. of Jesse [7] and Grace (Souther) Tower, b.
      Dec. 17, 1822; mar. John B. Barnes [8]
      Oct.   , 1842. He was b.
      Sept. 25, 1810, and was son of Peter [7] and Sibyl (Burbank)
      Barnes.

      BARNES, BEAL, BATES.   TOWER.
      John B. [8], Peter [7], Benjamin [6], Hannah [5], Rachel [4], Rachel [3], Ibrook [2],
      John [1].

Childr. born in Cohasset.

       I.   ELIZABETH [9]   born Feb. 2, 1843; died Feb. 6, 1843.
       II.   JOHN OTIS [9]   "   Sept. 20, 1846.
       III. PETER L. [9]   "   Jan.   , 1848; " June 22, 1853, ag. 5 y. 5 m.
       IV.   GEORGE HENRY [9]   "   April 18, 1850.
       V.   JOHN TOWER [9]   "   Jan. 21, 1853.
       VI.   PETER [9]   "   Jan. 23, 1855; died Nov 23, 1856, ag. 1 y. 10 m.
       VII. JOANNA H. [9]   "   April 22, 1857; mar. George Crocker, of Co-
                                     hasset.
       VIII. JESSE TOWER [9]   "
       IX.   ABBY [9]   "

1174. Souther.   **Ninth Generation.**   **Tower.**

674. ABIGAIL K. [8], JESSE [7], JESSE [6], ROBERT [5], DAVID [4], HEZEKIAH [3],
      IBROOK [2], JOHN [1].

Abigail K.[8], dau. of Jesse[7] and Grace[6] (Souther) Tower, b.
Sept. 29, 1826 ; mar. John Souther[7]
Oct. 9, 1846. He was b.
May 4, 1824, and was son of Nathan[6] and Sally (Wilson)
Souther.

SOUTHER.   TOWER.
John[7], Nathan[6], Joseph[5], Joseph[4], Content[3], Ibrook[2], John[1].

Child born in Cohasset.

I. WILLIAM OTIS[9] born July 4, 1851.

1175. Osgood.   Ninth Generation.   Tower.

677. MARY H.[8], ABRAHAM H.[7], ABRAHAM H.[6], ABRAHAM[5], DANIEL[4],
DANIEL[3], IBROOK[2], JOHN[1].
Mary H.[8], dau. of Abraham H.[7] and Mary L. (Brown)
Tower, b.
Oct. 30, 1852 ; mar. Edmund Q. S. Osgood, of Cohasset,
Sept. 23, 1879. He was b. in Cohasset, Mass.,
Feb. 26, 1851, and was son of Joseph and Ellen D. (Sewall)
Osgood.

Childr.

I. ETHEL LEWIS[9]   born June 21, 1880.
II. RONALD SEWALL[9] "   Sept. 10, 1883.

1176.   Ninth Generation.   Tower.

677. ABRAHAM H.[8], ABRAHAM H.[7], ABRAHAM H.[6], ABRAHAM[5],
DANIEL[4], DANIEL[3], IBROOK[2], JOHN[1],
Abraham H.[8], son of Abraham H.[7] and Mary L. (Brown)
Tower, b.
Sept. 8, 1858 ; mar. Mary Fogg Osgood, of Cohasset, Mass.,
Oct. 28, 1880. She was b. in Cohasset
May 9, 1857, and was dau. of Joseph and Ellen D. (Sewall
Osgood.

Childr.

I. MARY LEWIS[9]   born June 10, 1882.
II. ABRAHAM HOBART[9] "   Jan. 26, 1884.

1177. Wheelwright. Ninth Generation.   Tower.

678. LAURA S.[8], HENRY C.[7], ABRAHAM H.[6], ABRAHAM[5], DANIEL[4],
DANIEL[3], IBROOK[2], JOHN[1].
Laura S.[8], dau. of Henry C.[7] and Martha D. (Joy) Tower, b.
Jan. 4, 1864 ; mar. Charles W. Wheelwright, of Boston,
April 27, 1887. He was b. in Roxbury, Mass.,
March 14, 1863, and was son of Josiah and Lucinda Orne
(Chapin) Wheelwright.

WHEELWRIGHT.   TOWER.
Charles W.[9], Josiah [8], Josiah [7], Lot [6], Silence [5], John [4], Johu [3], Ibrook [2], John [1].

1178.   **Ninth Generation.**   **Tower.**

680. GEORGE P.[8], NEWCOMB B.[7], ABRAHAM H.[6], ABRAHAM [5], DAN-
      IEL [4], DANIEL [3], IBROOK [2], JOHN [1].
      George P.[8], son of Newcomb B.[7] and Sophronia L. (Parker)
      Tower, b.
      Feb. 1, 1865; mar. Laura Kincaid Richardson, in Winona,
      Dec. 28, 1887. She was b. in Winona, Minn.,
      Aug. 7, 1862, and was dau. of William H. and Mary J.
      Richardson.

1179.   **Ninth Generation.**   **Tower.**

683. FRED E.[8], IBROOK [7], ABRAHAM [6], ISAAC [5], DANIEL [4], DANIEL [3],
      IBROOK [2], JOHN [1].
      Fred E.[8], son of Ibrook [7] and Mary (Wheeler) Tower, b.
      Feb. 22, 1845; mar. Belle Shepard
      Aug. 13, 1866.

        Childr. born in Milford, Oakland Co., Mich.

I.   MARY B.[9]   born April 23, 1867.
II. THOMAS E.[9]   "   Dec. 9, 1868.
III. CARRIE L. FOOT, an adopted daughter, born April 9, 1874, in Ithaca,
      Mich.

1180.   **Ninth Generation.**   **Tower.**

683. DECKER F.[8], IBROOK [7], ABRAHAM [6], ISAAC [5], DANIEL [4], DANIEL [3],
      IBROOK [2], JOHN [1].
      Decker F.[8], son of Ibrook [7] and Mary (Wheeler) Tower, b.
      Dec. 27, 1848; mar. Cornelia H. Chrittenden
      Jan. 20, 1869. She was born in White Lake, Mich.

                        Childr.
I.   LEWIS D.[9] born Aug. 20, 1870, in White Lake.
II. ALBERT C.[9]   "   Feb. 19, 1872, in Carthage, Texas.
III. WALTER [9]   "   Jan. 12, 1877, in Milford, Mich.

1181. **Woodward.** **Ninth Generation.**   **Tower.**

683. IDA M.[8], IBROOK [7], ABRAHAM [6], ISAAC [5], DANIEL [4], DANIEL [3],
      IBROOK [2], JOHN [1].
      Ida M.[8], dau. of Ibrook [7] and Mary (Wheeler) Tower, b.
      Aug. 13, 1853; mar. Harlow W. Woodward
      Dec. 8, 1874.

Child.

I. MARY L.[9] born Oct. 4, 1876, in Milford, Mich.

1182. Eastman. Ninth Generation. Tower.

698. ALICE M.[8], DAVID [7], ISAAC [6], ISAAC [5], DANIEL [4], DANIEL [3], IBROOK [2], JOHN [1].
Alice M.[8], dau. of David [7] and Sarah D. (Chapin) Tower, b. Sept. 7, 1859; mar. George Eastman Jan. 17, 1883.

Childr.

I. LEON C.[9]   born Nov. 22, 1883.
II. CLAUD [9]   "   Nov. 26, 1884; died Jan. 5, 1888.
III. ALICE MAUD [9]   "   Oct. 21, 1886.

1183. Ninth Generation. Tower.

711. SAMUEL D.[8], EDWARD [7], LEVI [6], LEVI [5], DANIEL [4], DANIEL [3], IBROOK [2], JOHN [1].
Samuel D.[8], son of Edward [7] and Elizabeth B. (Delano) Tower, b.
March 31, 1838; mar. Fanny B. Downs Sept. 15, 1860. She was b.
1842, and was dau. of Loring and Elizabeth Downs.

Childr. born in Cohasset.

I. EDWARD CLARENCE [9] born Jan. 9, 1864.
II. ABBY FRANCES [9]   "   June 1, 1873.

1184. Chamberlain. Ninth Generation. Tower.

711. HANNAH E. D.[8], EDWARD [7], LEVI [6], LEVI [5], DANIEL [4], DANIEL [3], IBROOK [2], JOHN [1].
Hannah E. D.[8], dau. of Edward [7] and Elizabeth B. (Delano) Tower, b.
March 11, 1849; mar. Warren Bradley Chamberlain, of Bath, N. H.,
Nov. 28, 1876. He was b. in Bath 1854, and was son of Isaac and Jane (Lang) Chamberlain.

1185. Ninth Generation. Tower.

712. EDWARD E.[8], LEVI [7], LEVI [6], LEVI [5], DANIEL [4], DANIEL [3], IBROOK [2], JOHN [1].
Edward E.[8], son of Levi [7] and Rebecca (Bates) Tower, b.
Feb. 1, 1834; mar. Charlotte M. B. Tower [7], of Cohasset,

Jan. 18, 1860. She was b. in Cohasset, Mass.,
Feb. 25, 1836, and was dau. of Abraham H.[6] and Charlotte[8]
(Bates) Tower.

Tower.   Tower.
Charlotte M. B.[7], Abraham H.[6], Abraham[5], Daniel[4], Daniel[3], Ibrook[2],
John[1].

Childr. born in Cohasset.

I.	Grace Everett[9]	born June 1, 1861; mar. Henry F. Furber, of Boston, April 4, 1887.	
II.	Edward[9]	" March 15, 1863.	
III.	Edith Josephine[9]	" Feb. 18, 1867.	
IV.	Henry Earl[9]	" March 26, 1868; died Aug. 19, 1868.	
V.	Burgess Clifford[9]	" Jan. 26, 1874.	
VI.	Russell Bates[9]	" Oct. 30, 1876.	

1186. **Ninth Generation.** **Tower.**

712. Levi[8], Levi[7], Levi[6], Levi[5], Daniel[4], Daniel[3], Ibrook[2],
John[1].

Levi[8], son of Levi[7] and Rebecca (Bates) Tower, b.
June 8, 1836; mar. Mary Rebecca Tower[8], of Cohasset,
Aug. 18, 1862. She was b. in Cohasset, Mass.,
Aug. 18, 1840, and was dau. of Daniel and Susan S. (Bates)
Tower.

Tower.   Tower.
Mary R.[8], Daniel[7], Nichols[6], Levi[5], Daniel[4], Daniel[3], Ibrook[2], John[1]

Child.

I. Margaret Bates[9] born June 19, 1864.

1187. **Ninth Generation.** **Tower.**

716. George B. N.[8], David B.[7], Nichols[6], Levi[5], Daniel[4],
Daniel[3], Ibrook[2], John[1].

George B. N.[8], son of David B.[7] and Elizabeth (Bates)
Tower, b.
1834; mar. Abby C. Nickerson
Jan. 8, 1858. She was b.
Oct. 20, 1840, and was dau. of George L. and Harriet
(Oakes) Nickerson.
Abby C. (Nickerson) Tower died in Cohasset, Jan. 25, 1858,
ag. 17 y. 3 m. 5 d.

1188. **Ninth Generation.** **Tower.**

717. Benjamin L. M.[8], George[7], Nichols[6], Levi[5], Daniel[4],
Daniel[3], Ibrook[2], John[1].

Benjamin L. M.[8], son of George[7] and Adeline (Lane)
Tower, b.

1848; mar. Eliza A Kneeland, of Cohasset, Mass.,
July 3, 1878. She was b. in Boston
1853, and was dau. of Samuel and Eliza M. (Curtis)
Kneeland.

1189. Lincoln.   Ninth Generation.   Tower.

718. ELIZABETH H.[8], THOMAS N.[7], NICHOLS [6], LEVI [5], DANIEL [4],
DANIEL [3], IBROOK [2], JOHN [1].
Elizabeth H.[8], dau. of Thomas N.[7] and Jane B.[7] (Bates)
Tower, b.
July 17, 1841 ; mar. James Davis Lincoln, of Cohasset,
Nov. 26, 1868. He was b. in Cohasset, Mass.,
April   , 1838, and was son of Martin and Ruth Lincoln.

Childr. none.

Elizabeth H.[8] (Tower) Lincoln died in Cohasset, Aug. 4, 1870,
ag. 29 y. 18 d.

1190.   Ninth Generation.   Tower.

718. NICHOLS [8], THOMAS N.[7], NICHOLS [6], LEVI [5], DANIEL [4], DANIEL [3],
IBROOK [2], JOHN [1].
Nichols [8], son of Thomas N.[7] and Jane B.[7] (Bates) Tower, b.
July 20, 1844 ; mar. Maud Theresa Gardner
Nov. 27, 1867.

Childr.

I. EUGENE NICHOLS [9] born Oct. 28, 1868.
II. FREDERICK BATES [9] " Aug 17, 1873.

1191.   Ninth Generation.   Tower.

719. CLEMENT B.[8], DANIEL [7], NICHOLS [6], LEVI [5], DANIEL [4], DANIEL [3],
IBROOK [2], JOHN [1].
Clement B.[8], son of Daniel [7] and Susan S. (Bates) Tower, b.
March 13, 1848; mar. Adeline B. Bates [9], of Cohasset,
July 7, 1872. She was b. in Cohasset, Mass.,
Feb. 20, 1851, and was dau. of Loring and Catherine (Clarra)
Bates.

BATES.   TOWER.
Adeline B.[9], Loring [8], Phineas [7], Zealous [6]. Joshua [5], Joshua [4], Rachel [3],
Ibrook [2], John [1].

Child.

I. CLEMENT BATES [9] born Aug. 6, 1873.

1192. Giddings, Bartlett.   Ninth Generation.   Tower.

734. WEALTHY T.[8], STEPHEN [7], STEPHEN [6], PETER [5], PETER [4], JERE-
MIAH [3], JEREMIAH [2], JOHN [1].

Wealthy T.[8], dau. of Stephen [7] and Milley (Bartlett) Tower, .
Jan. 18, 1805 ; mar. Peter Bartlett, of Worthington, Mass.,
July 1, 1823.   He was b. in Easton, Mass.,
            1800, and was son of Peter and Bethia (Morse)
    Bartlett.

Childr.

I.   WILLIAM EUSTIS [9] born Feb. 5, 1825; mar. Corrinth Winching; mar.,
                2d, Rebecca Kyle.
II. HORACE AMES [9]   "   Oct. 20, 1826.
III. OTIS BOYS [9]   "   May 15, 1828.
IV. ANGELINE B.[9]   "   Feb. 6, 1835; died July 20, 1835.

Peter Bartlett died in Worthington, July 30, 1836, ag. 36.
Wealthy T. (Tower) Bartlett [8] mar., 2d, William Giddings,
    of Chesterfield, Mass.,
    April 6, 1842.   He was born
        1804.

Child.

V. CHARLES B.[9] born Aug 10, 1843; died Jan. 17, 1847, ag. 3 y. 5 m. 7 d.

1193.   **Ninth Generation.**   **Tower**

734. CALVIN B. [8], STEPHEN [7], STEPHEN [6], PETER [5], PETER [4], JERE-
    MIAH [3], JEREMIAH [2], JOHN [1].
    Calvin B.[8], son of Stephen [7] and Milley (Bartlett) Tower, b.
    Nov. 4, 1808 ; mar. Amanda M. Higgins, of Worthington,
        Mass.,
    May 28, 1835.   She was b. in Chesterfield, Mass.,
    Aug. 28, 1815, and was dau. of Luther and Lydia (Ring)
        Higgins.

Childr. born in Worthington.

1391.   I.   LYDIA A.[9]   born July 20, 1836.
        II. ELVIRA N.[9]   "   Sept. 17, 1839.
1392.   III. ANGELINA D.[9]"   May 3, 1843.
        IV. GRACE [9]   "   July 14, 1849.

1194. Bartlett.   **Ninth Generation.**   **Tower.**

734. PERMELIA [8], STEPHEN [7], STEPHEN [6], PETER [5], PETER [4], JERE-
    MIAH [3], JEREMIAH [2], JOHN [1].
    Permelia [8], dau. of Stephen [7] and Milley (Bartlett) Tower, b.
    Nov. 24, 1811 ; mar. Tillson Bartlett, of Worthington, Mass.,
    July 8, 1830.   He was b.
    Feb. 28, 1801, and was son of Edward and Polly (Barr)
    Bartlett.

Childr. born in Worthington.

I.	MILLEY [9]	born April 3, 1831; died Nov. 16, 1831.	
II.	MILLEY ELIZABETH [9]	" Oct. 18, 1832.	
III.	NOYES COLT [9]	" Oct. 18, 1834.	
IV.	JACOB MANLEY [9]	" June 26, 1837.	
V.	CALVIN TOWER [9]	" June 11, 1841.	
VI.	ZILPAH JANE [9]	" Oct. 2, 1843.	
VII.	HORACE FRANKLIN [9] } Twins	" Aug. 20, 1845; Howard F. mar.	
VIII.	HOWARD FRANCIS [9] }	Helen Hoyt, July 2, 1878.	
IX.	CHARLES T. [9]	" March 25, 1848.	
X.	ELLEN M. [9]	" June 26, 1850.	
XI.	JOHN [9]	" June 26, 1856.	

Tillson Bartlett died in Worthington, Jan. 28, 1877, ag. 75 y. 10 m. 28 d.

Permelia (Tower) Bartlett died in Worthington, Sept. 25, 1867, ag. 55 y. 10 m. 1 d.

1195. **Ninth Generation.** **Tower.**

734. LUTHER B, [8], STEPHEN [7], STEPHEN [6], PETER [5], PETER [4], JERE-MIAH [3], JEREMIAH [2], JOHN [1].

Luther B. [8], son of Stephen [7] and Milley (Bartlett) Tower, b. Dec. 13, 1819; mar. Sabrina Tower [7], of Cummington, Mass., Nov. 25, 1841. She was b. in Cummington May 29, 1820, and was dau. of Warren [6] and Rhoda [7] (Tower) Tower.

Childr. born in Cummington.

	I.	MARY ADELINE [9]	born Jan. 14, 1843.
1393.	II.	HENRY LEWIS [9]	" March 27, 1845.
	III.	EUNICE AMELIA [9]	" April 22, 1848.
	IV.	CHARLES WESLEY [9]	" May 16, 1852.
	V.	SIDNEY HERBERT [9]	" May 30, 1855; died Oct. 6, 1861, ag. 6 y. 4 m. 7 d.
	VI.	MARIA ELIZABETH [9]	" Oct. 26, 1858; died June 12, 1878, ag. 19 y. 7 m. 17 d.
	VII.	ADELLA AGNES [9]	" Feb. 15, 1861.

1196. **Ninth Generation.** **Tower.**

735. JOHN M. [8], JOHN [7], STEPHEN [6], PETER [5], PETER [4], JEREMIAH [3], JEREMIAH [2], JOHN [1].

John M. [8], son of John [7] and Ruth (Reed) Tower, b. April 5, 1810; mar. widow Rebecca (Burroughs) Pickard She was b. in Nova Scotia March , 1813, and was dau. of John Burroughs.

Childr. born in Wilson, N. Y.

I. JOHN MADISON [9] born Oct. 31, 1844; died April 2, 1846, ag. 1 y.
5 m. 2 d.
II. EMMA [9] 　　　" Nov. 28, 1847.
III. STEPHEN [9] 　　" Sept. 17, 1849.
IV. REBECCA [9] 　　" Aug. 7, 1851.
V. LAURA [9] 　　　" Sept. 4, 1854; died

Rebecca (Burroughs) (Pickard) Tower died
John M. Tower [8] mar., 2d, Fanny Bills
Dec. 11, 1855. She was b. in Sharon, Vt.,
Dec. 9, 1815, and was dau. of Alfred and Betsey (Fuller)
Bills.

Childr.

VI. ESTHER [9] 　born May 6, 1857; died Aug. 14, 1858, ag. 1 y. 3 m. 8 d.
VII. HARMON F. [9] " Nov. 13, 1859; died 　　1886.

1197. Bartlett.　　Ninth Generation.　　　Tower.

735. CELEMNA [8], JOHN [7], STEPHEN [6], PETER [5], PETER [4], JEREMIAH [3],
JEREMIAH [2], JOHN [1].
Celemna [8], dau. of John [7] and Ruth (Reed) Tower, b.
May 5, 1815 ; mar. Hiram Bartlett, of Worthington, Mass.
Int. pub.
May 6, 1835. He was b.
1809, and was son of Edward and Mary (Farr)
Bartlett.

Childr. born in Worthington.

I. JOHN EDWARD [9] born Dec. , 1836; died June 22, 1837.
II. MARTHA [9] 　　　" June 3, 1839.
III. JOHN TOWER [9] 　" May 9, 1845; died Aug. 19, 1849, ag. 4 y. 3 m. 10 d.
IV. VENILA [9] 　　　" ; mar. Charles Rockwell, of Pittsfield, Mass.
V. VIRGIL [9] 　　　" Jan. 15, 1851; mar. Maria Gleason, of Hinsdale,
Mass.

Celemna (Tower) Bartlett died in Worthington, Oct. 26,
1853, ag. 38 y. 5 m. 21 d.
Hiram Bartlett died in Worthington, Jan. 8, 1877, ag. 68.

1198.　　　　Ninth Generation.　　　　Tower.

735. DEXTER [8], JOHN [7], STEPHEN [6], PETER [5], PETER [4], JEREMIAH [3],
JEREMIAH [2], JOHN [1].
Dexter [8], son of John [7] and Ruth (Reed) Tower, b.
March 12, 1817 ; mar. Irene B. Pierce [8], of Windsor, Mass.,
Nov. 30, 1847. She was b. in Windsor
Sept. 1, 1825, and was dau. of Isaac and Joanna [7] (Bailey)
Pierce.

PIERCE, BAILEY. TOWER.

Irene B.[8], Joanna[7], Lucy[6], Peter[5], Peter[4], Jeremiah[3], Jeremiah[2], John[1].

Childr.

1394.	I.	CLINTON BAILEY[9]	born March 1, 1858.
	II.	CLIMENA BELL[9]	" July 26, 1861; mar. ; 2 childr.
	III.	ELIZABETH JOANNA[9]	" July 30, 1863.
	IV.	PURLEY DEXTER[9]	" Nov. 28, 1867.

1199. Thayer. Ninth Generation. Tower.

735. LAURA[8], JOHN[7], STEPHEN[6], PETER[5], PETER[4], JEREMIAH[3], JEREMIAH[2], JOHN[1].

Laura[8], dau. of John[7] and Ruth (Reed) Tower, b.

May 13, 1819; mar. Cephas Thayer, of Chesterfield, Mass., March 6, 1850. He was b.

Jan. 30, 1824, and was son of Chapin and Tryphena (Montague) Thayer.

Childr. none.

1200. Ninth Generation. Tower.

735. ROSWELL[8], JOHN[7], STEPHEN[6], PETER[5], PETER[4], JEREMIAH[3], JEREMIAH[2], JOHN[1].

Roswell[8], son of John[7] and Ruth (Reed) Tower, b.

Sept. 4, 1821; mar. Elizabeth Bryant, of Chesterfield, Mass., April 8, 1851. She was b.

Sept. 19, 1833, and was dau. of Patrick and Bricea (Dumpleton) Bryant.

Childr. born in Windsor, Mass.

	I.	Infant[9]	born ; died
1395.	II.	ADA C.[9]	" March 5, 1854.
	III.	JOHN CLARENCE[9]	" July 2, 1855; died May 5, 1876, ag. 20 y. 10 m. 3 d.
	IV.	GEORGE MARTIN[9]	" April 15, 1857.
	V.	CLIFFORD RUSSELL[9]	" Nov. 23, 1858.
	VI.	LAURA IDA[9]	" Oct. 29, 1860; died April 16, 1865, ag. 4 y. 5 m. 18 d.
	VII.	FANNY AMANDA[9]	" Aug. 8, 1864.
	VIII.	FRED ELLIS[9]	" Feb. 10, 1867; died Dec. 28, 1867.
	IX.	Infant[9]	" ; "
	X.	ALICE MAUD[9]	" Sept. 2, 1870; " April 17, 1872, ag. 1 y. 7 m. 15 d.
	XI.	Infant[9]	" ; died

Roswell Tower[8] died in Windsor, Mass.

1201. Ninth Generation. Tower.

735. RUSSELL[8], JOHN[7], STEPHEN[6], PETER[5], PETER[4], JEREMIAH[3], JEREMIAH[2], JOHN[1].

Russell [8], son of John [7] and Ruth (Reed) Tower, b.
May 31, 1826 ; mar. Rebecca S. Granger, of Worthington,
July 2, 1865. She was b. in Worthington, Mass.,
Jan. 12, 1838, and was dau. of Abraham and Jane Granger.

. Childr.

I. CELEMNA EDITH [9] born March 17, 1867.
II. MARY ETTA [9]   " Sept. 26, 1868.
III. RUTH WINIFRED [9]   " Oct. 3, 1870; died Dec. 3, 1876, ag. 6 y. 2 m.

1202.   Ninth Generation.   Tower.

736. DAVID D.[8], DAVID [7], STEPHEN [6], PETER [5], PETER [4], JEREMIAH [3],
JEREMIAH [2], JOHN [1].
David D.[8], son of David [7] and Elsie M. (Dean) Tower, b.
Nov. 14, 1814 ; mar. Achsah E. Farrar [8]
Sept. 20, 1838. She was b. in Russell, N. Y.,
Aug. 7, 1820, and was dau. of Peter [7] and Lydia (Williams)
Farrar.

FARRAR.   TOWER.
Achsah E.[8], Peter [7], Lucy [6], Peter [5], Peter [4], Jeremiah [3], Jeremiah [2],
John [1].

Childr. born in Wilson, N. Y.

1396.	I. ELSIE [9]	born Jan. 15, 1840.
1397.	II. OLIVE [9]	" Aug. 4, 1841.
1398.	III. LYDIA [9]	" Aug. 23, 1843.
1399.	IV. DAVID A.[9]	" Aug. 8, 1845.
	V. SALEM [9]	" Nov. 6, 1847; mar. Jane Bowker.
	VI. ALPHORETTA [9]	" Sept. 6, 1849; died Aug. 8, 1870, ag. 24 y. 11 m. 2 d.
	VII. FRANK H.[9]	" Dec. 24, 1853.
1400.	VIII. EDGAR DEAN [9]	" July 11, 1858.
	IX. CHRISTOPHER E.[9]	" April 11, 1862.
	X. NORMA MAY [9]	" May 11, 1866.

David D. Tower [8] died in Wilson, April 30, 1887, ag. 72 y.
5 m. 16 d.

1203.   Ninth Generation.   Tower.

736. CHRISTOPHER M.[8], DAVID [7], STEPHEN [6], PETER [5], PETER [4], JERE-
MIAH [3], JEREMIAH [2], JOHN [1].
Christopher M.[8], son of David [7] and Elsie M. (Dean) Tower, b.
Sept. 20, 1818 ; mar. Mary E. A. Vinton, of Southbridge,
Mass.,
June 8, 1848. She was b.
Oct. 16, 1821, and was dau. of Lyman and Lucinda (Eddy)
Vinton.
Childr. none.

1204. **Ninth Generation.** **Tower.**

736. LUKE B.[8], DAVID[7], STEPHEN[6], PETER[5], PETER[4], JEREMIAH[3], JEREMIAH[2], JOHN[1].

Luke B.[8], son of David[7] and Elsie M. (Dean) Tower, b.
May 21, 1820; mar. Lucinda ———.
Luke B. Tower[8] died Oct. 2, 1859, ag. 39 y. 4 m. 12 d.
Lucinda ( ) Tower died 1872?

1205. **Ninth Generation.** **Tower.**

736. STEPHEN A.[8], DAVID[7], STEPHEN[6], PETER[5], PETER[4], JEREMIAH[3], JEREMIAH[2], JOHN[1].

Stephen A.[8], son of David[7] and Elsie M. (Dean) Tower, b.
Sept. 27, 1824; mar. Eliza Jane Martin, of New York,
June 20, 1861. She was b. in New York
Jan. 28, 1844, and was dau. of George W. and Susan A.
(Berrian) Martin.

Childr.

I. GEORGE W.[9] born Feb. 22, 1862.
II. EMMA[9] " May 24, 1865; died June 7, 1865.
III. HARRY C.[9] " Aug. 8, 1867; " Dec. , 1868, ag. 1 y. 4 m.
IV. GERTRUDE[9] " May 11, 1869.
V. ALANSON B.[9] " Dec. 10, 1871.

Stephen A. Tower[8] died in New York, Feb. 13, 1883, ag.
58 y. 4 m. 16 d.

1206. **Ninth Generation.** **Tower.**

736. LEVI L.[8], DAVID[7], STEPHEN[6], PETER[5], PETER[4], JEREMIAH[3], JEREMIAH[2], JOHN[1].

Levi L.[8], son of David[7] and Elsie M. (Dean) Tower, b.
Oct. 15, 1826; mar. Sophronia M. Thayer, of Windsor, Mass.,
Sept. 15, 1852. She was b.
Dec. 12, 1832, and was dau. of Timothy and Morandy Thayer.

Childr.

I. EMMA THAYER[9] born Feb. 13, 1854.
II. ANN ADELLA[9] " Dec. 25, 1855.
III. ADA ELIZA[9] " Oct. 3, 1857.
IV. GEORGE MARTIN[9] " Oct. 6, 1859.
V. LILLIAN ESTELLA[9] " July · 6, 1861.
VI. WALTER LINCOLN[9] " June 24, 1864.
VII. EDITH MABEL[9] " April 8, 1868.

1207. **Ninth Generation.** **Tower.**

736. JOHN W.[8], DAVID[7], STEPHEN[6], PETER[5], PETER[4], JEREMIAH[3], JEREMIAH[2], JOHN[1].

John W.[8], son of David [7] and Elsie M. (Dean) Tower, b.
Oct. 20, 1828 ; mar. Lizzie Peavey
Dec. 28, 1851.   She was b. in Tuftonsborough, N. H.,
May   4, 1832, and was dau. of Joseph L. and Mary (Drew)
    Peavey.

Childr.

	I.	WALTER HAZEN [9]	born	Oct. 5, 1852, in North Adams, Mass. ; died June 24, 1853.
	II.	MINNIE E.[9]	"	July 12, 1855, in Boston.
1401.	III.	GERTRUDE ANNIE [9]	"	April 25, 1858, "
1402.	IV.	LOUISA MATILDA [9]	"	Dec. 30, 1863, in Melrose, Mass.
	V.	BESSIE MAUD [9]	"	Feb. 23, 1871, in Boston.
	VI.	JOHN W.[9]	"	April 5, 1876, "

1208.   **Ninth Generation.**   **Tower.**

736. DANIEL T.[8], DAVID [7], STEPHEN [6], PETER [5], PETER [4], JEREMIAH [3], JEREMIAH [2], JOHN [1].

Daniel T.[8], son of David [7] and Elsie M. (Dean) Tower, b.
Aug. 13, 1831 ; mar., 2d, Georgia A. Patten
June 25, 1862.   She was b. in Newburyport, Mass.,
May 15, 1837, and was dau. of William C. and Mary A.
    (Lambert) Patten.

Childr.

I.	ANNIE GERTRUDE [9]	born	Jan. 5, 1865.
II.	MARY SANDERS [9]	"	Dec. 20, 1867.

Daniel T. Tower [8] died March 13, 1870, ag. 38 y. 7 m.

1209.   **Robinson.**   **Ninth Generation.**   **Tower.**

740. LYANDA [8], PETER [7], STEPHEN [6], PETER [5], PETER [4], JEREMIAH [3], JEREMIAH [2], JOHN [1].

Lyanda [8], dau. of Peter [7] and Hannah (Bailey) Tower, b.
Oct. 19, 1819 ; mar. Samuel Robinson
May 14, 1839.   He was b. in Kingston, Canada,
April 9, 1813, and was son of Samuel and Tamson (Field)
    Robinson.

Childr. born in Genesee Co., Mich.

	I.	EDWIN T.[9]	born	March 16, 1841; died Sept. 11, 1843, ag. 2 y. 5 m. 26 d.
	II.	CHARLES E.[9]	"	April 29, 1846.
1414.	III.	SAMUEL P.[9]	"	July 13, 1849.
	IV.	TAMSON LYANDA [9]	"	Jan. 16, 1854; died March 18, 1855, ag. 1 y. 2 m. 2 d.
	V.	GEORGE A.[9]	"	Aug. 17, 1856.
	VI.	THEODORE FRANK [9]	"	Dec. 13, 1861.

1210.   **Ninth Generation.**   **Tower.**

740.   JOHN E.[8], PETER [7], STEPHEN [6], PETER [5], PETER [4], JEREMIAH [3], JEREMIAH [2], JOHN [1].

John E.[8], son of Peter [7] and Hannah (Bailey) Tower, b.
Jan. 3, 1821; mar. Mary Jane Eggleston, of Porter, N. Y.,
Feb. 20, 1841. She was b.
Feb. 19, 1822, and was dau. of John and Huldah (Warren)
Eggleston.

Childr. born in Wilson, N. Y.

	I.	MORTIMER [9]	born June 1, 1843; died Dec. 10, 1864, ag. 21 y. 6 m. 9 d.
1403.	II.	OSCAR [9]	" Nov. 3, 1844.
1404.	III.	CHARLES G.[9]	" Sept. 7, 1846.
1405.	IV.	DE WITT CLINTON [9]	" Aug. 25, 1848.
1406.	V.	EUGENE HORTENSE [9]	" March 3, 1850.
1407.	VI.	BYRON EDWIN [9]	" Feb. 2, 1853.
1408.	VII.	MARY JOSEPHINE [9]	" Jan. 15, 1855.

1211.   **Ninth Generation.**   **Tower.**

740.   WILLIAM [8], PETER [7], STEPHEN [6], PETER [5], PETER [4], JEREMIAH [3], JEREMIAH [2], JOHN [1].

William [8], son of Peter [7] and Hannah (Bailey) Tower, b.
Oct. 1, 1822; mar. Anna L. Knowles, of Porter, N. Y.,
Oct. 1, 1849. She was b. in Wilson, N. Y.,
April 22, 1826, and was dau. of William and Olive (Davis)
Knowles.

Childr. born in Porter.

1409.	I.	GERTRUDE [9]	born May 21, 1851.
1410.	II.	ELLETTA [9]	" April 4, 1853.
1411.	III.	ALBERT KNOWLES [9]	" Aug. 3, 1855.
1412.	IV.	GLYCIE E.[9]	" June 6, 1857.
	V.	ELMER ELLSWORTH [9]	" Nov. 23, 1859; died Sept. 12, 1878, ag. 18 y. 9 m. 19 d.
	VI.	GLENWOOD L.[9]	" June 4, 1863.
	VII.	JESSIE B.[9]	" June 19, 1865; died.

1212.   **Ninth Generation.**   **Tower.**

740.   JAMES M.[8], PETER [7], STEPHEN [6], PETER [5], PETER [4], JEREMIAH [3], JEREMIAH [2], JOHN [1].

James M.[8], son of Peter [7] and Hannah (Bailey) Tower, b.
Oct. 1, 1824; mar. Mary Jane Huffman, of Michigan,
Jan. 14, 1847.

Child.

I. SARAH E.[9]

Mary J. (Huffman) Tower died in Davison, Mich.,
James M. Tower [8] mar., 2d, Elizabeth Hall, of Davison,
Oct. 2, 1858.

Childr.

II. JAMES MADISON [9] born   III. JANE ELIZABETH [9] born

James M. Tower [8] died in Davison, Feb. 6, 1880, ag. 55 y.
4 m. 5 d.

1213.   Ninth Generation.   Tower.

740. LUKE [8], PETER [7], STEPHEN [6], PETER [5], PETER [4], JEREMIAH [3],
JEREMIAH [2], JOHN [1].

Luke [8], son of Peter [7] and Olive (Baldwin) Tower, b.
May 24, 1834 ; mar. Bessie Hosmer
Dec. 15, 1868. She was. b.
May 18, 1841, and was dau. of Albert and Sarah (Palmer)
Hosmer.

Childr. born in Porter, N. Y.

I.   LUKE [9]   born May 15, 1872.
II.   PAUL [9]   "   Dec. 6, 1874 ; died April 15, 1875.
III. JENNIE CHURCHILL [9] "   July 6, 1877.

1214.   Ninth Generation.   Tower.

740. GEORGE P. [8], PETER [7], STEPHEN [6], PETER [5], PETER [4], JEREMIAH [3],
JEREMIAH [2], JOHN [1].

George P. [8], son of Peter [7] and Olive (Baldwin) Tower, b.
May 19, 1836 ; mar. Elizabeth Peet, of Lewiston, N. Y.,
May 23, 1860. She was b.
1838, and was dau. of Cyrus and Sally (Vanderlin)
Peet.

Childr. born in Porter, N. Y.

I.   FRANK R. [9]   born March 26, 1861 ; died Oct. 16, 1865, ag.
                               4 y. 6 m. 21 d.
II.   FRED P. [9]   "   March 16, 1863.
III. SARAH E. [9]   "   Sept.   7, 1864.
IV.   CYRUS P. [9]   "   Oct.   19, 1866.
V.   JENNIE S. [9]   "   June   3, 1868.
VI.   PETER B. [9] } Twins "   May 23, 1870.
VII. PORTER V. [9] }

Elizabeth (Peet) Tower died Dec. 15, 1879, ag. 41.
George P. Tower mar., 2d, widow Maria (Woolson) Holden,
Oct. 30, 1882. She was born
Aug. 1, 1846, and was dau. of Isaac and Elizabeth (Maxfield)
Woolson.

1215.   **Ninth Generation.**   **Tower.**

740. HARMON B.[8], PETER[7], STEPHEN[6], PETER[5], PETER[4], JERE-
MIAH[3], JEREMIAH[2], JOHN[1].

Harmon B.[8], son of Peter[7] and Olive (Baldwin) Tower, b.
Aug. 28, 1838; mar. Harriet M. Henry
June 10, 1861. She was b.
Jan. 13, 1845, and was dau. of Lewis and Isabel (Hosmer)
Henry.

Childr. born in Porter, N. Y.

I.	CLARENCE JEROME[9]	born March 4, 1862.
II.	ZERUAH ALLIE[9]	" March 21, 1864; mar. G. Elmer Manning, of Cambria, N.Y., Dec. 15, 1886.
III.	HARMON EUGENE[9]	" Dec. 6, 1865.
IV.	HATTIE BELL[9]	" Aug. 25, 1867.
V.	EMMA LYANDA[9]	" April 1, 1869.
VI.	FLORENCE M.[9]	" March 29, 1870; died July 11, 1871, ag. 1 y. 3 m. 13 d.
VII.	MAY[9]	" Dec. 25, 1871.
VIII.	LEWIS CLARK[9]	" Oct. 5, 1873.
IX.	WALTER CLEMENT[9]	" March 19, 1875.
X.	GERTRUDE GLYCENE[9]	" Aug. 22, 1876.
XI.	FLOSS[9]	" Aug. 2, 1877; died Aug. 26, 1877.
XII.	JESSIE FREMONT[9]	" Aug. 31, 1878.
XIII.	GRACE PEARL[9]	" July 11, 1880; died Sept. 9, 1880.
XIV.	ISA MECKIE[9]	" Aug. 31, 1881.
XV.	PETER[9]	" Jan. 13, 1883.

1216. Cowan.   **Ninth Generation.**   **Tower.**

740. EMUGENE[8], PETER[7], STEPHEN[6], PETER[5], PETER[4], JEREMIAH[3],
JEREMIAH[2], JOHN[1].

Emugene[8], dau. of Peter[7] and Olive (Baldwin) Tower, b.
Oct. 9, 1840; mar. John W. Cowan, of Porter, N. Y.,
April 21, 1860. He was b.
March 27, 1834, and was son of John and Sarah (Johnson)
Cowan.

Childr. born in Porter, N. Y.

I.	LILLIE BELL[9]	born March 30, 1861.
II.	BESSIE ELLA[9]	" Oct. 21, 1862; died.
III.	OLIVE A.[9]	" Jan. 1, 1864; mar. Linn Swain, Nov. 24, 1886.
IV.	SARAH E.[9]	" Sept. 30, 1865.
V.	EMUGENE[9]	" April 26, 1867.
VI.	RUBY ALICE[9]	" Nov. 29, 1868.
VII.	ELTON T. R.[9]	" Dec. 11, 1870

Emugene (Tower) Cowan died in Porter, Jan. 6, 1873, ag.
32 y. 2 m. 28 d.

1217.　　　　**Ninth Generation.**　　　　**Tower.**

740. PETER S.[8], PETER [7], STEPHEN [6], PETER [5], PETER [4], JEREMIAH [3], JEREMIAH [2], JOHN [1].

Peter S.[8], son of Peter [7] and Olive (Baldwin) Tower, b.

March 22, 1843 ; mar. Lizzie McConkey, of Lewiston, N. Y., Sept. 26, 1868. She was b. in West Guillimbury, Province of Ontario,

Sept. 6, 1848, and was dau. of John and Catherine J. (Johnson) McConkey.

Childr. born in Porter, N. Y.

   I. MARY BELLE [9] born Dec. 16, 1869.
  II. VICTORINE [9]　　" 　Dec. 3, 1872.
 III. DAN P.[9]　　　" 　Aug. 8, 1874.
 IV. RAY CLARKSON [9] " 　April 18, 1883.
  V. NELLIE [9]　　　" 　　　　1886.

1218.　Hosmer.　　　**Ninth Generation.**　　　**Tower.**

740. OLIVE A.[8], PETER [7], STEPHEN [6], PETER [5], PETER [4], JEREMIAH [3], JEREMIAH [2], JOHN [1].

Olive A.[8], dau. of Peter [7] and Olive (Baldwin) Tower, b.

June 15, 1846 ; mar. Lewis C. Hosmer, of Porter, N. Y., Feb. 13, 1869. He was b.

April 10, 1836, and was son of Prentice and Helen (Brown) Hosmer.

Childr. born in Porter, N. Y.

   I. HARRY [9]　　　born Nov. 18, 1869.
  II. LEWIS CASS [9]　" 　Sept. 1, 1871.
 III. GLEN P.[9] } Twins " 　Oct. 29, 1873; Ben R. died Oct. 7, 1874.
 IV. BEN R.[9] }
  V. MERRITT [9]　　" 　Aug. 1, 1876.
 VI. LOUIE [9]　　　" 　Sept. 28, 1881.

1219.　Wendell.　　　**Ninth Generation.**　　　**Tower.**

741. LUCETTA [8], OTIS [7], STEPHEN [6], PETER [5], PETER [4], JEREMIAH [3], JEREMIAH [2], JOHN [1].

Lucetta [8], dau. of Otis [7] and Susanna (Bowker) Tower, b.

Jan. 18, 1818 ; mar. Everett Wendell, of Rose, Mich., May 12, 1836. He was b. in Saratoga Co., N. Y.,

Jan. 14, 1816, and was son of John A. and Elizabeth (Bedford) Wendell.

Childr.

   I. MARY JANE [9]　　born Jan. 8, 1838.
  II. MARGARET [9]　　" 　Oct. 19, 1840.
 III. ANDREW FRANKLIN [9] " 　May 20, 1845.

Lucetta (Tower) Wendell died in Rose, Mich., Oct. 13, 1881, ag. 63 y. 8 m. 26 d.

1220. Allen. Ninth Generation. Tower.

741. MARY[8], OTIS[7], STEPHEN[6], PETER[5], PETER[4], JEREMIAH[3], JEREMIAH[2], JOHN[1].
Mary[8], dau. of Otis[7] and Susanna (Bowker) Tower, b.
Dec. 19, 1821 ; mar. Palmer Allen, of Wilson, N. Y.

Child.

I. NORMAN O.[9] born Dec. 25, 1839.

Mary (Tower) Allen died in Wilson, Jan. 12, 1849, ag. 27 y. 24 d.

1221. Hamlin. Ninth Generation. Tower.

741. ANNA[8], OTIS[7], STEPHEN[6], PETER[5], PETER[4], JEREMIAH[3], JEREMIAH[2], JOHN[1].
Anna[8], dau. of Otis[7] and Susanna (Bowker) Tower, b.
Oct. 15, 1823 ; mar. William Hamlin
Oct. 15, 1841. He was b.
May 6, 1821, and was son of Enos and Susanna (Smith) Hamlin.

Childr. born in Wilson, N. Y.

1398. I. ELI NELSON[9] born May 17, 1842.
II. GEORGE O.[9] " Feb. 11, 1845.
III. MARY ANNA[9] " Feb. 13, 1848.

Anna (Tower) Hamlin died in Wilson, March 30, 1854, ag. 30 y. 5 m. 15 d.

1222. Ninth Generation. Tower.

741. JOHN[8], OTIS[7], STEPHEN[6], PETER[5], PETER[4], JEREMIAH[3], JEREMIAH[2], JOHN[1].
John[8], son of Otis[7] and Susanna (Bowker) Tower, b.
Sept. 23, 1827; mar. Emery P. Aiken, of Wilson, N. Y.,
June 13, 1848. She was b.
July 12, 1827, and was dau. of Peter and Lucinda (Cleveland) Aiken.

Childr. born in Porter, N. Y.

1413. I. OTIS FRANKLIN[9] born July 20, 1850.
1414. II. MARY ETHELDA[9] " July 31, 1852.
1415. III. CHARLES DEWEY[9] " Nov. 6, 1854.

Emery P. (Aiken) Tower died in Porter.

1223. Adams.   Ninth Generation.   Tower.

741. CAROLINE[8], OTIS[7], STEPHEN[6], PETER[5], PETER[4], JEREMIAH[3]
     JEREMIAH[2], JOHN[1].

Caroline[8], dau. of Otis[7] and Susanna (Bowker) Tower, b.
April 6, 1830; mar. John Q. Adams, of Wilson, N. Y.,
April 17, 1853. He was b. in Lockport, N. Y.,
March 3, 1831, and was son of Amos and Leah (McDonald)
     Adams.

Childr. born in Wilson.
  I.   SUSAN EMMA[9]   born Jan. 18, 1854.
  II. ADA JOANNA[9]   "   Feb. 9, 1857.
  III. CARIE EMARETT[9]   "   Jan. 6, 1860.

1224. Vosburg.   Ninth Generation.   Tower.

741. ADELINE S.[8], OTIS[7], STEPHEN[6], PETER[5], PETER[4], JEREMIAH[3],
     JEREMIAH[2], JOHN[1].

Adeline S.[8], dau. of Otis[7] and Susanna (Bowker) Tower, b.
July 16, 1832; mar. Edward Vosburg, of Wilson, N. Y.,
Oct.   , 1852. He was b.
Feb. 1, 1830, and was son of Abraham and Mary Ann
     Vosburg.

Childr. born in Wilson.
  I.   ANNA EDNEY[9]   born Dec. 29, 1853.
  II. HATTIE ANNEMEL[9]   "   Jan. 25, 1859; died Aug. 18, 1867, ag. 8 y.
                                 6 m. 24 d.
  III. LILLIAN LAZETTE[9]   "   Oct. 25, 1861.

Adeline S. (Tower) Vosburg died in Wilson, Oct. 15, 1864,
ag. 32 y. 2 m. 30 d.

1225. Pierce.   Ninth Generation.   Tower.

743. BETSEY[8], ASA[7], ASA[6], PETER[5], PETER[4], JEREMIAH[3], JERE-
     MIAH[2], JOHN[1].

Betsey[8], dau. of Asa[7] and Clarissa (Bates) Tower, b.
Sept. 12, 1816; mar. Almond T. Pierce, of Windsor, Mass.,
Nov. 17, 1836. He was b.
Feb. 17, 1814.

Childr. born in Windsor.
  I.   MARION J.[9]   born Sept. 19, 1837.
  II. ORLANDO W.[9]   "   Aug. 30, 1839.
  III. EUGENE W.[9]   "   May 28, 1841; died March 22, 1863, ag. 21 y.
                                 9 m. 25 d.
  IV. LUCRETIA TOWER[9]   "   June 15, 1843.
  V.   SARAH I.[9]   "   May 26, 1845.
  VI. ALMOND O.[9]   "   June 24, 1847.

VII.   EDGAR H.[9]   born Nov. 20, 1850.
VIII. ROSCOE W.[9]   "   May 15, 1858.

1226.   **Ninth Generation.**   **Tower.**

743. WILLIAM [8], ASA [7], ASA [6], PETER [5], PETER [4], JEREMIAH [3], JERE-
      MIAH [2], JOHN [1].
      William [8], son of Asa [7] and Clarissa (Bates) Tower, b.
      May 20, 1818; mar. Mary A. Stetson, of Plainfield, Mass.,
      Nov. 17, 1842. She was b.
      Oct. 14, 1824, and was dau. of Judson and Abigail (Thayer)
      Stetson.

                        Childr.

      1416.   I.   HARRIET E.[9]   born July 25, 1844.
      1417.   II.   MARY E.[9]   "   Aug. 10, 1846.
      1418.   III. WILLIAM WESLEY [9]   "   Dec. 26, 1848.
              IV.   WILLIS F.[9]   "   March 4, 1855.
      1419.   V.   JETSON A.[9]   "   Feb.   5, 1857.

1227. Hamilton.   **Ninth Generation.**   **Tower.**

743. CLARISSA [8], ASA [7], ASA [6], PETER [5], PETER [4], JEREMIAH [3], JERE-
      MIAH [2], JOHN [1].
      Clarissa [8], dau. of Asa [7] and Clarissa (Bates) Tower, b.
      Jan. 19, 1822; mar. John O. Hamilton, of Becket, Mass.
      Int. pub.
      Nov. 9, 1845.

                   Childr. none.

      Clarissa (Tower) Hamilton died   1847, ag. 25.

1228.   **Ninth Generation.**   **Tower.**

743. ALMOND J.[8], ASA [7], ASA [6], PETER [5], PETER [4], JEREMIAH [3],
      JEREMIAH [2], JOHN [1].
      Almond J.[8], son of Asa [7] and Clarissa (Bates) Tower, b.
      May 18, 1828; mar. Mary U. Corwin, of Lockport, Ill.,
      Sept. 28, 1852. She was b. in Lima, Ill.,
      Nov. 21, 1834, and was dau. of Nathan and Sophia (Jewell)
      Corwin.

                        Childr.

              I.   EVA LELIA [9]   born Jan. 21, 1854.
              II.   WILLIAM THOMAS [9]   "   Oct. 30, 1855.
      1420.   III. NATHAN EUGENE [9]   "   Aug. 2, 1858.
              IV.   GEORGE HENRY [9]   "   Dec. 2, 1860.
      1421.   V.   LILA ALICE [9]   "   Nov. 3, 1862.
              VI.   ALMON FRANK [9]   "   Nov. 2, 1866.
              VII. MARY SOPHIA [9]   "   Feb. 12, 1869.

Almond J. Tower [8] died Sept. 28, 1869, ag. 41 y. 4 m. 11 d.

1229. Tucker.   Ninth Generation.   Tower.

743. MARY S.[8], ASA [7], ASA [6], PETER [5], PETER [4], JEREMIAH [3], JERE-
      MIAH [2], JOHN [1].

Mary S.[8], dau. of Asa [7] and Clarissa (Bates) Tower, b.
April 24, 1834 ; mar. Edwin Herbert Tucker, of Windsor,
      Mass.,
March 4, 1854.   He was b. in Cummington, Mass.,
      1832, and was son of Francis and Docian Tucker.

Childr.

I.   ALICE M.[9] born April 25, 1857.
II. NETTIE M.[9] " Jan.   , 1860.
III. CLARA [9]   "   1862; died
IV. Infant [9]   "   1865; "

1230. Phillips.   Ninth Generation.   Tower.

748. LYDIA [8], DYER [7], ASA [6], PETER [5], PETER [4], JEREMIAH [3], JERE-
      MIAH [2], JOHN [1].

Lydia [8], dau. of Dyer [7] and Lydia (Wilkes) Tower, b.
March 16, 1838 ; mar. Lewis E. Phillips in Plainfield, Mass.,
Oct. 20, 1853.   He was b. in Ashfield, Mass.,
Feb. 13, 1831, and was son of Abiram and Lucretia Phillips.

Childr.

I.   MINNIE E.[9] born June 15, 1856, in Oshkosh, Wis.
II. LUCY E.[9]   " March 9, 1859, in Bear Creek, Wis.
III. RUFUS [9]   " Dec. 10, 1865,   "   "
IV. RALPH [9]   " Oct. 27, 1867,   "   "

Lewis E. Phillips died in Bear Creek, Jan. 21, 1870, ag. 38 y.
      11 m. 5 d.

1231.   Ninth Generation.   Tower.

748. CYRUS R.[8], DYER [7], ASA [6], PETER [5], PETER [4], JEREMIAH [3], JERE-
      MIAH [2], JOHN [1].

Cyrus R.[8], son of Dyer [7], and Lydia (Wilkes) Tower, b.
May 23, 1843 ; mar. Julia S. Smith, of Worthington, Mass.,
May 23, 1867.   She was b. in Worthington
May 24, 1845, and was dau. of Joseph M. and Orrel R. Smith.

Childr. none.

1232.   Ninth Generation.   Tower.

749. DAVID H.[8], STEPHEN D.[7], ASA [6], PETER [5], PETER [4], JEREMIAH [3],
      JEREMIAH [2], JOHN [1].

David H.[8], son of Stephen D.[7] and Esther E. (Beals) Tower, b.

March 7, 1832; mar. Margaret Young in Huntington, Mass.,
July 2, 1859. She was born in Glasgow, Scotland,
May 30, 1838, and was dau. of James and Agnes (Allen)
Young.

Childr.

I. Son [9] born May 4, 1866; died in infancy.
II. WALTER [9] " Dec. 26, 1868, in Dalton, Mass.

1233. **Ninth Generation.** **Tower.**

749. JARVIS E.[8], STEPHEN D.[7], ASA [6], PETER [5], PETER [4], JEREMIAH [3],
JEREMIAH [2], JOHN [1].
Jarvis E.[8], son of Stephen D.[7] and Esther E. (Beals) Tower, b.
Sept. 18, 1834 ; mar. Julia C. Grover, of Lee, Mass.,
April 18, 1862. She was b.
1843, and was dau. of Elijah and Martha Grover.

Child.

I. MARY ESTHER [9] born March 28, 1863; died April 6, 1863.

1234. **Ninth Generation.** **Tower.**

749. HENRY A.[8], STEPHEN D.[7], ASA [6], PETER [5], PETER [4], JEREMIAH [3],
JEREMIAH [2], JOHN [1].
Henry A.[8], son of Stephen D.[7], and Esther E. (Beals) Tower, b.
May 27, 1836 ; mar. Sylvia Howland Hussey in Cornwall,
N. Y.,
Dec. 26, 1858. She was b. in New Bedford, Mass.,
Dec. 15, 1834, and was dau. of William and Jane (Perry)
Hussey.

Childr. born in Newburg, N. Y.

I. ROBERT H.[9] born May 6, 1863, died Jan. 14, 1865, ag. 1 y. 8 m. 8 d.
II. WILLIAM A.[9] " Feb. 20, 1865; " Oct. 22, 1866, ag. 1 y. 8 m. 2 d.
III. JOHN TUCKER [9] " July 11, 1867.
IV. MARY A.[9] " May 25, 1872.
V. BESSIE H.[9] " July 16, 1874.

Sylvia H. (Hussey) Tower died Jan. 7, 1878, ag. 43 y. 23 d
Henry A. Tower[8] mar., 2d, Annie McGuigan in Newburg
March 20, 1879. She was b. in County of Antrim, Ireland,
Nov. 30, 1834, and was dau. of Robert and Bridget (Mullen)
McGuigan.

Child.

VI. LIZZIE [9] born May 25, 1880.

1235. Congdon. Ninth Generation. Tower.

749. EMMA E.[8], STEPHEN D.[7], ASA [6], PETER [5], PETER [4], JEREMIAH [3], JEREMIAH [2], JOHN [1].

Emma E.[8], dau. of Stephen D.[7] and Esther E.(Beals) Tower, b. Aug. 22, 1838; mar. Isaac Congdon, of Pomfret, Conn., Dec. 11, 1853. He was b. in Pomfret Jan. 23, 1833, and was son of Hezekiah and Elizabeth (Medbury) Congdon.

Childr.

I.	ELLEN ELIZABETH [9]	born June 12, 1854, in Windsor, Mass.
II.	IDA ESTHER [9]	" Nov. 29, 1855, in Dalton,	"
III.	SARAH JANE [9]	" Aug. 25, 1857,	"	"
IV.	HARRIET LOUISA [9]	" July 31, 1859,	"	"
V.	EDWIN HORATIO [9]	" Oct. 26, 1861,	"	"
VI.	WILLIS AUGUSTUS [9]	" Aug. 27, 1866,	"	"
VII.	EDGAR EUGENE [9]	" July 14, 1868,	"	"

1236. Newell. Ninth Generation. Tower.

749. ELMA L.[8]. STEPHEN D.[7], ASA [6], PETER [5], PETER [4], JEREMIAH [3], JEREMIAH [2], JOHN [1].

Elma L.[8], dau. of Stephen D.[7] and Esther E. (Beals) Tower, b. May 8, 1840; mar Benjamin Franklin Newell, of Dalton, Mass., Nov. 12, 1862. He was b. in South Berwick, Me., Jan. 7, 1818, and was son of David and Abigail Newell.

Childr.

I.	ROBERT BRUCE [9]	born Oct. 1, 1863
II.	MARY A.[9]	" Sept. 1, 1865, died April 3, 1872, ag. 6 y. 7 m 2 d.
III.	MAGGIE MINNIE [9]	" Feb. 14, 1867; " Sept. 23, 1871, ag. 4 y. 7 m. 7 d.
IV.	GEORGE STEPHEN [9]	" May 1, 1868; " Sept. 2, 1870, ag. 1 y. 4 m. 1 d.
V.	NELLIE ELIZA [9]	" Jan. 23, 1875.

1237. Newell. Ninth Generation. Tower.

749. LUCIA D. D.[8], STEPHEN D.[7], ASA [6], PETER [5], PETER [4], JEREMIAH [3], JEREMIAH [2], JOHN [1].

Lucia D. D.[8], dau. of Stephen D.[7] and Esther E. (Beals) Tower, b. Sept. 29, 1844; mar. William F. Newell, of Westfield, Mass., Dec. 16, 1867. He was b. 1844, and was son of Benjamin F. and Margaret (Larrabee) Newell.

Childr.

I. WILLIAM WALLACE [9] born Nov. 23, 1871, in Dalton, Mass.
II. GEORGE STEPHEN [9] " May , 1873, in Hinsdale, "

1238. **Ninth Generation.** **Tower.**

749. ASHLEY B.[8], STEPHEN D.[7], ASA [6], PETER [5], PETER [4], JEREMIAH [3],
JEREMIAH [2], JOHN [1].
Ashley B.[8], son of Stephen D.[7] and Esther E. (Beals)
Tower, b.
June 26, 1847 ; mar. Pamela Jane Fritt, of Holyoke, Mass.,
March 10, 1875. She was b. in Chicopee, Mass.,
Jan. , 1847, and was dau. of Sylvester and Maria Fritt.

Childr. none.

1239. Hitt. **Ninth Generation.** **Tower.**

749. MAHALA J.[8], STEPHEN D.[7], ASA [6], PETER [5], PETER [4], JEREMIAH [3],
JEREMIAH [2], JOHN [1].
Mahala J.[8], dau. of Stephen D.[7] and Esther E. (Beals)
Tower, b.
March 21, 1850 ; mar. Harry W. Hitt, of Dalton, Mass.,
May 29, 1873. He was b. in Devonshire, England,
Feb. 5, 1841, and was son of John and Mary Ann (West)
Hitt.

Child.

I. CORA MAY [9] born April 14, 1877.

1240. Allen. **Ninth Generation.** **Tower.**

750. MARY J.[8], MOSES [7], MALACHI [6], MALACHI [5], PETER [4], JERE-
MIAH [3], JEREMIAH [2], JOHN [1].
Mary J.[8], dau. of Moses [7] and Mary (Binney) Tower, b.
Feb. 24, 1810 ; mar. Ralph W. Allen in Hingham, Mass.,
Aug. 10, 1835. He was b. in Enfield, Conn.,
Feb. 16, 1812, and was son of Chester and Margaret (Shaw)
Allen.

Childr.

I. MARY JANE [9] born Sept. 16, 1836, in Southbridge, Mass.
II. SARAH BINNEY [9] " Jan. 4, 1838, " Manchester, Conn.; died
Oct. 4, 1838.
III. SARAH BINNEY [9] " March 26, 1839, " " "
IV. WILLARD SPENCER [9] " May 12, 1841, " Eastford, "
V. ANNA SOPHIA [9] " Nov. 3, 1842, " New London, " ; died
Oct. 3, 1843.

VI.   Thomas Jones [9]   born Jan. 10, 1846, in Norwich, Conn.
VII. Ella Anna [9]   "   Sept. 5, 1847, " Providence, R. I.
VIII. Charles Fabyan [9] "   Dec. 1, 1848, "   "   "

Mary J. (Tower) Allen died in Malden, Mass., Nov. 25, 1883, ag. 73 y. 8 m. 29 d.

1241.   **Ninth Generation.**   **Tower.**

750. Moses B.[8], Moses [7], Malachi [6], Malachi [5], Peter [4], Jere-
      miah [3], Jeremiah [2], John [1].
      Moses B.[8], son of Moses [7] and Mary (Binney) Tower, b.
      April 26, 1814 ; mar. Olive Gould Cushing, of Hull, Mass.,
      June 10, 1838. She was b. in Hull
      May 12, 1816, and was dau. of Pyam and Olive (Lovell)
      Cushing.

                    Childr. born in Hull.

1422. I.   Mary Binney [9]   born July 13, 1839.
1423. II.   Lydia Cushing [9]   "   Sept. 1, 1841.
1424. III. Olive Gould [9]   "   Oct. 29, 1844.
1425. IV.   Moses Spencer [9]   "   Jan 31, 1848.
       V.   Abner Jones [9]   "   June 27, 1851 ; mar. Caroline Morse, of
                                      Easton, Mass.
      VI.   Florence Estelle [9] "   Oct. 21, 1856.

1242.   **Ninth Generation.**   **Tower.**

750. Thomas J.[8], Moses [7], Malachi [6], Malachi [5], Peter [4], Jere-
      miah [3], Jeremiah [2], John [1].
      Thomas J.[8], son of Moses [7] and Mary (Binney) Tower, b.
      Sept. 29, 1818 ; mar. Mary Wilder Lane [8], of Hingham,
      July 9, 1843. She was b. in Hingham, Mass.,
      Oct. 18, 1821, and was dau. of Elias N.[7] and Mary (Hatch)
      Lane.

Lane.   Tower.
Mary W.[8], Elias N.[7], Peter [6], Lucy [5], Peter [4], Jeremiah [3], Jeremiah [2],
John [1].

                    Childr. none.

Thomas J. Tower [8] died in Hingham, April 6, 1847, ag. 28 y. 6 m. 7 d.
Mary W.[8] (Lane) Tower mar., 2d, Joseph P. Dunbar [6], of Weymouth, Mass.,
May 13, 1848. He was b. in Weymouth
Aug. 14, 1821, and was son of Joseph [5] and Sarah (Turner) Dunbar.

Dunbar.   Tower.
Joseph P.[6], Joseph [5], Rachel [4], Joseph [3], Samuel [2], John [1].

Childr.

I. MARY PORTER [9] born Feb. 16, 1849.
II. S. E.[9] (Daughter) " Dec. 31, 1852; died Aug. 18, 1854, ag. 1 y.
7 m. 18 d.
III. SARAH ABBY TURNER [9] " July 15, 1859.
IV. LIZIETTA [9] " Dec. 17, 1860.

1243. Ninth Generation. Tower.

750. JOHN W.[8], MOSES [7], MALACHI [6], MALACHI [5], PETER [4], JERE-
MIAH [3], JEREMIAH [2], JOHN [1].
John W.[8], son of Moses [7] and Mary (Binney) Tower, b.
Aug. 11, 1821; mar. Jane Binney Reed, of Hull, Mass.,
Feb. 13, 1848. She was b. in Hull
July 24, 1819, and was dau. of John and Amy (Dill) Reed.
Jane B. (Reed) Tower died in Hull, Aug. 3, 1866, ag. 47 y.
10 d.

1244. Ninth Generation. Tower.

751. MARTIN W.[8], PETER [7], MALACHI [6], MALACHI [5], PETER [4], JERE-
MIAH [3], JEREMIAH [2], JOHN [1].
Martin W.[8], son of Peter [7] and Susan (Churchill) Tower, b.
Nov. 10, 1806; mar. Eleanor Lancaster Spencer, of Orono,
Me.,
Oct. 30, 1828. She was b. in Orono
April 4, 1811, and was dau. of Asa and Sarah Spencer.

Childr.

I. ELIZABETH BATHSHEBA [9] born May 14, 1832.
II. SARAH ANN [9] " Nov. 14, 1833.
III. MARY ELEANORIA [9] " Aug. 27, 1835.
IV. CAROLINE VICTORIA [9] " Sept. 8, 1838.
1426. V. MARTIN VAN BUREN [9] " Oct. 5, 1841.
VI. FRANCIS MARION [9] " March 6, 1843.
VII. WASHINGTON IRVING [9] " Oct. 11, 1844; died March 17,
1850, ag. 3 y. 5 m. 6 d.
VIII. PRINCE ALBERT [9] " June 21, 1846.
IX. HENRY SNOW [9] " Sept. 27, 1849; died April 1,
1850.
X. ELLA MARION [9] " May 30, 1851.
XI. ADA ASORIA [9] " April 11, 1856; died Aug. 10,
1856.

1245. Ninth Generation. Tower.

751. MALACHI [8], PETER [7], MALACHI [6], MALACHI [5], PETER [4], JERE-
MIAH [3], JEREMIAH [2], JOHN [1].
Malachi [8], son of Peter [7] and Susan (Churchill) Tower, b.

June 30, 1808 ; mar. Ruth Hunt, of Belmont, Me.,
Sept.　, 1828.　She was b. in Belmont
　　　　and was dau. of Seth and Rachel (Brooks) Hunt.

Child.

I.　WARREN [9] born　　　　　　　; died Aug. 10, 1838.

Malachi Tower [8] died in Lincolnville, Me., Aug. 10, 1838, ag.
　30 y. 1 m. 10 d.

1246.　Elms.　　Ninth Generation.　　　　Tower.

751.　EUNICE C. [8], PETER [7], MALACHI [6], MALACHI [5], PETER [4], JERE-
　　　MIAH [3], JEREMIAH [2], JOHN [1].

Eunice C. [8], dau. of Peter [7] and Susan (Churchill) Tower, b.
May 12, 1810 ; mar. Nathaniel Elms in Belmont, Me.,
Jan. 21, 1830.　He was b. in Searsmont, Me.,
　　　　1807, and was son of Benjamin and Sarah Elms.

Childr.

I.　JOHN [9]　　　born
II.　SARAH E. [9]　　"　Dec. 31, 1840, in Searsmont, Me.
III.　LUCY A. [9]　　"　Dec. 31, 1842, "　　"　　"
IV.　WILLIAM M. [9] "　Mar. 23, 1845, "　　"　　"

Nathaniel Elms died in Searsmont, Me., May 17, 1845, ag. 38.
Eunice C. (Tower) Elms died in Searsmont, June 17,
　1853, ag. 43 y. 1 m. 5 d.

1247.　　　　　Ninth Generation.　　　　Tower.

751.　WARNER C. [8], PETER [7], MALACHI [6], MALACHI [5], PETER [4], JERE-
　　　MIAH [3], JEREMIAH [2], JOHN [1].

Warner C. [8], son of Peter [7] and Susan (Churchill) Tower, b.
Jan. 2, 1814 ; mar. Mary Ann Jones in Lincolnville, Me.,
Jan. 2, 1841.　She was b. in Lincolnville
July 14, 1817, and was dau. of Rev. Benjamin and Mary
　Jones.

Childr. born in Lincolnville.

I.　RUEL WARNER [9]　　born Oct. 31, 1843; died April 4, 1850,
　　　　　　　　　　　　　　　ag. 6 y. 5 m. 4 d.
1427.　II.　ELISHA JONES [9]　　"　June 1, 1846.
III.　HANNAH VERONA [9]　　"　March , 1849.
IV.　RUEL [9]　　　　　"　Aug. 10, 1852; died Dec. 31, 1865,
　　　　　　　　　　　　　ag. 13 y. 4 m. 21 d.
V.　FLORENCE NIGHTINGALE [9] "　Nov. 13, 1854.

1248. **Ninth Generation.** **Tower.**

751. PETER [8], PETER [7], MALACHI [6], MALACHI [5], PETER [4], JEREMIAH [3], JEREMIAH [2], JOHN [1].
Peter [8], son of Peter [7] and Susan (Churchill) Tower, b.
April 24, 1816 ; mar. Huldah Frohawk, of Searsmont, Me.,
Dec. 4, 1837. She was b. in Searsmont
July 10, 1818, and was dau. of Solomon and Nancy
Frohawk.

Childr.

I. FRANCIS AUGUSTUS [9] born Feb. 6, 1840; mar.; childr. Frank, Percy.
II. MARY ALLEN [9] " July 1, 1842.
III. ALTHEA ELIZABETH [9] " Aug. 4, 1845.
IV. CHARLES [9] " Aug. 2, 1847.
V. JULIA [9] " Jan. 30, 1856.

1249. **Ninth Generation.** **Tower.**

751. ELBRIDGE G. [8], PETER [7], MALACHI [6], MALACHI [5], PETER [4], JERE-
MIAH [3], JEREMIAH [2], JOHN [1].
Elbridge G. [8], son of Peter [7] and Susan (Churchill) Tower, b.
March 29, 1818 ; mar. Mary G. Edgecomb in Belfast, Me.,
March 9, 1845. She was b. in Hartford, Me.,
Sept. 26, 1824, and was dau. of Aaron and Sarah (Tink-
ham) Edgecomb.

Childr. born in Belmont, Me.

1428. I. GEORGE WASHINGTON [9] born Oct. 22, 1846.
1429. II. GEORGIANA [9] " Oct. 9, 1848.

Elbridge G. Tower [8] died in Belmont, Me., Nov. 18, 1848, ag.
30 y. 7 m. 20 d.

1250. **Warren.** **Ninth Generation.** **Tower.**

751. SUSAN G. [8], PETER [7], MALACHI [6], MALACHI [5], PETER [4], JERE-
MIAH [3], JEREMIAH [2], JOHN [1].
Susan G. [8], dau. of Peter [7] and Susan (Churchill) Tower, b.
Dec. 16, 1819 ; mar. Nathaniel Gerrish Warren
Oct. 31, 1846. He was b. in Brookfield, N. H.,
May 7, 1818, and was son of John and Sarah (Brown)
Warren.

Childr.

I. IRENA FRANCES [9] born Aug. 22, 1847, in Boston.
II. MARIA ISABELL [9] " July 21, 1849, " " ; died April 6,
1851, ag. 1 y. 8 m. 16 d.
III. PHILEMON DUGAN [9] " June 26, 1850, in Boston.

IV. CHARLES EDDY[9]   born April 1, 1852, in Charlestown ; died Aug.
                           11, 1854, ag. 2 y. 4 m. 10 d.

V. JESSE[9]   " Aug. 11, 1855, in Charlestown ; died Aug.
                           22, 1855.

1251.   **Ninth Generation.**   **Tower.**

751. NEHEMIAH H.[8], PETER[7], MALACHI[6], MALACHI[5], PETER[4], JERE-
MIAH[3], JEREMIAH[2], JOHN[1].
Nehemiah H.[8], son of Peter[7] and Susan (Churchill) Tower, b.
July 31, 1822 ; mar. Mary Ann Buttler in Lincolnville, Me.,
May 2, 1853. She was b. in Union, Me.,
          and was dau. of George W. and Eleanor (Collins)
Buttler.
          Childr. born in Belmont, Me.

     I. WASHINGTON WELLS[9] born Jan. 17, 1856.
    II. JOHN PHINEAS[9]   " Aug. 1, 1858.
   III. SUSAN ANN[9]   " March 9, 1861.
   IV. MENDORA FRANCES[9]   " Sept. 30, 1865.
    V. MABEL RACHEL[9]   " Dec. 3, 1871.
   VI. HARRIET BERTHA[9]   " Jan. 27, 1873.

1252.   **Ninth Generation.**   **Tower.**

751. JOHN C[8], PETER[7], MALACHI[6], MALACHI[5], PETER[4], JERE-
MIAH[3], JEREMIAH[2], JOHN[1].
John C.[8], son of Peter[7] and Susan (Churchill) Tower, b.
April 24, 1825 ; mar. Carrie M. Clark in Rockland, Me.,
          She was dau. of George and   (Flagg) Clark.
                       Child.
   I. Daughter[9] born   in Rockland, Me.
John C. Tower[8] died in Rockland, April   , 1870, ag. 45.

1253. Curtis.   **Ninth Generation.**   **Tower.**

752. SARAH E.[8], COMFORT[7], MALACHI[6], MALACHI[5], PETER[4], JERE-
MIAH[3], JEREMIAH[2], JOHN[1].
Sarah E.[8], dau. of Comfort[7] and Priscilla (Hobart) Tower, b.
May 15, 1834 ; mar. Samuel Cushing Curtis, of Hingham,
Oct. 15, 1854. He was b. in Hingham, Mass.,
Jan. 26, 1827, and was son of Enoch and Betsey (Cushing)
   Curtis.
          Childr. born in Hingham.

   I. JULIA ELIZABETH[9] born Oct. 15, 1855 ; died Dec. 31, 1860, ag. 5 y.
                           2 m. 16 d.
  II. WILBUR CUSHING[9]   " Feb. 21, 1860.
 III. JULIETTA[9]   " June 9, 1862; died Sept. 10, 1862.
 IV. JULIETTA[9]   " June 11, 1863; " Sept. 11, 1863.
  V. Child[9] } Twins   " March 3, 1866; March 4, 1866.
 VI. Child[9] }

1254.   Ninth Generation.   Tower.

752. JOHN M.⁸, COMFORT⁷, MALACHI⁶, MALACHI⁵, PETER⁴, JERE-
        MIAH³, JEREMIAH², JOHN¹.
      John M.⁸, son of Comfort⁷ and Priscilla (Hobart) Tower, b.
      July 21, 1836; mar. Harriet Atwood Souther⁷, of Hingham,
      Nov. 23, 1860. She was b. in Hingham, Mass.,
      Aug. 29, 1829, and was dau. of Daniel⁶ and Rebecca⁷ (Tower)
      Souther.

SOUTHER.   TOWER.

Harriet A.⁷ ˒ ⁸ { Daniel⁶, Daniel⁵, Joseph⁴, Content⁸
                  Rebecca⁷, Jesse⁶, Robert⁵, David⁴, Heze- } Ibrook², John¹.
                  kiah⁸

                Childr. born in Hingham.

      I.   JOHN BURLEY⁹   born Oct. 15, 1861; died April 25, 1868, ag.
                                6 y. 6 m. 11 d.
1430. II. FRANK ATWOOD⁹   "   April 13, 1863.
      III. HERBERT STARR⁹ "   Oct. 7, 1865; died April 27, 1868, ag.
                                2 y. 6 m. 21 d.
      IV. FLORENCE LOUISE⁹ "   July 1, 1869.

1255.   Ninth Generation.   Tower.

753. JOHN H.⁸, JOHN H.⁷, MALACHI⁶, MALACHI⁵, PETER⁴, JERE-
        MIAH³, JEREMIAH², JOHN¹.
      John H.⁸, son of John H.⁷ and Phebe (Poland) Tower, b.
      March 1, 1819; mar. Jane Adelia Woodruff, of Underhill, Vt.,
      Sept. 26, 1843. She was b. in Essex, Vt.,
      Aug. 10, 1822, and was dau. of Nathan and Annie (Camp-
      bell) Woodruff.

                        Childr.

1431. I. CORNELIUS POLAND⁹ born Sept. 30, 1844, in Underhill.
1432. II. WILLIAM HANCOCK⁹ "   July 27, 1859, in Towerville, Wis.
          Three other children who died in infancy.

1256.   Ninth Generation.   Tower.

753. JOSEPH P.⁸, JOHN H.⁷, MALACHI⁶, MALACHI⁵, PETER⁴, JERE-
        MIAH³, JEREMIAH², JOHN¹.
      Joseph P.⁸, son of John H.⁷ and Phebe (Poland) Tower, b.
      Aug. 18, 1821; mar. Lydia Woodburn, of Underhill, Vt.,
      Oct.   , 1841. She was b. in Rutland, Vt.,
      March , 1820, and was dau. of David and Sarah (Anderson)
      Woodburn.

Childr.

I.   WILLIAM LORING⁹ born May 21, 1845.
II. ELLEN⁹   " April 22, 1849; mar. G. Jenkins; 2d, C.
                          Sherman.
III. MARION⁹   " June 6, 1851; mar. Samuel Walker.

1257. Brooks.   Ninth Generation.   Tower.

756. ROSALIE⁸, EDWIN W.⁷, GAD H.⁶, LYNDE⁵, JAMES⁴, BENJA-
     MIN³, BENJAMIN², JOHN¹.
     Rosalie⁸, dau. of Edwin W.⁷ and Mary A. (Deering) Tower, b.
     Oct. 28, 1840; mar. Aretas Fleuniken Brooks
     April 30, 1867.   He was b. in Clarksburg, W. Va.,
     June 4, 1831, and was son of Asa and Hannah (Fleuniken)
     Brooks.
                Childr. born in Pittsburg, Penn.

I.   EDWIN TOWER⁹   born Nov. 10, 1869; died Feb. 19, 1871, ag. 1 y.
                       3 m. 11 d.
II. ROSALIE⁹   " June 20, 1871; " Oct. 24, 1878, ag. 7 y.
                       4 m. 3 d.
III. JOHN JENNINGS⁹ " March 28, 1875.

1258. Williams.   Ninth Generation.   Tower.

756. MARY M.⁸, EDWIN W.⁷, GAD H.⁶, LYNDE⁵, JAMES⁴, BENJA-
     MIN³, BENJAMIN², JOHN¹.
     Mary M.⁸, dau. of Edwin W.⁷ and Mary A. (Deering) Tower, b.
     May 8, 1842; mar. Robert Williams in Monongahela City,
     Penn.,
     March 3, 1864.   He was b.
         1836, and was son of James and Nancy (Manown)
     Williams.
                       Childr.

I.   MARY TOWER⁹   born Jan. 30, 1866, in Pittsburg, Penn.; died Feb. 21,
                       1871, ag. 5 y. 22 d.
II. NANNIE MANOWN⁹ " Sept. 3, 1867, in Monongahela City; died Feb.
                       21, 1877, ag. 9 y. 5 m. 18 d.

     Robert Williams died Feb. 17, 1869, ag. 33.
     Mary M. (Tower) Williams mar., 2d, John Forehope
     Jan. 1, 1880.   He was b. in Adams Co., Penn.,
         1824, and was son of Godfrey and Eva (Smith)
     Forehope.
                   Childr. none.

1259. Lapsley.   Ninth Generation.   Tower.

756. CAROLINE J.⁸, EDWIN W.⁷, GAD H.⁶, LYNDE⁵, JAMES⁴, BENJA-
     MIN³, BENJAMIN², JOHN¹.

Caroline J.[8], dau. of Edwin W.[7] and Mary A. (Deering) Tower, b.
March 30, 1844; mar. Rev. James E. Lapsley
Jan. 20, 1865. He was b. in Indiana Co., Penn.,
March 16, 1839, and was son of James and Eleanor (Changhey) Lapsley.

Childr.

I. MARY T.[9]   born July 16, 1866, in Pittsburg, Penn.
II. ELEANOR F.[9]   "   Oct. 22, 1867, in Illinois.
III. CARRIE S.[9]   "   Aug. 15, 1869,   "
IV. JAMES E.[9]   "   Oct. 23, 1872, in Alleghany City, Penn.

1260. Dorrington.   Ninth Generation.   Tower.

756. ANNA L.[8], EDWIN W.[7], GAD H.[6], LYNDE[5], JAMES[4], BENJAMIN[3], BENJAMIN[2], JOHN[1].

Anna L.[8], dau. of Edwin W.[7] and Mary A. (Deering) Tower, b.
Dec. 11, 1850; mar. James Calvin Dorrington, in Pittsburg,
Feb. 17, 1870. He was b. in Pittsburg, Penn.,
Aug. 17, 1844, and was son of Joseph and Eliza (Long) Dorrington.

Childr.

I. HARRY TOWER[9]   born Oct. 18, 1872, in Pittsburg.
II. GRACE ANNA[9]   "   March 30, 1875, in Blairsville, Penn.
III. ELIZA GLEN[9]   "   Sept. 30, 1877, in Pittsburg.
IV. ROSALIE BROOKS[9]   "   Aug. 7, 1880, in Franklin, Penn.

1261.   Ninth Generation.   Tower.

756. HARRY G.[8], EDWIN W.[7], GAD H.[6], LYNDE[5], JAMES[4], BENJAMIN[3], BENJAMIN[2], JOHN[1].

Harry G.[8], son of Edwin W.[7] and Mary A. (Deering) Tower, b.
July 5, 1856; mar. Ida A. Cochran in Denver, Col.,
Dec. 4, 1881. She was b. in Effingham Co., Ill.,
June 3, 1858, and was dau. of Shepley and Susannah (Ralston) Cochran.

Childr.

I. JESSIE ELLICOTT[9] born July 26, 1882.
II. CARRIE ESTELLA[9]   "   Feb. 22, 1884.

1262. Cable.   Ninth Generation.   Tower.

759. ADA MAY[8], GAD H.[7], GAD H.[6], LYNDE[5], JAMES[4], BENJAMIN[3], BENJAMIN[2], JOHN[1].

Ada May[8], dau. of Gad H.[7] and Rebecca H. (Smith) Tower, b.
; mar. Daniel J. Cable, of Pittsburg, Penn.,

May 14, 1876.   He was b.

and was son of Dr. H. W. and Matilda (Jackson) Cable.

Child.

I.   GUSTINE TOWER[9] born May 1, 1877, in Franklin.

Daniel J. Cable died

1263.   Wood.   Ninth Generation.   Tower.

762. JENNIE A.[8], LYNDE[7], JAMES[6], LYNDE[5], JAMES[4], BENJAMIN[3], BENJAMIN[2], JOHN[1].

Jennie A.[8], dau. of Lynde[7] and Almeda (Fairbanks) Tower, b.

April 13, 1850; mar. Henry A. Wood, of Langdon, N.H., Jan. 17, 1874.   He was b.

1845, and was son of Gardner L. and Mary A. Wood.

Child.

I.   WALTER L.[9] born Dec. 15, 1878.

1264.   Ninth Generation.   Tower.

766. JAMES S.[8], BENJAMIN[7], BENJAMIN T.[6], BENJAMIN[5], JAMES[4], BENJAMIN[3], BENJAMIN[2], JOHN[1].

James S.[8], son of Benjamin[7] and Lucy[6] (Tower) Tower, b. Jan. 8, 1833; mar.

Child.

I. MARY ELLEN[9] born   ; mar.   Parker, of Brattleboro, Vt.

James S. Tower[8] died in Westmoreland, N. H.

1265.   Ninth Generation.   Tower.

767. JOHN T.[8], WASHINGTON[7], BENJAMIN T.[6], BENJAMIN[5], JAMES[4], BENJAMIN[3], BENJAMIN[2], JOHN[1].

John T.[8], son of Washington[7] and Marcia (Chaffee) Tower, b. Nov. 24, 1825; mar. Jane Foster, of Rochester, Vt., March 16, 1846.   She was b. in Rochester Dec. 22, 1829, and was dau. of Hiram and Prudence (Ammidon) Foster.

Childr. born in Rochester.

I.   HIRAM FOSTER[9] born April 15, 1848; died July 9, 1853, ag. 5 y. 2 m. 24 d.

1433.	II.	SCOTT[9]	"	July 9, 1852.
1434.	III.	CHARLES C.[9]	"	March 18, 1854.

IV. ADDIE E.⁹   born Jan.   23, 1858.
V. ESTELLA C.⁹   "   Oct.   23, 1861.
VI. FRANK M.⁹   "   Dec.   24, 1865.

1266.   **Ninth Generation.**   **Tower.**

767. BENJAMIN F.⁸, WASHINGTON⁷, BENJAMIN T.⁶, BENJAMIN⁵, JAMES⁴, BENJAMIN³, BENJAMIN², JOHN¹.

Benjamin F.⁸, son of Washington⁷ and Marcia (Chaffee) Tower, b.

April 5, 1828; mar. Charlotte M. Metcalf
         She was b. in Irasburg, Vt.,
Sept. 29, 1825.

Childr.

I. AMOS M.⁹ born Sept. 29, 1852.
II. JENNIE E.⁹   "   Dec. 23, 1856; mar. Charles Stowell, April 18, 1882.
III. GEORGE C.⁹   "   March 23, 1860.

1267. Huntington.   **Ninth Generation.**   **Tower.**

767. JANE⁸, WASHINGTON⁷, BENJAMIN T.⁶, BENJAMIN⁵, JAMES⁴, BENJAMIN³, BENJAMIN², JOHN¹.

Jane⁸, dau. of Washington⁷ and Marcia (Chaffee) Tower, b.
June 6, 1830; mar. Joseph Huntington, of Irasburg, Vt.,
Nov. 26, 1848. He was b.
July 2, 1825, and was son of John and Mary (Hutchinson) Huntington.

Childr.

I. WILLIAM⁹ born Dec. 8, 1850.   IV. GEORGE⁹ born Aug. 25, 1860.
II. ELLA⁹   "   May 23, 1853.   V. ANNA⁹   "   Aug. 27, 1862.
III. JENNIE⁹   "   April 24, 1857.

Joseph Huntington died in Virginia, May 4, 1864, ag. 38 y. 10 m. 2 d.

1268.   **Ninth Generation.**   **Tower.**

767. LYMAN C.⁸, WASHINGTON⁷, BENJAMIN T.⁶, BENJAMIN⁵, JAMES⁴, BENJAMIN³, BENJAMIN², JOHN¹.

Lyman C.⁸, son of Washington⁷ and Marcia (Chaffee) Tower, b.
May 19, 1832; mar. Julia A. Hamilton
April 24, 1852. She was b. in Waterbury, Me.,
May 6, 1830, and was dau. of Ephraim and Elizabeth (Carl) Hamilton.

Childr.

1435.   I. MARCIA I.⁹   born June 11, 1852, in Biddeford, Me.
1436.   II. MYRA A.⁹   "   Dec. 6, 1854, in Bethel, Vt.
      III. MINNIE A.⁹   "   July 4, 1860, in Barnard, Vt.
      IV. CHARLES HENRY⁹ "   July 2, 1865, in Rochester, Vt; died
                       April 24, 1867, ag. 1 y. 9 m. 22 d.

1269. Paul.   Ninth Generation.   Tower.

767. ELLEN [8], WASHINGTON [7], BENJAMIN T.[6], BENJAMIN [5], JAMES [4], BENJAMIN [3], BENJAMIN [2], JOHN [1].

Ellen [8], dau. of Washington [7] and Marcia (Chaffee) Tower, b. April 24, 1839; mar. Irving Paul, of Rochester, Vt., Sept. 5, 1858. He was b. in Rochester
1838, and was son of John Paul.

Child.

I. HERBERT IRVING [9] born Sept. 22, 1860.

Ellen (Tower) Paul died

1270. Emerson.   Ninth Generation.   Tower.

768. MARY [8], AMASA [7], BENJAMIN T.[6], BENJAMIN [5], JAMES [4], BENJAMIN [3], BENJAMIN [2], JOHN [1].

Mary [8], dau. of Amasa [7] and Lucy (Warrington) Tower, b.
1848; mar. Edward Emerson, of Rockingham, Vt., Nov. 22, 1865. He was b. in Alstead, N. H.,
1844, and was son of Perley and Roxa Emerson.

1271. Bingham.   Ninth Generation.   Tower.

768. RHODA [8], AMASA [7], BENJAMIN T.[6], BENJAMIN[5], JAMES [4], BENJAMIN [3], BENJAMIN [2], JOHN [1].

Rhoda [8], dau. of Amasa [7] and Lucy (Warrington) Tower, b.
1857; mar. Frederick Bingham, of Washington, Ill., Jan. 27, 1876. He was b. in Spencer, Mass.,
1856, and was son of Thomas A. and Marion P. Bingham.

1272.   Ninth Generation.   Tower.

769. JOEL M.[8], GARDNER [7], BENJAMIN T.[6], BENJAMIN [5], JAMES[4], BENJAMIN[3], BENJAMIN [2], JOHN [1].

Joel M.[8], son of Gardner [7] and Mary A. (Darling) Tower, b.
June 8, 1836; mar. Mary Ann Adom, of Mississippi,
She was b. in Tuscaloosa, Ala.,
Sept. 22, 1835, and was dau. of Thomas and Lizzie Ann (Babb) Adom.

Child.

I. LUCINDA H.[9].

1273.   Ninth Generation.   Tower.

769. JULIUS [8], GARDNER [7], BENJAMIN T.[6], BENJAMIN [5], JAMES [4], BENJAMIN [3], BENJAMIN [2], JOHN [1].

Julius [8], son of Gardner [7] and Mary A. (Darling) Tower, b.
June 16, 1839; mar. Ella E. Gamble in Woodhull, Ill.,
Dec. 31, 1866. She was b.
April 9, 1847, and was dau. of Samuel and Isabella B.
(Wilson) Gamble.

Childr.

I. CHARLES B.[9] born Feb. 21, 1868.
II. FREDERICK J.[9] " May 29, 1870.

1274.   **Ninth Generation.**   **Tower.**

769. GEORGE R.[8], GARDNER [7], BENJAMIN T.[6], BENJAMIN [5], JAMES [4],
     BENJAMIN [3], BENJAMIN [2], JOHN [1].
George R.[8], son of Gardner [7] and Mary A. (Darling) Tower, b.
Jan. 8, 1844; mar. Emma Frances Chaffee, of Charlemont,
Mass.,
Oct. 11, 1865. She was b.
Feb. 18, 1847, and was dau. of Constant and Huldah (Hawes)
Chaffee.

Childr. born in Rockingham, Vt.

I. ANNA [9] born Dec. 2, 1866; died July 21, 1878, ag. 11 y. 7 m. 19 d.
II. BELL [9] " Dec. 18, 1867.
III. ELOISE [9] " Jan. 1, 1871.

1275.   **Smith.**   **Ninth Generation.**   **Tower.**

769. MARY E.[8], GARDNER [7], BENJAMIN T.[6], BENJAMIN [5], JAMES [4],
     BENJAMIN [3], BENJAMIN [2], JOHN [1].
Mary E.[8], dau. of Gardner [7], and Mary A. (Darling) Tower, b.
Nov. 8, 1846; mar. William Smith, of Putney, Vt.,
Jan. 29, 1865. He was b.
1825, and was son of John Smith.

Childr.

I. EDITH LOUISA [9] born   1866.
II. AUSTIN GARDNER [9] " Aug. 8, 1873.
III. CLARA A.[9] " Aug. 26, 1878.

1276.   **Merrill.**   **Ninth Generation.**   **Tower.**

771. LIZZIE [8], LYNDE [7], EPHRAIM D.[6], BENJAMIN [5], JAMES [4], BEN-
     JAMIN [3], BENJAMIN [2], JOHN [1].
Lizzie [8], dau. of Lynde [7] and Cynthia M. (Blood) Tower, b.
April 6, 1847; mar. Frank Mortimer Merrill, of Lowell,
Feb. 3, 1870. He was b. in Lowell, Mass.,
Feb. 27, 1846, and was son of Benjamin and Abby (Holt)
Merrill.

Childr. none.

1277. Currier.   Ninth Generation.   Tower.

771. Lucy [8], Lynde [7], Ephraim D. [6], Benjamin [5], James [4], Benjamin [3], Benjamin [2], John [1].

Lucy [8], dau. of Lynde [7] and Cynthia M. (Blood) Tower, b.
Feb. 27, 1849 ; mar. Henry William Currier
June   8, 1876. He was b. in Dracut, Mass.,
March 12, 1849, and was son of William H. and Alice B.
   (Gardiner) Currier.

Childr.

    I. Alice Gardiner [9] born July 6, 1878.
   II. Amy Elizabeth [9]   "   May 4, 1880.

1278. Simpkins.   Ninth Generation.   Tower.

773. Ada E. [8], Warren J. [7], Jacob [6], Benjamin [5], James [4], Benjamin [3], Benjamin [2], John [1].

Ada E. [8], dau. of Warren J. [7] and Elizabeth H. (Freeman)
   Tower, b.
Oct. 20, 1855 ; mar. Wilson A. Simpkins, of Manchester,
   N. H.,
Sept. 11, 1875. He was b. in Bath, England,
Nov. 18, 1854.

Child born in Manchester

    I. M. Herbert [9] born June 12, 1876.

1279. Taylor.   Ninth Generation.   Tower.

795. Emma V. [8], Sanford M. [7], Jonathan H. [6], Jonathan [5], Jonathan [4], Benjamin [3], Benjamin [2], John [1].

Emma V. [8], dau. of Sanford M. [7] and Jane R. (Crane) Tower, b.
Oct.   24, 1833 ; mar. John Henry Taylor
Oct.   16, 1854. He was b. in Boston
March 16, 1833.

Child.

I. John Walter [9] born Aug. 12, 1855; died Feb. 19, 1863, ag. 7 y. 6 m. 10 d.

Emma V. (Tower) Taylor died in Brooklyn, N. Y., Nov. 17,
   1860, ag. 27 y. 24 d.

1280.   Ninth Generation.   Tower.

795. Oscar M. [8], Sanford M. [7], Jonathan H. [6], Jonathan [5], Jonathan [4], Benjamin [3], Benjamin [2], John [1].

Oscar M. [8], son of Sanford M. [7] and Jane R. (Crane) Tower, b.
Nov. 1, 1835 ; mar. Mary Georgiana Pietch
April 9, 1857.

Child.

I. EDWARD CAMERON [9] born Aug. 4, 1863.

1281. Taylor. Ninth Generation. Tower.

795. SARAH A.[8], SANFORD M.[7], JONATHAN H.[6], JONATHAN [5], JONA-
THAN [4], BENJAMIN [3], BENJAMIN [2], JOHN [1].
Sarah A.[8], dau. of Sanford M.[7] and Jane R. (Crane) Tower, b.
Oct.   4, 1843 ; mar. John Henry Taylor
Nov. 13, 1861. He was b. in Boston,
March 16, 1833.

Child.

I. EVELINE I.[9] born March 1, 1865.

John H. Taylor died.

1282. Eldred. Ninth Generation. Tower.

795. PHEBE A.[8], SANFORD M.[7], JONATHAN H.[6], JONATHAN [5], JONA-
THAN [4], BENJAMIN [3], BENJAMIN [2], JOHN [1].
Phebe A.[8], dau. of Sanford M.[7] and Jane R. (Crane) Tower, b.
April 8, 1848 ; mar. D. Joseph Eldred
April 11, 1869.

Child.

I. GEORGE CLARENCE A.[9] born Dec. 6, 1869.

1283. Young. Ninth Generation. Tower.

805. MARY A.[8], JOB S.[7], GRENVILLE [6], JONATHAN [5], JONATHAN [4],
BENJAMIN [3], BENJAMIN [2], JOHN [1].
Mary A.[8], dau. of Job S.[7] and Mary (Crane) Tower, b.
June 14, 1846 ; mar. William H. Young.

Childr.

I. LEWIS [9]   III. HERBERT [9]
II. EDWARD [9]   IV. MARY ALICE [9]   , died June   , 1875.

Mary A. (Tower) Young died in Newark, N. J., Dec. 18,
1874, ag. 28 y. 7 m. 3 d.

1284. Chapman. Ninth Generation. Tower.

816. SARAH AMELIA [8], ALDEN [7], NATHANIEL [6], NATHANIEL [5],
NATHANIEL [4], THOMAS [3], BENJAMIN [2], JOHN [1].
Sarah A.[8], dau. of Alden [7] and Laura (Everett) Tower, b.
June 15, 1835 ; mar. Albert J. Chapman, of Detroit, Mich.

Childr.

I. GRACE[9]. II. AMANDA[9]. III. GERTRUDE[9]. died.

1285. Matthews. Ninth Generation. Tower.

816. AMANDA[8], ALDEN[7], NATHANIEL[6], NATHANIEL[5], NATHANIEL[4], THOMAS[3], BENJAMIN[2], JOHN[1].

Amanda[8], dau. of Alden[7] and Laura (Everett) Tower, b. Sept. 6, 1840 ; mar. Newell Matthews, of Princeton, Ill.

Child.

I. AMANDA[9] born March 7, 1866.

Amanda (Tower) Matthews died in Peoria, Ill., March 13, 1866, ag. 25 y. 6 m. 7 d.

1286. Bates. Ninth Generation. Tower.

816. NELLY A.[8], ALDEN[7], NATHANIEL[6], NATHANIEL[5], NATHANIEL[4], THOMAS[3], BENJAMIN[2], JOHN[1].

Nelly A.[8], dau. of Alden[7] and Mary (Pierce) Tower, b. Jan. 10, 1858 ; mar. Shepard F. Bates[9]

Feb. 9, 1878. He was b.

Feb. 8, 1855, and was son of Gordyce[8] and Corrinth (Wing) Bates.

BATES. TOWER.

Shepard F.[9], Gordyce[8], Quincy[7], Lebbeus[6], Sarah[5], Peter[4], Jeremiah[3], Jeremiah[2], John[1].

Child born in Worthington, Mass.

I. CLARENCE KIMBALL[9] born Feb. 17, 1879.

1287. Ninth Generation. Tower.

817. OSMOND S.[8], OSMOND[7], NATHANIEL[6], NATHANIEL[5], NATHANIEL[4], THOMAS[3], BENJAMIN[2], JOHN[1].

Osmond S.[8], son of Osmond[7] and Martha (Gallagher) Tower, b.

May 27, 1840 ; mar. Sarah Bartholemew, of Ypsilanti, Mich.

Childr.

I. FREDERICK[9] born Sept. 21, 1863.
II. MARION[9] " July , 1867.
III. ELSIE[9] " April , 1873.

1288. Ninth Generation. Tower.

817. ANGELO E.[8], OSMOND[7], NATHANIEL[6], NATHANIEL[5], NATHAN-
IEL[4], THOMAS[3], BENJAMIN[2], JOHN[1].
Angelo E.[8], son of Osmond[7] and Martha (Gallagher) Tower, b.
Aug. 16, 1842; mar Abby Lovell.

Childr.

I. ADA B.[9] born Oct. , 1865. II. CARRIE S.[9] born 1867.
III. LOUIS L.[9] born 1871.

1289. Ninth Generation. Tower.

817. JAMES F.[8], OSMOND[7], NATHANIEL[6], NATHANIEL[5], NATHANIEL[4],
THOMAS[3], BENJAMIN[2], JOHN[1].
James F.[8], son of Osmond[7] and Martha (Gallagher) Tower, b.
May 26, 1849; mar. Florence Holmes.

Child.

I. OSMOND H.[9] born April , 1873.

1290. Stephens. Ninth Generation. Tower.

824. EDITH M.[8], WARREN E.[7], WARREN[6], NATHANIEL[5], NATHAN-
IEL[4], THOMAS[3], BENJAMIN[2], JOHN[1].
Edith M.[8], dau. of Warren E.[7] and Agnes (Lyman) Tower, b.
April 22, 1857; mar. Alfred C. Stephens, of Worthington,
Mass.,
Feb. 14, 1877. He was b.
May 31, 1856, and was son of Lafayette and Laura (Pack-
ard) Stephens.

Child.

I. WALTER LEROY[9] born Dec. 14, 1877.

1291. Ninth Generation. Tower.

828. CHARLES F.[8], HORACE[7], THOMAS[6], THOMAS G.[5], SHADRACH[4],
THOMAS[3], BENJAMIN[2], JOHN[1].
Charles F.[8], son of Horace[7], and Lucinda (Witt) Tower, b.
Aug. 10, 1837; mar. Ellen M. Ward, of Sand Lake, N. J.,
Sept. 8, 1865. She was b. in Sand Lake,
June 4, 1840, and was dau. of Russell T. and Ruth J.
(Allen) Ward.

Childr.

I. NELLIE[9] born July 6, 1866; died July 13, 1866.
II. ALBERTA RUTH[9] " Sept. 24, 1867; died July 5, 1872, ag. 4 y.
9 m. 11 d.
III. FREDERICK RUSSELL[9] " April 19, 1869.

IV.	WILLIAM HENRY[9]	born Feb. 14, 1871; died Nov. 26, 1876, ag. 5 y. 9 m. 11 d.
V.	MARK WINFIELD[9]	" March 16, 1874 ; died Oct. 28, 1876, ag. 2 y. 7 m. 12 d.
VI.	ANNA MABEL[9]	" May 10, 1878 ; died Dec. 18, 1880, ag. 2 y. 7 m. 8 d.
VII.	MABEL ALBERTA[9]	" April 18, 1880.

1292.   **Ninth Generation.**   **Tower.**

828. HENRY A.[8], HORACE[7], THOMAS[6], THOMAS G.[5], SHADRACH[4], THOMAS[3], BENJAMIN[2], JOHN[1].

Henry A.[8], son of Horace[7] and Lucinda (Witt) Tower, b. Oct. 14, 1839 ; mar. Ann Eliza Walker June 19, 1858. She was b. Nov. 30, 1841, and was dau. of Thomas and Cynthia Walker.

Childr.

I.	JULIA ANGIE[9]	born Oct. 14, 1859.
II.	HERBERT[9]	" Dec. 26, 1861; died.
III.	LILIAN MAUD[9]	" July 12, 1865.
IV.	MINNIE[9]	" Dec. 9, 1867; died Sept. 19, 1868.

1293.   **Ninth Generation.**   **Tower.**

828. EDWARD A.[8], HORACE[7], THOMAS[6], THOMAS G.[5], SHADRACH[4], THOMAS[3], BENJAMIN[2], JOHN[1].

Edward A.[8], son of Horace[7] and Lucinda (Witt) Tower, b. March 5, 1842 ; mar. Mary E. Parks, of North Adams, Mass., May 18, 1862. She was b. May 25, 1845, and was dau. of John and Caroline Parks.

Childr.

I.	LINIE M.[9]	born Aug. 15, 1863.
II.	CAROLINE IMOGENE[9]	" Sept. 1, 1865.
III.	HORACE LINWOOD[9]	" Dec. 18, 1870.

1294.   **Ninth Generation.**   **Tower.**

828. HORACE A.[8], HORACE[7], THOMAS[6], THOMAS G.[5], SHADRACH[4], THOMAS[3], BENJAMIN[2], JOHN[1].

Horace A.[8], son of Horace[7] and Lucinda (Witt) Tower, b. Feb. 3, 1845 ; mar. Georgiana Preston, of Whittingham, Vt., April 26, 1870. She was b. Nov. 21, 1851, and was dau. of Lorenzo and Lucy (Clark) Preston.

Childr. none.

1295. Ninth Generation. Tower.

829. AUSTIN[8], EPHRAIM[7], THOMAS[6], THOMAS G.[5], SHADRACH[4], THOMAS[3], BENJAMIN[2], JOHN[1].
Austin[8], son of Ephraim[7] and Minerva (Brown) Tower, b. Sept. 24, 1845; mar. Alice M. Kemp, of Florida, Mass., Sept. 2, 1868. She was b. in Florida Oct. 24, 1847, and was dau. of Kendall and Dorcas P. (Comstock) Kemp.
Childr.
I. LULA A.[9]   born July 30, 1870; died May 26, 1871.
II. CLIFFORD K.[9] } Twins " March 8, 1875; died March 22, 1875.
III. CLENTON A.[9] }

1296. Ninth Generation. Tower.

829. RUSSELL B.[8], EPHRAIM[7], THOMAS[6], THOMAS G.[5], SHADRACH[4], THOMAS[3], BENJAMIN[2], JOHN[1].
Russell B.[8], son of Ephraim[7] and Minerva (Brown) Tower, b. Aug. 27, 1846; mar. Delcy M. Cain, of Savoy, Mass., May 23, 1872. She was b. in Savoy Aug. 17, 1855, and was dau. of Senaca T. and Melissa A. (Bliss) Cain.
Child.
I. ELWIN NEWMAN[9] born May 9, 1873; died Nov. 23, 1874, ag. 1 y. 6 m. 15 d.

1297. Davis. Ninth Generation. Tower.

829. JANE[8], EPHRAIM[7], THOMAS[6], THOMAS G.[5], SHADRACH[4], THOMAS[3], BENJAMIN[2], JOHN[1].
Jane[8], dau. of Ephraim[7] and Sally M. (Bushnell) Tower, b. Sept. 18, 1853; mar. John E. Davis, of Florida, Mass., July 9, 1875. He was b. June , 1853, and was son of Rev. J. and Harriet (Humphrey) Davis.
Childr.
I. ROY ALLISON[9] born April 11, 1876.
II. NETTIE T.[9] " March 10, 1878.
III. FLOYD E.[9] " March 17, 1880.

1298. Sherman. Ninth Generation. Tower.

831. MARYETTE[8], ALVIN[7], MARTIN[6], THOMAS G.[5], SHADRACH[4], THOMAS[3], BENJAMIN[2], JOHN[1].
Maryette[8], dau. of Alvin[7] and Mary B. (Roberts) Tower, b. Feb. 23, 1845; mar. David Henry Sherman, of Monroe,

May 4, 1862. He was b. in Monroe, Mass.,
June 11, 1834, and was son of Jacob and Lucy (Goodell)
Sherman.

Childr. born in Monroe.

I.	MARY LUCY[9]	born April	29,	1863.
II.	NETTIE VIOLA[9]	" May	20,	1866.
III.	DAVID OLIN[9]	" Aug.	26,	1868.
IV.	ELSIE IDELL[9]	" Sept.	11,	1870.
V.	MERRITT HENRY[9]	" Oct.	15,	1872.
VI.	ELLA ESTELLA[9]	" Oct.	3,	1874.
VII.	SYLVIE IRENA[9]	" March	1,	1877.
VIII.	CORA BELL[9]	" Oct.	25,	1878.
IX.	ADA[9]	. " June	21,	1881.

1299. Sherman. Ninth Generation. Tower.

831. NANCY E.[8], ALVIN[7], MARTIN[6], THOMAS G.[5], SHADRACH[4],
THOMAS[3], BENJAMIN[2], JOHN[1].
Nancy E.[8], dau. of Alvin[7] and Mary B. (Roberts) Tower, b.
July 27, 1847; mar. Jacob Sherman, of Rowe, Mass.,
June 19, 1864. He was b. in Rowe
1846, and was son of Jacob and Lucy (Goodell)
Sherman.

Child.

I. Daughter[9]   ; died

Jacob Sherman died

1300. Burnett. Ninth Generation. Tower.

833. LUCY E.[8], ORRIN[7], MARTIN[6], THOMAS G.[5], SHADRACH[4],
THOMAS[3], BENJAMIN[2], JOHN[1].
Lucy E.[8], dau. of Orrin[7] and Florinda (Granger) Tower, b.
Oct. 23, 1850; mar. Alfred W. Burnett, of Savoy, Mass.,
March 23, 1871. He was b. in Cheshire, Mass.,
1851, and was son of Willis W. and Susan A.
Burnett.

Child.

I. Daughter[9] born Dec. 30, 1871; died Dec. 30, 1871.

Lucy E. (Tower) Burnett died in Savoy, Dec. 30, 1871, ag.
21 y. 2 m. 7 d.

1301. Ninth Generation. Tower.

833. GILBERT J.[8], ORRIN[7], MARTIN[6], THOMAS G.[5], SHADRACH[4],
THOMAS[3], BENJAMIN[2], JOHN[1].
Gilbert J.[8], son of Orrin[7] and Florinda (Granger) Tower, b.

April 1, 1854; mar. Laura Ella White
Dec. 25, 1872. She was born in Savoy, Mass.,
Oct. 31, 1856, and was dau. of Wolcot L. and M. Jane
(Haskins) White.

Childr.

I. CLINTON GUY[9] born Oct. 12, 1873, in Savoy.
II. FLETA IRENE[9] " Aug. 18, 1877, "
III. CARL GARFIELD[9] " Nov. 14, 1879, in Buckland, Mass.

1302. **Ninth Generation.** **Tower.**

843. ALONZO D.[8], DENNIS[7], WILLIAM[6], THOMAS G.[5], SHADRACH[4],
THOMAS[3], BENJAMIN[2], JOHN[1].
Alonzo D.[8], son of Dennis[7] and Abigail (Alden) Tower, b.
Oct. 4, 1839; mar. Sophia D. Ballard, of Charlemont, Mass.,
Nov. 25, 1869. She was b. in Charlemont
1843, and was dau. of Jonathan and Sophia (Brown)
Ballard.

Child.

I. JOHN BALLARD[9] born July 28, 1873, in Florida, Mass.

1303. Nelson. **Ninth Generation.** **Tower.**

843. SARAH A.[8], DENNIS[7], WILLIAM[6], THOMAS G.[5], SHADRACH[4],
THOMAS[3], BENJAMIN[2], JOHN[1].
Sarah A.[8], dau. of Dennis[7] and Abigail (Alden) Tower, b.
Jan. 23, 1842; mar. Lewis Nelson, of Florida, Mass.,
March 12, 1861. He was b. in Florida
1842, and was son of David and Mary (Kemp)
Nelson.

Childr.

I. MINNIE E.[9] born July 19, 1862.   III. HENRY L.[9] born Nov. 21, 1876.
II. MARY A.[9] " Oct. 4, 1874.

1304. **Ninth Generation.** **Tower.**

843. SYLVANUS C.[8], DENNIS[7], WILLIAM[6], THOMAS G.[5], SHADRACH[4],
THOMAS[3], BENJAMIN[2], JOHN[1].
Sylvanus C.[8], son of Dennis[7] and Abigail (Alden) Tower, b.
Feb. 17, 1844; mar. Mary E. Stackhouse
May 26, 1879. She was b.
July 26, 1858.

Childr. none.

1305. Pike. **Ninth Generation.** **Tower.**

843. SELINA L.[8], DENNIS[7], WILLIAM[6], THOMAS G.[5], SHADRACH[4],
THOMAS[3], BENJAMIN[2], JOHN[1].
Selina L.[8], dau. of Dennis[7] and Abigail (Alden) Tower, b.

July 23, 1846; mar. James Pike, of Florida, Mass.,
April 7, 1867. He was b. in Florida
Nov. 20, 1841, and was son of Jeremiah and Abigail (Witt)
Pike.

Childr.

I.	FLORA E.[9]	born June 29, 1868.
II.	WILLIE BURTON [9]	" Dec. 19, 1870; died Oct. 10, 1876, ag. 5 y. 10 m. 1 d.
III.	ARTHUR H.[9] } Twins	" Jan. 17, 1873; { died March 20, 1873.
IV.	ALICE M.[9] }	" May 1, 1873.
V.	WALTER E.[9]	" Feb. 17, 1881.

1306. Davis.   Ninth Generation.   Tower.

843. RIZPAH A.[8], DENNIS [7], WILLIAM [6], THOMAS G.[5], SHADRACH [4],
THOMAS [3], BENJAMIN [2], JOHN [1].
Rizpah A.[8], dau. of Dennis [7] and Abigail (Alden) Tower, b.
May 4, 1853; mar. George Davis, of Cambridge, Mass.,
Nov. 22, 1876. He was son of Rev. Jacob and Harriet
(Humphrey) Davis.

1307.   Ninth Generation.   Tower.

849. HOBART C.[8], CHESTER L.[7], CHESTER [6], THOMAS G.[5], SHADRACH [4],
THOMAS [3], BENJAMIN [2], JOHN [1].
Hobart C.[8], son of Chester L.[7] and Mary A. (Nelson) Tower, b.
Sept. 16, 1852; mar. Esther M. Kilbourn, of Clarksburg,
Oct. 14, 1874. She was b. in Clarksburg, Mass.,
and was dau. of George F. and Lydia (Nor-
cross) Kilbourn.

Child.

I. AMY ELOISE [9] born Feb. 2, 1879.

1308. Kemp.   Ninth Generation.   Tower.

849. LIDA E.[8], CHESTER L.[7], CHESTER [6], THOMAS G.[5], SHADRACH [4],
THOMAS [3], BENJAMIN [2], JOHN [1].
Lida E.[8], dau. of Chester L.[7] and Mary A. (Nelson) Tower, b.
Sept. 23, 1858; mar. Barney S. Kemp, of North Adams,
Mass.,
Aug. 5, 1875. He was son of Sylvester A. and Almira
(Brown) Kemp.

Childr.

I.	BURDELLE [9]	born Oct. 30, 1876.
II.	EDWARD ELMWOOD [9]	" March 12, 1881.

1309. **Ninth Generation.** **Tower.**

880. ISAIAH F.[8], ISAIAH G.[7], ISAIAH [6], ISAIAH [5], ISAIAH [4], PETER [3],
BENJAMIN [2], JOHN [1].
Isaiah F.[8], son of Isaiah G.[7] and Mary A. (Fearing) Tower, b.
Nov. 24, 1838; mar. Mary Catherine Traman Downs, of
Dayton, Ohio,
Aug. 4, 1862. She was b. in New York city
Nov. 13, 1843, and was dau. of Cornelius H. and Anna
(Sherwood) Downs.

1310 **French.** **Ninth Generation.** **Tower.**

880. MARY A.[8], ISAIAH G. [7], ISAIAH [6], ISAIAH [5], ISAIAH [4], PETER [3],
BENJAMIN [2], JOHN [1].
Mary A.[8], dau. of Isaiah G.[7] and Sally (Higgins) Tower, b.
Aug. , 1841; mar. Jacob W. French [9]
Dec. 30, 1861. He was b.
Oct. 16, 1836, and was son of Jacob and Lucinda B.[8] (Bicknell) French.

FRENCH, BICKNELL. TOWER.
Jacob W.[9], Lucinda B.[8], Stephen [7], Ezra [6], Patience [5], Peter [4], Jeremiah [3],
Jeremiah [2], John [1].

Child born in Weymouth.
I. ARTHUR WHITON [9] born Sept. 26, 1863.

Mary A. (Tower) French died in Weymouth, Oct. 25, 1881,
ag. 40 y. 2 m.

1311. **Ninth Generation.** **Tower.**

888. REUBEN E.[8], REUBEN [7], REUBEN [6], ISAIAH [5], ISAIAH [4], PETER [3],
BBNJAMIN [2], JOHN [1].
Reuben E.[8], son of Reuben [7] and Hannah D. (Snow) Tower, b.
April 12, 1847; mar. Anna E.

Child.
I. WALTER LEAVITT [9] born June 11, 1886; died in Chelsea, Mass, Dec.
26, 1887.

1312. **Waite.** **Ninth Generation.** **Tower.**

888. HANNAH L.[8], REUBEN [7], REUBEN [6], ISAIAH [5], ISAIAH [4], PETER [3],
BENJAMIN [2], JOHN [1].
Hannah L.[8], dau. of Reuben [7] and Hannah D. (Snow) Tower, b.
Oct. 5, 1848; mar. Thomas Edward Waite, of Charlestown,
Mass.,
May 1, 1870. He was b. in Malden, Mass.,
1839, and was son of Peletiah and Mary O. Waite.

Child.

I.   GRACE EVELYN [9] born Feb. 13, 1871.

1313. Burrell.   Ninth Generation.   Tower.

891. NELLIE J.[8], WILLIAM S.[7], REUBEN [6], ISAIAH [5], ISAIAH [4], PETER [3], BENJAMIN [2], JOHN [1].

Nellie J.[8], dau. of William S.[7] and Mary A. (Wilder)Tower, b. Feb. 7, 1863 ; mar. Frank W. Burrell, of Weymouth, Mass., Nov. 5, 1882.

Childr. born in Hingham, Mass.

I.   MARION GILMAN [9] born March 27, 1884 ; died July 10, 1885, ag. 1 y.
                     3 m. 14 d.
II. HELEN RUSSELL [9]   "   Feb. 22, 1887.

1314. Swift.   Ninth Generation.   Tower.

895. ALICE M.[8], HENRY T.[7], REUBEN [6], ISAIAH [5], ISAIAH [4], PETER [3], BENJAMIN [2], JOHN [1].

Alice M.[8], dau. of Henry T.[7] and Drucilla (Swift) Tower, b. Aug. 15, 1857 ; mar. Thomas Swift, of East Bridgewater, Mass.,
June 7, 1874. He was b. in Plymouth, Mass.,
Nov. 24, 1851, and was son of Thomas and Lucretia S. (Cahoon) Swift.

Childr.

I.   HENRY T.[9]   born   ; died
II. HARRY T.[9]   "   ; "
III. HARRY LINCOLN[9] "   May 16, 1876.
IV. HATTIE L.[9]   "   June 11, 1880; died Sept. 25, 1880.

1315. Howell.   Ninth Generation.   Tower.

901. MARY A. B.[8], PHILO [7], ISAAC [6], ISAAC [5], JOSEPH [4], AMBROSE [3], BENJAMIN [2], JOHN [1].

Mary A. B.[8], dau. of Philo [7] and Cynthia (Beecher)Tower, b. Oct. 12, 1841 ; mar. Andrew Howell in Rochester, N. Y., June 16, 1859. He was son of Joseph and Lutetia (Van Dyur) Howell.

Childr. born in Adrian, Mich.

I.   PARK DUDLEY [9] born May 15, 1860; died Sept. 29, 1860.
II. ROBERT BEECHER [9] " Jan. 22, 1864.
III. CHARLES ARTHUR [9] " March 20, 1865.

1316. Pierce.   Ninth Generation.   Tower.

906. SUSAN L.⁸, ISAAC⁷, JOB⁶, ISAAC⁵, JOSEPH⁴, AMBROSE³, BEN-
JAMIN², JOHN¹.

Susan L.⁸, dau. of Isaac⁷ and Mary E. (Ackerman) Tower, b.
June 2, 1857; mar. Charles Calhoun Pierce, of Boston
(Neponset),
June 2, 1881. He was b. in Dorchester, Mass.,
March 1, 1852, and was son of John F. and Mary G. (Tucker)
Pierce.

Childr. born in Yonkers, N. Y.,

I.	HERBERT TOWER⁹	born July 5, 1882; died Sept. 18, 1884, ag. 2 y. 2 m. 13 d.
II.	FRANCIS BOWMAN⁹	" Feb. 3, 1885.
III.	EDYTHE DE MILT⁹	" Jan. 22, 1887.

1317.   Ninth Generation.   Tower.

910. SAMUEL D.⁸, JOSHUA C.⁷, SAMUEL⁶, ISAAC⁵, JOSEPH⁴, AM-
BROSE³, BENJAMIN², JOHN¹.

Samuel D.⁸, son of Joshua C.⁷, and Charlotte (Nash) Tower, b.
June 10, 1852; mar. Addie S. Mather, of Belchertown,
Nov. 3, 1876. She was b. in Belchertown, Mass.,
1857, and was dau. of James and Sarah R. Mather.

1318.   Ninth Generation.   Tower.

914. CHARLEMAGNE⁸, CHARLEMAGNE⁷, REUBEN⁶, JEDUTHUN⁵, JO-
SEPH⁴, AMBROSE³, BENJAMIN², JOHN¹.

Charlemagne⁸, son of Charlemagne⁷ and Amelia Malvina
(Bartle) Tower, b.
April 17, 1848, in Philadelphia; mar. Helen Smith in Oak-
land, Cal.,
Feb. 8, 1888. She was b. in San Francisco, Cal.,
Sept. 2, 1858, and was dau. of G. Frank and Susan (Rising)
Smith.

Childr.

I.	CHARLEMAGNE⁹	born March 19, 1889, in Philadelphia.
II.	GEOFFREY⁹	" July 1, 1890, in Germantown, Philadelphia.

1319. Lee.   Ninth Generation.   Tower.

914. DEBORAH T.⁸, CHARLEMAGNE⁷, REUBEN⁶, JEDUTHUN⁵, JOSEPH⁴,
AMBROSE³, BENJAMIN², JOHN¹.

Deborah T.⁸, dau. of Charlemagne⁷ and Amelia M. (Bartle)
Tower, b.

Feb. 4, 1851 ; mar. Richard Henry Lee in Pottsville, Penn.,
July 16, 1875. He was b. in Pottsville
Feb. 16, 1850, and was son of Richard and Isabella (Fletcher)
Lee.

1320. Snyder.　　Ninth Generation.　　Tower.

914. EMMA [8], CHARLEMAGNE [7], REUBEN [6], JEDUTHUN [5], JOSEPH [4], AM-
BROSE [3], BENJAMIN [2], JOHN [1].

Emma [8], dau. of Charlemagne [7] and Amelia M. (Bartle)
Tower, b.
June 15, 1852 ; mar. Benjamin Cummings Snyder, of Potts-
ville, Penn.,
Oct. 18, 1875. He was b. in Pottsville
June 30, 1851, and was son of George W. and Isabella
(Cummings) Snyder.

Childr. born in Pottsville.

I. RUTH [9]　　　 born Nov. 20, 1876.
II. EMMA TOWER [9] " March 10, 1878 , died in Brighton, Eng., July 4,
1890, ag. 12 y. 3 m. 25 d.

Benjamin C. Snyder died in Pottsville, Nov. 26, 1884, ag. 33 y.
4 m. 26 d.
Emma (Tower) Snyder mar., 2d, Thomas Alexander Reilly
in Waterville, N. Y.,
June 24, 1889. He was b. in Philadelphia
Nov. 28, 1838, and was son of Bernard and Mary (McCleary)
Reilly.

1321. Putnam.　　Ninth Generation.　　Tower.

914. GRACE W. [8], CHARLEMAGNE [7], REUBEN [6], JEDUTHUN [5], JOSEPH [4],
AMBROSE [3], BENJAMIN [2], JOHN [1].

Grace W. [8], dau. of Charlemagne [7] and Amelia M. (Bartle)
Tower, b.
May 15, 1859 ; mar. Earl B. Putnam [8]
Oct. 17, 1882. He was b.
Dec. 31, 1855, and was son of George [7] and Sarah M. (Bill)
Putnam.

PUTNAM, WHEELER.　　　　　　　　　　TOWER.
Earl B. [8], George [7], Betsey [6], Thankful [5], Joseph [4], Ambrose [3], Benjamin [2],
John [1].

Childr. born in Rochester, N. Y.

I. AMELIA [9]　　　　　born Aug. 26, 1883.
II. GRACE TOWER [9]　　 " May 5, 1886.
III. CHARLEMAGNE TOWER [9] " Feb. 16, 1888 ; died Feb. 17, 1889, ag 1 y.
1 d.
IV. EARL BILL [9]　　　　 " Feb. 1, 1890.

1322.   **Ninth Generation.**   **Tower.**

915. WALTER S.[8], JULIUS [7], REUBEN [6], JEDUTHUN [5], JOSEPH [4], AMBROSE [3], BENJAMIN [2], JOHN [1].
Walter S.[8], son of Julius [7] and Delia (Hearsey) Tower, b.
May 10, 1834; mar. Catherine L. Whiting, of Dedham, Mass.
                    She died May 18, 1861.
He mar., 2d, Sarah A. Griffin, of Boston,
Oct. 21, 1863. She was dau. of John Griffin.

1322 a.   **Ninth Generation.**   **Tower.**

917. LAWRENCE [8], FAYETTE B. [7], REUBEN [6], JEDUTHUN [5], JOSEPH [4],
AMBROSE [3], BENJAMIN [2], JOHN [1].
Lawrence [8], son of Fayette B.[7] and Ann R. (Phelps) Tower, b.
Oct. 16, 1845 ; mar. Anna Maria Hodgins
Oct. 19, 1870.

Child.

I. ADELINA DU BOIS [9] born Feb. 19, 1874, in Brooklyn, N. Y.

1322 b.   Wood.   **Ninth Generation.**   **Tower.**

917. EMILY [8], FAYETTE B.[7], REUBEN [6], JEDUTHUN [5], JOSEPH [4], AMBROSE [3], BENJAMIN [2], JOHN [1].
Emily [8], dau. of Fayette B.[7] and Anna L. (Frary) Tower, b.
Nov. 12, 1854 ; mar. Walter C. Wood.

Childr.

I. CLARA [9].   II. GRACE [9].

Emily (Tower) Wood died   Dec. 29, 1878.

1323.   Bebee.   **Ninth Generation.**   **Tower.**

918. BLANCHE [8], DE WITT C.[7], REUBEN [6], JEDUTHUN [5], JOSEPH [4],
AMBROSE [3], BENJAMIN [2], JOHN [1].
Blanche [8], dau. of De Witt C.[7] and Anne (Williams) Tower, b.
June 22, 1845; mar. Munson H. Bebee, of Brooklyn,
Dec. 5, 1872. He was b. in Brooklyn, N. Y.,
Aug. 4, 1845, and was son of William J. and Elizabeth
    (Hinman) Bebee.

Childr.

I.   ELIZABETH [9] born March 6, 1875; died Aug. 22, 1875, in Passaic, N. J.
II.   EUGENE H.[9]   "   Oct. 29, 1876, in Brooklyn.
III. ETHEL [9]   "   June 23, 1881, " Chicago.

1324.   **Ninth Generation.**   **Tower.**

918. DE WITT C.[8], DE WITT C.[7], REUBEN [6], JEDUTHUN [5], JOSEPH [4], AMBROSE [3], BENJAMIN [2], JOHN [1].

De Witt C.[8], son of De Witt C.[7] and Anne (Williams)Tower, b. Sept. 27, 1856; mar. Emma Louise English, of Brooklyn, Nov. 2, 1882. She was b.
Sept. 27, 1857, and was dau. of William C. R. and Catherine (Groesbeck) English.

1325.   **Ninth Generation.**   **Tower.**

923. FRANK C.[8], CHARLES [7], DANIEL [6], JEDUTHUN [5], JOSEPH [4], AMBROSE [3], BENJAMIN [2], JOHN [1].

Frank C.[8], son of Charles [7] and Elvira (Whitney) Tower, b. Sept. 21, 1846; mar. Virginia Adeline Harding, of Binghampton, N. Y.,
Jan. 10, 1872. She was b.
Jan. 30, 1847, and was dau. of Augustus L. and Sarah M. (Marshall) Harding.

Childr.

I. FRANK AUGUSTA [9]   born May 17, 1873, in Wenona, Ill.
II. MAX ELSER [9]   "   Nov. 25, 1880, " Malden, "

1326.   **Ninth Generation.**   **Tower.**

924. JAMES A.[8], LENTHEL [7], DANIEL [6], JEDUTHUN [5], JOSEPH [4], AMBROSE [3], BENJAMIN [2], JOHN [1].

James A.[8], son of Lenthel [7] and Cornelia M. (Hull) Tower, b. July 29, 1843; mar. Laura E. Simons, of Evanston, Ill., Nov. 18, 1873. She was b.
Sept. 7, 1852, and was dau. of Leonard and Elizabeth(Bowen) Simons.

Childr.

I. EDITH M.[9] born Oct. 9, 1874.   III. LYMAN H.[9] born May 8, 1881.
II. JAMES A.[9]   " Nov. 16, 1875.   IV. BESSIE S.[9] " May 23, 1883.

1327.   **Ninth Generation.**   **Tower.**

924. LYMAN H.[8], LENTHEL [7], DANIEL [6], JEDUTHUN [5], JOSEPH [4], AMBROSE [3], BENJAMIN [2], JOHN [1].

Lyman H.[8], son of Lenthel [7] and Cornelia M. (Hull) Tower, b. July 11, 1845; mar. Amelia A. Dent, of Ottawa, Ill.,
May   9, 1866. She was b. in La Salle Co., Ill.,
March 28, 1846, and was dau. of Rawley E. and Rebecca (McCallam) Dent.

1328. Ninth Generation. Tower.

929. HENRY M.⁸, AMBROSE M.⁷, LUKE⁶, JONATHAN⁵, JOSEPH⁴, AMBROSE³, BENJAMIN², JOHN¹.

Henry M.⁸, son of Ambrose M.⁷ and Rosamond D. (Adams) Tower, b.

July 23, 1847; mar. Sarah Maria Woodbury, of Spencer, Mass.,

Nov. 24, 1870. She was b. in Southborough, Mass.,

March 13, 1853, and was dau. of Lucien C. and Harriet N. (Hudson) Woodbury.

Childr.

I.	BERTHA HUDSON⁹	born Sept. 9, 1871;	died March 10, 1872.	
II.	BEULAH MAY⁹	" Feb. 8, 1873;	" June 8, 1874, ag. 1 y. 4 m.	
III.	DE WITT⁹	" Dec. 17, 1874.		
IV.	IDA BEULAH⁹	" Sept. 3, 1878.		
V.	ARTHUR MENDELL⁹	" Oct. 1, 1887.		

1329. Ninth Generation. Tower.

933. WILLIAM S.⁸, HORACE W.⁷, HORACE D.⁶, JUSTUS⁵, JOSEPH⁴, AMBROSE³, BENJAMIN², JOHN¹.

William S.⁸, son of Horace W.⁷ and Cornelia S. (Stafford) Tower, b.

July 13, 1850; mar. Eliza Moyes

May 28, 1874. She was b.

July 24, 1853, and was dau. of Rev. Edward and Maria (Peters) Moyes.

Childr.

I.	CORNELIA MARIA⁹	born March 6, 1875.	
II.	EDWARD CLARENCE⁹	" July 13, 1876.	
III.	MARIA MOYES⁹	" July 31, 1880.	

1330. Allen. Ninth Generation. Tower.

933. CLARA S.⁸, HORACE W.⁷, HORACE D.⁶, JUSTUS⁵, JOSEPH⁴, AMBROSE³, BENJAMIN², JOHN¹.

Clara S.⁸, dau. of Horace W.⁷ and Caroline S. (Stafford) Tower, b.

Oct. 8, 1854; mar. George Allen, of Waterville, N. Y.,

Jan. 20, 1881. He was b. in Poultney, Vt.,

Sept. 16, 1853, and was son of John and Ellen (Winchester) Allen.

Child.

I. GLADYS⁹ born Feb. 22, 1882, in Waterville.

1331.   **Ninth Generation.**   **Tower.**

962. JUSTUS D.[8], GEORGE[7], ABEL[6], ABEL[5], AMBROSE[4], AMBROSE[3],
BENJAMIN[2], JOHN[1].

Justus D.[8], son of George[7] and Mary A. (Castle) Tower, b.
Jan. 18, 1830; mar. Mary Carnes
Jan. 18, 1853. She was b. in Lenox, Canada,
Jan. 25, 1826, and was dau. of Andrew and Elizabeth (Mc-
Gee) Carnes.

Childr. born in Clarion, Ill.

	I.	GEORGE D.[9]	born Oct. 31, 1853.
1437.	II.	ANDREW J.[9]	" July 29, 1855.
	III.	MARY ANN[9]	" June 15, 1857; died Aug. 21, 1857.
	IV.	HENRY[9]	" Nov. 2, 1858.
	V.	ANNIE E.[9]	" July 7, 1860.
	VI.	CARRIE[9]	" July 18, 1862.
	VII.	JENNIE[9]	" July 8, 1865.
	VIII.	DANIEL C.[9]	" Dec. 29, 1868.
	IX.	WILLARD G.[9]	" Nov. 8, 1872; died Aug. 3, 1873.

1332.   **Ninth Generation.**   **Tower.**

962. AUGUSTUS C.[8], GEORGE[7], ABEL[6], ABEL[5], AMBROSE[4], AM-
BROSE[3], BENJAMIN[2], JOHN[1].

Augustus C.[8], son of George[7] and Mary A. (Castle) Tower, b.
July 4, 1833; mar. Amanda M. James
Dec. 15, 1853. She was b. in Corrine, Me.,
April 6, 1833, and was dau. of Jonathan and Sophia (Bun-
ker) James.

Childr.

1438.	I.	CHARLES A.[9]	born Oct. 23, 1854.
	II.	CLARA EMMA[9]	" June 29, 1857.
	III.	LOUIS J.[9]	" July 1, 1864.

1333. Dix.   **Ninth Generation.**   **Tower.**

962. MARY J.[8], GEORGE[7], ABEL[6], ABEL[5], AMBROSE[4], AMBROSE[3],
BENJAMIN[2], JOHN[1].

Mary J.[8], dau. of George[7] and Mary A. (Castle) Tower, b.
May 4, 1840; mar. Samuel Dix, of Wilmington, Vt.,
March 7, 1870.

Childr. none.

Mary J. (Tower) Dix died in Mendota, Ill., Aug.   , 1877,
ag. 37 y. 3 m.

1334. Blanchard.   Ninth Generation.   Tower.

962. CAROLINE E.⁸, GEORGE⁷, ABEL⁶, ABEL⁵, AMBROSE⁴, AM-
      BROSE³, BENJAMIN², JOHN¹.
      Caroline E.⁸, dau. of George⁷ and Mary A. (Castle) Tower, b.
      July 2, 1843; mar. George L. Blanchard in Mendota, Ill.,
      Dec. 31, 1864. He was b. in Lunenburg, Vt.,
      Feb. 27, 1827, and was son of Lemuel and Diantha (Temple)
      Blanchard.

Childr.

I.	ALICE JENETTE⁹	born Nov. 27, 1865.	
II.	WARREN W.⁹	" May 18, 1867; died June 15, 1867.	
III.	GEORGE ESLI⁹	" May 28, 1868.	
IV.	MARILLA DIANTHA⁹	" July 21, 1870.	
V.	JULIA JUSTINA⁹	" Oct. 28, 1872.	
VI.	LUCY ANN⁹	" March 19, 1876; died May 28, 1877, ag. 1 y.	
		2 m. 9 d.	
VII.	FRANK EDGAR⁹	" Oct. 15, 1878.	

1335.   Ninth Generation.   Tower.

965. GEORGE W.⁸, DAVID⁷, ABEL⁶, ABEL⁵, AMBROSE⁴, AMBROSE³,
      BENJAMIN², JOHN¹.
      George W.⁸, son of David⁷ and Mary A. (Daily) Tower, b.
      Sept. 22, 1853; mar. Caroline Lanan, of Sycamore, Ill.
      April 11, 1876.

Childr.

    I. HENRY DAVID⁹ born Jan. 28, 1877.
    II. CARRIE BELL⁹ " Jan. 11, 1881.

1336. Goodenow.   Ninth Generation.   Tower.

982. IDA F.⁸, GEORGE F.⁷, DANIEL⁶, JONATHAN⁵, JONATHAN⁴,
      AMBROSE³, BENJAMIN², JOHN¹.
      Ida F.⁸, dau. of George F.⁷ and Sarah J. (Warren) Tower, b.
      Jan. 15, 1856; mar. Frank Goodenow
      April 29, 1875. He was b.
      April 17, 1852, and was son of Albert and Mary (Brown)
      Goodenow.

Childr. none.

Ida F. (Tower) Goodenow died Jan. 8, 1877, ag. 20 y. 11 m.
24 d.

1337. Bryant.   Ninth Generation.   Tower.

982. EVA A.⁸, GEORGE F.⁷, DANIEL⁶, JONATHAN⁵, JONATHAN⁴,
      AMBROSE³, BENJAMIN², JOHN¹.

Eva A.[8], dau. of George F.[7], and Sarah J. (Warren) Tower, b.
April 9, 1858; mar. William Bryant
Sept. 11, 1875.   He was b. in Bristol, Me.,
        1850, and was son of Charles and Cordelia (Morton)
Bryant.
                              Child.
      I.   FRANK WARREN [9] born   1878.

1338.   Ninth Generation.   Tower.

983.   GEORGE A.[8], DANIEL A.[7], DANIEL [6], JONATHAN [5], JONATHAN [4],
          AMBROSE [3], BENJAMIN [2], JOHN [1].
      George A.[8], son of Daniel A.[7] and Frances M. (Chase)
          Tower, b.
      Aug. 11, 1853; mar. Lusie Hollis, of Cohasset, Mass.,
      Nov. 4, 1880.   She was b. in Boston
      July 15, 1856, and was dau. of John B. and Susan (Stod-
          dard) Hollis, and adopted daughter of Thomas M. and
          Mary H. Smith.

1339. Fongeres.   Ninth Generation.   Tower.

988.   MARY E.[8], HENRY C.[7], CALVIN [6], JONATHAN [5], JONATHAN [4],
          AMBROSE [3], BENJAMIN [2], JOHN [1].
      Mary E.[8], dau. of Henry C.[7] and Eliza A. (Paine) Tower, b.
      March 4, 1851; mar. Louis Fongeres, of Wabash, Ind.,
      Feb. 4, 1867.   He was b. in Charlestown, W. Va.,
          and was son of ——— and Jane (Gibbs) Fongeres.

                     Childr. born in Wabash.

   I. LOUIS [9] born Jan. 9, 1880.   II. TOMMY [9] born Dec. 20, 1882.

1340.   Ninth Generation.   Tower.

988.   CHARLES [8], HENRY C.[7], CALVIN [6], JONATHAN [5], JONATHAN [4],
          AMBROSE [3], BENJAMIN [2], JOHN [1].
      Charles [8], son of Henry C.[7] and Eliza A. (Paine) Tower, b.
      Sept. 19, 1852; mar. Ruth Hampson, of Wabash, Ind.,
      Sept. 17, 1875.   She was b. in Wabash
          1853, and was dau. of James and Ruth (Sprague)
      Hampson.

1341. Rounds.   Ninth Generation.   Tower.

989.   GRACE E.[8], CALVIN D.[7], CALVIN [6], JONATHAN [5], JONATHAN [4],
          AMBROSE [3], BENJAMIN [2], JOHN [1].
      Grace E.[8], dau. of Calvin D.[7] and Sarah J. (Richardson)
          Tower, b.

Sept. 30, 1858; mar. Parker Sterling Rounds, of Chicago,
Sept. 29, 1878.   He was b. in Chicago
and was son of P. S. and Martha Rounds.

Child.

I. MARIA ZOULETTE [9] born June 26, 1880.

1342.   Ninth Generation.   Tower.

1002. DEXTER [8], ELI [7], RUEL [6], PETER [5], BENJAMIN [4], AMBROSE [3],
BENJAMIN [2], JOHN [1].

Dexter [8], son of Eli [7] and Susan (Farrington) Tower, b.
Oct. 22, 1851; mar. Abbie Fowle, of South Conway, N. H.,
1874. She was b. in Parsonfield, Me.,
March 6, 1856, and was dau. of Thomas and Elizabeth
(Philbrook) Fowle.

Childr.

I. LIZZIE A. [9]   born Dec. 25, 1877.
II. GUY E. LEWIS [9]   "   June 14, 1880; died July 19, 1881.
III. JESSIE E. [9]   "   Sept. 25, 1882.

1343.   Ninth Generation.   Tower.

1002. EDGAR C. [8], ELI [7], RUEL [6], PETER [5], BENJAMIN [4], AMBROSE [3],
BENJAMIN [2], JOHN [1].

Edgar C. [8], son of Eli [7] and Susan (Farrington) Tower, b.
Aug.   , 1853; mar. Matilda Lord, of Lovell, Me.,
July 29, 1879.   She was b. in Waterford, Me.,
1850, and was dau. of Orren and Achsah (Tarbox)
Lord.

Childr.

I. BERTY [9] born Jan. 5, 1880.   II. SUSIE [9] born June 5, 1882.

1344.   Ninth Generation.   Tower.

1018. DAVID B. [8], MATTHEW [7], MATTHEW [6], MATTHEW [5], MATTHEW [4],
SAMUEL [3], SAMUEL [2], JOHN [1].

David B. [8], son of Matthew [7] and Lydia (Brookhart)
Tower, b.
July 27, 1823; mar. Louisa B. Kline
Oct. 3, 1854.   She was b. in Osnaburg, Ohio,
Sept. 11, 1837, and was dau. of David and Susan (Miller)
Kline.

Childr. born in Marshall, Ill.

I. JAMES ALLEN [9]   born Nov. 10, 1855.
II. WILLIAM EDGAR [9] "   March 21, 1862.

1345. Handy. Ninth Generation. Tower.

1018. SAVINA⁸, MATTHEW⁷, MATTHEW⁶, MATTHEW⁵, MATTHEW⁴,
SAMUEL³, SAMUEL², JOHN¹.
Savina⁸, dau. of Matthew⁷ and Lydia (Brookhart) Tower, b.
; mar. Stephen P. Handy.

Childr.

I.   LYDIA I.⁹ born Nov. 27, 1847.
II. MARY⁹   "   ; mar. Frank Cronic. Child, son. She died.

Stephen P. Handy died in California   1856.
Savina (Tower) Handy mar., 2d, Alfred Rariden.
Savina (Tower) Rariden died   1877.

1346. Patrick. Ninth Generation. Tower.

1019. JULIA A.⁸, COTTON⁷, MATTHEW⁶, MATTHEW⁵, MATTHEW⁴,
SAMUEL³, SAMUEL², JOHN¹.
Julia A.⁸, dau. of Cotton⁷ and Hannah (Edson) Tower, b.
July 19, 1817; mar. Jackson Patrick, of Crawford Co., Ind.,
Feb. 12, 1837. He was b. in Crawford Co.,
July 7, 1816, and was son of Brice and Elizabeth (Hager-
man) Patrick.

Childr.

I.   DANIEL ABDELBERT⁹ born Dec. 28, 1837, in Crawford Co.
II.   LUTHER⁹   "
III. SARAH ROSALTHA⁹   "   ; died in Louisville, Ky.
IV.   CHARITY ELIZABETH⁹ "   ;   "

Jackson Patrick died in Crawford Co., Dec. 16, 1869, ag.
53 y. 5 m. 9 d.
Julia A. (Tower) Patrick died in New Albany, Ind., Feb. 1,
1857, ag. 39 y. 6 m. 13 d.

1347. Neal. Ninth Generation. Tower.

1019. ELIZABETH⁸, COTTON⁷, MATTHEW⁶, MATTHEW⁹, MATTHEW⁴,
SAMUEL³, SAMUEL², JOHN¹.
Elizabeth⁸, dau. of Cotton⁷ and Hannah (Edson) Tower, b.
Dec. 31, 1827; mar. Joel Neal in Crawford Co., Ind.,
Nov. 5, 1846. He was b. in Crawford Co.,
Aug. 9, 1826, and was son of John and Nancy (Houghton)
Neal.

Childr. born in Crawford Co.

I. HARRIET J.[9] born Oct. 7, 1847; died Jan. 22, 1849, ag. 1 y. 3 m. 15 d.
II. SAMUEL A.   "   Feb. 17, 1849.
III. SARAH E.[9]   "   Oct. 23, 1850; died Dec. 7, 1862, ag. 12 y. 1 m. 15 d.
IV. MARY M.[9]   "   Nov. 19, 1852;   "   Jan. 24, 1870, ag. 17 y. 2 m. 4 d.

Joel Neal died in Crawford Co., Sept. 15, 1853, ag. 27 y. 1 m. 6 d.

DOOLITTLE.   TOWER.

1348. Elizabeth (Tower) Neal mar., 2d, Nelson Doolittle in Crawford Co.,
Feb. 28, 1856. He was b. in Canada
March 18, 1817, and was son of Samuel and Sabra (Scott) Doolittle.

Childr.

V. MARTHA R.[9] born Oct. 3, 1857; died May 11, 1860, ag. 2 y. 7 m. 8 d.
VI. JULIA A.[9]   "   Jan. 9, 1863.
VII. CHARLES I.[9]   "   March 1, 1866 ; died Aug. 26, 1868, ag. 2 y. 5 m. 25 d.
VIII. ELLA[9]   "   Sept. 4, 1868 ; died Oct. 25, 1880, ag. 12 y. 1 m. 21 d.

Nelson Doolittle died in Leavenworth, Ind., March 30, 1876, ag. 59 y. 12 d.

1348. Doolittle.   Ninth Generation.   Tower.

1020. MARY A.[8], ABRAHAM B.[7], MATTHEW[6], MATTHEW[5], MATTHEW[4], SAMUEL[3], SAMUEL[2], JOHN[1].
Mary A.[8], dau. of Abraham B.[7] and Delilah (Lynch) Tower, b.
; mar Nelson Doolittle.

Childr.

I. SARAH JANE[9].   III. HARRIET SOPHIA[9]
II. ALONZO[9].   IV. JOHN[9].

Mary A. (Tower) Doolittle died
1347. Nelson Doolittle mar., 2d, widow Elizabeth[8] (Tower) Neal.

1349. Scott.   Ninth Generation.   Tower.

1020. NANCY J.[8], ABRAHAM B.[7], MATTHEW[6], MATTHEW[5], MATTHEW[4], SAMUEL[3], SAMUEL[2], JOHN[1].
Nancy J.[8], dau. of Abraham B.[7] and Delilah (Lynch) Tower, b.
mar. Walter Scott.

Childr.

I. MIRANDA⁹.   II. MARGARET⁹.   III. WILLIAM⁹.

1350. Gorman, Burt, Howe.   Ninth Generation.   Tower.

1020. HARRIET S.⁸, ABRAHAM B.⁷, MATTHEW⁶, MATTHEW⁵, MAT-
THEW⁴, SAMUEL³, SAMUEL², JOHN¹.
Harriet S.⁸, dau. of Abraham B.⁷ and Delilah (Lynch)
Tower, b.
mar. Joseph Howe. He died
She mar., 2d, Amos Burt. He died
She mar., 3d, Jackson Gorman.

1351. Ferguson, Shores.   Ninth Generation.   Tower.

1022. SARAH J.⁸, HULL⁷, MATTHEW⁶, MATTHEW⁵, MATTHEW⁴,
SAMUEL³, SAMUEL², JOHN¹.
Sarah J.⁸, dau. of Hull⁷ and Sarah (Edson) Tower, b.
Sept. 28, 1822; mar. Elmer Shores in Harden Co., Ky.,
Feb. 18, 1842.
Childr.

I. Infant⁹ born   ; died in infancy.
II. SARAH E.⁹ " June 29, 1845.

Elmer Shores died Sept. 25, 1847.
Sarah J. (Tower) Shores mar., 2d, William F. Ferguson in
Cumberland Co., Ill.
Nov. 3, 1849. He was son of Stephen and Mary A. (At-
wood) Ferguson.
Childr.

III. LYDIA ELLEN⁹   born April 1, 1851, in Coles Co., Ill.
IV. MYRON ALONZO⁹   " Aug. 15, 1853, " Oregon Ter.
V. MARY ARLOA⁹   " Aug. 9, 1855, " Douglas Co., Oregon.
VI. STEPHEN HULL⁹   " Oct. 31, 1857, "   "   "   " ; died
in Walla Walla, Wash. Ter., Jan. 6,
1884, ag. 26 y. 2 m. 4 d.
VII. DANIEL GUSTAVUS⁹ " Dec. 15, 1859, in Douglas Co.
VIII. WILLIAM ARTHUR⁹ " June 6, 1862, "   "   "
IX. ARVILLA JANE⁹   " Sept. 25, 1863, "   "   "
X. WALTER SCOTT⁹   " June 15, 1866, "   "   "

1352. Smith.   Ninth Generation.   Tower.

1022. ABIGAIL B.⁸, HULL⁷, MATTHEW⁶, MATTHEW⁵, MATTHEW⁴,
SAMUEL³, SAMUEL², JOHN¹.
Abigail B.⁸, dau. of Hull⁷ and Sarah (Edson) Tower, b.
Nov. 6, 1826; mar. David Smith

Nov. 6, 1849. He was b. in Licking Co., Ohio,
Aug. 31, 1828, and was son of Thomas and Mary (Siger)
Smith.

Childr.

I.	MARY MELISSA [9]	born Dec.	9, 1850.
II.	HANNAH LOUISA [9]	" Oct.	21, 1856.
III.	MARTHA ADA [9]	" Dec.	9, 1858.
IV.	LUCINDA [9]	" Feb.	11, 1861; died Sept. 20, 1862, ag. 1 y. 7 m. 7 d.
V.	LA FAYETTE [9]	" Nov.	21, 1863 ; died Oct. 5, 1865, ag. 1 y. 10 m. 14 d.

David Smith died Nov. 21, 1863, ag. 35 y. 2 m. 21 d.
Abigail (Tower) Smith mar. William Smith, brother of
David,
Dec. 13, 1866. He was b. in Licking Co.,
Oct. 4, 1832.

Childr.

VI.	ELMER CORNELIUS [9]	born Oct.	23, 1867.
VII.	SARAH WELTHEA [9]	" Jan.	3, 1869.

1353.   **Ninth Generation.**   **Tower.**

1022. WASHINGTON L. [8], HULL [7], MATTHEW [6], MATTHEW [5], MAT-
THEW [4], SAMUEL [3], SAMUEL [2], JOHN [1].
Washington L. [8], son of Hull [7] and Sarah (Edson) Tower, b.
Feb. 27, 1831 ; mar. Ellen Smith in Cumberland Co., Ill.,
April 6, 1851. She was b. in Ohio
Jan. 8, 1834, and was dau. of John S. and Sarah A.
(Cooley) Smith.

Childr.

1439.	I.	SARAH TRIFENIA [9]	born April 15, 1852, in Iowa.
1440.	II.	LYDIA BELLE [9]	" June 5, 1855, " Oregon.
	III.	MARTHA JANE [9]	" June 25, 1858, " " ; mar. Sam Whittaker, Sept. 23, 1881.
	IV.	LUELLA FLORENCE [9]	" March 21, 1863, in Oregon ; died Aug. 29, 1867, ag. 4 y. 5 m. 8 d.
	V.	HERBERT MILTON [9]	" March 4, 1867, in Oregon.

1354. Powers.   Ninth Generation.   Tower.

1022. HARRIET N. [8], HULL [7], MATTHEW [6], MATTHEW [5], MATTHEW [4]
SAMUEL [3]. SAMUEL [2], JOHN [1].
Harriet N. [8], dau. of Hull [7] and Sarah (Edson) Tower, b.
Oct. 12, 1837 ; mar. Winslow Phelps Powers
Dec. 14, 1854. He was son of James and Anne (Phelps)
Powers.

Childr.

I.	SARAH VIOLA [9]	born	Dec. 18, 1855, in Oakland, Oregon.
II.	WILLIAM B. [9]	"	May 9, 1857, " " "
III.	MARY CATHERINE [9]	"	Nov. 3, 1859, " " ; died Nov. 27, 1871, ag. 12 y. 24 d.
IV.	ANNE JANE [9]	"	Sept. 17, 1861, in Oakland, Oregon.
V.	FRANCES ASBURY [9]	"	Jan. 14, 1864, " " "
VI.	JAMES W. [9]	"	July 16, 1869, " " "
VII.	HARRIET RACHEL [9]	"	Oct. 2, 1870, " " "
VIII.	LOREN TOWER [9]	"	April 16, 1874, " Wallowa, "
IX.	EDWIN DANIEL [9]	"	April 23, 1877, " Lagrande, "
X.	IDA MARTHA [9]	"	Feb. 8, 1880, " Wallowa, "

1355. De Baun.   Ninth Generation.   Tower.

1022. HANNAH [8], HULL [7], MATTHEW [6], MATTHEW [5], MATTHEW [4], SAMUEL [3], SAMUEL [2], JOHN [1].

Hannah [8], dau. of Hull [7] and Sarah (Edson) Tower, b. March 16, 1841 ; mar. Edwin De Baun in Douglas Co., Oregon,

Oct. 26, 1856. He was b.

Oct. 26, 1833, and was son of John and Margaret (Collyer) De Baun.

Childr.

I.	MARGARET ALVIRA [9]	born	Nov. 25, 1857, in Douglas Co., Oregon; Died in Walla Walla, Wash. Ter., Dec. 3, 1880, ag. 23 y. 8 d.
II.	VIOLA ELIZABETH [9]	"	Oct. 1, 1859, in Douglas Co.
III.	MELVINA GERTRUDE [9]	"	Sept. 3, 1861, " " " ; died in Walla Walla, Aug. 15, 1883, ag. 21 y. 11 m. 12 d.
IV.	GARRETT LINCOLN [9]	"	Nov. 8, 1863, in Douglas Co.
V.	MARTHA LIBERTY [9]	"	Jan. 8, 1866, " " " ; died in Walla Walla, Dec. 31, 1880, ag. 14 y. 11 m. 23 d.
VI.	MARY VICTORIA [9]	"	April 28, 1868, in Walla Walla.
VII.	SARAH JANE [9]	"	Sept. 15, 1870, " "
VIII.	FRANCENA BELLE [9]	"	Dec. 10, 1873, " "
IX.	JOHN EDWIN [9]	"	July 29, 1876, " "
X.	GRACE TOWER [9]	"	Sept. 1, 1879, " "

1356. Bramlet.   Ninth Generation.   Tower.

1022. MARTHA E. [8], HULL [7], MATTHEW [6], MATTHEW [5], MATTHEW [4], SAMUEL [3], SAMUEL [2], JOHN [1].

Martha E. [8], dau. of Hull [7] and Sarah (Edson) Tower, b. May 25, 1844 ; mar. Francis Clayton Bramlet, of Franklin Co., Ga.,

June 27, 1867. He was b. in Georgia
June 26, 1827, and was son of Nathan and Jane (Gober)
Bramlet.

Childr.

I.	NATHAN HULL [9]	born March 17, 1869, in Douglas Co., Oregon.
II.	WILLIAM HENRY [9]	" Nov. 25, 1870, " " " "
III.	SARAH JANE [9]	" July 17, 1873, " Union Co., "
IV.	GEORGE EDWIN [9]	" Feb. 19, 1875, " " " " ; died

Jan. 8, 1878, ag. 2 y. 10 m. 17 d.

V.	MARY NANCY [9]	" Dec. 28, 1876, in Union Co., Oregon.
VI.	MARTHA ELLEN [9]	" Feb. 17, 1879, " " " "
VII.	LEWIS FRANCIS [9]	" April 30, 1880, " " " "
VIII.	CHARLES DAVID [9]	" May 31, 1883, " " " "

1357.   **Ninth Generation.**   **Tower.**

1024. MATTHEW [8], JONATHAN W.[7], MATTHEW [6], MATTHEW [5], MAT-
THEW [4], SAMUEL [3], SAMUEL [2], JOHN [1].

Matthew [8] son of Jonathan W.[7] and Sarah V. (Munroe)
Tower, b.
March 25, 1832; mar. Sarah J. Long
Sept. 5, 1852. She was b. in Harrison Co., Ind.,
Dec. 4, 1835, and was dau. of Thomas and Nancy (Days)
Long.

Childr.

1441.	I.	ARMENTA REBECCA [9]	born May 20, 1855.
1442.	II.	PHILO HUSTIN [9]	" June 16, 1857.
1443.	III.	SAMUEL BENSON [9]	" June 17, 1859.
1444.	IV.	MARY LEORA [9]	" Aug. 9, 1861.

Matthew Tower [8] died in Crawford Co., Ind., Jan. 10, 1863,
ag. 30 y. 9 m. 16 d.
Sarah J. (Long) Tower died in Crawford Co., Ind., Feb. 7,
1869, ag. 33 y. 2 m. 3 d.

1358.   **Bates.**   **Ninth Generation.**   **Tower.**

1024. LOUISA C.[8], JONATHAN W.[7], MATTHEW [6], MATTHEW [5], MAT-
THEW [4], SAMUEL [3], SAMUEL [2], JOHN [1].

Louisa C.[8], dau. of Jonathan W.[7] and Sarah V. (Munroe)
Tower, b.
June 22, 1834; mar. Henry G. Bates
Nov. 15, 1866. He was b.
July 3, 1829, and was son of Oliver and Anna (Greene)
Bates.

Childr.

I.   HENRY ALBERT [9]   born Jan. 1, 1868.
II. GEORGE WARREN [9]   " May 4, 1869; died Aug. 27, 1869.
III. ROBERT FRANKLIN [9]   " July 22, 1870.
IV. AUSTIN LEWIS [9]   " Feb. 22, 1872.

Henry G. Bates died Nov. 4, 1873, ag. 44 y. 4 m. 1 d.

1359.   Ninth Generation.   Tower.

1024. ABRAHAM B.[8], JONATHAN W.[7], MATTHEW [6], MATTHEW [5],
MATTHEW [4], SAMUEL [3], SAMUEL [2], JOHN [1].
Abraham B.[8], son of Jonathan W.[7] and Sarah V. (Munroe)
Tower, b.
Oct. 16, 1837; mar. Nancy Angeline Long
Oct. 28, 1858. She was b. in Harrison Co., Ind.,
May 2, 1840, and was dau. of Thomas and Nancy Ann
(Daggs) Long.

Childr.

I.   LAURA A.[9]   born Sept. 29, 1859, in Crawford Co., Ind.
II.   ERASTUS LABAN [9]   "   Aug. 7, 1861,   "   "
III. MARY LOUISA [9]   "   July 31, 1866, in Linn Co., Mo.; mar.
                                Peter R. Newton, of Bird's Eye, Ind.
IV.   SARAH ALICE [9]   "   April 9, 1868, in Linn Co.
V.   WILLIAM WARREN [9]   "   Aug. 31, 1870,   "
VI.   VIOLA MATILDA [9]   "   Feb. 3, 1873,   "
VII. ZACHEUS [9]   "   March 2, 1875,   "   ; died March
                                5, 1875.
VIII. REUBEN THEODORE [9]   "   May 13, 1876,   "
IX.   MELISSA ANGELINE [9] "   Nov. 14, 1878,   "
X.   EMMA LILLIAN [9]   "   Sept. 26, 1881, in Perry Co., Ind.

1360. Osman, Bellcrist.   Ninth Generation.   Tower.

1024. ROSANNAH C.[8], JONATHAN W.[7], MATTHEW [6], MATTHEW [5],
MATTHEW [4], SAMUEL [3], SAMUEL [2], JOHN [1].
Rosannah C.[8], dau. of Jonathan W.[7] and Sarah V. (Munroe) Tower, b.
May 10, 1840; mar. William Bellcrist
March 29, 1867.

Childr. born in Crawford Co., Ind.

I. SARAH LOUISA BELL [9] born Dec. 14, 1867.
II. JOHN WARREN [9]   "   July 18, 1869; died Sept. 30, 1876, ag. 7 y.
                                2 m. 12 d.

Rosannah C. (Tower) Bellcrist mar., 2d, Daniel Osman
May 29, 1874. He was b. in Allegany Co., N. Y.,
Sept. 30, 1828, and was son of James and Polly (South well) Osman.

Childr. born in Leavenworth, Ind.

III. LOUISA GIFFORD[9] born July 30, 1875; died Aug. 13, 1876, ag. 1 y. 14 d.
IV. JAMES MADISON[9] " Sept. 4, 1877; " July 27, 1879, ag. 1 y.
10 m. 23 d.
V. FRANCES APASIA[9] " Dec. 24, 1879.
VI. DANIEL GARDNER[9] " Jan. 23, 1882.

1361. Williams. Ninth Generation. Tower.

1024. CHARLOTTE T.[8], JONATHAN W.[7], MATTHEW[6], MATTHEW[5],
MATTHEW[4], SAMUEL[3], SAMUEL[2], JOHN[1].
Charlotte T.[8], dau. of Jonathan W.[7] and Sarah V. (Munroe) Tower, b.
Sept. 3, 1845; mar. John F. Williams
Oct. 20, 1870. He was b. in Crawford Co., Ind.,
1827, and was son of Horace Z. and Lois (Stone)
Williams.

Childr. born in Crawford Co.

I. ELLA L.[9] born Oct. 8, 1872. IV. OWEN H.[9] born Aug. 30, 1879.
II. ROVILLA C.[9] " March 9, 1875. V. LILLA A.[9] " June 22, 1883.
III. HENRY O.[9] " Feb. 26, 1877.

1362. Ninth Generation. Tower.

1024. JONATHAN W.[8], JONATHAN W.[7], MATTHEW[6], MATTHEW[5],
MATTHEW[4], SAMUEL[3], SAMUEL[2], JOHN[1].
Jonathan W.[8], son of Jonathan W.[7] and Sarah V. (Munroe)
Tower, b.
Aug. 21, 1848; mar. widow Nancy Peabody
dau. of Henry and Nancy (Trainer) Bird.

Childr. born in Crawford Co., Ind.

I. ETHEL G.[9] II. JESSE P.[9]

1363. Hanger. Ninth Generation. Tower.

1024. SARAH J.[8], JONATHAN W.[7], MATTHEW[6], MATTHEW[5], MATTHEW[4], SAMUEL[3], SAMUEL[2], JOHN[1].
Sarah J.[8], dau. of Jonathan W.[7] and Sarah V. (Munroe)
Tower, b.
Sept. 17, 1853; mar. Martin F. Hanger
April 15, 1875. He was b. in Crawford Co., Ind.,
Oct. 19, 1854, and was son of John and Rebecca T. (Green)
Hanger.

Childr. born in Crawford Co.

I. LAURA F.[9] born Feb 15, 1876.
II. JOHN WARREN[9] " July 25, 1877.
40

III.	Denzil L.[9]	born March 22, 1879.
IV.	Theodore O.[9]	" Feb. 9, 1881.
V.	Willard Herman[9]	" Nov. 21, 1883.
VI.	Harry Edgar[9]	" Feb. 20, 1884.

1364.   Ninth Generation.   Tower.

1024. Levi G.[8], Jonathan W.[7], Matthew[6], Matthew[5], Matthew[4], Samuel[3], Samuel[2], John[1].

Levi G.[8], son of Jonathan W.[7] and Sarah V. (Munroe) Tower, b.

Sept. 27, 1856; mar. Harriet Isabel Patrick.

Childr. born in Crawford Co., Ind.

I. Hattie V.[9]   II. Sylvia O.[9]   III. Brice[9].

1365. Graves. Ninth Generation.   Tower.

1027. Ellen O.[8], Loren L.[7], Luther[6], Abner[5], Joseph[4], Joseph[3], Samuel[2], John[1].

Ellen O.[8], dau. of Loren L.[7] and Sophronia (Bates) Tower, b.

Sept. 4, 1843; mar. Charles H. Graves, of Northampton, Mass.,

Oct. 20, 1870. He was b. in Williamsburg, Mass.,

Sept. 18, 1845, and was son of Elam and Eunice (Graves) Graves.

Childr.

I.	Son[9]	born April 7, 1874; died April 11, 1874.
II.	Bertha[9]	" April 17, 1878; died May 10, 1879, ag. 1 y. 23 d.
III.	C. Harry[9]	" Sept. 4, 1881.

1366. Edwards. Ninth Generation.   Tower.

1027. Alice L.[8], Loren L.[7], Luther[6], Abner[5], Joseph.[4], Joseph[3], Samuel[2], John[1].

Alice L.[8], dau. of Loren L.[7] and Sophronia (Bates) Tower, b.

Oct. 15, 1845; mar. Henry M. Edwards, of Chesterfield, Mass.,

Nov. 7, 1866. He was. b. in Cummington, Mass.,

Sept. 9, 1842, and was son of William A. and Maria C. Edwards.

Childr. born in Peru, Mass.

I.	Etta Alice[9]	born Oct 20, 1867.
II.	Charles Henry[9]	" Aug. 8, 1869.
III.	Infant[9]	" July 23, 1875; died July 26, 1875.

1367. Ninth Generation. Tower.

1027. WALTER M.[8], LOREN L.[7], LUTHER [6], ABNER [5], JOSEPH [4],
JOSEPH [3], SAMUEL [2], JOHN [1].
Walter M.[8], son of Loren L.[7], and Sophronia (Bates)
Tower, b.
Sept. 19, 1847; mar. Ida M. Mann, of Northampton, Mass.,
Aug. 14, 1869. She was b. in Northampton
1853, and was dau. of Henry and Elizabeth (Wol-
cot) Mann.
Childr. born in Northampton.
I. LOREN H.[9] II. ELLA MAUD [9].

1368. Bradford. Ninth Generation. Tower.

1027. VIETTA E.[8], LOREN L.[7], LUTHER [6], ABNER [5], JOSEPH [4], JOSEPH [3],
SAMUEL [2], JOHN [1].
Vietta E.[8], dau. of Loren L.[7] and Sophronia (Bates)
Tower, b.
Dec. 20, 1849; mar. Herbert L. Bradford
Dec. 21, 1874. He was son of Levi and ———— (Mann)
Bradford.
Childr.
I. WENDELL [9]. II. LILLA [9]. III. FRED.[9]

1369. Rhodes. Ninth Generation. Tower.

1027. ANN E. V.[8], LOREN L.[7], LUTHER [6], ABNER [5], JOSEPH [4], JOSEPH [3],
SAMUEL [2], JOHN [1].
Ann E. V.[8], dau. of Loren L.[7] and Sophronia (Bates)
Tower, b.
June 13, 1852; mar. Willie H. Rhodes, of Hillsborough,
Feb. 25, 1875. He was b. in Hillsborough, N. H.,
Oct.   , 1852, and was son of Franklin W. and ————
(White) Rhodes.

TENTH GENERATION.

1370. Webster. Tenth Generation. Tower.

1102. IDA A.[9], HANNIBAL [8], DAVID [7], THOMAS [6], NATHANIEL [5],
JOSEPH [4], BENJAMIN [3], JOHN [2], JOHN [1].
Ida A.[9], dau. of Hannibal [8] and Polly E. (Potter) Tower, b.
July 31, 1852; mar. Ace Webster
May 19, 1874. He was born in Palatine, Ill.,
May 19, 1853, and was son of Joseph P. and Phebe (Sta-
ples) Webster.

Child.

I. EARL M.[10] born July 21, 1882.

1371.   **Tenth Generation.**   **Tower.**

1115. GEORGE O.[9], WILLIAM E.[8], JAMES [7], MEHITABLE [6], JOHN [5],
       JOHN [4], JOSEPH [3], JOHN [2], JOHN [1].

George O.[9], son of William E.[8] and Urania M. (Wakefield)
Tower, b.
Feb. 28, 1849 ; mar. Ellen Pierce in Milford, Mass.,
March 12, 1871. She was b. in Hopkinton, Mass.,
May 16, 1854, and was dau. of John and Mary (Ward)
Pierce.

Childr.

I. FRANK OSCAR [10]   born Dec. 16, 1872, in Milford, Mass.
II. GEORGE HERBERT [10] " Feb. 1, 1875, in Hopkinton, Mass.

1372. Kemp.   **Tenth Generation.**   **Tower.**

1115. MARY M.[9], WILLIAM E.[8], JAMES [7], MEHITABLE [6], JOHN [5],
       JOHN [4], JOSEPH [3], JOHN [2], JOHN [1].

Mary M.[9], dau. of William E.[8] and Urania M. (Wakefield)
Tower, b.
July 18, 1852 ; mar. Fred W. Kemp in Woonsocket, R. I.,
March 28, 1869. He was b. in Hopkinton, Mass.,
Jan. 14, 1849, and was son of Ezekiel and Mary K. (Morey)
Kemp.

Childr.

I.   CHARLES H.[10]   born Jan. 13, 1870, in Hopkinton, Mass.
II. WILLIAM E.[10]   " Aug. 7, 1872, in Milford, Mass.
III. FREDERICK W.[10]   " April 30, 1874, in Hopkinton ; died Sept. 2, 1877,
                            ag. 3 y. 4 m. 2 d.
IV. EVA U.[10]   " Nov. 6, 1875, in Hopkinton.
V.   EFFIE M.[10]   " Dec. 5, 1877,   "

1373. Ward.   **Tenth Generation.**   **Tower.**

1115. EVA V.[9], WILLIAM E.[8], JAMES [7], MEHITABLE [6], JOHN [5], JOHN [4],
       JOSEPH [3], JOHN [2], JOHN [1].

Eva V.[9], dau. of William E.[8] and Urania M. (Wakefield)
Tower, b.
May 3, 1860 ; mar. Wilbur Ward in Westborough, Mass.,
May 7, 1882. He was b. in Hopkinton
Jan. 12, 1858, and was son of Almond and Ellen (Temple)
Ward.

Child.

I. VERNON CARLOS [10] born Feb. 26, 1883, in Hopkinton.

1373 a. Nickerson.   Tenth Generation.   Tower.

1118. EUNICE A.⁹, ISAAC A.⁸, ISAAC P.⁷, ALEXANDER⁶, JOHN⁵, JOHN⁴, JOSEPH³, JOHN², JOHN¹.

Eunice A.⁹, dau. of Isaac A.⁸ and Eunice (Roberts) Tower, b. Oct. 27, 1851; mar. James H. Nickerson¹⁰ Aug. 6, 1868. He was b. May 21, 1848, and was son of Edmund L. and Lydia A.⁹ (Bicknell) Nickerson.

NICKERSON.   TOWER.

James H.¹⁰, Lydia A.⁹, James⁸, James⁷, Zechariah⁶, Patience⁵, Peter⁴, Jeremiah³, Jeremiah², John.¹

Child.

I. LILIAN¹⁰ born   ; mar.

1374. Dodge.   Tenth Generation.   Tower.

1118. ELIZABETH S.⁹, ISAAC A.⁸, ISAAC P.⁷, ALEXANDER⁶, JOHN⁵, JOHN⁴, JOSEPH³, JOHN², JOHN¹.

Elizabeth S.⁹, dau. of Isaac A.⁸ and Eunice (Roberts) Tower, b. May   , 1853; mar. Charles A. Dodge, of Braintree, Mass., May   , 1869. He was b. in Danvers, Mass., 1847, and was son of Osian and Martha (Miller) Dodge.

1375. Bailey.   Tenth Generation.   Tower.

1119. REBECCA E.⁹, CHARLES L.⁸, ISAAC P.⁷, ALEXANDER⁶, JOHN⁵, JOHN⁴, JOSEPH³, JOHN², JOHN¹.

Rebecca E.⁹, dau. of Charles L.⁸ and Rebecca M. (Stetson) Tower, b. Jan. 16, 1854; mar. Orentes L. Bailey, of Hanover, Mass., Feb. 17, 1878. He was b. in Maine 1847, and was son of Ambrose and Julia Bailey.

Child.

I. ALICE LORING¹⁰ born Oct. 17, 1879, in Chattanooga, Tenn.

1376.   Tenth Generation.   Tower.

1145. CHARLES P.⁹, CHARLES B.⁸, ELISHA⁷, ELISHA⁶, ELISHA⁵, ELISHA⁴, RICHARD³, IBROOK², JOHN¹.

Charles P.⁹, son of Charles B.⁸ and Harriet L. (Putnam) Tower, b.

Feb. 6, 1854 ; mar. Martha Ann Weeks in Rutland, Vt.,
May 7, 1879. She was b. in Clarendon, Vt.,
June 13, 1852, and was dau. of Newman and Rebecca
(French) Weeks.

1377.   Tenth Generation.   Tower.

1165. THOMAS [9], THOMAS [8], ASA C.[7], JESSE [6], ROBERT [5], DAVID [4],
HEZEKIAH [3], IBROOK [2], JOHN [1].
Thomas [9], son of Thomas [8] and Rebecca [8] (Lambert)Tower, b.
Feb. 19, 1832 ; mar. Elizabeth B. Williston [9], of Cohasset,
Jan. 15, 1853. She was b. in Cohasset, Mass.,
Dec. 31, 1834, and was dau. of Henry and Charlotte [8]
(Tower) Williston.

Child born in Cohasset.

1445. I. ALICE ANN [10] born May 2, 1854.

WILLISTON.   TOWER.
Elizabeth B.[9], Charlotte [8], Asa C.[7], Jesse [6], Robert [5], David [4], Hezekiah [3], Ibrook [2], John [1].

1378. Souther.   Tenth Generation.   Tower.

1165. SARAH J. [9], THOMAS [8], ASA C.[7], JESSE [6], ROBERT [5], DAVID [4],
HEZEKIAH [3], IBROOK [2], JOHN [1].
Sarah J. [9], dau. of Thomas [8] and Rebecca [8] (Lambert)
Tower, b.
Feb. 25, 1834 ; mar. Samuel C. Souther [7]
May 31, 1851. He was b.
July 8, 1824, and was son of Daniel [6] and Rebecca (Tower)
Souther.

SOUTHER.   TOWER.
Samuel C.[7], Daniel [6], Daniel [5], Joseph [4], Content [3], Ibrook [2], John [1].

Childr. born in Hingham, Mass.

I.	NATHAN TOWER [10]	born July 11, 1852; mar. Lida S. Smith, Feb. 24, 1887.	
II.	ELEANOR [10]	" Aug. 25, 1853 ; died Sept. 11, 1854, ag. 1 y. 17 d.	
III.	ELEANOR [10]	" Aug. 25, 1855.	
IV.	SAMUEL CUSHING [10]	" Sept. 5, 1857.	
V.	DODARAH LESTER [10]	" July 21, 1859 ; died Sept. 15, 1863, ag. 4 y. 1 m. 25 d.	
VI.	ARTHUR WILBUR [10]	" June 13, 1861; died Sept. 14, 1863, ag. 2 y. 3 m. 1 d.	
VII.	SARAH JANE [10]	" Dec. 24, 1862; died Sept. 4, 1863.	
VIII.	LESTER WILBUR [10]	" April 1, 1865.	
IX.	ARTHUR ELMER [10]	" May 25, 1867; died Aug. 22, 1867.	
X.	HENRY SPALDING [10]	" May 29, 1868.	

1379.   **Tenth Generation.**   **Tower.**

1165. LEVI C.⁹, THOMAS⁸, ASA C.⁷, JESSE⁶, ROBERT⁵, DAVID⁴, HEZEKIAH³, IBROOK², JOHN¹.

Levi C.⁹, son of Thomas⁸ and Rebecca⁸ (Lambert) Tower, b. Oct. 17, 1835 ; mar. Ellen Elizabeth Morse⁸, of Cohasset, June 16, 1861. She was b. in in Cohasset, Mass.,
     1845, and was dau. of Andrew⁷ and Lydia (Lincoln) Morse.

     MORSE, BEAL, BATES.   TOWER.

Ellen E.⁸, Andrew⁷, Catherine⁶, Joshua⁵, Rachel⁴, Rachel³, Ibrook², John¹.

Child born in Cohasset.

     I.   LEVI ELLSWORTH¹⁰ born May 12, 1862.

Levi C. Tower⁹ died Feb. 28, 1867, ag. 31 y. 4 m. 14 d.

Ellen E. (Morse) Tower mar., 2d, William Harrison Totman, of Hingham,
Nov. 20, 1869, and died

1380. Powers.   **Tenth Generation.**   **Tower.**

1165. RUTH C.⁹, THOMAS⁸, ASA C.⁷, JESSE⁶, ROBERT⁵, DAVID⁴, HEZEKIAH³, IBROOK², JOHN¹.

Ruth C.⁹, dau. of Thomas⁸ and Rebecca⁸ (Lambert)Tower, b.
     1839 ; mar. Henry Powers in Cohasset, Mass.,
June 25, 1857. He was b.
     1835.

Child born in Cohasset.

I.   RUTH HENRY¹⁰ born June 22, 1860; died Sept. 7, 1860.

Ruth (Tower) Powers died in Cohasset, March 5, 1863, ag. 24.

1381. Fish.   **Tenth Generation.**   **Tower.**

1165. POLLY N.⁹, THOMAS⁸, ASA C.⁷, JESSE⁶, ROBERT⁵, DAVID⁴, HEZEKIAH³, IBROOK², JOHN¹.

Polly N.⁹, dau. of Thomas⁸ and Rebecca⁸ (Lambert) Tower, b.
Feb. 10, 1841 ; mar. Elisha R. Fish in Cohasset, Mass.,
Nov. 10, 1859. He was b. in Marshfield, Mass.,
     and was son of Rufus and Joanna Fish.

1382. Ainslie.   Tenth Generation.   Tower.

1165. REBECCA [9], THOMAS [8], ASA C.[7], JESSE [6], ROBERT [5], DAVID [4], HEZEKIAH [3], IBROOK [2], JOHN [1].

Rebecca [9], dau. of Thomas [8] and Rebecca [8] (Lambert) Tower, b.

June 30, 1843; mar. Henry Ainslie, of Cohasset, Mass., Feb. 19, 1861.   He was b. in Halifax, N. S.,

1834, and was son of Garret and Margaret (Power) Ainslie.

Childr. born in Cohasset.

1430. I. EMMA FRANCES [10] born Dec. 1, 1861.

II. HARRIET TOWER [10] " Sept. 26, 1865; died Oct. 8, 1865.

Rebecca (Tower) Ainslie died in Cohasset, Oct. 25, 1865, ag. 22 y. 3 m. 25 d.

1383.   Tenth Generation.   Tower.

1165. ISAAC H.[9], THOMAS [8], ASA C.[7], JESSE [6], ROBERT [5], DAVID [4], HEZEKIAH [3], IBROOK [2], JOHN [1].

Isaac H.[9], son of Thomas [8] and Rebecca [8] (Lambert) Tower, b.

May 26, 1846; mar. Betsey Ann Treat

June 24, 1865. She was b.

1843, and was dau. of Aquilla and Sarah Treat.

Childr. born in Cohasset.

I. THOMAS A.[10]   born May   5, 1866.
II. CARRIE MATILDA [10]   " Dec.   4, 1867.
III. MARY REBECCA [10]   " Aug. 25, 1870.
IV. WILLIE RUSSELL [10]   " Sept. 13, 1872.
V. BETSEY ANN [10]   " Nov. 15, 1875.
VI. JOHN FRANKLIN [10]   " March 12, 1878.

1384. Taylor.   Tenth Generation.   Tower.

1165. HARRIET [9], THOMAS [8], ASA C.[7], JESSE [6], ROBERT [5], DAVID [4], HEZEKIAH [3], IBROOK [2], JOHN [1].

Harriet [9], dau. of Thomas [8] and Rebecca [8] (Lambert) Tower, b.

Oct. 26, 1848; mar. George Taylor, of Cohasset, Mass., Dec. 26, 1874.   He was b. in Norfolk Co., England,

1849, and was son of Stephen and Mary A. (Pycroft) Taylor.

1385. Sylvia.   Tenth Generation.   Tower.

1165. CAROLINE L.[9], THOMAS [8], ASA C.[7], JESSE [6], ROBERT [5], DAVID [4], HEZEKIAH [3], IBROOK [2], JOHN [1].

Caroline L.[9], dau. of Thomas [8] and Rebecca [8] (Lambert) Tower, b

Feb. 26, 1852; mar. Joseph Sylvia, of Cohasset, Mass.,
Jan. 12, 1875. He was b. in the Western Isles, Portugal,
1848, and was son of Antoine and Augusta Sylvia.

Childr. born in Cohasset.

I. GENEVA[10] born Feb. 10, 1871.
II. CLARENCE[10] " Jan. 9, 1876. ; died Dec. 30, 1876.

1386. Goodwin. Tenth Generation. Tower.

1167. SARAH C.[9], ASA C.[8], ASA C.[7], JESSE[6], ROBERT[5], DAVID[4],
HEZEKIAH[3], IBROOK[2], JOHN[1].
Sarah C.[9], dau. of Asa C.[8] and Sarah W.[8] (Lambert)
Tower, b.
June 6, 1840; mar. Isaac F. Goodwin
Nov. 26, 1857. He was b.
1836, and was son of Richard and Sarah Goodwin.

Childr. born in Hingham, Mass

I. WALTER F.[10]
II. NELLIE[10]
III. EUGENE W.[10] born Jan. 17, 1865.
IV. FREDERICK[10] " July 29, 1867.
V. EDITH MAY[10] " May 25, 1871.

Sarah C. (Tower) Goodwin died in Hingham, Oct. 10, 1886,
ag. 46 y. 4 m. 4 d.

1387. Tenth Generation. Tower.

1167. OLIVER[9], ASA C.[8], ASA C.[7], JESSE[6], ROBERT[5], DAVID[4],
HEZEKIAH[3], IBROOK[2], JOHN[1].
Oliver[9], son of Asa C.[8] and Sarah W.[8] (Lambert) Tower, b.
Dec. 25, 1848; mar. Ann Jane Moore, of Montreal, Canada,
Oct. 13, 1871. She was b.
1849, and was dau. of Stewart and Jane (Reed)
Moore.

Child born in Hingham, Mass.

I. ANNIE ELVIRA[10] born Nov. 27, 1872.

1388. Couillard. Tenth Generation. Tower.

1171. HARRIET E.[9], JESSE[8], JESSE[7], JESSE[6], ROBERT[5], DAVID[4],
HEZEKIAH[3], IBROOK[2], JOHN[1].
Harriet E.[9], dau. of Jesse[8] and Grace S.[7] (Souther)Tower, b.
March 15, 1838; mar. Ephraim M. Couillard, of Cohasset,

Dec.   8, 1859. 'He was b. in Cohasset, Mass.,
Jan.   30, 1836, and was son of William and Priscilla
    Couillard.

Childr. born in Cohasset.

   I.   FRANKLIN WILBUR [10] born Oct. 14, 1864.
  II. CLÁRENCE SUMNER [10]   "   March 27, 1870.

1389. Bates.   Tenth Generation.   Tower.

1171. GRACE E. [9], JESSE [8], JESSE [7], JESSE [6], ROBERT [5], DAVID [4],
    HEZEKIAH [3], IBROOK [2], JOHN [1].
    Grace E. [9], dau. of Jesse [8] and Grace S. [7] (Souther) Tower, b.
    March 25, 1844; mar. William H. Bates, of Cohasset, Mass.,
    Sept. 17, 1859. He was b. in Hanover, Mass.,
        1838, and was son of Abner and Jerusha Bates.

Childr. born in Cohasset.

    I.   ABNER NEWHALL [10]   born May 17, 1860.
   II.   WILLIAM HENRY [10]   "   July 2, 1861.
  III. JERUSHA ELLEN [10]   "   Feb. 28, 1863.
  IV.   MARTHA JANE [10]   "   Sept. 22, 1864.
   V.   STEPHEN TOWER [10]   "   April 23, 1867.
  VI.   Daughter [10]   "   Dec. 19, 1871.
 VII.   GRACE S. [10]   "   Feb. 28, 1875; died Aug. 17, 1875.
VIII.   JOHN [10]   "   Jan. 21, 1878.

1390.   Tenth Generation.   Tower.

1172. HELEN L. [9], JOHN [8], JESSE [7], JESSE [6], ROBERT [5], DAVID [4],
    HEZEKIAH [3], IBROOK [2], JOHN [1].
    Helen L. [9], dau. of John [8] and Susan (Dady) Tower, b.
            ; mar. Moses Pratt, of Cohasset, Mass.,
    Oct. 13, 1860. He was b. in Cohasset
            1838, and was son of Lewis and Dorcas (Wood)
    Pratt.

1391. Parsons.   Tenth Generation.   Tower.

1193. LYDIA A. [9], CALVIN B. [8], STEPHEN [7], STEPHEN [6], PETER [5],
    PETER [4], JEREMIAH [3], JEREMIAH [2], JOHN [1].
    Lydia A. [9], dau. of Calvin B. [8], and Amanda M. (Higgins)
        Tower, b.
    July 20, 1836; mar. Jason Parsons, of Pittsfield, Mass.,
    July 2, 1865. He was b.
    Aug. 5, 1797, and was son of Lemuel and Abigail Parsons.

1392. Haskins. Tenth Generation. Tower.

1193. ANGELINE D.[9], CALVIN B.[8], STEPHEN [7], STEPHEN [6], PETER [5], PETER [4], JEREMIAH [3], JEREMIAH [2], JOHN [1].
Angeline D.[9], dau. of Calvin B.[8], and Amanda M. (Higgins) Tower, b.
May 3, 1843; mar. Milo J. Haskins, of Chester, Mass.,
May 3, 1865. He was b.
1843, and was son of Joel and Mary Haskins.

Child.

I. EDITH ALMA [10] born Feb. 14, 1868.

1393. Tenth Generation. Tower.

1195. HENRY L.[9], LUTHER B.[8], STEPHEN [7], STEPHEN [6], PETER [5], PETER [4], JEREMIAH [3], JEREMIAH [2], JOHN [1].
Henry L.[9], son of Luther B.[8] and Sabrina(Tower)Tower, b.
March 27, 1845; mar. Cynthia Louisa Allen, of Worthington,
Jan. 19, 1876. She was b.
Sept. , 1856.

Child.

I. HERBERT LORENZO [10] born Nov. 1, 1879.

1394. Tenth Generation. Tower.

1198. CLINTON B.[9], DEXTER [8], JOHN [7], STEPHEN [6], PETER [5], PETER [4], JEREMIAH [3], JEREMIAH [2], JOHN [1].
Clinton B.[9], son of Dexter [8] and Irene B. (Pierce) Tower, b.
March 1, 1858; mar. Ida Salome Bartlett
Sept. 4, 1878. She was b.
Dec. 31, 1858, and was dau. of Spencer and Salome Bartlett.

Child.

I. ARTHUR CLINTON [10] born Feb. 17, 1880.

1395. Allen. Tenth Generation. Tower.

1200. ADA C.[9], ROSWELL [8], JOHN [7], STEPHEN [6], PETER [5], PETER [4], JEREMIAH [3], JEREMIAH [2], JOHN [1].
Ada C.[9], dau. of Roswell [8] and Elizabeth (Bryant) Tower, b.
March 5, 1854; mar. Emery Clement Allen, of Adams, Mass.,
June 1, 1880. He was b.
Dec. 6, 1851, and was son of Darwin D. and Anna (Sherman) Allen.

1396. Bowker. Tenth Generation.   Tower.

1202. ELSIE [9], DAVID D.[8], DAVID [7], STEPHEN [6], PETER [5], PETER [4],
JEREMIAH [3], JEREMIAH [2], JOHN [1].
Elsie [9], dau. of David D.[8] and Achsah E.[8] (Farrar) Tower, b.
Jan. 15, 1840; mar. Calvin Bowker [8]
Nov. 30, 1856. He was b.
Oct. 7, 1831, and was son of Franklin and Leah [7] (Tower)
Bowker.

BOWKER.   TOWER.
Calvin [8], Leah [7], Asa [6], Peter [5], Peter [4], Jeremiah [3], Jeremiah [2], John [1].

Child.

I. AULDEN FRANCIS [10] born June 10, 1866, in Wilson.

Calvin Bowker [8] died in Wilson, Jan. 27, 1883, ag. 51 y.
3 m. 20 d.

1397. Johnson. Tenth Generation.   Tower.

1202. OLIVE [9], DAVID D.[8], DAVID [7], STEPHEN [6], PETER [5], PETER [4],
JEREMIAH [3], JEREMIAH [2], JOHN [1].
Olive [9], dau. of David D.[8] and Achsah E.[8] (Farrar) Tower, b.
Aug. 4, 1841; mar. George W. Johnson, of Wilson, N. Y.,
July 2, 1857. He was b.
Aug. 7, 1832, and was son of Henry Johnson.

Childr.

I. LIZZIE [10].	III. FRANK [10].	V. MARY [10].
II. HENRY [10].	IV. ACHSAH [10].	VI. CALVIN B.[10].

1398. Hamlin. Tenth Generation.   Tower.

1202. LYDIA [9], DAVID D.[8], DAVID [7], STEPHEN [6], PETER [5], PETER [4],
JEREMIAH [3], JEREMIAH [2], JOHN [1].
Lydia [9], dau. of David D.[8] and Achsah E.[8] (Farrar) Tower, b.
Aug. 23, 1843; mar. Eli Nelson Hamlin, of Wilson, N. Y.,
July 4, 1864. He was b. in Wilson
May 17, 1842, and was son of William and Anna [8] (Tower)
Hamlin.

HAMLIN.   TOWER.
Eli N.[9], Anna [8], Otis [7], Stephen [6], Peter [5], Peter [4], Jeremiah [3], Jeremiah [2], John [1].

Childr. born in Wilson.

I.   WILLIAM [10] born April 29, 1865; died Nov. 4, 1865.
II. GERTIE [10]   "   Oct. 21, 1869; "   Sept. 16, 1870.
III. EDITH [10]   "   July 2, 1877.
IV. BESSIE [10]   "   Feb. 10, 1881.

1399. **Tenth Generation.** **Tower.**

1202. DAVID A.[9], DAVID D.[8], DAVID [7], STEPHEN [6], PETER [5], PETER [4], JEREMIAH [3], JEREMIAH [2], JOHN [1].

David A.[9], son of David D.[8] and Achsah E.[8] (Farrar) Tower, b.

Aug. 8, 1845; mar. Mary Lourie.

Child.

I. ANNA R.[10]

1400. **Tenth Generation.** **Tower.**

1202. EDGAR D.[9], DAVID D.[8], DAVID [7], STEPHEN [6], PETER [5], PETER [4], JEREMIAH [3], JEREMIAH [2], JOHN [1].

Edgar D.[9], son of David D.[8] and Achsah E.[8] (Farrar) Tower, b.

July 11, 1858; mar. Ida Perry, of Wilson, N. Y.,

April 18, 1875. She was b.

April 27, 1858, and was dau. of Harrison and Maria (Parish) Perry.

Childr. born in Wilson.

I. GERTIE C.[10] born May 14, 1876.	IV. AULDEN [10] born July 5, 1883.
II. MYRTIE [10] " July 17, 1877.	V. EFFIE F.[10] " Sept. 8, 1884.
III. MARION [10] " May 1, 1879.	

1401. Richardson. **Tenth Generation.** **Tower.**

1207. GERTRUDE A.[9], JOHN W.[8], DAVID [7], STEPHEN [6], PETER [5], PETER [4], JEREMIAH [3], JEREMIAH [2], JOHN [1].

Gertrude A.[9], dau. of John W.[8] and Lizzie (Peavey) Tower, b.

April 25, 1858; mar. William C. Richardson in Boston

Dec. 8, 1880. He was b.

April 28, 1855, and was son of Artemas C. and Celestia (Pease) Richardson.

Childr. born in Somerville, Mass.

I. WILLIE PEAVEY [10] born Nov. 21, 1881.
II. CLIFFORD TOWER [10] " Nov. 30, 1883.

1402. Wallace. **Tenth Generation.** **Tower.**

1207. LOUISA M.[9], JOHN W.[8], DAVID [7], STEPHEN [6], PETER [5], PETER [4], JEREMIAH [3], JEREMIAH [2], JOHN [1].

Louisa M.[9], dau. of John W.[8] and Lizzie (Peavey) Tower, b.

Dec. 30, 1863; mar. Fred E. Wallace in Boston, Mass.,
May 18, 1885. He was b. in Reading, Mass.,
May 31, 1863, and was son of Oliver and Martha N. (Rugg)
Wallace.

1403.   Tenth Generation.   Tower.

1210. OSCAR[9], JOHN E.[8], PETER[7], STEPHEN[6], PETER[5], PETER[4],
JEREMIAH[3], JEREMIAH[2], JOHN[1].
Oscar[9], son of John E.[8] and Mary Jane (Eggleston) Tower, b.
Nov. 3, 1844; mar. Emily A. Gifford in Sanborn, N. Y.,
Oct. 22, 1872. She was b. in Lockport, N. Y.,
May 20, 1848, and was dau. of Nathan and Sally (Hamlin)
Gifford.

Child.

I.   WILLARD OSCAR[10] born June 22, 1878, in Wilson, N. Y.

1404.   Tenth Generation.   Tower.

1210. CHARLES G.[9], JOHN E.[8], PETER[7], STEPHEN[6], PETER[5], PETER[4],
JEREMIAH[3], JEREMIAH[2], JOHN[1].
Charles G.[9], son of John E.[8] and Mary Jane (Eggleston)
Tower, b.
Sept. 7, 1846; mar. Sarah O. Bradley, of Wilson, N. Y.,
April 10, 1878. She was dau. of Martin and —— (Good-
enough) Bradley.

Child.

I.   LULU[10] born Dec. , 1882.

1405.   Tenth Generation.   Tower.

1210. DE WITT C.[9], JOHN E.[8], PETER[7], STEPHEN[6], PETER[5], PETER[4],
JEREMIAH[3], JEREMIAH[2], JOHN[1].
De Witt C.[9], son of John E.[8] and Mary Jane (Eggleston)
Tower, b.
Aug. 25, 1848; mar. Sarah Jennie Cobb, of Lockport, N.Y.,
Jan. 29, 1870. She was b. in Newfane, N. Y.,
Sept. 19, 1852, and was dau. of Crittenden and Janette
(Corwin) Cobb.

Childr.

I.   CORA MEDA[10] born March 9, 1871, in Wilson, N. Y.
II.   MERTIE DELL[10] " June 18, 1874, in Ada, Mich.
III. GRACIE MAY[10] " Sept. 16, 1878, in Wilson, N. Y.

1406. Sawyer. Tenth Generation. Tower.

1210. EUGENE H.[9], JOHN E.[8], PETER [7], STEPHEN [6], PETER [5], PETER [4], JEREMIAH [3], JEREMIAH [2], JOHN [1].

Eugene H.[9], dau. of John E.[8] and Mary J. (Eggleston) Tower, b.

March 3, 1850; mar. Charles F. Sawyer, of Newfane, N.Y., Dec. 17, 1879. He was b. in Newfane

Jan. 16, 1850, and was son of Amos and Betsey H. (Van Horn) Sawyer.

Childr. born in Batavia, N. Y.

I. EDWIN VAN RAY [10] born Oct. 2, 1881; died Dec. 17, 1881.
II. CLAUDE ALBERT [10] " May 16, 1884.

1407. Tenth Generation. Tower.

1210. BYRON E.[9], JOHN E.[8], PETER [7], STEPHEN [6], PETER [5], PETER [4], JEREMIAH [3], JEREMIAH [2], JOHN [1].

Byron E.[9], son of John E.[8] and Mary J.(Eggleston) Tower, b.

Feb. 2, 1853; mar. Nettie Robinson, of Porter, N.Y., Nov. 16, 1881. She was b. in Porter

April 15, 1860, and was dau. of George and Martha Robinson.

Child.

I. PERRY EDWARD [10] born Feb. 23, 1884.

1408. Sawyer. Tenth Generation. Tower.

1210. MARY J.[9], JOHN E.[8], PETER [7], STEPHEN [6], PETER [5], PETER [4], JEREMIAH [3], JEREMIAH [2], JOHN [1].

Mary J.[9], dau. of John E.[8] and Mary J. (Eggleston) Tower, b.

Jan. 15, 1855; mar. Charles F. Sawyer, of Newfane, N. Y., April 12, 1877. He was born in Newfane

Jan. 16, 1850, and was son of Amos and Betsey H. (Van Horn) Sawyer.

Childr. none.

Mary J. (Tower) Sawyer died in Wilson, N.Y., May 23, 1878, ag. 23 y. 4 m. 8 d.

1409. Piper. Tenth Generation. Tower.

1211. GERTRUDE [9], WILLIAM [8], PETER [7], STEPHEN [6], PETER [5], PETER [4], JEREMIAH [3], JEREMIAH [2], JOHN [1].

Gertrude[9], dau. of William [8] and Anna L. (Knowles) Tower, b.

May 21, 1851 ; mar. Frank E. Piper, of Charlotte, Mich.,
Jan. 6, 1871. He was b. in Ontario Co., N. Y.,
     1849, and was son of William S. and Lucinda
(Otley) Piper.
Childr.
I. EARL W.[10]   II. LEE L.[10]

1410. May.   Tenth Generation.   Tower.

1211. ELLETTA L.[9], WILLIAM [8], PETER [7], STEPHEN [6], PETER [5], PETER [4],
     JEREMIAH [3], JEREMIAH [2], JOHN [1].
Elletta L.[9], dau. of William [8] and Anna L. (Knowles)
Tower, b.
April 4, 1853 ; mar. Henry T. May
April 23, 1888. He was son of Thomas P. and Elizabeth
(Shear) May.

1411.   Tenth Generation.   Tower.

1211. ALBERT K.[9], WILLIAM [8], PETER [7], STEPHEN [6], PETER [5], PETER [4],
     JEREMIAH [3], JEREMIAH [2], JOHN [1].
Albert K.[9], son of William [8] and Anna L. (Knowles)
Tower, b.
Aug. 3, 1855 ; mar. Abbie M. Brown
Aug. 30, 1883. She was b. in Ionia Co., Mich.,
Nov.   , 1856, and was dau. of Leonard and Nancy (Smith)
Brown.
Child.
I. MAX L.[10] born Dec. 8, 1885.

1412. Grier.   Tenth Generation.   Tower.

1211. GLYCIE [9], WILLIAM [8], PETER [7], STEPHEN [6], PETER [5], PETER [4],
     JEREMIAH [3], JEREMIAH[2], JOHN [1].
Glycie [9], dau. of William [8] and Anna L. (Knowles) Tower, b.
June 6, 1857 ; mar. Charles J. Grier
Oct. 3, 1883. He was b. in Eaton Co., Mich.,
     1856, and was son of James and Elvira S. (Fields)
Grier.

1413.   Tenth Generation.   Tower.

1222. OTIS F.[9], JOHN [8], OTIS [7], STEPHEN [6], PETER [5], PETER [4], JERE-
     MIAH [3], JEREMIAH [2], JOHN [1].
Otis F.[9], son of John [8] and Emery P. (Aiken) Tower, b.
July 20, 1850 ; mar. Barbara Fletcher, of Lewiston, N. Y.,
March 15, 1870. She was dau. of Jacob and Emily (Chap-
man) Fletcher.

Childr. none.

Otis F. Tower[9] died   1886, in Laingsburg, Mich., ag. 36.

1414. Robinson.   Tenth Generation.   Tower.

1222.   MARY E.[9], JOHN[8], OTIS[7], STEPHEN[6], PETER[5], PETER[4], JERE-
MIAH[3], JEREMIAH[2], JOHN[1].
Mary E.[9], dau. of John[8] and Emery P. (Aiken) Tower, b.
1209.   July 31, 1852; mar. Samuel P. Robinson[9]
Sept. 2, 1883. He was b.
July 13, 1849, and was son of Samuel and Lyanda[8] (Tower)
Robinson.

ROBINSON.   TOWER.
Samuel P.[9], Lyanda[8], Peter[7], Stephen[6], Peter[5], Peter[4], Jeremiah[3],
Jeremiah[2], John[1].

1415.   Tenth Generation.   Tower.

1222.   CHARLES D.[9], JOHN[8], OTIS[7], STEPHEN[6], PETER[5], PETER[4],
JEREMIAH[3], JEREMIAH[2], JOHN[1].
Charles D.[9], son of John[8] and Emery P. (Aiken) Tower, b.
Nov. 6, 1854; mar. Henrietta M. Scott, of Lewiston, N.Y.,
Aug. 13, 1873. She was b,
Feb. 22, 1847, and was dau. of John Scott.

Childr. none.

Henrietta M. (Scott) Tower died in Lewiston, Sept. 10,
1880, ag. 33 y. 6 m. 17 d.

1416. Hunt.   Tenth Generation.   Tower.

1226.   HARRIET E.[9], WILLIAM[8], ASA[7], ASA[6], PETER[5], PETER[4],
JEREMIAH[3], JEREMIAH[2], JOHN[1].
Harriet E.[9], dau. of William[8] and Mary A. (Stetson)
Tower, b.
July 25, 1844; mar. Josiah T. Hunt
Aug. 14, 1862. He was b. in Cummington, Mass.,
Sept.   , 1843, and was son of Ebenezer and Maria Hunt.

Childr. born in Cummington.

    I.   OLA E.[10]   born May 7, 1865.
   II.   SUSIE A.[10]   "   Nov. 8, 1868.
  III.   BERTHA LENA[10] "   March , 1877; died July   1877.

1417.   Hunt.   Tenth Generation.   Tower.

1226. MARY E.⁹, WILLIAM ⁸, ASA ⁷, ASA ⁶, PETER ⁵, PETER ⁴, JERE-
MIAH ³, JEREMIAH ², JOHN ¹.

Mary E.⁹, dau. of William ⁸ and Mary A. (Stetson) Tower, b.
Aug. 10, 1846 ; mar. James H. Hunt, of Cummington,
Mass.,
Oct. 2, 1867. He was b.
1847, and was son of Ebenezer and Maria Hunt.

Childr.

I.   LILIAN MARIA ¹⁰ born Jan. 8, 1869.
II.   WILLIAM E.¹⁰   "   April 14, 1873.

1418.   Tenth Generation.   Tower.

1226. WILLIAM W.⁹, WILLIAM ⁸, ASA ⁷, ASA ⁶, PETER ⁵, PETER ⁴,
JEREMIAH ³, JEREMIAH ², JOHN ¹.

William W.⁹, son of William ⁸ and Mary A. (Stetson)
Tower, b.
Dec. 26, 1848 ; mar. Lucy M. Guilford in Cummington,
Mass.,
May 1, 1872. She was b.
1848, and was the adopted dau. of William Guilford.

Child born in Cummington.

I.   FLORA ¹⁰ born Jan.   , 1873.

1419.   Tenth Generation.   Tower.

1226. JETSON A.⁹, WILLIAM ⁸, ASA ⁷, ASA ⁶, PETER ⁵, PETER ⁴,
JEREMIAH ³, JEREMIAH ², JOHN ¹.

Jetson A.⁹, son of William ⁸ and Mary A. (Stetson) Tower, b.
Feb. 5, 1857 ; mar. Carrie M. Longley in Pittsfield, Mass.,
May 4, 1878. She was b.
1861, and was dau. of Lewis and Laura (Beals)
Longley.

Childr. none.

Carrie M. (Longley) Tower died in Cummington, Feb. 25,
1880, ag. 19.

1420.   Tenth Generation.   Tower.

1228. NATHAN E.⁹, ALMON J.⁸, ASA ⁷, ASA ⁶, PETER ⁵, PETER ⁴,
JEREMIAH ³, JEREMIAH ², JOHN ¹.

Nathan E.⁹, son of Almon J.⁸ and Mary U. (Corwin)
Tower, b.

Aug. 2, 1858; mar. Elizabeth Carroll in Homer, Ill.,
Oct. 15, 1879. She was b. in Orland, Ill.,
May 28, 1857, and was dau. of Amos and Ann (Wiles)
Carroll.

Childr.

I. ELVIR [10] born Dec. 12, 1880.   II. MORRIS [10] born June 3, 1882.
III. MERTON [10] born Oct. , 1884.

1421. Paddock.   Tenth Generation.   Tower.

1228. LILA ALICE [9], ALMON J. [8], ASA [7], ASA [6], PETER [5], PETER [4],
JEREMIAH [3], JEREMIAH [2], JOHN [1].
Lila Alice [9], dau. of Almon J. [8] and Mary U. (Corwin)
Tower, b.
Nov. 3, 1862; mar. Elmer Paddock in Homer, Ill.,
Dec. 21, 1881.

Child born in Homer.

1. Son [10] born Sept. 5, 1882; died Nov. 14, 1882.

Lila Alice (Tower) Paddock died in Homer, Nov. 14, 1882,
ag. 20 y. 11 d.

1422. Malcolm.   Tenth Generation.   Tower

1241. MARY B. [9], MOSES B. [8], MOSES [7], MALACHI [6], MALACHI [5],
PETER [4], JEREMIAH [3], JEREMIAH [2], JOHN [1].
Mary B.[9], dau. of Moses B.[8] and Olive G. (Cushing) Tower, b.
July 13, 1839; mar. Frederick Malcolm
July 30, 1862. He was b. in New York
Nov. 4, 1838, and was son of James and Anna M. (Fader)
Malcolm.

Childr. born in Boston.

I. FRANK WALLACE [10] born Dec. 9, 1862; died Feb. 7, 1863.
II. ERNEST EUGENE [10]   "   June 7, 1864.
III. EDITH LYDIA [10]   "   Dec. 3, 1869.
IV. GEORGE FREDERICK [10] "   Jan. 27, 1874.

1423. Hall.   Tenth Generation.   Tower.

1241. LYDIA C. [9], MOSES B. [8], MOSES [7], MALACHI [6], MALACHI [5],
PETER [4], JEREMIAH [3], JEREMIAH [2], JOHN [1].
Lydia C.[9], dau. of Moses B.[8] and Olive G. (Cushing)
Tower, b.
Sept. 1, 1841; mar. Rev. Linville John Hall in Boston
Sept. 21, 1871. He was b. in Springfield, Mass.,
July 8, 1822, and was son of John and Bathsheba S.
(White) Hall.

Childr. born in Boston.

I. LILIAN MAY[10]   born Dec. 21, 1872.
II. LINVILLE TOWER[10] " Jan. 21, 1877.

1424. Eager.   Tenth Generation.   Tower.

1241. OLIVE G.[9], MOSES B.[8], MOSES[7], MALACHI[6], MALACHI[5],
PETER[4], JEREMIAH[3], JEREMIAH[2], JOHN[1].
Olive G.[9], dau. of Moses B.[8] and Olive G. (Cushing)Tower, b.
Oct. 29, 1844 ; mar. George Russell Eager in Boston
June 10, 1868. He was b. in Weston, Mass.,
Dec. 10, 1843, and was son of Penuel B. and Harriet
(Austin) Eager.

Child born in Boston.

I. MABEL TOWER[10] born April 15, 1869.

1425.   Tenth Generation.   Tower.

1241. MOSES S.[9], MOSES B.[8], MOSES[7], MALACHI[6], MALACHI[5],
PETER[4], JEREMIAH[3], JEREMIAH[2], JOHN[1].
Moses S.[9], son of Moses B.[8] and Olive G. (Cushing) Tower, b.
Jan. 31, 1848 ; mar. Alma Wing Patterson in Belmont, Me.,
Nov. 24, 1872. She was b. in Belfast, Me.,
May 1, 1850, and was dau. of Hiram and Betsey (Farrar)
Patterson.

Childr. born in Newton, Mass.

I. MOSES BINNEY[10]   born Aug. 13, 1873.
II. BESSIE PATTERSON[10] " Oct. 2, 1874.
III. Son[10]   " Aug. 22, 1876.

1426.   Tenth Generation.   Tower.

1244. MARTIN V. B.[9], MARTIN W.[8], PETER[7], MALACHI[6], MALACHI[5],
PETER[4], JEREMIAH[3], JEREMIAH[2], JOHN[1].
Martin V. B.[9], son of Martin W.[8] and Eleanor L. (Spencer)
Tower, b.
Oct. 5, 1841 ; mar. Amarilla Reynolds in Clifton, Wis.,
Oct. 5, 1866. She was b. in Attica, N. Y.,
March 21, 1834, and was dau. of Silas C. and Susan D.
(Raymond) Reynolds.

Childr. born in Clifton, Wis.

I. FRED A.[10]   born May 27, 1868.
II. HENRY H.[10]   " April 29, 1870.
III. CLARENCE W.[10] " Oct. 24, 1873.
IV. RAYMOND N.[10]   " Nov. 5, 1877 ; died June 1, 1881, ag. 3 y. 6 m.
26 d.

1427. Tenth Generation. **Tower.**

1247. ELISHA J.[9], WARNER C.[8], PETER [7], MALACHI [6], MALACHI [5],
PETER [4], JEREMIAH [3], JEREMIAH [2], JOHN [1].

Elisha J.[9], son of Warner C. [8] and Mary Ann (Jones)
Tower, b.

June 1, 1846; mar. Celestia A. Moody in Belfast, Me.,
July 13, 1872. She was b. in Lincolnville, Me.,
July 8, 1852, and was dau. of James and Esther S. (Wallace) Moody.

Childr. born in Lincolnville.

I. AUBREY W.[10] born Nov. 25, 1875.
II. MARY E.[10] " March 27, 1878.

1428. Tenth Generation. **Tower.**

1249. GEORGE W.[9], ELBRIDGE G.[8], PETER [7], MALACHI [6], MALACHI [5],
PETER [4], JEREMIAH [3], JEREMIAH [2], JOHN [1].

George W.[9], son of Elbridge G.[8] and Mary G. (Edgecomb)
Tower, b.

Oct. 22, 1846; mar. Abbie Adams, of Cambridgeport, Mass.,
March 12, 1870. She was b. in East Unity, N. H.,
Jan. 10, 1848, and was dau. of Joseph M. and Abigail A.
(Weed) Adams.

Childr. born in Cambridge.

I. GEORGE WASHINGTON [10] born Oct. 27, 1871.
II. ELBRIDGE A.[10] " Dec. 5, 1873; died Feb. 5, 1875, ag.
1 y. 2 m.
III. ADELBERT A.[10] " June 10, 1878. -

1429. Cushing. Tenth Generation. **Tower.**

1249. GEORGIANA [9], ELBRIDGE G.[8], PETER [7], MALACHI [6], MALACHI [5],
PETER [4], JEREMIAH [3], JEREMIAH [2], JOHN [1].

Georgiana [9], dau. of Elbridge G.[8] and Mary (Edgecomb)
Tower, b.

Oct. 9, 1848; mar. Nathan Cushing in Boston, Mass.,
March 30, 1871. He was b. in Woodstock, Vt.,
Dec. 21, 1842, and was son of Nathan and Vernon (King)
Cushing.

1430. Tenth Generation. **Tower.**

1254. FRANK A.[9], JOHN M.[8], COMFORT [7], MALACHI [6], MALACHI [5],
PETER [4], JEREMIAH [3], JEREMIAH [2], JOHN [1].

Frank A.[9], son of John M.[8] and Harriet A.[8] (Souther)
Tower, b.

1382.   April 13, 1863 ; mar. Emma F. Souther [10] in Cohasset,
May 11, 1884. She was b. in Cohasset, Mass.,
Dec. 1, 1861, and was dau. of Henry and Rebecca[9]
(Tower) Ainslie

and adopted dau. of Samuel [7] and Sarah J.[9]
(Tower) Souther.

AINSLIE.   TOWER.

Emma F.[10], Rebecca[9], Thomas[8], Asa C.[7], Jesse[6], Robert[5], David[4],
Hezekiah[3], Ibrook[2], John[1].

Child born in Hingham.

I. NELLIE FRANCES [10] born Dec. 18, 1885.

Emma F. (Souther) Tower died in Hingham, Dec. 29, 1885,
ag. 24 y. 28 d.

Frank A. Tower [9] died in Hingham, June 21, 1887, ag. 24 y.
2 m. 8 d.

1431.   **Tenth Generation.**   **Tower.**

1255. CORNELIUS P.[9], JOHN H.[8], JOHN H.[7], MALACHI[6], MALACHI[5],
PETER[4], JEREMIAH[3], JEREMIAH[2], JOHN[1].

Cornelius P.[9], son of John H.[8] and Jane A. (Woodruff)
Tower, b.

Sept. 30, 1844 ; mar. Maria Rutter
Dec. 10, 1868. She was dau. of John and Mary Rutter.

Childr.

I. FREDERICK H.[10]	born Oct.	4, 1869.
II. MARY JANE [10]	"	April 29, 1870.
III. GEORGE WASHINGTON [10]	"	April 29, 1873.
IV. MINNIE BELL[10]	"	Jan. 2, 1875.
V. FLORENCE LOUISA [10]	"	Sept. 8, 1878.
VI. ERVITT CORNELIUS [10]	"	Aug. 7, 1883.

1432.   **Tenth Generation.**   **Tower.**

1255. WILLIAM H.[9], JOHN H.[8], JOHN H.[7], MALACHI[6], MALACHI[5],
PETER[4], JEREMIAH[3], JEREMIAH[2], JOHN[1].

William H.[9], son of John H.[8] and Jane A. (Woodruff)
Tower, b.

July 27, 1859 ; mar. Hannah Phebe Newton
May 16, 1881. She was dau. of Solomon and Eliza J.
Newton.

Childr.

I. FLOYD L.[10] born June 3, 1882.
II. ALMA JANE[10] " Sept. , 1884.

1433. **Tenth Generation.** **Tower.**

1265. SCOTT[9], JOHN T.[8], WASHINGTON[7], BENJAMIN T.[6], BENJAMIN[5], JAMES[4], BENJAMIN[3], BENJAMIN[2], JOHN[1].

Scott[9], son of John T.[8] and Jane (Foster) Tower, b.
July 9, 1852; mar. Marian Fassett, of Rochester, Vt.,
Aug. 24, 1874. She was b. in Hancock, Vt.,
Oct. 25, 1857, and was dau. of Augustus A. and Roxy
Fassett.

Childr. born in Rochester, Vt.

I. HARRY L.[10] born May 16, 1877.   III. EDITH N.[10] born Oct. 30, 1881.
II. ETHEL M.[10] " Nov. 2, 1878.

1434. **Tenth Generation.** **Tower.**

1265. CHARLES C.[9], JOHN T.[8], WASHINGTON[7], BENJAMIN T.[6], BEN-JAMIN[5], JAMES[4], BENJAMIN[3], BENJAMIN[2], JOHN[1].

Charles C.[9], son of John T.[8] and Jane (Foster) Tower, b.
March 18, 1854; mar. Dora Hammond, of West Derby, Vt.,
Jan. 1, 1878. She was b. in Derby,
June , 1857.

Childr.

I. ALTON F.[10] born Aug. 29, 1879.   II. Child[10] born March , 1882.

1435. Carter. **Tenth Generation.** **Tower.**

1268. MARCIA I.[9], LYMAN C.[8], WASHINGTON[7], BENJAMIN T.[6], BEN-JAMIN[5], JAMES[4], BENJAMIN[3], BENJAMIN[2], JOHN[1].

Marcia I.[9], dau. of Lyman C.[8] and Julia A. (Hamilton) Tower, b.
June 11, 1852; mar. William E. Carter, of East Ran-dolph, Vt.,
Feb. 19, 1870. He was b. in Randolph
Jan. 30, 1850, and was son of David and Harriet (Smith) Carter.

Childr.

I. CADDIE L.[10] born Jan. 15, 1871.   II. MYRA A.[10] born Aug. 10, 1872.

1436. Terry. **Tenth Generation.** **Tower.**

1268. MYRA A.[9], LYMAN C.[8], WASHINGTON[7], BENJAMIN T.[6], BEN-JAMIN[5], JAMES[4], BENJAMIN[3], BENJAMIN[2], JOHN[1].

Myra A.[9], dau. of Lyman C.[8] and Julia A. (Hamilton) Tower, b.

Dec. 6, 1854; mar. Marcellus C. Terry, of Cavendish, Vt., Nov. 16, 1880. He was b. in Saranac, N. Y.,

Feb. 4, 1856, and was son of Oman and Deborah (Baker) Terry.

Child.

I. MARCIA E.[10] born Dec. 15, 1881.

1437. Tenth Generation. Tower.

1331. ANDREW J.[9], JUSTUS D.[8], GEORGE [7], ABEL [6], ABEL [5], AMBROSE [4], AMBROSE [3], BENJAMIN [2], JOHN [1].

Andrew J.[9], son of Justus D.[8] and Mary (Carnes) Tower, b. July 29, 1855; mar. Sarah J. Porterfield

Dec. 28, 1876. She was dau. of Robert and Mary Porterfield.

Child.

I. MARY [10] born April 11, 1879.

Sarah J. (Porterfield) Tower died April 17, 1879.

Andrew J. Tower [9] mar., 2d, Nettie Bridge

Feb. , 1881. She was b.

Aug. 3, 1864, and was dau. of Sereno and Alice Bridge.

1438. Tenth Generation. Tower.

1332. CHARLES A.[9], AUGUSTUS C.[8], GEORGE [7], ABEL [6], ABEL [5], AMBROSE [4], AMBROSE [3], BENJAMIN [2], JOHN [1].

Charles A.[9], son of Augustus C.[8] and Amanda M. (James) Tower, b.

Oct. 23, 1854; mar. Clara A. Ives

Jan. 28, 1880. She was b.

June 6, 1857, and was dau. of Erastus B. and Harriet (Green) Ives.

Child.

I. LOUIS [10] born Oct. 3, 1881.

1439. Hickethier. Tenth Generation. Tower.

1353. SARAH T.[9], WASHINGTON L.[8], HULL [7], MATTHEW [6], MATTHEW [5], MATTHEW [4], SAMUEL [3], SAMUEL [2], JOHN [1].

Sarah T.[9], dau. of Washington L.[8] and Ellen (Smith) Tower, b.

April 15, 1852; mar. Augustus Hickethier

March 8, 1884. He was b. in Germany

Feb. 2, 1844, and was son of Daniel and Hannah (Magdeburg) Hickethier.

1440. Cole.   Tenth Generation.   **Tower.**

1353. LYDIA B.[9], WASHINGTON L.[8], HULL[7], MATTHEW[6], MATTHEW[5]
MATTHEW[4], SAMUEL[3], SAMUEL[2], JOHN[1].
Lydia B.[9], dau. of Washington L.[8] and Ellen (Smith)
Tower, b.
June 5, 1855; mar. Sidney Cole
May 1, 1876. He was b. in Douglas Co., Ore.,
Dec. 25, 1851, and was son of James and Louisa (Leeper)
Cole.

Childr. born in Douglas Co., Ore.

I. CARRIE[10] born April 16, 1877.   II. ELLEN LOUISA[10] born Jan. 29, 1879.

1441. Kimes.   Tenth Generation.   **Tower.**

1357. ARMENTA R.[9], MATTHEW[8], JONATHAN W.[7], MATTHEW[6], MAT-
THEW[5], MATTHEW[4], SAMUEL[3], SAMUEL[2], JOHN[1].
Armenta R.[9], dau. of Matthew[8] and Sarah J. (Long)
Tower, b.
May 20, 1855; mar. Daniel W. Kimes in Jennings, Ind.,
Jan. 15, 1873. He was b.
Dec. 27, 1850, and was son of Daniel and Elizabeth (Cosby)
Kimes.

Childr. born in Jennings.

I. THEODORE OTIS[10] born Dec. 17, 1873.
II. NORA ALICE[10]   "   Sept. 20, 1875; died Oct. 20, 1877, ag. 2 y. 30 d.
III. SAMUEL WESLEY[10]   "   Feb. 2, 1877; died March 23, 1882, ag. 5 y.
1 m. 21 d.
IV. FRANCIS MARION[10]   "   March 1, 1879.
V. MARY BERTHA[10]   "   July 9, 1882.

1442.   Tenth Generation.   **Tower.**

1357. PHILO H.[9], MATTHEW[8], JONATHAN W.[7], MATTHEW[6], MAT-
THEW[5], MATTHEW[4], SAMUEL[3], SAMUEL[2], JOHN[1].
Philo H.[9], son of Matthew[8] and Sarah J. (Long) Tower, b.
June 16, 1857; mar. Rebecca Harriet Hawkins
Sept. 21, 1879. She was b. in Whiskey Run, Ind.,
Oct. 2, 1859, and was dau. of Edmond and Nancy (An-
derson) Hawkins.

Childr. born in Whiskey Run.

I. NORA ALICE[10]   born Aug. 17, 1881.
II. EDMOND MATTHEW[10]   "   Feb. 12, 1883.

1443.   Tenth Generation.   Tower.

1357. SAMUEL B.[9], MATTHEW [8], JONATHAN W.[7], MATTHEW [6], MAT-
THEW [5], MATTHEW [4], SAMUEL[3], SAMUEL [2], JOHN[1].
Samuel B.[9], son of Matthew [8] and Sarah J. (Long) Tower, b.
June 17, 1859 ; mar. Saran Skiff.

Childr.

I.   MARY ISABEL [10].   II.   GEORGE MATTHEW [10]

1444. **Merriless.**   Tenth Generation.   Tower.

1357. MARY L.[9], MATTHEW [8], JONATHAN W.[7], MATTHEW [6], MAT-
THEW [5], MATTHEW [4], SAMUEL [3], SAMUEL [2], JOHN[1].
Mary L.[9], dau. of Matthew [8] and Sarah J. (Long) Tower, b.
Aug. 9, 1861 ; mar. Joseph Merriless
Aug. 3, 1879. He was born in Sunderland, England,
Jan. 28, 1857, and was son of James and Mary (McDonald)
Merriless.

Childr. born near Leavenworth, Ind.

I.   JESSIE [10]   born March 14, 1881.
II.   ELMER JOSEPH [10] "   March 5, 1883.

ELEVENTH GENERATION.

1445. **Worrick.**   Eleventh Generation.   Tower.

1377. ALICE A.[10], THOMAS [9], THOMAS [8], ASA C.[7], JESSE [6], ROBERT [5],
DAVID [4], HEZEKIAH [8], IBROOK [2], JOHN [1].
Alice A.[10], dau. of Thomas [9] and Elizabeth B.[9] (Williston)
Tower, b.
May 2, 1854 ; mar. Levi L. Worrick [9]
Dec. 18, 1877. He was b.
Nov. 3, 1852, and was son of Levi L.[8] and Mary E.[7] (James)
Worrick.

WORRICK, LINCOLN, WHITCOMB.   TOWER.
Levi L.[9], Levi L.[8], Levi L.[7], Sally [6], Elizabeth [5], Sarah [4], Daniel [3],
Ibrook [2], John [1].

INDEX TO TOWER NAMES.

The Numbers indicate the Pages in the Work.

Relief, 191, 208, 311.
Rene, 180.
Reuben, 173, 181, 184, 200, 271, 291, 295.
Rial, 136, 222.
Robert, 132, 133.
Rodney, 180.
Roxanna, 141, 231.
Roxy, 175. 279.
Ruel, 197, 321.
Rufus, 143, 162, 174, 260, 276.
Russell, 189. 305.
Ruth, 135, 137, 139, 164, 191, 228, 309.
Sabiah, 180. 287.
Sally, 139, 142, 147, 152, 154, 175, 177, 180, 191, 193, 197, 236, 245, 250, 255, 278, 288, 310, 321.
Sally A., 202. 326.
Salma, 179, 284.
Salmon P., 203, 328.
Samuel, 130, 153, 183, 196, 294.
Samuel G., 194, 315.
Samuel N., 180, 287.
Samuel S., 188, 304.
Sarah, 141, 153, 162, 172, 232, 268.
Sevia, 197.
Sherman B., 190.
Sibyl, 183, 294.
Silas D., 142.
Sile, 147.
Silence, 145.
Spencer, 203, 328.
Stephen, 162, 259.
Stoddard, 152, 251.
Sukey, 191, 308.
Susan, 208, 328.
Susanna, 145.
Sylvanus, 143, 239.
Thaddeus, 191, 309.
Theda, 180.
Theoda, 152.
Thomas, 136, 177, 200, 219, 280.
Uriah, 180.
Ursula, 185. 298.
Ursula C., 190, 307.
Varazina, 196, 319.
Wanton, 130, 204.
Warren, 171, 175, 268, 278.
Washington, 189, 229.
Wealthy, 203, 204.
Welcome, 136, 221.
William, 130, 137, 178, 179, 182, 189, 193, 281, 284, 291, 305.
William E., 204, 330.
Zerviah, 138, 226.
Zillah, 131, 209.

Seventh Generation.

Abbie, 320.
Abby, 251.
Abby F., 237, 254, 404.
Abby J., 269, 432.
Abial F., 301.
Abigail, 216, 253, 257, 353, 402, 409.
Abigail C., 254.
Abigail N., 256.
Abner L., 328.
Abraham, 248, 258, 259, 396, 410.
Abraham B , 325, 512.
Abraham H , 246, 393.
Abraham W., 237, 377.
Ackley, 305.
Ada, 297.
Adaline, 320, 504.
Addison, 285, 459.
Adeline, 257, 409.
Adeline E., 291.
Adeline F., 286, 462.
Adeline P., 268, 432.
Adeline R., 275, 441.
Alanson, 219, 355.
Alanson P., 207, 335.
Albert, 268, 297, 325, 431, 482, 512.

Albert R., 304, 492.
Albro W., 320.
Alden, 276, 443.
Alexander, 226.
Alfred, 214, 349.
Alfred L., 280.
Alfred O., 302.
Alfrida, 263.
Alice M., 293, 475.
Allen F., 285.
Alma, 215, 349.
Almira, 219, 273, 310, 356, 435.
Almira C., 277, 444.
Almon, 285.
Almon N., 268, 431.
Alonzo, 323, 509.
Alpha L., 216, 354.
Altheda, 216, 219.
Alvin, 280, 449.
Amanda, 214, 276, 293, 320, 349, 447, 503.
Amantha, 248.
Amasa, 265, 285, 428, 459.
Ambra, 253, 402.
Ambrose, 267, 276, 429, 444.
Ambrose M., 298, 484.
Amelia, 276, 305, 443, 493.
Amelia C., 209, 341.
Amelia E., 313.
Amos, 216, 353.
Amy, 320, 504.
Andrew, 291, 471.
Andrew J., 292, 474.
Angelina H., 290, 467.
Angeline, 276.
Angeline P., 264, 426.
Angeline W., 263, 423.
Anise, 244, 390.
Ann, 235, 243, 315, 375.
Ann E , 206, 333.
Ann M., 315.
Anna, 260, 413.
Anna C., 290.
Anna E., 313.
Anna H., 292.
Anna M., 315.
Anne H., 256, 405.
Annie E., 224, 366.
Anstis, 253.
Ariel, 204.
Arthur W., 270.
Asa, 261, 418.
Asa C., 245, 391.
Asa D , 244. 390.
Augustus, 209.
Aurelia M., 287, 464.
Austin W., 268.
Belinda B. B , 272, 434.
Benjamin, 239. 244, 265, 389. 427.
Benjamin F., 233.
Benjamin H., 243.
Betsey A , 264, 291, 426, 469.
Betsey M., 317. 322.
Betsey S., 288, 326, 457, 516.
Betty, 214.
Bradley C., 219, 359.
Caleb E., 313, 496.
Calista, 210, 281, 345, 452.
Calvin, 280, 450.
Calvin D., 317, 503.
Carlton T., 301.
Caroline, 249, 291, 470.
Caroline E., 273, 436.
Carrie A., 237.
Catherine, 310, 494.
Catherine L., 302.
Charlemagne, 295, 477.
Charles, 223, 242, 293, 296, 312, 317, 365, 476, 481, 494.
Charles A., 318, 322.
Charles B., 329, 519.
Charles C., 246, 271, 394.
Charles E , 269, 275, 441.
Charles F., 289, 467.

Charles H , 244, 292, 301, 303, 324, 388, 474, 489.
Charles M., 222, 365.
Charles N., 315.
Charles S., 291, 472, 473.
Charles W., 235.
Charlotte, 219, 357.
Charlotte M. B., 246, 565.
Chester L., 283, 456.
Chloe, 211, 346.
Cinderilla L., 216, 352.
Clarence, 271.
Claris, 224.
Clarissa, 214, 215, 260, 416.
Clarissa M., 244.
Clarissa T., 280, 449.
Comfort, 262, 422.
Cornelia N., 207, 340.
Cotton, 325, 512.
Cynthia, 206, 219, 332, 358.
Cynthia H., 264, 427.
Cyrus O., 285, 461.
Daniel, 239, 257, 381, 408.
Daniel A., 317, 501.
Daniel C., 315.
Daniel E., 268.
Daniel F., 249, 398.
Daniel J., 290.
Daniel N., 246, 395.
Daniel W., 234, 373.
Daniel W. P., 240, 382.
David, 206, 219, 249, 259, 260, 270, 312, 332, 357, 401, 414, 495.
David B., 257, 407.
David J., 243, 387.
Deborah, 239, 260. 261, 416.
Delia, 210, 242, 345, 386.
Delila, 211. 346.
Dennis, 281, 454.
De Witt C., 295, 479.
Diantha E., 222, 364.
Dyer, 261, 420.
Eben L., 304.
Edgar A., 286, 462.
Edgar D., 329.
Edmonds, 216.
Edward, 241, 256, 383, 406.
Edward C., 263, 424.
Edward H., 315, 499.
Edward J., 301, 487.
Edwin, 229, 290, 468.
Edwin M., 285, 460.
Edwin O., 289, 465.
Edwin R., 268, 432.
Edwin W., 263, 424.
Eleanor, 216.
Eleazer E., 267.
Electa, 219, 358.
Elephol O., 235.
Eli, 241, 281, 321, 384, 453, 507.
Elisha, 239, 240, 377, 381.
Elisha C., 329, 519.
Eliza, 243, 251.
Eliza A., 229, 234, 237, 238, 317, 370, 373, 377, 502.
Eliza M., 322, 508.
Elizabeth, 209, 239, 271, 276, 284, 305, 381, 441.
Elizabeth A., 223, 315.
Elizabeth A. V., 317.
Elizabeth B , 207, 245, 340, 391.
Elizabeth C., 254.
Elizabeth F., 241, 242, 383, 385.
Elizabeth H., 300, 486.
Elizabeth M., 291, 473.
Elizabeth S., 249, 397.
Ellen, 305.
Ellen B., 251.
Ellen C., 326.
Ellen F., 238.
Ellen M., 295.
Ellen R., 301, 490.
Elmina, 277, 278, 446.
Elsey, 206, 334.

INDEX TO NAMES OTHER THAN TOWER.

The Numbers indicate the Pages in the Work.